A Moonlight Massacre: The Night Operation on the Passchendaele Ridge, 2 December 1917

The Forgotten Last Act of the Third Battle of Ypres

Wolverhampton Military Studies No. 34

Second Edition

Michael LoCicero

Helion & Company Limited

This edition is dedicated to the late Jon Cooksey.
With Great Uncle Albert, "In hearts at peace under an English heaven."

Helion & Company Limited
Unit 8 Amherst Business Centre
Budbrooke Road
Warwick
CV34 5WE
England
Tel. 01926 499 619
Email: info@helion.co.uk
Website: www.helion.co.uk
Twitter: @helionbooks
Visit our blog at blog.helion.co.uk

Published by Helion & Company 2014. Second Edition published 2021
Designed and typeset by Mach 3 Solutions (www.mach3solutions.co.uk)
Cover designed by Paul Hewitt, Battlefield Design (www.battlefield-design.co.uk)

Text © Michael LoCicero 2014, 2021
Images © as individually credited
Uniform plates drawn by Giorgio Albertini © Michael LoCicero 2021
Maps © Barbara Taylor 2014

Front cover: Hill 52, Vat Cottages Ridge and environs oblique aerial photograph abstract, 17 October 1917. (Author); Inserts (L to R): British 8th Division, Second Army and 32nd Division formation insignias.

Every reasonable effort has been made to trace copyright holders and to obtain their permission for the use of copyright material. The author and publisher apologize for any errors or omissions in this work and would be grateful if notified of any corrections that should be incorporated in future reprints or editions of this book.

ISBN 978-1-911628-72-9

British Library Cataloguing-in-Publication Data.
A catalogue record for this book is available from the British Library.

All rights reserved. No part of this publication may be reproduced, stored in a retrieval system, or transmitted, in any form, or by any means, electronic, mechanical, photocopying, recording or otherwise, without the express written consent of Helion & Company Limited.

For details of other military history titles published by Helion & Company Limited contact the above address or visit our website: http://www.helion.co.uk.

We always welcome receipt of book proposals from prospective authors.

Praise for *A Moonlight Massacre*

"This meticulously researched account of the last forgotten phase of the Third Battle of Ypres, utilising German as well as British sources, provides detailed insight into why First World War battles were launched, how they were organised at every level and why they so often disappointed the hopes of their planners."

Professor John Bourne, Hon. Vice President of the Western Front Association

"In this fine book, Michael LoCicero has painstakingly reconstructed a hitherto forgotten episode of First World War history. Thanks to him, we are able to look at the Passchendaele campaign through new eyes."

Gary Sheffield, Professor of War Studies, University of Wolverhampton & Hon. President of Western Front Association

"A scholarly and highly detailed new operational study of a little-known action which was a postscript to the Third Battle of Ypres. With this book, Michael LoCicero has shed much fresh light on the BEF's command, planning and tactics in late 1917."

Peter Simkins, Hon. Professor of Western Front Studies, University of Wolverhampton

"An impeccably researched and highly detailed account of the Third Ypres campaign's forgotten final act."

Richard van Emden, author of *The Road to Passchendaele: The Heroic Year in Soldiers' own Words and Photographs*

"One book adds to the story of the lamentable last days at Passchendaele. Michael LoCicero has discovered an abortive and futile action after the battle had been formally closed down."

Robin Prior & Trevor Wilson, *Passchendaele: The Untold Story Third Edition*

" … a mightily impressive book. It sets a standard for anyone wishing to describe and analyse a military operation …"

The Long, Long Trail website

"… a unique study which is exhaustively researched, lavishly illustrated, and extensively footnoted. It is a dense work that will appeal to academics and those interested in the mechanics of how the British planned and carried out operations. The author achieves his goal of delivering a full appreciation of an operation, its execution and its consequences from the highest command levels down to individuals."

Canadian Military History

" … Michael LoCicero does not ignore the human side, whether it is the nervous breakdown of a battalion commander or the death of a lowly private soldier. The overall result is, therefore, not simply a dry academic account of a little-known tailpiece. This book is an in-depth, thoughtful, and, at times, moving study of the BEF and the German Army in action in late 1917. It certainly merits careful study."

Journal of the Society for Army Historical Research

"… an excellent example of the possibilities opened by fastidious use of a wide spectrum of sources … Where this work is atypical is that it manages to be a rare thing – a genuinely operational study … Perhaps the greatest success of this book, notwithstanding its deft mastery of narrative and sources both well-known and obscure is that the author always maintains balance … It demands – and deserves – your close attention. At the risk of sounding evangelical or repetitive, again Helion bring the best modern research to market at an accessible price and beautifully produced. Wholeheartedly recommended."

Newsletter of the Society of Friends of the National Army Museum

Recordabor Semper

For Sergeant H.J. Cuff 8th Canadian MG Company, Captain C. Cundall MC 2nd Royal Inniskilling Fusiliers, Private G. Holman, Private F.J. Wakely 2nd Royal Berkshire Regiment, Lieutenant R.H. Parker 2nd Lincolnshire Regiment, Captain H.R. Forde MC, Private A. Cooksey 2nd King's Own Yorkshire Light Infantry, Private H. Cairns, Private W. Gilmour 16th Highland Light Infantry, 2nd Lieutenant W.T. Ridgway, 2nd Lieutenant W.B. MacDuff 11th Border Regiment, 2nd Lieutenant R.H. Reid, Sergeant R.B. Milligan MM 17th Highland Light Infantry, 2nd Lieutenant J.E. Baskott 193rd Siege Battery RGA and Lieutenant R.V. Facey No. 7 Squadron RFC.

Contents

List of Illustrations and Maps within the text	ix
List of Plates	xiv
List of Abbreviations and Terms	xv
Series Editor's Preface	xix
Foreword to 2021 Edition	xxi
Foreword	xxii
Acknowledgements	xxv
Note to the Reader	xxvii
Introduction	xxviii

1 Antecedents — 37
- 1.1 Setting the Stage — 37
- 1.2 Aspinall's Appreciation — 52
- 1.3 German Defensive Measures — 62
- 1.4 Corps & Division Commanders — 76
- 1.5 Tactical Controversy — 92
- 1.6 A New Zealand Gambit — 104
- 1.7 Preparations & Preliminaries — 105

2 Divisional Instructions & Orders — 118
- 2.1 Standard Operating Procedure & Formulaic Approach — 118
- 2.2 8th Division — 122
- 2.3 32nd Division — 137
- 2.4 Upset: Loss of Teall Cottage — 163
- 2.5 Final Hours — 167

3 A Moonlight Massacre — 174
- 3.1 Assembly — 174
- 3.2 A Moonlight Massacre — 207
- 3.3 25 Brigade — 208
- 3.4 97 Brigade — 221

4 Dawn & Dénouement — 243
- 4.1 Loss of Southern Redoubt & Hill 52 — 243
- 4.2 Dawn — 252
- 4.3 25 Brigade — 254
- 4.4 97 Brigade — 264

		4.5 Dénouement	283

5 Counterblow & Aftermath — 292
    5.1 Counterblow — 292
    5.2 Aftermath — 311
    5.3 Tactical Debrief — 333

6 Conclusion — 356
    6.1 Operational, Strategic & Political Consequences — 356
    6.2 Costs — 369
    6.3 Epilogue — 375

Appendices

I	Second Army Infantry Orders of Battle: II Corps & VIII Corps: November/December 1917	381
II	Infantry Orders of Battle: 25th Division & 38th Division	384
III	Second Army Order No. 14	385
IV	VIII Corps Orders No. 52 & No. 54	388
V	II Corps Operation Orders No. 167 & No. 168	390
VI	8th Division Instructions No. 1	393
VII	32nd Division Instructions No. 1: Outline Plan of Operations	394
VIII	32nd Division Instructions No. 11: Special Instructions to GOC Brigade in Divisional Support [14th Infantry Brigade] and GOC Brigade in Divisional Reserve (96th Infantry Brigade)	399
IX	100th Brigade Order No. 293	403
X	97 Brigade Operation Order No. 181	404
XI	97 Brigade Operation Order No. 182	406
XII	97 Inf. Bde. Operation Order No. 183	408
XIII	Battalion Commanders' Response to 25 Brigade Questionnaire G 1/79	410
XIV	GHQ Instructions for the Defence of the Flesquières and Passchendaele Salients	414
XV	Lieutenant-General Aylmer Hunter-Weston's Confidential Correspondence	416
XVI	Night Operation on the Passchendaele Ridge: The German Experience from Published Regimental Accounts	419
XVII	Casualties: KIA & DOW (30 November – 10 December 1917)	442
XVIII	German Interrogation Report, 8 December 1917	471
XIX	Lieutenant-Colonel T.F. Tweed War Office Correspondence	476
XX	Official History Correspondence: General Cameron Shute	479
XXI	How Untrained were the Troops in Late 1917?	480

Bibliography — 486
Index — 503

List of Illustrations and Maps within the text

Passchendaele December 1917. (IWM Q56257)	xxxvi
British POWs at *Hessisches Infanterie-Regiment Nr. 116* HQ near Gheluvelt, 26 September 1917. (Author)	43
General Sir Henry Rawlinson. (Author)	45
Vicinity of Paddebeek and Lekkerboterbeek December 1917. (McMaster University)	47
The mudflats west of Westroosebeke: British dead from the air November 1917. (Author)	51
Brigadier-General Cecil Faber Aspinall BGGS VIII Corps. (National Portrait Gallery 59919)	51
Passchendaele Salient and vicinity wet map December 1917. (Library of Congress)	54
Venison Trench winter 1917-18. (Author)	64
Defence Organisation of a German Regiment on the Passchendaele Ridge November 1917	66
Venison Trench and redoubts summer 1917. (Memorial Museum Passchendaele 1917)	69
Detail from *Gruppe Staden* situation map 1 December 1917. Shaded areas denote inundated parts of the battlefield. (BA-MA PH3)	72
German pillboxes autumn 1917. (Author)	73
German KTK headquarters winter 1917-18. (Author)	76
Lieutenant-General Sir Claud Jacob GOC II Corps. (IWM HN82158)	77
Lieutenant-General Sir Aylmer Hunter-Weston GOC VIII Corps and Major-General Reginald John Pinney GOC 33rd Division. (IWM Q6543)	80
Major-General Cameron Deane Shute GOC 32nd Division. (IWM HN82157)	85
Major-General William Charles Giffard Heneker GOC 8th Division. (IWM Q114384)	90
Pillbox HQ of 2nd East Lancashire Regiment, Passchendaele Salient December 1917. (Lancashire Infantry Museum)	99
Brigadier-General Clifford Coffin VC GOC 25 Brigade. (Author)	107
Brigadier-General Cyril Aubrey Blacklock GOC 97 Brigade. (IWM HN82159)	111
German heavy gun. (Author)	115

8th Division communications scheme diagrams. (TNA: WO/95/1677: 8th Division War Diary)	129
8th Division machine-gun barrage map. (TNA: WO/95/1677: 8th Division War Diary)	131
8th Division field artillery barrage map. (TNA: WO/95/1677: 8th Division War Diary)	136
32nd Division Instructions No. 3 liaison scheme. (TNA: WO/95/2370: 32nd Division War Diary)	143
32nd Division communications scheme diagram. (TNA: WO/95/2370: 32nd Division War Diary)	145
'B' Flight No. 7 Squadron RFC. (Peter Facey)	148
32nd Division objective map depicting yellow, green and red lines. (TNA: WO/95/2370: 32nd Division War Diary)	150
32nd Division area concentration barrage map. (TNA: WO/95/2370: 32nd Division War Diary)	152
32nd Division machine-gun barrage map. (TNA: WO/95/2370: 32nd Division War Diary)	154
Dispositions of 1st RIR and 2nd Royal Berkshire on the night of 30 November/ 1 December 1917. (TNA: WO/95/1677: 8th Division War Diary)	168
Passchendaele to Vat Cottages Ridge: British aerial photograph/German map overlay. (Memorial Museum Passchendaele 1917)	170
25 Brigade diagram showing company and platoon dispositions and formations. (TNA: WO/95/1677: 8th Division War Diary)	176
Duckboard track skirting boggy terrain. (Author)	177
Private F.J. Wakely. (Memorial Museum Passchendaele 1917)	178
Lieutenant R.H. Parker. (Wellington College)	180
2nd Lieutenant J. Nettleton. (John Nettleton, *The Anger of the Guns: An Infantry Officer on the Western Front* (London: William Kimber, 1979))	183
Captain H.R. Forde MC. (Anonymous, *The Roll of Honour of the Empire's Heroes* (London: Queenhithe Publishing Co., 1919))	188
Private A. Cooksey. (Jon Cooksey)	190
Private H. Cairns. (Dr Joanne Coyle)	193
Lieutenant-Colonel T.F. Tweed MC. (Michael Stedman)	194
W.T. Ridgway attestation document September 1914. (Ridgway Family)	196
Acting Lieutenant-Colonel J. Inglis. (J.W. Arthur & I.S. Munro (eds), *The Seventeenth Highland Light Infantry (Glasgow Chamber of Commerce Battalion): Record of War Service 1914–1918* (Glasgow: David J. Clark, 1920))	198
Sergeant R.B. Milligan 17th HLI KIA 1 December 1917. (Neill Gill & Colin Milligan)	201
Zero hour 1:55 a.m. Pen and ink drawing by A.M. Burnie. (Thomas Chalmers (ed), *A Saga of Scotland: History of the 16th Battalion Highland Light Infantry (City of Glasgow Regiment)* (Glasgow: John M'Callum & Co, 1930))	206

List of Illustrations   xi

Exert Farm from the air November 1917. (Memorial Museum Passchendaele 1917)	209
Lieutenant H.A.V. Wait 2nd Royal Berkshire Regiment KIA 2 December 1917. (Private collection)	210
Looking south from site of Southern Redoubt toward Exert Farm and Passchendaele church. (Rob Thompson)	211
Pre-war boxing photograph of Private A. Sturgess. (Trustees of the Rifles Wardrobe Museum Trust)	211
Panorama looking SE from site of Southern Redoubt. (Rob Thompson)	213
Lance Corporal T.H. Cooper 2nd Lincolnshire Regiment KIA 2 December 1917. (Don Roach & Lyn Schulz)	213
Captain W.F. Somervail. (University of Edinburgh, *University of Edinburgh Roll of Honour 1914-1919* (London: Oliver & Boyd, 1921))	216
Northern Redoubt from the air summer 1917. (Memorial Museum Passchendaele 1917)	218
Panorama looking west from site of Northern Redoubt. (Rob Thompson)	219
Private W. Hanson 2nd KOYLI KIA 2 December 1917. (Stephen Wilson)	225
View north across present-day site of Hill 52. (Rob Thompson)	226
Vox and Vocation farms from the air. (Memorial Museum Passchendaele 1917)	228
Captain G.L. Davidson. (George Heriot's School, *George Heriot's School Roll of Honour 1914-1919* (Edinburgh: War Memorial Committee, 1921))	230
Captain A.F. Sandeman 11th Border Regiment KIA 2 December 1917. (University of Edinburgh, *University of Edinburgh Roll of Honour 1914-1919* (London: Oliver & Boyd, 1921))	232
2nd Lieutenant W.B. MacDuff 11th Border Regiment KIA 2 December 1917. (Andrew Arnold)	232
Watt Brothers: George right, John centre. (Colin Bardgett, *The Lonsdale Battalion 1914-1918* (Melksham: Cromwell Press, 1993))	232
2nd Lieutenant P.N. Cunnigham 17th HLI KIA 2 December 1917. (Society of Telegraph Engineers, *The Roll of Honour of the Institution of Electrical Engineers* (London: W.A.J. O'Meara, 1924))	235
2nd Lieutenant R.H. Reid 17th HLI KIA 2 December 1917. (University of Glasgow Archives)	235
2nd Lieutenant J. Miller 17th HLI KIA 2 December 1917. (Bellahouston Academy, *Bellahouston War Memorial Volume August 4th 1914 – 28 June 1919* (Glasgow: J. Cossar, 1919))	235
2nd Lieutenant W. Morland 17th HLI KIA 2 December 1917. (Hillhead High School, *Hillhead High School War Memorial Volume* (Glasgow: William Hodge & Co., 1919))	235
Wallemolenstraat from Tournant Farm looking north: Approximate site of jumping-off line boundary between 17th HLI and 15th LF. (Rob Thompson)	237
Tournant Farm from the air. (Memorial Museum Passchendaele 1917)	237
2nd Lieutenant J.S. Scrivener. (*De Ruvigny's Roll of Honour 1914-1918* (London: Naval & Military Press reprint of 1922 edition))	239

2nd Lieutenant Charles Buchan 15th LF KIA 2 December 1917. (Mabel Desborough Allardyce (ed), University of Aberdeen, *Roll of Service in the Great War 1914-1919* (Aberdeen: Aberdeen University Press, 1921))   239
Panorama looking north from Vat Cottages Ridge. (Author)   241
Panorama of low-lying region NW of Vat Cottages Ridge. (Author)   241
News from the firing line: A contemporary illustration. (*The War Illustrated*, 16 March 1918)   256
Lieutenant-Colonel N.M.S. Irwin MC (centre). (IWM 1100)   257
Captain A. Cowe. (University of Edinburgh, *University of Edinburgh Roll of Honour 1914-1919* (London: Oliver & Boyd, 1921))   261
October 1917: Hauptmann von Arnim at the head of *III Battalion, IR117* during a regimental parade. (Hauptmann Kurt Offenbacher, *Die Geschichte des Infanterie-Leibregiments Grossherzogin (3. Grossherzoglich Hessisches) Nr. 117* (Oldenburg: Gerhard Stalling, 1931))   261
Captain J.A. Alexander. (University of Glasgow Archives)   268
Site of Mallet Copse looking from southern to northern edge. (Rob Thompson)   268
Panorama looking east to north towards Vat Cottages and Veal Cottages. (Rob Thompson)   272
German infantrymen Flanders December 1917. (Author)   278
German map abstract of the Passchendaele – Westroosebeke sector. (Memorial Museum Passchendaele 1917)   284
Brigadier-General Frederick William Lumsden VC. (Author)   285
Valuation Houses and vicinity from the air December 1917. (McMaster University)   290
Passchendaele battlefield late November 1917. (Eleonore von Bojanowski, et al, *Thüringen im Weltkrieg: Vaterländisches Kriegsgedenkbuch im Wort und Bild für die Thüringischen Staaten Vol. 2* (Leipzig: Verlag der Literatur "Minerva" R. Max Lippold, 1919))   290
Panorama looking south from site of Mullet Farm towards Vat Cottages Ridge. (Rob Thompson)   294
Map showing direction of the 4:15 p.m. German counter-attack. (TNA: WO/95/2370: 32nd Division War Diary)   297
Lieutenant-Colonel A.J. Scully MC. (Captain C.H. Cooke, *Historical Records of the 16th (Service) Battalion Northumberland Fusiliers* (Newcastle-upon-Tyne: Council of the Newcastle and Gateshead Incorporated Chamber of Commerce, 1923))   297
Map showing 8th Division final positions prior to relief by 14th Division. (TNA: WO/95/1677: 8th Division War Diary)   313
Private W. Gilmour (George Gilmour)   314
Polderhoek Chateau grounds from the air. (Author)   324
Map showing 32nd Division final line on 5 December 1917. (TNA: WO/95/2370: 32nd Division War Diary)   330

17th HLI church parade: Hill Top Farm 16 December 1917. Watercolour by Fred Farrell. (Glasgow Life Photo Library)	334
"Graves"; "In memory of Officers, NCOs, 16th Bn. HLI killed in action on Passchendaele Ridge 2nd/12/17"; "Not in Vain"; "Sgt Colin Turner", 19 December 1917. Watercolour by Fred Farrell. (Glasgow Life Photo Library)	334
Observation denied: site of Venison Trench looking east from new British outpost line. (Rob Thompson)	340
Pillbox, winter 1917-18. (*The Outpost*, January 1918)	355
Area north and NW of Passchendaele January 1918. (Memorial Museum Passchendaele 1917)	364
German cartoon: The British Lion "After sixteen Flanders battles, At least they have left me my growl." (*Simplicissimus*, 1 January 1918)	366
Passchendaele Ridge late December 1917: 2nd East Lancashire Regiment officers in the salient. (Lancashire Infantry Museum)	370
Passchendaele 2 December 1917: British prisoners pose with their German captors. (Eleonore von Bojanowski, et al, *Thüringen im Weltkrieg: Vaterländisches Kriegsgedenkbuch im Wort und Bild für die Thüringischen Staaten Vol. 2* (Leipzig: Verlag der Literatur "Minerva" R. Max Lippold, 1919))	374
Tyne Cot Cemetery: Gravesite of Captain Henry Rawson Forde MC. (Rob Thompson)	377
The Ridgway family remembers: Tyne Cot Memorial to the Missing 2003. (Author)	378
Junction of *Haringstraat* and *Goudbergstraat* 11 August 2004: A hazel sapling commemorating Private Hugh Cairns is ceremonially planted by niece Joanne Coyle. (Author & Wereldoorlog 1 in de Westhoek <www.wol.be>)	379
Second Army Objective Map: The area between "EXISTING LINE" and "FORMING-UP LINE" was to be secured in a preliminary operation (subsequently cancelled) scheduled for the night of 21/22 November. (TNA: WO/95/643: II Corps War Diary)	387

List of Plates

In colour section

Third Battle of Ypres: Second & Fifth Army Operations June-December 1917	i
German Flanders Positions July 1917	ii
Forecast of the Stages of the Campaign GHQ 22 September 1917	iii
II Corps Proposed Operations 9 November 1917	iv
Second Battle of Passchendaele 26 October-10 November 1917	v
Passchendaele Salient	vi
Second Army Objectives 2 December 1917	vii
Lance Corporal of 'B' Company 2nd KOYLI as equipped on 2 December 1917. (Giorgio Albertini)	viii
Musketier of *Infanterie-Regiment Grossherzog von Sachsen (5. Thüringisches) Nr. 94* as equipped on 2 December 1917. (Giorgio Albertini)	ix
2 December 1917: Illuminated by discharged Verey lights, advancing worm columns of 11th Border Regiment are detected by German defenders on Vat Cottages Ridge. (Peter Dennis)	x
Positions prior to Zero 2 December 1917	xii
Positions taken up after dawn 2 December 1917	xiii
Ultimate positions reached 2 December 1917	xiv
Situation evening 3 December 1917	xv
Polderhoek Chateau 3 December 1917	xvi

List of Abbreviations and Terms

Archives

BA-MA	Bundesarchiv-Militärarchiv
BL	British Library
CAC	Churchill College Archives
DCRO	Durham County Record Office
GHA	Bayerisches Geheimes Hausarchiv
IWM	Imperial War Museum
JSCSC	Joint Services and Command Staff College
KA	Bayerisches Kriegsarchiv
LHCMA	Liddell Hart Centre for Military Archives
NRO	Newport Record Office
TNA	The National Archives of the United Kingdom

Military

AAA	Message/telegram full-stop
ADC	Aide de Camp
ADMT	Assistant Director of Military Training
ADS	Advanced Dressing Station
AMS	Assistant Military Secretary
ANZAC	Australian New Zealand Army Corps
APM	Assistant Provost Marshal
Bde	Brigade
BEF	British Expeditionary Force
BGGS	Brigadier-General General Staff
BGRA	Brigadier-General Royal Artillery
BGRE	Brigadier-General Royal Engineers
CCS	Casualty Clearing Station
CGS	Chief of the General Staff
CHA	Commander Heavy Artillery
C-in-C	Commander and Chief

CID	Committee of Imperial Defence
CIGS	Chief of the Imperial General Staff
CMDS	Corps Main Dressing Station
CMGO	Corps Machine-gun Officer
CO	Commanding Officer
CQMS	Company Quartermaster Sergeant
CRA	Commander Royal Artillery (divisional artillery commander)
CRE	Commander Royal Engineers
CSM	Company Sergeant Major
CW	Continuous Wave
DAAG	Deputy Assistant Adjutant General
DAA & QMG	Deputy Assistant Adjutant & Quartermaster General
DADOS	Deputy Assistant Director Ordnance Services
DCGS	Deputy Chief of the General Staff
DDMS	Deputy Director Medical Services
DGT	Director General of Training (GHQ)
Div.	Division
DMGO	Division Machine-gun Officer
DMO	Director of Military Operations
DMT	Director of Military Training
DoW	Died of Wounds
DSO	Distinguished Service Order
FA	Field Ambulance
FOO	Forward Observation Officer
FSC	Field Service Company (mapping and survey)
FSR	Field Service Regulations (1909)
GHQ	General Headquarters
GOC	General Officer Commanding
GOCRA	General Officer Commanding Royal Artillery (corps artillery commander)
GSO 1 (I) /(O)	General Staff Officer, Grade 1 belonging to the (I) Intelligence or (O) Operations branch of the staff
GSO2 (I) /(O)	General Staff Officer, Grade 2 belonging to the (I) Intelligence or (O) Operations branch of the staff
GSO 3 (I) /(O)	General Staff Officer, Grade 3 belonging to the (I) Intelligence or (O) Operations branch of the staff
HAG	Heavy Artillery Group
HBMGC	Heavy Branch Machine Gun Corps
HE	High Explosive
how.	howitzer
HQ	Headquarters
HV	High Velocity
ID	*Infanterie Division*

Inf.	Infantry
IO	Intelligence Officer
IR	*Infanterie Regiment*
MC	Military Cross
MEF	Mediterranean Expeditionary Force
MG	Machine-gun
MGGS	Major General General Staff
MGO	Machine-gun Officer
MGRA	Major General Royal Artillery (advisor for that arm at Army HQ)
MM	Military Medal
MS	Military Secretary
NCO	Non-commissioned Officer
NZ	New Zealand
OCB	Officer Cadet Battalion
OC	Officer Commanding
OHL	*Oberste Heeresleitung* (German Commander-in-Chief, General HQ Higher Command)
OR	Other Rank
OTC	Officer Training Corps
pdr.	pounder
POW	Prisoner of War
QMS	Quarter Master Sergeant
RAMC	Royal Army Medical Corps
RAP	Regimental Aid Post
RD	*Reserve Division*
RE	Royal Engineers
RFA	Royal Field Artillery
RIR	*Reserve Infanterie Regiment*
RND	Royal Naval Division
RSM	Regimental Sergeant Major
SAA	Small Arms Ammunition
SD	Service Dress
SOS	Call or coloured flare signal for immediate assistance by prearranged defensive artillery on previously surveyed approaches to the frontline
TM	Trench Mortar
TMB	Trench Mortar Battery
VC	Victoria Cross

German Ranks and British Equivalents

General-Leutnant — Lieutenant-General
Oberstleutnant — Lieutenant-Colonel

Major — Major
Hauptmann — Captain
Leutnant — Lieutenant
Feldwebel — Sergeant Major
Vizefeldwebel — Staff Sergeant
Sergeant — Sergeant
Unteroffizier — Corporal
Gefreiter — Lance Corporal
Musketier, Fusilier, Schütze, Ersatz-Reservist — Private (infantry)

The Wolverhampton Military Studies Series
Series Editor's Preface

As series editor, it is my great pleasure to introduce the *Wolverhampton Military Studies Series* to you. Our intention is that in this series of books you will find military history that is new and innovative, and academically rigorous with a strong basis in fact and in analytical research, but also is the kind of military history that is for all readers, whatever their particular interests, or their level of interest in the subject. To paraphrase an old aphorism: a military history book is not less important just because it is popular, and it is not more scholarly just because it is dull. With every one of our publications we want to bring you the kind of military history that you will want to read simply because it is a good and well-written book, as well as bringing new light, new perspectives, and new factual evidence to its subject.

In devising the *Wolverhampton Military Studies Series*, we gave much thought to the series title: this is a *military* series. We take the view that history is everything except the things that have not happened yet, and even then a good book about the military aspects of the future would find its way into this series. We are not bound to any particular time period or cut-off date. Writing military history often divides quite sharply into eras, from the modern through the early modern to the mediaeval and ancient; and into regions or continents, with a division between western military history and the military history of other countries and cultures being particularly marked. Inevitably, we have had to start somewhere, and the first books of the series deal with British military topics and events of the twentieth century and later nineteenth century. But this series is open to any book that challenges received and accepted ideas about any aspect of military history, and does so in a way that encourages its readers to enjoy the discovery.

In the same way, this series is not limited to being about wars, or about grand strategy, or wider defence matters, or the sociology of armed forces as institutions, or civilian society and culture at war. None of these are specifically excluded, and in some cases they play an important part in the books that comprise our series. But there are already many books in existence, some of them of the highest scholarly standards, which cater to these particular approaches. The main theme of the *Wolverhampton Military Studies Series* is the military aspects of wars, the preparation for wars or their prevention, and their aftermath. This includes some books whose main theme is the technical details of how armed forces have worked, some books on wars and battles, and some books that re-examine the evidence about the existing stories, to show in a different light what everyone thought they already knew and understood.

As series editor, together with my fellow editorial board members, and our publisher Duncan Rogers of Helion, I have found that we have known immediately and almost by instinct the kind of books that fit within this series. They are very much the kind of well-written and challenging books that my students at the University of Wolverhampton would want to read. They are books which enhance knowledge, and offer new perspectives. Also, they are books for anyone with an interest in military history and events, from expert scholars to occasional readers. One of the great benefits of the study of military history is that it includes a large and often committed section of the wider population, who want to read the best military history that they can find; our aim for this series is to provide it.

Stephen Badsey
University of Wolverhampton

Foreword to 2021 Edition

The Belgian city of Ypres is indelibly associated with the First World War. As the site of intense fighting in every year of the conflict except 1916, Ypres holds a place in British and Commonwealth memory that invites comparisons to the way which Verdun has become a lodestone for French and German remembrance.

In 1914 control of Ypres had clear strategic value for it barred the German advance towards the Channel Ports. The "Old Contemptibles" of the British Expeditionary Force and the professionals of the Indian Expeditionary Force held the line here and fought the Germans to a standstill at the First Battle of Ypres in October and November 1914. Yet victory came at a terrible cost. First Ypres was proportionately the bloodiest battle fought by the BEF in the First World War. The stubborn defiance of the Regular army became a touchstone of heroism and gave Ypres psychological importance which matched its strategic value. This was apparent when the Germans launched a new offensive, the Second Battle of Ypres, in April 1915. Notorious for marking the first large scale use of poison gas on the Western Front, the battle is also remembered for the terrible casualties suffered by British, Indian and Canadian forces as they struggled to protect the city. The Allied line held, but only after another great bloodletting. Yet the defensive battles of 1914 and 1915 are overshadowed by the maelstrom of the British attack at the Third Battle of Ypres in 1917. Third Ypres shook the British Army in a way which no other battle of the war did. The impossible conditions of the battlefield created a quagmire which swallowed men, animals, machines and, crucially, morale. By the end of the year the British Army was close to exhaustion. The mood was perhaps exemplified by a German cartoon of 1 January 1918, reproduced in this volume, which portrayed a mutilated British lion, shorn of its fur and its crown, with nothing to show for its efforts.

The controversies around Third Ypres would animate generals and statesmen for the remainder of their lives, with the arguments being renewed by successive generations of historians. The long and bitter debate is perhaps best encapsulated by the intense arguments which surrounded publication of the relevant volume of the *Official History*. Compiled during the Second World War and published soon after, it could be reasonably assumed that the debate over the 1917 battle would have been diminished by the events of a second global conflict. This was not to be the case. The volume would be dogged by difficulties from its inception to its publication. Far from providing an authoritative account and the final word on the battle, the *Official History* instead added further controversy. That controversy continues, largely unabated, to the present day. A century after the guns fell silent on the Western Front there seems to be little sign that debate has concluded.

Given the century long discussion of the topic, a student of conflict may be forgiven for assuming that all that can be said has already been said. Yet this is not the case. Indeed, for almost a century a significant aspect of the Third Battle of Ypres lay forgotten: the night attack on the Passchendaele Ridge which marked the final act of the offensive. Fortunately, the work of Dr Michael LoCicero uncovered this story, and the book which you now hold describes it in the detail which it deserves.

This is the second edition of the volume and I was delighted when Michael asked me to write a new foreword. The first edition was a book which I deeply admired. It was a rare combination of both breadth and depth. It showcased Michael's ability to examine a battle at its highest level before diving down to the front line and studying the actions of individual battalions, companies, and platoons in the kind of detail which is normally reserved for micro-histories. Above all else, Michael has an eye for the human side of war, exemplified by his skilful descriptions and use of veteran accounts. There is an unfortunate tendency in 21st century academia to reject vivid descriptions of battle as distasteful, but to do so hides the heroism and the horror of conflict. This book reveals both and is all the better for it.

There is more to the book than recounting the story of the forgotten battle. What is particularly striking is Michael's determination that the men who fell in the fighting should be remembered. By telling the story of the night assault the book itself serves as a tribute, but Michael went a step further in 2017 when he dedicated a memorial to the battle near Westrozebeke. The site has since become a place of pilgrimage for those with a connection to the affair.

Interest in the memorial shows that Ypres retains its power as a place of remembrance, defined by the white headstones of Tyne Cot and the haunting sound of the Last Post at the Menin Gate. Thanks to Michael's care and dedication, the soldiers who fell on 2 December 1917 are now commemorated alongside their comrades.

Dr Spencer Jones
University of Wolverhampton
March 2021

Foreword

They are nothing much to look at but on the desk where I am writing these few lines lie two of my most prized possessions. One is a battered metal cigarette case bearing crossed flags and Chinese characters which, when translated, reads "Long live Taiwan". The other is a metal snuff box engraved with a blazing sun motif. I can't remember now how I got them – my father passed them on to me, I think – but they belonged to his father's brother, his Uncle Albert; killed somewhere in France and Belgium during the First World War. I can remember, however, that it was more than thirty-five years ago – long before the study of military history became my career – that I first became interested in Great Uncle Albert and how and where he died. This was a time long before "digitization" and "online archives". I knew precious little then of medal index cards, medal rolls, unit war diaries or trench maps. Records were all index cards and 'hard copy' and any research – quite literally in the case of the National Archives – was all "pencil and paper". I asked around the family, wrote to his younger sister Auntie Lilian, who lived in Australia and got a few family snippets. Albert had been a professional soldier before the war started; he had served overseas with the Yorkshire Light Infantry; the family had called him "the man with the teddy bear". No one knew why.

Little by little, by much trial and error, I pieced together a story of sorts. Albert Cooksey was serving with the 2nd Battalion of the King's Own Yorkshire Light Infantry when he was killed on 2 December 1917 near a town called Ypres in Belgium. He had no known grave but his name was inscribed on a wall at a cemetery called Tyne Cot. I found a war diary and read what had happened to his battalion on 2 December 1917. I studied the maps and sketches in it and found the place where the attack in which he was killed took place that winter's day in 1917. Yet I was puzzled. First, the attack did not take place in the day at all, it started at 1.55 a.m. Second, if, as various books told me, the great offensive known as The Third Battle of Ypres – always "Passchendaele" to those who fought it and survived – had ended on 10 November after more than 100 days of bitter and bloody fighting and Passchendaele itself had been taken, why then was the British Army still incurring heavy casualties in night operations north of the village? I looked for answers and found none.

The fighting on that sector at that time – and the heavy losses incurred – at the fag end of what was a highly controversial campaign of a highly controversial year – was then, and remains today, almost entirely unknown and unmentioned in the literature. Even the British official historian and the committee charged with bringing spatial and temporal order to the confused and chaotic nature of the fighting on the ground by first naming battles and then dating them, seemed to have overlooked the struggles on the northern quarter of the Passchendaele Ridge. The Germans, however, knew something that the British appeared to forget over the years; that the night-attack at Passchendaele was the last significant assault of Third Ypres.

I visited Uncle Albert's name on the memorial to the Missing at Tyne Cot and walked the ground but life moved on; my questions were left hanging in the air, unanswered.

Thankfully Michael LoCicero has changed all that, for he resolved to do something about it when he too was driven to ask similar questions regarding the December 1917 fighting. It has taken almost a century for the full story of those fateful days to be told but here, at last, the result of his labours is in your hands. LoCicero's rigorously researched yet accessible narrative provides us with the first detailed study of this long-neglected, yet compelling aspect of the "Passchendaele" campaign, an event that has never been evaluated within its proper historical context. Guided by his depth of scholarship and his skill at conveying the experience of the "men in the mud" in those "haunted acres" south of Westroosebeke – he moves deftly between the doings on the great strategic stage and the worm's eye view of events – we at last come to understand the significance and import of what happened and why. Above all we come to know the men; their strengths, their weaknesses, their trials and tribulations. Through these individuals LoCicero has done us all a great service in helping to shape and extend our understanding of the entire sweep of the Third Ypres or Passchendaele campaign. We now have answers to those questions.

It has been my great privilege, over the last two decades or more, to accompany groups of adults and young people around the First World War battlefields of France and Belgium. On the vast majority of tours an almost obligatory stop has been made at Tyne Cot Cemetery where, after I have done my "bit" and I have given time for the group to reflect on the awesome impact of seeing roughly the equivalent of the infantry component of a British infantry division lying under the serried ranks of white headstones, I slink off towards the southeastern apse of the memorial. There, often alone, I say "hello again" to Uncle Albert and the men who fought and died with him on that cold, wet, December night in 1917 just a few kilometres to the northeast. Next time I'm there I'll tell him about this book. I'll tell him about how the battle in which he and his comrades fought has finally been accorded the attention it deserves and how their role in one of the most momentous battles in British military history has finally been acknowledged.

As a pre-war Regular and an "old sweat" who had fought on the Western Front since November 1914 and as someone who had undoubtedly seen it all and had probably done a lot more, Albert, if he had still been alive, may well have shrugged his shoulders at the news that what he and his mates had done would appear in a book. I cannot begin to imagine what that final fight must have been like for Albert on that cold, damp, featureless quagmire of a battlefield, but as one of the almost sixty men of his battalion who were killed or died of wounds as a result of the attack – most of whose names appear on the panels of the memorial like his – I'll bet he'd be proud that their story was being told at last.

Jon Cooksey
Stratford-upon-Avon, July 2014

Acknowledgements

I should like to express my gratitude to the following institutions and people in the United Kingdom, France, Belgium, Germany, Canada and the United States for their generous support and assistance with this book: the extremely helpful staffs at the National Archives, British Library, National Portrait Gallery, Imperial War Museum, National Army Museum, Royal Air Force Museum, Liddell Hart Centre for Military Archives, Churchill College Archives, University of Glasgow Archives, Prince Consort's Library (Aldershot), Isle of Wight Public Record Office, Trustees of the Rifles Wardrobe Museum Trust, Lancashire Infantry Museum, Glasgow Life Photo Library, Memorial Museum Passchendaele 1917, US Army Heritage and Education Center and Bundesarchiv-Militärarchiv; Adam Hutek and Reinhard Kirner Bayerisch Kriegsarchiv, Dr C.S. Knighton Clifton College, Judith Curthoys Christ Church College Oxford, Ben Lewsley and Jill Shepherd Wellington College; individuals in the UK: Andrew Arnold, Chris Baker, Chris, Marianne, Julian and Olivia Barker, Stephen Barker, Malcolm Barrass, Dr James Beach, Dr Joanne Coyle, Tom Donovan, Brenda Eastaff, Paul Edgerton, Peter Facey, Sue Floyd, Neill Gill, Clive Harris, Anthony and Lois Houghton, Paul Humphriss, Paul Johnson, Matthew Lucas, Phil McCarty, Michael McLaren, the late Charles Messenger, Colin Milligan, Carl Mitchley, Captain Christopher Page RN (Rtd), Dr Lucian and Dr Aurelia Pascut, Andrew Payne, Paul Reed, Peter and David Roberts, Alan Ridgway, David Ridgway, Michael Stedman, Gillian Towers, Brian Turner and Stephen Wilson; in France, Belgium and Germany: Alfons Dedeyne, Wim Degrande, Madeleine Demuynck, Josue Denoo, Bram Depoorter and the Depoorter family, Emiel and the late Alice Depuydt, De Wissel School and Art School Lima teachers and students, Dr Mandy Diskar, Anne Hansen, Johan de Jonghe, Markus Klauer, Jo Lottegier, Colonel Dr Jack Sheldon (Rtd), Tamara Staelens and Bart Terryn of Tganzengoed Staden, Gilles Uijtterhaegen, Jan Vancoillie, Kristien Vandenaweele, Pierre Vandervelden, Claude Verstraete, Wilfred and Rose Anne Caroloen Vierkelst, Antony Thibaut van Wallengham, Andre Winne; in Canada and the United States: the late Richard Baumgartner, Marianne Brochhagen, Lieutenant-Colonel Lou Brown US Army (Rtd), Dr David and the late Helen Cuff, Alexander Falbo, Dr Janice Florey, Randall Gaulke, Dr George Gilmour, Jeff Holder, Jon Kulaga, Barbara Kulp, Tim Kuntz, George Nafziger, Steve Raby, Chris Simmons, James Taub and

Ron Turfitt; my former University of Birmingham colleagues: Dr Jonathan Boff, Dr Derek Clayton, Nigel Dorrington, Dr Aimée Fox, John Freeman, James and Fabiénne Gordon-Cumming, Air Commodore Dr Peter Gray RAF (Rtd), Dr Armin Grünbacher, Dr Peter Hodgkinson, Andy Lonergan, Dr Ross Mahoney, Dr Stuart Mitchell, Dave Molineux, Liz Morris, Dr Geoffrey Noon, Dr Steffen Prauser, Sophie Schrubsole, Dr Michael Snape, Dr Alun Thomas, Rob Thompson, Major-General Dr David Zabecki US Army (Rtd). And finally, a very special thanks to Giorgio Albertini, Dr Stephen and Dr Phylomena Badsey, Dr Niall Barr, Professor John Bourne, the late Dr Bob Bushaway, Arséne Carrein and Christine Dierynck-Carrein, Georgia Cooksey, the late Jon Cooksey, Peter Dennis, Derik Hammond, Dr Geoffrey Haywood, Dr Victoria Henshaw, Paul Hewitt, Colonel Dr Alison Hine (Rtd), Dr Spencer Jones, Kim McSweeney, Nicholas A. Panos, Wilf and Jan Rogers, Professor Gary Sheffield, Professor Peter Simkins MBE, Barbara Taylor, Dr David Valuska, Bart Vandeputte, Heidi Carrein-Vandeputte, Wouter and Amber Vandeputte, the late Marcel Vandeputte and Maria Cappelle-Vandeputte, Dr Richard Wertime; my esteemed publisher Duncan Rogers; my immediate family: late grandparents Philip "Kingy" and Irene DeRea, Benedetto and Rosina LoCicero; John and Gail DeRea, the late Father Philip DeRea, Stephen and Sylvia DeRea, the late Ben and late Pia LoCicero, Joe and Gale LoCicero, Mario and Rose Marcozzi, Mario Marcozzi and Lynn Cheddar-Marcozzi, Ray and Marisa Mecchi; my parents Salvatore and Eileen, brother Scott, YZ and Elena Claudia.

Note to the Reader

Some of the stylistic conventions found in this volume have been adopted from the relevant British Official History [OH].[1] Officers are described by the rank they held during the winter of 1917-18. Troop and place locations are normally written from right to left of the respective British and German forces. Thoroughfares running through the frontline are described with the names of towns or villages in British hands taking precedence, thus: Passchendaele – Westroosebeke Road. OH emulation of standard BEF conventions for distinguishing numbers of Army, Corps, Division and Brigade has also been adhered to, thus: Second Army, II Corps, 32nd Division, 97 Brigade. German formations and units are reproduced in italics, thus: *Fourth Army, Gruppe Ypern, 25th Division, 49 Infanterie-Brigade, Infanterie-Regiment [IR] 117*. Exceptions and adjustments to these conventions have been made with the following: Reference to artillery brigades, which, in contravention of the army-wide practice of using Arabic figures for units numbered higher than 100, will be described 161 Field Artillery Brigade, etc. Formal unit titles, exclusive of direct quotations, have been adopted, thus: 2nd Royal Berkshire Regiment, 11th Border Regiment, etc. Commonly recognised regimental abbreviations are also employed: 1st RIR for 1st Royal Irish Rifles and 16th HLI for 16th Highland Light Infantry, etc. These titles will, on first appearance, be reproduced in full with the intended abbreviation in squared brackets. See list of abbreviations and terms for all other acronyms, etc. Recurring terms strategic, operational, tactical and related forms are loosely defined, with the exception of direct quotes, throughout as follows: Strategic concerns the application of military resources to achieve political objectives; operational concerns the activities of armies and corps in the conduct of large-scale military operations; tactical concerns the conduct of military operations at divisional level and below.

---

1 See Sir J.E. Edmonds, *Military Operations: France and Belgium 1917 Vol. 2* (London: HMSO, 1948), pp. xxi-xxii.

Introduction

The Third Battle of Ypres (31 July–10 November 1917) epitomises the suffering and perceived futility of the First World War. Images of mud-covered Tommies foundering through impassable bogs under shot and shell in vain attempts to seize unobtainable objectives will always remain an indelible aspect of popular British folk memory relating to the conflict. There was, however, more to the strategically ambitious offensive to expel Imperial Germany from Belgium than this tendentious perspective would have us believe. Operationally effective British fighting methods, based on a combination of overwhelming artillery support and limited infantry advances adopted mid-way through the stalled offensive, forced a desperate German high command to seriously consider a strategic withdrawal they could ill-afford. Subsequent heavy autumnal rainfall rescued the hard-pressed defenders by transforming large portions of the battlefield into a swamp. This unwelcome development, coupled with British failure to recognise and meet consequent logistical challenges, preceded the campaign's often misunderstood post-strategic phase where capture of the northern extremity of the strategically important Passchendaele Ridge became the primary objective before winter set in. It was in the immediate aftermath of this final phase that one more major assault was, following approval of a tactically novel albeit highly controversial attack plan, launched during the icy pre-dawn hours of 2 December 1917. This volume examines the consequent night operation against formidable German defences astride the Passchendaele Ridge; its origins lay in the mixed operational outcome of an unsuccessful British and ostensibly successful Canadian assault that in reality failed to achieve all of its objectives. Set in motion three weeks later, the resultant nocturnal gamble – subsequently referred to in classic British understatement by one mentally and physically exhausted battalion commander participant as a "bad show" – remains almost entirely unknown and unmentioned in most standard works on Third Ypres or what is commonly known as "Passchendaele", a highly controversial campaign of which it was the notable last act.[1]

A decade has passed since I first came across a clearly rendered operational battle map entitled "PASSCHENDAELE RIDGE 1/2 December 1917" whilst leafing

---

1 TNA: WO 339/21553: Lieutenant-Colonel Thomas Frederic TWEED. The Lancashire Fusiliers, Officers' Service File.

through a dog-eared 1926 edition of *The Eighth Division 1914-1918* by Lieutenant-Colonel J.H. Boraston and Captain C.E.O. Bax. This surprising discovery occurred during a leisurely shelf-browse at the popular "Shell Hole" bed and breakfast/antiquarian bookshop not far from the *Grote Markt* in Ypres. Baffled, I contemplated the date: "December 1917? Surely Passchendaele had finished by then?" Initial investigation provoked two primary research questions: First, why was another attack on the Passchendaele Ridge deemed important and necessary following the official conclusion of the seemingly inconclusive Third Battle of Ypres? Second, was there more to this perceived lunatic and "futile" operation than "attacks on meaningless fragments of trench, barbed wire, and pillboxes …"?[2] Subsequent examination of key archives and available printed sources led to the formulation of six detail-specific queries into the action/affair – a military engagement involving less than four divisions: First, was Field Marshal Sir Douglas Haig wise to sanction the operation given prevailing political and strategic circumstances? Second, could the extremely vulnerable Passchendaele Salient have been secured without having to resort to further offensive measures? Third, did an unpropitious full moon and/or enemy foreknowledge directly contribute to the barren operational outcome? Fourth, how was it that the right and left battalions of the assaulting 8th and 32nd divisions only discovered the loss of a tactically vital strongpoint just hours before the attack? Fifth, were the attackers detected on the forming-up tape prior to the advance? And sixth, what sort of tactical/operational conclusions were reached in the subsequent unit and formation after-action reports? The relevance of the topic lies in these general and specific enquiries and their direct correlation to an event that has never been appraised within its proper historical context. From a broader perspective, evaluation of the attack's planning and preparations also clearly demonstrates, despite the obvious failure, a fit for purpose operational/tactical template (circa late 1917) adopted by the BEF following a period of intense fighting.

The chosen analytical framework is that of in-depth battle account with a considered attempt to mesh the detailed narrative with rigorous academic enquiry. Such proceedings, it must be admitted, are an unapologetically atypical format for a work offering a necessary corrective to the accepted chronology of the Third Ypres campaign. "A crucial and unavoidable feature of narrative history is the fact of selectivity. The narrative historian is forced to make choices and selections at every stage: between 'significant' and 'insignificant', between 'sideshow' and 'main event', and between levels of description."[3] For example, is a First World War offensive best

2   See John Nettleton, *The Anger of the Guns: An Infantry Officer on the Western Front* (London: William Kimber, 1979), p. 115, Robin Prior & Trevor Wilson, *Command on the Western Front: The Military Career of Sir Henry Rawlinson 1914-18* (Oxford: Blackwells, 1992), p. 273 and William Moore, *See How They Ran: The British Retreat of 1918* (London: Sphere Books, 1975), p. 31.

3   'Narrative History', Understanding Society: Innovative Thinking About Social Agency and Structure in a Global World <understandingsociety.blogspot.com/2008/11/narrative-

described at the level of policy-makers and generals or infantrymen and artillerymen? Is it possible to place these varied participant perspectives into a readable interpretive account? The decision to engage and blend these contextual conundrums – thus conceivably illuminating complex and varied aspects of a somewhat arcane event – has been my ultimate goal from the start. While primary focus is on operations and the interaction of mid-level commanders, tactical, strategic and political determinants are also investigated in order to facilitate understanding of what amounts to a three-week period culminating in a large-scale night attack on a front still active in the immediate aftermath of a great campaign. Operational narrative with accompanying analysis is seldom taken to this level. Recent scholarship focusing on complexities of a particular style of set-piece attack circa September-November 1917 [4] is further substantiated by detailed enquiry into the genesis, planning (especially in regard to employment of standard operating procedure guidelines related in contemporary *S.S. 135, Instructions for the Training of Divisions for Offensive Action* and *S.S.143, Instructions for the Training of Platoons for Offensive Action, 1917* General Staff training manuals) and execution of what was widely viewed as a "dud show" or "half-success." What follows, therefore, is an original combination of strategic, operational and tactical analysis, recent related and complementary academic viewpoints/perspectives on BEF and *Westheer* (Westfront Army) leadership and organisation coupled with applicable first-hand accounts. The human cost is also poignantly explored by focus on the personal experience and varying tangible legacies of six British participant fatalities. Thus this volume, in addition to reconstructing for the first time in a wide-ranging accessible narrative format, the background, course of events and outcome of a forgotten attack that cost approximately 1,689 British officers and men killed, wounded and missing, also highlights the accompanying sacrifice whilst contributing to further understanding of the Third Battle of Ypres and its aftermath in particular and First World War scholarship in general.

The dearth of published accounts concerning what I have christened "The Night Operation on the Passchendaele Ridge" has no doubt contributed to its relative obscurity. Indeed, Sir Douglas Haig, in his wartime despatch covering the 1917 campaign, made only vague reference to the event in a brief statement of post-strategic phase policy: "These operations [Second Battle of Passchendaele] concluded our Flanders offensive for the time being, *although considerable activity was still continued for another fortnight…*" (My emphasis).[5] Lieutenant-Colonel Reginald Bond DSO subsequently

history.html>

4   For example, see Andy Simpson, *Directing Operations: British Corps Command on the Western Front 1914-18* (Stroud: Spellmount, 2006), p. 106 and John Lee, 'Command and Control in Battle: British Divisions on the Menin Road Ridge, 20 September 1917' in Gary Sheffield & Dan Todman (eds), *Command and Control on the Western Front: The British Army's Experience 1914-1918* (Staplehurst: Spellmount, 2004), pp. 119-39.

5   See Fourth Despatch, 25 December 1917 in Lieutenant-Colonel J.H. Boraston, *Sir Douglas Haig's Despatches: December 1915- April 1919* (London: J.M. Dent & Sons, 1919),

recognised in his post-war history of the King's Own Yorkshire Light Infantry that the only large-scale night attack associated with the lengthy Third Ypres campaign had been understandably overshadowed by the concurrent Cambrai offensive: "There was yet an incident on the Passchendaele front, dismissed in half-a-dozen lines in contemporary history, which involved a handful of battalions in dire distress ... It is the affairs of the battalions and with the lives of the gallant soldiers that this regimental record is concerned. In devoting a few pages to this incident, therefore, it can hardly be said that the treatment of the affair is bringing it out of its perspective."[6] Bond's appreciation that the general public remained unaware of the so-called affair was substantiated by the *Report of the Battles Nomenclature Committee* [BNC], which determined "what were officially the actions of the war and what were the geographical and chronological limits of those actions and their relative importance." This select government panel completely ignored the operation in its published findings. Appointed by the War Office immediately after the armistice, the BNC (presided over by Major-General Sir John Headlam) consisted of representatives of all the forces. Its guiding principle in selection and allotment of battle honours was based on the determination that headquarters and at least 50% of a unit's effective strength must have been present during an engagement. Lieutenant E.A. James (CID Historical Section) subsequently observed in a *RUSI* article listing BNC approved British battles and engagements that the number of troops involved in earlier operations were "relatively small" compared with later episodes of the war. "For example, during the retreat from Mons, battalion fights are mentioned, while an attack carried out north of Passchendaele on 2nd December 1917, by two divisions, 8th and 32nd, is not mentioned in the report."[7] Major A.F. Becke, compiler (1935-45) of *Order of Battle of Divisions*, eventually bestowed the unofficial battle honour "Assault of Southern Redoubt, Passchendaele" to 8th Division; 32nd Division, tasked with carrying out the most challenging part of the two-division assault, was inexplicably awarded nothing for the 1917 campaign beyond "Defence of Nieuport."[8] Becke's curious selectivity was, in order "to allow inclusion of actions of which a division was particularly proud", likely determined by a personal appeal from the former GOC 8th Division. The fact that "Each divisional story was submitted for comment to the general officer who

p. 133.

6   Lieutenant-Colonel Reginald C. Bond DSO, *The King's Own Yorkshire Light Infantry in the Great War Vol. 3* (London: Percy Lund, Humphries & Co., 1929), pp. 909-10.
7   House of Lords, *The Parliamentary Debates: Official Report, Fifth Series – Volume XLIX* (London: HMSO, 1922), column 127, Lieutenant E.A. James, 'A Record of the Battles and Engagements of the British Armies in France and Flanders, 1914-1918', *Royal United Service Institute Journal*, 68:1 (February 1923), p. 458 and Captain E.A. James, *A Record of the Battles and Engagements of the British Army in France and Flanders 1914-1918* (Aldershot: Gale & Polden, 1924), p. 1.
8   See Najor A.F. Becke, *Order of Battle of Divisions, Part 1 – The Regular British Divisions* (London: HMSO, 1934), p. 95 and *Order of Battle Divisions, Part 3B – New Army Divisions (30–41); and 63rd (RN) Division* (London: HMSO, 1945), p. 28.

commanded…" and Southern Redoubt and its immediate environs represented the only tangible – albeit short-lived – territorial gain made by 8th Division during the ill-fated attack lends credence to this supposition.⁹

Brigadier-General Sir James Edmonds, in his Official History of the Third Battle of Ypres, also overlooked the Passchendaele night operation by noting that the "intention to complete the capture of the main ridge northward to Westroosebeke as a winter position could not be put into effect", regardless of the fact that a large-scale attempt was made a fortnight after the official conclusion (20 November) of the Flanders campaign.¹⁰ A surviving correspondence relating to the second volume for 1918 reveals that Major-General C.D. Shute (GOC 32nd Division) once expressed particular interest in what Edmonds and his team of historians had – in addition to the other "rather big shows" under his direct command – to say about the attack, although work on the relevant volume for 1917 did not commence until three years after the former's death in 1936.¹¹ His not unreasonable assumption that the night operation would be included in the official narrative appears to have been based on concerns for personal reputation relative to posterity. The absence of any sort of similar correspondence from surviving officer participants is indicative of an apparent dearth of advocates for inclusion.¹² Subsequent exclusion, notwithstanding the fact that

---

9   Becke, *Order of Battle of Divisions, Part 1*, p. iv. Regiments were bestowed with the generic 'Theatre of War' honour 'Ypres 1917', which ostensibly represented the campaign's nine distinct phases (Pilkem Ridge, Capture of Westhoek, Battle of Langemarck, Battle of Menin Road, Battle of Polygon Wood, Battle of Broodseinde, Battle of Poelcappelle, First Battle of Passchendaele, Second Battle of Passchendaele). Unofficial battalion 'Battle Honours' were more phase specific ('Pilkem 1917', etc. for 1st Battalion Coldstream Guards, etc.). Thus general acknowledgement of a battalion's role in the night operation on the Passchendaele Ridge, whilst not officially recognised as part of Third Ypres, could technically fall within the parameters of allotted theatre of war honours.

10   Sir J.E. Edmonds, *Military Operations: France and Belgium 1917 Vol. 2* (London: HMSO, 1948), pp. 359-60. Casualties (killed, wounded and missing) sustained during the night operation, William Moore observed, are not included in the official history's (pp. 364-65) 'final figures for Passchendaele.' See Moore, *See How They Ran*, p. 32. That British troops were called upon to carry on the work of Canadian Corps following its withdrawal from the Passchendaele sector is, taking into account parochial former Dominion perspectives about Third Ypres, indicative that the campaign should, amongst others, be viewed in an 'Imperial' context.

11   See Appendix XX for a typescript facsimile of Shute's 1930 letter. Brigadier-General Edmonds submitted first narrative drafts to 'as many survivors as possible (down to battalion commanders) and all replies acknowledged and responded to where necessary.' Andrew Green, *Writing the Great War: Sir James Edmonds and the Official Histories 1915-1948* (London: Frank Cass, 2003), pp. 57 and 168. No doubt Shute, Edmonds' reply having been lost, was assured that the listed engagements would be covered in future volumes.

12   Conversely, official historians sometimes deliberately overlooked comparatively successful local operations despite earnest advocacy for inclusion. In 1938, Brevet-Major I.S.O. Playfair pleaded – 'a splendid example of bold tactics' the novelty of which 'should be a

similar sized or much smaller affairs were recounted, however briefly, in other series monographs, may have been influenced by the operation's occurrence outside the nine BNC adopted phases (31 July to 10 November) that comprised what is officially known as the Third Battle of Ypres.[13] Edmonds' ready adherence to this officially adopted chronologic construct is still accepted by historians, normally critical of his Passchendaele volume's perceived pro-Haig bias, to this day. Published accounts of what was most recently referred to as a "futile sideshow",[14] therefore, remain limited to a miscellaneous assortment of personal memoirs, one divisional and a dozen or so battalion histories primarily but not exclusively produced during the inter-war period, which, by their very nature, focus on individual experience or a particular unit without, more often than not, any sort of broad perspective or contextual evaluation. General historical focus on Cambrai and the succession of German offensives that followed in 1918 has, in addition to the BNC and Official History, thoroughly consigned the intervening local Passchendaele affair to almost complete obscurity, as perusal of even the most comprehensive available chronologies of the First World War will attest.[15] Moreover, given the understandably parochial focus of post-war Dominion accounts, a smaller operation (3 December 1917) in which two New Zealand battalions participated in a failed daytime attack, has received far more attention in related Antipodean military literature. Conversely, the comperatively large-scale nocturnal attack, involving nine British battalions, remains relatively unknown to this day. It is also curious to note that the relevant German official campaign monograph makes, unlike its British equivalent twenty years later, particular mention – albeit in a few short lines – of the early December night operation. This in itself clearly demonstrates the author's accurate perception of what was deemed the last major "English" effort in Flanders for the year 1917.[16]

    refreshing contrast to the prevailing stereotyped methods and I feel that readers would be glad to know that ingenuity and imagination were not entirely lacking in those days' – with Captain Cyril Falls to include an account of the capture of 'Infantry Hill' by 76 Brigade (3rd Division) on 14 June 1917. 'His plea went unanswered. The Official History makes no mention of activities on the Monchy front after 30 May.' See Colin Fox, *Monchy le Preux* (Barnsley: Leo Cooper, 2000), p. 100.

13 For example, see Captain Cyril Falls, *Military Operations: France and Belgium 1917 Vol. 1* (London: Macmillan & Co., 1940), pp. 525-32 for 'Events Outside the Arras Battlefield' during spring 1917. Indeed, given its somewhat vague operational connection (see Chapter 1, pp. 57-58) with Third Army's offensive, the Passchendaele night attack would not have been out of place in the relevant volume covering the Battle of Cambrai.

14 Michael Stedman, *Salford Pals: A History of the Salford Brigade – The 15th, 16th, 19th, and 20th (Service) Battalions the Lancashire Fusiliers 1914-19* (London: Leo Cooper, 1993), p. 157.

15 See Major-General Lord Edward Gleichen, *Chronology of the Great War* (London: Greenhill, 1988 omnibus reprint of 1918-20 editions) and Randall Gray & Christopher Argyle, *Chronicle of the First World War Vol. 2 1917-1921* (Oxford: Facts on File, 1991).

16 Werner Beumelburg, *Flandern 1917* (Oldenburg: Gerhard Stalling, 1928), p. 167. A more recent work also acknowledges this late resumption of British offensive operations. See

A wide range of primary source documents from the National Archives' extensive WO series, a fundamental starting point for scholars wishing to understand the British Army during the First World War, provided the essential formation/unit war diaries, operation orders, intelligence and after-action reports on which this study is based. Analysis of their contents revealed, besides comprehensive operational and tactical details, a reasonably efficient bureaucratic process for dissemination of information at all levels and general encouragement, by written report, questionnaire and personal interviews, of subordinate commanders to frankly communicate their thoughts and actions to immediate superiors. In addition, surviving VIII Corps and 32nd Division telephone and telegraph transcripts provided valuable "fly on the wall" retrospective insight into the prevailing chaos and consequent impact of contradictory and erroneous messages at corps and division level throughout the attack. Subsequent examination of the available diaries and/or papers of Field Marshal Sir Douglas Haig (C-in-C BEF), General Sir Henry Rawlinson (GOC Second/Fourth Army), Major-General A.A. Montgomery (MGGS Second/Fourth Army), Lieutenant-General Sir Aylmer Hunter-Weston (GOC VIII Corps) and Major-General W.C.G. Heneker (GOC 8th Division), among others, disclosed the thoughts and actions of over a dozen participants from GHQ to platoon level. New material relating to the character and command style of Major-General C.D. Shute and additional Passchendaele night operation documents unavailable in the equivalent Kew files, were also discovered in the seemingly unrelated personal paper collections of Major-General A.H. Marindin and Brigadier-General T.S. Lambert respectively. Exploration of the *Bayerisch Kriegsarchiv's* extensive *Heeresgruppe Kronprinz Rupprecht* (HKR) collection put paid to the general assumption that coeval operation orders, telegraph/wireless messages, situation reports, etc. were lost forever following the 1945 air raid that reduced the Reich's central military archive to ashes.[17] In addition, six relevant Hessian and Thüringian regimental histories provided the principal source for understanding sharp end perspectives, collective experience and course of events relating to the "other side of the hill." The factual gulf between these accounts and the wealth of British primary documents was, in comparison, very limited, the former sources, more often than not, complimenting the latter.

Chapter 1 considers Third Ypres' general course up to the capture (6 November 1917) of Passchendaele village. Sir Henry Rawlinson's succession as Second Army commander and the subsequent Anglo-Canadian attack (10 November) to gain additional ground north and NW of Passchendaele follows. The decision to attack in early December, enemy defensive measures, biographical portraits of participating

---

    Jack Sheldon, *The German Army at Passchendaele* (Barnsley: Pen & Sword, 2007), pp. 310-12.
17 See introduction in Mark Osborne Humphries & John Maker (eds), *Germany's Western Front: Translations from the German Official History of the Great War 1914 Part 1. The Battle of the Frontiers and Pursuit to the Marne* (Waterloo, Ontario: Wilfred Laurier University Press, 2013).

British formation commanders, consequent tactical planning and resultant controversy, infantry training and artillery preparations are examined next in order to set the stage for the contemplated night assault. Part one of Chapter 2 compares and contrasts the plethora of related divisional instructions and orders. Part two explores the partially successful German riposte (30 November) that ultimately disrupted the painstakingly laid attack plan and the final hours leading up to Zero. Chapter 3 chronicles the assembly and initial assault. Chapter 4 continues the narrative from sunrise on 2 December to the commencement of the afternoon German counterattack. Chapter 5 relates events and immediate consequences of the hostile retaliatory thrust, resultant British consolidation of ground gained and GHQ's decision to terminate further offensive measures within ten hours of Zero. This is followed by a detailed tactical analysis. The concluding chapter analyses the operational, strategic, political and, utilising data that sheds a new light on combined British losses, human consequences as they directly or indirectly relate to this opaque episode of the First World War. First conceived as a lasting tribute to the men of 8th and 32nd divisions, this volume attempts to embrace the sombre tale in its entirety.

The passage of seven years since publication has resulted in the acquisition of additional material, none of which substantially alters the narrative or conclusions. Nevertheless, it has been included to ensure that *A Moonlight Massacre* second edition is as comprehensive as possible. To this end, the bibliography also contains some previously overlooked or unavailable at the time entries. Readers interested in sharing related material culture, images and supplementary sources are urged to contact me at thirdypres@hotmail.com.

Michael LoCicero
Birmingham, April 2021

Passchendaele December 1917. (IWM Q56257)

1

Antecedents

Any further offensive on the Flanders front must be at once discontinued though it is important to keep this fact secret as long as possible.[1]

1.1 Setting the Stage

Great Britain and her Empire went to war in August 1914 to prevent a German hegemony of Europe and, in particular, to prevent the Low Countries and channel ports from falling into the hands of a hostile power. The cost of achieving these ends rose exponentially. Britain was the world's premier maritime power, but by the middle of 1916, the exigencies of the Anglo-French alliance and the strength of the Imperial German Army had compelled the nation to create an enormous army to match that of its primary continental foe. Exigencies of the French alliance also compelled the employment of this largely extemporized force before it was fully trained and equipped. The subsequent long-drawn-out Battle of the Somme (July–November 1916) was the bloody template from which the British Army developed and applied emerging operational methods and technologies that would be effectively adapted and adjusted throughout 1917–18.

On 1 December 1917 the First World War passed into its fortieth month. Three years' deadlock on the Western Front had taken its toll. Imperial Germany was hard-pressed but defiant in the west. Victorious on the Eastern Front in the immediate aftermath of the Bolshevik Revolution, the *Kaiserreich* prepared for an all-out offensive designed to bring France and Great Britain to terms before the influx of millions of reinforcements from the United States tipped the military balance. France, reeling from internal unrest and the tremendous human and material costs sustained during the fighting of 1914–17, anticipated a previously agreed upon takeover by its British

---

1 Sir Douglas Haig to Sir William Robertson 15 November 1917, Robert Blake (ed), *The Private Papers of Douglas Haig 1914-1919* (London: Eyre & Spottiswoode, 1952), p. 267.

ally of a forty-mile swath of battlefront south of the Somme as the campaign season drew to a close. The ability of the British Expeditionary Force [BEF] to continue offensive operations in the west would be further reduced by the Lloyd George government's insistence that five divisions be dispatched to support the beleaguered Italian Army in the aftermath of the Caporetto defeat. Meanwhile, Britain's civil and military leadership, having sanctioned three costly and seemingly unproductive western offensives commencing with the Battle of Arras the previous April, further exacerbated prevailing strategic/political contentions by engaging in heated debate over a growing manpower shortage that appeared to seriously threaten the Empire's capacity to continue the conflict.

It was against this alarming strategic and political backdrop that Field Marshal Sir Douglas Haig (C-in-C BEF) officially terminated his great Flanders offensive; the "Third Battle of Ypres" or what is still popularly known as "Passchendaele", on 20 November 1917. The very real danger of *Kaiserliche Marine* destroyer and U-boat flotillas contesting Royal Navy dominance of the English Channel from the occupied Belgian ports of Ostend and Zeebrugge – a serious threat to cross-channel communications since late 1914 – made Germany's expulsion from Flanders a cornerstone of British war policy. Confronting this threat was deferred until spring 1917 in order to support the offensive schemes of Britain's main continental ally, France. The vaunted "Nivelle Offensive" (16 April–9 May 1917) and the series of widespread mutinies that affected the French Army afterwards left the BEF to shoulder the main burden of offensive operations on the Western Front. This provided Haig with the opportunity to confront the menace in Flanders. Thus the West Flanders market town of Ypres, the last major Belgian municipality remaining in Allied hands, and its notorious salient became the starting point for what would be the principal British military effort of 1917. Haig aimed at nothing less than driving the enemy from Belgian soil. Clearance of the dominating Messines, Passchendaele and Klercken ridges would be the requisite precursor to a north-easterly drive against the key railway centres at Roulers and Thourout. The second and penultimate phase of the projected offensive, assisted by a hazardous amphibious landing behind enemy lines at Middlekirke and successive coastal advance from Nieuport on Ostend and Zeebrugge, would follow in due course.[2] Thus the hard-pressed defenders, unable to disengage without having their vital lateral rail communications severed, were to be worn down in a campaign to force the abandonment of occupied Belgium.[3]

By this time the BEF, bolstered by the full mobilization of British industry which was producing not only colossal quantities of established weaponry, but also new weapons such as the tank and trench mortar, had honed its fighting skills to conduct offensive operations that caused growing anxiety at all levels of the German high

---

2   See Andrew Weist, 'The Planned Amphibious Assault' in Peter Liddle (ed), *Passchendaele in Perspective: The Third Battle of Ypres* (London: Leo Cooper, 1997), pp. 201-12.
3   See Edmonds, *Military Operations: France and Belgium 1917 Vol. 2*, Frontispiece and Sketch 6.

command. At the strategic level, Sir Douglas Haig failed to curb his overriding ambition, some say over-ambition, to expel Germany from Flanders in 1917. This still debatable strategic design was, nevertheless, accompanied by an increasingly effective operational approach that challenged the stark realities of position warfare with a lethal combination of massed artillery providing overwhelming fire support for limited infantry attacks. Tactical level developments were characterized by an increase in the amount of firepower through automatic rifles such as the Lewis Gun and rifle grenades, and a return to fire and manoeuvre that devolved initiative to platoon level under the auspices of an innovative GHQ-inspired infantry training manual.

Seizure of the Messines Ridge, a necessary preliminary to a northern offensive aimed at Passchendaele Ridge, Roulers and Thourout, was accomplished by Second Army on 7 June. Grudging sanction for the next stage of Haig's campaign was authorised by the Lloyd George government on 20 July. The main offensive by General Sir Hubert Gough's Fifth Army, supported by Second Army and French First Army on the right and left respectively, opened against the German *Fourth Army* on 31 July. Three and a half months severe fighting resulted in the capture of over three-quarters of Passchendaele Ridge by the offensive's official close date. Another major offensive, launched that very day by General Sir Julian Byng's Third Army, broke through the vaunted "Hindenburg Line" defences on a six-mile front near Cambrai. A devastating German counter-offensive, opening on 30 November, succeeded in recapturing most of the British territorial gains. These events, occurring 60 miles south of Ypres, did not completely distract Haig from sanctioning a relatively large-scale attack by Second Army (GOC General Sir Henry Rawlinson).[4] Its subordinate VIII Corps (GOC Lieutenant-General Sir Aylmer Hunter-Weston) and II Corps (GOC Lieutenant-General Sir Claud W. Jacob) were tasked with overseeing a night operation near the almost obliterated village of Passchendaele on 2 December. The objective was to make a short advance from a dangerously exposed salient on a 2,870-yard front north and NW of Passchendaele. On the right, the 8th (Regular) Division would assault with one brigade; on the left, the 32nd (New Army) Division, utilising a reinforced brigade, was to prolong the left flank. The operation, if successful, would secure important observation points while expanding the salient for projected winter operations and increased defensive security.[5] Rawlinson had, by the time the December operation was under

---

4   Sir Henry Seymour Rawlinson Bt. GVCO KCB (1864-1925). Educated Eton and Sandhurst; commissioned Rifle Brigade 1884; ADC to Lord Roberts 1885; Burma 1886; Staff College 1892-93; Sudan 1898; South Africa 1899-1902; Commandant Staff College 1904-06; GOC 2 Infantry Brigade, Aldershot. 1906-09; GOC 3rd Division, Aldershot 1910-14; GOC IV Corps 1914-16; GOC Fourth Army 1916-18; GOC Second Army November-December 1917. See Major-General Sir Frederick Maurice, *Soldier, Artist, Sportsman: The Life of General Lord Rawlinson of Trent* (Boston & New York: Houghton Mifflin Co., 1928) and Prior & Wilson, *Command on the Western Front*.
5   The projected attack was one of four contemplated during the winter months; only two of the four actually took place.

consideration, taken over the embattled Second Army from the Italy-bound General Sir Herbert Plumer on 8 November.[6] The new commander, having been sidelined to command subsidiary operations on the Flanders coast the previous June,[7] arrived just in time to oversee the next operational phase of the Third Battle of Ypres.

The massive sixteen-day preliminary bombardment preceding the opening of the great northern offensive three months earlier all but eradicated the series of streams (*beeks*) channelling drainage from the heights east of Ypres. A collateral consequence of the discharge of 4.3 million shells,[8] the destruction of these man-made conduits inundated the high water table terrain west of Passchendaele Ridge. Six defensive zones of considerable depth,[9] bristling with MEBU fortifications[10] and protected by formidable artillery concentrations behind Gheluvelt Plateau and Passchendaele Ridge, coupled with the start of a horrendous aberrational rainfall lasting, with few clear days, for weeks on end, ensured Fifth Army achieved less than half its ambitious objectives on 31 July.[11] The deluge, continuing without pause for seven days, transformed a battlefield of broken, expanding watercourses and vast shell hole tracts into a treacherous quagmire. August evolved into one of the wettest months in decades, a total accumulation of 127 mm falling between the 1st and 31st.[12] Resultant low cloud cover hampered air and ground observation whilst the appalling ground conditions hindered rapid advances by infantry and tanks.[13]

---

6   Plumer had, at the insistence of the Lloyd George government, been chosen to command a British contingent of 5 divisions dispatched to assist the Italians following the Caporetto rout, regardless of the fact that Second Army was conducting major offensive operations in Flanders.

7   The contemplated amphibious landing and concurrent coastal advance under Rawlinson's command were dependent on measured offensive progress made by Second and Fifth armies. The scheme was abandoned in mid-October following the Second Battle of Passchendaele. See Andrew A. Wiest, *Passchendaele and the Royal Navy* (Westport, Connecticut: Greenwood Press, 1995), pp. 163-64.

8   Edmonds, *Military Operations: France and Belgium 1917 Vol. 2*, p. 138, fn. 2.

9   Consisting of 'Frontline', 'Second Line', 'Third Line', *Flandern I*, *Flandern II* and *Flandern III* positions extending to a depth of approximately 8 miles. For the genesis of these fortifications and applied defensive scheme see Captain G.C. Wynne, *If Germany Attacks: The Battle in Depth in the West* (Brighton: Tom Donovan unexpurgated edition, 2008), pp. 199-20 and Appendix I: German Fourth Army Order of 27th June 1917.

10   MEBU: *Mannshafts-Eisen-Beton-Unterstand* or reinforced concrete shelter for troops to stand under. The acronym was popular with the British until the familiar appellation 'pillbox' superseded it. See Peter Oldham, *Pill Boxes on the Western Front: A Guide to the Design, Construction and Use of Concrete Pill Boxes 1914-1918* (London: Leo Cooper, 1995), p. 20.

11   Fifth Army aimed at a maximum first day advance of 4,000-5,000 yards to the line Polygon Wood – Broodseinde – Langemarck. See Robin Prior & Trevor Wilson, *Passchendaele: the Untold Story* (New Haven/London: Yale University Press, 1996) pp. 73-77.

12   See John Hussey, 'The Flanders Battleground and the Weather in 1917' in Liddle (ed), *Passchendaele in Perspective*, pp. 140-58.

13   Prior & Wilson, *Passchendaele*, p. 97.

Gough's subsequent performance as principal army commander proved a disappointment throughout August and early September. Two large-scale (Capture of Westhoek 10 August, Battle of Langemarck 16-18 August) and dozens of piecemeal attacks, fiercely opposed by a resourceful, determined enemy relying on a staggered system of immediate and prepared counter-attacks, failed to capture significant amounts of strategically important ground in exchange for combined total losses of 81,325 officers and men killed, wounded and missing.[14]

On 25 August Haig, troubled by the perceived poor performance of Gough and his unpopular MGGS Major-General Neill Malcolm, decided to shift the stalled offensive's primary locus to Plumer's Second Army, which, heretofore, had played a secondary role in operations commencing on 31 July.[15] Second Army's main task after extending its left flank northward was to clear Gheluvelt Plateau of enemy battery concentrations engaging Fifth Army in enfilade farther north. Fifth Army was tasked with carrying out corresponding subsidiary advances on the left. Plumer and his efficient MGGS Major-General C.H. Harington required three weeks planning and preparation before launching the first of a series of step-by-step assaults dependent on the range and mobility of the supporting artillery; the overall aim was a combined maximum penetration of the German defences to a depth of 24,000 yards. To all of this Haig readily agreed.[16] The celebrated set-piece attacks between 20 September and 4 October (battles of Menin Road Ridge, Polygon Wood and Broodseinde), with their thorough preparations and strictly limited objectives, frustrated previously successful German attempts to retake lost ground by counter-attack.[17] Indeed, the seemingly relentless British gains, interrupted by pauses of four or five days to move supporting artillery forward, made under favourable weather conditions during 20 and 26 September were almost immediately followed by a consequent ill-considered attempt by *OHL* to bolster the once lightly held German forward area with additional troops. Their subsequent slaughter by massed British and Dominion batteries during the Broodseinde push contributed to *Fourth Army's* loss, in addition to what remained of the tactically vital Gheluvelt Plateau, of the southern extremity of the main Passchendaele Ridge from east of Polygon Wood to just beyond Broodseinde crossroads. Meanwhile, Fifth Army, keeping pace with its southerly neighbour's three drives, steadily pushed eastward toward Poelcappelle and, surmounted by the sprawling village of Westroosebeke, the remaining northern stretch of the extended Passchendaele plateau. Second and Fifth armies thus appeared poised for further

---

14 See Edmonds, *Military Operations: France and Belgium 1917 Vol. 2*, pp. 183-208, 364 and Prior & Wilson, *Passchendaele*, pp. 97-110.
15 For feint operations conducted by Second Army between La Basse Ville and Klein Zillebeke on 31 July see Edmonds, *Military Operations: France and Belgium 1917 Vol. 2*, pp. 149-50 and Sketch 11.
16 Prior & Wilson, *Passchendaele*, pp. 108-14.
17 See Edmonds, *Military Operations: France and Belgium 1917 Vol.2*, pp. x-xii for the strategic impact of these offensives.

success against a weakened and demoralized enemy. Australian official historian C.E.W. Bean, famously commenting on the notable territorial gains made between 20 September – 4 October, asked rhetorically: "Let the student, looking at the prospect as it appeared at noon on 4 October, ask himself: 'In view of the three step-by-step blows all successful, what will be the result of three more in the next fortnight?'"[18] These lauded victories were not cheap; combined total losses sustained by Second and Fifth armies amounting to approximately 56,375 men killed, wounded and missing.[19]

Against this novel "British approach to the battle, the Germans could find no remedy; the recapturing of ground once lost was impossible." *Gruppe Wijtschate* chief of staff Albrecht von Thaer remarked on 28 September: "We are going through a really awful experience. I do not know any more what to do in the face of the British."[20] By mid-October, *Heeresgruppe Kronprinz Rupprecht*, of which *Fourth Army* was part, seriously considered a "comprehensive withdrawal" to husband "men and material, which would have included the abandonment of the navy bases at Zeebrugge and Ostend."[21] Second Army was now prepared to launch its primary thrust opposite the swampy, low-lying area just below the northern portion of Passchendaele Ridge. This tapering extremity, with its constituent heavily-fortified, mutually supporting Passchendaele and Bellevue spurs protruding SW like extended fingers, presented a formidable obstacle. The attackers, driving NE instead of due east into a constricted salient, were unable to establish enough available sites for the deployment of batteries tasked with overwhelming the enemy's artillery and providing adequate fire support for the infantry. A fatal combination of sustained German resistance, narrowing assault frontages and recurring bad weather, which reduced the battlefield to the infamous folk memory nightmare of autumnal mud and floodwater in the days following Broodseinde, foiled further attempts to achieve a breakthrough. Rushed preparations to increase operational tempo and neglect of crucial "logistico-engineering" factors ultimately led to recognition that the strategic phase of the campaign had, in the immediate aftermath of the operationally barren follow-up battles of Poelcappelle (9 October) and First Passchendaele (12 October), run its course. This dolorous phase of the campaign cost 9,741 British, Australian and New Zealanders killed, wounded and missing for no appreciable gain. Meanwhile, Fifth Army, at the cost of a further 5,598 casualties, made some barely measurable territorial gains towards Westroosebeke whilst closing with the southern fringes of Houthulst Forest.[22]

18   C.E.W. Bean, *The Australian Imperial Force in France 1917 Vol. IV* (Sydney: Angus & Robertson, 1936), p. 881.
19   Prior & Wilson, *Passchendaele*, pp. 119, 131 and 137.
20   Hans Hagenlüke, 'The German High Command' in Liddle (ed), *Passchendaele in Perspective*, p. 53.
21   Ibid.
22   Edmonds, *Military Operations: France and Belgium 1917 Vol. 2*, pp. 323-41 and 364-65, Prior & Wilson, *Passchendaele*, pp. 138, 159-69, Rob Thompson, 'Mud, Blood and Wood: Logistico-Engineering during the Battle of Third Ypres', in Peter Doyle & Matthew

British POWs at *Hessisches Infanterie-Regiment Nr. 116* HQ near Gheluvelt, 26 September 1917. (Author)

British GHQ, having abandoned all thoughts of strategic breakthrough aimed at Roulers, Thourout and clearance of the Belgian ports, now brought in Lieutenant-General Sir Arthur Currie's Canadian Corps to seize Passchendaele village and its elevated environs before the onset of winter. The painstaking Currie insisted that sufficient guns should be brought forward and "adequate" preparations, by which he meant time to get battlefield communication routes in a proper state, were crucial before further attacks occurred. Granted a required two-week preparation period by Haig, Currie and his staff made certain that vital overland arteries were "pushed forward into the salient at a considerable cost of 1,500 casualties" before offensive operations were resumed.[23] The series of three methodically planned and "carefully scripted" 500 yard advances that followed during the period 26 October–6 November allowed assaulting Canadian divisions to "gobble up the ridge, piece by methodical piece", until pulverized, corruption-strewn Passchendaele village and Bellevue Spur

---

Bennett (eds), *Fields of Battle: Terrain in Military History* (Dordrecht, Boston, London: Kluwer Academic Publishers, 2002), pp. 237-55. A staff officer attached to *Heeresgruppe Kronprinz Rupprecht* was assigned the specific duty of estimating British losses based on *The Times* casualty lists. No doubt the newspaper was obtained from neutral channels. See KA HKR 189: 'ENGLISCHE VERLUSTE' 24 November, 1 December 1917, et al.

23 Ian Malcolm Brown, *British Logistics on the Western Front 1914-1919* (Westport, Connecticut: Praeger, 1998), p. 168.

were overrun.²⁴ Fifth Army's neighbouring corps (XVIII and XIV), foundering in horrific, swamp-like conditions below Westroosebeke and opposite Houthulst Forest, made little headway during 26–30 October. As a result, GHQ instructed Second Army to take over XVIII Corps' front on the 31st, "so that the forthcoming further operations should be under one command." Fifth Army, once the primed spearhead of a great northern offensive, was left with a single corps under its command. II Corps replaced the tired XVIII Corps two days later on 2 November.²⁵ In the meantime, almost bloodless minor operations perpetrated by the exchanging corps' right-hand 63rd (Royal Naval) Division during the nights of 1/2 and 3/4 November successfully secured a number of seemingly impregnable German strongpoints.²⁶ These small, company-level enterprises, carried out by stealth, would influence the operational planning of the only large-scale night attack to occur in Flanders during 1917. Prior to this, Haig, his great campaign having lapsed into an uncertain post-strategic phase during which clearance of the northern part of Passchendaele Ridge was paramount, had determined to launch one more offensive (what would become known as the Battle of Cambrai), employing massed tanks accompanied by a revolutionary predicted artillery barrage, before the long and bloody campaign season ended.²⁷ The semi-distracted field marshal would nonetheless continue to contemplate theatre strategic designs centring on Flanders well into the first quarter of 1918.

Sir Henry Rawlinson was left to conduct waning offensive operations on the Ypres front. The northern extremity of Passchendaele Ridge still remained in enemy hands and, as the newly-arrived GOC Second Army observed the next two attacks would be "very difficult [,] but the 1st and 32 divisions are available and which I hope [to] get Westroosebeke."²⁸ This diary entry clearly reveals his intention to press on in the immediate aftermath of the Second Battle of Passchendaele. Thus Second Army would, with the capture of Westroosebeke, secure the ridge portion currently beyond

24   Dean Oliver, 'The Canadians at Passchendaele' in Liddle (ed), *Passchendaele in Perspective*, p. 257.
25   Edmonds, *Military Operations: France and Belgium 1917 Vol. 2*, pp. 351-52 and 354. Second Army was ordered to take over the remainder of Fifth Army's front on 10 November. See TNA: WO/158/251: 'S.G. 657/608', 1 November and 'C.A. 271', 10 November 1917, Fifth Army Operations File.
26   Launched following crippling losses sustained whilst carrying out daylight attacks beyond the Canadian left on 26 and 30 October respectively, 63rd RND suffered the bulk of its 2,514 casualties killed, wounded and missing during the late October operations. See Leonard Sellers (ed), 'Western Front: Report on Operations During the Third Battle of Ypres: Passchendaele, 24th October to 5th November 1917', *R.N.D.: Royal Naval Division. Antwerp, Gallipoli & Western Front 1914-1918*, Issue Number 22 (September 2002), p. 2179.
27   See Captain Wilfred Miles, *Military Operations: France and Belgium 1917 Vol. 3* (London: HMSO, 1948), pp. 1-16 for the operational and technological genesis of the Battle of Cambrai.
28   CAC: RWLN 1/9: Rawlinson Diary, 8 November 1917.

General Sir Henry Rawlinson. (Author)

its grasp. The ground, still relatively firm on the heights, was in direct contrast to the swampy flats east of Poelcappelle where Fifth Army remained bogged down some 4,000 yards distant from the ridgeline's northern verge.[29] A recent II Corps intelligence report revealed all that was known about the state of the battlefield:

> The ground in the valleys is at present practically impassable and consequently an attack against the TOURNANT FARM spur from the west across the valley of the PADDEBEEK can be considered at present impracticable. For the same reasons, under present weather conditions it is essential that the assembly for any attack on the TOURNANT FARM – VAT COTTAGES spur should be made on the northern side of the stream to as far east as VAPOUR FARM. Patrol reports on the state of the ground east of the latter farm have not yet been received but a study of the most recent air photographs of the area show that the valley is very wet indeed to as far east as GOUDBERG COPSE.
>
> The VAT COTTAGES RIDGE in itself appears comparatively dry and should be fairly good going even though 'Z' day be rainy. To the north of the spur

---

29 The 58th (London) Division (left of II Corps since 2 November) was responsible for this sector as far as the Lekkerboterbeek stream, which was the former formation's boundary with 1st British Division.

the 35-metre contour forms approximately the southern limit of the marshes of the LEKKERBOTERBEEK. The slopes of the ridge are regular – if anything slightly convex, though not sufficiently so to afford any cover to troops advancing from the south.[30]

Thus the only remaining avenue of approach to Westroosebeke and its environs was on a narrow front northwards astride the Passchendaele plateau and adjacent Vat Cottages Ridge.

II Corps submitted (9 November) a document to Second Army that outlined "approximate objectives proposed for future stages of the operations northwards along the Passchendaele – Westroosebeke ridge."[31] Six operational objectives/objective contingencies were articulated. First: "it would not be known definitely what the state of the ground is like between Veal Cottages and Westwood House" until Canadian Corps and II Corps achieved their objectives.[32] These distant enemy strongpoints, overlooking marshy territory south of Spriet, were part of stalwart ridge defences dominating the flooded plain below. This low-lying area, inundated by the Paddebeek and Lekkerboterbeek streams, was the site of a diffuse number of fortified farms, pillboxes and four wooded localities known as West Wood, Middle Copse, Double Copse and Mallet Wood.

Second: it remained "to be seen whether after the capture by us of tomorrow's objective the enemy will, or will not, continue to hold his positions between Sourd Farm and Veal Cottages."[33] In other words, it was hoped the Germans would evacuate these positions following the capture of the high ground (main ridge in vicinity of Void Farm and Vat Cottages Ridge) overlooking their defences from the east.

Third: if the Germans were unwilling to withdraw, it would be "necessary to undertake subsidiary operations to clear him [sic] out of this area" and establish a line 600 yards to the north. This was, once again, dependent on the success of the next operation, which, if successful, would allow for the commencement of subsidiary operations on the night of 10/11 November. "In the meantime, the proposed objectives and left flank of the attack … must be regarded as very tentative."[34]

Fourth: if "determined German resistance was not met with and operations progress satisfactorily" it was hoped that "1st Imperial Division"[35] would gain the line Valuation Houses, Mullet Farm, Westwood House, Mullet Wood and Veal Cottages.

---

30 TNA: WO/95/643: 'Summary of Information About the Area Concerned and the Probable Enemy Dispositions', 8 November 1917, II Corps War Diary.
31 Ibid: 'G.S. 6/5, 9 November' [1917].
32 Ibid.
33 Ibid. Sourd Farm was approximately 1,400 yards west of Veal Cottages.
34 Ibid.
35 The 1st British Division was given the sobriquet 'Imperial' in order to avoid confusion with the neighbouring 1st Canadian Division. Henceforth, it will be referred to as '1st Division'. See 5 November entry in TNA: WO/95/643: II Corps War Diary.

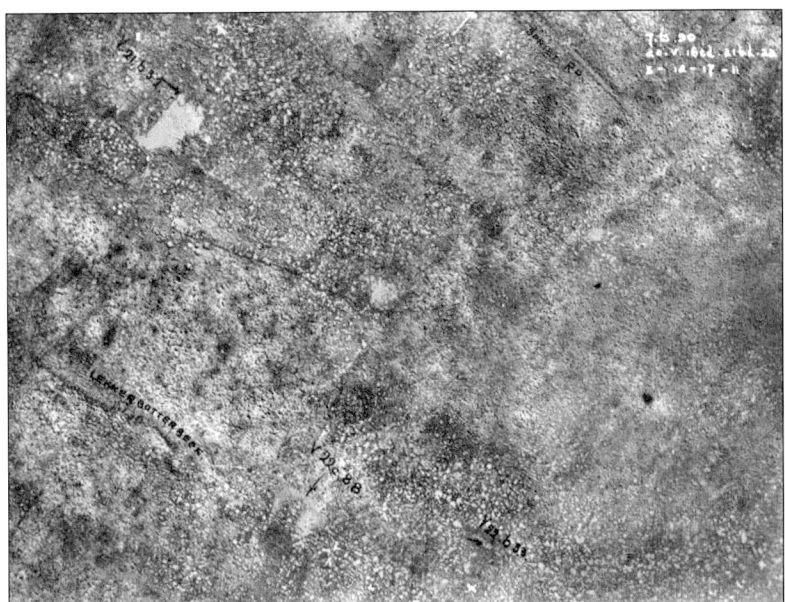

Vicinity of Paddebeek and Lekkerboterbeek December 1917. (McMaster University)

The most northerly point of this line would be just 800 yards from the southern environs of Westroosebeke; 32nd Division would relieve 1st Division at the conclusion of these operations.[36]

Fifth: 32nd Division would carry on operations by advancing an additional 300 yards on the right in order to secure the high ground at Hill 50, while on the left a further advance of approximately 400 yards would extend the line along the Spriet – Westroosebeke Road. Another advance, "in conjunction with a minor operation from the west along the Poelcappelle – Spriet road", was to be made "by whatever division was holding the line in front of Poelcappelle at the time."[37]

Sixth: all proposed operations were dependent on the forward movement of the artillery. Projected dates for further advances were "dependant on the speed with which it is found possible to move the guns forward." To support 1st Division's assault against Valuation Houses and Mullet Farm, it was necessary to move within 5,000 yards of the former, "11 batteries of each of the two divisional [field] artillery groups on the II Corps front." It would also be necessary to relocate "sufficient medium howitzers and heavy batteries forward to positions where they can deal with the enemy's batteries in what will probably be their positions after tomorrow's attack if successful."[38]

36 TNA: WO/95/643: 'G.S. 6/5', 9 November [1917].
37 Ibid.
38 Ibid.

The document concluded by stating that the forward movement of batteries could not be "done in sufficient time to allow the [second] attack to take place earlier than the 17th of November and even then [,] the time taken must to a great extent depend on the weather and the enemy's artillery activity." Nevertheless, he believed the artillery situation could "be modified if the Canadian Corps find it practicable to give the II Corps any artillery support for the proposed operation." Assistance had been requested, but a definite reply had "not been received on this point from Canadian Corps."[39]

It is noteworthy – regardless of Rawlinson's previously articulated desire to "get Westroosebeke" – that II Corps contemplated a step-by-step northern advance only as far as the environs of the heavily fortified town. The capture of Hill 50, along with the establishment of a line along the Spriet – Westroosebeke road, would make the position of Westroosebeke's German garrison untenable. This gradational scheme, however, still adhered to the general outline of the previous forecast report, forwarded by British GHQ to Second and Fifth armies on 22 September, of projected stages of the Flanders campaign.[40] Progressive operations bent on securing Passchendaele Ridge as far as Westroosebeke were, Robin Prior and Trevor Wilson have observed, nonetheless, "almost certain to fail: the narrow front of attack (the ridge was less than 500 yards in this area) would allow the Germans, employing their artillery concentrations behind the ridge on the right and in the Houthulst Forest on the left, to pour heavy enfilade fire into both flanks of the attacker."[41]

The next Anglo-Canadian assault was launched on both sides of the Passchendaele – Westroosebeke Road on 10 November. On the right, 1st Canadian Division gained 500 yards along the main ridge, although the summit and NE slope of Hill 52 (the highest tactical feature on the northern part of the ridge) was not secured. On the left, 1st British Division (II Corps), attacking with two battalions (1st South Wales Borderers [SWB] and 2nd Royal Munster Fusiliers [RMF]) covered the Canadian left flank.[42] Their objectives were the tongue-shaped outcrop of Vat Cottages Ridge[43] and two corresponding strongpoints on the Passchendaele plateau. A right-hand divergence by 1st SWB allowed counter-attacking German infantry to exploit a

---

39 Ibid. The imminent relief of the Canadian Corps precluded the involvement of its component artillery in the projected tenth stage of operations.
40 See Edmonds, *Military Operations: France and Belgium 1917 Vol. 2*, pp. 280-81.
41 Prior & Wilson, *Passchendaele*, p. 173.
42 'In consequence of the very bad condition of the low-lying country in the vicinity of the Paddebeek stream and Goudberg Copse [,] it was found impossible to attack across this, there being no room for forming up before attack, and arrangements were made by II Corps to take over from the Canadian Corps a portion of their left brigade front [opposite Vat Cottages Ridge], where the ground was better.' See TNA: WO/95/1232: 1st Division War Diary.
43 Referred to as such by Major-General E.P. Strickland (GOC 1st British Division) in his 4-page after-action report. See TNA: WO/95/1232: 'Appendix A, 1st (Imp) Division No. G', 15 November 1917, 1st Division War Diary.

considerable gap between the assaulting battalions; 2nd RMF was cut off and routed with heavy loss after seizing a number of strongpoints. 1st SWB, its left flank dangerously exposed, was thus compelled to fall back to the original jumping-off line situated in the marshy Paddebeek valley.[44] The attack frontage "narrow enough to begin with, and reduced by three-fifths by failure on the left, allowed the enemy to concentrate an unusual weight of artillery against the new line. In all, the counter-batteries of German corps were turned on the Canadian front."[45] That evening Sir Henry Rawlinson recorded a summation of the day's events in his diary:

> It has been a very disappointing day [.] After a wet blustery night the II and Canadian corps assembled for the attack at 6:5[0] am and went over the top [.] By 7:30 they had gained all their objectives and were [,] I hoped [,] well established [,] but soon after 9am the Bosch began concentrated hurricane artillery fire [,] which we could not hope to cope with [,] as no airmen were available to get into the air and the counter-battery work was ineffective [.] The Bosch has greatly strengthened his batteries opposite Passchendaele and until we can bring their fire under [,] I doubt [we] are making much progress [.] We shall be driven out every time. The Canadians have held on [,] but the Munsters and SWB have been driven back to their original line [.] It is very disappointing [.][46]

Sir Douglas Haig, in contrast to his new Second Army Commander, was satisfied with the results of the day:

> Attack launched at 6:5[0] am today on II and Canadian corps fronts extending from north of Passchendaele village to Tornaut farm [sic] on the west of the ridge. At 9:30 am Second Army reported all objectives taken. Very heavy rain had fallen in the night and the ground was very deep. At 3:30 pm Second Army reports our troops have been driven out of 'Veal Cottages' on the [Vat Cottages] spur northwest of Passchendaele and also from Vox and Vocation Farms, which are on the main ridge. 'Steps are being taken to retake these localities.' Notwithstanding these points being still in enemy hands, our troops have improved their position on the Passchendaele ridge very greatly.[47]

---

44 2nd RMF losses amounted to 13 officers and 400 ORs; 1st SWB 10 officers and 374 ORs; 1st Canadian Division 1,094 killed, wounded and missing. Canadian Corps combined casualties from 26 October to 11 November amounted to 12,924 killed, wounded and missing. See Edmonds, *Military Operations: France and Belgium 1917 Vol. 2*, pp. 358-59 and G.W.L. Nicholson, *Canadian Expeditionary Force: 1914-1919* (Ottawa: Queen's Printer, 1962), p. 326.
45 Nicholson, *Canadian Expeditionary Force*, p. 326.
46 CAC: RWLN 1/9: Rawlinson Diary, 10 November 1917.
47 Haig diary entry 10 November 1917 in 'The First World War Political, Social and Military Manuscript Sources: Series One: The Haig Papers from the National Library of

The ultimate result, despite this reserved optimism, was the creation of the narrow and extremely vulnerable "Passchendaele Salient", a deadly, jutting proboscis extended to a depth of "about three thousand yards to a width of only 1,000 yards."[48]

The southern shoulder of the salient began SW of Passchendaele near Broodseinde Crossroads. Two important tactical features lay in the immediate rear: Crest Farm, a "considerable eminence that served as a pivot point for the concentration of troops in the event of hostile counter-attacks from the north and the east", was situated near the western extremity of Passchendaele Village.[49] The pillbox-laden Bellevue Spur, a 50-metre promontory at its highest, carried the unswerving Gravenstafel Road (one of two major supply routes to the forward area) past the erased hamlets of Meetcheele and Mosselmarkt, towards the eastern acme of the salient. Between the vicinity of Crest Farm and the southern gradient of Bellevue lay the swampy depression, still littered with the mortal and material detritus from earlier fighting, of the Ravebeek Valley. The northern shoulder of the salient wound its way westward, from the vicinity of Vindictive Crossroads, across the main ridge and southern slopes of the Vat Cottages outcrop. Beyond lay the remainder of the Passchendaele plateau with the village of Westroosebeke topping its northern extremity. From Vat Cottages Ridge the British line continued NW, with few re-entrants, past the flattened village of Poelcappelle, before extending west once more to the southern fringe of Houthulst Forest. It was here that the autumn advance of Fifth Army ground to a halt when confronted by a foul expanse of mud, floodwater and the murky depths of the forest. Above this plain, acute German observers, ensconced in watchtowers and tree platforms among the leafless Houthulst boscage, concealed in the tumbledown ruins of Westroosebeke and aloft in observation balloon platforms provided target information to batteries massed within Houthulst Forest and east of Passchendaele Ridge.[50] Beyond the forest, to the north, lay Klercken Ridge; unattained and unattainable. The salient encompassing Broodseinde, Passchendaele, Crest Farm and Bellevue Spur, the combined responsibility of VIII and II Corps from 18 November, was also "overlooked by the enemy from Westroosebeke, and suffered from shellfire and gas of all descriptions continuously both night and day."[51] The overall position was so dire that Brigadier-General

---

Scotland, Part I Haig's Autograph Great War Diary', NLS Acc., 3155, Reel 5 (Brighton: Harvester Press Microfilm Publications LTD, 1987) and Gary Sheffield & John Bourne (eds), *Douglas Haig: War Diaries and Letters 1914-1918* (London: Weidenfeld & Nicolson, 2005), p. 340.

48   Lieutenant-Colonel Graham Seton Hutchison, *The Thirty-Third Division in France and Flanders 1915-1919* (London: Warlow & Sons, 1921), p. 76.
49   Ibid., p. 76.
50   TNA: WO/297/4903: 'Hostile Artillery Dispositions December 9th, 1917' (map), Sheet name and no.: Oostnieuwkerke Edition No: 1 Production: FS Co (1291).
51   See Prior & Wilson, *Passchendaele*, p. 45 and Hutchison, *The Thirty-Third Division in France and Flanders 1915-1919*, p. 75.

The mudflats west of Westroosebeke: British dead from the air November 1917. (Author)

Brigadier-General Cecil Faber
Aspinall BGGS VIII Corps.
(National Portrait Gallery 59919)

Cecil Faber Aspinall, the newly appointed BGGS VIII Corps,[52] prepared, ostensibly for Second Army HQ, a controversial appreciation that painted a grim picture of prevailing conditions within the salient.[53]

1.2 Aspinall's Appreciation

Brigadier-General Aspinall's report began with a topographic and logistic overview of the newly created salient. The British front, an exact semi-circle with a radius of 1,300 yards, extended from the vicinity of Goudberg Copse (NNW of Passchendaele Village) to Tiber (a captured German strongpoint south of the village).[54] Marching distance from the Menin Gate to the apex was 13,000 yards, and every yard of this approach was under the effective range of the German 5.9-inch howitzer from some portion of the enemy line;[55] "the last 8,000 yards, i.e. from the old German forward system" could be "reached by 5.9 fire from any point" in an arc of more than 180 degrees:

> For the last 3,000 yards, until duckboard tracks can be made in the present impassable valleys, troops must move either along the BELLEVUE spur or along the main Passchendaele Ridge. The first named route is nowhere more than 1,500 yards from the frontline of the [II] Corps on our left; the last named

---

52   Brigadier-General Cecil Faber Aspinall-Oglander ('Oglander' was added later to comply with terms of a family bequest) CMG DSO (1878-1959). 2nd Lieutenant 4th Volunteer Battalion East Surrey Regiment 1898; Lieutenant 7th Battalion Royal Fusiliers (Militia) 1899; commissioned Royal Munster Fusiliers 1900; Ashanti Operations 1900; South Africa 1901; Staff College and Mohmand Expedition 1908; General Staff India and War Office 1909-14. GSO1 MEF 1915; GSO 1 63rd (Royal Naval) Division 1916-17; DSO June 1917, Brigadier-General and BGGS VIII Corps November 1917. Aspinall subsequently authored the official history of the Gallipoli campaign. See Compton Mackenzie, *Gallipoli Memories* (London: Cassell & Company, 1929), pp. 97-98 for a revealing pen portrait of Aspinall.
53   TNA: WO/95/821: 'Appreciation of the Situation on the VIII Corps Front: November 1917', VIII Corps War Diary. An *ex post facto* notation on this document by an unknown hand states: 'General Aspinall-Oglander in Nov[ember] 1934, told us that this appreciation was discussed verbally with Fourth Army [sic] HQ's.' A puzzling aspect of Aspinall's paper concerns divided command responsibility for the salient: 'The VIII Corps front comprises the extreme NE extremity of the Passchendaele Salient, and from its left at V.29.a. 6. 5. to its right at Tiber, is an exact semi-circle of 1,300 yards.' These map references would put the left half of the salient under VIII Corps' aegis. II Corps had been responsible for this area since 2 November. It would appear, considering the two sectors were not mutually exclusive, that Aspinall could not disregard the neighbouring corps' portion of the salient.
54   Ibid. The right of VIII Corps was subsequently extended from Tiber approximately 1,000 yards south to Rhine. See LHCMA: 'Second Army No. 20/59 (G)', 19 November 1917, Montgomery-Massingberd Papers, File 7/15, King's College, London.
55   The 5.9-inch howitzer had a maximum range of 9,296 yards.

route is throughout within 1,000 yards of our own frontline. The necessity for us to use one of these routes is well known to the enemy, who can cut off all communication by the simple expedient of placing a barrage across them.

The right (33rd) division was "served by one passable road as far as Devil's Crossing, whence pack animals can be taken as far as Seine."[56] This point was "4,000 yards from the left flank of the Division's line." The left (8th) division's route was passable for wheeled transport only as far as the indispensable nodal point at Kansas Cross,[57] and for pack mules as far as Bellevue, "whence there is a 3,000 yard carry to the frontline."[58]

Accumulated artillery assets remained vulnerable and exposed: "Owing to the paucity of roads and tramlines, the artillery is at present dangerously bunched and casualties are heavy. This must continue until the guns can be separated, which can only be done when more lateral roads are completed." Light railway construction, to service gun platforms on Windmill Cabaret Ridge and Abraham Heights (west of the Passchendaele Ridge) was, with consequent difficulties, under way to ease a portion of the gunners' logistical nightmare:

LIGHT RAILWAYS
(3) In order to give adequate counter-battery support to the infantry it is essential to bring heavy artillery up to the WINDMILL CABARET Ridge. Guns can only be adequately supplied on this line when the loops between Y4 and Y8 spurs has [sic] been completed.

The situation on the Abraham Heights – Boeteleer Line would remain unsatisfactory for the ubiquitous British 18-pounder [pdr.] field gun[59] until light railway service could be extended. "Unfortunately, however, the construction of [rail] lines is hampered by hostile fire from our [VIII Corps] right flank, the shape of the salient

---

56 Devil's Crossing was situated on the Ypres – Roulers railway. Seine was a captured German strongpoint NE of Zonnebeke.
57 The Passchendaele Salient was serviced by two roads: 'Gravenstafel Road ran northeast along the Gravenstafel Ridge, bypassing Passchendaele to the north, whilst Zonnebeke Road ran from Ypres eastwards via Potijze and the Frezenberg Ridge to Zonnebeke and thence northeast into Passchendaele. Three other roads (Oxford and Cambridge roads, Godley Road and Kansas Cross-Zonnebeke Road) laterally connected the two main roads, allowing material to be transported from the Ypres-Roulers railway (which ran southwards from the main axis of the attack) to the north-eastern sector.' See Thompson, 'Mud, Blood and Logistico-Engineering during the Battle of Third Ypres' in Doyle & Bennett (eds), *Fields of Battle*, pp. 243-45.
58 TNA: WO/95/821: 'Appreciation of the Situation on the VIII Corps Front: November 1917', VIII Corps War Diary.
59 The 18 pdr. field gun had a maximum range of 7,000 yards.

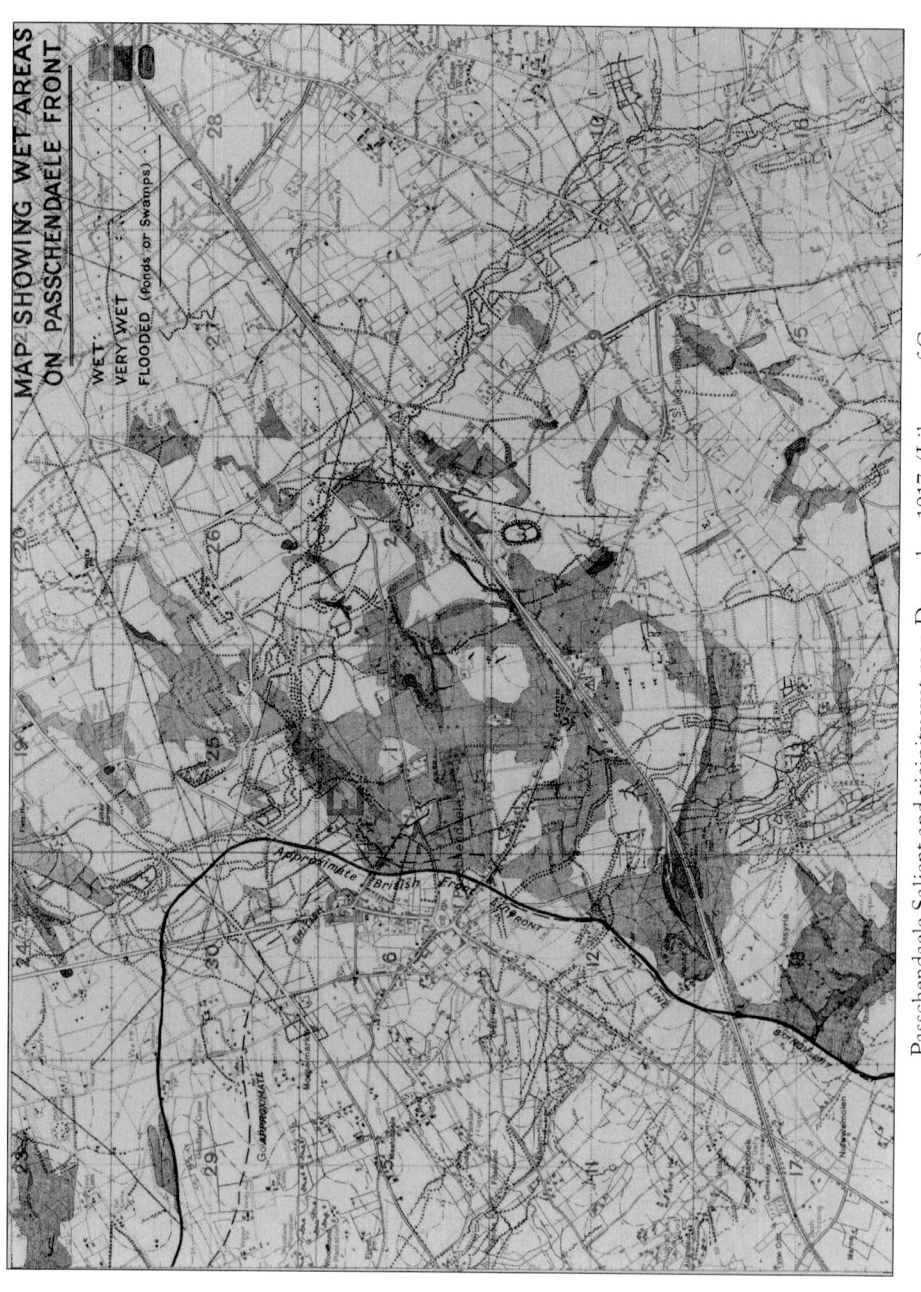

Passchendaele Salient and vicinity wet map December 1917. (Library of Congress)

being such that railways in our area, when still 5,000 yards from our own frontline, are within 2,000 yards of the front of the [II ANZAC] Corps[60] on our right."[61]

Clearly there was a great deal of work to be done: "The backward state of communications necessitates a very large amount of labour, and the constant heavy shelling necessitates a further large number of men for maintenance alone." Manpower, however, was in short supply: "It is estimated that the total number of battalions required for work in VIII Corps area is eight, of this number it is at present impossible to provide more than three battalions from within the Corps."[62]

A carefully considered appraisal of "advantages" and "disadvantages" of retaining such a poor position followed in parts 6 and 7:

ADVANTAGES OF OUR POSITION
6. The main advantages to be derived from our position in the salient are:
    (a) <u>MORAL</u>. Passchendaele was one of the main objectives of our summer offensive, and was captured despite the enemy's most strenuous efforts.
    (b) It denies to the enemy close observation of some portion of our back areas.
    (c) It would greatly assist a spring offensive either from Poelcappelle towards Westroosebeke, or eastwards towards Moorslede and Menin.

As regards (b), it will be noticed that only negative advantages are claimed on the score of observation. The present British position offers few facilities for observation N or NE, and up to the present no satisfactory OP has been established in the salient.

DISADVANTAGES OF OUR POSITION
7. The disadvantages of our position are:
    (a) The frontline troops can be shelled from any point on an arc of 240 degrees.
    (b) There is no cover for supports or close reserves, and distances are so great that material can only be carried up with great difficulty.
    (c) The approaches are such that, with a very small effort, the enemy can make it impossible for us to reinforce the frontline by troops kept outside the salient. Conversely the area comprised within the salient is so small that the enemy could blot out the whole garrison by artillery fire at will, and the larger the garrison the greater would our losses be.

---

60 On 8 November, II ANZAC Corps relieved the I ANZAC Corps along the Passchendaele Ridge from Tiber southwards, as far as the Reutelbeek stream (SE of Polygon Wood). See Lieutenant-Colonel H. Stewart, *The New Zealand Division 1916-1919: A Popular History Based on Official Records* (Auckland: Whitcombe & Tombs, 1921), p. 298.
61 TNA: WO/95/821: 'Appreciation of the Situation on the VIII Corps Front: November 1917', VIII Corps War Diary.
62 Ibid.

(d) The "rent" in casualties which we pay for the occupation of the salient is extremely severe.
(e) Troops holding the frontline have so arduous a time that they will have little chance of "picking up" for a spring offensive
(f) The line has to be strongly supported by artillery. This necessitates a large proportion of available artillery being kept in the line without rest, and the guns are so far forward that they are subjected to close range fire from their flanks.

A contentious strategic poser followed this careful survey:

IS THE SALIENT WORTH KEEPING?
8. A consideration of the foregoing paragraphs leads to the question of whether it is worthwhile to maintain a position which was fought for and gained as a means to an end, and which, since the end was not achieved, has in itself so few advantages.

The answer to this question is largely dependant on whether or not there is to be a British offensive in the spring, and it can therefore be given only by the high command. It would appear, however, that if the British forces in Flanders are to be on the defensive in 1918, the moral and political advantages of remaining at Passchendaele are more than outweighed by the military disadvantage of clinging to so unfavourable a position.[63]

RECOMMENDATION
9. It is strongly urged, therefore, that unless a British offensive is to take place in this area in the spring, a policy of withdrawal [westward] to the Westhoek – Pilckem Ridge Line should be decided on, and that preparation of a strong defensive system in that neighbourhood be commenced at once.

It is further urged that if the policy of withdrawal from the salient be accepted, the retirement should take place as soon as a defensive position in the rear was prepared. Such a retirement, carried out in our own time, and as a surprise, could almost certainly be completed without loss. If, on the other hand, it was decided to postpone the withdrawal until the enemy should attack, there would be a great risk of our only two roads being destroyed by his fire and a very large number of guns being sacrificed.

A deliberate retirement 8,000 yards westwards to the Westhoek – Pilckem Ridge Line would relinquish the northern portion of the "eleven miles of the main ridge east

---

63 Aspinall was presentient in regard to the BEF's adoption of a defensive policy during the first half of 1918. British GHQ would not reveal this change of strategy until the following month.

of Ypres, including the village of Passchendaele and high ground of importance to the north of it" secured during three and a half months costly fighting. The suggested withdrawal, based on the logical outcome of pure attrition, made military sense. On the other hand, the "moral and political advantages of remaining at Passchendaele" could not be ignored.[64]

To give up territory seized after immense expenditures of both men and material during an offensive that was the British Empire's main effort for the year 1917 would, in addition to demonstrating the failure of Haig's preferred strategy, have adverse morale effects on the army, the civilian population at home and Great Britain's allies. Moreover, already strained relations between the Lloyd George Government and British GHQ would be further exacerbated if the meagre gains in Flanders were relinquished before year's end. Third Ypres was never just an attritional battle, so political and psychological factors took equal precedence for consideration as the campaign drew to a close. Strategic determinents were nevertheless of equal importance: British GHQ still planned to resume the offensive in early 1918. Second Army expected, come spring, to jump-off from advantageous positions on Passchendaele Ridge and push on to Roulers – a downhill advance of approximately five miles –Thourout and the Belgian coast. Prevailing logistical infrastructure difficulties would be improved and expanded throughout the winter months, whilst retention of the possessed heights provided desirable dry ground on which to spend the winter.[65]

Sir Henry Rawlinson, taking into consideration plans to clear the main ridge before 1917 ended, future plans for 1918 and the dismally obvious points made in Brigadier-General Aspinall's Appreciation concluded the Passchendaele Salient would have to be retained. It was, in any case, not BEF policy to sanction withdrawals of the kind contemplated by the BGGS VIII Corps; a decision of this magnitude was the exclusive purview of GHQ. The salient could, however, be rendered less vulnerable if satisfactory observation posts could be established over valleys to the north and NE. GHQ, Rawlinson noted in his diary, provided further incentive: "Tavish [Brigadier-General J.H. Davidson DMO GHQ] was here today but I missed him. He says that if D[ouglas] H[aig] considers the Third Army attack [at Cambrai] sufficiently

---

64 TNA: WO/95/821: 'Appreciation of the Situation on the VIII Corps Front: November 1917', VIII Corps War Diary and War Cabinet, *Report for the Year 1917* (London: HMSO, 1918), p.42.
65 The projected 1918 offensive was outlined by Lieutenant-General Sir L.E. Kiggell (CGS GHQ) during a conversation with the influential *Times* Military Correspondent Colonel Repington the previous October: 'We [British] should take the rest of the [Passchendaele] ridge and then continue next April, threatening the Hun coast defences on our left and Lille on our right, and extending our hold gradually until we reach the Dutch frontier, which was only 18 miles from Roulers. We should then clear the two ports (Zeebrugge and Ostend), establish railway communication with them, destroy the Hun aerodromes, and menace the right of the whole German line.' See Lieutenant-Colonel C. À Court Repington, *The First World War 1914-1918 Vol. 2* (London: Constable & Co., 1920), p. 102.

successful he will want me to have a further go at the ridge [,] so I am to prepare for it about the end of this month."⁶⁶

Sir Henry Rawlinson convened a conference, attended by Lieutenant-Generals Jacob, Hunter-Weston and Currie (GOC of the out-going Canadian Corps), at II Corps HQ on 18 November:

> I gave them their objectives for the next operation [,] which will go as far as the edge of Westroosebeke [.] The 32 will protect and prolong the flank [.] I left it to them to discuss the details [.] If we can get enough guns forward we shall do all right [,] but the II Corps command are the difficulty [.] Everyone is crying out for labour and there is none to be had [.] All help is required for II Corps [,] which I hope [will] be allowed to keep the 2 [British] Division [.] I will discuss this with DH tomorrow when I meet him at 9:45.⁶⁷

Thus the GOC Second Army dispensed with any designs to capture Westroosebeke and thereby clear the northern portion of Passchendaele Ridge; an advance as far as the environs of that town was all that was contemplated. Formal orders were issued on 21 November.⁶⁸ Following this, planning and preparations for the second phase of a step-by-step northern drive along the main ridge toward what was termed the "Passchendaele – Westroosebeke – Spriet Position" were set in motion. On 26 November 8th Division (VIII Corps) would make a short (100 to 300 yards) advance on a front of 1,020 yards from the apex of the salient; 32nd Division (II Corps) was chosen to safeguard and extend the flank by advancing 400 yards (on the right and left) to 700 yards (centre) on a front of 1,850 yards from the northern shoulder of the salient. The limited nature of the proposed advance bears comparison with the four 500-yard bounds (two made on narrow frontages) accomplished by Canadian

---

66 CAC: RWLN 1/9: Rawlinson Diary, 17 November 1917.
67 Ibid, 18 November 1917. GHQ did not allow II Corps to retain 2nd (Regular) Division (GOC Major-General C.E. Pereira), the latter formation was sent south to join Third Army reserve for the imminent offensive at Cambrai instead. Major Earl Stanhope (GSO 2 II Corps) subsequently remarked: 'It had been intended, should the weather permit, that a further big advance should be made and that we should endeavour before the winter to seize Westroosebeke and Stadenberg, our line then being designed to run westward through or north of the Forest of Houthulst. Such a line would have given us the whole of the high ground east and north of Ypres overlooking most of the Flanders plain. Owing, however, to the Caporetto disaster in Italy whither the British Army had to send seven [sic] divisions, and to our tank attack at Cambrai on November 20th our beloved 2nd Division, which had been returned to us to take part in this attack, was withdrawn again, and all further attacks in the Ypres Salient were abandoned [sic].' See Brian Bond (ed) *The War Memoirs of Earl Stanhope: General Staff Officer in France 1914-1918* (Brighton: Tom Donovan Editions, 2006), p. 149 and TNA: WO/95/643: 'II Corps G.S. 6/5', 9 November 1917, II Corps War Diary.
68 See Appendix IIIa.

Corps from 26 October to 10 November. These previous efforts, despite horrendous conditions and heavy losses, demonstrated what could be achieved following reasonable time allotments and methodical preparation.[69]

Major-General Shute (GOC 32nd Division) received a warning order for pending operations from II Corps on 16 November:

> Early in November, the 32nd Division, at that time resting around Lederzeele, were informed that they would move into the line at an early date in the neighbourhood of BELLEVUE and would attack northward with a view to improving our position at PASSCHENDAELE.[70]

The forwarded document clearly outlined Rawlinson's intention to flesh-out Second Army's position within the Passchendaele Salient:

> So far as can be foreseen, it will be necessary for your division to relieve the 1st Division on the front between approximately Vocation Farm on the right and the Paddebeek on the left.
>
> Further operations will then probably have to be undertaken to drive the enemy from the PASSCHENDAELE – HILL 50 – SPRIET position and so widen out the front and gain observation east of the WESTROOSEBEKE – STADEN Ridge.
>
> Though no definite orders have been received on the subject it is possible either –
> a) That the VIII Corps may operate on the right of the II Corps and be responsible for forming a flank down the slopes of the hill towards WRANGLE FARM and RACKET WOOD.
> b) That the II Corps (32nd Division) may have to take over the front as far as the PASSCHENDAELE – WESTROOSEBEKE Road and may itself be responsible for forming a right flank to the advance towards VALUATION HOUSES – HILL 50.

II Corps concluded by asking Shute to relate "briefly how in either of the above eventualities you would propose employing your division to gain the approximate line VALUATION HOUSES – HILL 50 – MULLET FARM – WESTWOOD HOUSE – and thence a line along the western edge of the WESTROOSEBEKE

---

69 A preliminary operation (scheduled for the night of 21/22 November) to establish strong posts on Hill 52 and at Vox Farm 'before the bigger attack is made' was subsequently cancelled. See CAC: RWLN 1/9: Rawlinson Diary, 20 November 1917, LHCMA: 'Notes of Army Commander's Conference at Chateau Lovie', 20 November 1917, Montgomery-Massingberd Papers, File 7/15, King's College, London and appendices IIIa b & c, IV a & b, V a & b.
70 TNA: WO/95/2370: After-action report, 'Part II, Plan of Operations, Section 1, General', 11 December 1917, 32nd Division War Diary.

Ridge in the vicinity of TOURNANT FARM."[71] Expectations of what awaited the Ypres front newcomers were based on previous battle reports, operation orders and frontline excursions by advanced parties of officers. One subaltern recalled provisional orders for an attack in the direction of Westroosebeke. This sobering document, issued the previous October, gave companies "eight minutes for every 100 yards, but even this pace proved in the course of the month to be far beyond the capacity of men in the prevailing conditions."[72]

Major-General Heneker (GOC 8th Division) considered the imminent Passchendaele relief a less than "alluring prospect." Somewhat perturbed, he petitioned – as acting GOC VIII Corps during Hunter-Weston's absence on leave – Second Army HQ to keep Canadian Corps in place "while the battle is on for the Passchendaele ridges." Sir Henry Rawlinson remained non-committal, although he promised to "go into it."[73] On the afternoon of 18 November Heneker, his division now responsible for VIII Corps' left sub-sector, met with Aspinall (BGGS VIII Corps), who related there was to be "another and rather more considerable local operation, in which troops of the VIII and II corps were to be engaged."[74] The attack, according to Heneker's diary, would occur on 26 November; the objective was to "drive [the] Boche off the edge of the plateau we are on."[75] Subsequent conference minutes relate that offensive operations would be resumed by Second Army "about the end of the month" on the fronts of II Corps and VIII Corps: "The objective of the VIII Corps will be the capture of VENISON TRENCH, thus obtaining observation to the east, while at the same time the II Corps will capture the line VOLT FARM – V.23 central (vicinity of Mallet Wood)[76], improving our position on the ridge, and making

---

71 TNA: WO/95/643: 'II Corps G.S. 6, 16 November 1917', II Corps War Diary.
72 Charles Douie, *The Weary Road: Recollections of a Subaltern of Infantry* (Stevenage: Tom Donovan Publishing, 1988 reprint of 1929 edition), p. 181.
73 IWM: 66/541/1: Heneker Diary, 1-7 and 8-13 November 1917. Heneker, all hopes of deployment to Italy dashed, first received notice to take over the line near Passchendaele in mid-October: 'If we don't go we stay in this Corps, and about the middle of December, move up and take over the line about Passendael [sic], east of Ypres, for about a month, and then come out to train for the spring offensive.' Sir Julian Byng (GOC Third Army) had, according to Lieutenant-Colonel Beddington (GSO 1), requested 8th Division's transfer to the Cambrai sector. GHQ 'had taken the view that we were not fit for battle yet. Byng pressed so hotly for us that it was decided to see what we ourselves thought … Our view that end of November was the date [for battle preparedness] made us rather too late for Third Army attack and so Byng was told he could not have us.' See Edward Beddington, 'My Life'(UK: Privately Printed, 1960), pp. 117-18.
74 Lieutenant Colonel J.H. Boraston & Captain Cyril E.O. Bax, *The Eighth Division: 1914-1918* (London: Naval & Military Press reprint of 1926 edition), p. 163.
75 IWM: 66/541/1: Heneker Diary, 18 November 1917.
76 'From VOLT FARM a very good view on the ground to the east and SE of WESTROOSEBEKE' could 'be obtained and the 'capture of this locality' was deemed to be of 'considerable importance.' Hostile 'sniping fire' from Mallet Wood (situated in low-lying ground just north of Vat Cottages Ridge) inflicted heavy losses on 2nd RMF

our hold on PASSCHENDAELE doubly secure."⁷⁷ The proposed operation would, if successful, open out the west side of the salient whilst simultaneously carrying the British line "sufficiently far northward along the ridge to give us observation into the valleys running up to the Passchendaele plateau from the north and east." Occupation of these new vistas would also prevent the enemy from massing troops along the ridge line's reverse slope thus reducing potential threats throughout the winter months.⁷⁸

Sir Douglas Haig, keeping one strategic eye on Flanders as the opening of the Cambrai offensive approached, made one important tactical suggestion during a meeting with Sir Henry Rawlinson on 19 November:

> At 9:45 a.m. I saw Sir H. Rawlinson commanding Second Army. He told me of his views to extend the front northwards of Passchendaele. He does not wish to take Westroosebeke. I suggested attack by small units at night, because up to the present nothing of this nature has been attempted by us at the Ypres battlefront. I directed Rawlinson to work out his plan, but not to give effect to them until the result of tomorrow's attack is known, and I can decide on our future plans.⁷⁹

Rawlinson, writing in his diary that evening, remarked: "DH is not in any hurry [for a continuance of operations], but if we wait [,] I shall have no fresh troops."⁸⁰ His concern was no doubt engendered by the dispatch of British divisions to Italy and requirements for Third Army's forthcoming offensive. These factors, combined with a politically contentious manpower shortage, would limit the number of troops available for any subsequent operations intended to improve the situation on the Passchendaele

---

during the 10 November assault. It was, therefore, 'desirable' that the shattered woodland strongpoint 'be cleared if possible.' TNA: WO/95/2370: 'Notes to Accompany Special Intelligence: Maps of the Area V.15 – V.30' November 1917, 32nd Division War Diary.

77 LHCMA: 'Notes of Army Commander's Conference at Chateau Lovie', 20 November 1917, Montgomery-Massingberd Papers, File 7/15, King's College, London.

78 Boraston & Bax, *The Eighth Division*, p. 163. Conversely, Sir Douglas Haig, writing in his diary in the immediate aftermath of the proposed operation, observed: 'The object [of the attack] was to obtain certain points which gave the Enemy observation westwards on to our communications.' See Haig diary entry 2 December 1917 in 'The First World War Political, Social and Military Manuscript Sources: Series One: The Haig Papers from the National Library of Scotland, Part I Haig's Autograph Great War Diary', Reel 5, and Sheffield & Bourne (eds), *Douglas Haig*, p. 355.

79 Haig diary entry 19 November 1917 in 'The First World War Political, Social and Military Manuscript Sources: Series One: The Haig Papers from the National Library of Scotland, Part I Haig's Autograph Great War Diary', Reel 5 and Sheffield & Bourne (eds), *Douglas Haig*, p. 345. Haig's evident desire to resume operations at this time was in keeping with the post-strategic policy 'to progress as far as Passchendaele' related in his official despatch of 25 December 1917. See Lieutenant-Colonel J.H. Boraston, *Sir Douglas Haig's Despatches: December 1915- April 1919* (London: J.M. Dent & Sons, 1919), pp. 130, 132.

80 CAC: RWLN 1/9: Rawlinson Diary, 19 November 1917.

Ridge before year's end.[81] Thus the projected night attack, all schemes to capture the Passchendaele – Hill 50 – Spriet Position abandoned, was subsequently downgraded – a sideshow to on-going offensive operations at Cambrai – on 25 November from "tenth phase" to that of "local operation" conducted by VIII Corps and II Corps.

1.3 German Defensive Measures

Two German army corps (*Gruppe Staden* and *Gruppe Ypern*) were situated opposite the Passchendaele Salient and its environs.[82] *Gruppe Staden* was organised and established between *Gruppes Diksmuide* and *Ypern* following the First Battle of Passchendaele after it was recognised that the British offensive was being directed northwards in an attempt to clear the ridge as far as Westroosebeke.[83] The boundary between the *Staden* and *Ypren Gruppes* ran NE along the road from Vindictive Crossroads to Oostnieuwkerke.[84] By mid-November, the left division of *Gruppe Staden* and right division of *Gruppe Ypern* were responsible for the Passchendaele plateau from Passchendaele village to Vat Cottages Ridge. Adjoining defensive arrangements for both divisions were, nonetheless, somewhat contradistinctive.[85] *Gruppe Ypern's* right

---

81   See Keith Grieves, 'The 'Recruiting Margin' in Britain: Debates on Manpower during the Third Battle of Ypres' in Liddle (ed), *Passchendaele in Perspective*, pp. 390-405.
82   A *Gruppe* [Group] was a fixed corps command assigned, as circumstances directed, a greater or lesser number of infantry divisions. 'The previous year, during the battle of the Somme, it had become clear to the German Army that the Corps level of command was critical to the conduct of the contact battle and that the pressures of modern major battles required a flexible approach. Each of the corps was renamed a 'Group' and was so organised as to be able to take under command varying numbers of divisions as they rotated through the battle area. From time to time they themselves would be relieved, but they were expected to carry out longer tours of duty, to build up expertise over a particular area and thus provide essential continuity.' The Fourth Army was divided into three *Gruppe* sectors (*Diksmuide, Ypern, Wijtschate*) during July 1917. See Hermann Cron, *Imperial German Army 1914-18: Organisation, Structure, Orders-of-Battle* (Solihull: Helion & Company, 2002), pp. 87-88 and Sheldon, *The German Army at Passchendaele*, p. 40.
83   Bean, *The Australian Imperial Force in France 1917 Vol. IV*, p. 928.
84   See TNA: WO/95/643: 'Map A. Showing Enemy Dispositions, Line of Resistance and assembly Positions of Reserve Battalions to Accompany II Corps O.O. 167', 22 November 1917, II Corps War Diary.
85   The German defences are described as they were following the Anglo-Canadian assault of 10 November. Captured German maps indicate the Passchendaele Salient was divided into a left 'Passchendaele Sector' and right 'Westroosebeke Sector.' The line of *Gruppe Staden's* left division extended from the Lekkerboterbeek stream inclusive to Vindictive Crossroads; the line of *Gruppe Ypern's* right division continued from the vicinity of Vindictive Crossroads to south of Passchendaele Village. Divisional rotation in the former's left sub-sector during 11-30 November was as follows: *199th Reserve* (to night of 16/17 November), *4th* (night of 16/17 November to night of 21/22 November), *199th Reserve* (night of 21/22 to night of 30 November/1 December). Divisions rotating in and out of the latter's right sub-sector during the same period were: *44th Reserve* (to 14

division (responsible for *Abschnitt A* or sub-sector A) occupied two breastworks – known to the British as Southern Redoubt and Northern Redoubt respectively – north of Passchendaele.[86] Venison Trench, a shallow, muddy furrow extending in an undeviating line for approximately 600 yards, conjoined both redoubts in a conventional trench configuration.[87] The continued defence of what was more or less an orthodox linear defensive system, a conspicuous deviation from the conceived position warfare doctrine at this stage of the campaign, was based on local tactical necessity.

Defensive dispositions known as *die Leer des Gefechtsfeldes* (invisible garrison) were first introduced by *Fourth Army* as one of a number of *OHL* inspired amendments on 23 October.[88] This was part of the update to established defence doctrine adopted in the aftermath of British "bite and hold" attacks from 20 September to 4 October. The vaunted *Eingreifdivisionen* (counter-attack divisions), heretofore an often decisive component to the staggered counter-attacks that blunted repeated British assaults, no longer encountered an overextended enemy pressing forward beyond the range of supporting artillery. Deadly protective barrages and a solidly established defence of captured objectives foiled German attempts to exploit the attackers' weakness with large-scale counter-strokes.[89] The new defensive measures, in a carefully considered response to this disquieting operational development, called for *Eingreifdivision* to be "brought up wholly or in part so close" behind each line-holding or *Stellungsdivision* that the former would be within the zone of the enemy's long-range fire and could, if necessary, intervene at once in the battle. German military authorities estimated that under "normal conditions, and with divisions at full strength, two divisions assembled in depth in this manner should be able to hold a frontage of 5,000 yards." Severe weather conditions, intense bombardments

---

November), *25th* (14 November to 20 November), *44th* (20 to 26 November), *25th* (26 November). See TNA: WO/157/120 and 121: Intelligence Summaries, November 1917, Second Army Intelligence File.

86 Excavated in late 1916 and early 1917, the redoubts were part of the *Flandern II* defences. A large German war cemetery, destroyed during subsequent fighting, was situated just south of Northern Redoubt along the present-day *Grote Roeselarestraat*.

87 Discrepancies occur when attempting to delineate divisional sector responsibilities of *Gruppe Staden's* left and *Gruppe Ypern's* right. Contemporary British intelligence maps show Northern Redoubt in occupation by *Gruppe Ypern's* right division while a sketch map found in the relevant German regimental history places the redoubt under the aegis of *Gruppe Staden's* left Division. See various 'Situation' maps in TNA: WO/95/643: II Corps War Diary, WO/157/287 and 288, II Corps Intelligence Files and Alexander von Hartmann, *Das Infanterie Regiment Grossherzog von Sachsen (5. Thüringisches) Nr. 94 im Weltkrieg* (Berlin: Verlag von Klasing & Co., 1921), *Skizze 32*.

88 Wynne, *If Germany Attacks*, pp. 222-23.

89 Robert T. Foley, 'The Other Side of the Wire: The German Army in 1917' in Peter Dennis & Jeffrey Grey (eds), *1917: Tactics, Training and Technology* (Commonwealth of Australia, Australian History Military Publications, 2007), pp. 174-75. See also, Jonathan Boff, *Haig's Enemy: Crown Prince Rupprecht and Germany's War on the Western Front* (Oxford: Oxford University Press, 2018), pp. 178-83 for a novel reassessment of *Fourth Army's* defensive arrangements during Third Ypres.

Venison Trench winter 1917-18. (Author)

and "the failing quality and quantity" of manpower had halved the originally proposed frontage to 2,500 yards by the close of the campaign.[90]

The application of the new defence organisation led to the creation of a new "defence unit of two divisions, one close up behind the other", under the front divisional (*Stellungsdivision*) commander. This arrangement permitted command and control cohesion to continue once a *Stellungsdivision* became heavily engaged. Subsequent *Gegenstoss* (formal, deliberate counter-stroke supported by artillery) was, if deemed necessary; to be carried out by an *Eingreifdivision* echeloned to the rear. Thus *Eingreifdivisionen* would be placed, on arrival in the forward area, under operational control of the *Stellungsdivision* commander whose proximity to events allowed for on-the-spot decision making.[91] Available artillery batteries remained, as per doctrine adopted in late 1916, under his authority: "The commander of a *Stellungsdivision* was assisted by a newly created divisional artillery commander. Prior to the new doctrine, artillery was primarily a corps-level asset. With the shift to the division as the primary tactical unit, came a redistribution of artillery assets."[92]

---

90 Wynne, *If Germany Attacks*, pp. 222-23. Wynne also observed that the 'invisible garrison' was 'only rendered practicable in such conditions by inter-battalion reliefs within the front division every two days, and by inter-divisional reliefs every six days; so that each battalion of the two divisions was in the front line for only two days in twelve.'
91 Ibid. pp. 222-24.
92 Foley, 'The Other Side of the Wire' in Dennis & Grey (eds), *1917*, pp. 167-68.

The new two-division formation had its origins in a 9 October 1917 *OHL* memorandum – inspired by *Generalquartiermeister* Erich Ludendorff – detailing the desired method of *Eingreifdivisionen* deployment. *Stellungsdivisionen* were now, in principal, to use organic reserves to drive the enemy from areas of responsibility.[93] The Germans were thus faced with the problem of concealing two divisions, deployed 8,000 yards in depth, on the barren, shell-swept Passchendaele Ridge. Their immediate solution was to adopt the aforementioned *die Leer des Gefechtsfeldes* arrangements. Shell holes provided the necessary cover:

> There was no entrenched position or anything resembling a connected trench system, which the enemy's artillery could have destroyed in a few hours; our lines were such that they were unrecognisable to the enemy's ground or air observers. There was no lack of accommodation, wet and filthy though it was; for every crater made by the heavy shells was a potential shelter for a machine-gun nest or a few men, with a tent or a strip of corrugated iron as their only head-cover and a few planks as their only chairs or beds.[94]

Eingreifdivisionen units were expected to shelter in the cellars of villages and farms in areas immediately behind designated *Stellungsdivisionen*.

The *Westheer* began organising its defences into two zones (*Vorfeldzone* and *Grosskampfzone*) at the close of 1916..[95] This general arrangement remained, with

---

93 'If this was not possible, counter-strokes by *Eingreif* troops are only possible if the operations are launched by powerful forces (both infantry and artillery), are concentrated and swift (within a few hours) and well supported by artillery. To facilitate this it is important that the troops are placed in good accommodation outside the range of the mass of the enemy artillery. They should be concentrated by regiments and have good communications with the artillery.' KA HKR 90: 'Chefs de Generalstabs des Feldheers 1 a Nr. 67059 op. Gr. H. Qu., den 9. Oktober 1917' quoted in Sheldon, *The German Army at Passchendaele*, p. 227.

94 Wynne, *If Germany Attacks*, p. 223. This quote was gleaned from the history of *Reserve Infanterie Regiment Nr. 10*. (*11th Reserve Division*), which was deployed near Passchendaele from November 1917 to January 1918. See Intelligence Section of the General Staff, American Expeditionary Forces, *Histories of Two Hundred and Fifty-One Divisions of the German Army Which Participated in the War 1914-1918* (London: London Stamp Exchange, 1989 reprint of 1920 edition), p. 203.

95 "The concepts of flexible defence and the centrality of the Division were incorporated into a new manual, 'Grundsatze für die Führung in der Abwehrschlacht im Stellungskrieg' ('Principles of Command in the Defensive Battle in Position Warfare'), issued on 1 December 1916, and into 'Allegemeines über Stellungsbau' (Principles of the Construction of Positions') issued on 15 December 1916. These two manuals, together the new doctrine for defensive warfare, enshrined the ideas of elastic area defence." See Foley, 'The Other Side of the Wire' in Dennis & Grey (eds), *1917*, pp. 164-65. For contemporary documents relating to the development and organisation of the German defence during the closing weeks of Third Ypres see KA HKR 229: Sixt von Armin memorandum 'Armee-Oberkommando 4: Abt. Ia/g. Nr. 51/Nov. A. Hq. den 2.11.17', Kronprinz

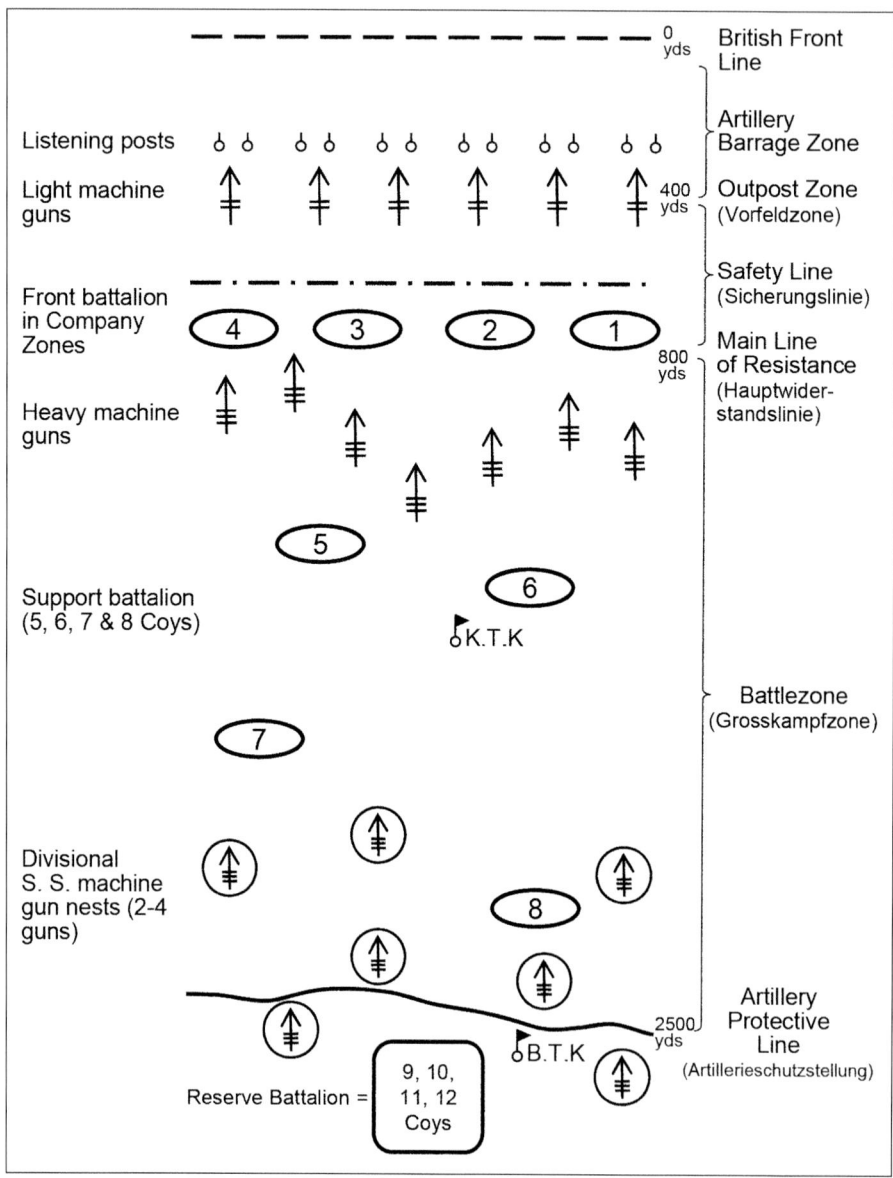

Defence Organisation of a German Regiment on the Passchendaele Ridge November 1917

periodic adjustments in organisation and application, in place throughout the *Flandernschlacht*. The recent attempt to counter effective British tactics by packing the forward area with additional troops had, nonetheless, proved disastrous on 4 October. Frontline battalions were now, in the aftermath of consequent catastrophic losses, arranged in groups of shell holes. These formed a *Vorfeldzone* (outpost zone or what Ludendorff described as a "narrow strip of territory") of double sentry posts some 300-500 yards in depth and 400 yards or less from the British outpost line. Companies defending this area were "given areas or zones, instead of lines to hold …"[96] At the immediate rear of this foremost zone was the *Sicherungslinie* where the outpost garrison would, if pressed by the enemy, retire first. This safety or security line was, as an additional defensive measure, only occupied at night. Approximately 400 yards behind lay the *Hauptwiderstandslinie* (main line of resistance), which was normally "some defined bank or track across the regiment's sector" fronting the mutually supporting fortified farms, pillboxes and shell hole positions of the *Grosskampfzone*.[97] Troops driven into the *Sicherungslinie* were, if unable to contain a hostile assault, supposed to retire and reinforce the *Hauptwiderstandslinie* defenders against a rapidly developing large-scale attack. General von Kuhl (*Chef des Generalstabes Heeresgruppe Kronprinz Rupprecht*) wrote of this elastic arrangement:

> The foremost shell crater area to a depth of 500 to 1,000 yards was to be considered merely a Vorfeld and only to be occupied by a thin line of sentries with a few machine-guns. In face of a big offensive these few troops were to retire to the Hauptwiderstandslinie at the back of the advanced zone, while the artillery were at once to lay down and maintain a dense barrage of shell in front of it.[98]

Vorfeldzone garrisons were expected to withdraw only if pressed by a major attack. Kuhl recognised the inherent tactical conundrum that beset the defenders of Ludendorff's so-called "narrow strip of territory" from the start: Was it possible to differentiate a hostile patrol or local attack from a large-scale attack? "Was it always possible to tell one from the other? And was it not possible that a thin line of men, who could count on no support, would feel that they had been abandoned and so tend

---

Rupprecht memorandums 'Ia/II Nr. 69778 op. Gr.Hq.U den 10.11.17', 'Iad Nr. 101 Nov. Geh. A.H.Qu. 16.11.17' and Ludendorff memorandum '11. Nr. 71 191 op. Gr. H. Qu., 24 November 1917'.
96 Wynne, *If Germany Attacks*, p. 222.
97 Ludendorff *op.cit.* in Sheldon, *The German Army at Passchendaele*, p. 226, Wynne, *If Germany Attacks*, p. 222 and KA HKR 244: 'Kampfuerfahren bei englischen Angriffen: Lehren und Folgerumgen aus den Kämpfen des letzen Schlachttages (Kampf um Passchendaele am 6.11.17)'.
98 Wynne, *If Germany Attacks*, p. 220.

to withdraw even earlier?" This part of the scheme had an "artificial air" that the men never fully comprehended.[99]

The *Grosskampfzone* extended 2,500 yards from the *Hauptwiderstandslinie* to *Artillerieschutzstellung* (artillery protective line). A *Stellungsdivision's* support and reserve battalions were positioned thereabouts for *Gegenangriff* (automatic counter-attacks) toward the embattled main line of resistance the moment word was received of an enemy breakthrough. A clear distinction was maintained between local *Gegenangriff* and formal, deliberate *Gegenstoss*; the variance was in timing. *Gegenangriff* by support and reserve battalions would only be sanctioned if the defensive barrage failed to halt advancing British infantry within the *Vorfeldzone*; a *Stellungsdivision* commander set the designated *Eingreifdivision* in motion for *Gegenstoss* only if the earlier *Gegenangriff* failed to achieve its objective.[100]

Venison Trench and its redoubts, although provided with the prescribed *Vorfeldzone*, evolved into a doctrinally anomalous linear *Hauptwiderstandslinie* position following Canadian gains on 10 November. Situated where a firm hold could be maintained on the sloping eastern contours of Passchendaele Ridge, its reverse slope defences prevented direct observation into valleys to the north and east. Thus the British were denied a corresponding panoramic view, seized after so much blood and effort from 4 October to 6 November, available southward along the ridge from Broodseinde to Passchendaele village.

The left sub-sector (*Abschnitt B*) of *Gruppe Staden's* left division continued along dry ground west of Northern Redoubt. Astride the east side of the straight Passchendaele – Westroosebeke road was a concrete pillbox designated on British maps as "Teall Cottage".[101] This tiny shell-scarred edifice was ideally placed to cover the northern approach to the Venison Trench defences. Beyond the main thoroughfare lay numerous outworks blocking the ridge route to Westroosebeke. Defences in this sector differed from those of Venison Trench: in keeping with the idea of *die Leere des Gefechtsfeldes*, there was no definite line, but "a series of fortified localities and improved shell holes."[102]

Hill 52, a local promontory 200 yards west of Teall Cottage, was the key position in *Abschnitt B*. The Germans knew this elevation, along with the flat-topped high ground

---

99 General Hermann von Kuhl, *Der Weltkrieg 1914-1918 Vol.2* (Berlin: Verlag Wilhelm Kolk, 1929), pp. 128-29.
100 KA HKR 244: 'Kampfuerfahren bei englischen Angriffen: Lehren und Folgerungem aus den Kämpfen des letzen Schlachttages (Kampf um Passchendaele am 6.11.17)' and Foley, 'The Other Side of the Wire', Dennis & Grey (eds), *1917*, p 163.
101 Teall Cottage was likely named after Captain G.H. Teall who subsequently became A/AA & QMG of 32nd Division on 27 November 1917. The site is now occupied by a brick utility tower and nearby pig farm.
102 See TNA: WO/95/2370: After-action report, 'Part II, Plan of Operations, Section I, General', 11 December 1917, 32nd Division War Diary.

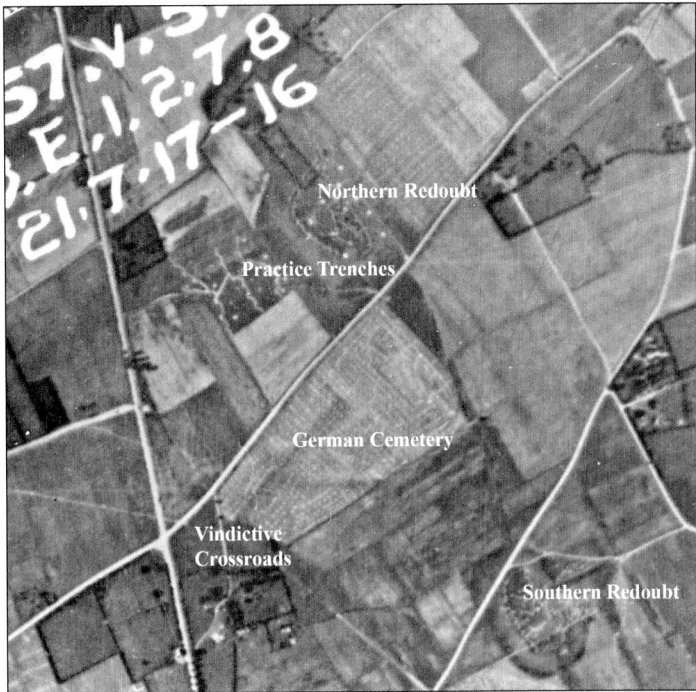

Venison Trench and redoubts summer 1917. (Memorial Museum Passchendaele 1917)

around it, as *Höhenrücken* (high ridge) *Passendale*.[103] It provided good observation of the British forward area "from almost any part of the [Passchendaele] ridge north of Vindictive Cross Roads…"[104] British maps designated this rise (an objective of 1st Canadian Division on 10 November) as the highest point on the northern extremity of the Passchendaele Ridge. Some, according to David Schurman, viewed the use of the word "ridge" to describe their high ground objectives as a misnomer – an illusion gradually dispelled during the Canadian advance:

> Strictly speaking, the expression is geographically accurate, but to Canadian eyes the slope was so imperceptible that the advancing troops almost doubted its existence, until they were on top and looked back over the slowly undulating sea of mud toward Ypres.[105]

---

103 See Hartmann, *Das Infanterie Regiment Grossherzog von Sachsen (5. Thüringisches) Nr. 94 im Weltkrieg*, p. 238.
104 TNA: WO/157/287: 'II Corps Summary of Information, 13 November 1917', II Corps Intelligence File.
105 David Schurman, 'Passchendaele: The Final Phase', *History of the First World War*, London: BPC Publishing, Vol. 6 No. 5 (1971).

This deceptive upland contributed to post-operational uncertainties about the actual situation at Hill 52. Historian Daniel Dancocks asserts, based on statements found in the battalion after-action report that 10th Canadian Battalion secured the tactically important elevation on the evening of 10 November.[106] Post-war published official accounts also generally avouch, regardless of contrary contemporary evidence, that 1st Canadian Division captured Hill 52 along with its other assigned objectives. Nevertheless, a Second Army intelligence summary, written immediately after the Second Battle of Passchendaele, stated: "The left flank of the Canadians is thrown back in the *vicinity of Hill 52* (My emphasis) and rests on Venture Farm."[107] A II Corps intelligence summary outlined what was known by 13 November:

> It is almost certain that the enemy's main defensive line prior to the 10th inst. was on the reverse, or northeastern slope of Hill 52, and so far beyond immediate local counter-attacks, he has made no great effort to prevent us from reaching the southwestern slopes, or possibly the top of this hill.
>
> To obtain command over the area which lies in the triangle Westroosebeke – Vindictive Crossroads – Oostnieuwkerke, and to discover the enemy's battery positions [,] it would be necessary for us to advance to the false crest on the northeastern slope of Hill 52. It is apparently on, or near this false crest that the enemy's line runs [,] and he appears to be organising artillery so that he can deny it to us by artillery fire.[108]

Thus this vital hillock remained, notwithstanding earlier Canadian gains on its SW slope, an important topographical asset to the German defenders.[109] *Fourth*

---

106 Daniel G. Dancocks, *Gallant Canadians: The Story of the Tenth Canadian Infantry Battalion 1914-1919* (Calgary: Calgary Highlanders Regimental Funds Foundation, 1990), p. 151.
107 TNA: WO/157/120: 'Second Army Daily Intelligence Summary, 10 November 1917', Second Army Intelligence Files.
108 TNA: WO/157/287: 'II Corps Summary of Information, 13 November 1917', II Corps Intelligence File.
109 The British Official History provides a general summary of Canadian Corps and II Corps objectives for 10 November; Hill 52 is not specifically referred to. The Canadian Official History states that 1st Canadian Division advanced the line to the final objective. Dancocks observed by 'dawn next morning [11 November], Hill 52 was in Canadian hands.' To substantiate this he quotes a report claiming 'that we [Canadians] commanded the whole slope to our right front.' The slope in question, most likely the southwestern one, placed the Canadian line below the hill's summit. Exhaustive efforts to ascertain if Hill 52 was seized in its entirety on 10 November or lost in the days leading up to the night operation, led to the discovery of contemporary intelligence reports that contradict the former and make no mention of the latter. It would appear that Hill 52 was never fully secured by 10th Battalion. Furthermore, its subsequent loss after 10 November is not recorded in the war diaries or intelligence summaries of Second Army, Canadian Corps, VIII Corps, II Corps or various attached divisions. It is unlikely, given the perceived tactical importance of the promontory that these formations would have failed to note the event. See Edmonds, *Military Operations:*

Army HQ was equally uncertain about the local situation in the aftermath of the last British attack, a secret situation map dated 1st December denoting the area extending from Hill 52 to the vicinity of Southern Redoubt in a line of question marks.[110] The remaining defences in this sector (the scene of 1st Division's debacle) extended in a loose collection of fortified farms across the protruding tongue of Vat Cottages Ridge. Strongpoints at Volt, Void, Vocation, Virile and Vox farms and Veal and Vat Cottages dotted the area.[111] There were also a number of pillboxes and fortified positions exclusive of these buttressed locales.[112]

Approximately 400 yards NE of the German forward posts on Vat Cottages Ridge lay a scarcely discernable spinney known as Mallet Copse. This shattered clump of fallen trees and overlapping shell holes, situated at the junction of the former outcrop with the western slope of the main Passchendaele Ridge, contained a cluster of battered trenches, dugouts and shelters to house supporting troops. Situated across a shallow valley just 300 yards to the north was a soggy, confused wilderness of bare and broken timberland known as Mallet Wood.[113]

The established *Vorfeldzone* was approximately 150 yards deep opposite Southern Redoubt and 400 yards opposite Venison Trench and Northern Redoubt. Its maximum depth from the vicinity of Hill 52 to Vat Cottages was 200 yards. Behind, comprising the established *Hauptwiderstandslinie*, were Venison Trench and its redoubts. II Corps intelligence officers encountered difficulties when trying to determine the exact course and depth of the comparatively indistinct *Vorfeldzone* and *Hauptwiderstandslinie* defences covering Hill 52 and Vat Cottages Ridge: the former appeared to extend (east to west) from below Hill 52 astride firm ground to Vox Farm and SW of Vat Cottages; the latter appeared to be situated north and east of Hill 52, just north of Vox Farm, along a contiguous trench line extending WNW for approximately 500 yards from just north of Vox Farm to south of Mallet Copse, Vat Cottages inclusive and the road south of Veal Cottages.[114]

France and Belgium 1917 Vol.2, pp. 358-59, Nicholson, *Canadian Expeditionary Force*, p. 326 and Daniel G. Dancocks, *Legacy of Valour: The Canadians at Passchendaele* (Edmonton: Hurtig Publishers, 1986), pp. 173-74. The summit of Hill 52 can be found in a field just south of a factory parking lot. Its immediate environs are also the site of a number of large greenhouses and a lovely white *huis* with beautifully manicured lawn.

110 See BA-MA PH3/Karte 36: 'Gruppe Staden Nahzielkarte', 1 December 1917.
111 An aerial photograph of Volt Farm, taken by the RFC 'at a very low altitude' on 15 November, 'shows the actual structure of the building to have completely disappeared…' See TNA: WO/157/287: 'II Corps Summary of Information', 17 November, 1917, II Corps Intelligence.
112 A prisoner captured on 10 November stated that Vat Cottages 'had several direct [artillery] hits and is uninhabitable.' See TNA: WO/157/287: 'II Corps Intelligence Summary', 12 November 1917, II Corps Intelligence File.
113 Both copse and wood no longer exist.
114 TNA: WO/95/2370: 'Notes to Accompany Special Intelligence Maps of the Area V.15 to V.30' November 1917, 32nd Division War Diary. There has, according to Robert Foley,

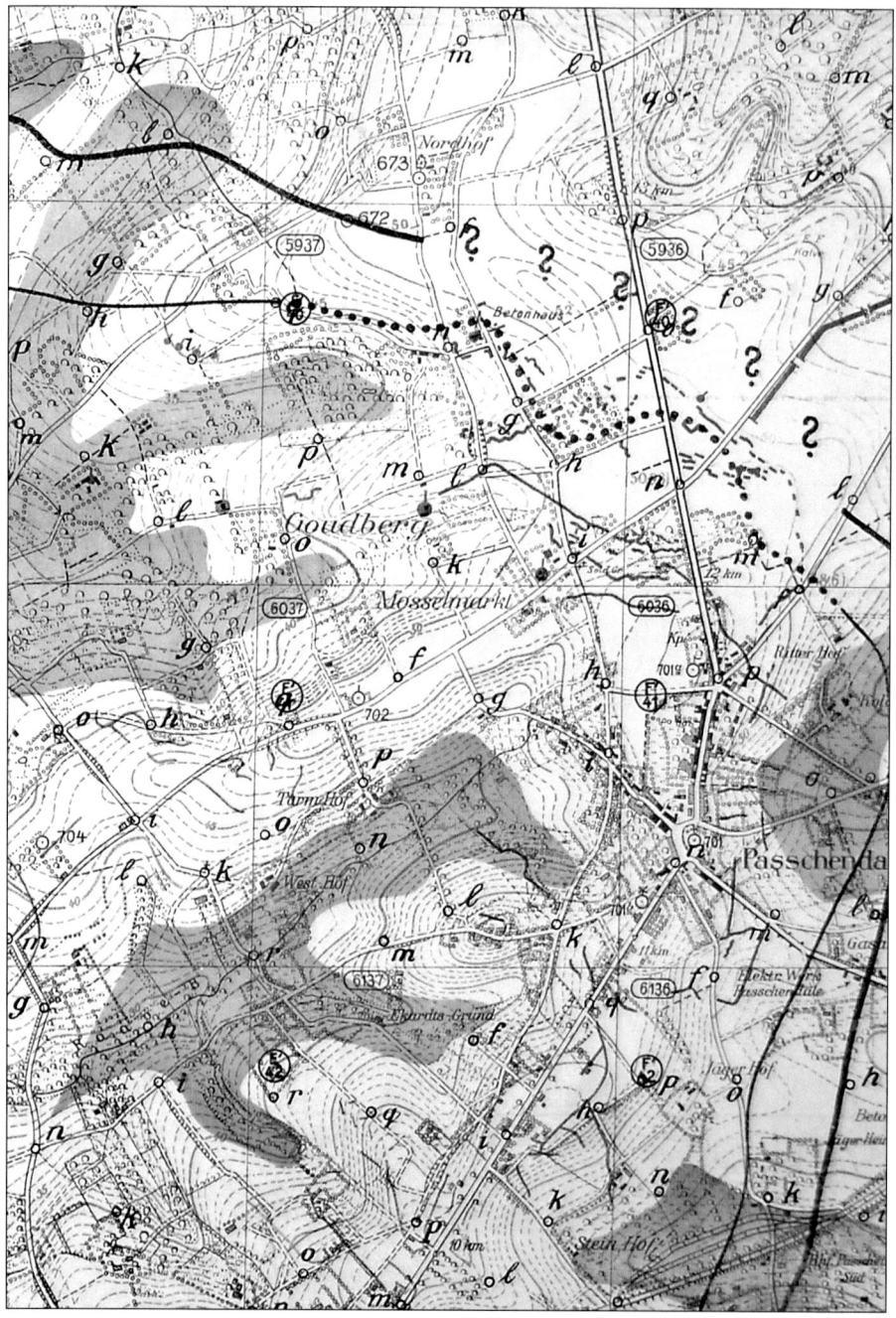

Detail from *Gruppe Staden* situation map 1 December 1917. Shaded areas denote inundated parts of the battlefield. (BA-MA PH3)

Antecedents 73

German pillboxes autumn 1917. (Author)

Three regiments of nine battalions of *Gruppe Staden's* left *Stellungsdivision*, along with one regiment of three battalions of *Gruppe Ypern's* right *Stellungsdivision*, were responsible for a line (extending from Southern Redoubt exclusive to north of Tournant Farm) 2,850 yards in length by 1 December.[115] The remaining two regiments of the latter clung to Southern Redoubt and low-lying positions east of Passchendaele village. Designated front, support and reserve battalions were echeloned the approximately 2,500 yards from the *Vorfeldzone* to the *Artillerieschutzstellung*.[116] Forward battalions defended *Vorfeldzone* and *Hauptwiderstandslinie* positions[117] whilst support battalions were deployed behind the *Grosskampfzone*. Reserve battalions garrisoned

"been a tendency in the historiography to introduce linearity to the new defensive system that was not the doctrine's intention. Although the doctrine discusses two separate combat zones, these were not necessarily designed to be completely separate areas. The new doctrine emphasised that the size and location of the *Vorfeldzone* and *Grosskampfzone* were dependent on the particular terrain of a sector and could actually overlap. In other words, the two zones did not have to be two completely separate areas. In many respects, the difference between the two zones was in function. The *Vorfeldzone*, which would be more exposed to enemy observation and hence knowledge, was designed to be strong enough for 'ordinary trench warfare.' It also prevented the enemy from seeing and knowing the features behind this forward zone. The new doctrine recognised that to hold this zone in the face of a determined large-scale offensive would be prohibitively costly in manpower terms. In the face of such an attack, the *Grosskampfzone* was to be the area in which the battle was fought. This area would be unfamiliar terrain to an enemy, who prior to a large-scale attack would not have been able to penetrate the *Vorfeldzone*." Indefinite aspects of this applied defence scheme were subsequently recognised in the 32nd Division's intelligence notes which concluded that boundaries of the main line of resistance (*Hauptwiderstandslinie*) were constantly changing. See Foley, 'The Other Side of the Wire', Dennis & Grey (eds), *1917*, pp. 166-67.

115 The average strength of a German battalion was approximately 640 men. This seemingly small complement was backed up by the increased firepower of 12 08/15 light machine-guns. See Wynne, *If Germany Attacks*, p. 207.
116 The German defences were sited north, NE, east and SE of where the *Flandern I* and *Flandern II* lines intersected. Second Army penetrated the junction of both positions during October-November, thus forcing the defenders to echelon into a re-entrant from Goudberg Copse to Tiber.
117 II Corps intelligence observed that 32nd Division's proposed assault involved the 'capture of practically all the area occupied by the front battalions of the centre and left [German] regiments. It also effects [sic] the right regiment insomuch as it threatens the isolation of its forward battalion.' Prisoners related that 'support battalions are 500 yards to 600 metres in the rear, but they are probably distributed over considerable areas as the localities they occupy have been continuously and heavily shelled.' Detailed dispositions of companies were 'almost impossible to determine', but it appeared 'tolerably certain that all four companies of each battalion are forward and maintain groups pushed forward between main line of resistance and our frontline.' See TNA: WO/95/2370: Notes to Accompany Special Intelligence Maps of the Area V.15 to V.30' November 1917, 32nd Division War Diary.

the *Artillerieschutzstellung* and vicinity.¹¹⁸ Beyond this lay *Eingreifdivisionen* in immediate reserve.

A *Stellungsdivision's* three attached regiments, Jack Sheldon has observed, readily diversified and delegated command responsibilities amongst component battalion commanders throughout 1917. The *Kampftruppenkommandeur* or *KTK* (Commander of Forward Troops) deployed his battalion in the frontline. Approximately 600 to 800 metres behind was the support battalion under the command of the *Bereitschaftstruppenkommandeur* or *BTK* (Commander of Supporting Troops). The third battalion occupied reserve positions under command of the *Reservetruppenkommandeur* or *RTK*. The *BTK* was, in the event of an attack, to be sent forward "a further 300 yards or so, ready to participate in the defence in whatever way events dictated they were needed", whilst the *RTK* would reinforce if necessary. "Without any doubt, the key man in each sector was the *KTK*. His command responsibilities went well beyond that of a normal battalion commander. Whenever possible he and his small staff (including an artillery liaison officer) were located in a concrete blockhouse, preferably of reasonable size, between the main defensive line and the gun lines." Communications breakdowns experienced during Third Ypres dictated, "regimental, brigade and divisional commanders were not in a position to react swiftly enough in the face of enemy attacks. The supporting troops were always near at hand, at the disposal of the *KTK*, and the companies of the reserve battalion were usually within easy reach as well." Thus the *KTK* – more often than not of *Hauptmann's* rank – was, analogous with the aforementioned authorised responsibilities of a *Stellungsdivision* commander, delegated with the immediate command decision of when and where a *BTK's* support troops would be deployed. "From the moment they were committed, they came under his direct command. The same applied to the reserve battalion if it was called for, but the deployment of this unit was a decision for the regimental commander in the first instance."¹¹⁹

Dispersed bulwarks based on the *die Leer des Gefechtsfeldes* concept, the two-division defensive organisation, along with application of a flexible, mobile defence of the *Vorfeldzone* and *Hauptwiderstandslinie* undoubtedly assisted those tasked with maintaining a firm grip on Westroosebeke and the northern portion of Passchendaele Ridge. Nevertheless, by mid-November *Fourth Army* was "reduced to hanging on grimly, assisted by the weather, until winter came to their rescue."¹²⁰ Alert to all movement in their fortified shell hole outposts; peering through narrow embrasures

---

118 The British were well aware of changes to *Fourth Army's* defence scheme after 7 October, as their intelligence files and maps attest. Reserve battalions of *Gruppe Staden's* front left division were billeted along the Oostnieuwkerke – Roodkruis Road; reserve battalions of *Gruppe Ypern's* right division were quartered in the open near the Veldebrook (just south of the junction of the Moorslede-Roulers highway with the Ypres-Roulers railway) and in the villages of Vierkavenhoek, Zilverberg, La Cavalier and Magermeirie.
119 Sheldon, *The German Army at Passchendaele*, pp. xiii-xiv.
120 Ibid., p. xii.

German KTK headquarters winter 1917-18. (Author)

of concrete pillboxes and observation posts; seeking shelter in the cellars of ruined houses, farms and mined dugouts, vigilant German troops awaited the next British assault.

1.4 Corps & Division Commanders

Operational and tactical planning for the projected night attack rested on the shoulders of four experienced general officers: Confident, fearless and personally unambitious, Lieutenant-General Sir Claud W. Jacob (GOC II Corps) was a member of a renowned Indian Army family.[121] A practical level-headed and operationally progressive soldier, thorough in his methods and straightforward in approach, an innate modesty kept him out of the limelight, so that subsequent advancement was in recognition of perceived military aptitude combined with an exceptional talent for commanding men. Jacob, Major Earl Stanhope (GSO 2) observed, while not a clever man, demonstrated sound common sense and good judgment when dealing with subordinates. Ably served by an efficient staff, his "fat and cheery" BGGS,[122] Brigadier-General Samuel Herbert

---

121 Lieutenant-General Claud W. Jacob (1863-1948). Commissioned Worcestershire Regiment 1882; Indian Staff Corps 1884; Zhob Valley Expedition 1890; North-West Frontier 1901; GSO 1 Indian Corps 1914-15; GOC Dehra Dun Brigade, 7th (Meerut) Division 1915; GOC 21st (New Army) Division 1915-16; GOC II Corps 1916-18.

122 A BGGS or GSO 1, as chief staff officer of a Corps, 'would have wide-ranging and challenging responsibilities, including intelligence assessment and operational planning…' See Bond (ed), *The War Memoirs of Earl Stanhope*, p. viii.

Lieutenant-General Sir Claud Jacob GOC II Corps. (IWM HN82158)

Wilson,[123] "consulted his staff officers far more than did any of those holding the same position…" whilst the GSO Intelligence Major F.P. Nosworthy:

> [M]ade it a point of honour to discover and hand over to regimental officers every possible scrap of information which could be of use to them, with the result that units had confidence in the Corps. The objective to be gained in any attack was only decided upon after careful consideration of the information in regard to the enemy's trenches in the possession of our Intelligence Branch and also after consultation with our artillery staff in regard to the protective barrage they could put down in front of any line we might capture and the line from which the barrage would have to start for any attack we might make.[124]

---

123 Brigadier-General Samuel Herbert Wilson. Commissioned Royal Engineers 1893; Railway Pioneers South Africa 1899-1902; Captain 1904; General Staff WO 1906-10; General Staff RMC Sandhurst 1911; Assistant Secretary CID and Secretary Overseas Defence Committee 1911-14; Major 1913; General Staff 27 (Regular) Division and First Army 1914-16; Bt. Lieutenant-Colonel 1916; BGGS II Corps 1916-18; Bt. Colonel 1917.

124 Bond (ed) *The War Memoirs of Earl Stanhope*, p. 110 and 155. For intelligence organisation, leadership and personnel see James Beach, 'British Intelligence and the German Army, 1914-1918' (PhD Thesis. London: University College, 2004), pp. 88-134.

Jacob's "staff advised him, and divisional staffs liked and trusted him, as did the troops."[125] Visits to tributary formations seldom extended to the forward area. Command supervision, he believed, required a certain amount of detachment; so frequent sojourns to the frontline were avoided in order to maintain a broad operational outlook. Jacob refused to be browbeaten by superiors. This admirable quality was amply demonstrated, according to Stanhope, the previous year during preparations for an attack in the vicinity of Mouquet Farm:

> Sir Claud Jacob told me that when he sent in to General Gough his plans for his first attack, the [Fifth] Army Commander criticized them severely, so General Jacob replied that he must carry out his attacks in his own way or he had better resign and hand over command of II Corps to someone else. Sir Hubert Gough replied that this was the last thing that he wanted and let him carry out the attack as he had planned it. The attack was a wonderful success, over 1,000 yards of German trench being taken and many of the enemy killed at a cost of only about twenty casualties, far fewer than in any similar British attack.[126]

Gough, nevertheless, paid fulsome tribute to the GOC II Corps in his autobiography *Soldiering On*: "He [Jacob] was, perhaps, the soundest soldier in the British Army, his tactical ability was of a very high order, and this was based on solid foundations of a firm and honest character. It was his energy that won so many successes for Fifth Army" and "As I have been mentioning Sir Claud Jacob, I would like to add here that he displayed the best attributes of a great soldier again in the Passchendaele battle, operating under very adverse conditions."[127] Prior and Wilson, however, are critical of Jacob's seemingly "complacent" attitude toward disconcerting (bad weather and delays in the deployment of additional heavy artillery) developments whilst the preliminary bombardment for Third Ypres was in progress. This misplaced confidence was in contrast to that of Fifth Army's three other corps commanders who were grateful for a five-day extension of the crucial bombardment.[128] Brigade staff officer Walter Guinness concluded that Jacob was "a very good soldier", but remained dubious about his effusive forecast of victory in 1917:

> While we were at Fruges, Jacob came and addressed us one day and talked the most arrant nonsense I ever heard about the function of the 5th Army, who in the next few days were to drive the Germans right out of Belgium. He told us

---

125 Richard Holmes, *Tommy: The British Soldier on the Western Front 1914-1918* (London: Harper Perennial, 2005), p. 233.
126 Bond (ed), *The War Memoirs of Earl Stanhope*, p. 130.
127 General Sir Hubert Gough, *Soldiering On* (London: Arthur Barker, 1954), p. 132.
128 Prior & Wilson, *Passchendaele*, p. 86.

that we should go on living in shell holes until the war was brought to an end by the complete defeat of the Boche.¹²⁹

Such hopes were dashed during successive attacks against the Gheluvelt Plateau from 31 July to 23 August. II Corps was relieved by X Corps and I ANZAC Corps on 5 September. Jacob and his staff returned, as left corps of Second Army, on 2 November to replace XVIII Corps (Fifth Army) on the paludal frontage Goudberg to Poelcappelle.

A prominent division and corps commander during the Gallipoli campaign, Lieutenant-General Sir Aylmer Hunter-Weston (GOC VIII Corps) was a well-known soldier and eccentric.¹³⁰ Indeed, as official historian Sir James Edmonds retrospectively observed: "the whole Army knew who 'Hunter-Bunter' was."¹³¹ A Conservative Member of Parliament – he would deliver a much-anticipated maiden speech on manpower in January 1918 – his personal public addresses to troops under his command were often delivered in a bombastic rhetorical style associated with politicians of the day.¹³² Anecdotal evidence concerning this controversial Corps Commander is legion. Viewed by some contemporaries as an ambitious and erratic mountebank, Hunter-Weston, a self-described "financially independent, hardworking professional soldier" who had devoted "his life to the study of war", was a self-satisfied, buoyant and thoroughly loquacious individual who, it is claimed, was "never popular with his inferiors, equals or superiors." General Sir Ian Hamilton (C-in-C MEF) believed Hunter-Weston had "truly great qualities as a commander, although

---

129 Brian Bond & Simon Robbins, *Staff Officer: The Diaries of Walter Guinness (First Lord Moyne) 1914-1918* (London: Leo Cooper, 1987), p. 162.
130 Lieutenant-General Sir Aylmer Gould Hunter-Weston (1864-1940). Commissioned Royal Engineers 1884; Miranzai Expedition 1891; Waziristan Delimitation Escort and night action of Wana 1894; A/CRE Waziristan Field Force 1894-95; Dongola Expedition 1896; Staff College 1898-99; South Africa 1899-1901; CO Field Company RE Shorncliffe 1902-04; DAAG IV Army Corps 1904; General Staff Eastern Command 1904-08; General Staff Scottish Command 1908-11; ADMT 1911; Brigadier-General and GOC 11 Brigade, 4th Division February 1914; Mentioned in dispatches four times for service in France and Flanders August 1914 to February 1915; Major-General and GOC 29th Division February 1915; Gallipoli campaign April-July 1915; temporary Lieutenant-General and GOC VIII Corps May 1915; KCB August 1915; GOC VIII Corps Western Front 1916-18; MP for Ayrshire North 1916-18, MP for Bute and Northern 1918-35.
131 Ian Beckett (ed) *The Memoirs of Sir James Edmonds* (Brighton: Tom Donovan, 2013), p. 402.
132 See Keith Wilson (ed), *The Rasp of War: The Letters of H.A. Gwynne to the Countess Bathhurst 1914-1918* (London: Sidgwick & Jackson, 1988), pp.240-41. For a transcript of Hunter-Weston's manpower speech see House of Commons, *The Parliamentary Debates: Official Report, Fifth Series – Volume 101* (London: HMSO, 1918), columns 1234-40.

Lieutenant-General Sir Aylmer Hunter-Weston GOC VIII Corps and Major-General Reginald John Pinney GOC 33rd Division. (IWM Q6543)

he was also grasping, tiresome and talkative."[133] Other contemporary descriptions, Tim Travers notes, "reveal an officer of intelligence, but lacking mental balance, given to extravagant and flamboyant gestures, and far too interested in irrelevant detail, a romantic out of place in an industrial war." Severe sunstroke resulted in Hunter-Weston's evacuation from Cape Helles in July 1915. It can only be surmised whether or not the after-effects of this malady contributed to a heightening of the GOC VIII

---

133 BL: 48366: 'Letter from General Hunter-Weston to Sir Abe Bailey', 14 December 1917, Hunter-Weston Diary, Vol. XII, Colin Hughes introduction in Llewellyn Wyn Griffth, *Up to Mametz* (Norwich: Gliddon Books, 1988 reprint of 1931 edition), p. 23 and General Sir Ian Hamilton *op.cit.* in Tim Travers, *Gallipoli 1915* (Stroud: Tempus, 2001), p. 104. Hunter-Weston displayed, as an aggressive GOC 11 Brigade, sound tactical sense and timely personal leadership when seizing a valuable bridgehead during operations on the Aisne in September 1914. The official historian of the Gallipoli campaign also praised Hunter-Weston's operational grasp during planning for the Cape Helles landing. See Nikolas Gardner, *Trial by Fire: Command and the British Expeditionary Force in 1914* (Westport. Connecticut: Praeger, 2003), p. 18 and Brigadier-General Cecil F. Aspinall-Oglander, *Military Operations: Gallipoli Vo1.1* (London: Heinemann, 1929), pp. 220-21.

Corps' previous idiosyncratic behavior.¹³⁴ Nevertheless, the competent, well-connected and somewhat acerbic Major Cuthbert Headlam (GSO (I) VIII Corps) retrospectively recalled a superior who was brave, optimistic and kindhearted, although passage of time had certainly softened a jaundiced 1917 perspective:

> H[unter] B[unter] is getting wilder and wilder ... Men like HB who consider themselves tin Gods and lay down the law about everything never can get the best out of their underlings ... My plan with HB is to let him have his say, and then, if what he says is too ridiculous, simply not carry it out! So far the plan has worked well – but probably someday I shall be discovered and then the fat may be in the fire...

In some respects Hunter-Bunter was a preposterous figure, "fond of making dramatic entrances at staff conferences, rubicundly gruff, self-important and vain..." One of his least endearing traits "was to give orders to junior officers designed more to impress those within earshot, than to achieve any worthwhile end" or so it appeared. When this occurred, his BGGS (Brigadier-General E.L. Ellington) for most of 1917 would often take steps to see that such orders were countermanded or, like Headlam, ignored.¹³⁵ Captain Llewellyn Wyn Griffith, temporarily attached to VIII Corps during the winter of 1916-17, noticed that the "better soldiers despised" the lean, energetic corps commander with the bristling moustache who walked fast, "criticized everything and everybody" and turned tired officers out of their dugouts in order to address them.¹³⁶ This frenetic energy – no doubt some of this perception originated from the enthusiastic attention paid to seemingly unimportant aspects of minutiae – was often demonstrated during Hunter-Weston's frequent inspections and visits of a less formal nature. Whatever personal foibles, his voluminous diaries demonstrate that this aspect of a corps commander's duties was carried out in a whirlwind of indefatigable thoroughness.¹³⁷

---

134 Sun or heat stroke 'leads only rarely to permanent neurological deficits and the convalescence is almost complete. There are, however, some sporadic descriptions of disturbances that lasted for up to 4 months.' See M. Royburt, et al, 'Long-term Psychological and Physiological Effects of Heat Stroke', *Physiology & Behavior*, 54:2 (August 1993), pp. 265-67.
135 Brigadier-General E.L. Ellington, BGGS VIII Corps (January-November 1917).
136 See Travers, *Gallipoli 1915*, p. 104, Stuart Ball (ed), *Parliament and Politics in the Age of Churchill and Attlee: The Headlam Diaries 1935-1951* (Cambridge: Cambridge University Press, 2000), p.190, DCRO: D/He/167/10: Headlam Correspondence, 8 December 1917, Robert Rhodes James, *Gallipoli* (London: Pan Books, 1984), p. 210 and Hughes introduction in Griffth, *Up to Mametz*, pp. 23-24.
137 Hunter-Weston's diary records various meetings and meals (over which important business was often conducted) with neighbouring corps commanders and their staffs, along with meetings and meals with various subordinates (staff and division commanders) during the period 18 to 30 November. Inspection tours were also made to divisions, brigades, camps

Hunter-Weston's handling of military operations was less satisfactory. Andy Simpson has written that the GOC VIII Corps was "so hands-off as to be almost absent from the battle. Any reputation he has acquired since as a 'thruster' should be replaced with the image of a general drifting forwards with the steady plod of a sleepwalker."[138] This view is analogous with Nikolas Gardner's observation that while Hunter-Weston "valued such notions as honour and personal bravery, and was willing to lead his troops during mobile operations, he adopted a managerial style of command that emphasized planning and staff work following the advent of trench warfare in the fall of 1914."[139] Demonstrating occasional flashes of sound judgment and prescience, Hunter-Weston expressed pessimistic reservations – forecasts of "a second Crimea" – prior to the opening of the Gallipoli campaign that proved sadly prophetic. His operational response, along with that of his French counterpart, to the three disastrous battles of Krithia (April–June 1915) was the implementation of a sensible step-by-step approach against formidable Turkish defences before being invalided home.[140] Nevertheless, Sir Douglas Haig and Sir Henry Rawlinson, according to Tim Travers, considered Hunter-Weston and his staff rank "amateurs in hard fighting" because of their earlier Gallipoli experience.[141] Perceived callousness in regard to casualties earned him the sobriquet "Butcher of Helles" whilst the campaign was still in progress. Novelist Compton Mackenzie (attached to Hamilton's staff as an intelligence officer) challenged this acrimonious view of Hunter-Bunter with sympathetic comprehension of prevailing military logic: "Actually no man I have met brimmed over more richly with human sympathy. He was a logician of war, and as a logician he believed and was always ready to contend in open debate that, provided the objective was gained, casualties were of no importance. Did a more compassionate spirit animate the conduct of war on the Western Front?"[142] GHQ and Fourth Army

and the attached RFC corps squadron aerodrome during the same period. Major Graham Seton Hutchison recalled that during his time in the Passchendaele Salient Hunter-Weston was an active Corps Commander constantly seen in the forward area testing box respirator drill, inspecting sanitation arrangements and salvage organisation. On one occasion the GOC VIII Corps 'stood on top of a pillbox under shellfire and lectured to the universe – staff officers, fatigue men, Commanding Officers, batmen, subalterns, and drivers, with their pack animals, were all gathered into his audience by his stentorian voice.' See Lieutenant-Colonel Graham Seton Hutchison, *Footslogger: An Autobiography* (London: Hutchinson & Co., 1931), p. 207. Professor Gary Sheffield once observed in a correspondence with the author that Hunter-Weston's lessons were, despite the pedantic and bombastic delivery, 'eminently sensible and expressed in a form likely to be remembered.'

138 See Simpson, *Directing Operations*, p. 198.
139 Gardner, *Trial by Fire*, p. 19.
140 See Robin Prior, *Gallipoli: The End of the Myth* (New Haven/London: Yale University Press, 2009), pp. 80-81, 152-159.
141 Sir Douglas Haig, Sir Henry Rawlinson and Walter B. Wood *op.cit.* in Tim Travers, *The Killing Ground: The British Army, the Western Front and the Emergence of Modern Warfare 1900-1918* (London: Allen & Unwin, 1987), p. 157.
142 Mackenzie, *Gallipoli Memories*, p. 152.

prejudice appeared to be confirmed at the start of Somme offensive: Poor pre-assault decision-making and subsequent bloody repulse (14,000 men killed, wounded and missing) of VIII Corps on the infamous opening day of the campaign led to reserve status relegation, or command over what were deemed "quiet sectors" during major offensives. Indeed, Simpson, commenting on Sir Hubert Gough's selection of the four corps commands for Third Ypres, observed it was "unlikely that any Army commander would place his hopes of victory in the hands of Sir Aylmer Hunter-Weston of VIII Corps." The latter was removed from Fifth Army sector in mid-June 1917.[143]

This attitude did not prevent superiors from viewing Hunter-Weston as a safe pair of hands capable of entertaining and accompanying important visitors to parts of the forward area considered expedient for them to see. His guests, besides VIPs from Great Britain and the Empire, included the King of the Belgians, President Bernardino Machado of Portugal, French and Belgian politicians and generals, American congressmen and generals, foreign military attaches, clerics and journalists.[144] These important, albeit pleasant forays in domestic and inter-Allied cooperation and understanding – Prince Amoradhat, Military Attaché to the Siamese delegation in Paris was expected on 28 November – did not distract Hunter-Weston from the operational business at hand; he viewed the tenuous position held by VIII Corps since 18 November with trepidation and expressed genuine compassion and paternalistic concern for those enduring such miserable conditions:

> This Passchendaele position is an unpleasant one, for it is cramped, heavily shelled and difficult to maintain. However, there it is and I am very interested in doing my best in a position which was none of my making. If only I could get the officers and men in the front, who have to live in this horrible wet and mud, more comfortable I would be happy… [145]

Hunter-Bunter, taking into account prevailing circumstances, wasted no time; subordinates were immediately tasked with developing and implementing offensive/defensive schemes and measures.

---

143 Simpson, *Directing Operations*, p. 89. Hunter Weston's remarkable contemporary grasp of various strategic and operational issues still raised in the on-going historical debate over the Third Ypres campaign is demonstrated in a lengthy letter to Lady Hunter-Weston dated 18 December 1917. See BL: 48366: Hunter-Weston Diary, Vol. XII. See also Elaine McFarland, *'A Slashing Man of Action': The Life of Lieutenant-General Sir Aylmer Hunter-Weston MP* (Bern: Peter Lang, 2014) for a balanced modern biography.
144 Simpson relates (p. 197) that perhaps Hunter-Weston's 'finest hour' was during a visit by President Machado in October 1917: 'A Guard of Honour, two bands, and a four-course lunch for 20, with a different wine for each course', was provided. 'Afterwards, he and his staff took the President and his entourage to a part of the line captured at the battle of Messines, to show them the front and provide the opportunity for them to find some souvenirs, taking care to have the ground seeded with interesting items beforehand!'
145 BL: 48366: Hunter-Weston Diary, 2 December 1917, Vol. XII.

Major-General C.D. Shute (GOC 32nd Division) was a capable and aggressive soldier who frequented the frontline.[146] These attributes were often demonstrated whilst commanding a New Army infantry brigade during 1915-16. As one Sergeant who had direct contact with him near Guillemont in August 1916 subsequently related: "General Shute was the finest offensive officer I've ever come across and he was a man who wanted to be in line and know exactly what was going on."[147] Brigadier-General A.C. Girdwood (GOC 96 Brigade) reminisced to the official historian about a "Tiger" Shute, "who worked us hard but sensibly and who damned us all to heaps but whom we all adored all the same because he understood infantry and their funny ways as none of the others did. He had [Lieutenant-Colonel A.E.] McNamara [GSO 1][148] and [Brigadier-General F.W.] Lumsden [GOC 14 Brigade] to back him up and that is why the [32nd] Division did so brilliantly afterwards."[149] Indeed, official historian Captain Cyril Falls, writing of the period after Shute was appointed GOC, was very complimentary about 32nd Division's performance during fluid actions associated with the German retirement to the Hindenburg Line in March and April 1917: "The plan [capture of Holnon Wood] was the conception of Major-General C.D. Shute, commanding the 32nd, and the more important part of it was carried out brilliantly by his troops" and "The 32nd Division had admirably adapted itself to the present type of semi-open warfare, as is proved both by its artillery arrangements and by the speed which this attack [capture of Fayet] was launched."[150]

Shute was, as intimated by Girdwood, also a very demanding superior and somewhat of a martinet, his regimental obituary tactfully recollecting "a man of forceful and dominating personality, with a vehement and untiring energy and terrific drive."[151] One battalion history remarked that he was "reputed to be a tremendous strafer" who while holding the rank of Brigadier 'SOS (an odorous monosyllable)' was

---

146 Major-General Cameron Deane 'Tiger' Shute (1866-1936). Commissioned Welsh Regiment 1885; Staff College 1893-94; transferred to Rifle Brigade 1895; Sudan 1898; DAAG Malta 1899-1904; GSO2 Scottish Coast Defences 1905-09; CO 2nd Rifle Brigade 1910-14; GSO 1 Aldershot 1914; BGGS 1914-15; GOC 59 Brigade, 20th Division 1915-16; T/Major-General on assuming command of 63rd (Royal Naval) Division October 1916; GOC 32nd Division February 1917; temporary GOC 19th (Western) Division May-June; GOC 32nd Division and promoted Major-General June 1917.
147 Sergeant A.K. Paterson *op.cit.* in Lyn MacDonald, *Somme* (London: Michael Joseph , 1983), p. 230.
148 A/Lieutenant-Colonel A.E. McNamara DSO. Commissioned Royal West Surrey Regiment 1897; Lieutenant 1898; South Africa 1899-1902; Captain 1903; Major 1915; DSO awarded for gallantry at Delville Wood and Longueval July 1916.
149 See TNA: CAB/145/134: General A.C. Girdwood 1930 typescript letter to Brigadier-General J.E. Edmonds, Official History Correspondence (Somme 1916).
150 Falls, *Military Operations: France and Belgium 1917 Vol. 1*, pp. 156 and 528.
151 See Major H.G. Parkyn (ed), *The Rifle Brigade Chronicle for 1936* (London: The Rifle Brigade Club and Association, 1937), p. 332.

Major-General Cameron Deane Shute GOC 32nd Division. (IWM HN82157)

the code that passed from signal office to signal office" to warn of his approach.¹⁵² "Be a man. Hard as you like, but just" was his advice to those seeking senior command appointments.¹⁵³ Acting Lieutenant-Colonel I.H. MacDonell (CO 1st Dorsetshire Regiment), a pre-war Regular with previous service in West Africa and Mesopotamia, recorded a seemingly unjust verbal strafe by the peripatetic divisional commander at Nieuport in June 1917:

> You will remember that before I was in command of anything, I said that you might soon <u>have me home</u> when I heard of which Division I was going. The

---

152 J.C. Dunn, *The War the Infantry Knew: 1914-1919. A Chronicle of Service in France and Belgium with the Second Battalion His Majesty's Twenty-Third Foot, The Royal Welch Fusiliers: founded on personal records, recollections and reflections, assembled, edited and partly written by One of their Medical Officers* (London: Jane's, 1987 reprint of 1938 edition), p. 482.

153 JSCSC: Major-General A.H. Marindin Papers: 'Senior Officers' School: Lecture Delivered by Major-General Sir C.D. Shute, KCG, KCMG November 1920.'The contents of this unique document are a valuable representation of Shute's cumulative Great War military thought and experience. It is not unreasonable to assume, despite the post-war lecture date, that many of the ideas expressed were, as we shall see, *idées fixes* in the GOC 32nd Division's mind by late 1917. Shute has no traceable personal papers, so a very special thanks to Professor Gary Sheffield for bringing these long-forgotten lecture notes to my attention.

reason was this. It is commanded by one General Shute. The man has consistently sacked one commanding officer after another. It is only a question of time. This I foresaw that if I were under him my turn would come. Well it looks as if it's going to. As I say, we held a very difficult line. We took it over under <u>unusual</u> circumstances, in which I had to <u>fend</u> for myself with no orders at all from [14] Brigade. We held it. We were shelled – we lost men + we went on to stay it … One evening [,] after the trenches had been knocked about by bombardment during the night – General Shute came round – He only looked at a little piece of the line + was very nervous of shellfire + from start to finish he <u>damned me</u>.

Why, Shute enquired, weren't all the trenches secured? Why were they in a bad state and why had no system of fatigues been arranged for?

> We had but he would not listen to what it was – he swore + jumped – If I could do no better he would. If a shell had come + killed me, I would have welcomed it, if it had also killed him. He went away growling and cursing. He is said to be a very good General + it may be – I don't know that – but he is hated by everyone but his jackals.[154]

Viewed by others as "a great thruster" with "a rather ruthless nature", Stanhope recalled what appeared to be unconscionable methods during operations against Puisieux and River trenches from 3 to 5 February 1917:

> I was horrified, therefore, when General Shute sent in [to II Corps HQ] his so-called "suggestions to the Brigade Commander" who was to do the attack to find that although General Shute stated the Brigade would only be attacking two German battalions with a third available as reinforcement, the attack was to be carried out by, I think, four battalions while four others were to be concentrated in a hollow which the Germans always shelled when anything was happening in that neighbourhood. Unfortunately General Jacob was away on leave owing to the death of a relative and only returned the day before the attack was due to be launched when it was too late to radically alter the plans. General Shute was, therefore, temporarily commanding the Corps and General "Sammy" Wilson did not feel we could interfere, although he agreed that our attacking forces were unnecessarily large and would probably suffer severely from shellfire in consequence.

---

154 IWM: 88/39/1: MacDonell Papers, Letter dated 24 June 1917. MacDonell's short time with 32nd Division, where he was posted from one temporary job to another, was disheartening both professionally and personally, so his attitude toward Shute must be considered in context.

I was informed by a member of the 63rd Divisional staff that these "suggestions" for the attack which in effect were orders, were partly issued in consequence of General Shute not liking the brigadier in question, but the result was of course that the attack attained its objectives, but at an unnecessarily heavy price.[155]

Provided a General was successful GHQ never questioned, so far as my experience went, that casualties which the operation had entailed and General Shute then, as on other occasions, earned the reputation of being a good General because he always attained his objectives though he did so by using more troops than were necessary and so never risked the possibility of failure.[156]

Shute was, nonetheless, well aware, whatever the operational consequences, of his responsibilities as a commander. His personal views on leadership and accountability were clearly articulated in a post-war lecture: "No man will command unless he is prepared to accept full responsibility for his actions. Playing for safety is fatal. You may not get the safety and you will never gain success. As a general rule all commanders must accept responsibility for any operation ordered by them. Here is where the weak or lazy commander so often fails."[157]

Shute's unhappy appointment as GOC 63rd (Royal Naval) Division has left for posterity a well-known bit of ribald doggerel verse composed at his expense by a member of the Division's naval reservist element whose nautical traditions their new commander was loath to accept.[158] Douglas Jerrold, adjutant of Hawke Battalion, believed Shute's contentious and intimidating countenance undermined military efficiency:

---

155 According to the official history: 'The operation had been costly, the casualties of 189th Brigade being 24 officers and 647 other ranks, as against a comparatively small number of captures, 176 prisoners and two machine-guns.' See Falls, *Military Operations: France and Belgium 1917 Vol. 1*, p. 72.
156 Lieutenant-General Aylmer Haldane *op.cit.* in Simon Robbins, *British Generalship on the Western Front 1914-1918: Defeat into Victory* (London: Frank Cass, 2005), p. 16 and Bond (ed), *The War Memoirs of Earl Stanhope*, pp. 114-15.
157 JSCSC: Major-General A.H. Marindin Papers: 'Senior Officers' School: Lecture Delivered by Major-General Sir C.D. Shute, KCG, KCMG November 1920.'
158 The oft-quoted four-verse poem is attributed to humourist, novelist and playwright Alan Patrick Herbert (1890-1971), a serving officer in the RND. It was composed in response to the new divisional commander's splenetic reaction to what he deemed as filthy excreta-ridden trenches during an inspection tour in October 1916. The final verse is sufficient to gauge content:
For shit may be shot at odd corners
And paper supplied there to suit
But a shit would be shot without mourners
If somebody shot that shit Shute
MacDonald, *Somme*, p. 322.

> Once an officer gets into the state where he asks not "What ought I to do", but "What will the General say" he has ceased to function as a useful member of an army in the field. Our own Brigadier was a case in point.[159] Till Shute came he had been charming, efficient and courageously independent. After Shute arrived he just dithered and spoke in faltering prose the abuse which he felt that his superior officer would deliver in the finest poetry of invective. And the men, who after all, have to do the fighting with all this going on, lose confidence either in their officers or in their generals, or more probably both.[160]

Shute assumed command of 32nd Division in February 1917. This was followed by a brief spell as temporary GOC 19th (Western) Division, before resuming the former appointment in June. Sir Douglas Haig subsequently observed that he was unpopular, "very talkative and rather a gas bag", but "did splendidly" while in command of 19th Division at Messines.[161] His command style – a generally effective though flawed combination of adherence to the pre-war principal of "delegation to the man-on-the spot" and direct personal intervention – Stuart Mitchell contends in a recent study, cannot be regarded as an unequivocal success. It did, nonetheless, curb "the more urealistic excesses thrown up by his optimism and determination; it allowed subordinates room to tailor their tactics to the conditions and through his occasional direct intervention he reminded his subordinates of the wider objectives and possible tactical methods for achieving them." Shute's often harsh and divisive dealings with subordinates were, Mitchell also asserts, somewhat offset by application of "classical ideas of paternalism and trust" associated with the late Victorian/Edwardian officer establishment.[162]

One aspect of this positive approach to soldier morale and welfare was the institution of popular sporting events including division and brigade cups. Private Albert Elshaw, a stretcher-bearer in 17th HLI, fondly recalled successive victories over the divisional supply column and 2nd Royal Inniskilling Fusiliers in November 1917: "The [battalion] football team again won the [32nd] Divisional Cup – semi-final and final were played within the space of 48 hours, the former running into an exciting period of extra time. How would today's pros and managers react to such a state of affairs? 'Wembley' was an open field and the 'goals' made up of improvised materials.

---

159 Brigadier-General L.F. Philips (GOC 189 Brigade) was also the unfortunate recipient of Shute's 'suggestions' prior to the operations against Puisieux and River trenches.
160 Douglas Jerrold, *Georgian Adventure* (London: The 'Right' Book Club, 1938), p. 178.
161 Sir Douglas Haig *op.cit.* in Robbins, *British Generalship*, p. 59. Shute's regimental obituary observed that his 'battle-winning renown was so great that, while 32nd Division was out of the line in June 1917, he was sent temporarily by GHQ to command the 19th Division in the Battle of Messines.' See Parkyn (ed), *The Rifle Brigade Chronicle for 1936*, p. 332.
162 Stuart Mitchell, 'An Inter-disciplinary Study of Learning in the 32nd Division on the Western Front 1916-18' (PhD Thesis. Birmingham: University of Birmingham, 2013), pp. 209, 224-25, 264.

Enthusiasm was tremendous and the imagination baulked at the thought of any minor Prussian Warlord had he seen all ranks – brasshat to private – dancing about excitedly at the touch lines, rank forgotten in the mutual enjoyment of the game." Mutual obligations and expectations between leaders and led were reinforced the following day when Shute "addressed the Brigade, which was drawn up on the football field, and reminded the men of the sterner duties that now lay before them, and expressed the hope that they would maintain the honourable traditions associated with the name of the 97th Infantry Brigade …" [163]

Canadian-born Major-General W.C.G. Heneker was appointed GOC of the somewhat tired and demoralized 8th Division in December 1916.[164] Captain Sidney Rogerson (2nd West Yorkshire Regiment) recorded that his arrival was greeted by some with dismay: "One official document had arrived, and this turned out to be a series of rules and orders issued by the divisional commander, a new one whom we had not seen, but who was reputed to be a bit of a slave-driver", whilst Lieutenant-Colonel A.A. Hanbury-Sparrow (CO 2nd Royal Berkshire) recalled: "He came with the suddenness of a cyclone … the CO of the battalion in the adjacent village rang up hurriedly to warn us to look to our guard. The new man, he said, had just passed and raised hell, had hauled him over the coals and threatened to send the adjutant home in disgrace. 'Look out' he reiterated, as he rang off."[165] An able, thorough and exacting professional soldier, Heneker's years of distinguished service in West Africa and India provided the necessary experience and temperament for the rigours of command. Said to be "more at home in a rough house than in civilised discussion or speculation", this "courageous, tactically astute and humane commander" was never satisfied with incurring heavy losses unless there was no other alternative. Blunt speech and insistence for what were deemed necessary alterations to attack plans made concerns about needless casualties all too evident to superiors. His "leadership style was that of 'auditor'";

---

163 See IWM: PP/MCR 49: Elshaw unpublished memoir and J.W. Arthur & I.S. Munro (eds), *The Seventeenth Highland Light Infantry (Glasgow Chamber of Commerce Battalion): Record of War Service 1914-1918* (Glasgow: David J. Clark, 1920) p. 66.
164 Major-General Sir William Charles Giffard 'Billy' Heneker DSO, ADC (1867-1939). Commissioned Connaught Rangers 1888; traveling commissioner Niger Coast Protectorate, West Africa 1897-1899; Benin Territories Expedition 1899; CO Ubium and Ishan expeditions 1900; Aro Expedition 1901-02; CO Ibeku–Olokro, Afikpo and Igara expeditions 1902-03; DSO 1902; DAA & QMG Orange River Colony District 1906-10; Author *Bush Warfare* 1906; ADC to King Edward VII 1907; 2/ic South Nigerian Regiment, West Africa Force 1911-12; CO 2nd North Staffordshire Regiment 1912; T/GOC Rawalpindi Infantry Brigade 1913-14; GOC 1 Infantry Brigade, Quetta 1914. Returned to UK in 1915 as T/Brigadier-General and GOC 54 Brigade, 18th (New Army) Division. Wounded and invalided home December 1915; Colonel April 1916; GOC 190 Brigade, 63rd (Royal Naval) Division 29 October to 8 December 1916; GOC 8th Division 9 December 1916, Major-General (substantive) 3 June 1917.
165 Lieutenant-Colonel A.A. Hanbury-Sparrow, *The Land-Locked Lake* (London: Arthur Barker, 1932), p. 211.

Major-General William Charles Giffard Heneker GOC 8th Division. (IWM Q114384)

his job was to "expose faults and to make sure they were put right." This could not be accomplished unless he made himself known throughout the Division. "He was, therefore, not a remote figure, but a striking personality and a real commander."[166]

Heneker, in keeping with the ethos of the majority of dedicated pre-war Regular officer contemporaries, would not abide slackness. "The surest indicator of slackness was dirt. Dirty rifles, dirty uniform and webbing, dirty trenches, and unshaven chins indicated poor discipline."[167] As Hanbury-Sparrow approvingly wrote two decades later:

> In truth, the G.O.C.'s methods were very simple. He had one limited object, which he kept clearly in view, and that was to vivify the morale of the division by a martinet discipline and the most fastidious attention to turn-out. Once

---

166 Sidney Rogerson, *Twelve Days on the Somme: A Memoir of the Trenches 1916* (London: Frontline Books, 2009 reprint of 1933 edition), p. 151, Captain H. Essame *op.cit.* in Robbins, *British Generalship on the Western Front 1914-1918*, p. 13 and John Bourne, 'Major-General W.C.G. Heneker: A Divisional Commander of the Great War' in Matthew Hughes & Matthew Seligmann (eds) *Leadership in Conflict 1914-1918* (Barnsley: Leo Cooper, 2000), pp. 63,65.
167 Bourne, Major-General W.C.G. Heneker in Hughes & Seligmann (eds), *Leadership in Conflict 1914-1918*, p. 60.

this was gained, you gathered he thought the rest would come, and because you knew his methods were sound you swore by him. For what he was achieving was the liberation of the thinking mind from fear. Instead of having one's energies consumed by the struggle with fear, discipline was to take on the task and the energies could be set free to think how to beat the Germans.[168]

One staff officer, however, remarked that Heneker was "rather too keen on spit and polish and outward appearance at the expense of efficiency with the weapons with which the men were armed."[169]

Subordinates viewed as tired or lacking in fighting spirit were sent home on Heneker's recommendation. He had, on assuming divisional command, rapidly arrived at the conclusion that a number of senior officers would have to be replaced. As one battalion commander remarked: "Under General Heneker a commander's saddle is a slippery one"; indeed, the MGRA, GSO 2 and two brigade commanders were sacked in January 1917. The popular Brigadier-General E.A. Fagan (GOC 23 Brigade) followed after "a difference of opinion with the divisional general" in March.[170] Heneker expressed the desire to remove the GOC 24 Brigade in mid-October: "Am getting rid of Cobham under six-months [sic] rest rule[171] and hope to get Roly Haig for 24 Bde." Forty-four-year-old Brigadier-General Roland Haig had been a valued battalion commander in 25 Brigade. A "man of great courage and leadership", he assumed command of 24 Brigade on 21 November.[172]

Among a divisional commander's primary duties was to "identify, encourage and promote able subordinates." Heneker was fortunate to inherit acting Lieutenant-Colonel Edward "Moses" Beddington,[173] a "clever 34-year-old cavalryman who suffered fools no better than his GOC", as GSO 1.[174] Beddington retrospectively considered time spent with 8th Division to be "some of the happiest years of his life", and remarked on his good fortune to serve under such a qualified, if rather severe, divisional commander:

---

168 Hanbury-Sparrow, *The Land-Locked Lake*, p.216.
169 Brigadier-General G.R. Roupell VC *op.cit.* in Robbins, *British Generalship on the Western Front 1914-1918*, p. 92.
170 John Terraine (ed) *General Jack's Diary: The Trench Diary of Brigadier General J. L. Jack DSO* (London: Cassell, 2000), pp. 191,197.
171 The 'six-month rest rule' was a humane system of temporary firing instituted following summary dismissals of mid-level commanders during 1916. General officers sent home could, therefore, anticipate some sort of re-employment at a later date.
172 IWM: 66/541/1: Heneker Diary, 16 to 31 October 1917 and Bourne, 'Major-General W.C.G. Heneker' in Hughes & Seligmann (eds) *Leadership in Conflict 1914-1918*, p. 62.
173 Lieutenant-Colonel E.H.L. Beddington DSO. Educated Eton and Sandhurst; Commissioned 16th Lancers 1902; Lieutenant 1903; Captain 1914; Major 1916.
174 Bourne, 'Major-General W.C.G. Heneker' in Hughes & Seligmann (eds) *Leadership in Conflict 1914-1918*, p. 62.

I was very lucky; Heneker was a good tactician and a good man to serve so long as one stood up to him; he was also a good disciplinarian but a bit of a bully. Our relations were such that not only did we become friends, but he would let me during his bullying of someone pull his coat and whisper "That'll do, Sir, he has had enough."[175]

Heneker was generally well served by the appointments and promotions resulting from the purge of early 1917.[176] "His concern to maintain professional standards of duty and leadership among his subordinates was unrelenting. He never ceased to prize "smartness" and outward appearance as indicators of morale and efficiency." Indifferent to popularity and sparing of praise, his uncompromising stance toward the military amateurism sometimes found amongst the volunteer and conscript elements of the expanded BEF was not always welcome or appreciated.[177]

1.5 Tactical Controversy

Preparations for a narrow front attack to open out the Passchendaele Salient's western face and carry the frontline northwards in order to obtain observation into low-lying valleys situated north and east of the main ridge had been set in motion.[178] On the right, 8th Division[179] (VIII Corps) would advance on an approximate frontage of 1,020 yards east north-east to a varied depth of 100 to 300 yards. On the left, 32nd Division[180] (II Corps) was to protect and prolong the northern flank by advancing

---

175 Beddington, 'My Life', p. 119.
176 Most notably Brigadier-General G.W. St G. Grogan (GOC 23 Brigade) and Brigadier-General C. Coffin (GOC 25 Brigade).
177 Bourne, 'Major-General W.C.G. Heneker' in Hughes & Seligmann (eds) *Leadership in Conflict 1914-1918*, p. 62.
178 See appendices IV a & b, V a & b, VI and VII for VIII Corps, II Corps, 8th Division and 32nd Division operation orders respectively.
179 The 8th (Regular) Division sustained a combined total of 5,320 killed, wounded and missing during the opening stages of the Third Ypres campaign. Sent south to the comparatively quiet Ploegsteert sector for rest and refit, it was ordered to return north in November. See Boraston & Bax, *The Eighth Division*, pp. 156-61 and Appendix I for infantry orders of battle.
180 Known to the enemy as "the 'Red' Division, partly on account of the red tabs worn on the tunic sleeves of all ranks and partly for its full-blooded virility in battle", the 32nd (New Army) Division had been deployed on the Flanders coast, where it suffered heavy losses (10-11 July) during the German riposte at Nieuport, throughout the Third Ypres campaign. Estimated casualties killed, wounded and missing sustained in this sector during the period 19 June to 17 September 1917 were 186 officers and 4,126 ORs. The Division was ordered south to join II Corps the following October. See Thomas Chalmers (ed), *A Saga of Scotland: History of the 16th The Highland Light Infantry (City of Glasgow Regiment)* (Glasgow: John M'Callum & Co., 1930), p. 17, Becke, *Order of Battle Divisions Part 3B*, pp.

west and north on a frontage of 1,850 yards to a depth of 400 yards on the left and right and 700 yards in the centre.

Information gleaned from recently captured documents – outlining the new defence scheme ordered by *Generalquartiermeister* Ludendorff following *Fourth Army's* disastrous experience of 4 October – caused the commanders of both divisions a great deal of concern. The acquired papers revealed that the commencement of a British bombardment would be perceived as a sign of imminent attack. Formed up along engineer tape in preparation for the assault, the massed hostile infantry was to be dealt with by bringing an immediate artillery defensive barrage to bear on jumping-off positions inside the enemy frontline. This overwhelming curtain of fire would be withdrawn back across positions evacuated by the *Vorfeldzone* garrison minutes after the start of the enemy bombardment. Thus surviving British troops, traversing the hurriedly abandoned outpost zone in order to come to grips with the heavily defended *Hauptwiderstandslinie*, would encounter an intense curtain of annihilating-shellfire. *Fourth Army* began to put this method into effect on 13 October. The artillery was now the main line of defence. "It was hoped that the 'dense barrage of shell' in front of the main line of resistance would stop, or at least break up, an offensive before it covered the varying depths of the *Vorfeld*."[181] This tactic made it necessary for the attackers to get beyond the *Vorfeldzone* as quickly as possible. To this end, it was resolved to surprise the advanced hostile outpost zone before the supporting artillery could be brought to bear on the British forward line; 32nd Division faced the most difficult task in the projected night attack, so the planning and preparations of 8th Division were influenced and constrained by the tactical schemes of the former.[182]

Shute recognised it was impossible for a brigade to form up below Vat Cottages Ridge during daylight owing to the unpleasant fact that any such movement would be in full view of the enemy. A dawn or night attack offered the only prospect of achieving surprise: "As so many recent attacks have been made at dawn [,] it was decided to risk the inherent dangers of a night attack on a big scale and to attack at night."[183] No doubt Haig's earlier recommendation to Rawlinson that Second Army should "attack by small units by night, because up to the present nothing of this nature

---

21-29, TNA: WO/95/2370: '32nd Division; Summary of Reliefs Showing Casualties for each period', 32nd Division War Diary and Appendix I for infantry orders of battle.

181 TNA: WO/95/1677: 'Narrative of Operations Carried Out by 8th Division on 1st/2nd December 1917', 13 December 1917, 8th Division War Diary and Wynne, *If Germany Attacks*, p.222.

182 32nd Division was scheduled to relieve 1st Division on the night of 23/24 November.

183 See TNA: WO/95/2370: After-action report, 'Part II, Plan of Operations, Section I, General', 11 December 1917, 32nd Division War Diary. Shute composed his night operation narrative in the form of an *ex post facto* general report of eighteen pages and eight appendices. His concern about a kind of 'wooden' approach to operations was previously articulated by Brigadier-General Shoubridge (GOC 54th Brigade) during the Somme offensive, when the dangers of 'trying to do every attack by barrage and relying on stereotyped tactics which meant that the Bosch always knows by our barrage

has been attempted by us at the Ypres battle front" had made its way down the chain of command to the GOC 32nd Division.[184] Shute, however, would substitute the idea of nocturnal assaults by small units suggested by Haig with a large-scale set-piece night attack involving a reinforced brigade from his division. With this tactical approach he hoped to secure the formidable defences of Hill 52 and Vat Cottages Ridge.

Two primary factors caused Shute concern during planning for the proposed operation. First, supporting artillery could only fire from west to east in support of an infantry brigade assaulting along the ridge from south to north. The failure of 1st SWB on 10 November had been attributed to the same difficulty.[185] Perennial (bad weather, poor roads, mud, hostile shelling) difficulties encountered whilst shifting batteries forward continued to be exacerbated by the diminishing number of dry sites available for heavy and field guns. Such locations that did exist were limited to the waterlogged ground in the west, and within the confines of the Passchendaele Salient.

Second, how to avoid the defensive barrage that would surely be brought down on 32nd Division's jumping-off positions the moment British artillery commenced its bombardment? Shute succinctly outlined his carefully considered solution:

> The idea of an advance under a creeping barrage was therefore abandoned, and it was decided to advance for the first 200 yards without artillery fire, except of course, preliminary artillery bombardment within safety limits, and to attempt to surprise the enemy's most advanced posts and to overwhelm them with the bayonet.[186]

Thus the usual procedure was to be dispensed with; batteries would not open fire at Zero. As the unfortunate tactical situation facing the gunners dictated: fire – to assist an advance with a creeping barrage that would "perforce be in enfilade, and experience had shown that such a barrage was difficult to manipulate, was often inaccurate and tended to mislead the infantry as to their direction"[187] – was to commence at "Zero plus 8 with all available artillery and machine-guns in a series of area concentrations,[188]

---

where we are going to attack and when we are.' See Brigadier-General T.H. Shoubridge *op.cit.* in Robbins, *British Generalship on the Western Front 1914-1918*, p. 108.
184 Haig diary entry 19 November 1917 in 'The First World War Political, Social and Military Manuscript Sources: Series One: The Haig Papers from the National Library of Scotland, Part I Haig's Autograph Great War Diary', Reel 5 and Sheffield & Bourne (eds), *Douglas Haig*, p. 345.
185 Only one part of the 3 Brigade's barrage was fired in enfilade during 10 November. Shute could only contemplate a similar barrage along the *entire* front of his assaulting brigade.
186 TNA: WO/95/2370: After-action report, 'Part II, Plan of Operations, Section I, General', 11 December 1917, 32nd Division War Diary.
187 Boraston & Bax, *The Eighth Division*, p. 164.
188 Area concentrations, fired in lieu of a creeping barrage by the supporting artillery, would have been the most effective method in targeting the dispersed German defences along Vat Cottages Ridge.

those inside the objective to lift as the infantry advanced."[189] This hybrid tactical approach to the set-piece attack, with its delayed artillery scheme and employment of area concentration fire as a creeping barrage substitute, would hopefully allow the *Vorfeldzone* garrison to be surprised and overwhelmed. A more effective bombardment (although the necessary pre-attack dominance of enemy batteries was hardly realised) of the dispersed targets on Vat Cottages Ridge would also be obtained. Conversely, Shute's assaulting brigade would be exposed to the direct fire of German machine-guns for 6 to 8 minutes.

Shute recognised the danger of allowing men to be exposed to machine-gun and rifle fire for 6 to 8 minutes – a seemingly interminable passage of time given the risks involved – "but it was considered preferable running this risk to drawing the enemy's intense artillery barrage on us by opening our own barrage."[190] In this way, the dangerous area could be traversed and German forward posts rushed to a depth of 200 yards before hostile batteries brought down the expected defensive barrage. "Playing for safety" was not an option if desired objectives were to be achieved. Shute later expressed strong views on the necessity for such tactical risk-taking:

> Try to be versatile and strive to invent some new plan. Remember that your effort should always be to "mystify and mislead the enemy"– Stonewall Jackson. Don't be contented time after time to follow the same old plan. No two military problems are exactly the same. A line of action which succeeded once under one set of circumstances may be the worst possible one to follow in the next battle. Don't hesitate to take risks. Don't dread defeat. Feel sure of victory. Your optimism will communicate itself to those under you. Remember that the man who takes no risks will never get great results and does not deserve them. Fortune favours the bold. The enemy does not know your risk. Then when you have made your plan see red and go all out.[191]

The current plan, given the problematic tactical circumstances, was the best that could be devised and the GOC 32nd Division was a confident soldier: "The strong man in war is an OPTIMIST. He won't allow himself that he is going to fail." Night attacks, Shute also observed "almost invariably succeeded."[192]

---

189 TNA: WO/95/2370: After-action report, 'Part II, Plan of Operations, Section I, General', 11 December 1917, 32nd Division War Diary.
190 Ibid. Shute also noted that his 'decision was further strengthened by the fact that in previous attacks on this front the enemy had disclosed such a superiority in artillery fire that the assaulting troops suffered very heavy casualties in reaching their objectives.'
191 JSCSC: Major-General A.H. Marindin Papers: 'Senior Officers' School: Lecture Delivered by Major-General Sir C.D. Shute, KCG, KCMG November 1920.'
192 Ibid. Shute's insistence on a pragmatic tactical approach was supported in principal by Lieutenant-General H.C.C. Uniacke (CRA Fifth Army) in a report on artillery operations during Third Ypres: 'As the enemy changes … his methods of defence … so we

A night operation is always a difficult undertaking. Shute found it necessary to attack during the *relative* darkness of a moonlit night in order to ensure direction and rapidity of advance across the almost featureless battlefield.[193] Thus coordination was deemed more important than concealment. Indeed, the GOC 32nd Division subsequently stated without reservations: "Night Attacks: Moonlight best – not worst."[194] A moon at full sphere would therefore, in Shute's view, expedite the first operational stage by providing the attackers with just enough light to traverse wet and broken ground quickly to overrun the *Vorfeldzone* before Zero + 8.

Heneker related during the nascent planning stage that he preferred to attack at dawn because "the difficulties of assembly leave no choice for the hour of attack."[195] Brigadier-General Aspinall stated, in his reply on 21 November, that II Corps was "anxious for the attack to take place at night [,] and since you [Heneker] are in agreement with this [aspect of the] plan, the [VIII] Corps commander is concurring with the II Corps proposal."[196] Heneker also expressed grave concerns about other aspects of Shute's plan. He was not in complete agreement in regard to the immediate danger

> must modify ... our methods of artillery attack in order to break down that defence, allow our infantry to assault with a reasonable prospect of success, and gain their objective with the minimum of loss – *always bearing in mind that the final decisive factor is the bayonet of the infantry soldier*'(My emphasis). See Uniacke, *op.cit.* in Sanders Marble, '*The Infantry Cannot Do with a Gun Less': The Place of the Artillery in the British Expeditionary Force 1914-18* (New York: Columbia University Press, 2003), p. 105.

193 Shute's operations against Puisieux and River Trenches (3-5 February 1917) are case in point: 'With the object of surprise, so far as that was possible, on ground covered with snow and in bright moonlight, the attack was launched at 11 p.m.' See Falls, *Military Operations: France and Belgium 1917 Vol. 1*, p. 71.

194 JSCSC: Major-General A.H. Marindin Papers: 'Senior Officers' School: Lecture Delivered by Major-General Sir C.D. Shute KCG, KCMG November 1920.' Failure to take into account the crucial relationship between nocturnal operations and astronomic projections was amply demonstrated during the disastrous large-scale night attack by Fifth, Third and First armies (Third Battle of the Scarpe) on 3 May 1917. GHQ adjusted zero hour, at Fifth Army's request, just before the assault. 'A night attack was therefore carried out, based on dispositions suited to an attack at dawn. The sun did not rise till 5:22 [a.m.] and it was impossible to distinguish a line of men at a distance of fifty yards until 4.5 a.m. – the original Third Army Zero. Nor was this all. The moon, approaching the full, set 16 minutes before the new zero hour. On large stretches of the front the troops assembling for the assault were silhouetted against its light as it sank behind them, their appearance giving warning of the attack and drawing heavy fire, which caused serious loss and confusion.' Official historian Cyril Falls gloomily concluded: 'That British troops, with their traditional skill in estimating the effect of the lights of the heavens and turning it to their own advantage, should have suffered to fall into this trap is one of the most melancholy features of a melancholy episode...' See Falls, *Military Operations: France and Belgium 1917 Vol. 1*, pp. 430-33.

195 TNA: WO/95/1677: '8th Division No. G. 97/1/1, 18th November 1917', 8th Division War Diary.

196 Brigadier-General Aspinall added that the 'actual time of Zero will be decided on after trials of the time required for forming-up have been carried out by the divisions

of the German defensive barrage or the necessity of dispensing with a creeping barrage on 8th Division's front. This is not to say he dismissed the necessity of a surprise advance without a creeping barrage or the inherent threat of the defensive barrage employed by enemy gunners. On the nights of 18/19, 20/21 and 24/25 November, 8th Division advanced its line by stealth, thus narrowing the distance to the *Hauptwiderstandslinie*, and seized portions of the *Vorfeldzone* opposite the Venison Trench defences. It was during the latter operation that a new line, offering an uninterrupted view for approximately 400 yards, was dug on the ridge crest.[197] Obviously there was something to be said for this tactic. Shute, however, envisaged the opening phase of the forthcoming night attack as only the precursor to a larger operation that would be carried out on hitherto established lines with artillery assistance once the *Vorfeldzone* was overrun. Ominously, one of Heneker's battalions suffered a number of casualties during the small advance on the night of 24/25 November. These losses were sustained when alert German machine-gunners discerned obvious movement under the bright moonlight.[198]

Assaulting enemy positions on a small scale under cover of darkness without a barrage became fairly routine in the Passchendaele – Westroosebeke sector following the successful operations carried out west of the Paddebeek by 63rd Division on the evenings of 1/2 and 3/4 November. Lessons learned during these attacks were elaborated in a lengthy after-action report – lessons clearly recognised by Shute:

MINOR OPERATIONS

- Minor night operations and surprise tactics as employed on the nights 1st/2nd and 3rd/4th November are most effective against enemy outpost lines in marshy country, and are infinitely less costly than set-piece attacks under a barrage.
- A policy of minor night enterprises when holding battle lines is strongly advocated. Those enterprises increase the morale of our troops, and the constant

concerned.' See TNA: WO/95/1677: 'VIII Corps G.1990, 21st November 1917', 8th Division War Diary.
197 2nd Devonshire and 2nd West Yorkshire (23 Brigade) participated in this minor attack. On the left, 1st Division carried out, prior to its relief by 32nd Division on the night of 23/24 November, similar small-scale operations on the nights of 16/17 and 17/18 November. These modest enterprises succeeded in advancing the frontline along the western slope of Vat Cottages Ridge. Two important (Vocation and Virile farms) strongpoints were thus secured; the hostile garrison occupying Vox Farm continued to hold out. 1st Division's measurable gains reduced overall distances to the *Hauptwiderstandslinie* opposite and strengthened the boundary between II Corps and VIII Corps. See TNA: WO/95/1712: 'Report of Minor Operation carried out by this Battalion on night of 24/25 November', 26 November 1917, 2nd Devonshire War Diary, WO/95/1714: 2nd West Yorkshire War Diary, C.T. Atkinson, *The Devonshire Regiment 1914-1918* (London: Eland Brothers, 1926), pp. 318-19 and WO/95/1232: 1st Division War Diary.
198 Boraston & Bax, *The Eighth Division*, pp. 162-63.

movement of our posts prevents their being accurately located by the enemy's artillery

- Further, if a set-piece attack is contemplated soon after a series of such enterprises, the enemy will be in ignorance of the exact position of his own outpost line. This will cause him to place his initial barrage at a greater distance from his line than would otherwise be the case and minimize the risk of this barrage opening on our troops.
- To make minor enterprises successful special attention must be paid to the training of subordinate commanders in night work, minor tactics, and reconnaissance, as the success of such enterprises entirely depends on the initiative of subordinate commanders.
- The new German tactics as described in a captured order of the 11th Infantry Division received since these notes were written appears to make night enterprises of a kind advocated above more than ever valuable.
- The few men that the enemy employs to hold his forward zone and the uncertainty that must exist in their minds as to how much resistance they are to offer should render posts in this zone particularly liable to capture by such enterprises. Further if a set-piece attack is contemplated it is more than ever necessary to get as close as possible to the "line of resistance of the forward zone" prior to the attack. Unless this is done our troops may be caught by the enemy counter-barrage when it is brought back at Zero plus 15 minutes.

NIGHT OPERATIONS VERSUS DAY OPERATIONS
- In the case of a strong position such as TOURNANT FARM [captured by 1st Division on 10 November] there is little chance of a minor enterprise succeeding unless the enemy is taken by surprise. In such situations the attack must be supported by artillery fire. It is, however, suggested that in swampy ground a night attack on a large scale following a preliminary bombardment will have more chance than a set-piece daylight attack, the success of which largely depends on the ability of the assaulting infantry to keep up to the barrage.[199]

The terrible battlefield conditions that limited movement and decreased creeping barrage effectiveness combined with excellent observation capabilities afforded the Germans during daylight hours, made it necessary to isolate and overwhelm with small assault parties by night, certain pillboxes and strongpoints that remained unapproachable without severe loss by day. Thus "individual pill-boxes would be on their

---

199 Leonard Sellers (ed), 'Western Front: Report on Operations During the Third Battle of Ypres: Passchendaele, 24th October to 5th November 1917', *RND: Royal Naval Division. Antwerp, Gallipoli & Western Front 1914-1918*, Issue Number 22 (September 2002), pp. 2181-82.

Pillbox HQ of 2nd East Lancashire Regiment, Passchendaele Salient December 1917. (Lancashire Infantry Museum)

own [at night], and not mutually supporting as by day; they would have fewer targets, and would be vulnerable to surprise attacks."[200]

It was the thought of what a luminous moon would allow the Germans to observe that vexed Heneker most when considering application of this tactic on a large scale: "How was I to protect the infantry from the enemy's MG and rifle fire between Zero and Zero plus 8 in case the enemy becomes alarmed before the latter hour, and opened on the attacking infantry?"[201] He had originally requested a conventional creeping barrage:

---

200 Christopher Page, *Command in the Royal Naval Division: A Military Biography of Brigadier General A.M. Asquith DSO* (Staplehurst: Spellmount, 1999) p. 162.
201 TNA: WO/95/1677:'Narrative of Operations Carried out by 8th Division on 1/2 December, 1917', 13 December 1917, 8th Division War Diary. Heneker advanced the assault date for an operation between Bouchavesnes and Moislains the previous winter after careful consideration of moon phase data. See Alun Thomas, 'British 8th Infantry Division on the Western Front 1914-18' (PhD Thesis. Birmingham: University of Birmingham, 2010), p. 241.

The barrage should move fairly quickly as the advance is short: I hope to be able to ask for lifts of 100 yards in four minutes, but naturally this depends on reconnaissance [and] the state of the weather and ground. If this can be managed, the attacking troops should be past the main German defences [Venison Trench] before the enemy barrage comes down on them.[202]

Gunners responsible for 8th Division's barrage were not hampered by the difficulties confronting 32nd Division batteries. As the former division's assaulting brigade advanced NE, its supporting artillery *would* be capable of firing an orthodox creeping barrage. Aspinall's response was, at first, somewhat equivocal: "II Corps is suggesting that there should be no creeping barrage. The Corps Commander is deferring an answer to this point until you have formed your opinions on it."[203] It was, however, deemed necessary – regardless of the fact that both divisions were expected to attack in different directions – to have a homogeneous artillery timetable. Thus 8th Division had to conform to the 8-minute interregnum prescribed by its neighbour. Consequently, Heneker was required by VIII Corps to adhere to Shute's scheme so as not to alert by the opening of a preliminary barrage, an already vigilant enemy obstinately clinging to the northern portion of the much-contested ridge.

Heneker proposed two ways to minimize the risk: First, he suggested that a protective artillery barrage should immediately be brought down on to the enemy line if the German defenders opened fire before Zero + 8. The assaulting battalions could then form up under the cover of this fire. As the barrage lifted forward, the infantry would rush the enemy line in the prescribed manner. "Had this been agreed to I [Heneker] would have had my outpost line all along the front withdrawn at Z − 1 hour to a line 150 yards from the enemy trenches", the GOC 8th Division adding that he had applied this method on previous occasions with success.[204] Vital signalling liaison between infantry and artillery could be arranged with Lieutenant-Colonel N.M.S. Irwin MC (CO 2nd Lincolnshire Regiment),[205] whose HQ would be at Mosselmarkt, to discharge an SOS rocket "as soon as he considered it advisable, between Z[ero] and Z[ero] plus 8." This officer would be in a position "to see and hear how soon the enemy's fire opened"; his signal would alert supporting British gunners to begin the necessary protective barrage. 32nd Division HQ, unwilling to adjust its preferred

---

202 TNA: WO/95/1677:'8th Division No. G. 97/1/1, 18 November 1917', 8th Division War Diary.
203 Ibid: 'VIII Corps G.1990, 21 November 1917'.
204 Ibid.
205 A/Lieutenant-Colonel Noel Mackintosh Stuart Irwin (1892-1972). RMC Sandhurst; commissioned Essex Regiment 1912; Lieutenant1914; Captain and MC 1915; A/Major and A/Lieutenant-Colonel 1917. Irwin's short autobiography makes no mention of this operation. See Hubert C. Fox (ed), *Infantry Officer 1914-1918: The Record of Service as a Young Officer in the First World War of Lt. General N.M.S. Irwin, CB, DSO, MC, Member of the British Legion* (Southampton: Pearson & Lloyd, 1995), pp. 14-15.

artillery scheme, summarily rejected Heneker's latest contingency plan by claiming it would lead to confusion.[206]

The denial of Heneker's first recommendation was immediately followed by a suggestion that the barrage start time be reduced from Zero + 8 to Zero + 6 or Zero + 4, "for in my [Heneker] experience [,] I felt much more fearful of the enemy's MG fire from prepared positions on a bright moonlight [sic] night then I did of any artillery barrage." The brigadier and battalion commanders of 25 Brigade (the formation chosen to carry out 8th Division's part of the night operation) expressed total agreement with this latest proposal. "This idea was overruled, for the 32nd Division which had to carry out the major operation [sic] were against curtailing the time."[207] Boraston and Bax, authors of 8th Division's post-war history, noted that Heneker's suggestions "were overruled, as the 32nd Division considered that it was impossible to organise an effective creeping barrage to cover an infantry advance on their front…"[208]

Heneker, unconvinced and perturbed, subsequently wrote: "I did not feel justified in refusing to attack although I felt very doubtful of success and I said so."[209] He was even more candid in his diary: [Shute] "wishes to do a surprise attack by moonlight and have no covering fire to protect the advance from hostile machine-gun fire before Z + 8. I don't agree and protested but my protest was overruled.[210] I told the Corps Commander that neither we nor the 32nd would succeed in consequence. However, I was ordered to attack."[211] The apprehensive Heneker also expressed little confidence in his infuriatingly irrepressible Corps Commander: "Hunter-Weston is mad and very trying. Such Corps Commanders should not be allowed out here."[212] As Lieutenant-Colonel Beddington (GSO1 8th Division) recollected decades later: "Both the General and I hated this operation, and suggested amendments, all of which were turned down. It was a night attack over horribly churned up ground three nights after a full moon and we considered that even if we were not seen advancing

---

206 TNA: WO/95/1677: 'Narrative of Operations Carried out by 8th Division on 1/2 December 1917', 13 December 1917, 8th Division War Diary.
207 Ibid.
208 Boraston & Bax, *The Eighth Division*, p. 164.
209 TNA: WO/95/1677: 'Narrative of Operations Carried out by 8th Division on 1/2 December 1917', 13 December 1917, 8th Division War Diary.
210 A then Brigadier-General Heneker previously expressed what appears to be intellectual disdain towards Shute during a short spell (29 October-8 December 1916) as GOC 190 Brigade, remarking on 18 October 1916: 'All four divisional commanders [Shute, Harper, Walker, Deverell] had dinner at [V] Corps HQ this evening and attended a conference on the attack [planning for the Battle of the Ancre] after dinner … I was not impressed with the knowledge or power of mind of either the Corps Commander [Lieutenant-General Sir Edward Fanshawe] or any of the div. comdrs at this conference' and, writing somewhat cryptically on 29 October, 'The [190] Bde is in 63rd Royal Naval Division and Shute commands. Funny being under him.' See IWM: 66/541/1: Heneker Diary, 18 and 29 October 1916.
211 IWM: 66/541/1: Heneker Diary, 19-29 November 1917
212 Ibid, 16 to 31 October 1917.

to the attack, which was highly improbable, we were certain to be heard squelching through the mud."[213]

Sir Henry Rawlinson harboured some pre-disposed views about lunar impact on night operations. The foundation of his approach, based on military history, recent experience in South Africa and careful study of the Russo-Japanese War, were related by the then Brigadier-General Rawlinson during a lecture at Aldershot in December 1907:

> In all military operations the weather often influences the situation. In night work it is probably the most important and perhaps the most unstable factor which calls for our consideration. I fancy there is a good deal of conflict of opinion even amongst soldiers as to the ideal night for a night march, but again I find it impossible to generalise, and must leave each particular occasion to be judged on its merits. There is, however, no doubt that a bright, clear, moonlight night very much facilitates the movement of troops…[214]

Rawlinson still retained this outlook nine years later when planning for the second phase of the Somme campaign. Two of five Fourth Army assault divisions were successfully assembled in no man's land under the light of a full moon to reduce a 1,500-yard gap opposite the heavily defended German second line. The subsequent Battle of Bazentin Ridge led to the seizure, "on the heels of a truly devastating bombardment", of formidable German positions during a surprise dawn attack on 14 July 1916.[215] It is probable, based on theoretical disposition and previous battle experience that the GOC Second Army heartily approved of Shute's large-scale moonlight scheme regardless of perceived risks, although final sanction was certainly the administrative purview of II Corps.[216] Enemy battery groups caused Rawlinson greater concern: "Shute is very confident of bringing off a good success [.] The only

---

213 Beddington, 'My Life', p. 119.
214 Brigadier-General Sir H.S. Rawlinson, Bart., CVO, CB, psc, commanding 2nd Infantry Brigade, Aldershot Command, 'Night Operations', *RUSI: Royal United Services Institute Journal*, 52:1 (June 1908), p. 810.
215 See Prior & Wilson, *Command on the Western Front*, p. 202.
216 Passages found in FSR (1909) shed further light on the tactical mindset of those involved with the complex decision making process: 'Night operations may be undertaken to … pass over an area of ground which it has been found difficult or impossible to traverse in daylight … Surprise in some form is usually an object of night operations … Night assaults, that is to say assaults delivered in the dark, should rarely be attempted by a force larger than an infantry brigade against a single objective unless the conditions are exceptionally favourable … In all night operations the maintenance of connection is of the first importance.' Lunar effect was not directly addressed in the contents, although its relative value, when considering maintenance of coordination, would have been assumed by contemporaries. See War Office, *Field Service Regulations Part 1: Operations 1909 (Reprinted with Amendments, 1912)* (London: HMSO, 1914), pp. 176-77.

thing I am anxious about is the guns of which the Bosch has concentrated in large numbers in that area."[217]

The date finally chosen for the forthcoming night operation was based on meteorological data indicating the next period when the moon would be full.[218] It was, as we have seen, recognised by Sir Henry Rawlinson, Major-General Shute and 32nd Division staff among others, that assaulting troops would – in order to facilitate coordination, direction and rapidity of advance on the barren desolate ridge – be better able to discern objectives in the relative darkness of a moonlit night.[219] Examination of meticulously prepared and distributed documents like Second Army's "Moonlight Chart for October, November & December" imparted the moon was certain to be full or just past full sphere during the nights of 26 November to 1 December.[220] The original (26 November) date was shelved because of the need for additional preparation time by both divisions. A new (night of 1/2 December) attack date was later agreed upon by all concerned.[221] Zero had to be fixed for an hour that would ensure "time to assemble and yet assault as early as possible in order to give the maximum number of hours of darkness in which to consolidate ground gained." 1:55 a.m. was subsequently chosen as the hour "best meeting" desired operational requirements.[222]

217 CAC: RWLN 1/9: Rawlinson Diary, 19 November 1917. Rawlinson was probably aware that Second Army HQ had requested that subordinate corps commanders should 'carefully consider the advisability of carrying out the attack by moonlight … in order to launch the attack before the enemy expects it' three days before the Broodseinde offensive. Unfortunately, the full moon was obscured by clouds on the day of the assault. See TNA: WO/95/275-9: Second Army War Diary, 1 October 1917.
218 See National Schools Observatory, Universe Now: A Month of the Moon, National Grid for Learning. <http://www.schoolsobservatory.org.uk/ngfl.htm> for phases of the moon during November/December 1917.
219 A different response to this operational approach is clearly evident in the account of a failed attack by 29th Division east of Monchy-le-Preux on 30 May 1917: 'The operation was carried out by the 86th Brigade with two of its own battalions and one, the 8/East Lancashire, detached from the 37th Division … Major-General de Lisle's first intention was that there should be no artillery fire unless it were called for; the troops were simply to crawl forward in the darkness and rush the trench. Unfortunately, a man, possibly a deserter, walked into the enemy's lines. Fearing that the secrecy of the plan was compromised, Major-General de Lisle decided to postpone the attack from 12:40 a.m. on the 30th of May until 11:30 p.m. that night. He also concluded that owing to the moonlight it was no longer feasible to dispense with artillery support. The Germans evidently saw the troops leave their trenches a quarter of an hour before Zero and brought down their barrage within five minutes. On the greater part of the front the attack broke down. In the centre, a party of the 16/Middlesex got in, but was not reinforced, and, assailed next morning from all sides, was compelled to surrender.' See Falls, *Military Operations: France and Belgium 1917 Vol. 1*, p. 517.
220 Second Army: 'Moonlight Chart for October, November and December' 1917, Author's collection.
221 CAC: RWLN 1/9: Rawlinson Diary, 20 and 29 November 1917. See Appendix III c.
222 TNA: WO/95/2370: After-action report, 'Part II, Plan of Operations, Section I, General', 11 December 1917, 32nd Division War Diary. 'Another factor governing the hour of Zero

1.6 A New Zealand Gambit: Polderhoek Chateau

Sir Henry Rawlinson convened a conference at II ANZAC Corps HQ on 22 November in order to discuss another contemplated operation approximately 7,500 yards SW of the Passchendaele Salient. South of the boundary between II ANZAC Corps and IX Corps lay a prominent spur; an eastern outcrop of the Gheluvelt Plateau. "On it were perched the piled ruins of Polderhoek Chateau and groups of pillboxes which occupied sites of the attached buildings amid the shattered trees of the once luxuriant pleasances."[223] This bleak outcrop stronghold had successfully withstood four previous assaults since the capture of strategically important high ground from Tower Hamlets Spur to Broodseinde on 4 October.[224] Owing to a sharp re-entrant in II ANZAC Corps' line, the frontline of and approaches to the New Zealand Division were "exposed to continuous and pressing discomfort caused by enfilade fire" from chateau grounds just beyond the left flank of the neighbouring IX Corps.[225] "For the satisfactory occupation of the Divisions' sector, it was highly desirable that a fresh effort should be made to capture the Polderhoek Spur."[226]

was that experience proved that the enemy shelled the tracks in front of the line KANSAS – HUBNER FARM [east of the Steenbeek valley] most heavily between 6 p.m. and 8 p.m. Zero hour had therefore to be so timed that that troops would not enter the shelled area until after 8 p.m.'
223 Stewart, *The New Zealand Division 1916-1919*, p. 305. Polderhoek Chateau was reduced to a mound of rubble by shellfire, 'but below ground level the large cellar had been turned into a reinforced concrete bunker with many concealed entrances and tunnels to various strongpoints. Viewed from our [British] lines it stood out like an island amid a sea of mud; a veritable fortress. Dotted here and there in what was once the chateau grounds were concrete pillboxes, perhaps from ground level they may have appeared to be positioned higgledy-piggledy, but each one was sited with deadly precision. They each provided covering fire to others and the whole of no man's land could be raked with lethal machine-gun fire.' See Terry Carter, *Birmingham Pals: 14th, 15th & 16th (Service) Battalions of the Royal Warwickshire Regiment: A History of the Three City Battalions Raised in Birmingham in World War One* (Barnsley: Pen & Sword, 1997), p. 231.
224 X Corps' efforts to secure Polderhoek Spur were repulsed on 4, 9, 26 October and 6 November respectively, after which it was replaced by IX Corps. See Chris McCarthy, *Passchendaele: The Day-by-Day Account* (London: Arms & Armour Press, 1996) and Becke, *Order of Battle Divisions, Part 4*, p. 196. For first-hand accounts of the repeated attempts against Polderhoek Chateau see H.V. Drinkwater, 'Heartbreak Attack on Polderhoek Chateau: A Ghastly Memory of a Duckboard Track in the Salient' and Major C.A. Bill, 'At the Chateau of Evil Omen: My Stretcher-Bearers Were Killed' in Sir John Hammerton (ed), *'The Great War... I Was There!' Undying Memories of 1914-1918* (London: Amalgamated Press, 1939), pp. 1305-11 and 1371-74.
225 Stewart, *The New Zealand Division 1916-1919*, p. 305.
226 A combined attack on both Gheluvelt village and Polderhoek Spur was initially contemplated 'as one of various local operations designed to continue our offensive during the winter, to add depth to our defence along the Army front, and to facilitate the initial phases of a resumed offensive on a large scale in the spring.' The scope of this operation

Local commanders thought it fitting, despite the fact that the chateau and its cratered grounds lay opposite IX Corps' front, that the New Zealand Division, constantly suffering from the most galling flanking fire, "should strike the blow for its capture." To this end, Lieutenant-General Alexander Godley (GOC II ANZAC Corps) submitted a proposal to Second Army HQ "that the New Zealanders, immediately affected, should carry out the attack and, on the conclusion of the operation, hand over the territory won to the IX Corps." A projected advance of only 600 yards on a 400 yard front would carry the line down the reverse slope of Polderhoek Spur, thus depriving the enemy of a commanding and enfilading position. "Further examination also showed that, owing to the height of the spur and general configuration of the ground, the new lines proposed about the chateau would not to a like degree be exposed to similar enfilade fire from the Gheluvelt Spur to the south."[227] Rawlinson observed that this operation required "hearty good will on the parts of IX and II ANZAC corps [,] and this I found to exist to a very satisfactory degree and I think all will be amicably arranged [.] I was well pleased with the conference."[228]

Rawlinson and his corps commanders considered launching the much smaller Polderhoek enterprise simultaneously with the operation scheduled for the night of 1/2 December. "The tactical objects in view, however, bore no correlation, and in addition the zero hours selected were different."[229] The II ANZAC Corps operation, II Corps and VIII Corps having previously agreed on a night assault, was scheduled to occur at 12:00 p.m. on 3 December. The midday hour was deemed preferable because the obvious disadvantages of a daylight attack would be more than compensated for by an assault delivered at a time when the Germans least expected it. "In the end, therefore, it was decided that the 2 operations should be executed independently."[230]

1.7 Preparations & Preliminaries: 18–30 November

The ghastly routine was maintained on both sides of the Passchendaele – Westroosebeke sector whilst the Battle of Cambrai was in progress. Life in the forward area consisted of improving and extending foremost positions, and taking cover in shell holes and any other available shelter during the almost incessant bombardments. Patrols probed

was eventually reduced to an attack on Polderhoek Chateau and the formidable pillboxes situated on its grounds. Ibid. p. 305.
227 Ibid. p. 305.
228 CAC: RWLN 1/9: Rawlinson Diary, 22 November 1917 and LHCMA: 'Second Army No. 1 (G).', 22 November 1917, Montgomery-Massingberd Papers, File 7/15, King's College, London.
229 The original intention that the four proposed minor operations should be carried out 'so as to attack on a wide front, thus preventing the concentration of hostile artillery fire on an isolated minor operation' appears to have been abandoned as impracticable. See LHCMA: 'Second Army No. 57 (G), Organisation of Army Front During Winter of 1917-18', 18 November 1917, Montgomery-Massingberd Papers, File 7/15, King's College, London.
230 Stewart, *The New Zealand Division 1916-1919*, pp. 307-08.

no man's land and approaches to the enemy line where the ground was dry enough to allow a firm footing.[231] Lieutenant A.B. Scott (32nd Division Artillery Reconnaissance Officer) recalled a somewhat disjointed frontline in his diary:

> Went up the line daily. Our line was north of Passchendaele and the front system consisted of a series of posts at irregular intervals over a front of about a mile. Drained shell holes or remnants of old "pillboxes" were generally the abodes of the brave men who watched there day and night. This was the chief concrete pillbox area – no other refuge was of use owing to the high water level. Cornish and I reconnoitered the posts by night to see if all were on the alert, and knew where their nearest neighbour was so that all the posts were in touch not only with their own men but with the flanking divisions' posts.[232]

Night-time in the salient, always a period of heightened activity, was recalled with retrospective dread by Hanbury-Sparrow: "Rifle bullets crack and whistle; machine-guns clatter; every track and road back to Hell-fire Corner and even Ypres is under intermittent fire; every hollow's being filled with gas, and invisible night raiders are droning in the sky. Ceaselessly the German Very lights rise, burst into cold light, and die. As far as a man can behold, east, west, south and north, there is no safety."[233] Ammunition, ration, fatigue and relief parties made their way forward after dark to battalion and battery positions and numerous other rendezvous on tramways, along corduroy roads or treacherous duckboard avenues extending across the seemingly endless sea of water-filled shell holes. Owing to extreme conditions, the average tour of the frontline by an British infantry brigade was just 48 hours: "Reliefs were hazardous operations and they would not have taken place every other night if it had not been absolutely necessary. But two days at Passchendaele in winter was enough for the most earnest seeker of austerity and a great deal too much for most men."[234] Vigilant German observers searched for signs of another British attack, while artillery, communication and training preparations proceeded in VIII Corps, II Corps and attached divisions.[235]

---

231 See TNA: WO/297/4903: 'Wet and Marshy Ground: Showing Normal State of Ground in Winter' (map winter 1917-18), Sheet name and no: Oostnieuwkerke Edition No: 1 Production: FS Co (1291)
232 A.B. Scott, R.E. Grice-Hutchison, et al., *Artillery & Trench Mortar Memories: 32nd Division* (London: Unwin Brothers, 1932), p. 84.
233 Hanbury-Sparrow, *The Land-Locked Lake*, pp. 312-13
234 Nettleton, *The Anger of the Guns*, p. 110. For harrowing accounts of frontline conditions experienced by the infantry during this period see Boraston & Bax, *The Eighth Division*, pp. 161-62, Dunn, *The War the Infantry Knew*, pp. 416-19 and IWM 569: Burke, Ulick Bernard (interview) Reel 16 <http://www.iwm.org.uk/collections/item/object/80000565>
235 8th Division took over VIII Corps' left sub-sector on a single brigade frontage from 3rd Canadian Division on 18 November. Brigade rotation in and out of the frontline up to 30 November was as follows: 25th Brigade (night of 17-18 to night of 19/20 November),

Brigadier-General Clifford Coffin VC GOC 25 Brigade. (Author)

Heneker requested that VIII Corps find suitable training grounds, adding that Brigadier-General Coffin, whose 25 Brigade would carry out 8th Division's part in the night operation, "says this area is essential" for attack preparation.[236] Brigadier-General Clifford Coffin VC DSO led by example.[237] Possessing a "cool analytical

---

24 Brigade (night of 19/20 to night of 23/24 November), 23 Brigade (night of 23/24 November). 32nd Division took over II Corps' right sub-sector on a single brigade frontage from 1st British Division on the night of 23/24 November. Brigade rotation in and out of the frontline to 30 November was: 97 Brigade (night of 23/24 to night of 26/27 November), 96 Brigade (26/27 November) See TNA: WO/95/1677: 8th Division War Diary and WO/95/2370: 32nd Division War Diary.

236 TNA: WO/95/1677: '8th Division No. G. 97/1/1.', 18 November 1917, 8th Division War Diary.

237 Brigadier-General Clifford Coffin (1870-1959). Commissioned Royal Engineers 1888; Submarine Miners, Jamaica 1891-94; 1st Fortress Company, Cork Harbour 1896-99; Captain and Staff College 1899; South Africa 1899-1902; Intelligence Department, War Office 1904-07; Major 1907; GSO2 Sierra Leone 1911-14; CRE 21st Division 1914; T/Lieutenant-Colonel 1915; T/Brigadier-General and GOC 25 Brigade January 1917; VC (citation 14 September) January 1918.

mind with a taciturn manner", he was, a battalion commander later observed, "religious to a degree, brave beyond words, not the bravery of excitement, but the cool steadfastness of faith, seemingly not to be diverted from the straight and narrow path by either imagination or humour."[238] Brigade staff officer Lieutenant Philip Ledward recalled the austere mess where, displaying the attributes of Oliver Cromwell's "plain russet-coated captain that knows what he fights for, and loves what he knows", the modest and dour Coffin presided:

> The meals were brief and silent affairs and terribly frugal and General Coffin was much more distant with his staff than [Brigadier-General] Grogan [GOC 23 Brigade], but on the rare occasions when he opened his mouth he was usually worth hearing. He used to wear an old tunic for dinner, which was without rank badges or medal ribbons and his clothes were always faded.[239]

A recent recipient of the Victoria Cross – the first awarded to an officer of general rank – for "very gallant conduct" during the opening stages of the Third Ypres campaign, Coffin's "personal courage and example" during the battles of Pilckem Ridge and Langemarck prevented a serious rout of overextended battalions shaken by severe shelling, fierce counter-attacks and mounting losses.[240]

Confirmation of a designated training site was received on 21 November.[241] Coffin's brigade was in divisional reserve near Brandhoek by this time.[242] His HQ diarist noted: "All battalions were bathed today. Battalions are situated in camp all round Brigade Headquarters. Headquarters are in the same camp as the 2nd Royal Berkshire Regiment. A field is being taped out for the Brigade to practice the attack." Practice manoeuvres on the assigned acreage were duly carried out over the next five days.[243] This sort of thorough pre-battle preparation was *de rigueur* throughout the BEF by

---

238 Fox (ed), *Infantry Officer 1914-1918*, p. 14.
239 IWM: 76/120/1: Ledward unpublished memoir.
240 See Stephen Snelling, *VCs of the First World War: Passchendaele 1917* (Gloucestershire: Sutton Publishing, 1998), pp. 8-18 and Hanbury-Sparrow, *The Land-Locked Lake*, pp. 247-79.
241 TNA WO/95/1677: 'VIII Corps. G.1990, 21st November 1917', 8th Division War Diary.
242 IWM IWM: 66/541/1: Heneker Diary, 19 to 29 November 1917.
243 25 Brigade's training schedule was as follows: '22 November: Battalions started training their companies on the taped out field. Weather rather wet; 23 November: Weather fine. Very strong wind. Battalions carried on training on the taped out field. Instructions were issued today for the coming offensive to be resumed by the VIII Corps; 24 November: Battalions carried on training according to training programme; 25 November: Training was carried on as usual according to the training programme; 26 November: The whole Brigade practiced the attack today on the taped field. The Divisional Commander and Corps Commander were there to watch it too. Very wet and cold night; 27 November: Weather fine. All the tapes were gathered in from the training area.' See TNA: WO/95/1727: 25 Brigade War Diary.

1917. Maintenance of signal communications between corps and division, division and brigade and brigade and battalion proved problematic under the inexorable stress of battle. Intense shellfire, which often disrupted the established communications infrastructure, led to the development of various standard operating procedures that helped maintain assault impetus and organisation while an attack was in progress: "If generals accepted that they had little chance to "control" the battle once it had started", John Lee has observed, "their solution was to do everything in their power to create the conditions for success before it began. This included the careful training of the infantry so that all ranks understood the task ahead and the battle drill that would see them achieve success."[244] Designated assault troops were withdrawn a few miles to the rear "and given intensive study of maps, air photos and models of the terrain." Participation in 1:1 reenactments of their duties in a field specially taped out to correct proportions followed. "An attempt would be made to simulate such aspects as creeping barrages, the loss of key personnel at critical moments, or the enemy's expected counter-attack during the consolidation period."[245]

Shute chose Brigadier-General C.A. Blacklock's 97 Brigade to carry out 32nd Division's part in the night operation.[246] The youthful – he was only 37 years old – clean-shaven brigadier had all of the qualities Shute most admired: courage, energy, resource, optimism and aggression. These attributes were clearly demonstrated during joint Anglo-French operations near St Quentin in April 1917:

> In the first instance the [Fourth] Army command had declined to accede to the French Army's request that Fayet should be attacked by us in conjunction with their first attack. However, on the comparative failure of the French attack General C.D. Shute was ordered to take Fayet as soon as possible. The three Brigadiers and Brigade Majors were hurriedly summoned to a conference at Division HQ. Two of the brigadiers stressed the impossibility of carrying out

---

244 Lee, 'Command and Control in Battle' in Sheffield & Todman (eds) *Command and Control on the Western Front*, p. 120 and Paddy Griffith, *Battle Tactics on the Western Front: The British Army's Art of Attack 1916-18* (New Haven/London: Yale University Press, 1994), pp. 188-89.
245 Griffith, *Battle Tactics on the Western Front*, pp. 188-89.
246 Brigadier-General Cyril Aubrey Blacklock DSO (1880-1936). Commissioned KRRC from Royal Warwickshire Militia 1901; South Africa 1901-02. Resigned commission and emigrated to Canada 1904; recommissioned KRRC 1914. "One of a small number of 'exotics' who managed to reach generals' rank despite their civilian status at the start of the First World War", Blacklock experienced rapid promotion: 2/ic and CO 10th KRRC 1915; DSO and Bar 1916; Brigadier-General and GOC 182 Brigade January 1917; GOC 97 Brigade March 1917. See John Bourne, 'The BEF's Generals on 29 September 1918: An Empirical Portrait with Some British and Australian Comparisons' in Peter Dennis & Jeffery Grey (eds), *1918: Defining Victory: Proceedings of the Chief of Army's History Conference Held at the National Convention Centre, Canberra 29 September 1998* (Canberra: Army History Unit, 1999), p. 102, fn. 20.

the operation in the time available, but Brigadier-General Blacklock volunteered to undertake the job, although in the ordinary rotation it would have been the job of one of the other two brigades.

The conference lasted until well into the afternoon, and it was somewhere about four O'clock before we got back to Brigade HQ. General Blacklock outlined his orders and left to give personal instructions to the commanding officers, ordering me to take the written orders personally by hand as soon as they were ready. The [97] Brigade was very scattered and had no idea an operation was pending. In spite of this, the whole Brigade was in position and lined up on tapes, laid for the assault at 2 a.m. No previous reconnaissance by the commanding officers had been possible.

The assault was carried out at 4:30 a.m. [on 14 April], and was a complete success, many prisoners being taken and casualties being comparatively small. Later in the day trouble developed from two copses on the left flank of the Brigade. This flank had of necessity become very exposed. General Blacklock decided to use his reserve battalion to capture these copses. The operation entailed a long approach march, deployment in the open, and an attack over very exposed ground. It was most successfully carried out by the 11th Border Regiment with great speed and dash, in fact it was only because of the speed and dash, coupled with surprise that the operation was so successful.[247]

Blacklock, no doubt appreciative of the high regard in which he was held, appeared, unlike so many contemporaries, unafraid of his formidable division commander. An exponent of calculated aggression, his corollate advocacy of "careful planning and proper preparation against facsimile objectives before carrying out attacks" was in keeping with contemporary best practice.[248] To this end, "special measures were taken to ensure that every officer and man not only understood the object of the scheme of operations [,] but also knew the definite part he himself had to play." A specially constructed plasticine model, "which represented with great accuracy and detail" the entire area of operations was also put on display at Division HQ, where "officers, NCOs and men were daily lectured, not only by their own officers, but by their Divisional Commander, Brigadier, and their respective staffs, on the forthcoming operations." Each man was issued a map, "and it may be safely said", Shute subsequently observed "that as far as explanation went on the ground and on the model, little was left undone

---

247 Captain R.C. Chichester-Constable (Brigade Major 97 Brigade) correspondence dated 28 February 1939, TNA: CAB/45/116: Post-war Official History Correspondence (Arras 1917). For 32nd Division's operations around St Quentin during the spring of 1917 see Falls, *Military Operations: France and Belgium 1917 Vol 1*, pp. 526-28.
248 Captain V.F. Inglefield, *The History of the Twentieth (Light) Division* (London: Nisbet, 1922), p.55.

Brigadier-General Cyril Aubrey
Blacklock GOC 97 Brigade.
(IWM HN82159)

to ensure each man knowing his part."²⁴⁹ 97 Brigade began its training following relief by 96 Brigade on the night of 26/27 November. The former, withdrawing to billets at Dambre Camp near Vlamertinghe, "rested and completed preparations for the forthcoming offensive at Passchendaele." Brigadier-Generals Coffin and Blacklock, in common with many of their BEF contemporaries, placed great value on pre-attack briefings and practice exercises that ensured staffs and subordinate officers "were efficient and also well briefed on the content and nuances of orders and battle plans", so they could direct operations in a brigade commander's place "should he become a casualty or lose contact through a failure in communications."²⁵⁰

The platoon²⁵¹ had been transformed into the BEF's basic sub-unit of manoeuvre by the distribution of *S.S. 143 Instructions for the Training of Platoons for Offensive Action*

---

249 TNA: WO/95/2370: After-action report, 'Part II, Plan of Operations, Section III, Preliminary Measures', 11 December 1917, 32nd Division War Diary.
250 Arthur & Munro (eds), *The Seventeenth Highland Light Infantry*, p. 67, TNA: WO/95/2370: 32nd Division War Diary and Peter Simkins, 'Building Blocks': Aspects of Command and Control at Brigade Level in the BEF's Offensive Operations 1916-1918', in Sheffield & Todman (eds). *Command and Control on the Western Front*, p. 146.
251 A British infantry battalion consisted of four companies of four platoons each. A full-strength platoon was organised as follows:

in February 1917.²⁵² Its authors provided the infantry with a basis for platoon reorganisation whereby the integration of firepower technology with small unit tactical independence and flexibility permitted the coordination of "Lewis Gun, rifle grenade and trench mortar fire with the advances carried out by riflemen and bombers." Sophisticated "fire and movement" drills carried out by these four component sections of specialists – operating as platoon firepower and manoeuvre elements – were now applied to overcome any resistance. "Great emphasis was placed on seeking out and turning the enemy's flank in any circumstance and the initiative of the platoon commander was favoured."²⁵³ This was, as Tim Cook points out, "never that easy, as there were often no gaps within the interlocking defensive fields of fire, but infantrymen had a more flexible organisation and system of weapons which better allowed them to fight their way forward when the artillery barrage broke down, as it often did." All of this, nevertheless, "blended with an increasing confidence in the gunner's ability to lay down effective creeping barrages", thereby transforming British low-level tactics and battle performance in 1917-18.²⁵⁴

S.S. 143 was based on battle experience gained during the Somme offensive in 1916.²⁵⁵ Instruction in the prescribed platoon battle drills – debate over their complete acceptance and standardization throughout the BEF continued well into 1918 – became the foundation of routine pre-assault training. Thus the battalions of 25 and

> HQ 1 Officer 4 ORs
> Bombing Section 1 NCO 8 ORs 8 men including two expert throwers and two bayonet men.
> Lewis Gun Section 1 NCO 8 ORs 8 men including two gunners
> Rifle Section 1 NCO 8 ORs 8 men including two marksmen and two scouts
> Rifle Bomb Section 1 NCO 8 ORs 8 men, four of them bomb firers.
> Total: 1officer and 40 ORs

252 See also General Staff training manuals *S.S. 144 The Normal Formation for the Attack* (February 1917) and *S.S.185 Assault Training* (September 1917).
253 Lee, 'Command and Control in Battle' in Sheffield & Todman (eds) *Command and Control on the Western Front*, p. 120.
254 John Lee, 'Some Lessons of the Somme: The British Infantry in 1917' in Brian Bond, et al, *'Look to Your Front:' Studies in the First World War* (Staplehurst: Spellmount, 1999), p. 80 and Tim Cook, 'Storm Troops: Combat Effectiveness and the Canadian Corps in 1917' in Dennis & Grey (eds), *1917*, p. 48.
255 Controversy over S.S. 143 continued throughout 1917. Lieutenant-General Ivor Maxse (GOC XVIII Corps) observed in a letter (9 December 1917) to Brigadier-General Charles Bonham Carter (DGT GHQ) that its authors 'had not grasped what kind of men were commanding platoons. They try to cram a Staff College education into a pamphlet … it is a fine performance but bewilders our platoon commanders and people like me. If they would be simple and teach a few points in each pamphlet I think they would produce better results.'Nevertheless, Brigadier-General Arthur Solly-Flood's (Bonham-Carter's predecessor and chief author of *S.S. 143*) pamphlet contributed to stabilization of the BEF's tactical structure and the shift of Lewis Gun assets from company to platoon level. See Shelford Bidwell & Dominic Graham, *Fire-Power: The British Army Weapons & Theories of War 1904-1945* (Barnsley: Pen & Sword, 2004), p. 127.

97 brigades, simulating attacks across specially prepared practice fields in waves or lines of columns, rigorously rehearsed manoeuvres against mock objectives in the days leading up to Zero. The increased proficiency gained during these exercises would, perhaps, also mitigate infantry apprehension about the absence of an orthodox artillery barrage from the impending operation's first stage.[256]

That stage, it will be recalled, was not subordinate to an artillery plan; it was up to the infantry to surprise and overrun the German advanced posts before the inevitable defensive barrage was called for. Batteries of VIII Corps, II Corps and attached divisions were, however, still an important component to this hybrid set-piece assault. Field artillery was tasked with providing fire support after the *Vorfeldzone* was overwhelmed, whilst heavy guns searched approach roads, bombarded assembly areas, and places where support and reserve battalions were disposed. Counter-battery groups were expected to continue with their main task: suppression of deadly artillery concentrations opposite the Passchendaele Salient.

Eight field artillery brigades and one Heavy Artillery Group[257] would support 8th Division's attack.[258] Heneker requested that the "Northern Bombardment Group" (62nd HAG) – a Corps artillery asset, be placed under his orders for required artillery preparations prior to the assault: "This arrangement had worked excellently on several occasions this year when I [Heneker] was operating in similar conditions under the orders of the G.O.C XV Corps."[259] VIII Corps acquiesced, but required the GOC 8th Division to submit his orders to Brigadier General H.D.O. Ward (GOCRA VIII Corps) for coordination.[260]

---

256 For a detailed survey of the new platoon tactics see General Staff Training Manual SS 143, *Instructions for the Training of Platoons for Offensive Action* (14 February 1917) and Lee, 'Some Lessons of the Somme' in Bond, et al, *'Look to Your Front'*, pp. 79-87.

257 Heavy Artillery Groups (typically of five batteries each) were organised and reorganised as best suited the situation in the sector they were deployed. These regiment-sized units consisted of siege (6 in., 8 in., 9.2 in or 12 in. howitzers, or 12 in. or 14 in. railway guns) batteries or a mixed or double grouping (60 pdr.) of siege and heavy batteries. See Dale Clarke & Brian Delf, *British Artillery 1914-19: Heavy Artillery* (Oxford: Osprey Publishing, 2005), pp 12-14.

258 The field artillery (18 pdr. and 4.5 in. howitzer) consisted of 4 brigades from 8th and 14th divisions and 4 Army field artillery brigades. See TNA: WO/95/1677: '8th Division Instruction No. 1, 22 November 1917', '8th Division Instructions No. 8, 25 November 1917', '8th Division Order No. 247, 26 November 1917', '8th Division No. G.97/1/2A, 29 November 1917' and 'Addendum No. 1 to 8th Division Order No. 247', 29 November 1917', 8th Division War Diary.

259 Attached to XV Corps in early 1917, 8th Division participated in a night attack near Bouchavesnes (4 March) and followed up the German withdrawal to the Hindenburg Line (24 March to 5 April). It was during the latter operations that it successfully launched a series of night attacks to secure Sorel and Fins (30 March) and, marching by compass 'during a wild and snowy night', the big village of Gouzeaucourt (12 April). See Becke, *Order of Battle of Divisions*, p. 95, Boraston & Bax, *The Eighth Division*, Chapter VIII and Falls, *Military Operations: France and Belgium 1917 Vol. 1*, pp. 120-22, 154-55 and 526.

260 See TNA: WO/95/1677: '8th Division. No. G.97/1/1.', 18 November 1917 and 'VIII Corps G.1990', 21 November 1917, 8th Division War Diary.

Work continued with all available labour on repairing and extending VIII Corps roads and tramlines under deadly enfilade fire from the right flank. This effort greatly improved supply routes to field batteries on the Abraham Heights – Boeteleer Line and the newly positioned heavy guns on Windmill Cabaret Ridge. The guns (the maximum range of the 18-pounder field gun and 4.5-inch howitzer was 7,000 yards) on the former position were now approximately 3,000 yards from Venison Trench and its environs. Both field and heavy batteries, however, still remained dangerously bunched and vulnerable to shelling by German counter-batteries.

The eight field artillery brigades directly supporting 32nd Division's attack were designated "Right" or "32nd Divisional Group", which consisted of sixteen batteries from 1st, 32nd, 63rd divisions and two attached army brigades.[261] Divisional batteries were under orders of Brigadier-General A.D. Kirby (GOCRA II CORPS) for the stated purpose of coordination and distribution of instructions and barrage tables.[262]

A formidable array of siege and heavy batteries were also deployed to support 32nd Division's attack. The guns were laboriously shifted forward along corduroy roads and rail lines intersecting the devastated area west of the Langemarck – Winnipeg Road. Conveying them away from these avenues to carefully prepared off-road emplacements was the most trying ordeal.[263] As November drew to a close, II Corps' accumulated siege and heavy artillery assets consisted of (1) 15-inch howitzer served by a crew of Royal Marine Artillery, (4) 12-inch howitzers, (12) 9.2-inch howitzers, (24) 8-inch howitzers, (88) 6-inch howitzers, (42) 60 pdrs, (8) 6-inch Mark VII guns and (1) 9.2-inch gun.[264] Kirby and his staff, surmounting all difficulties of transporting east, across very bad ground, the required number of field artillery brigades, ensured the newly sited batteries were now approximately 5,000 yards from targets on and about Vat Cottages Ridge. This accumulation of field and heavy guns, as in VIII Corps, remained clustered and exposed to concentrated German artillery fire from the north, NW and east.

Much of the hostile shellfire encountered on the northern part of Second Army front originated from artillery situated in the dead ground behind the Passchendaele – Westroosebeke portion of the main ridge. Flat terrain, westerly winds, foul weather, poor ground conditions, continuous bombardments and enemy employment of dummy

---

261 TNA: WO/95/643: 'Summary of Arrangements for Attack by II Corps, 29th November 1917', II Corps War Diary. 32nd Division artillery HQ distributed the necessary artillery instructions and amendments to field artillery brigades concerned during the period 28 November-1 December 1917. See TNA: WO/95/2370: '32nd Division Artillery Instructions No. 7', 28 November, '32nd Divisional Artillery Group Instructions No. 15', 30 November and '32nd Divisional Artillery Group Instructions No. 18', 1 December, 32nd Division War Diary.
262 Ibid: 'II Corps Operation Order No. 167', 22 November 1917.
263 See Major G. Goold Walker DSO (ed), *The Honourable Artillery Company in the Great War 1914-1919* (London: Seeley, Service & Co., 1930), pp. 378-79.
264 TNA: WO/95/1643: 'Summary of Arrangements for Attack by II Corps, 29 November 1917', II Corps War Diary.

German heavy gun. (Author)

batteries precluded effective use of sound ranging and flash spotting technology (responsible for detecting 75 percent of all German batteries by mid-1917)[265] to locate hostile guns for British counter-batteries.[266] The efficacy of flash spotting groups was also reduced by the dearth of observation posts between Houthulst Forest and Hill 60. Such posts that did exist were situated in captured pillboxes offering views to the NE. Providing the only available shelter for personnel and sensitive equipment, these pervasive structures were frequently defiladed by shellfire from the ridge; "That closest to the enemy was 5,000 yards from Passchendaele."[267] Consequently, the counter-battery efforts of VIII Corps and II Corps relied primarily on RFC flights to provide hostile battery intelligence. The airmen's concerted efforts were often hampered by bad visibility and mist.[268]

265 David John Jordan, 'The Army Co-operation Missions of the Royal Flying Corps/Royal Air Force 1914-1918' (PhD Thesis. Birmingham: University of Birmingham, 1997), p. 185.
266 Air and ground lines for these units were also frequently cut by constant traffic across the battlefield.
267 See Peter Chasseaud, 'Field Survey in the Salient: Cartography and Artillery Survey in the Flanders Operations in 1917' in Liddle (ed), *Passchendaele in Perspective*, pp. 117-39 for an excellent account of British sound ranging and flash spotting efforts during Third Ypres.
268 Ibid and Jordan, 'The Army Co-operation Missions of the Royal Flying Corps/Royal Air Force 1914-1918', pp. 172-203 for RFC developments in air-artillery co-operation during

Rawlinson had been "anxious" about massive concentrations of enemy batteries opposite the Passchendaele Salient. He was also aware of the need – primarily in II Corps – of obtaining the necessary labour to "get enough guns forward."[269] Much progress had been made by subordinates to improve the unsatisfactory artillery situation on VIII Corps and II Corps fronts in the weeks leading up to the next attack. Nevertheless, mastery of the enemy's artillery had not been achieved during the second half of November. Gun losses to hostile counter-battery fire in the vicinity of the salient remained high – 58 heavy and 248 field guns being "knocked out" between 14 and 29 November.[270]

Second Army Artillery Instructions No. 28 was distributed to all corps HQs on 20 November. This considered change in previously applied artillery tactics was scheduled to commence during the lead-up to what was still regarded as the tenth stage of operations commencing with the Battle of Menin Road on 20 September: "Whereas artillery attacks recently have taken the form of a series of continuous barrages, the attacks to be developed in the future will be in the nature of heavy concentrations upon areas and communications."[271] In addition, corps BGRAs and their staffs were to make advanced arrangements to meet any heavy bombardment launched against the Passchendaele front. All corps were to maintain vigorous counter-battery work, the artillery of XIX Corps to pay special attention to enemy concentrations[272] capable of bombarding Passchendaele Ridge from the north and NW. Daily intense bombardments would occur on the fronts of II ANZAC Corps, VIII Corps and II Corps during dawn or dusk. Targets to be engaged were probable places of assembly and roads leading to and from these locales. Pillboxes proved particularly difficult to penetrate, one siege battery history noting: "Well to do men recall the supposed consequences of a shoot we took one day on a Boche pillbox near Westroosebeke. This was visible to us, even with the naked eye, and we had the almost unique experience

---

    1916-17.
269 CAC: RWLN 1/9: Rawlinson Diary, 18 and 19 November 1917. The initial German defensive barrage, II Corps intelligence surmised, would 'probably come down on the general line VENTURE FARM – GOUDBERG COPSE – TOURNANT FARM and a later period (between zero plus 15 min[ute]s and zero plus 1 hour) will be brought back to the line VAT COTTAGES – VOX FARM – TEALL COTTAGE, the shelling on the TOURNANT FARM – GOUDBERG COPSE sector coming from the west of WESTROOSEBEKE [;] on the GOUDBERG COPSE – TEALL COTTAGE sector from the east of WESTROOSEBEKE and later from the SE.' See TNA: WO/95/2370: 'Notes to Accompany Special Intelligence Maps of the Area V.15 to V.30' November 1917, 32nd Division War Diary.
270 CAC: RWLN 1/10: Rawlinson Papers, '1917 & 1918 Documents Found Loose in War Journal.'
271 LHCMA: 'Second Army Artillery Instructions No. 28', 20 November 1917, Montgomery-Massingberd Papers, File 7/15, King's College, London.
272 Ibid. The British knew these concentrations as 'Houthulst Forest', 'Stadenreke' and 'Brim Polders Luike' groups.

of seeing each of our twelve rounds burst. Several seemed to be O.K.'s, but the pillbox was still there at the end of the shoot."[273] The German forward area was to be searched simultaneously with shrapnel and machine-gun fire. "The time at which these attacks are developed and the localities against which they are directed" would be "varied frequently."[274] Corps artillery schemes were to be based on all available intelligence. It was the "duty of those responsible for drawing up the plans to constantly think out the possible and probable action of the Germans if intending to attack on any particular day and to direct the fire accordingly."[275] In the meantime, batteries were dispatched south from Second Army to Italy or in support of the Cambrai offensive with increased frequency. Sir Henry Rawlinson lamented the loss of further artillery assets: "Today we got an order to send away 22 Brigade Field Artillery ... This will reduce us greatly [,] but still will leave us enough for defensive purposes. They are also reducing us very much in heavies."[276] Adequate artillery support for pending operations at Passchendaele and Polderhoek Chateau had been arranged for; only a bare minimum of guns, constantly reduced by enemy action and breakage, remained to defend the Army front.

Second Army had committed to two local operations (Passchendaele – Westroosebeke front and Polderhoek Chateau) designed to improve adverse sector-specific situations along Passchendaele Ridge by late November. Units designated to carry out the fast-approaching large-scale night assault, regardless of having to jump off from disadvantageous positions inside the Passchendaele Salient, were tasked with seizing proximate objectives that appeared, given ready acceptance of a novel, albeit highly controversial hybrid attack plan, obtainable in the eyes of both Army and Corps HQs. Sir Henry Rawlinson confidently expressed this conviction one day prior to the assault: "I visited the XIX, II and VIII Corps today and was satisfied with the plans for the attack tomorrow night."[277]

---

273 W.R. Kingham, *London Gunners: The Story of the HAC Battery in Action* (London: Methuen & Co., 1919), p. 77.
274 LHCMA: 'Second Army Artillery Instructions No. 28', 20 November 1917, Montgomery-Massingberd Papers, File 7/15, King's College, London.
275 Ibid.
276 CAC: RWLN 1/9: Rawlinson Diary, 28 November 1917.
277 Ibid, 30 November 1917.

2

Divisional Instructions & Orders

It is a beastly operation.[1]

2.1 Standard Operating Procedure & Formulaic Approach

British and Dominion infantry divisions trained for offensive operations in three ways after December 1916. Attacks on prepared trench positions; "the semi-open warfare of subsequent attacks on an enemy turned out of his main positions; and the longed for return to open warfare when the enemy was finally "on the run." Pre-attack preparations and practice assault exercises on prepared positions were based on guidelines found in *S.S.135 Instructions for the Training of Divisions for Offensive Action* issued by GHQ in December 1916.[2] This manual of "Standard Operating Procedure" was an update of *S.S.119 Preliminary Notes of the Tactical Lessons of Recent Operations* (July 1916). By disseminating the operational methodology found in *S.S.135*, "it was intended to get all British divisions working in a similar pattern of experience based on the Somme fighting" of the previous year.[3]

S.S.135 contained thirty-three section headings and two appendices. It serves, John Lee has observed, as a "useful reminder of just how complex an organisation was an infantry division of the period 1916–18 and how much work had to go into the planning of an attack by its many component parts." Each section of *S.S.135* was a means of addressing the problem of command and control on the battlefield. Commanders' intentions had to be clear and properly communicated to all component parts of an attacking force. Units were expected, following commencement of an assault, to make

---

1 IWM: 66/541/1: Heneker Diary, 30 November 1917.
2 *Field Service Regulations 1-Operations* (1909) still applied to open warfare. See Simpson, *Directing Operations*, p. 64.
3 Lee, 'Command and Control in Battle' in Sheffield & Todman (eds), *Command and Control on the Western Front*, p. 120.

the passing of accurate and timely information to command centres their highest priority. This kept superiors fully up to date as the battle unfolded. Development of an effective communications infrastructure that could, as cables were cut by hostile bombardments and runners reduced by casualties, withstand collapse in battle thus became a crucial aspect of pre-assault planning and organisation. Standardised signal preparations at division level called for the forward extension of buried cable systems and the adoption of brigade lines of communication manned by signallers organised into brigade forward parties. Wireless technology was still in its infancy; so telephones, telegraph, signal lamps, semaphore, carrier pigeons and runners were all utilised in order to provide multiple communication avenues.

Clarity of purpose during preparations was achieved before the issue of final operation orders by the distribution of a series of "instructions" covering seventeen categories of preliminary organisation and work. These documents dealt with artillery organisation and scheme, the action of massed machine-guns, tanks, signal communications, boundaries and liaison with neighbouring formations, rights of passage on communication routes to the frontline, location of HQs, tasks to be assigned to pioneer battalions and Royal Engineers [RE], medical arrangements, handling of prisoners, cooperation with Royal Flying Corps [RFC] contact aircraft and other myriad details that needed to be addressed prior to any set-piece assault.[4]

S.S. 135 also outlined the relationship and responsibilities of corps and division. Section I ("Issue of Orders by Divisional and Brigade Commanders") stated that Corps HQ would assign tasks, after which division would draw up the infantry assault plan. Division could issue schemes to subordinates after evaluation and approval by Corps. The procedure was expanded in Appendix A: "The Corps allots the task to be executed by Division. The Division Commander will be informed of the frontage, objectives, and assembly area allotted to his Division, as well as the artillery support he may expect and the action of the Divisions on his flank." Artillery plans were under the aegis (except for minor operations) of Corps. Barrage schemes would be coordinated by the Corps GOCRA after consultation with division, although the latter "were enjoined to suggest any modifications to the plan which might make success more likely."[5]

Section II ("Objectives") articulated the criteria divisions were to utilise when selecting objectives for the infantry in any one operation. Such proceeding usually precluded corps involvement. "But in the next section ("Co-Operation Between Artillery and Infantry") it became clear that artillery planning was very much the province of corps."[6] The control of virtually all artillery assets involved transformed corps HQs the highest operational unit within the BEF: "Army was mentioned in so

---

4 Ibid. p. 122.
5 Simpson, *Directing Operations*, p. 64.
6 Ibid.

far as it retained "general control" and would attend to the liaison between corps in consequence."[7]

Second Army HQ updated *S.S.135* with the army-wide distribution of *Notes on Training and Preparations for Offensive Operations* on 31 August 1917.[8] This pamphlet addressed in particular German defensive measures encountered since the opening of the campaign on 31 July. "The defence in depth was to be overcome by an attack itself organised in great depth, with fresh formations leap-frogging forward to take each successive objective line, always covered by massive creeping and standing barrages, and with each subsequent advance to an objective being shorter than the one before it." Assigned objectives were based on the infantry's ability to carry out the task.[9]

Plumer stressed the need for tactical flexibility: "The enemy has deliberately substituted flexibility for rigidity in his defence, and I think the response should be a corresponding flexibility in our attack."[10] Gaps in the line did not worry the methodical GOC Second Army: "The old linear tactics were thoroughly redundant by the autumn of 1917." New emphasis was also placed on the "need for every commander down to company level to keep a reserve in hand to meet and defeat the inevitable counter-attacks."[11] The usual stress was placed on the need to pass on a steady stream of reliable information to command centres during attacks. Continued application of the guidelines found in *S.S.135* and the further amelioration of these methods in the booklet circulated by Second Army, provided a template for measured operational success.[12] Deviations from certain aspects of this template (rushed preparations, unrealistic objectives, dilution of artillery fire support, etc.) combined with bad weather, unsatisfactory ground conditions and consequent logistical difficulties, contributed to the failures of 9 and 12 October. The return to the methodical pre-battle preparations and limited but realistic objectives agreed upon at a conference on 13 October led to the capture of Passchendaele, but also underlined the diminished post-strategic expectations of British GHQ.[13]

The reduction of Second Army's manpower and artillery assets limited further efforts to improve the local tactical situation on the Passchendaele Ridge after 20 November. Nevertheless, a pattern of tactical experience and increased operational tempo had evolved by the close of the offensive. Though the operations of 20

---

7   Ibid.
8   See Edmonds, *Military Operations: France and Belgium 1917 Vol. 2*, Appendix XXV.
9   Lee, 'Command and Control in Battle' in Sheffield & Todman (eds), *Command and Control on the Western Front*, p. 125.
10 Ibid. p.126.
11 Ibid.
12 Ibid.
13 See Haig diary entry 13 October 1917 in 'The First World War Political, Social and Military Manuscript Sources: Series One: The Haig Papers from the National Library of Scotland, Part I Haig's Autograph Great War Diary', Reel 5 and Sheffield & Bourne (eds), *Douglas Haig*, p. 336.

September to 12 October were "conducted with increasing frequency, they became steadily less successful as the Second Army advanced into a salient and the ground got worse, so ... it was not possible to sustain a tempo higher than the enemy's. The set-piece attack, however, organised by corps, had been fully developed."[14] Corps HQs acted as conduits of information from army to division. This was a direct result of an increasingly formulaic operational approach by Second and Fifth Armies after 20 September. Orders from Army HQ almost invariably began with the words "Ref. 'Attack Map' and objectives were marked on this map, as well as the stages of the attack being described in relation to it. Other than that, the orders were terse statements of the timetable, which corps were involved, any corps movements and when the attack should take place."[15]

Although corps remained the principal level of command responsible for the organisation of the battle, a trend, which began at Messines, toward allowing divisions more latitude with their artillery arrangements continued throughout the campaign.[16] This type of arrangement was demonstrated when VIII Corps agreed to allow 62nd HAG to be placed under Heneker's command during artillery preparations for the Passchendaele night attack, although oversight was maintained with the stipulation that the GOC 8th Division was required to submit his orders for review by the Corps GOCRA.[17]

Captain Guy Chapman (adjutant 13th Royal Fusiliers) subsequently observed that "the winter of 1917-18 was more prolific of paper than any other period earlier or later."[18] This evident increase in foolscap "bumf" was indicative of complex operational/organisational details and the means to disseminate such information throughout the BEF. The headquarters of 8th Division and 32nd Division would subsequently issue a routine plethora of attack orders, instructions and amendments to subordinate units between 18 and 30 November. The contents of these documents were in keeping with the standard operating procedures found in *S.S. 135*, GHQ-generated manuals and pamphlets,[19] Second Army's *Notes on the Training and Preparations for*

---

14   Simpson, *Directing Operations*, p. 224.
15   Ibid. p.106. Third Army's offensive at Cambrai, groundbreaking use of massed tanks and predicted artillery barrage aside, was planned on similar lines: 'Army issued its draft scheme in three parts, and 'subject to such alterations as have already been approved by the Army Commander, the draft scheme will form the basis on which Corps will formulate their schemes ... Objectives were shown on attached maps and the principals of the operation ... were stressed.' Ibid p.116. See Appendix IIIa.
16   Ibid, pp. 80 and 105.
17   See Chapter 1, pp. 113.
18   Guy Chapman, *A Passionate Prodigality* (New York: Holt, Rinehart & Winston, 1966), p. 223.
19   *S.S.148 Forward Inter-Communication in Battle* (March 1917). Reprinted with amendments September 1917) and *S.S. 158 Notes on Recent Operations on the Front of First, Third, Fourth, Fifth Armies* (May 1917). The latter manual related lessons learned during the Battle of Arras.

Offensive Operations and lessons learned and disseminated during the summer and autumn fighting.

2.2 8th Division

Heneker forwarded an outline proposal to VIII Corps following a meeting with Brigadier-General Aspinall on 18 November. An accompanying map detailed objectives, boundaries, jumping-off line and opening barrage line. A short advance of 100 to 300 yards by 25 Brigade would bring about the capture of Venison Trench and Northern and Southern redoubts on a frontage of 1,020 yards. The GOC 8th Division believed three battalions would be sufficient to carry out this task: "right battalion holding the line and forming a defensive flank with about a company" south of Southern Redoubt, "centre and left battalions attacking." The remaining battalion "would be in close support behind the jumping-off line." Another full brigade would be in close support at Bellevue, Wieltje and St. Jean ready to take over the line on the evening following "Zero/Zero plus one if required."[20]

Heneker proposed that 8th Division's attached (23rd, 24th, 25th, 218th) machine-gun companies[21] should be employed in three ways, two companies detailed to form a covering barrage; one company with eight guns sited for close defence of the present frontline, whilst a further seven guns would be made ready for close defence of the captured area. A reserve company was to be retained at Wieltje "ready to take over the close defence of the forward area from the M.G. Company last referred to if required."[22] Speculation that the "present allotment of artillery" covering the divisional front was sufficient, was followed by a proposal that the forthcoming operation, supported by a barrage of "lifts of 100 yards in four minutes", should commence at dawn. VIII Corps HQ, as we have seen, subsequently denied this request after II Corps' insistence on a night attack.[23]

Heneker observed that "first essential" attack preparations would concern overland communications. The only traversable road to the forward area extended across the elevated spine of the Bellevue Spur. One shell-swept road could not possibly accommodate the traffic of two divisions preparing to attack from the narrow salient. The solution was to lay two extensions of "No. 5 [duckboard] track to run just south of the Meetcheele [Bellevue] Spur and parallel to it…" These extensions would, after

---

20   TNA: WO/95/1677: '8th Division No. G. 97/1/1', 18 November 1917, 8th Division War Diary.
21   A British machine-gun company consisted of 16 'Vickers .303 inch MK I' heavy machine-guns. A fourth company was added during 1917, thus providing 64 guns per division.
22   TNA: WO/95/1677: '8th Division No. G. 97/1/1', 18 November 1917, 8th Division War Diary.
23   See Chapter 1, pp. 96-97.

skirting the treacherous Ravebeek[24] quagmire's northern edge, be prolonged as far as the immediate vicinity of Vindictive Crossroads. As the prevailing dearth of available labour prevented this essential work and the construction of certain defended localities, the decision was therefore made "to give the duckboard tracks preference."[25]

Heneker next submitted a series of requests for VIII Corps' consideration.[26] He asked that the supporting barrage be extended over the front of II ANZAC Corps, VIII Corps and II Corps to mask the actual frontage of attack. To this end, it would be necessary for 33rd Division to cover 8th Division's right flank by placing a machine-gun barrage "down the spurs running N.E. and E. by S. from Passchendaele", whilst launching a Chinese attack[27] combined with gas and smoke discharges just south of Passchendaele.[28] The GOC 8th Division also expressed the view that a boundary adjustment with II Corps should take place at an early date "so that divisions may prepare their own front of attack." He followed this by requesting "as soon as possible, for a précis of all available information about the German defences and topography south of my [Heneker's] present boundary and within my future one." Access to this kind of intelligence would, besides determining the most favourable locale for establishment of a new defensive flank, provide a basis for further sector intelligence gathering in the days leading up to the assault. VIII Corps agreed to all Heneker's entreaties except those concerning time of attack and artillery barrage arrangements. The desired boundary adjustment was scheduled to occur, Brigadier-General Aspinall

---

24 This small watercourse, situated in a valley between the Passchendaele and Bellevue spurs, had, by 9 October, become a 'morass 30 to 50 yards wide, waist-deep in water in the centre.' See Edmonds, *Military Operations: France and Belgium 1917 Vol. 2*, p. 331.
25 TNA: WO/95/1677: '8th Division No. G.97/1/1', 18 November 1917, 8th Division War Diary.
26 Ibid. These requests concerned the pushing out of forward posts to hinder enemy work on the *Vorfeldzone* opposite designate attack objectives, the desired artillery scheme and organisation and aforementioned application for a dedicated training area.
27 'Chinese Attack' was contemporary parlance for a feigned assault. In this case, Heneker probably had in mind the employment of life-sized, plywood, cut-out figures representing advancing British infantry. These *faux* soldiers would be released to rise vertically with hand-manipulated wires or electrically discharged detonators during accompanying smoke screen, artillery, machine-gun and gas barrages. Such mechanical ruses were designed to convince the enemy that they were under direct attack. 8th Division had previously (20 September) carried out one of these 'dummy shows' in the Lys valley sector opposite Warneton to support Second and Fifth armies' offensive operations (Battle of Menin Road) further north. See Lieutenant-Colonel J. H. Dyer, 'A Holding Operation in September 1917' in *Gun Fire No. 6*, Series 2 (date unknown) reprint of June 1939 *Royal Engineers Journal* article, pp. 2-7 and the wonderful two-page illustration in Peter Barton, *Passchendaele: Unseen Panoramas of the Third Battle of Ypres* (London: Constable, 2007), pp. 376-77.
28 TNA: WO/95/1677: '8th Division No. G.97/1/1, 18 November 1917, 8th Division War Diary.

remarked, "as soon as you [Heneker] have completed the minor operation [to capture Hill 52 and Vox Farm] discussed at this afternoon's conference."[29]

8th Division Instructions No. 1 was issued the following day. This document, the first of a series drawn up by proficient GSO 1 Lieutenant-Colonel Beddington, related the contents of 'VIII Corps Order No. 52' i.e., the notification of the resumption of the offensive, designated objectives, boundary adjustment, etc., to various attached HQs. 25 Brigade's selection to carry out the attack – still scheduled for November 30/1 December – was also confirmed.[30]

8th Division Order No. 242 was distributed at 8:30 p.m. on 23 November. This document dealt with further organisational details and the forthcoming divisional boundary adjustment (scheduled for the night of 24/25 November) previously related in "VIII Corps Order No. 54".[31] DMGOs of the three divisions (8th, 32nd, 33rd) concerned were to arrange the relief of machine-gun companies during the night of 25/26 November. "Aeroplane photos, all intelligence details, and trench stores" were, as per the usual procedure, to be handed over to incoming MG companies.[32] Use of the single traversable road and distribution of limited available shelter to battalion HQs had already been negotiated between II Corps and VIII Corps: 32nd Division was to have "rights of traffic" along the Bellevue Spur – Vindictive Crossroads Road; 8th Division had exclusive traffic rights on the two yet to be extended duckboard avenues. The latter Division, however, was permitted to use the road "for pack transport except when otherwise ordered from divisional HQ." Such occasions would "be rare and ample notice" given; 8th Division would also retain three battalion HQs and an aid post in designated pillboxes situated at Bellevue, Meetcheele and Mosselmarkt.[33]

The first order of business in 8th Division Instructions No. 2 (25 November) announced the cancellation of preliminary operations to capture Hill 52 and Vox Farm. General information concerning the allotment of the two duckboard tracks, battalion HQs, etc., in the vicinity of the Bellevue Spur was then restated. Units were, however, not to use the road (previously allotted to 32nd Division) running the length of the spur "between dusk and zero hour on the night before the attack." Specific details concerning pre-attack boundaries between 8th Division, 32nd Division and

---

29 Ibid: 'VIII Corps G. 1990', 21 November 1917. See Chapter 1, p. 59, fn. 69.
30 See Appendix VI.
31 See Appendix III b, IV b and V b.
32 See TNA: WO/95/1677: '8th Division Order No. 242', 23 November 1917, 8th Division War Diary.
33 Ibid. Signaller Corporal Eric Rossiter (7th Canadian Battalion) described his unit's Mosselmarkt pillbox HQ as 'thick-walled and partitioned inside into four chambers …The walls were thick enough to withstand most light shells, but as it was a German construction the door and several slanted, narrow windows faced the German lines.' See Richard Baumgartner (ed), 'Death Fugue in Flanders', *Der Angriff: A Journal of World War I Military History* (November 1982) pp. 28-29.

33rd Division followed.³⁴ Liaison between brigades was spelled out in detail: 2nd Rifle Brigade (CO Lieutenant-Colonel Hon. Roger Brand DSO)³⁵, left-hand assault battalion of 25 Brigade, was required to maintain close touch with the battalion on its immediate left. To this end, Coffin was to "get in touch" with Brigadier-General Blacklock (GOC 97 Brigade), who would "insure that the O.C., 2nd Rifle Brigade, left company and platoon commanders of that Battalion have thoroughly discussed the operation and their part in it, with the O.C. 2nd Kings Own Yorkshire Light Infantry and the right company and platoon commanders of that battalion."³⁶ A liaison officer would also be detailed to make certain that "touch was maintained with 32nd Division throughout the operations."³⁷ Similar arrangements were to be made between the assault battalions of 25 Brigade.³⁸ In the event of Coffin becoming a casualty, "command of the brigade would devolve" on Brand. The GOC 25 Brigade, the instructions also stipulated, was to establish his HQ in one of the forlorn pillboxes astride Bellevue Spur. In keeping with Section 30 of *S.S.135*, a number of officers and men from each battalion were chosen to remain behind before the attack. These select personnel would, if necessary, provide the available nucleus for unit reconstruction and absorption of new drafts should heavy losses occur.³⁹

A single specially prepared and printed cartographic rendering ("Message Map No. 27 1/10,000"), *S.S. 135* advising that officers and men "should not be overburdened

---

34 TNA: WO/95/1677: '8th Division Instructions No. 2', 25 November 1917, 8th Division War Diary.
35 Lieutenant-Colonel Hon. Roger Brand (1880-1945). Fifth son of Second Viscount Hampden; Marlborough College, commissioned Rifle Brigade from the Militia 1900; South Africa 1899-1901; Resigned1910; Captain Special Reserve 1910-12; Lieutenant 2nd Rifle Brigade August 1914; Captain, Major, A/Lieutenant Colonel 1914-16; DSO 1916; Bar 1917.
36 CO and OC: Technically these terms are not interchangeable in the British Army, 'CO' being the officer in command of a battalion, artillery brigade, RE company, etc. 'OC' is the officer appointed to command a sub-unit or adhoc grouping. This was normally an infantry company or artillery battery or, for example, a body of men on a train i.e., 'OC troops' or 'OC train' nevertheless, anachronistic usage of OC in reference to battalion commanders is prevalent in a large number of consulted contemporary documents. The aforementioned accepted terminology will be used, exclusive of direct quotations, throughout this volume.
37 TNA: WO/95/1677: '8th Division Instructions No. 2', 25 November 1917, 8th Division War Diary.
38 Ibid. In addition, the 'G.O.C. 25th Inf. Bde' would 'arrange that units are especially told off to fill any gaps that may occur, especially at the flanks of battalions, and in particular on the left flank of the 2nd Rifle Brigade.'
39 'Officers and other ranks will be left out of the action in accordance with section XXX of *S.S.135* 'Instructions for the Training of Divisions in [sic] Offensive Action.' See Ibid: '8th Division Instructions No. 2', 25 November 1917.

with maps",⁴⁰ was issued to be carried forward into action.⁴¹ Red ground flares, originally chosen for communicating with designated RFC contact aircraft, were to be exchanged for green flares the following (26 November) day.⁴² POW arrangements were to be organised as follows, prisoner escorts from 25 Brigade were to hand over captives to an escort detail of two platoons of 22nd Durham Light Infantry [DLI] (8th Division Pioneers) near Waterloo Farm.⁴³ Captives would next "be escorted thence to the divisional cage … where they will be taken over by the APM." Escorts were to be of the following approximate strength: "Up to 5 prisoners – Escort of 1; From 5 to 19 – Escort of 2; Over 10 – In proportion of 1 escort to every 10 prisoners." Lightly wounded men were expected, "as far as possible", to act as escorts. No examination of prisoner documents was to occur forward of the divisional cage, where all captured officers and men would be searched under the supervision of the Division APM. All documents found on the person of a POW were to be "tied in separate bundles for each prisoner and docketed with labels stating the owner's name, rank and regiment. All such bundles were to be "handed over to the divisional IO for transmission to VIII Corps."⁴⁴

Instructions No. 2 also outlined the adopted casualty evacuation organisation. Standard practice allowed for an injured Tommy to be carried by stretcher-bearers (usually 32 per battalion) as far as a battalion medical officer's established regimental aid post [RAP], "where essential first aid was carried out, splints were applied as necessary, and the wounded sorted out as well as possible into groups for treatment."⁴⁵ This was followed by transport to the brigade field ambulance and beyond. "It was common to need eight men to carry a stretcher in the Ypres salient in 1917, and both

40 See Section XXXIII. 'Documents and Maps', General Staff Training Manual *S.S.135, Instructions for the Training of Divisions for Offensive Action* (December 1916).
41 The reverse side listed 11 pro forma situation statements that required completion by company and platoon commanders. Sample statements were as follows: 'My Company/Platoon has reached ____, My Company/Platoon has consolidated ____, I need Ammunition, bombs, rifle grenades, water, etc., Counter-attack forming up at ____, I am in touch on right/left at ____.' Annotated maps would be sent back by runner to Battalion HQ. The practice of issue of tactical maps to battalions was just one more attempt to facilitate communications with the sharp end of an assault. See TNA: WO/95/1677: 'Message Map No. 127, 1/10,000', 8th Division War Diary.
42 Ibid: 8th Division Instructions No. 3', 26 November 1917.
43 The prisoner escort detail from 22nd DLI was to be in position by Zero – 30 minutes, 'and will report their arrival to 25th Inf. Bde. HQ. [at] Bellevue. The OC party will post sentries…to direct escorts of 25 Inf. Bde. with prisoners of war to their positions.' See Ibid: '8th Division Instructions No. 5', 27 November 1917 and 'Amendment No. 1 to 8th Division Instructions No. 5', 28 November 1917.
44 Ibid: '8th Division Instructions No. 3', 26 November 1917. For a general outline of the POW handling organization at division and corps level see Beach, 'British Intelligence and the German Army, 1914-1918', pp. 28-29.
45 Geoffrey Noon, 'The Treatment of Casualties in the Great War' in Paddy Griffith (ed), *British Fighting Methods in the Great War* (London: Frank Cass, 1996), p. 97.

bearers and casualties – if they arrived at all – would be exhausted by the time they reached a suitable aid post."[46] The RAP's of the attacking left and centre battalions would be situated at Mosselmarkt. The right battalion's post was to be established in the northern outskirts of Passchendaele.[47] Stretcher-bearers of the left and centre battalions were made responsible for clearing the ground of casualties as far as the Mosselmarkt RAP; bearers of the right battalion were expected to "clear [casualties] from their regimental aid post to Mosselmarkt."[48]

The CO 25 Field Ambulance was responsible for evacuation of the wounded. To accomplish this Herculean task, a total of 260 stretcher-bearers were placed at his disposal. Transport of wounded from aid posts situated at Mosselmarkt would be achieved by "hand carriage" down the Bellevue Spur road, and along No. 5 track to Waterloo Farm. From there, stretcher parties would carry their charges westward along the road section Gravenstafel – Wieltje, as far as the advanced dressing station [ADS] at Somme Redoubt.[49] This insalubrious accumulation of trenches, tunnels and mined dugouts, retrospectively described along with Waterloo Farm as "dirty holes", was where "emergency primary surgery, particularly in arresting haemorrhage" would be carried out.[50] These complex medical procedures had, "after it became apparent that lack of delay was vital for many types of wounds", become routine undertakings for ADS personnel by 1917.[51] 8th Division's wounded would, following treatment at Somme Redoubt, be transported by motor ambulance to the VIII Corps Main Dressing Station [CMDS] at Ypres Prison.[52]

Instructions No. 2 concluded by providing brigade relief schemes before and after the attack: 25 Brigade was scheduled to relieve 23 Brigade the night before; a brigade from 14th Division was scheduled to relieve 25 Brigade the night after. Three assault battalions (2nd Royal Berkshire Regiment, 2nd Lincolnshire Regiment, 2nd Rifle Brigade) of the latter were to march to assembly positions from camps in the vicinity of Wieltje and St Jean on the eve of the attack. Assigned march routes extended along the "Wieltje – Bellevue Road, thence the northern extension of No. 5 Track, No. 5 Track and its southern extension" to frontline positions held by the remaining (1st Royal Irish Rifles [RIR]) battalion of the brigade.[53]

46 Ibid, p. 97.
47 TNA: WO/95/1677: '8th Division Instructions No. 2', 25 November 1917, 8th Division War Diary.
48 Ibid.
49 Ibid.
50 Anonymous, *With the Forty-Fourths: Being a Record of the doings of the 44th Field Ambulance (14th Division)* (London: Spottiswoode, Ballantyne & Co., 1922), p. 47 and Noon, 'The Treatment of Casualties in the Great War' in Griffith (ed), *British Fighting Methods in the Great* War, p. 98.
51 Noon, p. 98.
52 TNA: WO/95/1677: 8th Division Instructions No. 2', 25 November 1917, 8th Division War Diary.
53 Ibid.

Instructions No. 3 were issued on 26 November. 25 Brigade was informed that an RE 8 contact plane attached to No. 21 Squadron RFC would "fly over the attack area at 7:30 a.m. or as soon as the weather is sufficiently clear, and will call for flares by sounding its KLAXON HORN and by firing Very lights." This low-flying aircraft would be distinguished by placement of a "black plaque extending behind the lower planes and a dumbbell [the squadron sign] painted on the fuselage."[54] The most advanced infantry posts were, in response to a plane bearing these markings, "to light green flares and wave Watson Fans."[55] The discharge of coloured flares, which burned for approximately one minute, along the extreme front of a captured objective proved to be the most satisfactory means for troops to signal from newly captured positions. "So successful did this method prove, that it became part of operation orders for an attack, that flares were to be lighted by troops at intervals along their frontline, and in all blocks, sap-heads, and other advanced positions…"[56] A "Contact Counter-attack aircraft" would also be aloft the morning after the assault for the "special purpose of locating and notifying by wireless any enemy counter-attack."[57]

The establishment of a complex communications network facilitated the passing of reliable information to division, brigade, battalion and artillery commanders. Diagram A, attached to instructions No. 3, laid out the divisional scheme. Three cable routes (buried, ground, ladder) were to extend from 8th Division HQ (situated at Canal Bank) through brigade HQs at Wieltje, Gallipoli Dugouts and Korek (near Gravenstafel) as far as Bellevue.[58] A single ladder line was to be extended from Bellevue to left battalion HQ at Meetcheele. Two more ladder lines were to be run from Meetcheele to the south and east as far as battalion HQs situated near Passchendaele and Mosselmarkt. Three wireless stations would be established along the cable route Wieltje – Bellevue, while a VIII Corps continuous wave [CW] wireless set was to be installed in the forward area. Nine visual signal stations were to be

---

54   Ibid: '8th Division Instructions No. 3', 26 November 1917. No.21 Squadron was formed at Netheravon in July 1915. Dispatched to France in January 1916, it initially operated in an army role until converted to a corps reconnaissance squadron in February 1917. Attached to VIII Corps in November 1917, its aerodrome was situated near La Lovie. See Air of Authority – A History of RAF Organisation <http://www.rafweb.org/Sqn021-25.htm> and TNA AIR 1/1186/204/5/2595: 'Location of R.F.C. Units – 1st December, 1917', RFC War Diary.
55   Watson Signalling Fan: A visual shutter device apparatus designed for signaling over short distances. Inconspicuous when closed up, when spread out on the ground with its face uppermost, it was utilised to point out the presence of troops to contact planes. See R.E. Priestley, *The Signal Service in the European War of 1914 to 1918 (France)* (Chatham: The Institution of Royal Engineers & Signals Association, 1921), p. 139.
56   Air Historical Branch, *The Royal Air Force in the Great War* (Nashville, Tennessee: Battery Press, 1996 reprint of 1936 edition), p. 118.
57   TNA: WO/95/1677: '8th Division Instructions No. 3', 26 November 1917, 8th Division War Diary.
58   Telephone cable was extremely vulnerable to shellfire. Lines were laid above ground in a ladder pattern in order to provide multiple redundant paths.

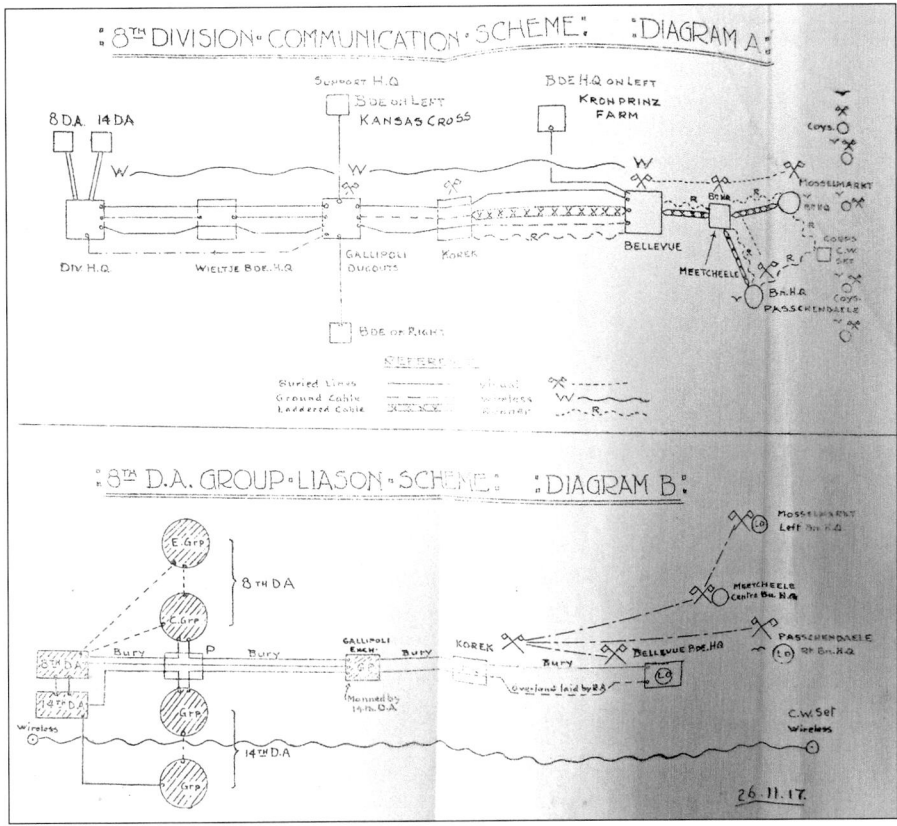

8th Division communications scheme diagrams. (TNA: WO/95/1677: 8th Division War Diary)

established at Gallipoli Dugouts, Bellevue, Meetcheele, and Mosselmarkt and with the five companies holding the frontline. Runner relay posts would also be established along routes extending from company HQs to Meetcheele, Bellevue and Korek.[59]

Diagram B illustrated the "8th Division Artillery Group" liaison scheme. Three buried cables were to be run eastward from 8th and 14th divisional artillery HQs at Canal Bank to Gallipoli Dugouts. Two more buried lines would be extended from the latter as far as Korek where additional buried and overland cable routes, put in place by

---

59　A buried lateral line ran north from Gallipoli Dugouts to the support brigade HQ of 32nd Division at Kansas Cross and south to the right brigade of 33rd Division. Another buried cable extended from Bellevue to the frontline brigade HQ of 32nd Division at Kronprinz Farm. See TNA: WO/95/1677: '8th Division Communication Scheme: Diagram A, 8th Division Instructions No. 3', 26 November 1917, 8th Division War Diary.

the gunners, had already been extended to Brigade HQ at Bellevue. The VIII Corps forward zone wireless station was also to be placed in direct touch with a station situated near divisional artillery HQs. Five visual signalling stations (established at Korek, Bellevue, Passchendaele, Meetcheele and Mosselmarkt) were assigned to support artillery communications. Lateral cable lines were also to be extended – from a junction situated between Canal Bank and the exchange at Gallipoli Dugouts – north and south to supporting batteries.[60] Subsequent intensive labour by signallers, engineers and working parties made certain that 8th Division's communications infrastructure was extended and expanded west to east for approximately 11,000 yards from Canal Bank to the apex of the Passchendaele Salient by late November.[61]

Instruction numbers 4 and 5 followed on 27 November. The former related detailed information concerning attack preparations by 8th Division's four attached machine-gun companies. Company commanders were to arrange for at least 15,000 rounds per gun to be concealed in positions constructed during a night selected by the DMGO. They would also ensure that new barrels were utilised and depression stops issued; wooden tripod stands were to be used for anti-aircraft work, whilst "calculations made for the error of the day" would be based on current meteorological reports. All machine-gun companies, excluding those designated for close defence of the captured area, were to be placed under the direct command of the DMGO throughout the attack. The seven designated close defence guns would be under orders of the GOC 25 Brigade. Four tables of data concerning earmarked machine-gun sites to be occupied before the attack and barrage scheme details were attached.[62]

Instructions No. 5 provided detailed schematic drawings of battle insignia worn by 2nd King's Own Yorkshire Light Infantry [KOYLI] (right battalion of 97 Brigade). Both 8th Division and 32nd Division had instituted a complex scheme of patches for identification purposes, so it was necessary for officers and men of 2nd Rifle Brigade to distinguish those worn on sleeves and below the collar of the neighbouring battalion. Information concerning the whereabouts of 97 Brigade HQ followed: "KANSAS at

---

60   Ibid: '8th D.A. Group Liason [sic] Scheme: Diagram B, 8th Division Instructions No. 3', 26 November 1917.
61   Communications during the attack were maintained as follows: 'Division to advanced Division: Buried cables, wireless and emergency ground line … Advanced Division to Brigade: Ground cable, visual and wireless … From Brigade to Battalions: Ladder cable lines, visual and Power Buzzers and runners … Artillery liaison established with separate system of ground cable and visual through their own forward exchanges which were soon connected with the Divnl exchanges whenever possible … At advanced Divnl. office a forward exchange for all two [sic] RA groups was established in connection with the Divnl. exchange, so that the information from Bdes to Bdes was forwarded direct to groups … During the hours of darkness W/T set with RFA groups were tuned to the Adv. Div. set in order that groups might obtain information immediately.' See TNA: WO/95/1701: 8th Division Signal Company War Diary, 1 December 1917.
62   Ibid: '8th Division Instructions No. 4', 27 November 1917.

8th Division machine-gun barrage map. (TNA: WO/95/1677: 8th Division War Diary)

present … at CANAL BANK" on the 28th.[63] Battalion HQs for 2nd Rifle Brigade and 2nd KOYLI would be established at Meetcheele. A liaison officer from 25 Brigade was to be attached to 97 Brigade HQ throughout the operation. Brigadier-General H.G. Lloyd DSO (GOC 8th Division Artillery) was also expected to detail "a senior liaison officer to be at Headquarters 25 Inf. Bde. during the operations, and for a liaison officer to be with each attacking battalion HQ."[64]

Special precautions, organised before the assault by "mutual arrangement" between 25 Brigade and 97 Brigade, were taken "to ensure that 2nd Rifle Brigade and 2nd K.O.Y.L.I. are in touch on [the] forming up line." A party of 2nd Field Company RE was to be placed at the disposal of the GOC 25 Brigade "to assist in placing the [jumping-off] tapes in position." All arrangements would be made directly between 25 Brigade and 2nd Field Company. In addition, the CRE was to deploy maintenance parties along assigned duckboard tracks on the night of assembly.[65]

Instructions No. 5 also addressed the on-going consolidation of positions currently held by 23 Brigade. Brigadier-General W. St. G. Grogan's infantry, whilst continuing to strengthen the forward line of posts, were to see that "three platoon posts in the frontline as taken over from 3rd Canadian Division are made strong with good firesteps, and inconspicuous wire put round them." Four additional mutually supporting platoon posts, covering gaps between front posts, were to be established some 300 yards to the rear. These positions would be constructed and wired on similar lines to the existing front posts. Coffin was required to supply garrisons for the posts "and will arrange that they carry up wire with them to strengthen that already put out." Captured ground was required to be "consolidated in depth in posts." The bulk of available Lewis Guns were to be pushed forward to the final objective as a deterrent to inevitable German counter-attacks.[66]

Coffin was, as per Instructions No. 5, also to arrange for one battalion (1st RIR), less one company, to be deployed south of Mosselmarkt and Meetcheele to "immediately counter-attack any enemy counter-attack." The most likely fronts where a strong enemy counter-attack would originate were listed in order of importance:

- WRANGLE FARM from low ground in W. 19 Central
- WRATH FARM – the approach is very narrow
- WRATH FARM – WRAP COTTAGE from about WRITTEN FARM

Immediate local counter-attacks could also be expected to emerge from shell-hole positions about Wrath Farm and Salter's Corner. All of these sites were situated on

63   The 2nd KOYLI were at Dambre Camp near Vlamertinghe.
64   TNA: WO/95/1677: '8th Division Instructions No. 5', 27 November 1917, 8th Division War Diary.
65   Ibid.
66   Ibid.

the gently sloping ground beyond Venison Trench and its redoubts. In conclusion, the assaulting infantry were reminded that they must "rely on their own rifles, bayonets, and Lewis Guns" when confronted by enemy counter-attack.[67]

Instructions No. 6 were issued on the 28th: Two battalions (2nd Lincolnshire Regiment and 2nd Rifle Brigade) were, on the eve of the attack, to proceed – via the Wieltje – Bellevue road and No. 5 track and its southern extension – from camp sites south of St Julian approximately 6,500 yards to jumping-off positions NE of Passchendaele. The remaining two (2nd Royal Berkshire would now deploy to the right of 1st RIR) battalions would take over the frontline two nights before the attack.[68] Overland routes assigned to machine-gun units and component mule transport was also detailed. Traffic control posts would be established by the Division APM at select points along assigned avenues of approach. The Division CRE was to arrange for additional notice boards to be erected as a guide to troops traversing duckboard tracks. In addition, Coffin had to make certain that the unplanked routes beyond the end of No. 5 Track and its extension were thoroughly reconnoitered and marked with white posts as far as the jumping-off line. German patrols were to be kept at arm's length: "Wherever forming up will take place within 250 yards of our [8th Division] present advanced line of posts, posts will be pushed out to cover it. This will be done nightly till the assault."[69]

Instructions No. 6 next addressed machine-gun communications, anti-aircraft measures and reports. The DMGO and his signal counterpart were to cooperate by organising runners and visual signaling stations for machine-gun companies. The experience on 10 November demonstrated the need for infantry to defend against marauding German aircraft: "The G.O.C. 25 Inf. Bde. will arrange that heavy rifle and Lewis Gun fire is brought to bear on all hostile low-flying aeroplanes. It is of the utmost importance that they should be brought down or driven off at once, as accurate and heavy hostile shelling of our position is sure to follow a successful reconnaissance at a low height." To facilitate this, one machine-gun per company was assigned

---

67 Ibid.
68 63rd RND's educative after-action report noted: 'It is suggested that when, as at present, objectives are strictly limited, the assaulting troops should only be brought into the line just before Zero, and should be withdrawn on the evening following the attack, their places in the new line being taken by troops holding the original line, who, during the attack, would act as a reserve. If this were done the assaulting troops could be relieved of much weight, and need only carry one day's rations.' See Leonard Sellers (ed), 'Western Front: Report on Operations During the Third Battle of Ypres: Passchendaele, 24th October to 5th November 1917', *RND: Royal Naval Division. Antwerp, Gallipoli & Western Front 1914-1918*, Issue Number 22 (September 2002), p. 2184.
69 See TNA: WO/95/1677: '8th Division Instructions No. 6', 28 November 1917, 8th Division War Diary, G.W.L. Nicholson, *Canadian Expeditionary Force: 1914-1919* (Ottawa: Queen's Printer, 1962), p. 326 and Lieutenant-Colonel H.S. Jervis, *The 2nd Munsters in France* (Aldershot: Gale & Polden, 1922), p. 39.

anti-aircraft duties during daylight hours.[70] Instructions No. 6 concluded by stressing the importance of maintaining communications throughout the attack. A confirmation report verifying the completion of the forming-up would be forwarded to 8th Division prior to Zero; situation reports were to follow at Zero + 40 minutes and every half-hour afterwards till Zero + 8 hours 45 minutes. Coffin was to impress on all ranks "the importance of frequent reports giving full information in writing or on situation maps."[71]

8th Division Order No. 247 was circulated the same day as Instructions No. 6.[72] The document opened with a statement that VIII Corps was to continue offensive operations on a date "which has been communicated to all concerned." This was followed by recapitulation of the operational details previously articulated in the series of instructions forwarded to subordinate formations since 22 November:

- The 32nd Division (II Corps) will attack on the left of and simultaneously with 8th Division. The 33rd Division, on the right of 8th Division [,] will not be attacking.
- The attack of the 8th Division will be carried out by 25th Inf. Bde., H.Q., Bellevue.
- The objective of the division and its boundaries, are shown on map G.31 issued with 8th Division Instructions No. 1 of 22 November.
- The attack will take place at an hour zero [sic]; which will be notified later.
- At zero hour the infantry will advance to the assault.

25 Brigade was tasked with advancing as far as the objective line; old enemy trenches were, "so far as possible", to be avoided, but final consolidation "must be in depth."[73]

Machine-gun companies attached to 23 and 25 Brigades were ordered to support the assault by indirect barrage[74] immediately behind Venison Trench and its redoubts

---

70 TNA: WO/95/1677: '8th Division Instructions No. 6', 28 November 1917, 8th Division War Diary.
71 Ibid.
72 Ibid. Orders No. 243 (Movement and billeting of machine-gun companies), 244 (Details of relief of 8th Division by 14th Division following the attack), 245 (Brigade reliefs from 29 November to 1 December) and 246 (Cancellation and substitution of Order No. 244) were issued during 24 to 28 November.
73 Ibid: '8th Division Order No. 247', 28 November 1917.
74 'The British began to develop use of MGs en masse to provide covering fire for their infantry as one solution to the enemy's own MGs.' Machine-guns were employed from the Somme onwards 'for overhead fire to cover advancing infantry, for establishing barrages against counter-attacks and for holding in advance captured trenches to cover consolidation' and to provide 'a machine-gun barrage in depth of 1000 yards', freeing the infantry to deal with the enemy infantry. Following the experiences of Fourth Army during the German withdrawal to the Hindenburg Line, GHQ noted in April 1917 'the value of machine-guns in covering the advance of troops with enfilade, oblique, or over-

at Zero + 8.⁷⁵ The barrage would lift to a "M.G. S.O.S barrage line" further forward at Zero + 9. Here it would remain until Zero + 25. Harassing fire was to be maintained on this line at intervals from Zero + 37 to Zero + 6 hours and 10 minutes, "and on the afternoon after the attack from 3:00 p.m. till 6:18 p.m."⁷⁶

24 Brigade's machine-guns – less seven guns – would engage German counter-attacks originating beyond the M.G. S.O.S barrage line by searching "all avenues of approach east of that line" from Zero + 15 to Zero + 16 hours and twenty minutes, "and on the afternoon after the attack from 3:00 p.m. till 6:20 p.m." The remaining seven guns would be "employed for close defence" of the captured area. Machine-gun companies of 32nd Division and 33rd Division would prolong the "M.G. S.O.S. barrage line to the south and north respectively, and would "be searching all enemy approaches on their fronts under similar arrangements." All machine-gun units were to be in "allotted positions for the attack by Zero – 2 hours."⁷⁷

Order No. 247 concluded with instructions for the synchronization of watches just prior to the attack.⁷⁸ Its last sentence informed subordinate formations that "8th Division Instructions No. 1-6 [,] which have been already issued are hereby confirmed and rendered operative as orders."⁷⁹

The artillery scheme (dated 29 November) was explained in Addendum No. 1 to 8th Division Order No. 247. Eight field artillery brigades and the "Northern Bombardment Group" of VIII Corps Heavy Artillery would carry out the complex fire support scheme. Field artillery brigades were to maintain the "usual harassing fire" prior to Zero + 8. "Occasional rounds" would be fired on the barrage start line throughout the night of the attack and the preceding nights, in order to mark the line where the barrage fell. Four field artillery brigades were to fire on "Line A" in

---

head fire was most marked' especially when employed well forward. See Robbins, *British Generalship on the Western Front 1914-18*, p. 105.
75 The 218th Machine Gun Company was attached to the '25 Inf. Bde. Group' throughout the operation. See TNA: WO/95/1677: '8th Division Order No. 246', 28 November 1917 and 'Addendum No. 1 to 8th Division Order No. 246', 29 November 1917, 8th Division War Diary.
76 Ibid: '8th Division Order No. 247', 28 November 1917.
77 Ibid.
78 'Watches will be synchronized as follows:
By Staff Officer from 8th Div. H.Q. with 32 Div. At their H.Q. at 12:30 p.m. and with 8th Div. Arty at 1p.m.
A Staff Officer from 8th Div. H.Q. with representatives of 2nd Lincoln Regt., 2nd Rifle Brigade, 25th and 218th machine gun companies, at the Brigade H.Q., WIELTJE, at 2 p.m.
By Staff Officer from 8th Div. H.Q. at 25th Inf. Bde. H.Q. at 2:45 p.m.
D.M.G.O. will arrange to synchronize watches with D.M.G.O., 33rd Division and with 23rd and 24th M.G. Cos.
The telephone will not be used for synchronization of watches except for artillery units.'
79 TNA: WO/95/1677: '8th Division Order No. 247', 28 November 1917, 8th Division War Diary.

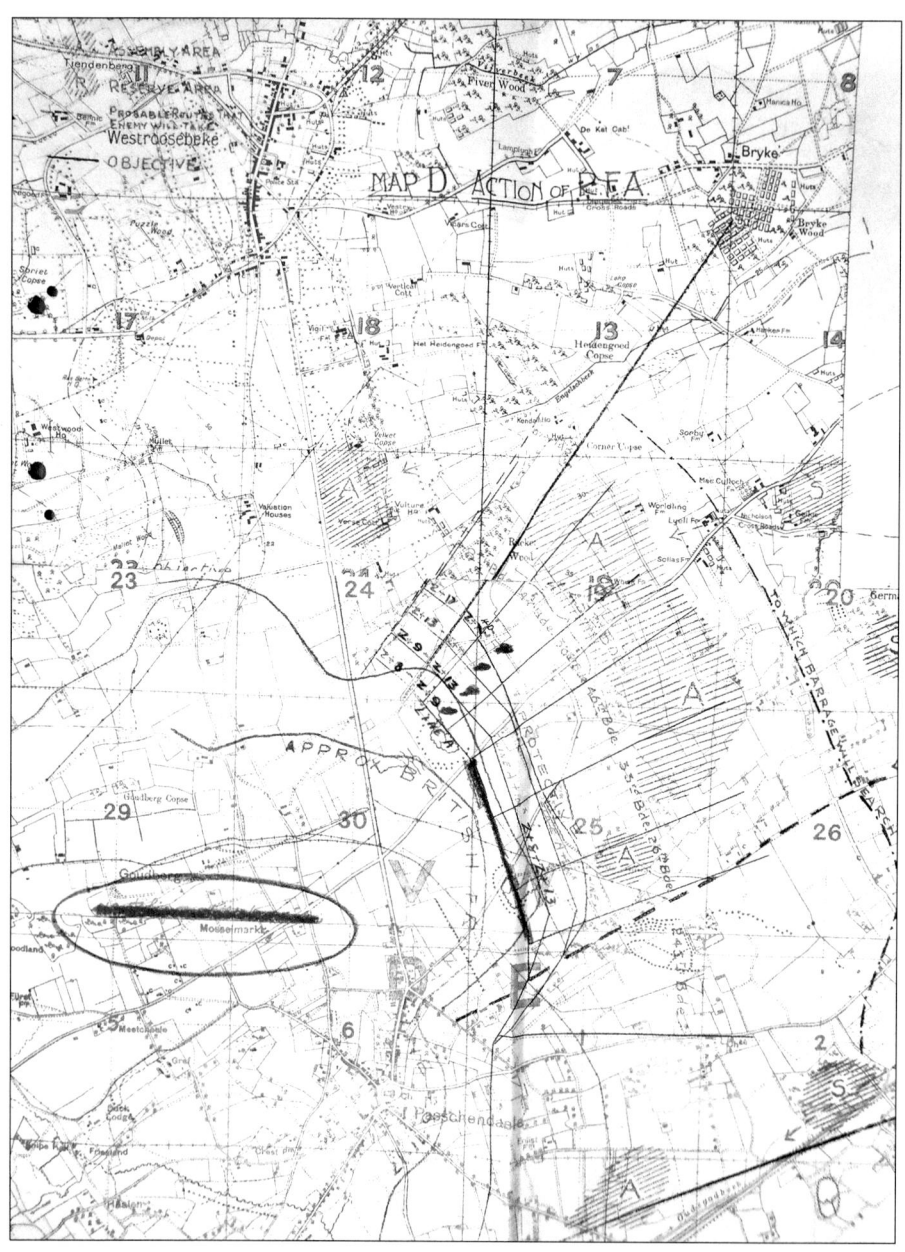

8th Division field artillery barrage map. (TNA: WO/95/1677: 8th Division War Diary)

the immediate rear of Venison Trench and redoubts at Zero + 8. All eight field artillery brigades would fire in combination at Zero + 9. The advancing curtain of fire, consisting of the 100% HE that Heneker "found best for night work", would proceed 100 yards to "Line A + 100" where it would remain until Zero + 13. From Zero + 13 to Zero + 40, the barrage would lift 100 yards every four minutes (lines "B" to "O") until reaching the protective barrage line ("Line P"), behind which the infantry would dig in and consolidate gains.[80] 4.5-inch howitzer batteries were to fire "with mean point of impact 200 yards in advance" of the protective line. From Zero + 90 to 6:00 a.m., bursts of fire would be placed on "Line P" at "irregular intervals." Additional bursts were to be placed 100 to 400 yards in advance of the same line.[81] Heavy guns were to commence fire at Zero + 15 "to search roads of approach and 200 yards each side of them, and to bombard assembly places and areas where German support and reserve battalions are located." Counter-batteries would open up after Zero + 8 "or prior to that hour if necessary", to engage German artillery concentrations; gas shells would be employed only if the "weather is suitable."[82]

2.3 32nd Division

32nd Division was entrusted with opening out the Passchendaele Salient to the west and north on a frontage of 1,850 yards. This would be accomplished by advancing the line to a depth of 400 yards on the right and left and 700 yards in the centre. Subsequent operational orders and instructions were based on the following factors governing the plan:

- Forming-up could not be achieved by day because the desired jumping-off area was in full view of the enemy.
- Previous attacks having commenced at dawn, the decision was made to risk the inherent dangers of a night attack on a large scale.
- The supporting artillery, operating from an extremity of range, could only fire from west to east in support of an attack along high ground from south to north. Approaches due west of the enemy positions were impassable.

---

80   The barrage would reach 'Line A + 200' at Zero + 17. Between Zero + 13 to 17, 18-pdr batteries were to fire 30% smoke shell on Line B if the 'wind lies between SW and NW.' This would 'produce a smoke screen lasting about ten minutes commencing about 100 yards beyond the objective.' If the wind was unfavourable, 'only one gun per battery will fire 30% smoke shell.' Utilisation of smoke projectiles, Heneker later observed, 'would prevent bodies of men from advancing too far and getting too much down on to the low ground to the east of the objective line.'
81   TNA: WO/95/1677: 'Addendum No. 1 to 8th Division Order No. 247', 29 November 1917 and 'Narrative of Operations Carried Out by the 8th Division on 1st/ 2nd December 1917', 13 December 1917, 8th Division War Diary.
82   Ibid.

- The idea of a creeping barrage having been dispensed with, the decision was taken to advance the first 200 yards without the customary (exclusive of a preliminary bombardment within safety limits) artillery support in order to achieve surprise and overwhelm the enemy's advanced posts with the bayonet.
- The supporting barrage was scheduled to open at Zero + 8 with all available artillery and machine-guns in a series of area concentrations, those engaging targets inside the objective to lift as the infantry pressed forward.
- Conceivable exposure of infantry to unsuppressed hostile machine-gun fire for six to eight minutes appeared preferable to running the risk of drawing, with the start of the anticipated British barrage, the enemy's intense defensive barrage. This controversial decision was further strengthened by the fact that hostile artillery concentrations displayed such superiority in firepower that previous attacks sustained crippling casualties before reaching the objective.
- Attacking at night decreased the risk of casualties from hostile machine-guns.
- Moonlight was perceived to be a critical element of this operation; thus the attack date was fixed for a night when the moon was certain to be full or just past full sphere.[83]

Division HQ issued the first instructions on 21 November.[84] 32nd Division Offensive Instructions No.1: Outline Plan of Operations provided general information to attached infantry brigades and other subordinate units regarding operational phases, tasks, troops to be employed, attack scheme, probable direction of enemy counter-attacks, artillery plan, machine-guns, etc.[85] This four-page draft, the first of a series prepared by Lieutenant-Colonel A.E. McNamara (GSO 1 32nd Division), were in keeping with recognised *S.S. 135* guidelines. II Corps' objective was to "continue operations at an early date to drive the enemy from the PASSCHENDAELE RIDGE"; VIII Corps was to "operate on the right of the II Corps." The red line objective (Hill 52 and Vat Cottages Ridge) would be captured by 32nd Division in the first phase, while 35th Division remained stationary on the immediate left.[86]

Instructions No. 1 originally entrusted the capture of these objectives to the four battalions (2nd KOYLI, 16th Highland Light Infantry, 11th Border Regiment, 17th Highland Light Infantry [HLI]) of 97 Brigade; two battalions of 14 or 96 brigades would be responsible for the frontline during the attack. This was later adjusted to an assault by 97 Brigade "with two battalions [15th Lancashire Fusiliers [LF] and 16th Northumberland Fusiliers [NF] of 96 Infantry Brigade attached." One detached battalion (16th NF) would be held in reserve as a "counter-counter-attacking force

---

83 Ibid. See Chapter 1, pp. 77-79.
84 See Appendix VII.
85 Amendments and updates to these offensive instructions followed on 24 and 25 November. These are included in the narrative review of the document issued on 21 November.
86 TNA: WO/95/2370: '32nd Division Offensive Instructions No. 1: Outline Plan of Operations', 21 November 1917, 32nd Division War Diary.

on the right flank in the vicinity of VIRILE FARM." Shute had thus concluded that an attack by a reinforced brigade of six battalions was necessary in order to provide the proportionate number of men to assault and consolidate dispersed objectives. Moreover, definite and distinct sub-units from each battalion were "to be told off to capture, garrison, and consolidate each known strongpoint and defended locality."[87]

The general scheme called for the capture of the red line by night attack; "the essence" of the operation was surprise. In order to meet this condition, the *Vorfeldzone* from Void Farm (dominating gently sloping ground as far as the western extremity of Vat Cottages Ridge) to Veal Cottages inclusive "had to be rushed at Zero without an artillery or machine-gun barrage." At Zero + 8 – the time the German outposts were expected to be overrun – the artillery would "open fire on all known and suspected strongpoints and machine-gun positions lying beyond…" The bombardment, timed to lift as the attacking troops reached the final objective, would "form a protective barrage which will be specifically thick on the enemy's most likely lines of counter-attack (i.e., Venison Farm – Verse Cottage – Valuation Houses – Mallet Wood (exclusive)" and assembly areas. Exact details concerning opening fire and lift-off times upon targeted strongpoints were, it was also related, still unavailable to Division HQ as of 21 November. This yet to be determined information was entirely dependent on orders received from II Corps, plans of the neighbouring VIII Corps and ground conditions at the time of the attack.[88]

Presumed locale and direction of German counter-attacks were addressed next. Examination of aerial photographs and other intelligence sources precluded the flooded low ground west of Mallet Wood as an avenue for defenders to emerge from, although small local ripostes might, it was surmised, originate from this area. The most probable direction would be north and NE from Racket Wood, Heidengod Copse and along the main ridge via Valuation Houses. Likely positions of enemy reserves at Roodkruis and Oostnieuwkerke (east of Westroosebeke) were also noted.[89]

32nd Division's four attached machine-gun companies were to be organised into two groupings: close defence weapons under the GOC 97 Brigade and barrage guns under the CMGO (II Corps).[90] 97th MG Company was to remain under Blacklock's orders for close defence of the captured line. The remaining (14th, 96th, 219th) three companies would contribute to the indirect barrage by providing protective fire in

87 Ibid: 'Amendment No. 1 to 32nd Division Offensive Instructions No. 1', 24 November 1917.
88 Ibid: '32nd Division Offensive Instructions No. 1: Outline Plan of Operations', 21 November 1917.
89 Ibid: After-action report, 'Part II, Plan of Operations, Section I, General', 11 December 1917.
90 It was unusual for a CMGO to be appointed commander rather than advisor. Officers acting in this capacity usually coordinated corps barrage arrangements. Control of machine-gun barrages on subordinate division fronts was normally placed in the hands of divisional commanders prior to an assault. See Simpson, *Directing Operations*, p. 66.

front of objective areas where counter-attacks in force were anticipated. They were also tasked with maintaining area concentration fire on likely assembly areas or over ground that hostile troops could pass. Targeted areas were to extend as far back into the enemy hinterland as possible. Defended localities on the left flank would be kept under fire, in order to engage machine-guns and snipers in areas beyond attack objectives.[91]

It was stressed that the infantry should immediately consolidate objectives. All available Vickers and Lewis guns would be "pushed up for the defence of the captured ground, the majority being advanced to the final objective." Strongpoints for all-round defence were to be constructed by 219th Field Company RE and 100 attached infantry in the vicinity of Hill 52, Void Farm, Volt Farm, Mallet Copse, Veal Cottages and the "enclosures" approximately 300 yards west of Veal Cottages. Two officers and eight sappers were specifically assigned to 2nd KOYLI and 16th HLI "for the purpose of siting and consolidating strongpoints at HILL 52 and VOID FARM."[92]

Battalions were to move forward from assembly positions at Wurst Farm (1 battalion), Irish Farm (2 battalions), and the dugout complex at Hilltop (1 battalion) on the night of the assault. "The problem of the assembly of troops prior to the attack was a serious one as even with extra [duckboard] tracks made, it would necessarily take a long time to move so large a body of troops in single file a distance of some 6 to 7 miles by night." This difficulty was further exacerbated by the fact that hostile batteries had carefully registered all tracks and shelled them almost continuously. Careful reconnaissance failed to identify billeting areas within close proximity to the start line. Proposed alternative sites "were waterlogged and it was decided that the exposure entailed on the men would militate more against their fitness for the assault than the march up."[93]

Possible delays while passing through the heavily shelled zone east and west of the flooded Steenbeek valley made it essential to determine the amount of time taken to traverse the approximately 2,000 yards from Wurst Farm and 8,000 yards from Irish Farm and Hilltop.[94] Brigades carrying out reliefs prior to the attack were thus required to record marching times and distances. This data would, after careful checking, be forwarded to Division HQ the following morning. Three available routes were avail-

---

91 TNA: WO/95/2370: '32nd Division Offensive Instructions No. 1: Outline Plan of Operations', 21 November 1917 and 'Addendum No. 1 to 32nd Division Offensive Instructions No. 1', 25 November 1917, 32nd Division War Diary.
92 Ibid, TNA: WO/95/2384: 219th Field Company RE War Diary, 1 December 1917 and IWM 4723: 'A.4/2', 6 December 1917, Brigadier-General T.S. Lambert Papers (Box 80/10/2). 32nd Division's 3 component field companies had 100 infantry permanently attached. Lieutenant-Colonel Pollard (CRE) subsequently observed: 'They live and work with, and are rationed by the RE, and are entirely under the control of the OC Field Coy.'
93 TNA: WO/95/2370: After-action report, 'Part II, Plan of Operations, Section IV, Assembly', 11 December 1917, 32nd Division War Diary.
94 It took 2nd RMF and 1st SWB 11 hours to traverse the same distance on 10 November. See Chapter 1, p. 39.

able as of 21 November: Mouse Trap and No. 3 duckboard tracks and the Gravenstafel Road. It was "hoped to get a fourth route constructed by the night of the attack", but this could not be relied on owing to the serious labour shortage in Second Army.[95]

The final section of Instructions No. 1 detailed sites where HQs were to be established: 32nd Division at Canal Bank, 97 Brigade advanced HQ at Kronprinz Farm and 14 Brigade (in support) inside a small pillbox near Kansas Cross. Blacklock was to identify potential battalion HQs after undertaking "necessary reconnaissance" of the forward area. The divisional signal officer was to ensure that buried cables reached brigade and battalion HQs before the attack.[96]

32nd Division Operation Order No. 134 followed at 7:00 p.m. on 23 November. Its contents dealt with specifics concerning the boundary adjustment (scheduled for the night of 24/25 November) between II Corps and VIII Corps. Rights of passage along the Bellevue Spur – Vindictive Crossroads Road "except between dusk and zero hour on the night before the attack" and the apportioning out of limited HQ accommodation astride Bellevue Spur were also clearly delineated on behalf of the neighbouring 8th Division.[97]

Order No. 135 was circulated at 8:30 p.m. on 24 November. 14 Brigade – now in reserve at Irish Farm, Canal Bank and Dambre Camp near Vlamertinghe respectively – was to dispatch a battalion to relieve 97 Brigade's close support battalion at Bellevue on 25 November. In addition, 96 Brigade would provide a battalion to relieve the reserve battalion at Wurst Farm on 26 November. The former brigade was scheduled to replace the latter opposite Vat Cottages Ridge on the night of 27/28 November: "The first two battalions of the 96 Infantry Brigade to go into the frontline will be prepared to stay in till the night 30 November/1 December." Days and nights spent in jumping-off positions and immediate vicinity allowed time for assault units to accustom themselves to unfamilar sectors, whilst direct observation of attack objectives by day and dispatch of reconnaissance patrols by night provided additional local intelligence. Subsequent reliefs by units from sister brigades would also allow time for further training and organisation in the rear. A table outlining brigade movements for the period 24-28 November was attached.[98]

Instructions No. 2 (24 November) dealt with vital preliminary work on railway and duckboard communications and further extension of buried cables. Two pioneer battalions and eight RE field companies with attached infantry (commanded by the CRE) were to carry out this task. General policy now called for the bulk of available labour

---

95 TNA: WO/95/2370: '32nd Division Instructions No. 1: Outline Plan of Operations', 21 November 1917 and After-action Report, 'Part II, Plan of Operations, Section IV, Assembly', 11 December 1917, 32nd Division War Diary.
96 Ibid: '32nd Division Instructions No. 1: Outline Plan of Operations', 21 November 1917 and Brigadier-General A.W. Pagan, *Infantry: An Account of the 1st Gloucestershire Regiment in the War 1914-1918* (Aldershot: Gale & Polden, 1951), p. 180.
97 TNA: WO/95/2370: '32nd Division Operation Order No. 134', 23 November 1917.
98 Ibid: '32nd Division Operation Order No. 135', 24 November 1917.

to extend two existing duckboard tracks whilst constructing two more. Brigade and battalion HQs were to be improved, tramways extended and roads repaired. Provision of additional shelter east of the canal was also to be undertaken by constructing a new forward camp at Wurst Farm. Extensions of an existing line of buried cable to Bellevue and an additional "main buried line" as far as 97 Brigade HQ at Kronprinz Farm was the responsibility of the CO Signals.[99]

Particulars concerning liaison between 97 Brigade and 25 Brigade were explained in Instructions No. 3 (26 November). Blacklock was ordered, as per instructions issued by 8th Division the previous day, to "arrange with the G.O.C. 25th Infantry Brigade, for the Commanding Officer, Company Commanders and Platoon Commanders of the 2nd K.O.Y.L.I. and 2nd Rifle Brigade to meet and discuss their various parts in the operations." Special mutual precautions were to be taken to ensure that both battalions were in touch on the jumping-off line prior to Zero, whilst "definite parties" from 97 Brigade were "detailed to join hands" with 25 Brigade in the vicinity of Teall Cottage and on the final objective. Liaison officers would be attached to brigade HQs throughout the attack. Battle insignia worn on the upper sleeves and below the collars of officers and ORs of 2nd Rifle Brigade and 2nd KOYLI were depicted in sketch diagrams to illustrate distinct unit identification schemes of battalions sharing the inner boundary between 25 Brigade and 97 Brigade; selected HQ locations for both brigades and 2nd Rifle Brigade followed.[100]

Order No. 136 (26 November) concerned the forthcoming relief – scheduled for the night of 27/28 November – of 97 Brigade. All details would be "arranged between the Brigadiers concerned."[101] Instructions No. 4 (Employment of RE and Pioneers) and No. 5 (Machine-guns) were distributed the following day. The former provided projected details and unit distribution particulars for preliminary work articulated in Instructions No. 2.[102] Instructions No. 5 stated that five additional machine-gun companies (80 guns) would be at 32nd Division's disposal.[103] Unfavourable ground conditions that hampered the deployment of field artillery on II Corps' front, made it necessary to reserve all available heavy machine-gun assets as a substitute force

---

99 Ibid: '32nd Offensive Instructions No. 2: Preparatory Work for Forthcoming Operations', 24 November 1917.
100 Ibid: '32nd Division Offensive Instructions No. 3: Liaison', 26 November 1917. One battalion commander appears to have made his own inter-battalion liaison arrangements, the CO 16th NF ('counter-attack counter attack' battalion) subsequently stating: 'I had liaison officers with Nos. 1 [2nd KOYLI], 2 [16th HLI] and 3 [11th Border] Battalions of 97th Bde.' See IWM 4723: '32nd Div. No.G.S.1499/3/33', 4 December 1917, Brigadier-General T.S. Lambert Papers (Box 80/10/2).
101 TNA: WO/95/2370: '32nd Division Order No. 136', 26 November 1917, 32nd Division War Diary.
102 Ibid: '32nd Division Offensive Instructions No. 4', 27 November 1917.
103 63rd Division would provide 64 of 80 additional guns.

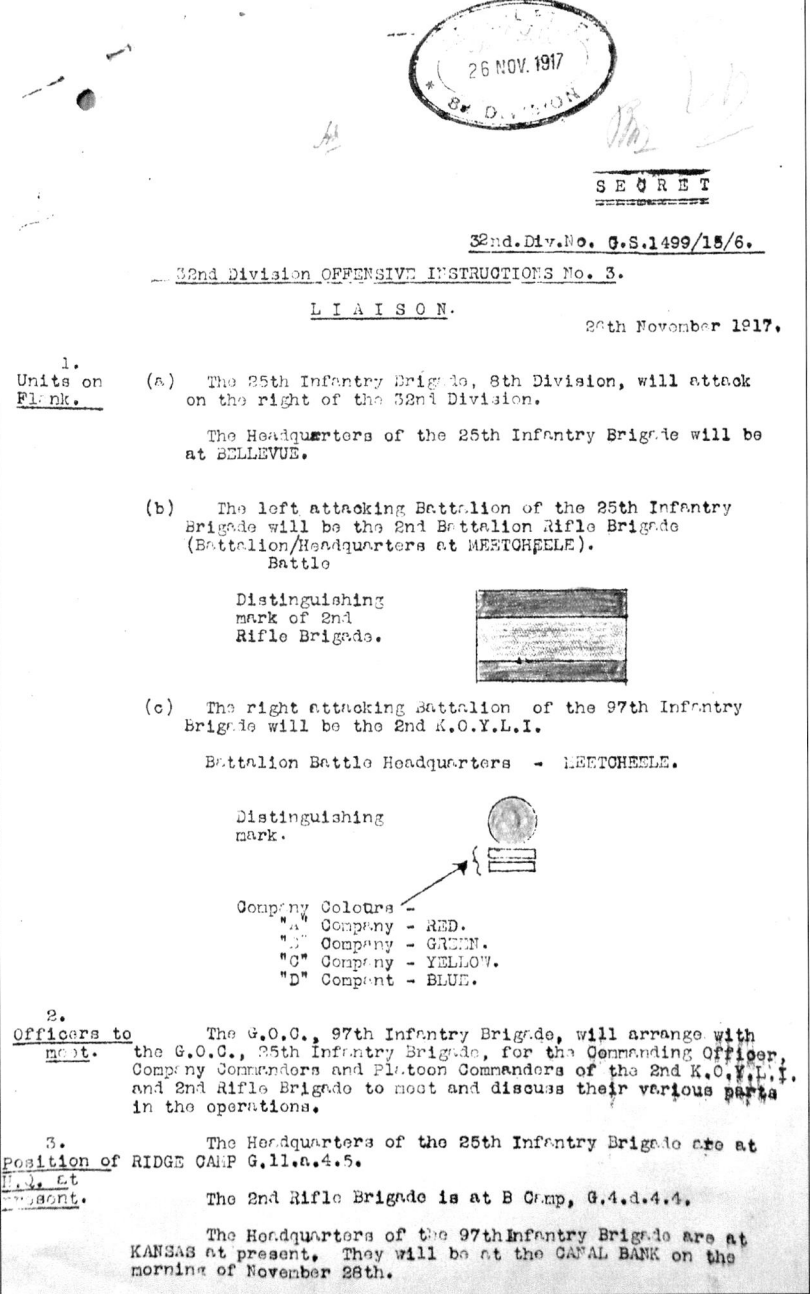

SECRET

32nd.Div.No. G.S.1499/15/6.

32nd Division OFFENSIVE INSTRUCTIONS No. 3.

LIAISON.

26th November 1917.

1. Units on Flank.

(a) The 25th Infantry Brigade, 8th Division, will attack on the right of the 32nd Division.

The Headquarters of the 25th Infantry Brigade will be at BELLEVUE.

(b) The left attacking Battalion of the 25th Infantry Brigade will be the 2nd Battalion Rifle Brigade (Battalion/Headquarters at MEETCHEELE).

Battle Distinguishing mark of 2nd Rifle Brigade.

(c) The right attacking Battalion of the 97th Infantry Brigade will be the 2nd K.O.Y.L.I.

Battalion Battle Headquarters - MEETCHEELE.

Distinguishing mark.

Company Colours -
"A" Company - RED.
"B" Company - GREEN.
"C" Company - YELLOW.
"D" Company - BLUE.

2. Officers to meet.

The G.O.C., 97th Infantry Brigade, will arrange with the G.O.C., 25th Infantry Brigade, for the Commanding Officer, Company Commanders and Platoon Commanders of the 2nd K.O.Y.L.I. and 2nd Rifle Brigade to meet and discuss their various parts in the operations.

3. Position of H.Q. at present.

The Headquarters of the 25th Infantry Brigade are at RIDGE CAMP G.11.a.4.5.

The 2nd Rifle Brigade is at B Camp, G.4.d.4.4.

The Headquarters of the 97th Infantry Brigade are at KANSAS at present. They will be at the CANAL BANK on the morning of November 28th.

32nd Division Instructions No. 3 liaison scheme. (TNA: WO/95/2370: 32nd Division War Diary)

multiplier tasked with carrying out offensive barrage and SOS fire support.[104] Two batteries (16 guns), under the GOC 97 Brigade's orders, would provide close defence of the captured line. Ten batteries (80 guns), under the II Corps MGO's orders, were to fire a protective barrage in front of the objective. The latter would also search and sweep areas where enemy reserves were sheltering. Six more batteries (48 guns), under the latter officer, were tasked with providing area concentration fire on select locales. Particulars about sites where this formidable array of 144 Vickers guns would be established prior to the assault, along with attached charts of the usual barrage data, were also included.[105]

Details concerning communications infrastructure were outlined in Instructions No. 6 (27 November). The cover letter to this four-page document stated: "The attached scheme of communications will be adhered to during forthcoming operations." General particulars indicated that 97 Brigade forward signal station would be established immediately behind the frontline at Virile Farm but would not follow up the advancing infantry, as laid down in *S.S. 148 Forward Inter-Communications in Battle* (March 1917), due to the limited nature of the operation "and of the ground over which it is being carried out…"[106] Every effort would be made to maintain telegraphic communications between assault battalions and artillery forward observation officers [FOO] and brigades and groups respectively. Liaison between infantry and artillery was to be centralized at Virile Farm and 6,500 yards farther back at Cheddar Villa. Visual signal and runner communications between battalion HQs and companies were to be thoroughly organised. Telephone lines would be extended forward as soon as possible after the start of the attack.[107] Of the "auxiliary means of communication" available, chief reliance would be placed on visual signalling organised to provide a "complete chain of communication in the event of the telegraphic system being destroyed." Communication by runners and aircraft was also to be arranged for. Contact between 97 Brigade and 25 Brigade would thus be maintained by a complex network of buried signal wire, visual signalling, runners and wireless."[108]

Use would be made of the already established "VIII Corps bury" system for communication between 32nd Division HQ at Canal Bank and artillery group and

---

104 Vickers machine-guns often 'assumed the role of light artillery' and 'were increasingly used for overhead fire to fill the gap between battalion weapons and the artillery.' See Bidwell & Graham, *Fire-Power*, p. 123.
105 TNA: WO/95/2370: '32nd Division Offensive Instructions No. 5', 27 November 1917, 32nd Division War Diary. Participating units, in addition to 32nd Division's component 14th, 96th, 97th and 219th MG companies, included 188th, 189th and 223rd (63rd Division) companies. See IWM 4723: 'G.188/4/1' (14th MG Company report), 14 December 1917 and 'Action December 2, 1917' (188th MG Company report), Brigadier-General T.S. Lambert Papers (Box 80/10/2).
106 TNA: WO/95/2370: '32nd Division Offensive Instructions No. 26', 27 November 1917, 32nd Division War Diary.
107 Ibid.
108 Ibid.

Divisional Instructions & Orders 145

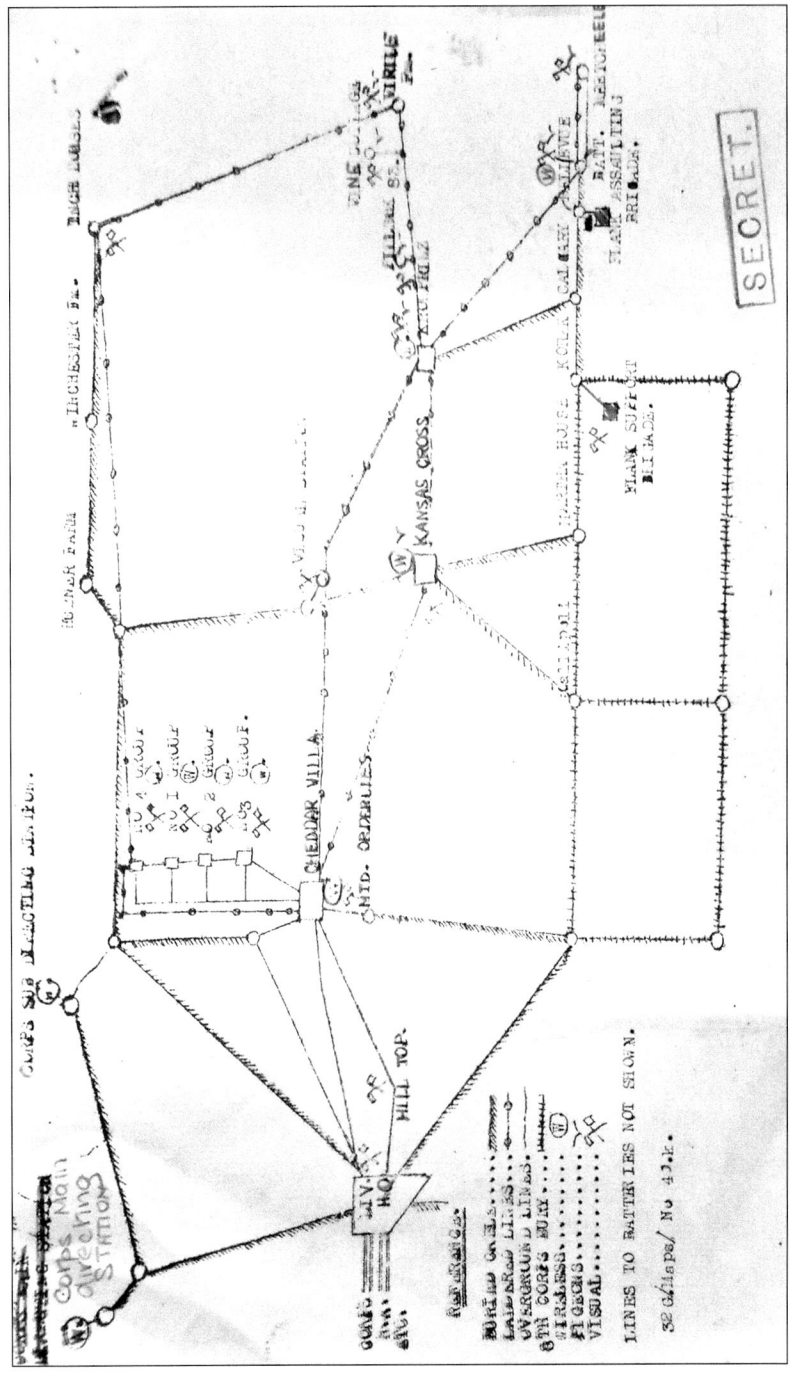

32nd Division communications scheme diagram. (TNA: WO/95/2370: 32nd Division War Diary)

infantry brigade HQs; this system was extended as far as Bellevue by 27 November. VIII Corps' bury was supplemented by an elaborate system of ladder lines "connecting the division to the artillery groups, infantry brigades with Cheddar Villa, also the artillery groups and infantry brigades with their batteries and battalions and with the brigade forward signal station at VIRILE FARM." Linemen and relay posts would be established at select points along ladder routes. These were to be arranged, "as far as possible, to coincide with visual stations and other points where auxiliary means of communication are available."[109] Spark wireless sets were to be employed throughout the assault.[110] Power Buzzer, amplifier and CW sets would not be utilised. Five wireless stations at Bellevue, Kronprinz Farm, Kansas Cross, Cheddar Villa and II Corps' Directing Station were to be in place and operative prior to the assault.[111] All messages, except in cases of emergency, had to be sent in code: "If handed in "in clear" they will be enciphered and deciphered by the wireless operators unless franked "in clear" by an officer. In all cases messages must be brief."[112] Wireless stations would, in order to communicate with supporting artillery groups, make direct contact with RFC receiving sets only during hours (4:30 to 6:30 p.m.) of darkness.[113] Special atten-

109 Ibid.
110 Use was probably made of the 50-Watt Spark transmitter and the newly adopted 'W/T Forward 20-Watt Spark Transmitter' at division and brigade HQs. The latter had a range of 2,000 to 3,000 yards. Major E.E. Evelegh (CO 32nd Division Signal School) subsequently remarked that 'Spark wireless was found very reliable on this occasion and good use was made of it.' See TNA: WO/95/2370: After-action report: 'Appendix 'I': Communications', December 1917, 32nd Division War Diary.
111 Any W/T station could communicate with any other. Set 1 was for communications with MG companies on Bellevue Spur, artillery observations posts and 25 Brigade; Set 2 was located at 97 Brigade HQ (Kronprinz Farm); Set 3 at 14 Brigade HQ (Kansas); Set 4 at Cheddar Villa for communication with artillery groups. Set 5 ('II Corps Directing Station') would be in 'close touch' with 32nd Division HQ and II Corps Heavy Artillery.
112 Divisional communications infrastructures were often hampered by institutionalized constraints. John Ferris notes that signals security 'fed from communications systems, and like all parasites, sapped the strength of its host. The purpose of these systems was to maintain command and control. Their success shaped operations.' The proliferation of listening sets by both sides to monitor enemy phone traffic up to 3,000 yards from the frontline, brought about measures whereby one's own telephone traffic also had to be monitored. Thus armies sought to minimize the security threat by limiting telephone usage. 'They often stripped telephones from their battalions, precisely where these were most needed, while the reluctance of personnel to face the lengthy process of enciphering messages hampered the adoption of radio until the armistice. As a senior British wireless officer noted in 1917: 'Ciphers have always been the bugbear of wireless. People don't like, or they have not the time, to do the encyphering [sic]. The result is that messages are sent by some other means than that which requires ciphers or code, such as runner.' By 1918, wireless provided the solution to the signals problem in the field, 'but the stranglehold of signals security throttled its use.' See John Ferris (ed), *The British Army and Signals Intelligence During the First World War* (Stroud: Allen Sutton & Army Records Society, 1992) pp. 5-6.
113 RFC wireless operators were permanently attached to artillery batteries and moved with them from the close of 1916. They remained under the control of the corps squadron with

tion was to be paid to this means of communication, "especially in the case of S.O.S messages and cancel S.O.S. messages."[114]

A network of seventeen visual signalling stations, for use by infantry battalions, machine-gun companies and artillery, was to be extended from the frontline to Canal Bank. Company runners were to deliver messages to battalion HQs. Runners dispatched from battalions and the brigade forward signal station would carry messages to the rear by a series of relay posts set up near established linemen posts at "intervals of 400 yards along duckboard tracks from VIRILE FARM to KRONPRINZ FARM … thence to KANSAS CROSS and CHEDDAR VILLA and on to artillery groups." Mounted orderlies, the last link in this chain, would then carry messages from artillery groups to Division HQ. Organisation of visual signals and runners was to be the sole responsibility of assault battalions, forward brigade, support brigade and artillery group signal officers.[115] Assault battalions were to be issued 8 pigeons each which, on release, would fly directly to a loft situated at Vlamertinghe. Artillery FOOs were expected to "draw on the nearest battalion for any birds they require." In addition, brigade HQs were issued 16 pigeons trained to home-in to a Watou-based loft. This means of communication, it was pointed out, was "not as reliable as usual owing to the time of year. Any messages of great importance must be sent by at least two birds." Messenger dogs would not be employed due to insufficient training.[116]

No. 7 Squadron RFC[117] was tasked with providing signal and "contact-counter-attack" aircraft throughout the assault. Fuselage mounted Klaxon horns would be sounded to "call attention and to signal to the infantry", while warnings of impending counter-attacks were to be signalled by "wireless and dropping a white parachute light." The designated aircraft was detailed to accept signals by lamp from brigade and battalion HQs "and will acknowledge the same by lamp." Lamp messages received from the ground were required to be air dropped at divisional HQ within five minutes of receipt.[118] Each battalion would be issued 15 signal rockets to be carried forward by battalion HQs and companies. Caution for placing too much reliance on this device

---

which the battery was working. See Air Historical Branch, *The Royal Air Force in the Great War*, p. 203.
114 TNA: WO/95/2370: '32nd Division Instructions No. 6', 27 November 1917, 32nd Division War Diary.
115 Ibid.
116 Ibid.
117 No. 7 Squadron was formed at Farnborough in May 1914. It remained in Great Britain carrying out experimental duties until April 1915. Subsequently dispatched to France, it served as a corps squadron throughout the remainder of the war. Attached to II Corps in November 1917, its aerodrome was located at Proven. See Air of Authority – A History of RAF Organisation <http://www.rafweb.org/Sqn021-25.htm> and TNA: AIR 1/1186/204/5/2595: 'Location of RFC Units – 1st December 1917', RFC War Diary.
118 TNA: WO/95/2370: '32nd Division Instructions No. 6', 27 November 1917 and '32nd Divisional Artillery Group Instructions No. 15', 30 November 1917, 32nd Division War Diary.

'B' Flight No. 7 Squadron RFC. (Peter Facey)

followed: "These rockets are unreliable owing to faulty manufacture."[119] Labouring under the most difficult of circumstances throughout what remained of November, consequent determined efforts by signallers, engineers and working parties ensured that 32nd Division's communications infrastructure was organised and extended west to east for approximately 10,000 yards from Canal Bank to the vicinity of Vat Cottages Ridge.

Order No. 137 (27 November) provided an updated table denoting routes and timetables for battalions marching to reserve and support positions at Dambre Camp, Hilltop Farm, Irish Farm and Wurst Farm. All movement would occur following the brigade exchange scheduled for the night of the 27/28. "The moves of battalions for 28th inst. as notified in table issued with 32nd Division Operation Order 135" were cancelled. Units would now commence their march on the 28th in accordance with the newly issued table.[120]

32nd Division Operation Order No. 138 – the entire seven-page attack plan in outline – was also forwarded on the 27th. Sections one to six related details of previously forwarded orders and instructions: The general attack objectives were Volt Farm which, along with neighbouring Void Farm, was situated on the 50-metre Y-shaped height overlooking the SW gradient of Vat Cottages Ridge, Mallet Copse and Veal

---

119 Ibid.
120 Ibid: '32nd Division Order No. 137', 27 November 1917.

Cottages. Map reference particulars concerning the boundary between II Corps and VIII Corps followed. Brigade tasks and organisation were as follows: 97 Brigade reinforced by two battalions from 96 Brigade to carry out the assault; 14 Brigade, in support with the two remaining battalions of 96 Brigade, to act as reserve. Assault troops would be distributed on a frontage of five battalions. An additional battalion would be held in reserve near Virile Farm to deal with German counter-attacks.[121]

Sections seven and eight dealt with attack methodology: Three objective lines (yellow, green, red) were delineated: "At Zero, the advanced posts of the enemy will be rushed without an artillery barrage to a depth of 200 yards" (yellow line). At Zero + 8, the artillery was to commence firing at all "known and suspected strongpoints lying outside the line 350 yards from the forming-up line. The bombardment would then pause on the "350 yards" or "dotted green line" intermediary objective for six minutes in order to allow the infantry to "close up". At Zero + 14, the artillery was to lift back at a rate of 100 yards in six minutes. Infantry detailed to capture strongpoints were to advance as close to the barrage as possible and "rush each defended locality when the artillery lifts." The gunners' final task was to place a protective barrage 300 yards outside the red line objective. This would be maintained until "Zero plus one hour 36 minutes unless ordered to continue." Definite and distinct units were expected to "capture and hold each known enemy strong point and defended locality." Troops were required to be "collected and company and battalion reserves reformed at the earliest possible moment after the capture of each position" in order to avoid confusion and straggling.[122]

Consolidation of objectives and deployment of RE field companies and divisional pioneer units were covered in sections nine and ten. The captured area was to be "consolidated in depth and all [Vickers] machine-guns detailed for close defence and Lewis Guns will be pushed up for the defence of the captured ground, the majority being advanced to the final objective." The position would be further strengthened by construction of six strongpoints extending from Hill 52 to the enclosures west of Veal Cottages; 219th Field Company would supervise construction with 100 attached infantry. This unit was also tasked with the responsibility for patrolling and maintaining "Mousetrap Track" forward of 97 Brigade HQ at Kronprinz Farm.[123] Four RE field companies (206th, 218th, 247th, 248th, 249th) and 14th Worcestershire Regiment (less two companies) were to be employed by the CRE "under special instructions" relating to track patrol and maintenance.[124]

---

121 Ibid: '32nd Division Operation Order No. 138', 27 November 1917.
122 Ibid.
123 IWM 4723: 'A.4/2', 6 December 1917, Brigadier-General T.S. Lambert Papers (Box 80/10/2).
124 TNA: WO/95/2370: '32nd Division Operation Order No. 138', 27 November 1917, 32nd Division War Diary and IWM 4723:'A.4/2', 6 December 1917, Brigadier-General T.S. Lambert Papers (Box 80/10/2). The 17th Northumberland Fusiliers (attached pioneer

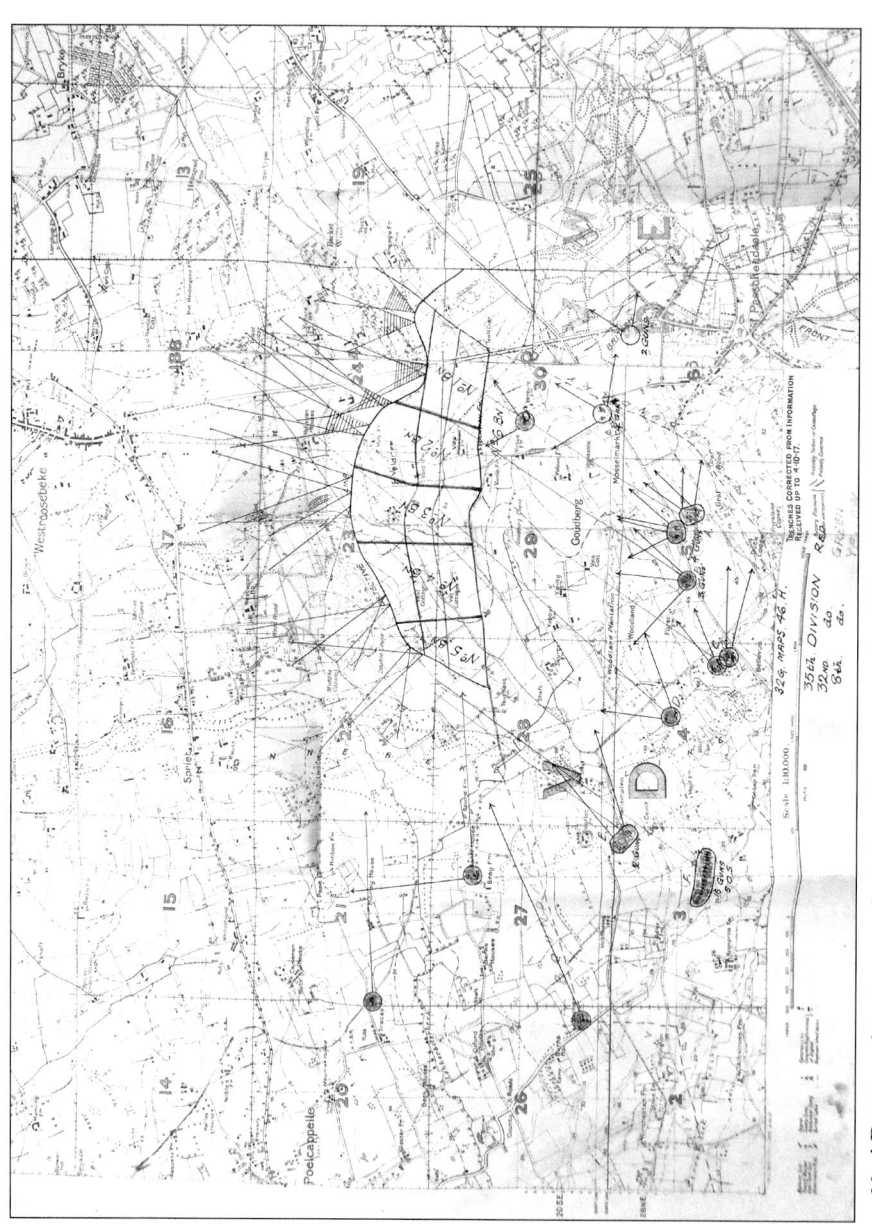

32nd Division objective map depicting yellow, green and red lines. (TNA: WO/95/2370: 32nd Division War Diary)

Section eleven indicated how attacking battalions were to deploy on the start-line prior to jumping-off. Section twelve provided more general forming-up instructions:

- The assaulting troops will form up close behind our frontline.
- The routes to the forming-up places are to be carefully reconnoitered and clearly pegged out and marked with white posts.
- The forming-up place of each platoon is to be marked with white posts and tapes.
- Patrols and Lewis Guns will cover the forming-up. These patrols must be pushed out every night previous to the assault so that the enemy may become accustomed to them.
- 97th Infantry Brigade will ensure that the forming-up is carried out in complete silence and that during the first rush there is no noise or shouting if possible.

"Every possible means and device for ensuring direction" needed to be employed. All officers and "as many N.C.O's as possible" would be issued with compasses and "know the compass bearing of their objective." Moreover, each company assembly area was to be provided with a luminous notice board on which would be painted "the bearing of the first company objective and the distance in yards to it."[125]

Section 13 provided additional information about when the barrage would open fire and lift on to targeted strongpoints. Fire was to remain normal on the eve of the attack until Zero + 8. From Zero + 8 onward; the action of the artillery would be as follows:

- The artillery firing on strongpoints in the area to be attacked will act as detailed in Paragraph 7 (i.e., on known and suspected enemy positions lying 350 yards from the forming-up line).
- All known strongpoints and machine-gun emplacements outside the area to be attacked will be kept under fire.
- A protective barrage will be maintained 300 yards in front of the objective until Zero + 1 hour 30 minutes (4/5 shrapnel, 1/5 smoke).[126]
- From Zero + 1 hour 30 minutes onwards a combing barrage will be put down on all enemy centres of activity and suspected assembly places for counter-attacks.
- North and west of the line LIND COT – CLEAR FARM – V. 17 central – V. 18 central (southern and eastern outskirts of Westroosebeke) [will be deluged with] a proportion of smoke and, if safe, gas shells. These projectiles will be mixed with other ammunition by guns firing on strongpoints, farms, etc., to blind machine-guns in this area and confuse the enemy as to the direction of the attack.

---

battalion) left Shute's command to be employed as 'GHQ Railway Construction Troops' on 13 November. See Becke, *Order of Battle Divisions, Part 3B*, pp. 24-26.

125 TNA: WO/95/2370: '32nd Division Operation Order No. 138', 32nd Division War Diary.
126 Ibid. Shute noted that it was 'advisable to keep this barrage well back on account of the long range at which the guns were firing.' See Ibid: After-action report, 'Part II, Plan of Operations, Section II, Detailed Plan', 11 December 1917, 32nd Division War Diary.

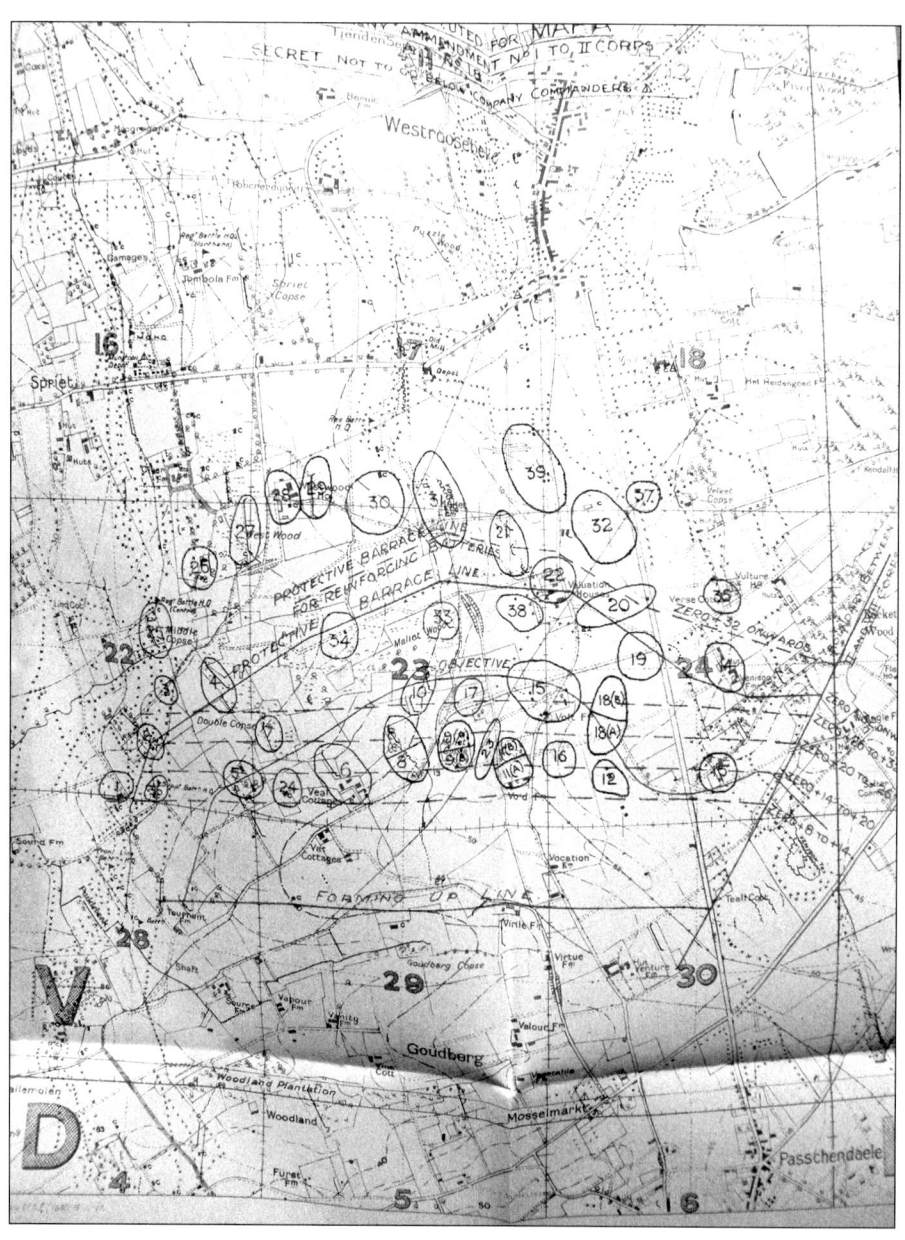

32nd Division area concentration barrage map. (TNA: WO/95/2370: 32nd Division War Diary)

Detailed artillery plans, it was added, were to be forwarded at a later date. Liaison with the supporting artillery was further facilitated in Section 14: The CRA would "detail a RFA battery commander to be attached to Headquarters of the 97th Infantry Brigade." This officer's battery was to be at Blacklock's direct disposal throughout the operation.[127]

Section 15 outlined details for the employment of Vickers machine-guns. Two close defence batteries would be tasked with moving forward to the vicinity of the final objective in order to provide direct fire support during consolidation. Ten batteries, tasked with engaging sites where enemy reserves were believed to be sheltered, were allocated for indirect barrage work beyond the objective. A further six batteries, furnished by 96 Brigade, were to be employed as area concentration guns targeting enemy assembly areas and likely threats from localities beyond the left flank. One battery allotted for area concentration work was to be withdrawn from this task at Zero + 1 ½ hours, and, following up the advancing infantry, position a half-section each at Hill 52, Void Farm, Mallet Copse and Veal Cottages respectively. Liaison would be further facilitated by having both II Corps and 32nd Division MGOs attached to 32nd Division and 97 Brigade HQs. "Careful arrangements" were necessary in order "to preserve communication with all machine-gun batteries by runners and all other means of communication."[128]

Section 16 related the deployment of Stokes Mortars in the event that all objectives had been attained. Ten tubes would be carried forward from Virile and Tournant farms to the vicinity of Hill 52 (six tubes), Volt Farm (2 tubes) and Veal Cottages (2 tubes) about one hour and thirty minutes after Zero. Their rapid indirect fire – 30 to 40 rounds per minute – was expected to provide considerable assistance during consolidation.[129] 14 Brigade would deploy two additional tubes against targets west of Tournant Farm "for the express purpose of being available to deal with strongpoints which might hold up our advance on the left flank."[130] They would also engage any counter-attack developing from inundated ground west and SW of Vat Cottages Ridge.[131]

Section 17 stated that "Every possible means of communication will be organised as laid down in *S.S. 148* and utilised to the fullest extent." The assaulting infantry would, as with 8th Division, utilise green ground flares and Watson Fans to communicate with designated contact aircraft. Two flares per man (Section 18) were to be

---

127 Ibid: '32nd Division Operation Order No. 138'.
128 Ibid.
129 Sixty rounds of ammunition were dumped at each Stokes Mortar position prior to the assault.
130 TNA: WO/95/2370: '32nd Division Operation Order No. 138', 27 November 1917 and after-action report 'Part II, Plan of Operations, Section II, Detailed Plan', 11 December 1917, 32nd Division War Diary.
131 See Appendix VIII.

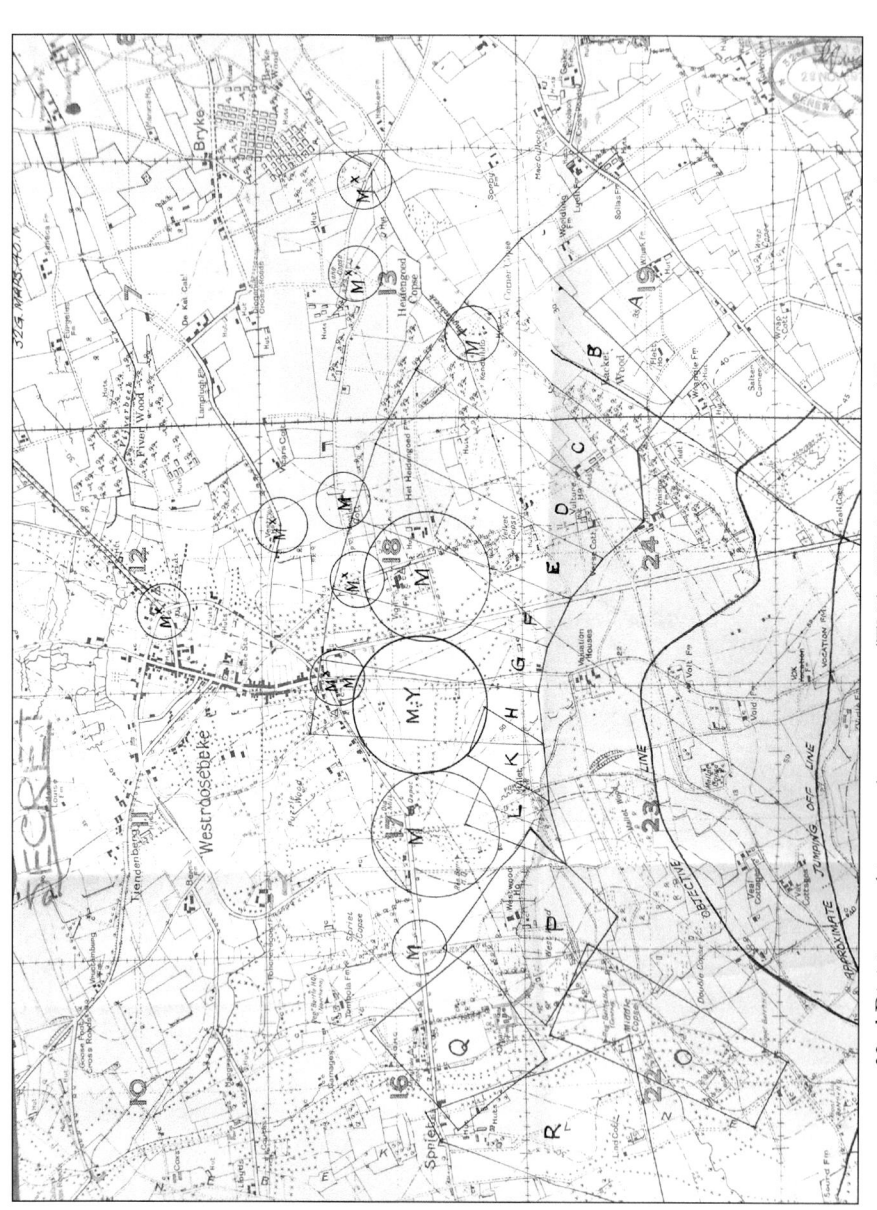

32nd Division machine-gun barrage map. (TNA: WO/95/2370: 32nd Division War Diary)

issued to carry forward.[132] Liaison arrangements (Section 19) were "as laid down in 32nd Division Instructions No. 3" (26 November). The placement of a senior artillery officer at 97 Brigade HQ and a junior artillery officer "with the headquarters of each assaulting battalion" would further facilitate communications with the infantry.[133] The infantry were to be equipped (steel helmet, rifle, bayonet, 170 rounds of standard .303 calibre ammunition carried in equipment pouches and issue cotton bandoleers, haversack, water bottle, mess tin, entrenching tool, box respirator and PH "tube" helmet) in "battle order". Each man would (Section 20) also carry a shovel. Leather jerkins and sheepskin waistcoats were to be worn over tunics as additional protection from the cold. Section 21 reminded officers and men to avoid carrying "any document likely to be of value to the enemy." German insignia and equipment denoting unit identity, captured documents, etc., were to be immediately sent back to Division HQ for examination.[134] Cadres from each of the six assault battalions' establishment of approximately thirty officers would (Section 22) remain behind during the attack as per *S.S. 135*: "No more than 21 officers will accompany their units into action." Select NCOs and specialists were also to be held back.[135]

Section 23 reminded all concerned that "Separate instructions have been issued as to medical arrangements, prisoners of war, positions of dumps, S.A.A., etc." Situation reports would (Section 24) be forwarded to Division HQ "at zero and at least every subsequent half-hour during the attack. Subordinates were reminded of the "importance of very frequent reports giving full information in writing or on situation maps must be impressed on the troops." Artillery liaison officers attached to assaulting battalions were responsible "for collecting all possible information from F.O.O.'s and forwarding it, through Infantry Brigade Forward Station and Infantry Brigade Headquarters to Divisional Headquarters."[136]

Section 25 stated that orders for the synchronization of watches would follow shortly. Section 26 confirmed the HQ locations for 32nd Division and its subordinate infantry brigades. A final note, almost identical to a section found in 8th Division Instructions No. 6, explained the expected response to German reconnaissance aircraft: "It must be impressed on all troops that it is of the utmost importance that the heaviest possible rifle and Lewis Gun fire must be brought upon all low-flying enemy areoplanes." All planes that escaped would, it ominously observed, "certainly report our positions and bring down a very heavy artillery concentration."[137]

A supplement to Offensive Instructions No. 1 was also issued on the 27th. 32nd Division Administrative Arrangements related the positions of ammunition, supply,

---

132 TNA: WO/95/2370: '32nd Division Operation Order No. 138', 27 November 1917, 32nd Division War Diary.
133 Ibid.
134 Ibid.
135 Ibid.
136 Ibid.
137 Ibid.

ordnance, water, salvage and RE dumps. Soup kitchens at St. Julian and south of Cheddar Villa would be established to serve up soup, tea, biscuits and cigarettes to men returning from the frontline. Hot food was to be "issued to the troops at the latest possible moment under brigade arrangements." Three straggler posts, manned by the military police, would be established west and SW of St. Julian. A straggler collection station would also be situated NW of Wieltje. All prisoners were to be escorted to the divisional cage at Canal Bank. A Division forward cage would be established NW of Wieltje, the APM arranging for escorts from this point to the enclosure at Canal Bank. The document concluded with instructions for the removal and burial of the dead.[138] These grim but necessary provisions were just one more part of routine pre-assault administrative arrangements.

32nd Division issued a further supplement to accompany Order No. 138 the following day: "Definite distinct and complete units would be detailed to capture, mop up, and garrison each known enemy strongpoint."[139] Careful arrangements were to be made for maintaining direction by ready knowledge of easily identifiable landmarks. All ranks were required to know distances from the jumping-off line to each strongpoint or trench. The direction – north, south, east or west – faced on the final objective was compulsory knowledge: "Every officer and as many N.C.O.s as possible must be in possession of compasses and know the compass bearing of their objective."[140] Hostile counter-attacks were expected to commence shortly after final objectives were obtained:

---

138 DIVISIONAL BURIAL PARTY 2nd Lieut. W. Thomson, 15th High. L. Infy., is Divisional Burial Officer, and with the Divisional Burial Party of 80 O.R., is located at Irish Farm; The Divisional Burial Party is responsible for burying all bodies up to the line ADLER FARM, D. 3. a. 7. 3, YETTA HOUSES, D. 3. d. 3. 7, BELLEVUE, D. 4. D. 7. 2. The responsibility for clearing forward of the above mentioned line rests on brigades; Bodies from the forward area placed by the [tramway] tracks at the limits of the area controlled by the Divisional Burial Party, will be brought back by them to the cemeteries and buried there; Rods and discs for marking graves may be had on application to Divisional Burial Officer; Special attention is drawn to the importance of keeping the Divisional Burial Officer informed of all burials carried out by units so that his records may be complete; Identity discs must not be removed from bodies left for burial by the Divisional Burial Party.' A main cemetery was already situated near Hill Top Farm. A forward and advanced cemetery would be established in the vicinity of Cheddar Villa and Yetta Houses respectively. Ibid: '32nd Division Administrative Arrangements: Supplementary to Offensive Instructions No. 1', 27 November 1917.

139 63rd RND's after-action report noted: 'In the majority of cases the enemy uses his pillboxes as a barrack, and defends them from neighbouring shell holes, or from a small trench just in rear. Pillboxes must therefore be approached from the flanks.' See Sellers (ed), 'Western Front: Report on Operations During the Third Battle of Ypres: Passchendaele, 24th October to 5th November 1917', *RND: Royal Naval Division. Antwerp, Gallipoli & Western Front 1914-1918*, Issue Number 22 (September 2002), p. 2184.

140 TNA: WO/95/2370: '32nd Division No. G.S. 1357/0/2', 28 November 1917, 32nd Division War Diary.

Troops must hold out against them [counter-attacks] <u>to the last man and no one must retire under any circumstances</u>. Should any individual or individuals retire [,] troops behind them <u>must never under any conditions</u> conform to the retirement. On the contrary [,] they must advance and counter-counter-attack the enemy at once."[141]

All ranks, it was further stressed, "must be made to realise that experience has proved that troops who retire invariably suffer 3 or 4 times greater losses than troops who advance."[142] This section of "cyclostyled sheet" was viewed by the post-war history of 16th HLI as indicative of a "desperate attack for important ground … Every inch on Passchendaele Ridge was valuable."[143]

Junior officers were reminded to prevent subordinates from scattering in search of souvenirs: "Every opportunity for reforming troops as reserves for repelling counter-attacks" was to be made use of. "Counter-counter-attacks must be delivered on the initiative of the officer on the spot." Success depended on "intelligence, dash and initiative of junior commanders."[144] Extreme care was also to be taken that adequate "moppers up" were detailed from "rear platoons to mop up the captured area." Secured ground was "not to be too thickly held." Formed bodies were to be carefully placed in the rear to engage enemy counter-attacks. It was necessary that close touch be maintained between the "O.C., counter-counter-attacking troops" and the frontline commander, "so that the former may have all arrangements made for a sudden move forward which must be made on his own initiative." Battle patrols would also be immediately pushed forward to "points of vantage where they can give early notice of approach of any counter-attacks."[145] The importance of maintaining an unbroken line and secure flanks was vital: "Touch must be maintained with units on the right and left and no gaps must be left." All units were to be prepared to form a defensive flank following attainment of objectives. "If the troops on their flanks are checked they must make every endeavour to join up with troops on either flank should there be a gap when the objective is reached." Flanking fire from neighbouring battalions could, it was also stressed, be expected to provide valuable assistance to units held up during the advance.[146]

All available Vickers and Lewis guns were to be brought forward to the final objective, "the main defences of the newly captured area entrusted to them while the men are digging in." Deployment some distance in advance or rear would ensure avoidance of hostile shelling. Work on defence organisation and consolidation "must be

---

141 Ibid.
142 Ibid.
143 Chalmers (ed), *A Saga of Scotland*, p. 110.
144 TNA: WO/95/2370: '32nd Division No. G.S. 1357/02', 28 November 1917, 32nd Division War Diary.
145 Ibid.
146 Ibid.

begun at once no matter how tired the men are"; the enemy, previous experience had demonstrated, would waste no time in preparing a strong counter-attack. Thus it was crucial that the consolidation period "be utilised to the utmost to get cover and prepare for the counter-attack which is certain to come and which can be easily beaten off if machine-gun defence is organised at once and our trenches are prepared with energy."[147] Timely information was essential if division and brigade HQs were to gauge the situation and provide the attackers with essential fire support: "Without such reports it is impossible for the commanders behind to organise efficient artillery support for the troops in front. Early information, although it may appear of little value to the sender, may be a great factor of success."[148]

Steps were to be taken to ensure all ranks had serviceable rifles despite muddy conditions that often rendered them useless: "It must be understood that rifle fire invariably wins the day." Wire to clear muzzles and brushes to clean breaches and bolts would be distributed; issue canvas breach covers would also be kept in place as long as possible.[149] The success of any assault was dependent on "lines of the assaulting troops being square on the objective to be attacked" during the forming-up. Jumping-off lines for each platoon had to be carefully marked by pegs and taped: "Failure to do this will lead to loss of direction which is fatal." Advancing troops were reminded to maintain touch with rear units: "Neglect of keeping this touch has lately resulted in failure."[150] Bypassed strongpoints that continued to resist were to be left "until the attacking troops have securely established themselves beyond them" and consolidated positions against inevitable counter-attack. "Then and not till then call on them to surrender." Prisoners were to be sent back immediately, as "the tide of battle may turn and the prisoners lost become a source of danger." The lengthy document concluded with an appeal to divisional *esprit*: "It must be remembered that it is a point of honour for every man in the 32nd Division that any position captured is held to the last and that not an inch of ground gained is ever given up."[151]

The final series of instructions and orders were issued during 28 to 30 November. Three instruction documents (7, 8, and 9) were forwarded on 28 November. Technical information (organisation, rates of fire, communication, equipment and rations, preparation and camouflage of emplacements) and pre-attack movements concerning deployment of the 128 barrage and area concentration machine-guns were related in Instructions No. 7.[152] Instructions No. 8 were based on the contents of II Corps

---

147 Ibid.
148 Ibid.
149 Ibid.
150 Ibid.
151 Ibid.
152 Ibid: '32nd Division Instructions No. 7: Machine-guns', 28 November 1917. Barrage and area concentration duties were to be carried out by MG companies: 14th, 96th, 219th (32nd Division); 188th, 189th, 233rd (63rd Division); 32 guns from 35th Division.

Operation Order No. 172 of 27 November.[153] "Part A" elaborated additional air to ground communication details: "A contact aeroplane will fly over the line at 7:30 a.m. on the morning of the attack and will call for flares by sending a succession of 'A's on the Klaxon Horn and dropping a white light." The most advanced line of infantry would burn green flares at that hour "as soon as called for by the aeroplane." Issue green flares were not to be expended unless specifically called for from the air or, accompanied by manipulated Watson Fans, at all other times on request. "Two oblong black panels fixed at right angles to the rear edge of the lower plane, one on each side of the fuselage and about three feet from it" would identify the contact aircraft. Ground flares were only to be lit for a machine bearing these markings. The "Contact Counter-attack Aeroplane" would, as with 8th Division's attack scheme, be in the air "from dawn on the morning of the day of the attack to watch for any indication of impending counter-attacks and to give warning of same by wireless and by dropping a WHITE PARACHUTE LIGHT." "Part B" provided additional instructions for watch synchronization.[154]

Instructions No. 9 stressed that "every officer and NCO and as many men as possible moving to position of assembly must know the details of the route he is to follow." Elaborate measures were to be taken to ensure that assault troops reached positions prior to Zero. 97 Brigade HQ, with attached infantry and engineers, would move to the assembly area on the night of 1/2 December. Routes were to be marked by noticeboards, which were not to be positioned by any other troops except road control and track maintenance parties. "Any individuals or parties meeting troops of 97th Infantry Brigade on any route will give way to them and get off the road or track" until clear. All duckboard tracks within the divisional area were reserved for the exclusive use of 97 Brigade from 4:00 p.m. on 1 December to 6:00 a.m. on the 2nd. Care was to be taken that carrying, artillery and signal parties were clear of these avenues during that time. Traffic control and reconnaissance of overland routes were the respective responsibilities of reserve and assault brigades: 14 Brigade was tasked with establishing a reliable traffic control post at the junction of "Peter Pan" track with the Gravenstafel – Bellevue Road to deny unauthorised access to 8th Division's allotted tracks. 97 Brigade was to see that all tracks and roads leading to assembly positions were carefully reconnoitered, while also ensuring traversable paths forward of established duckboard avenues were marked with whitewashed guide posts.[155]

---

153 See TNA: WO/95/643: 'II Corps Operation Order No. 172', 27 November 1917, II Corps War Diary.
154 TNA: WO/95/2370: '32nd Division Offensive Instructions No. 8', 32nd Division War Diary, 28 November 1917. The watch synchronization scheme called for an officer to be sent from Division HQ to infantry brigade, CRA and CRE HQs between 12:00 and 1 p.m. and 3:00 and 4:00 p.m. on the day of attack, the DMGO receiving the same information at 11:30 a.m. and 3:00 p.m. respectively.
155 Ibid: '32nd Instructions No. 9: Assembly', 28 November 1917 and 'Addendum No. 1 to 32nd Division Offensive Instructions No. 9', 29 November 1917.

Communication with the "Contact Counter-attack Aeroplane" was articulated in Instructions No. 10 (30 November). This machine was not to be confused with the contact aircraft referred to in Instructions No. 8. It would be identifiable by a single streamer attached to its tail. The observer was prepared to receive messages from the infantry by signal lamp. A chart containing thirty predetermined signal codes was attached. One example required the infantry to signal "CAR.CAR.CAR." This meant, "Enemy counter-attacking on our right flank." Confirmation of receipt from the air would be by repetition of any lamp signal received from troops on the ground.[156]

Brigadier-General F.W. Lumsden's 14 Brigade would be in divisional support.[157] Part "A" of Instructions No. 11 (30 November) explained its assigned role: "You [Lumsden] will be in command of the brigade in divisional support (14 Brigade, less 14th MG Company on barrage fire work) during the forthcoming operations." Arrangements were to be made to have his four battalions (5/6th Royal Scots, 1st Dorsetshire Regiment, 2nd Manchester Regiment, 15th HLI) deployed at Irish Farm, Hilltop, Wurst Farm and Bellevue for the immediate defence of the Bellevue Spur. These units must be prepared "to move at notice of ½ hour from Zero onwards." They were not to be employed "unless the enemy should make such a determined counter-attack as to endanger the present frontline." In any case, Lumsden was "to keep in close touch with the general situation and with the 97th Infantry Brigade, and have a liaison officer at the 97th Brigade Headquarters." 14 Brigade was also tasked with establishing observation posts in the vicinity of Bellevue in order to provide Division HQ with frequent reports "as to your [Lumsden's] view of the situation and all events that come to your knowledge." Lumsden would assume command of operations in the event of Blacklock becoming a casualty. He could "probably" expect to relieve 97 Brigade two nights after the assault, "but must be prepared to do so earlier if required." [158]

"Appendix A" of Instructions No. 11 outlined deployment of two detached 14 Brigade Stokes mortars against troublesome snipers, strongpoints and possible counter-attacks just beyond the left flank of 97 Brigade. At Zero + 2 hours, both tubes were to be brought forward to the vicinity of Tournant Farm to provide additional fire support assistance to the left (15th LF) battalion of 97 Brigade.[159] Part "B"

---

156 Ibid: '32nd Offensive Instructions No. 10: Communication with Contact Counter-attack Aeroplane', 30 November 1917.
157 Brigadier-General Frederick William Lumsden VC CB DSO (1872-1918). Commissioned Royal Marine Artillery 1888; Staff College 1910; GSO 2 Straits Settlements 1910-14; GSO 3 1915; Brigade Major 1915-16; GSO 2 1916-17; A/Brigadier-General and GOC 14 Brigade April 1917; DSO (2 bars) and VC January-April 1917. See Gerald Gliddon, *VCs of the First World War: Arras and Messines 1917* (Stroud: Sutton, 1998), pp. 33-38.
158 See Appendix VIII.
159 TNA: WO/95/2370: 'Instructions No. 11', 30 November 1917, 32nd Division War Diary.

informed Brigadier-General A.C. Girdwood (GOC 96 Brigade)[160] that his command – less two battalions and 96th MG Company attached to 97 Brigade – would be in divisional reserve. The remaining two battalions (2nd Royal Inniskilling Fusiliers and 16th Lancashire Fusiliers) were to remain in readiness for a move forward from Canal Bank and Irish Farm "at maximum notice of 2 hours from Zero onwards."[161]

Organisation for the evacuation of casualties was to be divided into two sectors: Wounded on the right front would be carried along the mule track by RAP stretcher-bearers at Mosselmarkt through relay posts at Meetcheele and Waterloo; wounded on the left front were to be carried – via duckboard and connecting timber track – from the RAP near Wallemolen through relay posts at Kronprinz Farm, Lump House and Kansas. The interim destination to parties traversing both routes was the ADS at Somme Redoubt. These paths, treacherous enough in the daytime, would be carefully flagged and night-lights placed "close to them to direct stretcher-bearers and walking wounded cases to the Advanced Dressing Station." All stretcher cases would, following treatment, be transported by ambulance car and Red Cross lorry westward along road section Gravenstafel – Wieltje, to the entraining point at Bridge House. Casualties, following transfer to light railway cars, would then be transported as far as the II Corps Main Dressing Station just north of Ypres. The DDMS II Corps was also to make arrangements for trains to be in place at Somme Redoubt at Zero + 2 and Zero + 3 hours. "Subsequent trains could be called up as required from the control point at BRIDGE HOUSE in 1½ hours."[162]

The CO 92nd Field Ambulance would be responsible for evacuation of casualties from RAPs to ADS. Stretcher-bearers from divisional field ambulances were to be placed at his disposal. "It was known the carrying of the wounded would be very arduous and arrangements were made with [the] General Staff, whereby 2 officers and 100 O.R. of infantry battalions of 14th Brigade could be called upon to act as stretcher-bearers after the R.A.M.C. bearers were too fatigued to carry on."[163]

Sir Henry Rawlinson expressed satisfaction with the pre-assault plans and preparations by both divisions:

> I went into details of their attack with the 32 and 8 and I was well satisfied with their preparations – Heneker's arrangements and plans were particularly good … Shute has an excellent model of the Passchendaele Ridge which he is going

---

160 A/Brigadier-General Austen Claude Girdwood DSO. Commissioned Northumberland Fusiliers 1896; Sudan 1898; Captain 1900; South Africa 1899-1902; Staff College; Mohmand Expedition 1908; Major 1915; DAAG 1916-17; A/Lieutenant-Colonel and CO 11th Border Regiment 1916-17; GOC 96 Brigade August 1917.
161 See Appendix VIII.
162 TNA: WO/95/2370: After-action report, 'Appendix 'G', Report on the Medical Arrangements During the Recent Operations: Night 1/2nd December 1917', 15 December 1917, 32nd Division War Diary.
163 Ibid.

to lecture his men on so that each and all may know exactly what is required of them – both divisions have been very thorough in the details of their barrages.[164]

Maintenance and prolongation of roads and tracks remained problematic. On 28 November Rawlinson wrote: "We are suffering much from the difficulty in communication from the frontline – the condition of Passchendaele is terrible with dead all over the place and no chance of burying them so long as the shelling continues."[165] Indeed, it is remarkable, given the dreadful conditions and almost impossible task of subduing active German battery concentrations ringing the salient that necessary preparation for, and consequent execution of any sort of coherent attack occurred during this time. This had much to do with the organisational and logistical aspects, as comparison of 8th Division and 32nd Division orders and instructions readily demonstrate, of *S.S. 135* and the formulaic operational approach adopted by Second Army as standard operating procedure after 20 September. Adequate advance dumps of rations, water, ammunition and HE stores were in place by late November. Overland communications infrastructures were maintained and extended.[166] Lieutenant-Colonel G.C. Pollard (CRE 32nd Division) outlined what had been accomplished in a report dated 6 December:

> On taking over from 1st Division work was pushed on with duckboard tracks toward the frontline. The following tracks were in existence: MOUSETRAP TRACK up to V.28.d.2.5 (vicinity of Source Farm), No. 6 TRACK up to D.3.d.9.9 (vicinity of Kronprinz Farm). It was decided to make a third track from WINNIPEG or its vicinity to KRONPRINZ [FARM] where it carried on along what had been No. 6 TRACK to direct through PETER PAN and on to VIRILE FARM, thus giving 3 distinct tracks to the frontline exclusive of the BELLEVUE ROAD. C.E., II Corps agreed to deliver 1,200 duckboards daily and this was found to be as much as could be carried up. The length of the track laid was decided by the strength of the carrying party. Dumps were a long way back and not more than one journey could be done at night. MOUSETRAP TRACK was got through to the frontline by 28/11/17. No. 6 Track through VIRILE FARM by 1/12/17. Cross tracks were also put in. The centre track (KRONPRINZ TRACK) was got to VAPOUR FARM by 1/12/17. Progress

164 CAC: RWLN 1/9: Rawlinson Diary, 27 November 1917.
165 Ibid. 28 November 1917.
166 '[I]n November 1917, the state of mapping of the British area in the Ypres Salient was so poor that the [4th Field Service] Company [FSC] had to obtain information about the roads constructed for and during the Flanders offensive of June to November by referring to captured German maps. The information had simply not been recorded by 2nd or 5th FSC [attached to Second and Fifth armies respectively] during the operations.' See Peter Chasseaud, *Artillery's Astrologers: A History of British Survey and Mapping on the Western Front 1914-1918* (Lewes: Map Books, 1999), p. 379.

was slow on this track as it was badly shelled and the ground was boggy in places. The new track from WINNIPEG to KRONPRINZ [FARM] was pushed through by 29/11/17, as much as 1,500 yards being laid in one night. Great credit is due to Major Waters of the 218th Field Coy. RE for his energy and determination in pressing on the work.[167]

The lengthening of vital duckboard tracks across impassable mud from Canal Bank to the forward area was duly noted by the often querulous Major-General Shute: "This extension reflects great credit on the R.E."[168] All such efforts were a triumph over extreme adversity.

2.4 Upset: Loss of Teall Cottage

Local German commanders, worried by three successful British efforts to reduce the depth of their established *Vorfeldzone,* planned a local operation to reclaim the strip of lost territory opposite 8th and 32nd divisions. Corporal George Ashurst (16th LF) first observed signs of enemy activity opposite his outpost on the left of 96 Brigade's two-battalion front during the moonlit night of 29/30 November: "The night was not too dark and I drew my officer's attention to moving figures just discernible on the ridge in front of us. Fritz seemed to be getting relieved or he was preparing for an attack. Thinking it was the latter, I fired at the figures. Others in the trench joined me and our officer ordered every man to stand to. However, no attack came…"[169]

30 November dawned misty with a drizzling rain.[170] Having been alerted for morning "Stand-to", men of 2nd Royal Inniskilling Fusiliers, holding the right sector of 96 Brigade's front, gazed across no man's land from a line that "consisted of small portions of trenches" extending from the vicinity of Vocation Farm to Teall Cottage. Each company ('A', 'B', 'C', 'D' from right to left) was responsible for 250 yards of front; touch being maintained with 2nd Devonshire (23 Brigade) on the right and

---

167 See TNA: WO/95/2370: After-action report, 'Part II, Plan of Operations, Section 1, General' 11 December 1917, and 'Appendix 'F', Report on RE Work during Operations by 32nd Division on 2/12/17', 6 December 1917, 32nd Division War Diary. Nine field companies (206th, 218th, 219th) of 32nd Division, 1 (23rd) of 1st Division, 3 (247th, 248th, 249th) of 63rd RND and 2 (446th and 447th) of 50th Division were employed to carry out road, track and tramway work. Two pioneer battalions (1/5th Welsh of 1st Division and 14th Worcestershire of 63rd RND) and 1 infantry battalion (Howe) of 63rd RND provided additional labour.
168 Ibid: After-action report, 'Part II, Plan of Operations, Section 1, General', 11 December 1917, and 'Map Showing Tracks Scale 1:20,000 32G/MAPS/46.M', 32nd Division War Diary.
169 George Ashurst, *My Bit: A Lancashire Fusilier at War 1914-18* (Ramsbury: Crowood Press, 1987), p. 128.
170 LHCMA: Second Army War Diary, 30 November 1917, Montgomery-Massingberd Papers, File 7/15, King's College, London.

164   A Moonlight Massacre

16th LF on the left respectively. Teall Cottage, in British hands since the night of 21/22 November, was occupied as an advanced post by a garrison of fourteen men.[171]

It was close to 6:00 a.m. when German howitzers and field guns commenced an intense barrage on the fronts of 8th and 32nd divisions.[172] The bombardment, lasting approximately thirty minutes, lifted beyond the forward British positions at 6:30 a.m. It was at approximately the same time that 2nd Devonshire's sentries observed an estmated 350 German infantry[173] press forward from Venison Trench and Northern Redoubt with great determination. Fifteen hostile aircraft, cooperating at low altitudes, machine-gunned outposts and tossed signal lights, the observers spotted shouting through megaphones to the infantry below. Small arms fire, supported by a timely SOS barrage, inflicted heavy losses, forcing the attackers to turn back or take refuge in nearby shell craters from which grenades were ineffectively tossed. Cut off and isolated, the majority of these survivors were mercilessly shot down in ones and twos whilst attempting to withdraw. Subsequent efforts to retrieve the wounded during the late morning were dispersed by rifle fire.[174]

On the left, the 2nd Royal Inniskilling Fusiliers sought cover under the same bombardment experienced by the neighbouring 2nd Devonshire. Parties of German infantry, previously massed behind Hill 52, were observed approaching their positions at 7:15 a.m. Scattered by the requested SOS barrage, the attackers pressed on through a deluge of shells only to be beaten off by rifle and Lewis Gun fire. Survivors went to ground in numerous surrounding shell holes before attempting to retire after nightfall.[175] Onset of darkness allowed time to take stock in the aftermath of the German assault. Twenty-one-year-old Captain Cecil Cundall MC (CO 'A' Company, 2nd Royal Inniskilling Fusiliers) visited his dispersed company line after nightfall.[176] Leaving cover to approach the advanced post at Teall Cottage, a full moon illuminated the distinctive shape of Cundall's Brodie steel helmet as he neared the squat

171 TNA: WO/95/2397: 2nd Royal Inniskilling Fusiliers War Diary.
172 On the right, 33rd Division experienced a heavy barrage 'along the Passchendaele Ridge, down the Ravebeek and on the tracks, smashing 'H' track up badly in some places.' Reports were also received that the Germans had left their trenches on the Keiberg Spur opposite the neighbouring II ANZAC Corps. See TNA: WO/95/2406: 33rd Division War Diary.
173 Comprised of elements from *I Battalion, RIR237 (199th Division)*. See TNA: WO/157/288: 'Annexe [sic] to II Corps Summary No. 30, Examination of Prisoner of I Battalion 237 R.I.R. (199 Div.) Captured at Teall Cottages About 5 p.m. 30/11/17, II Corps Summary of Information Received up to 9 p.m. on 1st December 1917', II Corps Intelligence File, WO/95/2370: 32nd Division War Diary and WO/95/2396: 96th Brigade War Diary.
174 TNA: WO/95/821: '8th Division No. G. .97/53. 23rd Infantry Brigade No. G. 33/49', 1 December 1917, TNA: WO/95/821: VIII Corps War Diary and Atkinson, *The Devonshire Regiment 1914-1918*, p. 319.
175 TNA: WO/95/2396: 96 Brigade War Diary and WO/95/2397: 2nd Royal Inniskilling Fusilier War Diary.
176 Captain Cecil Cundall (b.1896). Educated Dover College; enlisted 10th Royal Fusiliers 1914; commissioned Royal Inniskilling Fusiliers1915; MC *London Gazette* January 1917.

concrete structure; a sudden verbal challenge – "*Wer Da?*" – followed by a machine-gun fusillade at very short range, cut down the approaching company commander. This tragedy alerted the British to the fact that the 14 men occupying Teall Cottage had been surrounded and overpowered sometime during the morning attack. Unavoidable isolation of this post from the main line by day prevented the discovery of its loss until the unfortunate Cundall's fatal encounter the following night.[177] Acting Lieutenant-Colonel A.J. Scully MC (CO 16th NF)[178] recalled the immediate action taken to rectify the situation:

> The 16th Bn. North'd Fusiliers relieved the R. Innis. Fus. on the night of 30th/1st. On reaching Bn. Hd. Qrs. MEETCHEELE the OC 2nd R. Innis. Fus. reported to me that TEALL COTT. which had been occupied by them the previous night [,] had been retaken by the enemy. This was discovered when the right company commander was making his evening rounds. After completing the relief my right post was about 70 yards SW of TEALL COTT. On learning the situation I proceeded to my right company and ordered the company commander to attack and retake TEALL COTT.

The ad hoc counter-attack, supported by the Inniskillings, opened at 3:00 a.m. on 1 December:

> When this platoon had advanced a few yards a machine-gun opened fire on them from the left flank (probably N. of [HILL] 52). Fire was also opened from TEALL COTT. About 9 of the attacking platoon were hit and the officer in charge decided that TEALL COTT. was too strongly held to take with his force … As soon as I [Scully] received this report from my right company [,] I reported to Brigade Headquarters that my line was just S. of TEALL COTT. to about 50 yards N. of VENTURE FARM thence NW to VOCATION FARM thence to VIRILE FARM.[179]

---

177 Cundall has no known grave and is commemorated on the Tyne Cot Memorial to the Missing. The regimental history incorrectly states he was killed in an 'attempt to recapture the position [Teall Cottage] at nightfall.' See Frank Fox, *The Royal Inniskilling Fusiliers in the World War: A record of war service as seen by the Royal Inniskilling Regiment of Fusiliers, thirteen battalions which served* (London: Constable, 1928), p. 106.
178 A/Lieutenant-Colonel Arthur John Scully (1888-1937). Commissioned Manchester Regiment 1908; Lieutenant 1910; Captain and MC 1915, CO 16th NF March 1917.
179 Fox, *The Royal Inniskilling Fusiliers in the World War*, p. 106, TNA: WO/95/2397: 2nd Royal Inniskilling Fusilier War Diary, IWM 4732: '32nd Div. No.G.S.1499/3/33', 4 December 1917, Brigadier-General T.S. Lambert Papers (Box 80/10/2) and Capt. C.H. Cooke, *Historical Records of the 16th (Service) Battalion Northumberland Fusiliers* (Newcastle-upon-Tyne, Council of the Newcastle and Gateshead Incorporated Chamber of Commerce, 1923), p. 88. Inniskilling casualties during the period 27-30 November were recorded as follows: Officers: 1 killed, 2 wounded; ORs: 17 killed, 72 wounded, 29 missing.

16th NF's diarist wrote of the failed effort:

> Battalion on right of divisional sector holding line from south of Teall Cottage through Vocation and Virile Farms. During the early morning of the 1st Dec., [2nd Lieutenant] C.S. Sutherland and one platoon of 'A' Coy. attempted to capture Teall Cot. but were met by heavy MG fire and could not advance. Casualties: 2nd Lieutenant Sutherland [wounded] and 8 OR.[180]

The night attack was scheduled to start in 24 hours, but no further moves were made to reclaim the lost pillbox. Secured without opposition by a 1st Worcester (24 Brigade) patrol before daybreak on 21 November, Teall Cottage had been the responsibility of 32nd Division since the scheduled boundary adjustment with 8th Division on the night of 24/25 November. Belated discovery of its loss delayed further local counter-attacks.[181] *Fourth Army's* midday situation report for 1 December observed: "An operation was carried out yesterday in the *Vorfeldzone* on either side of the Westroosebeke – Passchendaele Road ... and improved the situation."[182] Unaware of the disquieting tactical implications, Second Army intelligence confidently noted the "easy repulse with no gains" of the German attacks, while the II Corps' intelligence summary for 1 December remarked:

> At 6:00 a.m. this morning [30 November] the enemy massed for attack behind the high ground at V.30.a and at the same time opened a heavy barrage in front of and immediately behind our frontline. Our artillery barrage prevented the attack from developing in force and only straggling parties advanced. They were easily driven off and several of the enemy were seen to be hit.[183]

---

180 TNA: WO/95/2398: 16th NF War Diary.
181 See TNA: WO/95/1677: 8th Division War Diary, WO/95/1718: 24 Brigade War Diary, WO/157/120-121: Disposition maps in 'Second Army Intelligence Summaries', 11 November to 5 December 1917, Second Army Intelligence File and Captain H. FitzM. Stacke MC, *The Worcestershire Regiment in the Great War Vol. 1* (Kidderminster: G.T. Cheshire & Sons, 1928), p. 300.
182 KA HKR 71, 'Lagge am 1.12. 1917 mittags'.
183 TNA: WO/157/289: II Corps Intelligence Summary, 1 December 1917, II Corps Intelligence File. This belated attempt to regain portions of the *Vorfeldzone* (secured by 8th Division on the nights of 18/19, 20/21 and 24/25 November) is indicative of the local German commander's elastic response – as opposed to adhering to any rigid tactical doctrine – to prevailing battlefield situations and conditions. This flexible approach, retained throughout 1914-18 as part of the Imperial German Army's pre-war cultural ethos, ignored, in this particular circumstance, doctrinal expectations that the *Vorfeldzone* would be regained quickly: 'The Outpost Zone – In a large attack a deep advanced zone prevents the enemy from destroying, with his artillery fire, great numbers of our garrisons and thereby penetrating our front. In local attacks, however, the troops must not withdraw from it without serious fighting. *If momentarily abandoned it will be retaken immediately*' (My emphasis). See Foley introduction in Wynne, *If Germany Attacks*, p.

The war diaries of VIII Corps, II Corps, 8th Division and 32nd Division also failed to register the loss of Teall Cottage, whilst 96 Brigade's diarist laconically observed: "It is surmised that during barrage in the morning enemy must have taken the post unnoticed." Subsequent events would soon demonstrate that the capture of this seemingly insignificant concrete pillbox had placed its hostile garrison (estimated at thirty men with one machine-gun) in a convenient position – 32nd Division side of the boundary with 8th Division – to disrupt at the very outset, the imminent night attack.[184]

2.5 Final Hours

Pre-arranged brigade reliefs commenced after dark on 30 November. On the right, two companies each from the 2nd Royal Berkshire Regiment and 1st RIR (25 Brigade) took over a frontline extending west of Exert Farm to Teall Cottage exclusive from 23 Brigade.[185] On the left, 16th NF and 15th LF (attached to 97 Brigade) relieved 2nd Royal Inniskilling Fusiliers and 16th LF (96 Brigade) from opposite Teall Cottage to Tournant Farm. Forward movements by 16th HLI and 11th Border Regiment to 97 Brigade support and reserve positions at Bellevue and Wurst Farm occurred simultaneously.[186]

1 December dawned with low clouds and thick mist; visibility remained very poor. The meteorological station at Vlamertinghe recorded temperature values of a 47° high during the day and 37° low after dark. Sunset was at 3:47 p.m.; moonrise at 6:21 p.m.[187] Rawlinson continued to express reserved optimism about the impending operation regardless of intelligence that the enemy was alert and expectant:

> The weather is better and I have great hopes that we shall do the trick at Passchendaele all right but the Bosch is expecting us. I visited the 32 & 8

---

xxvi and Historical Sub-section, General Staff, A.E.F., *A Survey of German Tactics 1918* (Washington DC: War Department, December 1918), p.33.
184 See TNA: WO/157/120: 'Second Army Intelligence Summary', 30 November 1917, Second Army Intelligence File, WO/157/288: 'II Corps Summary of Information', 1 December 1917, II Corps Intelligence File, WO/95/643: II Corps War Diary, WO/95/821: VIII Corps War Diary, WO/95/1677: 8th Division War Diary, WO/95/2370: 32nd Division War Diary, WO/95/2396: 96 Brigade War Diary and IWM 4732: '32nd Div. No.G.S.1499/3/33' (CO 16th NF after-action report), 5 December 1917, Brigadier-General T.S. Lambert Papers (Box 80/10/2).
185 TNA: WO/95/2370: 'Narrative of Operations Carried Out by 8th Division on 1st /2nd December 1917', 8th Division War Diary.
186 TNA: WO/95/2370: 32nd Division War Diary.
187 LHCMA: Second Army War Diary, Montgomery-Massingberd Papers, File 7/16, King's College, London, TNA: WO/95/15: 'Temperature Values during December 1917: Degrees Fahrenheit', GHQ War Diary and WO/157/288: 'Calendar for December 1917: Times Calculated for Second Army Front and Greenwich Mean Time', II Corps Intelligence File.

168 A Moonlight Massacre

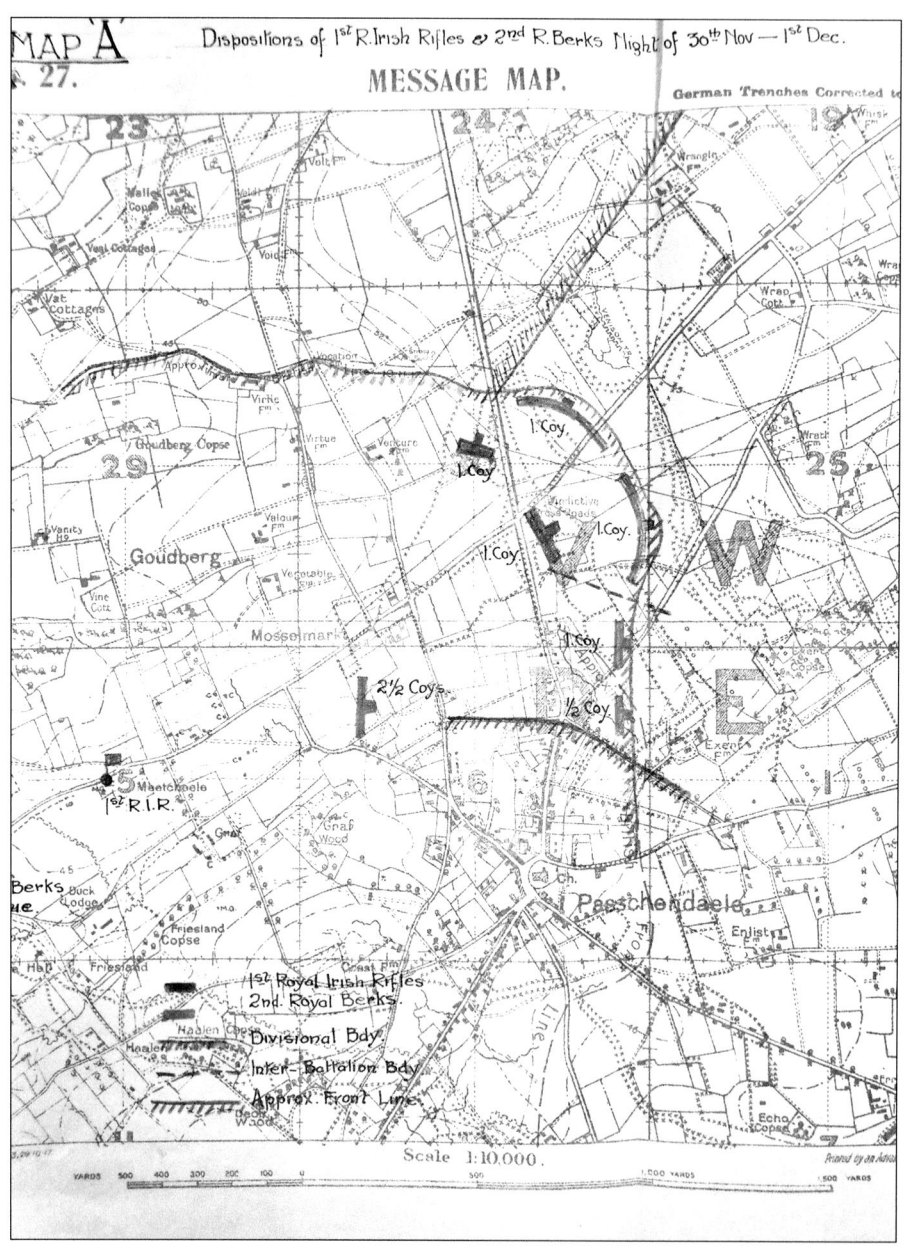

Dispositions of 1st RIR and 2nd Royal Berkshire on the night of 30 November/
1 December 1917. (TNA: WO/95/1677: 8th Division War Diary)

divisions this PM and was well satisfied with their arrangements – They are two very good divisions and will [,] I am sure [,] do all that is possible.[188]

Pre-battle preparations (priming Mills bombs, inspection of rifles, gas masks, Lewis guns, field dressings, iron rations, identity discs, etc.) by assault battalions of 25 and 97 brigades were carried out in dank dugout complexes, dismal hutted camps and shattered farms west of Passchendaele Ridge. Coffin's brigade, having previously (27 November) issued a final itemized list of issue equipment and ammunition, made certain that every combat necessity was provided for:

1. 1st and 2nd Line (a) <u>Riflemen</u>: Rifle and bayonet, 170 rounds of SAA, 1 shovel, valise, iron rations, rations for day of attack, water bottle full, 2 sandbags, 2 ground flares, Small Box respirator, leather jerkin, groundsheet, 1 Watson Fan per section.
   (b) <u>Bombers</u>: As for (a) except – 120 SAA only, 5 Mills grenades.
   (c) <u>Rifle Bombers</u>: As for (a) except – 50 rounds of SAA only, 8 rifle grenades, 16 cartridges for same.
   (d) <u>Lewis Gunners</u>: As for (a) except – Nos. 1 & 2 carry no rifle or bayonet, 50 rounds of SAA only, 20 drums SAA per gun, only two shovels per gun.
2. 3rd Wave: As for 1 except the following will be carried in addition: <u>Riflemen</u>: 100 rounds of SAA (i.e. 270 in all).
   <u>Bombers</u>: 2 men 16 L[ewis] G[un] drums, remainder 100 rounds of SAA (i.e. 270 in all).
   <u>Rifle Grenadiers</u>: 100 rounds of SAA (i.e. 270 in all).
   <u>Lewis Gunners</u>: 10 extra drums (i.e. 30 in all) SAA per gun.
   3.10 SOS grenades per company, divided between Company HQ, Platoon Commanders and Sergeants. 1 Box 'Very' Lights divided between companies.[189]

The long arduous journey to jumping-off positions was scheduled to begin after dark, time being allotted for battalions to arrive at destinations prior to zero hour at 1:55 a.m. on 2 December.

Aspinall submitted the weekly operations report on activity in VIII Corps' sector during 24–30 November to Second Army HQ on 1 December: "During the week harassing fire has been carried out on enemy's trenches and several concentration shoots on suspected areas." Ammunition dumps in the German rear were observed to be "blown up, and from prisoners statements, our artillery appears to have been successful." Enemy batteries were noted to be "extremely active" on Passchendaele Ridge, special attention being paid to Seine and Levi cottages. Hostile artillery

---

188 CAC: RWLN 1/9: Rawlinson Diary, 1 December 1917.
189 See TNA: WO/95/1727: '25th Infantry Brigade Instructions No. 3', 27 November 1917, 25 Brigade War Diary.

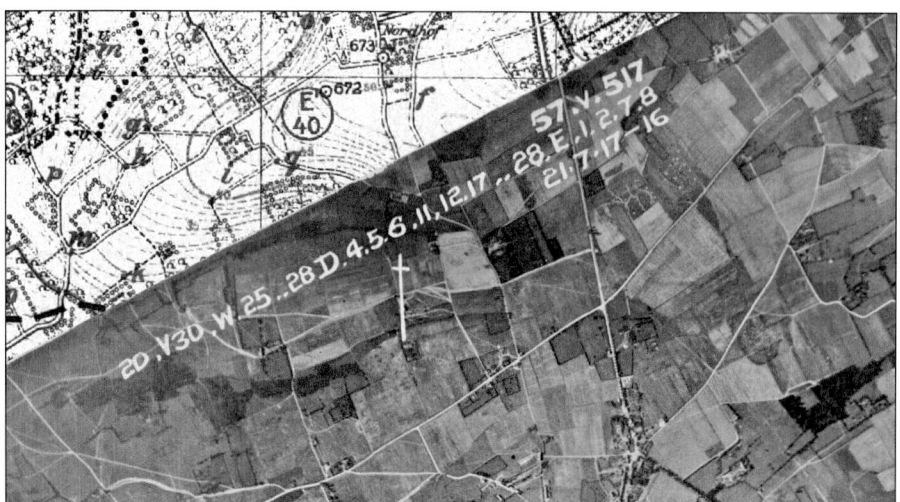

Passchendaele to Vat Cottages Ridge: British aerial photograph/German map overlay. (Memorial Museum Passchendaele 1917)

shoots of "short duration" were also directed on new 18-pounder battery positions near Abraham Heights. Enemy infantry, "though quiet, have shewn themselves to be alert and awaiting any signs of a renewal of the attack by our troops." 8th Division's steady success in narrowing the distance to Venison Trench and adjacent redoubts was also noted: "No minor operations have been undertaken, but the line of posts has been gradually pushed forward until the forward posts are now in close proximity to the enemy's main position, thus denying him the use of the defended zone in front of his main defences." German machine-guns, however, had been active by night throughout the previous week, "but have fired very little during the day." Active patrolling was nonetheless continued after dark; no enemy patrols were encountered.[190]

Heneker, suffering from a severe bout of lumbago and still harbouring extreme reservations about the impending "beastly operation", wrote tersely of "last preparations" in his diary. One detects a certain amount of fatigue, irritability and semi-fatalism in his correspondence prior to the attack; 1917 had been an arduous campaign year for the GOC 8th Division. Recurrent lumbago complaints, coupled with discomfort from a thigh wound sustained in December 1915, no doubt contributed to the pessimistic outlook.[191]

---

190 BL: 48359: 'VIII Corps, G. 2283, Weekly Report on Operations for week ending 6-0 p.m., Friday 30th Nov., 1917', 1 December 1917, VIII Corps Official War Diary with Appendices and Addenda, Hunter-Weston Papers, Vol. V.
191 TNA: WO/95/1677: 8th Division War Diary and IWM: 66/541/1: Heneker Diary, 1 December 1917.

II Corps' weekly operation report outlined a general policy of pre-attack preparations and activity. Patrols had been "very active throughout the week, with the idea of denying the superiority of no man's land to the enemy, and also to find out the nature of the ground over which we are to fight." Several machine-gun positions were also identified. British machine-guns carried out harassing fire each night. This took the form of "concentrated shoots on communications and occupied posts." British gunners concentrated "twice daily on enemy occupied areas and used tracks." Counter-preparation took place "at dawn for the first three days of period under review", after which concentrated bursts of fire were "directed on selected places in addition to harassing fire by day and night on enemy's approaches, roads, tracks, and centres of activity." Enemy activity varied in intensity, hostile patrols appearing to have diminished, whilst hostile artillery fire was "normal except that his [German] shelling of duckboard tracks and of the GRAVENSTAFEL – MEETCHEELE road has become intense." There were, however, few signs of a decrease in shellfire: "The WESTROOSEBEKE group has been most active. Little fire has been reported from HOUTHOULST [sic], but shelling from POLDERS WOOD and SHAW WOOD has been reported almost daily. Considerable decrease in gas shelling is noticeable, but there has been no active gas bombardment, merely gas shelling over wide areas."[192] "Very little activity" by German machine-guns was also noted: "On a few occasions our roads and tracks received attention, but generally speaking, the enemy appears to have confined himself to direct fire which has consisted of occasional sweeping of no man's land." Prompt fire was directed on probing British patrols, "but these bursts have been short."[193]

192   TNA: WO/95/643: 'II Corps No. 227 G., II Corps Summary of Operations for Week-ending 30. 11. 17', II Corps War Diary and IWM 4723: 'HARASSING FIRE MAP (To Accompany II Corps Artillery Instructions No. 10)', Brigadier-General T.S. Lambert Papers (Box 80/10/2). *Fourth Army's* weekly summary for 29 November – 5 December recorded 338 – out of total of 702 for the entire army front – hostile batteries identified by *Gruppes Staden* and *Ypern*: '[E]nemy artillery activity on both groups was, in general, of the same strength as the previous week and was particularly lively during the first half of the week. Frequent and strong destructive fire was experienced within the infantry zone along with numerous fierce, at times intense, bombardments. Sections of our positions, especially those of *38 I.D.* and *12. R.D.*, repeatedly came under strong and frequent destructive fire directed by aircraft. *Gruppe Ypern* notably experienced a large number of planned shoots on battle headquarters, some of which were destroyed …' See KA HKR 145: 'AOK 4 I/a MSO, AHQ 6.12.17, Fiendliche Artillerietätigkeit, Wochenzusammenstellung, Vom 29.11 bis 5.12.17', pp. 3-4.
193   TNA: WO/95/643: 'II Corps No. 227 G., II Corps Summary of Operations for Week-ending 30. 11. 17'.
  32nd Division casualties for the period covered by this report: Officers – 3 killed, 15 wounded; ORs – 97 killed, 337 wounded, 108 missing, 35th Division: Officers – 3 killed, 8 wounded; ORs – 18 killed, 116 wounded, 63rd Division: 4 ORs wounded, Corps Troops: Officers – 6 wounded; ORs – 17 killed, 66 wounded, 1 missing.

Enemy shellfire remained normal on 32nd Division's front during the remainder of the 1st. The divisional artillery responded with the usual concentration and harassing barrages on trenches, pillboxes, dugouts and tracks to the frontline. The following moves were to be carried out after dark "in accordance with table" attached to 32nd Division O.O. 139:

1. HQ 97 Infantry Brigade to move from Canal Bank to Kronprinz Farm.
2. All four battalions of 97 Infantry Brigade into the frontline.
3. HQ 14 Infantry Brigade from Canal Bank to Kansas relieving HQ 96 Infantry Brigade, with 16th Northumberland Fusiliers and 15th Lancashire Fusiliers assembled in accordance with 32nd Division Instructions No. 9, with 5 battalions in line.[194]

Dusk and the march forward to assembly tapes along allocated roads and slimy duckboard tracks were fast approaching. Time remained to consume one more hot meal and conduct final administrative and equipment checks. Battalion commanders discussed a myriad of last-minute details with HQ staff subordinates, whilst company and platoon officers, dressed like ORs with unobtrusive pips on shoulder straps and carrying service rifles, performed inspection parades of equipment-laden men; two heavy rain showers, occurring at 5:00 and 9:45 p.m. respectively, made the ground "greasy and difficult."[195] Previous tours of the horrific salient, serious reservations about the attack plan and consequent semi-fatalism left their mark, so a certain amount of pessimism appears to have prevailed at brigade and battalion level. The strain "beyond endurance" experienced by Lieutenant-Colonel Hanbury-Sparrow during his first tour of the area was compounded by the travails to come: "Your battalion … was under orders to do a local attack next time it was in; and the Germans were now said to be putting down barrages of 8-inch howitzers. It was all together too much to expect men to face, and be as good as before. They couldn't be. It was beyond flesh and blood." Gassed and near collapse, the veteran CO 2nd Royal Berkshire was finished: "As a result I was rather bad. Passchendaele broke me."[196] Major L. Heathcoat-Amory (Staff Captain 32nd Division Artillery) expressed serious doubts about the perceived operational necessity in a diary entry for 22 November: "Rode to Pop[eringhe] with General [Tyler] to a divisional conference. General Shute explained what we were going to take, and how. I wonder whether 500 yards of mud are worth all these lives and trouble. No one knows how hard we hit the Bosche each time – that's the worst of it. Our ground is always the worst to attack over."[197] As Lieutenant Charles Carrington

194 TNA: WO/95/2370: 32nd Division War Diary.
195 IWM 4723: 'Preliminary Report on Operations December 1st, 2nd and 3rd December', 4 December 1917, Brigadier-General T.S. Lambert Papers (Box 80/10/2).
196 See Nettleton, *The Anger of the Guns*, p. 115 and Hanbury-Sparrow, *The Land-Locked Lake*, pp. 315-17.
197 Scott, Grice-Hutchison, et al., *Artillery & Trench Mortar Memories*, p. 637.

(1/5th Royal Warwickshire Regiment) observed when recounting preparations for Broodseinde in his post-war memoir: "Men going into action support themselves by a sort of enforced hysterical cheerfulness, but no one could be cheerful in the Third Battle of Ypres." The official termination of that dreadful campaign on 20 November was of no consequence to the morale, cheerful or otherwise, of troops primed for another advance along Passchendaele Ridge.[198]

---

198 Charles Edmonds (Pseud.), *A Subaltern's War* (London: Anthony Mott, 1984 reprint of 1929 edition), p. 105. Edmonds/Carrington, while certainly not a member of the 'disenchantment school' of post-war literature, was writing over a decade after the war. Morale in Second Army was still reeling, albeit only temporarily, in the immediate aftermath of the Third Ypres campaign. Similar observations of troop despondency can be found in other inter-war memoirs. Gunner Aubrey Wade recalled a poignant scene during the autumn fighting: 'Reinforcements of the New Army shambled past the guns with dragging steps and the expressions of men who knew they were going to certain death. No words of greeting passed as they slouched along; in sullen silence they filed past one by one to the sacrifice', whilst a former Lieutenant-Colonel, writing to Lloyd George in the 1930s, recollected 'fresh divisions coming up, spick and span, from rest billets, but coming up hopelessly knowing what they had to face (the only time I have ever seen British soldiers anything but cheery and confident)…' See Aubrey Wade, *The War of the Guns* (London: Batsford, 1936), pp. 57-58 and the manifestly polemical David Lloyd George, *War Memoirs Vol. 2* (London: Odhams Press abridged edition, 1937), p. 343.

3

A Moonlight Massacre

Now I went forward for a space, and took heed not to look backwards; but to be strong of heart and spirit; for that which did lie before me had need of all my manhood and courage of soul…[1]

3.1 Assembly

Saturday 1 December 6:21 p.m.: A full moon rose with singular brilliance against an expansive backdrop of a starry winter sky. Scudding clouds, propelled westward by winds of 5 to 10 mph, interspersed the quasi-luminous atmosphere. Occasional flares cast an ephemeral gloss on swollen streams and the roily liquid surface of hundreds of shell holes. Afternoon showers failed to wash away a light coating of snow.[2] Heneker's after-action report noted: "The night was fine and clear and the moon was particularly bright. Individual figures could be distinguished at 100 yards, and bodies of men at 200 yards. The ground had been severely torn up by artillery fire, but was on the whole, unusually dry and the going was good", so earlier anxiety about being "heard squelching through the mud" was abated.[3]

Seven and one half assault companies from three battalions of Coffin's 25 Brigade were detailed to assemble in three waves inside the line of their advanced posts on a frontage of 1,020 yards from opposite Exert Farm to the vicinity of Northern Redoubt. Coffin hoped to reduce recognised dangers by having the attackers form up in rear of advanced positions:

---

1   William Hope Hodgson (1877-1918), *The Night Land*, Chapter VI.
2   TNA: WO/95/15: 'Weather Diary, December 1917', GHQ War Diary.
3   TNA: WO/95/1677: 'Narrative of Operations Carried Out by the 8th Division on 1st/ 2nd December 1917', 13 December 1917, 8th Division War Diary and Beddington, 'My Life', p. 119.

On account of our outpost line being close up to the enemy's advanced posts, and owing to the fact that it was only three days after a full moon and the nights were very light, forming up had to be carried out 200 yards inside our outposts on a line about 350 yards from the enemy's main position on the N[orth] and 250 yards from his main position on the S[outh] … The outpost line which was held by 2½ companies was to be responsible for covering the advance of the attacking troops by rifle and Lewis Gun fire until the attacking troops passed through it. We knew where the enemy's M.G.'s were and directly they opened, 2 Lewis Guns at least were to concentrate on to each M.G. and endeavour to neutralize it.[4]

The right battalion (2nd Royal Berkshire Regiment), tasked with forming a defensive flank in order to protect the "attacking battalions from an attack from a SE direction", would advance with one and one half companies. The "object was a line running from NW to SE, passing one hundred and fifty yards west of Wrath Farm to a point about two hundred yards north of Exert Farm, where it curved back towards the south-west. The left boundary of the battalion's area was directed NE towards Wrath Farm." Assault companies were organised in three waves: half of 'D' Company on the right, 'B' Company on the left, 'C' assigned to form a defensive flank "on the right in the latter part of the advance", while 'A' Company remained in reserve. The remaining half of 'D' was detailed to hold the outpost line.[5] "In the case of 2/Rifle Brigade and 2/Lincoln Regt. on the left and centre respectively, three companies were told off to do the attack while one company was told off to hold the outpost line and so cover forming up." One of 2nd Lincolnshire's three assault companies was assigned to fill an anticipated gap as the inner flanks of the former battalion (advancing due east) and 2nd Rifle Brigade (advancing NE) diverged. 2nd Rifle Brigade's left company was also detailed to "form up behind the left flank" to fill another anticipated gap on the left. The out-going 1st RIR would proceed to Brigade reserve at Meetcheele following relief of its companies in the outpost line. "Guides were provided from the head of the tracks under [25] Brigade arrangements to lead battalions to the right of their forming up tapes." Forming up was to be carried out "on a single tape laid from 150 yards SE of Teal [sic] Cottage" to west of Exert Farm. "This tape was laid on iron pickets each bearing a sign painted white denoting the frontage of various battalions." Direction

4   TNA: WO/95/1677: 'Narrative of Operations Carried Out by the 8th Division on 1st/2nd December 1917', 13 December 1917, 8th Division War Diary. See Neil Grant, *The Lewis Gun* (Oxford: Osprey Publishing, 2014) pp. 48-52 for the tactical employment of Lewis guns against hostile machine-guns.
5   BL: 48359: 'Report of Operations Carried Out by the VIII Army Corps on the Morning of 2nd December 1917, Official War Diaries with Appendices and Addenda, VIII Army Corps, Passchendaele Front, November 1917-April 1918', Vol. V, Hunter-Weston Papers and F. Loraine Petre, *The Royal Berkshire Regiment Vol. 2* (Reading: The Reading Barracks, 1925), p. 96

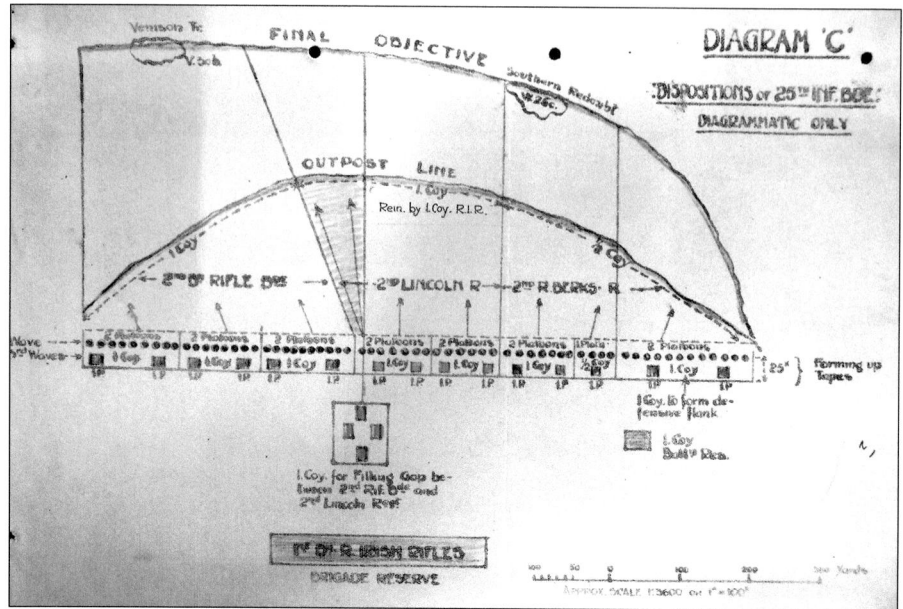

25 Brigade diagram showing company and platoon dispositions and formations.
(TNA: WO/95/1677: 8th Division War Diary)

tapes, "leading from the forming up tape in the direction of the advance [,] had also been laid" to aid assembly.[6]

The 2nd Royal Berkshire Regiment, responsible for the right half of 25 Brigade's line since the night of 30 November/1 December, began to deploy on a frontage of 200 yards as soon as darkness permitted. 'D' Company "took over the frontline on the frontage allotted to the battalion with one platoon of 'C' Company on the right in position as the beginning of the defensive flank, which was to be formed on the right." The remainder of the latter company was withdrawn from the line following relief "pending the time for it to form up on its tape later." 'A' Company, in reserve during the attack, began the march forward from the neighbourhood of Meetcheele just after dusk. "Owing to the extreme darkness" this company became lost and, suffering "numerous casualties" from shellfire whilst traversing the southern extension of No. 5 Track, did not reach its assigned reserve position, where it dug in, until about 9:00 p.m.[7]

---

6   TNA: WO/95/1677: 'Narrative of Operations Carried Out by the 8th Division on 1st/ 2nd December 1917', 13 December 1917, 8th Division War Diary and TNA: WO/95/1727: '25th Brigade No. G.1/1', 21 November 1917, 25 Brigade War Diary. See also WO/95/1677: '8th Division No. G.97/1/1', 18 November 1917 for Heneker's handwritten marginalia diagrams of proposed assembly tape layout.

7   TNA: WO/95/1929: 'Appendix B', 5 December 1917, 2nd Royal Berkshire War Diary.

Duckboard track skirting boggy terrain. (Author)

At 7:15 p.m., 'B' Company (left assault company of 2nd Royal Berkshire) and two platoons of 'D' Company (right assault company) marched from Meetcheele along No. 5 Track South under intermittent shelling. The going was rough and several men were lost:

> B Company [,] which was leading found great difficulty in getting across the gaps in the duckboards caused by shellfire and a great many men got badly stuck in the mud with the result that they and the leading half of D Company were [,] by the time they reached the head of the duckboards [,] in a state of disorganisation. 2nd Lieutenant Giddings (OC B Company) got together 1 platoon and led it forward to the tapes with one of the guides provided by Battalion HQ leaving 2nd Lieutenants Upton and Tremellan to get the remainder out of the mud and into their sections and platoons again. By 9:30 p.m. this re-organisation was complete [,] but 2nd Lieutenant Giddings has not returned. 2nd Lieutenant Rice and Lieutenant Francis (Brigade Intelligence Officer) went forward to look for him.[8]

Twenty-three-year-old acting Lieutenant-Colonel C.R.H. Stirling MC (CO 2nd Royal Berkshire since the broken Hanbury-Sparrow's recent departure)[9] extricated

---

8   Ibid.
9   Captain and A/Lieutenant-Colonel Colin Robert Hoste Stirling. Son of Brigadier-General J.W. Stirling CB CMG (CRA 59th Division 1917-18); commissioned

Private F.J. Wakely. (Memorial Museum Passchendaele 1917)

and took forward the stalled elements of 'B' and 'D' companies, "as the congestion at the head of the track was great, many men of the 2nd Lincolns and 2nd Rifle Brigade having arrived there." The forming up was carried out with "little further trouble", Stirling reporting to Brigade HQ that his battalion was ready to attack at 11:30 p.m.[10]

Hailing from Wimbledon, 21-year-old 38243 Private Frederick John Wakely was a gunner in the "Heavy Branch Machine Gun Corps" or recently designated – by Royal Warrant on 28 July 1917 – "Tank Corps", who somehow ended up in the ranks of 2nd Royal Berkshire. Military authorities, possibly influenced by manpower deficits, deemed "Fred" was required for service in a line infantry battalion. Fate thus necessitated that the experienced young veteran should find himself, in lieu of the noisome,

Cameronians 1913; Lieutenant 1914; Captain 1915; Staff Captain June-September 1916; A/Major September 1916-February 1917 and May-June 1917; A/Lieutenant-Colonel 2nd Cameronians June-July 1917 and 2nd East Lancashire from 17 October. A 'jolly decent chap' according to one 2nd Royal Berkshire subaltern, Stirling was appointed A/GOC 24 Brigade prior to Brigadier-General R. Haig's assumption of command on 21 November. See Loraine Petre, *The Royal Berkshire Regiment Vol. 2*, p. 96 and 2nd Lieutenant C. Morris *op.cit.* in Ian Cull, *The Second Battalion Royal Berkshire Regiment in World War One: The China Dragon's Tale* (Stroud: Tempus, 2005), p. 85.
10 TNA: WO/95/1929: 'Appendix B', 5 December 1917, 2nd Royal Berkshire War Diary.

stifling confines of a Mark IV tank, ensconced in a shell hole ready to advance with his company in the icy pre-dawn hours of 2 December.[11]

Numbed sentries of 'C' and 'D' companies 1st RIR, responsible for the left half of 25 Brigade's line since the night of 30 November/1 December, anticipated their imminent withdrawal to Brigade support whilst scanning a narrow no man's land irradiated by moonlight. German activity, other than the staccato rattle of a machine-gun, sharp report of a rifle or a bursting flare, appeared almost non-existent opposite the advanced line of outposts extending from the vicinity of Teall Cottage to the right boundary of 2nd Royal Berkshire. The relief would commence following the arrival of 2nd Lincolnshire and 2nd Rifle Brigade (centre and left assault battalions of 25 Brigade) the companies of which, burdened with Lewis Guns, hand grenades, ammunition, magnesium flares, picks, shovels, etc., made slow progress along scarcely discernable roads and serpentine duckboard tracks traversing the barren expanse of shell holes and swamp. "The journey, however, was ultimately accomplished and, once they arrived, the troops, assisted by Lieutenant O.S. Francis, M.C., Brigade Intelligence Officer, succeeded in getting into their correct forming-up positions without further difficulty."[12]

2nd Lincolnshire Regiment and 2nd Rifle Brigade commenced their march of approximately 6,500 yards shortly before nightfall. Exiting California Camp near Wieltje at 4:30 p.m., companies of 2nd Lincolnshire proceeded along Track No. 5 and the southern extension. 'C' Company, assigned to relieve 'A' Company 1st RIR in the outpost zone centre, had been dispatched earlier at 3:15 p.m. The march was especially onerous along the southern extension, which was "in a deplorable state":

> The boards [,] which had laid [sic] on trestles high up off the ground, were severely shelled and there were few cases of more than 20 yards in one stretch in good condition. The height of the boards from the ground and the bad state of the ground in the vicinity of the track made it very difficult to regain the track after passing a point where the boards had been blown away.[13]

To "step off the track was to become engulfed in deep clinging mud, and across country the 'going' was impossible." The battalion adjutant subsequently wrote: "The condition of the duckboard track No. 5 South was heartbreaking ... It took an unloaded man over 3 ½ hours to walk from WIELTJE to MOSSELMARKT instead of under 2 hours by road."[14]

---

11 Special thanks to Jan Van der Fraenen (Coordinator Passchendaele Archives Project 2005-07) for providing details about Pte. Wakely's war service.
12 Boraston & Bax, *The Eighth Division*, p. 165.
13 TNA: WO/95/1727: 'Report on Operation', 7 December 1917, 25 Brigade War Diary.
14 Major-General C.R. Simpson, *The History of the Lincolnshire Regiment 1914-1918* (London: Medici Society, 1931), p. 284 and TNA: WO/95/1730: 'Report on Action of Battn from 2:30 p.m. 1.12.17 – M.N. 2/3 .12. 17', 2nd Lincolnshire War Diary.

Lieutenant R.H. Parker.
(Wellington College)

Leading his toiling men forward along the broken and treacherous track was 22-year-old Lieutenant Rupert Hardy Parker, a twice-wounded veteran with over two years' active service experience. Born the only son of "Old Wellingtonian" (1880-84) Charles John Ernest Parker[15] of Beaconfield House, Harrowby, Grantham and his wife Louisa, née Dempsey, in July 1895, he attended his father's prestigious alma mater from 1909-13. An enthusiastic member of the Wellington OTC and crack marksman, Parker competed as a member of the school's representative "VIII" at Bisley. Matriculating at Christ Church College Oxford in August 1914, the nascent undergraduate joined, in lieu of taking up university residency, the 3rd (Reserve) Battalion Lincolnshire Regiment that autumn. Service at the front commenced in February 1915 when the newly-commissioned temporary 2nd Lieutenant was attached to 2nd Lincolnshire Regiment. Injured at Neuve Chapelle and Fromelles in March and May respectively, Parker ended the year in lengthy convalescence brought on by a serious bought of influenza. Having obtained a Regular commission in June 1916, his relatively recent promotion to full lieutenant carried with it the demanding responsibilities of company commander.[16]

---

15   A JP and late captain of the 3rd Lincolnshire Regiment, C.J.E. Parker was the son of Charles John Bullivant Parker JP, a Lieutenant-Colonel of Royal South Lincolnshire Militia and grandson of Lieutenant-Colonel William Parker, High Sheriff of Lincolnshire 1864-65.
16   See TNA: WO/339/24923: Lieutenant Rupert Hardy PARKER. The Lincolnshire Regiment. Special thanks to Ben Lewsley (College Historian) and Jill Shepherd (Archives Librarian) of Wellington College for providing additional details of Parker's brief life.

2nd Rifle Brigade, following departure from a campsite near Capricorn (a section of British frontline prior to 31 July) at 5:00 p.m., marched forward without mishap along the Wieltje – Gravenstafel – Bellevue Road as far as Waterloo Farm, and thence astride the northern extension of No. 5 track to its terminus near Mosselmarkt. 2nd Lincolnshire was not so fortunate, 'C' Company suffering heavy casualties from shellfire at the head of No. 5 Track. Twenty survivors eventually arrived to relieve two left posts and form a strongpoint approximately 150 yards in rear of the outpost line. Lieutenant-Colonel N.M.S. Irwin (CO 2nd Lincolnshire) took immediate steps to ensure his frontline was adequately defended by ordering 'D' Company, 1st RIR to remain in place, its spot in brigade reserve taken over by a company of 2nd West Yorkshire Regiment (23 Brigade).[17]

Forward outposts had already been occupied by what remained of 'C' Company, 2nd Lincolnshire and 'D' Company, 2nd Rifle Brigade, when 25 Brigade guides led the six remaining assault companies forward from the ends of the northern and southern tracks. The Lincolnshire regimental history recalled the exhausting ordeal: "Some idea of the terrible nature of moving up at that period may be gathered from the fact that it took the first ['C'] Company *five hours* to arrive at the head of the duckboard track." Shambling lines of encumbered men were then conducted across an unplanked gulf of approximately 700 yards that separated the two duckboard avenues eastern extremities from the near edges of carefully laid direction tapes. The Lincolnshire's adjutant observed: "For the attack men were not overloaded, although the condition of track No. 5 made the men dead tired before Zero." Direction tapes, connected at right angles every fifty yards with the single tape, were easily navigated to a jumping-off line 480 yards in length. "No difficulty was experienced in getting into position", though it was believed "that individual groups of men were observed by the enemy, their rifle fire being fairly severe, the hostile artillery, however, was unusually quiet."[18]

Close-range sniping was received from an unexpected quarter on the left, as taping-parties of 2nd Rifle Brigade prepared for the arrival of 'A', 'B' and 'C' companies at the designated 340 yard jumping-off line. Teall Cottage, it was almost immediately recognised, was still in enemy hands, 32nd Division having failed to secure the lost strongpoint during the early hours of 1 December.[19] Recaptured by the Germans on

17 TNA: WO/95/1677: 'Narrative of Operations Carried Out by the 8th Division on 1st/2nd December 1917', 13 December 1917, 8th Division War Diary, 'Report on Action of Battn from 2:30 pm. 1-12-17 – M.N. 2/3-12-17', 6 December 1917, WO/95/1730: 2nd Lincolnshire War Diary, Boraston & Bax, *The Eighth Division*, p. 164 and James W. Taylor, *The 1st Royal Irish Rifles in the Great War* (Dublin: Four Courts Press, 2002), p. 119.
18 TNA: WO/95/1677: 'Narrative of Operations Carried Out by the 8th Division on 1st/2nd December 1917', 13 December 1917, 8th Division War Diary and Simpson, *The History of the Lincolnshire Regiment*, p. 284.
19 2nd Lieutenant Alfred Haunsell Burman, 2nd Rifle Brigade, was subsequently awarded the MC for 'conspicuous gallantry and devotion to duty. He led his company up to the frontline under very heavy shellfire, and at once sent out patrols and established posts. It was chiefly to his skill in directing the guides of the incoming unit that the relief was

the morning of 30 November, the alert pillbox garrison still threatened the junction of 8th and 32nd divisions.[20] To add to this misfortune, Lieutenant-Colonel Roger Brand DSO (CO 2nd Rifle Brigade) was "wounded by a rifle bullet while reconnoitering the forming-up line"; Battalion adjutant Lieutenant G.H.G. Anderson MC immediately assumed command.[21] This inopportune incident, in addition to the many other trials and tribulations encountered during the wearisome march to the jumping-off line, did not disrupt 25 Brigade's deployment:

> The 2nd Lincolns Regt., the 2nd Royal Berks and the 2nd Rifle Brigade moved up into position on the tape ready for the attack on the morning of the 2nd December. The enemy was shelling rather heavily when the battalions were marching in [,] so they suffered some casualties. The weather was fine on the whole [,] though there was some occasional showers. Bde Hdqtrs moved up to Bellevue about 7 p.m. Lt. Col. the Hon. R. Brand [,] commanding the 2nd Bn Rifle Brigade [,] was wounded early in the evening. The 1st Royal Irish Rifles came out in to support. The relief was carried out according to Bde. Order No. 257.[22]

Two hundred yards inside the forward line of outposts, massed ranks of assault infantry hunkered down in the cursory shelter of disparate trench sections or shell holes of various shapes and sizes; others less fortunate lay prostrate on the cold earth. Fleeting figures of officers and NCOs were visible treading between companies, platoons and sections in the moonlight. The approach of zero hour was anticipated with customary apprehension compounded by fear that "Fritz" could not have missed their presence at the jumping-off tape.

Twenty-one-year-old Lieutenant John Nettleton (IO 2nd Rifle Brigade) had been detailed, as per 8th Division Instructions No. 2, to act as liaison officer with the neighbouring (2nd KOYLI) battalion of 97th Brigade for the attack's duration.[23] The boyish veteran – he volunteered for active service in 1914 – recalled a flawed attack scheme in a vitriolic post-war indictment:

---

carried out with very few casualties.' See *Supplement to the London Gazette*, 5 July 1918, p. 7899.
20 TNA: WO/95/1731: 'Report of the part played by the 2nd Battalion the Rifle Brigade in the recent operations at Passchendaele', 6 December 1917, 2nd Rifle Brigade War Diary and W.W. Seymour, *The History of the Rifle Brigade in the War of 1914-1918 Vol. 2* (London: Rifle Brigade Club, 1936), p. 165.
21 TNA: WO/95/1677: 'Narrative of Operations Carried Out by the 8th Division on 1st/2nd December 1917', 13 December 1917, 8th Division War Diary and Boraston & Bax, *The Eighth Division*, p. 165.
22 TNA: WO/95/1727: 25 Brigade War Diary.
23 See Chapter 2, p. 125.

2nd Lieutenant J. Nettleton. (John Nettleton, *The Anger of the Guns: An Infantry Officer on the Western Front* (London: William Kimber, 1979))

For this show, the staff put their great brains to work and decided on a surprise attack. It was to start at the unusual hour of 1:55 a.m., instead of just before dawn, and the troops were to dash forward and "overrun" the enemy's outposts before he knew what was happening. Then our barrage was to come down at zero plus 8 minutes and pulverize the enemy's main position.

This may have looked all right on paper back at GHQ but in fact was sheer raving lunacy under the existing conditions. To begin with, on the night of 1st/2nd Dec: the moon would be only just past full;[24] there was no cover of any sort, not even a blade of grass, to hide the advance from the enemy; and there was no possibility of rushing forward and "overrunning" anything; it was only with difficulty that one could advance at all at a dead slow stumble.

All these objections were put forward, to my certain knowledge, by battalion commanders to Brigade and by Brigade to Division. And our Divisional Commander is reported to have backed them up to the higher command, saying specifically that "hostile machine-gun fire from prepared positions on a bright moonlight night was more to be feared than any barrage" and making several

---

24 The moon was actually full. See National Schools Observatory, Universe Now: A Month of the Moon, National Grid for Learning. <http://www.schoolsobservatory.org.uk/ngfl.htm>

alternative suggestions. But he was over-ruled and, in the event, everything went exactly as anticipated; as anticipated, that is, by us and not by the staff.

Nettleton observed signs of low morale prior to the attack. He was certain the operation had been compromised:

> Everybody realised that the whole thing was going to be a shambles. That is not a good mood to start any operation. Then, in my opinion, the Boche knew all about it from the start. I feel sure he spotted the RE's laying out jumping-off tapes on the night before the show. Even if I'm wrong about this, he had many other chances to learn about it. There can seldom have been a "surprise" attack of which so much clear notice was given to the enemy.

The newly designated liaison officer's misgivings grew as he trudged, enfiladed by sporadic indirect machine-gun fire, up the corpse- and debris-strewn road from Gravenstafel to Mosselmarkt with 2nd KOYLI.[25]

Five assault battalions, four from Brigadier-General Blacklock's 97 Brigade and one attached from Brigadier-General A.C. Girdwood's 96 Brigade, formed up on a frontage of 1,850 yards below the barely perceptible summit of Hill 52 and the gently rising southern slope of Vat Cottages Ridge. Battalions deployed from right to left as follows: 2nd KOYLI with 3 assault companies and 1 support company; 16th HLI, 11th Border and 17th HLI "on a two company frontage with Nos. 3 and 4 companies in rear of Nos. 1 and 2 companies respectively", and 15th LF (holding the line with 16th NF since the night of 30 November/1 December) with 3 assault companies and 1 support company. 16th NF retired to Brigade reserve in the vicinity of Virile Farm following relief in the right sub-sector.[26]

---

25 Nettleton, *The Anger of the Guns*, p. 115.
26 Available intelligence related what was known about the organisation and state of the scattered enemy defences: "Points of Resistance. (a) General. All farms and buildings may be regarded as strong points. VALUATION HOUSES [north of Volt Farm], the district around them, the region between them and the WESTROOSEBEKE ROAD, also TOMBOLA FARM to CLEAR FARM, WESTWOOD HOUSE, MALLET FARM, VOLT FARM, MALLET COPSE and the houses just east of it (V.23.d.7.5.), VEAL COTTAGES and the 'Pill-boxes' west of it in V.25.c. are all points of resistance. VAT COTTAGES are held by posts at night and possibly by day. VOX FARM is strongly held. Although the main [Passchendaele – Westroosebeke] road in V.24.c. [,] east of the flooded portion (to which it acts as a dam) looks passable, it is probably commanded from many points, such as VALUATION HOUSES and the shell-holes just S.E. of them and from N.E. VOLT FARM probably commands the whole tongue of dry land [Vat Cottages Ridge] running S.W. from it. A new enemy strongpoint has been established on the southern side of the [Passchendaele – Westroosebeke] road in V.30.a.60.60. (East of VOCATION FARM). It is circular and 12 to15 feet across, manned by about 8 men, who appear to have a M.G. The enemy's defences immediately in rear and running from west to east have been worked upon and appear to be held with increased personnel.

Assembled on two or three company frontages forming four successive waves, Blacklock's battalions adopted a standardized small unit formation known as "worm" or "snake" columns to lead off and manoeuvre round the flank and rear of dispersed objectives:

> 1st wave: 3 sections of each of Nos. 1 and 2 platoons in line of sections in snake formation (i.e. not extended).
> 2nd wave: Lewis Gun sections and platoon H.Qrs. of Nos. 1 and 2 platoons in snake formation.
> 3rd wave: No. 3 Platoon in line of sections
> 4th wave: No. 4 Platoon in line of sections[27]

"In 1917 XVIII Corps[28] 'advocated a more elastic infantry formation for the attack' employing platoons 'working in depth rather than battalions stereotyped in waves' so that behind the initial assault wave 'worms' of 'little columns of units in depth' were

> (b) Front Line. The enemy has a line of outposts [*Vorfeldzone*] in shell-holes, running east from V.29.a. (S.W. of VAT COTTAGES) along the dry ground just north of the road [present-day *Goudbergstraat*] in V.29.a & b. towards VOX FARM and from VOX FARM in a S.E. direction in front of HILL 52 (V.30.a.). The line from V.29.b.d.7. to 7.9. (N.W. of VIRILE FARM) is probably held. In addition to farms and Pill-boxes in the forward zone, his main line of resistance [*Hauptwiderstandslinie*] (which is constantly changing) probably runs as follows: From VAT COTTAGES along the road in front of VEAL COTTAGES [;] the dotted trench in V.23.d., V.29.b., to a point just north of VOX FARM. Continuing east from that point as a line of small trenches or linked up shell-holes just north and east of HILL 52 (a prisoner stated that this line beyond HILL 52 is to be held). (c) Supports. The support line is very uncertain, but is thought to run approximately from V.17.b., west of the WESTROOSEBEKE – PASSCHENDAELE ROAD. Supports also line in ruins and pill-boxes just north of the SPRIET ROAD. There is also a line of occupied shell-holes or short trenches running S.E. from V.17.c.0.8. towards MILLET [sic MULLET] FARM.(d) Reserves. Reserves lie about OOSTNIEUWKERKE (W.3.) and can counter-attack within 3 hours or even less." See TNA: WO/95/2370: 'Notes to Accompany Special Intelligence Maps of the Area V.15 to V.30' November 1917, 32nd Division War Diary.

27 TNA: WO/95/2400: '97th Brigade Operation Order 178', 21 November 1917, 97 Brigade War Diary.
28 Lieutenant-General Sir (Frederick) Ivor Maxse (appointed GOC XVIII Corps in January 1917) was well known throughout the BEF as a progressive trainer of troops. His XVIII Corps was part of Fifth Army from the opening of Third Ypres until relieved by II Corps in early November. Historians have noted Maxse's considerable influence on BEF tactical development and training. Some junior contemporaries, however, were not impressed. Guy Chapman recalled a spirited lecture delivered by the GOC XVIII Corps in April 1917: "We stayed there for five days, in which the only diversion was a lecture by the Corps Commander, General Maxse. 'Infantry, gentlemen', he began, 'is a rectangular animal'; and then delighted with his trope, proceeded to draw a parallelogram on the blackboard. I glanced around the room. The rectangular animal sat with sullen face. Dim hopelessness settled on features as the Corps Commander warmed to his theme, a sullen resignation.

ready to 'stalk' the enemy on a narrow front' close to the barrage." Second Army also observed that attack waves employed by the end of Third Ypres "did not 'give sufficient elasticity' to counter the new conditions being experienced and abandoning linear formations advocated that the troops 'should move in small columns in file, the formation which the nature of the ground forces the men to adopt eventually." Common practice during 1917–18 called for two lines of skirmishers to act as an advanced guard for loose groups following in worm formation. "By early 1918 the platoon attacked with either one section thrown out as skirmishers and three sections advancing behind in single file or 'worms' of each section advancing in single file preceded by its two scouts." Coffin's 25 Brigade adapted the former battle formation (platoons of the 1st wave in a four section skirmish wave trailed by two platoons, in 2nd and 3rd waves, of four sections in column) to tackle what was a rudimentary linear defence. Shute and Blacklock chose the latter formation for the 1st and 2nd waves in order to apply the connate tactical flexibility of worm or snake columns advancing across broken ground against the enemy's diffused *die Leer des Gefechtsfeldes* positions. Distances between their attacking waves and companies were set at 20 and 40 yards respectively.[29]

Assembly areas had been "carefully reconnoitered and pegged out by the 97th Infantry Brigade when in the line between November 23rd and 27th." Battalion assembly areas were plotted with wire on the night of 30 November/1 December, and checked by compass bearing during the day. "On Z night [1/2 December] the assembly positions of each platoon were marked out with tapes and the position of its flanks marked with white discs." Luminous notice boards had also been "erected in company assembly areas on which were painted the bearing of the company objective and the distance in yards to it", while "tapes or wire on screw pickets" were placed to distinguish overland routes from duckboard track heads. Strong patrols and Lewis Gun teams entered no man's land, as per 32nd Division Operation Order No. 138, to cover the forming up after nightfall.[30]

'C' and 'D' companies of 16th NF [31] easily repulsed a small German attack with rifle and Lewis Gun fire at 5:15 a.m. on 1 December; a wounded prisoner was brought in after the enemy was driven off. Designated reserve or "Counter-counter-attacking Battalion" following relief by 2nd KOYLI and 16th HLI, its companies assembled on the right flank in the vicinity of Virile Farm, "as all available information indicated

> They felt they had little enough time to live: it was cruel to waste a spring afternoon listening to this high-falutin' chatter." See Chapman, *A Passionate Prodigality*, p. 153.
29 See Robbins, *British Generalship on the Western Front 1914-1918*, p. 101 and TNA: WO/95/1677: 'Map C, Dispositions of 25th Infantry Bde: Diagrammatic Only', 'Narrative of Operations Carried Out by the 8th Division on 1st/2nd December 1917', 13 December 1917, 8th Division War Diary.
30 TNA: WO/95/2370: After-action Report, 'Part II, Plan of Operations, Section 4, Assembly', 11 December 1917, 32nd Division War Diary.
31 The 16th (Service) Battalion NF was formed in Newcastle by the Newcastle and Gateshead Chamber of Commerce in September 1914.

that any serious counter-attack would come from this flank on account of the known dispositions of the enemy's reserves and the supposed impracticability of the ground west of MALLET WOOD." At 9:00 p.m., Battalion HQ shifted from Meetcheele to Virile Farm, whilst parties from 97 Brigade laid forming-up tape along the 1,850 yard front from Teall Cottage to NE of Tournant Farm.[32]

2nd KOYLI, billeted at Irish Farm throughout the 1st, had three hot meals served up during the day and "a final hot meal at 5:45 p.m …" Companies paraded at 6:55 p.m. before trekking 8,000 yards to the taped 400 yard jumping-off line. "Order of march was D, C, A, B companies, and Battalion Headquarters, at platoon intervals of 100 yards." The leading platoon passed the starting point (road junction north of Irish Farm) at 7:10 p.m. "and proceeded to the line via BUFFS ROAD – ROAD junction [NE of Wieltje] C.23.a.5.3 – No. 6 Track and PETER PAN SWITCH to BELLEVUE – MEETCHEELE – MOSSELMARKT – pillboxes at road junction [Gravenstafel Road with present-day *Osselstraat*] V.30.c.45.15 – VENTURE FARM – Assembly Position, a distance of about 8 kilometres altogether."[33] Lieutenant Nettleton recalled a nightmare journey:

> I was detailed as Liaison Officer with 32nd Division on our left, so I went up the metalled [Gravenstafel] road with them. We … had a sticky time and one incident must have given the Boche fair warning of what was happening, even if he hadn't known before. As we came up to the top of the ridge, a man carrying a sandbag full of Verey lights and SOS signals was hit by a machine-gun bullet, which set off the flares he was carrying. He blazed like a torch and though we rolled him in the mud, we couldn't stop the fire-work display, which must have been visible for miles.[34]

The post-war battalion history observed that the "element of surprise was all important for a successful attack. This night was bright with moonlight. The movement of troops before "Zero" hour had been only too easily observed."[35]

In command of 'D' Company was 22-year-old acting Captain Henry Rawson Forde MC, whose notable transformation from unpromising subaltern to decorated war hero no doubt astounded contemporaries. The only son of Henry James Forde Esq., a wealthy Waterford grain merchant, and Annie Catherine, née Rawson, Forde, he was educated (1909-11) at Clifton College where failure to advance beyond "3b", the middle of the lowest form for "Modern" subjects pointed, given the educational

---

32   TNA: WO/95/2370: After-action Report, 'Part II, Plan of Operations, Section 4, Detailed Plan', 11 December 1917, 32nd Division War Diary pp. 7-8, WO/95/2398: 16th NF War Diary and IWM 4732:'32nd Div. No.G.S.1499/3/33', 4 December 1917, Brigadier-General T.S. Lambert Papers (Box 80/10/2).
33   TNA: WO/95/2402: 2nd KOYLI War Diary.
34   Nettleton, *The Anger of the Guns*, p. 116.
35   Bond, *The King's Own Yorkshire Light Infantry in the Great War Vol. 3*, p. 911.

Captain H.R. Forde MC. (Anonymous, *The Roll of Honour of the Empire's Heroes* (London: Queenhithe Publishing Co., 1919))

expectations of the day, to a career with the armed forces.³⁶ Commissioned into the KOYLI following graduation from Sandhurst in January 1915, the still somewhat callow youth was posted to the 3rd (Reserve) Battalion depot at Hull. Immediate superiors appear to have formed a negative opinion of the immature and inexperienced officer during this time, although it was not until early June that he found himself in serious trouble. Observed engaging in public displays of affection with "an undesirable woman" at Hull's popular Tivoli Theatre, Forde was placed under arrest and confined to quarters for "disgraceful conduct" shortly afterwards. It was in a panicked state that the frightened subaltern exited through a window and disappeared later that evening. His whereabouts remained unknown until his father

---

36 One of Forde's Clifton record sheets (part of a series of brief term reports compiled by house/form masters and headmasters) states: '[Q]uite untrained – needs energy; good in House' but, despite further reference to perceived improvement, the most reoccurring word is 'lethargic' accompanied by a final disconcerting observation, 'slowly falling.' Special thanks to Dr C.S. Knighton (Clifton College Archives) for providing details of H.R. Forde's public school experience.

found him serving as a private in an Army Service Corps motor transport unit under an assumed name.[37]

Persuaded to return and take responsibility for his actions, Forde faced court martial or immediate dismissal until a number of well-connected individuals – amongst whom was Unionist leader Sir Edward Carson – intervened on his behalf.[38] Their concerted efforts bore fruit despite the obvious prejudice of the military authorities: "Forde", Major-General J.A. Ferrier (GOC Humber Garrison) disapprovingly observed, "I have not seen – I have no means of judging whether he would prove a gallant officer or not. I gather that he is thoughtless and irresponsible. His CO tells me he considers him careless and unreliable and not up to the standard of other young officers in the regiment. My opinion is that such an officer would be no accession to the strength of His Majesty's Forces." Found not guilty of the lesser charge of disgraceful conduct, he was convicted and sentenced "to take rank in precedence in the King's Own Yorkshire Light Infantry and in the Army as if his appointment as 2nd Lieutenant bore date the 6th day of July 1915" for the far greater offence of "When in arrest escaping."[39] Posted to 2nd KOYLI in October 1916, past critics were confounded and the stain on his military record all but expunged when, in addition to being promoted captain and company commander within two months of arrival, "He led his men in the attack with great gallantry, and captured an enemy line of strong posts, together with 40 prisoners."[40] Awarded the MC for his daring, Forde was a striking example of a rash and untried young officer making good.

9280 Private Albert Cooksey was a pre-war Regular who had enlisted in the KOYLI on the standard twelve-year contract – seven years with the colours followed by five in the reserve – in 1907. A middle son (six boys and five girls) of coal miner and subsequent day labourer John Cooksey and his wife Amelia, née Portman, Cooksey, he hailed from the bustling South Yorkshire manufacturing town of Barnsley. Left with three younger siblings to raise in the years after Albert's enlistment, John and Amelia's residence at 216 Midland Road, Royston was, as recorded in the 1911 census, indicative of economic hard times, some ten residents, including three male boarders, residing in a crowded five-bedroom terrace home. Albert's pre-war service took him to the Far East with 1st KOYLI. The outbreak of war put an end to his impending

---

37 TNA: WO/339/1191: J. Lindsay to R. Wallace correspondence 13 June 1915 and 'CONFIDENTIAL C.R.N.C. No. 59631/A.1' 17 June 1915, Captain Henry Rawson FORDE. The King's Own (Yorkshire Light Infantry).
38 Carson's intercession appears characteristic when considering his celebrated defence of falsely accused naval cadet George Archer-Shee, whose case was the basis for playwright Terence Rattigan's *The Winslow Boy*.
39 TNA: WO/339/1191: J. Lindsay to R. Wallace correspondence 13 June 1915; R. Wallace to Sir Edward Carson 15 June 1915; Sir Edward Carson to General Sclater 21 June 1915; 'CONFIDENTIAL C.R.N.C. No. 59631/A.1' 17 June 1915 and 'CONFIDENTIAL 1880.3. (A.G.3)' 22 July 1915, Captain Henry Rawson FORDE. The King's Own (Yorkshire Light Infantry).
40 *Supplement to the London Gazette* 17 April 1917, p. 3681.

Private A. Cooksey.
(Jon Cooksey)

discharge. Attached to 2nd KOYLI signal section, he had, since arrival as part of a reinforcement draft on 11 November 1914, already experienced a great deal of fighting. The strenuous march up the Gravenstafel Road was, in all likelihood, just one more taxing and dangerous episode in the old sweat's decade-long military career.[41]

Thirty-two-year-old acting Lieutenant-Colonel L. Lamotte (CO 2nd KOYLI since 26 November)[42] marched at the head of the battalion:

> The battalion was led by the commanding officer, Lieutenant Colonel L. Lamotte, and paused at KANSAS CROSS for a halt of ten minutes. The commanding officer personally guided the battalion to the "jumping-off" tape and saw each section of the battalion into its correct position and after synchronizing the watches of every officer, gave to each the correct angle of advance and made certain that it was perfectly understood by the platoon and section commanders. The march between BELLEVUE and MOSSELMARKT was rendered difficult owing to congestion, but energetic measures prevailed, and

---

41 *Stand To!* No. 98, September 2013 and email correspondence with Jon Cooksey 2 July 2014.
42 A/Lieutenant-Colonel Lewis Lamotte: Commissioned Royal Sussex Regiment 1905; Lieutenant 1909; A/Major March-June and August-December 1917; appointed CO 2nd KOYLI the following December.

plenty of time was allowed for assembly, and every man was in his proper position by 1:20 a.m., or thirty-five minutes before ZERO. The commanding officer reported this fact [from his newly-established HQ at Meetcheele] to brigade headquarters accordingly.[43]

Nettleton, unlike the 2nd KOYLI war diary, recollected surprise and consternation engendered by the discovery that Teall Cottage was still in enemy hands:

> This [Teall Cottage] was supposed to have been captured by the 32nd Division two days previously and it had been so reported. But when we got there we were met with machine-gun fire and found the Boche were still in possession. This fairly put the cat among the pigeons, because this position was the hinge between the two attacks and could enfilade either one of them.[44]

The right flank peril still unsubdued, a single 2nd KOYLI platoon was detailed to tackle Teall Cottage during the main attack.[45]

How was it that the left and right battalions of 8th and 32nd divisions were unaware of the failure to regain Teall Cottage until just prior to the assault? Post-operation reports and diary entries only recount resultant disruption and heavy casualties caused by machine-gun fire from the hostile strongpoint, while two battalion war diaries (2nd Royal Innsikilling Fusiliers and 16th NF) record a single unsuccessful attempt to recapture the position during the early hours of 1 December. Its loss was not revealed until the night of 30 November/1 December; time remained for one abortive counter-attack before daybreak. It appears, if Nettleton's post-war recollections are correct, that some sort of command and control deficiency contributed to assumed division and brigade-level ignorance of the threat, although, given the circumstances, a second counter-attack was out of the question until the following night. Perhaps it was hoped the situation could be cleared up – one more obstacle to overcome – during the main advance. This is a reasonable hypothesis when one considers the rapid course of events, Blacklock's subsequent admission that communications forward of brigade were "intermittent" because of shellfire, consequent available intelligence and confused nature of the battlefield. The battalions concerned, in any case, would no doubt be expected to adapt and "get on with it."[46]

---

43 TNA: WO/95/2402: 2nd KOYLI War Diary and WO/95/2400: '97th Brigade Operation Order No. 178', 27 November 1917, 97 Brigade War Diary.
44 Nettleton, *The Anger of the Guns*, p. 116.
45 TNA: WO/95/2402: 2nd KOYLI War Diary.
46 IWM 4723: 'Preliminary Report on Operations December 1st, 2nd and 3rd December', 4 December 1917, Brigadier-General T.S. Lambert Papers (Box 80/10/2).

192   A Moonlight Massacre

16th HLI,[47] in 97 Brigade support at Bellevue since the 30 November, spent the daylight hours of 1 December at rest despite "frequent bursts of hostile shell-fire" that failed to inflict casualties. Its nominal strength at the time was 16 officers and 404 ORs. Numbers changed with the arrival – during the distribution of "a hot meal of tea and rum" – of reinforcements consisting of 4 officers and 65 ORs at 5:30 p.m. The new drafts, hurriedly amalgamated, increased the Battalion's strength to 20 officers and 469 ORs. The designated taping party (Lieutenant J. McLellan MC and 18 ORs) departed to lay engineer tape from the vicinity of Mosselmarkt "to frontline position via VENTURE FARM" one hour later.[48] McLellan, assisted by Corporals Hilley, Gilmour and four NCOs per company, managed to extend the march line tape to the forming-up area. "They then taped the assembly position and erected luminous numbered boards to mark the right of each platoon." The jumping-off tape was set along a battalion frontage of 300 yards and "within a depth of 30 yards as experience had shown that this position was forward of the enemy's S.O.S. Barrage lines."[49]

Ordered and ready, 16th HLI moved forward – order of march: 'D', 'B', 'C', 'A', companies – from Bellevue with distances of 100 yards maintained between platoons at 9:30 p.m. Among their numbers was twenty-year-old 350220 Private Hugh Cairns, a native of Glasgow's poverty-stricken east end where he was raised, along with nine siblings, in a two-room tenement. Displaying an enthusiasm for military service, he had, according to family lore, emulated three older brothers by enlisting, much to his father's fury, while under age. Subsequent service with the 1st and 10th (Works) battalions Royal Scots Fusiliers was succeeded by posting to the 16th HLI. Was he a member of the newly arrived and swiftly assimilated draft? Whatever the circumstances, there is no doubt the young Glaswegian volunteer kept pace with equally burdened comrades as they slogged up Bellevue Spur toward the battalion jumping-off position.[50]

The first leg of 16th HLI's journey was complete by 9:25 p.m.; Bellevue crossroads was cleared at approximately 10:10 p.m. A guide provided by battalion HQ led the column "up to the position of assembly where the tape leaves the [GRAVENSTAFEL –] MOSSELMARKT road." Five men were lost to enemy shellfire before companies deployed along the jumping-off tape at 11:10 p.m. The Battalion diarist recorded that 16th HLI was now "in line with 11th Borders on its left. The 2nd KOYLI had taken up a position on a parallel line to our right 100 yards in rear. Liaison was obtained with both units." Advanced HQ had (10:30 p.m.) already been established at Vocation

47   The 16th (Service) Battalion HLI was formed in Glasgow by the Lord Provost and City on 2 September 1914. Many of its original recruits came from the Glasgow Boy's Brigade.
48   TNA: WO/95/2404: 16th HLI War Diary.
49   Ibid and TNA: WO/95/2370: 'Table to accompany Addendum No. 3 to 97th Inf. Bde. C.C. 178' and 'Addendum No. 4 to 97th Infantry Brigade Operation Order No. 178', 29 November 1917, 32nd Division War Diary.
50   TNA: WO/95/2404: 16th HLI War Diary and telephone interview with Dr Joanne Coyle (Pte. Cairns' niece) 29 May 2010.

Private H. Cairns.
(Dr Joanne Coyle)

Farm and connected, by the efforts of Battalion Signal Officer Lieutenant S.M. Roberts, with Battalion HQ at Bellevue. Meanwhile, the CO 'B' Company detailed two guides to meet the attached heavy machine-gun detachment near Bellevue. The rendezvous did not occur until, as directed, 2nd KOYLI passed up the Gravenstafel Road, after which the Vickers Gun teams were guided to allocated positions.[51]

The 11th Border Regiment (CO Lieutenant-Colonel T.F. Tweed MC),[52] in 97 Brigade reserve at Wurst Farm since the 30th, arrived, after a 2,000 yard tramp (platoons separated by 100-yard intervals) via "MOUSETRAP TRACK – SOURCE

---

51 TNA: WO/95/2404: 16th HLI War Diary and WO/95/2400: '97th Brigade Operation Order No. 178', 27 November 1917, 97 Brigade War Diary.
52 The 11th (Service) Battalion Border Regiment (Lonsdales) was formed in Penrith (HQ), Carlisle, Kendal and Workington by the Earl of Lonsdale and an executive committee in September 1914.

Lieutenant-Colonel T.F. Tweed MC. (Michael Stedman)

FARM" at the 300 yard jumping-off line without loss. Battalion HQ was established near Bellevue at Point 83. "The initial stages of the attack, assembling, etc., were successfully carried through", the battalion diarist observed, "but the enemy – as was afterwards learned – had been appraised of our intentions and had made strong preparation against them."[53]

Over two years' continuous active service had taken its toll on Lieutenant-Colonel Tweed.[54] Consistently favourable personal reports emanating from superior officers contributed to his steady rise from lieutenant to one of the youngest lieutenant-colonels in the British Army. Previously awarded the MC for bravery at Thiepval on 1 July 1916, further military accolades followed with a mention in despatches for services

---

53 TNA: WO/95/2403: 11th Border War Diary, WO/95/2400: '97th Brigade Operation Order No. 178', 27 November 1917, 97 Brigade War Diary, WO/95/2370: 'Table to accompany Addendum No. 3 to 97th Inf. Bde. C.C. 178', 32nd Division War Diary and IWM 4273: 'Preliminary Report on Operations, December 1st, 2nd and 3rd [1917]', Brigadier-General T.S. Lambert Papers (Box 80/10/2).

54 29-year-old A/Lieutenant-Colonel Thomas Frederic Tweed MC (1888-1940). Educated at Liverpool Institute and Liverpool University; underwriting member of Lloyd's; Liberal agent for Eccles at the outbreak of war; commissioned 15th LF (1st Salford Pals); transferred 16th LF (2nd Salford Pals) November 1914; Captain and CO 'B' or 1st Eccles Company 1915-16; Major and 2/ic 1916-17; MC January 1917; CO 11th Border Regiment from 25 August.

rendered whilst in temporary command of 16th LF at Nieuport on 10 July 1917.[55] The subsequent appointment to command 11th Border Regiment appears to have been the catalyst for a gradual descent into nervous strain and depression, further exacerbated by growing professional tensions with Brigadier-General Blacklock:

> The difficulties with that unit [11th Border Regiment] were very great. It had suffered very severe losses at Nieuport & when I took it over, my Company Commanders [,] with one exception [,] were all 2nd Lieutenants with under 12 months commissioned service. My 2nd in Command was only just promoted from Adjutant & my Adjutant a very junior 2nd Lieutenant. During the period of my command through casualties my Adjutant was changed 3 times & my RSM also 3 times … Though these difficulties were great, while I had the sympathy of the Brigadier, they were not inoperable, but when differences caused his sympathy to lessen, it was necessary for me to work night and day to keep the Unit's end up … [56]

Determined to carry out duties prescribed by achieved rank and responsibility, Tweed soldiered on despite periodic headaches, memory loss, irregular sleep patterns and a noticeable stammer.[57] It was in this undiagnosed neurasthenic condition resulting from acute anxiety and exhaustion that the CO 11th Border Regiment, final administrative details having been attended to, anxiously anticipated signs – immediate outbreak of hostile machine-gun fire or relative silence extending until Zero + 8 – of the night attack's opening stage.

Twenty-two-year-old 2nd Lieutenant William Thomas Ridgway (attached 11th Border Regiment), armed with revolver, rifle and bayonet and garbed in OR's Service Dress [SD] like the other company officers, awaited the approach of zero hour with his platoon. "Will" hailed from the picturesque rural village of Tingewick, where his father was parish clerk, in North Buckinghamshire. Graduation from Tingewick Council School was succeeded by the ambitious pursuit of a career in journalism. Eighteen months at the National Union of Journalists (Northampton and Peterborough) Typographical School led to employment as a young sports reporter for the *Cambridge Advertiser*. A qualified former member of the St John Ambulance Brigade, short service enlistment with the RAMC was attested at the busy East

---

55 Tweed was portrayed by actor Mike Rogers in the BBC's 2006 docudrama *The Somme: Defeat into Victory*.
56 TNA: WO/339/21553: Tweed to Military Secretary War Office, 27 February 1918, Lieutenant-Colonel Thomas Frederic TWEED. The Lancashire Fusiliers.
57 Ibid: 'Army Form W3436: Report to be rendered in the case of Officers and other ranks who, without any visible wound, become non-effective from physical conditions claimed or presumed to have originated from effects of British or enemy weapons in action', 14 December 1917 and 'Army Form A.45: Medical Board Report on Disabled Officer', 17 January 1918.

W.T. Ridgway attestation document September 1914. (Ridgway Family)

Anglia railway town of March on 12 September 1914. Six month's training was followed by eighteen month's service with the BEF. Promoted to local acting sergeant in January 1916, the temporary rank was reverted to corporal five months later during rear echelon employment at No. 18 General Hospital Camiers. It was not until late August 1916 that Will, having regained his sergeant's stripes, applied for a temporary Regular Army commission. Accepted for officer training at home, RAMC comrades expressed their admiration for the departing NCO by presenting him with a cigarette case inscribed: "Presented to Sergeant Wm. T. Ridgway, ROYAL ARMY MEDICAL CORPS, as a mark of respect and esteem, from His Brother Members No. 18 General Hospital British Ex. Force, France. Oct. 3rd 1916." [58]

Sergeant Ridgway embarked from France for instruction at Cambridge University. Training at No. 5 Officer Cadet Battalion [OCB], accommodated amidst the aristocratic precincts of Trinity College, began on 4 November 1916. No. 5 OCB, one of twenty-three facilities established throughout Great Britain, was "a mixture of boot camp and public school or Oxbridge college", where ex-rankers and other potential officer material learned, besides military skills, to emulate the ethos of pre-war Regular officers.[59] Will spent the holidays with his parents, two sisters and 6-year-old brother Fred: "I remember him coming home on leave during Christmas 1916", Fred recalled; "He looked very smart in his officer's uniform." One can almost visualize the upright, enthusiastic cadet, white-banded service cap in hand, attired as "on parade" in tailored khaki tunic, polished Sam Browne belt, whipcord breeches, carefully wrapped puttees and gleaming ankle boots, joining in hymns with his kindred during celebration services at St Mary Magdalene Church.[60]

Graduation from No. 5 OCB was succeeded by a posting to the Border Regiment in February 1917. His commission duly confirmed by the *London Gazette* on 23 March, orders for the front arrived shortly afterwards. It had, by early December, been almost one year since the youthful subaltern, formed up with 11th Battalion opposite the shell-churned southern slope of Vat Cottages Ridge, last visited with his family at their residence on Buckingham Road just outside Tingewick.

58 Special thanks to Ms Sue Floyd, Ms Brenda Eastaff (William Ridgway's niece) and Mr Alan Ridgway for providing material concerning 2nd Lieutenant Ridgway's background and war service.
59 Gary Sheffield, *Leadership in the Trenches: Officer-Man Relations, Morale and Discipline in the British Army in the Era of the First World War* (Basingstoke: Macmillan Press, 2000), p. 55. 'At a time when there were very few students at Cambridge University, the members of the three OCBs housed in the colleges provided a semblance of normal undergraduate life, playing sports, indulging in amateur dramatics, and producing magazines. Billeted in gracious surroundings very different from their peacetime environment, living a relatively carefree life far removed from the drudgery of the office or factory, many lower-class cadets proved particularly responsive to the need to play the role that was demanded of them.' Ibid, pp. 55-57.
60 Angela Foster, 'Fred Paid His Final Tribute', *Buckinghamshire Advertiser* (November 2000).

Acting Lieutenant-Colonel J. Inglis. (J.W. Arthur & I.S. Munro (eds), *The Seventeenth Highland Light Infantry (Glasgow Chamber of Commerce Battalion): Record of War Service 1914–1918* (Glasgow: David J. Clark, 1920))

Having "rested all day" at Hill Top Farm, 17th HLI[61] marched off with platoons at 100 yard intervals by way of "MOUSETRAP TRACK – SOURCE FARM" to its assembly position approximately 8,000 yards distant. The Battalion (CO acting Lieutenant-Colonel J. Inglis),[62] passing by Wurst Farm at 8:55 p.m., arrived at the 400-yard-long jumping-off tape without serious incident. Battalion HQ was, as with 11th Border Regiment, established at Point 83. Companies were to deploy at the start of the advance "from a two platoon frontage to snake formation – this method having been adopted owing to the shell torn nature of the ground …"[63]

61 The 17th (Service) Battalion HLI (3rd Glasgow) was formed by the Glasgow Chamber of Commerce in September 1914.
62 A/Lieutenant-Colonel John Inglis. RMC Sandhurst; Commissioned HLI 1900; South Africa 1901-02; Lieutenant 1906; Adjutant 1st HLI 1911; Captain 1912; Major 1916; CO 17th HLI July 1917.
63 TNA: WO/95/2405: 17th HLI War Diary, WO/95/2400: '97th Brigade Operation Order No. 178', 27 November 1917, 97 Brigade War Diary, WO/95/2370: 'Table to accompany Addendum No. 3 to 97th Inf. Bde. C.C. 178', 32nd Division War Diary and Arthur & Munro (eds), *The Seventeenth Highland Light Infantry*, p. 68.

Led by an attached American Medical Officer[64] – a "rational and very welcome acquisition" for 17th HLI – Private Elshaw and his fellow stretcher-bearers trekked from Hill Top Farm to the forward area. All were encumbered by a "white man's burden of ropes, ladders, spades, etc." and standard infantrymen's kit:

> After a full briefing we set off again a day or two later – armed with rifles, grenades, picks, shovels, ladders, ropes and Uncle Tom Cobley and all. We carried all but the arms, but had in addition, stretchers, extra dressings and huge Red Cross armbands. "Jerry" was not to be trusted to respect anything less and even that was no guarantee of immunity, for stretcher-bearers trying to get at casualties became casualties themselves.
>
> Struggling "up by" that night each human pack mule, not only due to his burden, but also due to the necessity of keeping "eyes down" to avoid floundering in the mud was very nearly nose to the ground. A halt was called where the duckboards wound between heavy batteries – owing mainly to the fact that we had progressed so well as to be in front of schedule. This provided a welcome break for those who may have been at liberty to avail themselves of the hospitality of the gunners – but the rest of us merely stood and waited, waited for what we deemed inevitable – and sure enough over came "John's" souvenirs intended presumably for the discomfort of the artillery personnel – though perhaps with an eye on a passerby. They were in the shape of 5.9 HV shrapnel. I never heard the one that hit me, raised a bump under my tin hat and left me with a helpless left arm. That shell sprayed its "bull's eyes" down one side of the halted column and inflicted wounds – all on the left side – from hand to toe on a dozen to twenty men.
>
> After first-aid treatment I set off with a limping squad back down the line, being fully aware that "Zero" and its accompanying barrage was due all too soon. I hustled my fellow patients past local aid posts and our recently left billets – stopping only to report – and made for the Corps Main Dressing Station. This involved a five-mile tramp in anything but ideal conditions and I marvelled at the stoicism of those with foot and leg wounds – but none wished to dally in the vicinity of the "hate" that was due to break out once our guns opened up – communications [routes], especially unprotected ones would be decidedly unhealthy – besides having "touches" for a spell out who wanted to be greedy and stop another one? The journey took us nearly three hours.

---

64 The American medical officer was Captain D.E. Pugh, Medical Officer's Reserve Corps (MORC). On 7 April 1917 the United States government agreed to attach 1,000 medical officers to the British forces. 1,649 subsequently served with the BEF at one time or another. See *The Outpost* (17th HLI journal), December 1917 and Michael Rauer, 'Yanks in the King's Forces: American Physicians Serving With the British Expeditionary Force During World War I' (Paper. Washington DC: Office of Medical History, Office of the Surgeon General United States Army, date unknown).

Elshaw, wounded seriously enough to avoid the impending embrace with "Johnnie" on the Westroosebeke ridge, was dispatched with his injured companions by motor ambulance to a CCS.[65]

Sometime after 10:30 p.m. companies of 15th LF,[66] holding the 97 Brigade's left front since the night of 30 November/1 December, began to concentrate opposite their objective following relief on a frontage of 700 yards by Lewis Gun teams of the incoming 11th Border Regiment and 17th HLI.[67] The forming-up line of 450 yards was reconnoitered and, as per brigade instructions, marked out with wire by 2nd Lieutenant J.S. Scrivener ('A' Company) before dawn on the 1st. Confirmation of its accurate placement was ascertained by compass the following morning. On the night of 1/2 December the "wire was replaced with tape and the flank of each platoon's position was marked with a white disc." Companies ('A' on the right, 'B' in centre, 'C' on the left) were thus redeployed without difficulty or loss along the assigned three-company frontage of 450 yards: "Since any sort of landmark had been utterly obliterated by the colossal weight of shellfire which pulverised this area for months beforehand, the Fusiliers' company objectives were identified by boards at the start lines, each one giving a compass bearing and distance to be covered with the details in luminous paint." 'D' Company remained in support immediately behind 'A'. The Battalion was formed up without loss and ready to move by 1:30 a.m. HQ was established under cover in a vacant pillbox SW of Tournant Farm. Blacklock later observed: "The assembly of No. 5 Battalion involved the relief and concentration of 2 companies holding the line, but was very well carried out."[68]

Approximately 2,000 yards to the SW, Brigadier-General Blacklock and the red-tabbed staff of 97 Brigade settled into their large pillbox HQ just east of the swampy Stroombeek at Kronprinz Farm. Sheltering beyond narrow entry-ways screened by heavy, solution-saturated anti-gas blankets in cramped, fuggy, coke fume permeated ferro-concrete recesses where odorous paraffin lamps and flickering candles cast spectral shadows on clammy walls; they patiently awaited confirmation that each assault battalion had taken its designated place along the attack frontage of 1,850 yards. These prearranged messages – "Assembly Complete CONTACT" – dispatched either by wireless or runner from sundry low-roofed, largely windowless battalion HQs, crowded to capacity by colonels, adjutants, artillery liaison officers, signallers,

---

65   IWM: PP/MCR 49: Elshaw unpublished memoir.
66   The 15th (Service) Battalion (1st Salford Pals) LF was raised in Salford by Mr Montague Barlow MP and the Salford Brigade Committee on 11 September 1914.
67   TNA: WO/95/2370: 'Addendum No. 4 to 97th Brigade Operation Order No. 178', 29 November 1917. 32nd Division War Diary.
68   TNA: WO/95/2397: 15th LF War Diary, Major-General J.C. Latter, *The History of the Lancashire Fusiliers in Two Volumes Vol. 1* (Aldershot: Gale & Polden, 1949). p. 276, Stedman, *Salford Pals*, p. 154 and IWM 4723: 'Narrative of Operations 2/3rd December 1917, 15th (S) Battalion Lancashire Fusiliers', 4 December 1917, Brigadier-General T.S. Lambert Papers (Box 80/10/2).

Sergeant R.B. Milligan 17th HLI KIA
1 December 1917.
(Neill Gill & Colin Milligan)

runners, medical officers and stretcher-bearers, duly arrived one by one during the hours leading up to Zero: "Units reported assembly complete and direction boards and guiding tapes in position …"[69] At 1:40 a.m. 97 Brigade verbally reported to Division HQ: "Forming up complete. All quiet." Casualties sustained by the five battalions during this period amounted (2nd KOYLI (15); 16th HLI (7); 11th Border Regiment (0); 17th HLI (15); 15th LF (0) to 37 men.[70]

Rawlinson's diary entry for 1 December: "I have great hopes that we shall do the trick at Passchendaele all right but the Bosch is expecting us", implies some foreknowledge of British intentions by the enemy.[71] Available war diaries, post-war unit accounts and memoirs also express the conviction that surprise was not achieved due to lack of available cover and increased visibility in the prevailing moonlight. Were the Germans aware of the impending night attack? Were the attackers detected on the forming-up tape prior to Zero? The history of *IR115* (responsible for the left sector of

---

69 Advanced report centres were situated at Point 83 and Virile Farm. Prearranged battalion messages arrived at the following times: 2nd KOYLI (1:20 a.m.), 16th HLI (12:00 a.m.), 11th Border (12:05 a.m.), 17th HLI (1:25 a.m.), 15th LF (1:33 a.m.).
70 See TNA: WO/95/2400: '97th Brigade Operation Order No. 178', 27 November 1917, 97 Brigade War Diary, WO/95/2370: After-action Report, 'Appendix 'J', 32nd Division: Telephone and Telegraph Messages 2 December 1917', 11 December 1917, 32nd Division War Diary and IWM 4723: 'Preliminary Report on Operations, December 1st, 2nd and 3rd, 4 December 1917, Brigadier-General T.S. Lambert Papers (Box 80/10/2).
71 CAC: RWLN 1/9: Rawlinson Diary, 1 December 1917.

25th Division) noted: "From the relief of opposing infantry, the possibility of attacks in this sector was assumed; for 28 November, heightened readiness was ordered", but added "these by-the-book precautions proved premature." This precipitate alert is confirmed by a Second Army intelligence summary dated 3 December: "Two prisoners of 6th Coy., 117th Inf. Regt. captured in E.1.a [vicinity of Exert Farm] at 1:30 a.m. on 2nd inst., state: A big attack by the British was expected on the 28th Nov[ember]. The advanced posts to retire on frontline and supports were to reinforce."[72] A captured *Feldwebel* of *3rd Company*, *IR94* (left regiment of the recently arrived *38th Division*) subsequently related during interrogation:

Dispositions.
The III Battalion has been holding the line since 30/1st [December] and the I Battalion was ordered to the support positions last night with a view of relieving III Battalion in the frontline tonight [2 December]. Subsequent orders were, however, issued at 10 p.m. last night [1 December] resulting in the 2nd and 3rd companies being sent forward to reinforce the frontline. The 1st Company was at VELDT FARM. From this statement it seems apparent that an attack was expected this morning, but the time and method was a complete surprise to the enemy.

Prisoner's Opinion of This Morning's Battle.
It seems that although the higher command expected an attack on our front today, the men of the foremost posts [*Vorfeldzone*] had either not received timely warning or did not act upon it. Prisoner states that too many men were asleep and that a large majority were running back from the line instead of putting up any resistance.[73]

---

72 Victor von Frankenberg und Ludwigsdorff, *Das Leibgarde Infanterie Regiment (1. Grossherzoglich Hessisches Nr. 115) im Weltkrieg 1914-1918* (Stuttgart: Verlagsbuchhandlung, 1921), p. 163 and TNA: WO/157/121: 'Annexe to Second Army Summary, Dated 3rd December 1917: Information Obtained from Prisoners', Second Army Intelligence Files.

73 TNA: WO/157/288: 'Annexe to II Corps Summary No. 31, Examination of Sergt. Major of the 3rd Company, 94th I.R. 38th Division, Captured at V.30.a on the morning of the 2nd Inst.', II Corps Summary of Information, 2 December 1917, II Corps Intelligence File. The circumstances of this POW's capture were as follows: 'Prisoner was ordered, as part of his training, to go forward during last night and ascertain the exact positions of the infantry, machine-guns and artillery in his regimental sector. He chose the period from midnight onwards as being the most suitable and left ROULERS about this time, proceeding direct to the frontline, intending to work his way back. He had only been in the line about five minutes before our attack started and was captured very shortly afterwards.' See TNA: WO/157/120: 'Annexe to Second Army Summary Dated 3rd December 1917, Information from Prisoners', Second Army Intelligence File.

POW interrogations between 24 November and 1 December only provided local German commanders with speculatory statements concerning a projected attack in the Passchendaele – Westroosebeke sector. Two men of 2nd KOYLI, captured near *Nordhof* (Void Farm) on the evening of 24 November, claimed to have no knowledge of pending offensive operations, but "they suppose further attacks are not excluded because, in their opinion, it is impossible to maintain the position they are now in over the winter." The 32nd Division, they also surmised, "after a long period of rest could be considered for an attack … This is even more likely, as it has proven itself a good attack formation." Seven men of 2nd Devonshire Regiment, captured north of Passchendaele on the morning of 25 November, stated there "was no need to attack, the general opinion of the troops is that they are to maintain [current] positions." Three men from the same Battalion, 2 (1 officer and 1 OR) of which were seized in the same area that evening, alleged that "on the night of 27/28 November, front battalions [of 23 Brigade] will be relieved by 25 Brigade, which will attack to capture the ridge in its entirety. According to [prisoner] statements, the anticipated attack will occur on the morning of 28 November. What the scope of the attack is none can say." No doubt *25th Division*'s precipitate alert of 28 November had its origin in the latter 2nd Devonshire prisoner interrogation report. Finally, 9 men of 2nd Royal Inniskilling Fusiliers and 16th NF, taken captive just prior to and during the German riposte of 30 November, collectively claimed to possess no information concerning a forthcoming assault, "but they would not completely rule out the possibility of an advance to improve the position." Carefully scrutinized for intelligence, the contents of these reports hardly inspired confident predictions of enemy intent.[74]

Moreover, perusal of *Heeresgruppe Kronprinz Rupprecht* and *Fourth Army* daily situation reports, telegraph and wireless messages for 30 November and 1 December make no mention, other than recording numerous bombardments of varying intensity, identification/confirmation of hostile formations opposite and other activities occurring along the now static front, of an anticipated British attack.[75] Thus it appears, despite the conclusion reached by British intelligence officers, that the German defenders remained, as a matter of course, especially vigilant in sectors (Venison Trench and its redoubts, the ridge route towards Westroosebeke, Vat Cottages Ridge) where British

74 See BA-MA PH 3/586:'A.O.K. 4. 131. VERNEHMUNG von 2 Gefangenen vom II/KO Yorks LI, 97 Brigade', 26 November 1917, '132. Vernehmung von VII Mann des II/Devon R.' and 'Vernehmung von 1 Offizier und 1 Mann des II/ Devon R.', 27 November 1917 and '141. VERNEHMUNG: 1. von 1 Gefangene vom II/R. Innis. Fus. 2. von 1 Gefangenen vom XVI/North'd Fus. gefangen genomnen am abend des 29.XI westlich Nordhof (atwa bei Fotop 1, Planq L. 39) von der 199.I.D. 3. vom 6. Gef (daven 3 verwundet) vom II/R. Innis. Fus. und 1 Gefangenen vom XVI/North'd Fus. gefangen genommen von 199.I.D. östl. Rotp n (Planq E.40) beidem deutschen Unternehmen am Morgen des 30.XI', 3 December 1917, Vernehmungsprotokolle französischer & englischer Kriegsgefangener im Bereich des AOK 4, Bd. 3 Oct.-Dez. [1917].
75 See KA HKR 71'Lagge am 1.12.1917 mittags' and 99 telegraph/wireless pro formas, 30 November and 1 December 1917.

assault troops could expect reasonably good going across vital traversable high ground (see map on p. 54). The determination reached by II Corps intelligence that "the German higher command had received information of our intentions, for at 10 p.m. on the night of the 1st a warning order was issued stating an attack was expected and at least one of his frontline battalions was reinforced by two companies of the battalion in support", was likely based on enemy reaction to "important disclosures" made by "three Englishmen" captured opposite *IR94* sometime after dark on 1 December. The content of these revelations are, unfortunately, not related in the post-war regimental history, but their relation to the subsequent action taken by the Thüringian Regiment's support battalion can be inferred. Furthermore, other relevant German unit histories, whilst acknowledging surprise, fail to mention any prior notice of the night attack, so it is possible that the shifting of two support companies to the frontline was a local response to recent POW declarations.[76] An argus-eyed officer of *IR95* also detected enemy patrol activity on the immediate (German) left:

> A light blanket of snow covered the landscape and a full moon illuminated the night sky, so one had to be careful. At around 11:00 p.m [German time][77] on the evening of 1 December, not long after the Regiment settled into [new] positions, the commander of *7th Company* discovered approximately 30 to 40 English opposite the *Vorfeldzone*. Believed to be ration carriers who lost their way, they were immediately shot down.[78]

It must, therefore, be generally assumed that the attackers were not discerned opposite either divisional sector until just before 1:00 a.m. (British time), and even then enemy intentions were only realised in *38th Division's* sector just minutes before zero hour:

---

76 TNA: WO/157/288: 'II Corps Summary of Information', 2 December 1917', II Corps Intelligence File and Hartmann, *Das Infanterie Regiment Grossherzog von Sachsen (5. Thüringisches) No. 94 im Weltkrieg*, p. 236. For German interrogation methods and British POWs see Christopher Duffy, *Through German Eyes: The British and the Somme 1916* (London: Weidenfeld & Nicolson, 2006), pp. 36-45. An interrogation report conveying the aforementioned POW declarations was not found in the BA-MA PH 3/586: Vernehmungsprotokolle französischer & englischer Kriegsgefangener im Bereich des AOK 4, Bd. 3 Oct.-Dez. [1917] file.
77 Relevant German regimental accounts record continental time, i.e., one hour ahead of British time. See Appendix XVI.
78 Major A.D. Buttmann, *Kriegsgeschichte des Koninglich Preusischen 6. Thüringischen Infanterie Regiment Nr. 95: 1914-1918* (Zeulenroda, Thüringen: Verlag Bernhard Sporn, 1935), p. 251. '32nd Division Operation Order No. 138' (27 November) stated: 'Patrols and Lewis Guns will cover the forming up. These patrols must be pushed out every night previous to the assault so that the enemy may become accustomed to them.' The unfortunate British patrol encountered by *IR95* was probably carrying out this portion, a standard pre-operation procedure by late 1917, of the previously issued order. See TNA: WO/95/2370: '32nd Division Operation Order No. 138', 27 November 1917, 32nd Division War Diary

Shortly before 2:00 a.m. an English patrol [either from 2nd Rifle Brigade or 2nd KOYLI] approached the right of *2nd Company* and was shot down. The *Vorfeldzone* reported much activity and moving about in the enemy line. At first this was thought to be only a relief in progress. Shortly before 3:00 a.m., *9th Company* recognised that an English assault was imminent. Annihilation [artillery] fire was immediately called for.[79]

At 2:15 a.m. on 2 December, a strong twenty-man patrol was sighted opposite the *Vorfeldzone* and easily dispersed. Suddenly, in the moonlight, an unbroken enemy line was discovered approaching the *Feldherrnhügel*.[80] Shortly before 3:00 a.m., they attacked through the deep mud. Abruptly, artillery fire, approaching the level of drumfire, bombarded the [divisional] hinterland where all the light and heavy guns were deployed.[81]

Blacklock subsequently wrote: "[T]here was no congestion or confusion and in spite of the brightness of the moon [,] I am confident that the assembly was carried out without detection. This has been further corroborated from prisoners taken who were holding the enemy advanced line … At Zero the whole attack was launched simultaneously. The moon was out and the attacking waves showed up very plainly."[82] Outposts comprising *25*th *Division's Vorfeldzone* failed to distinguish the imminent threat. A prisoner of *2nd Company, IR116* later informed his captors: "Our [British]

---

79 Hartmann, *Das Infanterie Regiment Grossherzog von Sachsen (5. Thüringisches) No. 94* im *Weltkrieg* , pp. 236-37.
80 *Feldherrnhügel*, or 'General's Hill', situated on the southern outskirts of Westroosebeke, was known to the British as 'Hill 50'. The *Feldherrnhügel*, according to a post-war Bavarian regimental history, 'got its high-sounding name during the first months of the Flanders campaign. From here, the top brass had acquired a commanding view over the battlefield when our most advanced units were 6 to 8 kilometres further forward. From here, imaginative War Correspondents had sent their lively reports to the waiting world. But the *Feldherrnhügel* has had its day. An insignificant regimental staff inhabiting it amidst the tumult of battle and the War Correspondents have disappeared. The breakthrough on the Italian front near Tolmein and Karfreit [Caporetto] and the crossing of the Tagliamento: these were more worthy stories. Wonderful countryside, victory after victory, immeasurable amounts of war booty, supplies and prisoners. Even the military communiqués had almost nothing but the most meagre reports of the violent events amidst the desolation and ravaged battlefields of Flanders… Only in the Flanders Positions were a few dugouts to be found, one on the *Feldherrnhügel*, which had to be continually pumped out in order to render it usable.' See Major a.D. Ernst Demmler, et al, *Das K. B. Reserve-Infanterie-Regiment 12* (Munich: Verlag Max Schid, 1934) pp. 238,240 and accompanying pocket map in Beumelburg, *Flandern 1917*.
81 Buttmann, *Kriegsgeschichte des Koninglich Preusischen 6. Thüringischen Infanterie Regiment Nr. 95*, p. 251.
82 IWM 4723: 'Preliminary Report on Operations December 1st, 2nd and 3rd December', 4 December 1917, Brigadier-General T.S. Lambert Papers (Box 80/10/2).

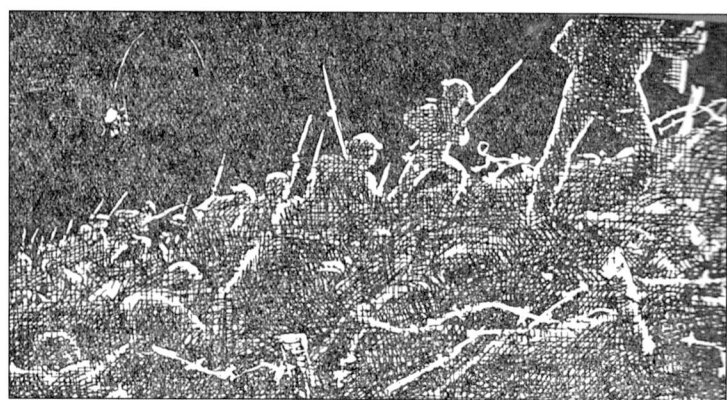

Zero hour 1:55 a.m. Pen and ink drawing by A.M. Burnie. (Thomas Chalmers (ed), *A Saga of Scotland: History of the 16th Battalion Highland Light Infantry (City of Glasgow Regiment)* (Glasgow: John M'Callum & Co, 1930))

attack was a surprise. Half his Company (including the Company Commander) ran away and the rest were overwhelmed."[83]

Identification of new formations (8th Division and 32nd Division) opposite contributed to anticipation of further efforts to seize more ground on Passchendaele Ridge,[84] so Sir Henry Rawlinson's view of an expectant enemy was most likely based on intelligence reports conveying augmented German vigilance.[85] It can also be speculated that the *Vorfeldzone* garrison, no doubt chilled and weary by the early hours of 2 December, received no warning of imminent attack because, as stated above, the exact day and hour could only be surmised. The absence of the expected opening barrage and shortened distance to the foremost outposts, especially opposite 8th Division, also increased the vulnerability of those attempting to make the most of uncomfortable "rabbit hole" positions comprising the *Vorfeldzone*.

---

83 TNA: WO/157/121: 'Annexe to Second Army Summary Dated 5th December 1917: Information Obtained from Prisoners', Second Army Summary of Information, 5 December 1917, Second Army Intelligence Files.
84 The 32nd Division's presence opposite Hill 52 and Vat Cottages Ridge was confirmed by German intelligence on 25 November 1917. See KA HKR 775: 'Lagenkarte der 4. Armee u. Feind Gleichseittog Stellungkarte. AOK 4 (Ia/c 99 (Hgr. Ia 5053)', 7 January 1918.
85 Shute observed afterwards: 'It must also be remembered that an intercepted German message [from which the II Corps intelligence determination was reached] shows that an attack by us was expected by the enemy on the night December 1/2, and that although his frontline of posts had not been warned, his main line of defence had been reinforced, and his machine-guns were ready for our advance.' See TNA: WO/95/2370: After-action Report, 'Part V, Reasons for the Failure of the Operation', 11 December 1917, 32nd Division War Diary.

3.2 A Moonlight Massacre

Elements of nine battalions, arrayed in depth along a jumping-off line of 2,870 yards, made final preparations and adjustments as zero hour approached. Pallid exhale vapours, dissipating as rapidly as they appeared, were momentarily visible in the bitterly cold air. The enemy, situated across a broken, cratered no man's land permeated by moonlight, appeared relatively quiet and unsuspecting. Officers, glancing at previously synchronized luminescent wristwatch dials, gave the order to fix bayonets[86] minutes before zero hour: a collective metallic clatter of blade hilts fitted to rifle nose caps succeeded whispered commands along the attack frontage extending from west of Exert Farm on the right to NE of Tournant Farm on the left.

Zero hour: Sunday 2 December 1:55 a.m. The attackers, organised in waves and columns, silently rose from their forming-up positions. Keeping to narrow, frozen crater rims separating innumerable shell hole cavities, they passed through friendly outposts and embryonic barbed wire obstacles, rifles at the port, to enter a constricted no man's land in the pre-dawn semi-darkness. Extreme haste whilst negotiating the pulverized, pockmarked landscape in the half-light was necessary in order to close with dispersed *Vorfeldzone* outposts as quickly as possible. Collective and individual focus was thus devoted to reaching the *Hauptwiderstandslinie* before the enemy's defensive barrage started.

The prevailing silence did not last long: unwelcome glinting muzzle flashes[87] – a deadly multiple display of direct fire – being readily discerned as the distinctive mechanical din from at least a half dozen *Maschinen-Gewehr 08/15* erupted opposite the left of 25 Brigade immediately after Zero. "Two were seen firing from TEALL COTTAGE and three from the front trench of the NORTHERN REDOUBT, but there were certainly others firing direct fire from the left flank." On the right and centre, "where the shadow of a passing cloud momentarily veiled the front", the German machine-guns "did not open fire until Zero + 3 minutes [1:58 a.m.]. A few coloured lights were sent up at this time." By Zero + 5 (2:00 a.m.) a withering rifle and machine-gun fusillade "had been opened up by the enemy along the whole front of attack and lights of various colours and designs were sent up in great numbers by him."[88] The onrushing battalions of 97 Brigade received an identical shock. Captain A. Fraser MC, a nearby observer, remembered:

---

86 Bayonet blades were blackened prior to the assault. See TNA: WO/95/1727: '25th Infantry Brigade Instructions No.3', 27 November 1917, 25 Brigade War Diary.
87 A muzzle-mounted flash suppressor or hider, like the conical-shaped attachment affixed to heavy 08 or light 08/15 machine-guns, redirects discharged incandescent gases to both sides of a barrel thus preserving a machine-gunner's night-time vision. The belief that such devices were developed to mask a shooter's position from the enemy remains a commonly held misconception.
88 TNA: WO/95/1677: 'Narrative of Operations Carried Out by the 8th Division on 1st/2nd December 1917', 13 December 1917, 8th Division War Diary and Boraston & Bax, *The Eighth Division*, p. 165.

> Those of us who stood on the high ground near Bellevue at zero hour on that memorable morning will always retain a very vivid impression of the fight. It was a fine night with everything quiet on the front. The hillside on which we stood was bathed in moonlight so that it was difficult to realise that within a few moments some five battalions would be advancing across that dark patch down the valley and that the stillness of the night air would be shattered by the rat-tat-tat of machine-guns and the whine of high explosives. At 1:55 a.m. we knew our men had started and we were glad that for the next two minutes everything was quiet.
>
> Suddenly, at three minutes to two, came the sound of several enemy rifle shots followed immediately by the ripple of machine-guns all along the front; up went the SOS on both flanks of the attack. Still our artillery was silent! We knew that we could hope for no assistance from them until three minutes after the hour, and, meantime, the enemy was having a free hand for five minutes on a target that looked grotesquely big against the bright moon.[89]

Lieutenant-Colonel Scully, watching and waiting in the immediate vicinity of his pillbox HQ at Virile Farm, recalled: "About zero plus ¼ minute enemy lights were sent up and MGs opened fire but I do not consider that the fire was heavy enough to stop the attack." Shute's subsequent after-action report disagreed: "By Zero + 7" (2:02 a.m.), "the enemy's machine-guns opened on all portions of the front with great intensity and held up the advance of our troops at nearly all points."[90] Heneker's worst fear was realised: the hoped-for surprise had been lost in the crucial minutes following zero hour. Captain Fraser lamented the fate of junior leaders charged with tactical command and control during the desperate enterprise: "Some of the finest officers that ever wore the King's uniform went to their deaths with brave faces, well knowing that their chances of success were frail."[91]

3.3 25 Brigade

Lieutenant-Colonel Stirling accompanied the advancing 'B' and 'D' companies of 2nd Royal Berkshire through the forward outpost line into a no man's land temporarily shrouded by darkness:

> At zero hour 1:55 a.m. B & D companies moved forward to the attack in touch with 2nd Lincolnshire Regiment on my left and until 1:58 apparently remained

---

89 Chalmers (ed), *A Saga of Scotland*, pp. 109-10.
90 IWM 4732: '32nd Div. No.G.S.1499/3/33', 4 December 1917, Brigadier-General T.S. Lambert Papers (Box 80/10/2) and TNA: WO/95/2370: After-action Report, 'Part III, Narrative of Events', Section 9, 11 December 1917, 32nd Division War Diary.
91 Chalmers (ed) *A Saga of Scotland*, p.110.

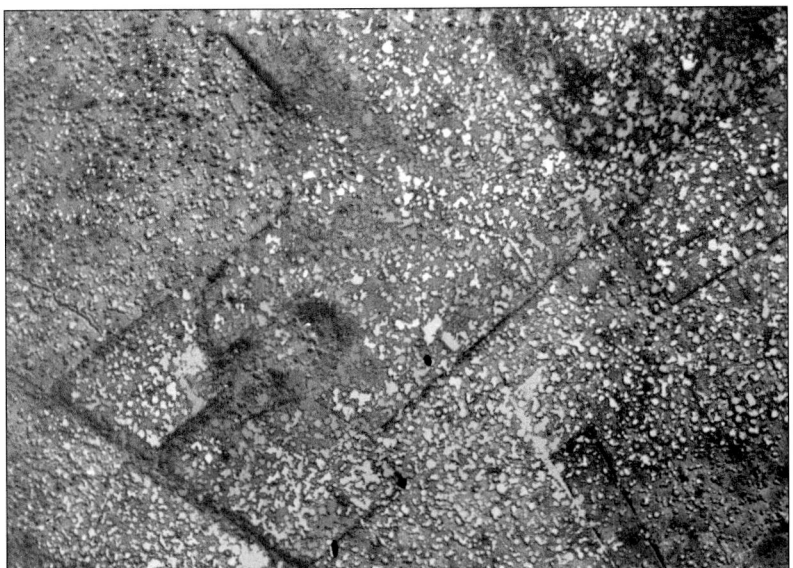

Exert Farm from the air November 1917. (Memorial Museum Passchendaele 1917)

unobserved by the enemy. The moon was at this time behind some clouds. At 1:58 the enemy put up a large number of red, green and golden lights[92] and opened a heavy but hurried and ill-aimed rifle and MG fire, which did not cause heavy casualties.[93]

The aroused defenders' wildly misdirected bursts, aimed far too high despite increased visibility from discharged flares, failed to halt the momentum of the Berkshire onslaught. One platoon of 'D' Company pressed on down the gentle gradient opposite Exert Farm and Exert Copse, while the left platoon of 'D' and two platoons of 'B' traversed the slight rise toward Southern Redoubt. Surprised *Vorfeldzone* outposts were immediately overrun, the recumbent occupants bayoneted. Sustaining the necessary impetus was one thing; maintaining proper direction was

---

92 German Verey light signal instructions were previously revealed in a II Corps intelligence report prepared by Major Nosworthy: 'A captured order of the 204th Division (LEKKERBOTERBEEK northward) dated 24/11/17 gives the following: Upon request being received for a barrage, it will be put down close in front of our own (i.e. German) line of posts, but white lights, with pearls being put up, the barrage will, at once, be put down in front of the main line of resistance. Green lights bursting into 2 stars only mean 'Lengthen Range' and NOT 'our own artillery falling short (Note: This signal appears to be in use along the whole of the [British] Second Army front.' See TNA: WO/157/287: 'II Corps Summary of Information, 29 November 1917', II Corps Intelligence File.

93 TNA: WO/95/1929: 'Appendix B', 5 December 1917, 2nd Royal Berkshire War Diary.

Lieutenant H.A.V. Wait 2nd Royal Berkshire Regiment KIA 2 December 1917. (Private collection)

to prove more difficult: "At this time" [1:58 a.m.], Stirling wrote, "it appeared that the Battalion on my left was easing off to its left and in consequence the left of B Company led by 2nd Lieutenant Upton bore off to maintain touch."[94] The opening of the British barrage beyond Vension Trench at 2:03 a.m. succeeded 'B' company's unfortunate divergence to maintain touch with 2nd Lincolnshire. The anticipated German defensive barrage erupted one minute later:

> The enemy's artillery barrage came down on the PASSCHENDAELE – VINDICTIVE crossroads road one minute after our guns opened fire, namely at zero plus 9. On the left our troops were well clear of the line of the enemy's barrage, but unfortunately on the right the support platoons of the attacking companies were caught in the barrage and suffered heavy casualties.[95]
>
> At 2:04 a.m. the enemy's barrage came down along the the VINDICTIVE CROSSROADS – PASSCHENDAELE road very heavily. It also caught the reserve and support platoons of B Company who suffered heavy casualties. Company HQ of this Company was also blown up at this point and 2nd Lieutenant Giddings knocked over and dazed.[96]

---

94 Ibid.
95 TNA: WO/95/1677: 'Narrative of Operations Carried Out by the 8th Division on 1st/2nd December 1917', 13 December 1917, 8th Division War Diary.
96 TNA: WO/95/1929: 'Appendix B', 5 December 1917, 2nd Royal Berkshire War Diary. 2nd Lieutenant Giddings' subsequent death appears to have gone unobserved. Lieutenant S.H. Troup and 2nd Lieutenant H.A.V. Wait are recorded as the remaining officer fatalities sustained by 2nd Royal Berkshire during the attack. 2nd Lieutenants W.A. Grove, H.E.E. Osborne and C.S. Morris were wounded. 21-year-old 2nd Lieutenant Frank Giddings MM, 25-year-old Lieutenant Stewart Houghton Troup and 19-year-old 2nd Lieutenant Herbert Alfred Vincent Wait have no known grave and are commemorated on the Tyne Cot Memorial to the Missing.

Looking south from site of Southern Redoubt toward Exert Farm and Passchendaele church. (Rob Thompson)

Pre-war boxing photograph of Private A. Sturgess. (Trustees of the Rifles Wardrobe Museum Trust)

Deprived of reinforcements from the shattered reserve and support platoons and lacking ready assistance from Upton's deviating platoon, 'B' Company's No. 5 Platoon stormed Southern Redoubt with a platoon from 'D' Company.[97] "A large number of the enemy advanced out of the Southern Redoubt to meet the attack of this battalion. Severe hand to hand fighting ensued, but the Berkshires killed them all with the bayonet…" The remaining platoon of 'D' "dug themselves in on a line extending to the south-east edge" of the redoubt. On the right 'C' Company (CO Captain Flint), forming a defensive flank opposite the marshy depression in the vicinity of Exert Farm,[98] "had succeeded in their task without much difficulty; though in getting into touch with 'D' company their left platoon under 2nd Lieutenant Smith had some brisk fighting and took 30 prisoners, including an officer and a machine-gun."[99]

8536 Sergeant A. Sturgess DCM, a reliable and celebrated NCO, led his No. 5 Platoon into the shallow excavations comprising Southern Redoubt.[100] The forlorn party, joined by the left platoon of 'D' Company, engaged the defenders with bomb and bayonet along dark, narrow confines of rudimentary trenches. Drifting barrage smoke further obscured the dim panoramic view – a low-lying Flemish hinterland of leafless spinneys, snow-coated fields, Gothic church steeples and tiled rooftops north of elevated Moorslede – from the rectangular reverse slope earthwork during the hours before dawn. Retention of such corresponding high ground would place Oostnieuwkerke village, the billeting and supply dump hamlets of Vierkavenhoek, Zilverberg, Magermeirie, Kalve, Roodkruis, De Ruiter and dozens of outlying farms west of Roulers under direct observation from Passchendaele Ridge.[101] Resistance by *IR116* (*Oberstleutnant* von Westernhagen) and *IR117* (*Oberstleutnant* Klotz) of *25th*

---

97 6259 Cpl Arthur Chivers ('B' Company, 2nd Royal Berkshire) was subsequently awarded (*London Gazette* 4 March 1918) the DCM for 'conspicuous gallantry and devotion to duty in rushing forward by himself when the advance was held up by machine-gun fire, shooting the gunner and capturing the gun and five prisoners.'

98 Opposite Passchendaele, a swampy morass (*sumpf*) extended NNE and SE of Exert Farm (*Kolonnenhof*). See Ludwigsdorff, *Das Leibgarde Infanterie Regiment (1. Grossherzoglich Hessisches Nr. 115) im Weltkrieg 1914-1918*, Skizze 17.

99 See TNA: WO/95/1677: 'Narrative of Operations Carried Out by the 8th Division on 1st/ 2nd December 1917', 13 December 1917, 8th Division War Diary, Boraston & Bax, *The Eighth Division*, p. 165 and Loraine Petre, *The Royal Berkshire Regiment Vol. 2*, p. 97. 2nd Lieutenant and former CQMS F.J. Smith was awarded the MC for this action.

100 Sergeant Albert Sturgess, a pre-war India service Regular, marksman and prominent Battalion boxer, was subsequently awarded a Bar to the DCM 'for conspicuous gallantry and devotion to duty in leading his platoon forward although wounded [arm and left side], capturing a [Southern] redoubt by a bayonet charge and himself killing many of the enemy. The success of this part of the attack in which the enemy suffered heavy casualties was due to him.' See Cull, *The Second Battalion Royal Berkshire Regiment in World War One*, pp. 134-35.

101 See TNA: WO/297/4903: 'Artillery Target Map: Enemy Rear Line Organisation Billets and Dumps 14 October 1917', Sheet name and no: Oostnieuwkerke Edition No: 1 Production: FS Co (1291).

A Moonlight Massacre   213

Panorama looking SE from site of Southern Redoubt. (Rob Thompson)

Lance Corporal T.H. Cooper 2nd Lincolnshire Regiment KIA 2 December 1917. (Don Roach & Lyn Schulz)

Division, responsible for *Gruppe Ypern*'s northern sector since 26 November, was fierce; the Germans could not afford to lose the skyline.[102] A sustained breach at the boundary of *IR116* and *IR117*[103] was expanded by 'B' Company's stray platoon under 2nd Lieutenant Upton who, with 2nd Lieutenant Tremellan, led his men to seize the portion of Venison Trench (an objective of 2nd Lincolnshire) approximately 50 yards to the north of Southern Redoubt.[104]

Six companies of 2nd Lincolnshire and 2nd Rifle Brigade, deployed on the immediate left of 2nd Royal Berkshire, rushed forward at Zero with fixed bayonets to storm Venison Trench and Northern Redoubt. The three Lincolnshire assault companies, in position at the battalion jumping-off line since 12:20 a.m., had not yet cleared their line of forward posts when, having been observed, four light machine-guns opened fire on exposed skirmish waves and trailing worm columns at 1:58 a.m.: "The advance continued, although all the officers of assaulting companies became casualties before our own outpost line was reached…"[105] Survivors pressed on as the astonished *Vorfeldzone* garrison abandoned their shell hole outposts and fled towards the main line of resistance at Venison Trench. Momentum was lost when the advance inexplicably stopped just 30 yards short of the objective and 2nd Lincolnshire dug in. The subsequent battalion after-action report related varied motivations for the halt:

> On investigation some men state that they were under the impression they had gained the objective – others that they were forced to dig in by hostile M.G. fire.

102 The *25th Hessian Großherzoglichen Division* (commanded by *General-Major* von Dresler und Scharfenstein), a pre-war formation attached to *XVIII Armeekorps*, entrained for Flanders from the St Quentin sector in mid-September. Its 1917 intelligence 'value estimate' stated: 'The XVIII Army Corps has been considered one of the best corps in the German Army. In September 1917 the morale of the 25th Division appeared good. At this time, as the division had not taken part in any important actions since September 1916, it was difficult to form a judgement as to the combat value of this organisation. Its local operation on the salient of Moulin des Tous Vents (July 18, 1917) was carried out energetically.' See Intelligence Section of the General Staff American Expeditionary Forces, *Histories of Two Hundred and Fifty-One Divisions of the German Army Which Participated in the War 1914-1918* (London: London Stamp Exchange, 1989 reprint of 1920 edition), p. 353 and Appendix II for infantry orders of battle.
103 See Appendix XVI Part B (para. 14) and Part C (paras. 10 and 11).
104 TNA: WO/95/1929: 'Appendix B', 5 December 1917, 2nd Royal Berkshire War Diary, Loraine Petre, *The Royal Berkshire Regiment Vol. 2*, p. 97 and Cull, *The Second Battalion Royal Berkshire Regiment in World War One*, p. 87. The dispositions of *25th Division's* regiments were, from right to left, roughly: *IR117:* Venison Trench to Southern Redoubt; *IR116*: Southern Redoubt (inclusive) to *Kolonnenhof* (Exert Farm); *IR115*: *Kolonnenhof* (exclusive) to the Ypres-Roulers railway. See Hartmann, *Das Infanterie Regiment Grossherzog von Sachsen (5. Thüringisches) Nr. 94 im Weltkrieg, Skizze 32* and Ludwigsdorff, *Das Leibgarde Infanterie Regiment (1. Grossherzoglich Hessisches Nr. 115) im Weltkrieg 1914-1918, Skizze 17.*
105 TNA: WO/95/1730: 'Report on Action of Battn from 2:30 p.m. 1.12.17 – M.N. 2/3 .12. 17', 6 December 1917, 2nd Lincolnshire War Diary.

The impression that the advanced line had reached their objective was probably caused by the fact that the advance had overcome enemy shell hole posts driving back the enemy + these shell hole posts were mistaken for the enemy trench. All men were informed in training that in the event of all officers becoming casualties, they must know where to stop by capturing the first <u>continuous</u> enemy trench they came to + then digging in about 50 yards in front of it or as close up to our barrage as they could get.[106]

The Lincolnshire's attack had already stalled when the British barrage started. Described in the aforementioned report as "efficient"; charting its progress proved difficult: "Owing to the advance being held up by M.G. fire from M.G.s on our side of the barrage line it is not possible to determine whether the pace of the barrage was suitable." Friendly fire also caused a certain amount of difficulty: "One or two howitzers were repeatedly firing short in S + T zones as far back as VINDICTIVE CROSSROADS."[107]

2nd Rifle Brigade faced an uncertain situation during the few remaining hours prior to Zero. The enemy held Teall Cottage in strength and Lieutenant-Colonel Brand had been seriously wounded. Lieutenant Nettleton (IO detached for liaison duty with 2nd KOYLI) turned back just prior to Zero:

> I went off at once to our own battalion HQ to report this [loss of Teall Cottage] bad news, only to find that they had some more of their own. Roger Brand, our CO, had been wounded and Anderson, the Adjutant, had just got back to HQ after seeing him carried off. Normally, when the CO becomes a casualty, the next senior officer of the battalion takes charge. But in this show, because of the difficulty of getting hold of any officer from the companies, it had been specifically laid down that the chain of command would go down the people normally at battalion HQ i.e., first to Anderson, then to me and then the Regimental Sergeant Major.
>
> We were still pondering this news about Teall Cottage when the Brigade Major came in and gave us his advice. I was struck by the way he kept on insisting that it was only advice that he was giving. Although Anderson was only a Lieutenant and the Brigade Major [Captain W.F. Somervail] was, besides being a Major [sic],[108] also, in effect, the GSO 1 of the Brigade and the direct representative of the Brigadier, he kept on saying, "Now, I am not giving you orders. You are in command of the battalion. I am only saying that, if I were in

---

106 Ibid.
107 Ibid.
108 Lieutenant A/Captain William Fulton Somervail MC (2nd Cameronians) functioned as brigade major during the operation. He was killed near Joncourt in October 1918. See IWM: 02(41).221[British Expeditionary Force]/3-2, 'Composition of the British Army Headquarters 1914-1918.'

Captain W.F. Somervail. (University of Edinburgh, *University of Edinburgh Roll of Honour 1914-1919* (London: Oliver & Boyd, 1921))

your position, I would try and echelon your left companies behind Teall Cottage etc., etc., but this is not an order." But of course Anderson was very glad of his advice and immediately went out to try and put it into effect, while the Brigade Major went back to Brigade HQ to report what had happened. For myself, I sat on in the pillbox and prayed that Anderson would not be hit, because I definitely did not want to take over command of the battalion in these circumstances.[109]

The original intent, according to Heneker's after-action report, was to run the forming-up tape to Teall Cottage. This no longer being possible, 2nd Rifle Brigade were "compelled to at once throw back a defensive flank" on a front of 150 yards "so as to keep touch with the 32nd Division operating on our [8th Division] left, Teal Cottage being in the hands of the enemy."[110] Nettleton remained under cover at 2nd Rifle Brigade's pillbox HQ throughout the battalion adjutant's absence; it was a very crowded affair:

---

109 Nettleton, *The Anger of the Guns*, pp. 116-17. Nettleton's counterpart, 2nd Lieutenant H.L. Brigham (detached for liaison duty with 2nd Rifle Brigade) was wounded one half-hour before Zero. A Sergeant Davies took his place. See Bond, *The King's Own Yorkshire Light Infantry in the Great War Vol.3*, p. 910.
110 TNA: WO/95/1677: 'Narrative of Operations Carried Out by the 8th Division on 1st/2nd December 1917', 13 December 1917, 8th Division War Diary. A 2nd Rifle Brigade company commander, Captain C.E. Pegram, was subsequently awarded an MC for establishing the defensive flank. See *Supplement to the London Gazette*, 5 July 1918, p. 7919.

The pillbox was about the size of a smallish kitchen, though of course with a very much lower ceiling; you couldn't stand upright in it. This small space had to contain two battalion HQ (2nd Rifle Brigade and 2nd Lincolns) and later a third, as the CO [Major T.H. Ivey][111] of the [1st Royal] Irish Rifles, which were in reserve, came forward from his reserve position and remained with us. Only the officers of the three battalion HQ and some signallers could be accommodated inside the pillbox and even then it was congested. The rest of the personnel had to find what cover they could in the trench outside. The runners of the Royal Irish Rifles, who always were an undisciplined mob, got at the rum ration and made themselves uproariously drunk and quite useless.[112] When their CO wanted to send messages to his companies, he had to borrow runners from us.[113]

Anderson returned just before zero hour "having done what he could to adjust our line, which wasn't very much…"[114] What had been accomplished was a provisional arrangement for the left flank to be thrown back from "the point where the tapes ended on the left (i.e. about 250 yards from the MOSSELMARKT – WHISK FARM road) to join hands with 32nd Division." Anderson and Nettleton passed the remaining minutes prior to Zero glancing at their watches and waiting. "Promptly at 1:55 a.m. we heard the Boche machine-guns open up and knew that the attack had started."[115]

The subsequent advance of 2nd Rifle Brigade (attacking NE from the gap at the top of the X that comprised Vindictive Crossroads) was almost over before it started, as deadly machine-gun fire from enemy outposts, Northern Redoubt and Teall Cottage wreaked havoc on stumbling skirmish lines and worm columns.[116] Anderson and Nettleton immediately understood what the fearful din signified:

111 A/Major Thomas Henry Ivey. Sergeant Coldstream Guards August-November 1914; Despatches 9 December 1914; Gazetted 2nd Lieutenant RIR October 1914; Lieutenant March 1915; Captain January 1917; joined 1st RIR April; 2/ic and A/Major June; Temp. CO 1-9 August and from 9 October.
112 Two riflemen (A. Hooton and W. Lee) were later sentenced to 56 days Field Punishment No. 1 after being found guilty of 'drunkenness' by a field general court martial. See Appendix V: Courts Martial and Discipline in Taylor, *The 1st Royal Irish Rifles in the Great War*, p. 195.
113 Nettleton, *The Anger of the Guns*, p. 117.
114 Ibid., p. 117.
115 TNA: WO/95/1731: 'Report of the part played by the 2nd Battn. The Rifle Brigade in the Operations at Passchendaele', 6 December 1917, 2nd Rifle Brigade War Diary and Nettleton, *The Anger of the Guns*, pp. 117-18.
116 Northern Redoubt and Teall Cottage were defended by the *IR94* (*38th Division*). The division's *Vorfeldzone* garrison was, unlike that of the neighbouring *25th Division*, alert and expectant. Interrogators of a captive taken near Void Farm noted: 'Prisoner captured in advanced post states that our men were seen to advance, but retired when they opened fire with their rifles and machine-guns. Prisoner imagined it was a patrol and did not realise that they [British] were attacking until our barrage opened. He calculated that this fell

218   A Moonlight Massacre

Northern Redoubt from the air summer 1917. (Memorial Museum Passchendaele 1917)

And within a very few minutes after that we knew that it had failed. When our barrage came down at Zero plus 8, it was a magnificent one – I think the most tremendous I ever heard. But long before that, the show was over. The Boche machine-guns had eight minutes in which to play unhindered on our troops advancing in bright moonlight and had simply wiped them out. We had advanced about 100 yards and lost ten officers out of twelve in those few minutes and there was nothing to be done except pick up the pieces.[117]

about 400 metres behind his post. He ran back in accordance with orders to the main line where he was captured.' See Hartmann, *Das Infanterie Regiment Grossherzog von Sachsen (5. Thüringisches) Nr. 94 im Weltkrieg*, Skizze 32 for boundaries between *IR94* and *IR117* and TNA: WO/157/288: 'Notes on Examination of Prisoners of 5th Coy., 95th I.R. (38th Div.) captured south of VOID FARM on the morning of 2nd December, II Corps Summary of Information', 2 December 1917, II Corps Intelligence File.

117 Nettleton, *The Anger of the Guns*, p. 118. Officer casualties for 2nd Rifle Brigade were as follows: Killed: Captain E.F. Ratliff MC, 2nd Lieutenants W. Morrison and J. Brooker; Wounded: 2nd Lieutenants J.B. MacGeorge, D.P. Jones, L.M. King-Harman, D.F.W. Baden-Powell, H.F. Cranswick, W. Bridgeman. See TNA: WO/95/1731: 2nd Rifle Brigade War Diary. Captain Edward Francis Ratliff MC (age unknown), 26-year-old 2nd Lieutenant William Morrison and 26-year-old 2nd Lieutenant James Brooker have no known grave and are commemorated on the Tyne Cot Memorial to the Missing.

Panorama looking west from site of Northern Redoubt. (Rob Thompson)

Desperate men sought shelter in any available shell hole or former German practice trench sections SW of the redoubt, while others flung themselves down and dug frantically to escape the murderous stream of bullets.[118] Additional defensive fire support was provided by a plunging indirect machine-gun barrage originating, approximately 500 yards beyond the *Hauptwiderstandslinie*, from the line Wrangle Farm – Wrath Farm. Consolidation of the meagre bit of ground gained – "about 100 yards in advance of their original line" – proceeded, as posts of 3 to 6 men each were formed in shell holes under the almost continuous hail of bullets.[119] Anderson later recalled that the supporting artillery barrage as "efficient" with few shorts and "suitable" pace. "Visibility in the moonlight", he also observed, "was up to 500 yards. The moon was behind us. It seems obvious that the enemy observed our forming up, but instead of interfering with it, pushed forward posts and machine-guns in front of our barrage line. Consequently, when our barrage commenced the machine-gun fire commenced rather than lessened."[120] The relevant German regimental history appears to partially

---

118 Inexplicably jumping-off seven minutes before Zero, part of the left company of 2nd Rifle Brigade appears to have strayed across the front of the neighbouring 2nd KOYLI. See below.
119 TNA: WO/95/1731: 'Report of the part played by the 2nd Battn. The Rifle Brigade in the Operations at Passchendaele', 6 December 1917, 2nd Rifle Brigade War Diary and Boraston & Bax, *The Eighth Division*, p. 166
120 TNA: WO/95/1731: 'Report of the part played by the 2nd Battn. The Rifle Brigade in the Operations at Passchendaele', 6 December 1917, 2nd Rifle Brigade War Diary.

confirm Anderson's speculation: "The English were very strong, attacking *IR 94* with three battalions.¹²¹ The men in the outpost line opened strong fire with rifles and machine-guns."¹²²

Fortifying small lodgments in and near Southern Redoubt or forced to seek cover opposite the enemy's main defensive position, 25 Brigade's assault had almost completely broken down minutes after Zero: "The enemy were holding TEAL COTTAGE, the NORTHERN and SOUTHERN REDOUBTS and the [VENISON] trench connecting them in considerable strength. Isolated groups of men had also been pushed well out in front. These were occupying shell hole positions."¹²³ Stalled elements of 2nd Lincolnshire and 2nd Rifle Brigade persevered with the arduous task of improving – by sustained digging and scraping – upon any available cover under ferocious hostile machine-gun fire. Anderson and Nettleton did what they could in the aftermath of the shambles:

> After the noise had died down, we went out to find out what we could. Men had grouped themselves in shell holes to get what shelter they could, but there was no organisation left and all we could do was to get the groups in touch with each other and pull some back and push others forward to make some sort of coherent line and evacuate as many wounded as we could find. Even this activity had to stop when dawn came, as one could not move about in daylight up at front.¹²⁴

A diversionary barrage, as per Heneker's request, by Major-General Pinney's 33rd Division (responsible for the right sub-sector of VIII Corps) was discharged to cover 8th Division's right flank. Brigadier-General A.W.F. Baird's 100 Brigade held the line as divisional artillery and machine-gun batteries opened up simultaneously with the main bombardment at Zero + 8.¹²⁵ Retaliation amounted to a "few shells in the vicinity of Brigade HQ."¹²⁶ On the left, German batteries commenced their dreaded protective barrage at Zero + 9 by targeting the Vindictive Crossroads – Passchendaele Road. This fire was, as previously anticipated, afterwards shortened to Venison Trench and the redoubts. Meanwhile, two platoons of 2nd Royal Berkshire fought desperately to maintain their hold on Southern Redoubt.¹²⁷

---

121 2nd Rifle Brigade, 2nd KOYLI and elements of 16th HLI. See below.
122 Hartmann, *Das Infanterie Regiment Grossherzog von Sachsen (5. Thüringisches) No. 94* im *Weltkrieg*, p. 237.
123 TNA: WO/95/1677: 'Narrative of Operations Carried Out by the 8th Division on 1st/2nd December 1917', 13 December 1917, 8th Division War Diary.
124 Nettleton, *The Anger of the Guns*, p. 118.
125 Plans to make use of dummy decoy figures, if even contemplated, were not mentioned in orders issued on 1 December. See Appendix IX.
126 TNA: WO/95/2429: 100 Brigade War Diary.
127 BL: 48359: 'Report of Operations Carried Out by the VIII Army Corps on the Morning of 2nd December 1917, Official War Diaries with Appendices and Addenda, VIII Army Corps, Passchendaele Front, November 1917-April 1918', Vol. V, Hunter-Weston Papers.

3.4 97 Brigade

Five assault battalions, companies organised into two distinct frontages, of 97 Brigade jumped-off with the final red line objective as their goal: 2nd KOYLI and 15th LF (far right and left battalions) attacked on a "three company frontage with one company in support moving in rear of No. 2 Company"; 16th HLI, 11th Border Regiment and 17th HLI (centre battalions) attacked on a two-company frontage "with Nos. 3 and 4 companies in rear of Nos. 1 and 2 companies." Companies were assembled on the taped line in varied (snake formation and line of sections) platoon frontages forming four waves. Anticipated frontages for each battalion on reaching the final objective were, from right to left: 2nd KOYLI (520 yards), 16th HLI (450 yards), 11th Border (400 yards), 17th HLI (500 yards) and 15th LF (700 yards). All units were expected be on the final objective by Zero + 32 (2:27 a.m.) [128]

Available intelligence concerning anticipated German tactics and probable counter-attack assembly areas in the sector Vat Cottages – Hill 52 was explained in concise terms prior to the assault:

> Enemy Tactics. Enemy makes use of immediate counter-attack, which generally speaking comes from N and NE.
>
> Assembly Places. Probably in low ground and woods on the E[ast] side of the ridge i.e. from NNE and E. He can see our advanced positions.

Enemy machine-guns, it was also noted, were "generally echeloned according to the field of fire in shell holes. The light MGs [*Maschinen-Gewehr 08/15*] are usually all forward."[129] All dry shell holes are potential MG emplacements. Some of the heavy MGs are possible [sic] fired from elephant dugouts."[130] Barbed wire obstacles were almost unknown on this part of the front, but a formidable belt just beyond the final objective was believed to exist "parallel to and west of the main street of WESTROOSEBEKE, running north and south and there is possibly a belt of wire running from NW to SE in front of WESTROOSEBEKE on high ground."

---

128 TNA: WO/95/2400: '97 Brigade Operation Order No. 178', 27 November 1917, 97 Brigade War Diary and IWM 4723: 'Summary of the attack of the 97th Inf. Bde. with 2 Battalions of the 96th Inf. Bde. on December 2 [1917]', Brigadier-General T.S. Lambert Papers (Box 80/10/2).

129 A prisoner of *IR96*, captured near Houthulst Forest on 25 November, informed his captors that 'since they [*38th Division*] left the Monchy front, the number of M.G's per battalion has been raised from 12 to 18. 6 of these guns were with each platoon of the M.G. Coy. in the main line of resistance, and each infantry company had three of the light pattern guns [08/15], which were about 60/70 m[etres] further forward in shell holes.' See TNA: WO/157/120: 'Annexe to Second Army Summary Dated 26th November 1917: Information Obtained from Prisoners', Second Army Intelligence Files.

130 'Elephant Dugouts': Splinter-proof shelters constructed from corrugated iron.

Another belt was definitely discerned "running from NW to SE across V.12. central (WESTROOSEBEKE)." The intelligence report concluded with the optimistic observation that 'Experience on this front show that there is nothing to be feared from the enemy so long as he is resolutely tackled.'[131]

Aligned along the jumping-off tape since 1:20 a.m., 2nd KOYLI promptly advanced at 1:55 a.m. Its final objective extended for 520 yards from NW of Northern Redoubt to just opposite the large, water-filled depression just west of the Passchendaele – Westroosebeke road.[132] From right to left, 'A', 'C' and 'D' companies moved forward in good order to secure "all localities and strongpoints occupied by the enemy between our assembly positions and the final objective." The "denial of Hill 52 to the enemy", Brigade orders emphasised, was "essential to the success of the operations." 'B' Company, following immediately behind 'C', was to be prepared for two likely tactical contingencies: "Support any of the leading companies should it become necessary to do so to enable these companies to reach their final objectives" or "Give assistance to the left [2nd Rifle Brigade] battalion of the [25] Brigade on our right in the event of its being held up by forming a defensive flank on the east"; 'B' Company, should neither of these eventualities occur, was to consolidate captured ground behind 'C' Company.[133]

Captain J.H. Howard (Adjutant 2nd KOYLI) was responsible for compiling an account of the operation for the Battalion war diary. His efforts were, unlike the majority of war diaries consulted, remarkably forensic in methodology and scope. "The subsequent action of the battalion", Howard explained, "is best described in narrative form by companies, the descriptions being those given by the surviving officers and non-commissioned officers. The essence of the attack", he added, "was the element of surprise. The night was very bright and moonlight [sic] and there is no doubt that all movement could be seen at a short distance."[134] 2nd KOYLI's advance was almost immediately followed by "very heavy machine-gun fire, owing to which the casualties, particularly among officers and NCOs, were very heavy." Intense enfilade fire was also experienced from the direction of Venison Trench, Teall Cottage and Volt

---

131 TNA: WO/95/2400: 'Notes to Accompany Special Intelligence Maps of the Area V.15. – V.30' November 1917, 97 Brigade War Diary. Westroosebeke, the report added, 'contains about 40 cellars, a strongly built church and two breweries. There is good visibility from V.12.a.3.6 [NE of Westroosebeke] The soil is said to be mostly sandy and dry.'

132 The road acted as a dam on the east side of this depression. See p. 184, fn. 26 above for part a of 32nd Division intelligence report: 'Notes to Accompany Special Intelligence Maps of the Area V.15 to V.30' November 1917.

133 TNA: WO/95/2400: '97 Brigade Operation Order No. 178', 27 November 1917, 97 Brigade War Diary. Lieutenant-Colonel Scully (CO 16th NF) subsequently wrote: 'I am of the opinion that the tape laid by the 2nd KOYLI was run along our frontline so that at least half of the Battalion were formed up facing NE instead of N[orth].' See IWM 4723: '32nd Div. No.G.S.1499/3/33', 5 December 1917, Brigadier-General T.S. Lambert Papers (Box 80/10/2).

134 TNA: WO/95/2402: 2nd KOYLI War Diary.

Farm. Wayward elements of flanking (2nd Rifle Brigade and 16th HLI) battalions "lost direction and, crossing our [2nd KOYLI] front, caused much confusion."[135] 2nd Lieutenant H.J. Knight (CO 'A' Company), all hope of obtaining surprise gone, led his four platoons forward in the face of fierce enemy resistance:

> This ['A'] company was on the right of the battalion and left the tape in good order at Zero. 2nd Lieutenant H.L. Brigham was wounded half an hour before Zero. He was the right platoon commander and detailed for keeping touch with the 2nd Bn. Rifle Brigade on our right. Sergeant Davies [acting liaison officer with 2nd Rifle Brigade] then took command of his platoon; before 'A' Company moved off they noticed the troops on our right were on the move 7 minutes before ZERO. The company at first, under the impression that these were hostile troops, nearly fired on them but discovered that that they were 2nd Bn. Rifle Brigade advancing in a NORTHERLY direction across our front.[136] The commander of 'A' Company (2nd Lieutenant H.J. Knight) endeavoured to redirect these troops but the officer he saw became a casualty almost immediately. This caused confusion amongst 'A' Company. The Rifle Brigade crossed the PASSCHENDAELE – WESTROOSEBEKE road at V.30.b.30.05 [vicinity of Teall Cottage]. The enemy opened fire less than a minute after ZERO; this fire appeared to come from TEALE COTT [sic], VENISON TRENCH and VOID FARM. 2nd Lieutenant C.P. Halliday MC, 2nd Lieutenant J.V. Webb (who joined the battalion late on the night of November 30) and the Company Sergeant Major became casualties in the first five minutes. The company progressed in spite of this until our artillery barrage came down, causing the men to hold up. At this time it is believed the 2nd Rifle Brigade lost heavily. No. 1 Platoon, which had been told off to capture TEALE COTTAGE, had lost its platoon commander and platoon sergeant and was reduced to 7 men. Sergeant Pannett from No. 3 Platoon was detailed to do this work; only the company commander and 1 NCO now remained to lead the company. The enemy artillery fire was very dispersed and not in the nature of a barrage. 'A' Company's commander found his men closing to the right and he tried to re-organise his men as best he could in spite of the fact that he had been severely shaken by a shell burst and was grazed above the eye by a bullet. The men at this point dug in groups with the 2nd Bn. Rifle Brigade…[137]

Remnants of 'A' Company laboured at converting shared shell hole positions, situated east of the Passchendaele – Westroosebeke road, into outposts. Lieutenant Knight

---

135 Ibid.
136 No reference to the early jumping-off and subsequent divergence appears in 2nd Rifle Brigade, 25 Brigade or 8th Division war diaries.
137 TNA: WO/95/2402: 2nd KOYLI War Diary.

subsequently stated that his company's failure to reach the objective "was entirely due to his being mixed up with 2nd Bn. Rifle Brigade and the fact that he had lost all his officers and NCOs in the early stage of the advance."[138] Owing to the troops on his right moving forward before ZERO the element of surprise was frustrated."[139]

In the centre, 'C' Company (CO Captain P. Lambert) sustained devastating leadership losses after proceeding just fifty yards:

> 'C' Company left the tape in perfect order. After going some 50 yards they came under heavy machine-gun fire and all the officers and senior NCOs became casualties.[140] The fire appeared to come from directly from our front and flanks. In spite of this they pushed on. Sergeant Hayward was then in command of the company and reports that he went a distance of 500 yards (?)[141] At one point he crossed the PASSCHENDAELE – WESTROOSEBEKE road about V.30.b.0.08 and found some derelict field guns and shelters, the occupants of which were killed. He then found himself in front of a line of trees, which were held by the enemy in force.

Hayward, the only company leader left standing, chose to remain under cover where he was with 7 men who accompanied him up to that point.[142]

On the left, 'D' Company (CO Captain H.R. Forde MC) was tasked with seizing Hill 52 before pushing on to the final objective opposite the water-filled depression west of the Passchendaele – Westroosebeke road. Heavy losses amongst company officers and NCOs left a Sergeant Horne the sole remaining company leader to interview:

> 'D' Company, No. 3 or left company … recounted by Sergeant Horne: 'D' Company left the tape in perfect order and immediately came under heavy machine-gun fire. He [Sergeant Horne] lost twelve men before going twenty yards. He was in touch with the 16th Highland L.I. on his left the right company of which advanced across his front and the two companies became

---

138 'A' Company officer casualties: 2nd Lieutenants H.J. Knight, H.L. Brigham, C.P. Halliday and J.V. Webb wounded.
139 TNA: WO/95/2402: 2nd KOYLI War Diary.
140 'C' Company officer casualties: Captain Lambert, 2nd Lieutenants T.S. Goode and C.S. Allen wounded, 2nd Lieutenant G.W. Asquith missing. 2nd Lieutenant Gordon William Asquith (age unknown) has no known grave and is commemorated on the Tyne Cot Memorial to the Missing.
141 Captain Howard also observed: 'It is extremely difficult to give a the exact position to which this NCO reached and dug himself in; I am of the opinion that he crossed the PASSCHENDAELE – WESTROOSEBEKE road and dug in between VENISON TRENCH and TEALE [sic] COTT[AGE].'
142 TNA: WO/95/2402: 2nd KOYLI War Diary and Bond, *The King's Own Yorkshire Light Infantry in the Great War Vol.3*, p. 911.

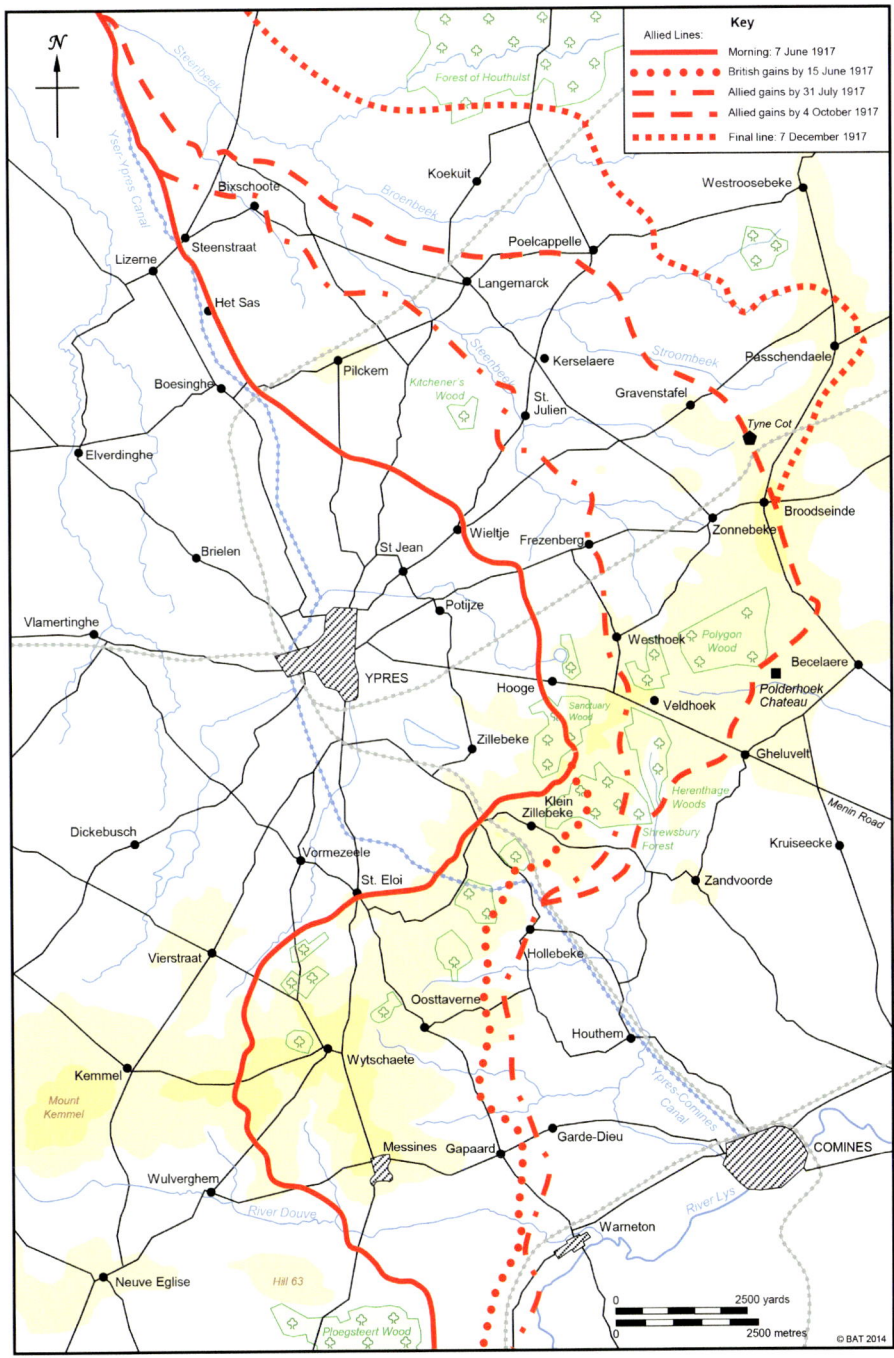

Third Battle of Ypres: Second & Fifth Army Operations June–December 1917

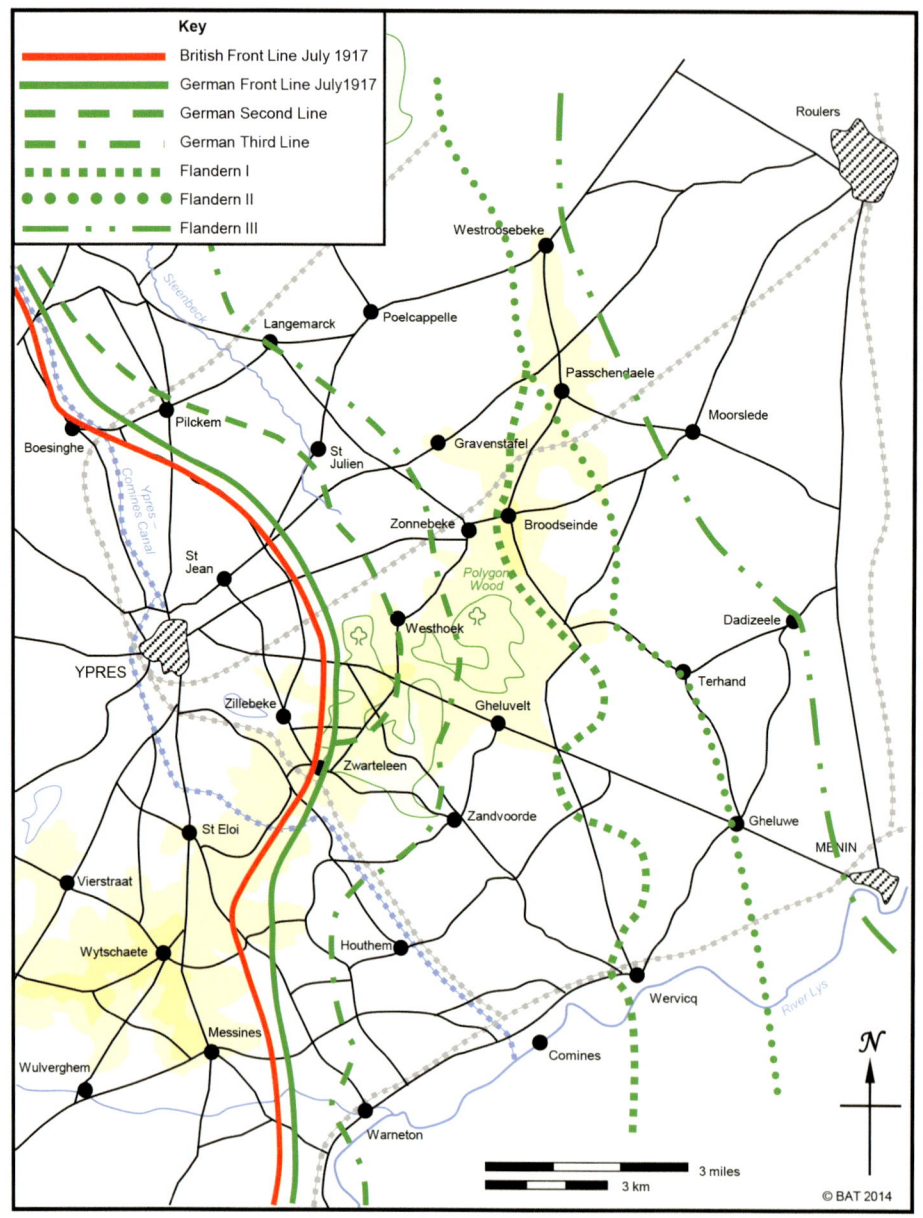

German Flanders Positions July 1917

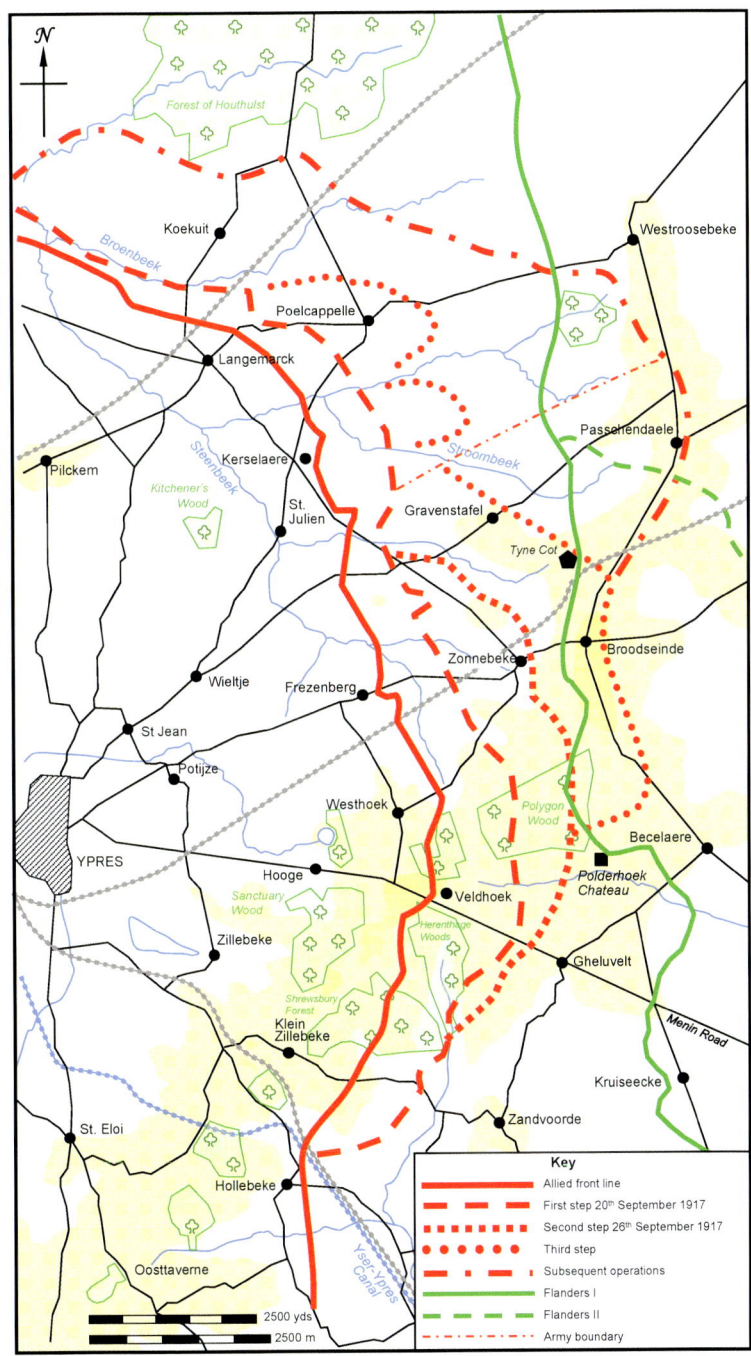

Forecast of the Stages of the Campaign GHQ 22 September 1917

II Corps Proposed Operations 9 November 1917

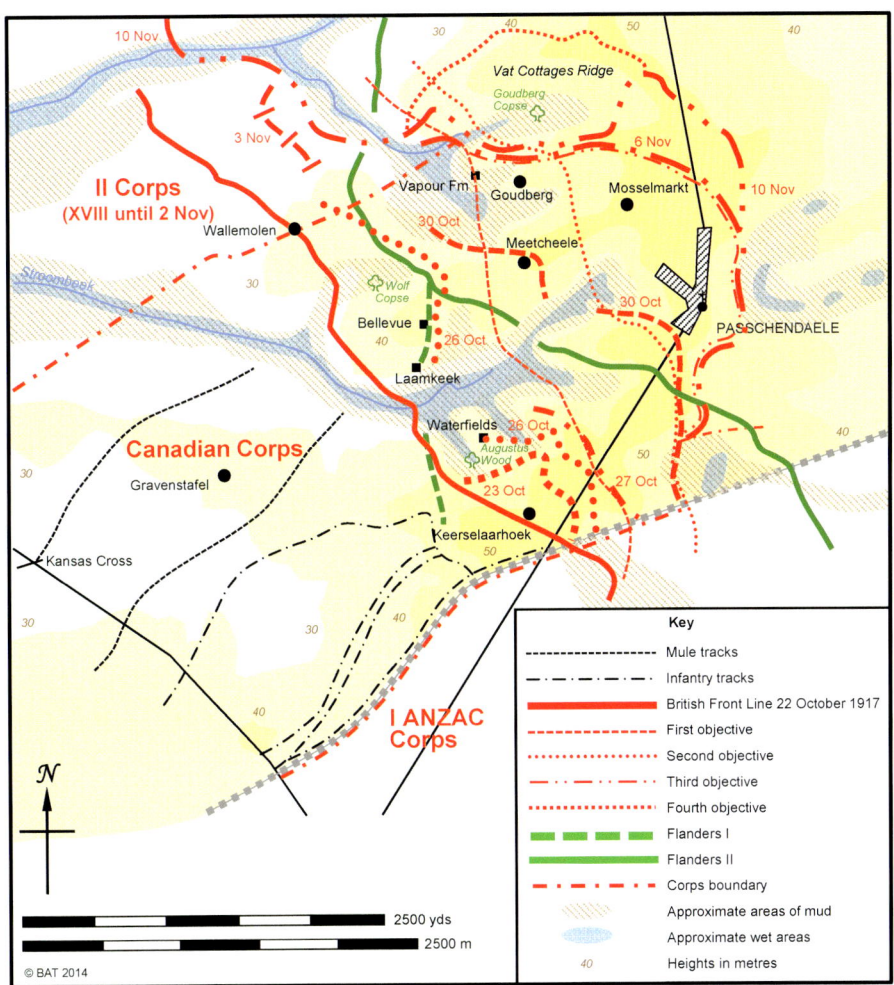

Second Battle of Passchendaele 26 October–10 November 1917

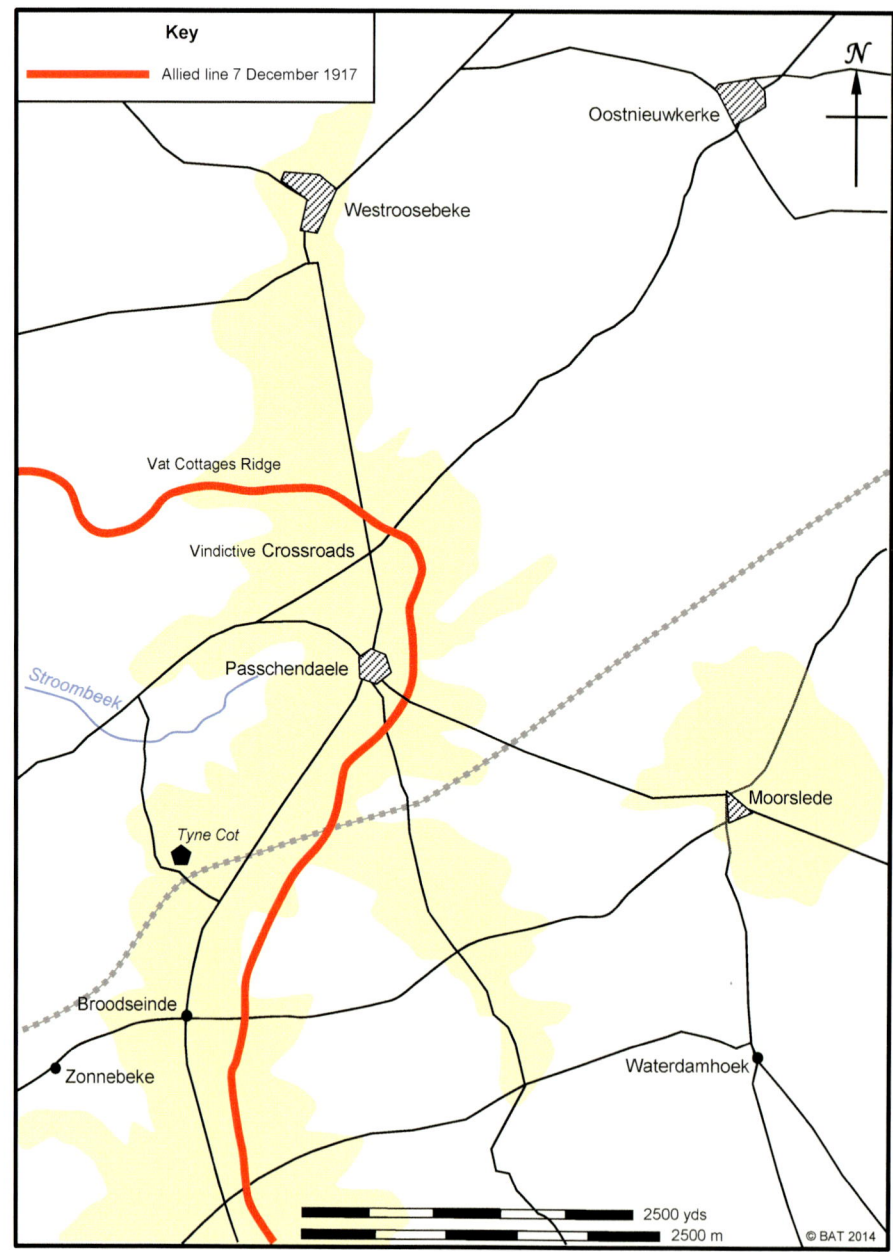

Passchendaele Salient

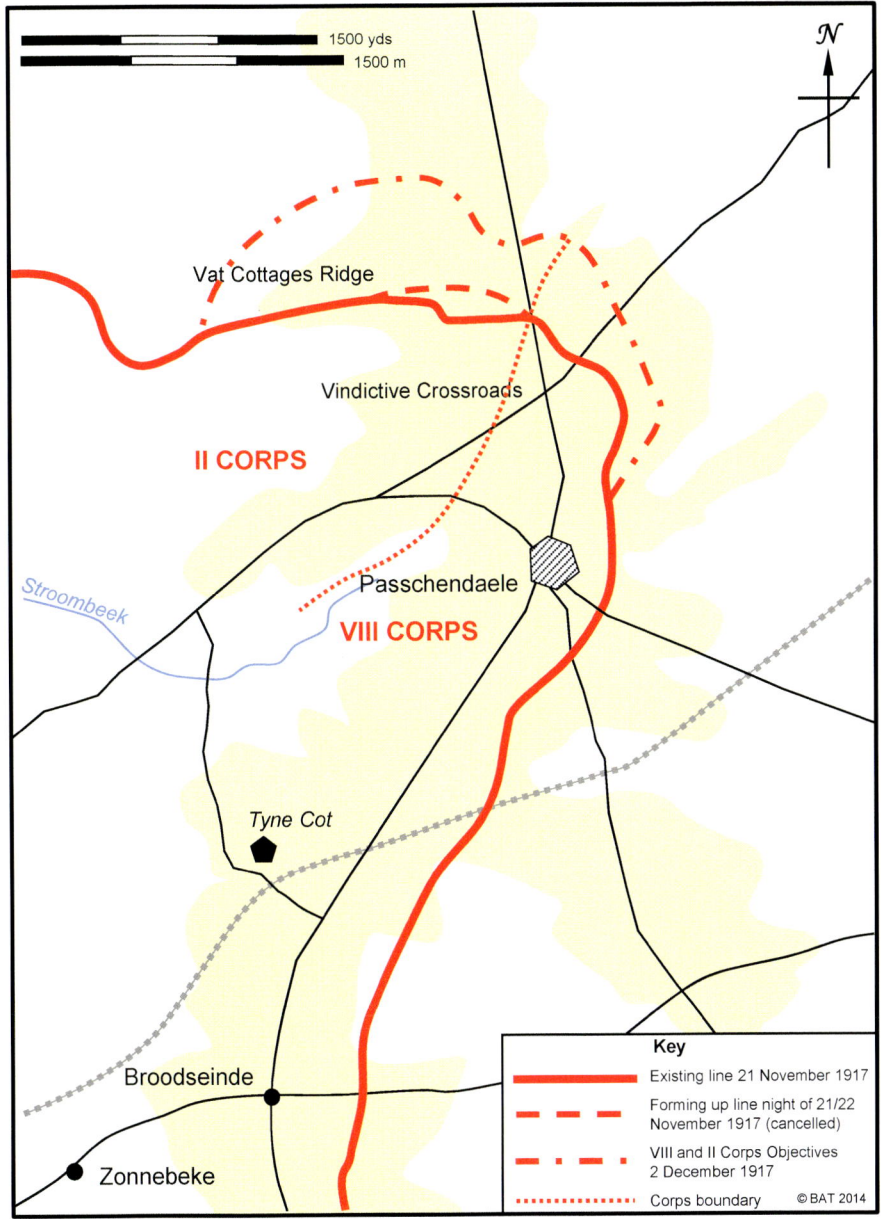

Second Army Objectives 2 December 1917

Lance Corporal of 'B' Company 2nd KOYLI as equipped on 2 December 1917.
(Giorgio Albertini)

Musketier of *Infanterie-Regiment Grossherzog von Sachsen (5. Thüringisches) Nr. 94* as equipped on 2 December 1917. (Giorgio Albertini)

2 December 1917: Illuminated by discharged Verey lights, advancing worm columns of 11th Border Regiment are detected by German defenders on Vat Cottages Ridge. (Peter Dennis)

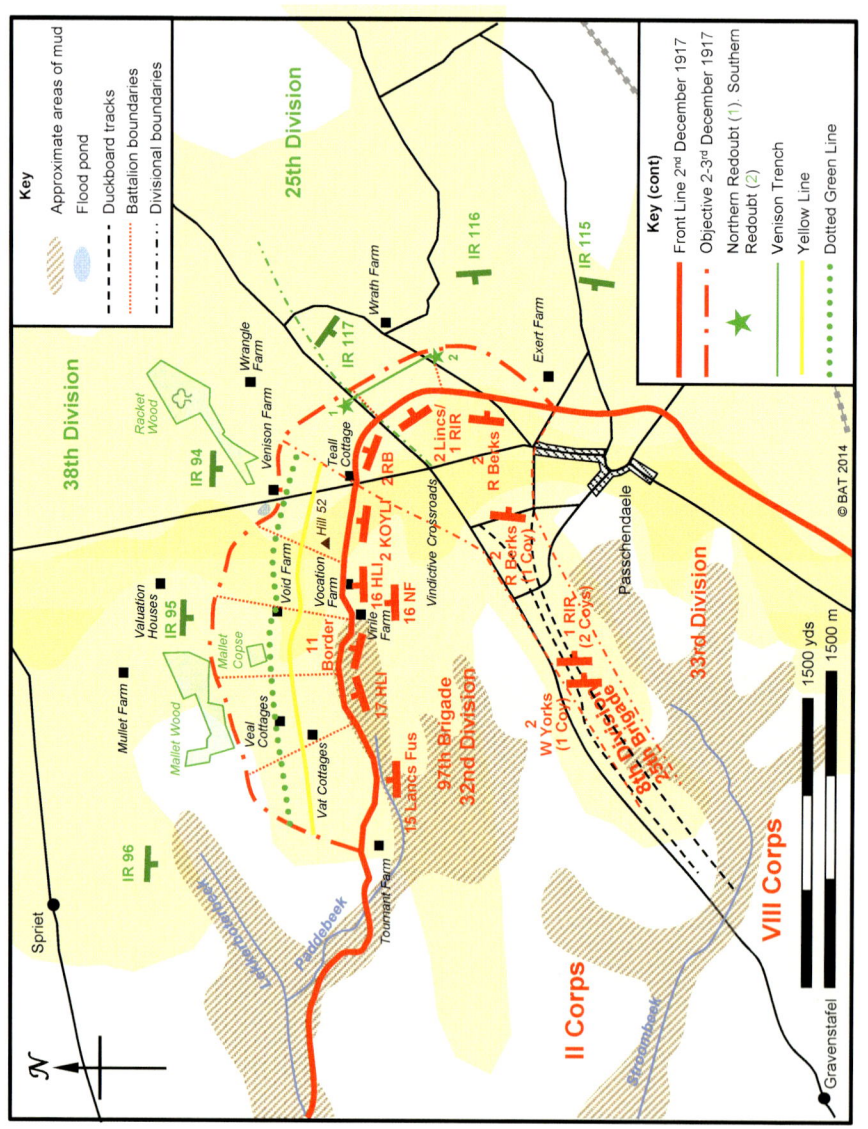

Positions prior to Zero 2 December 1917

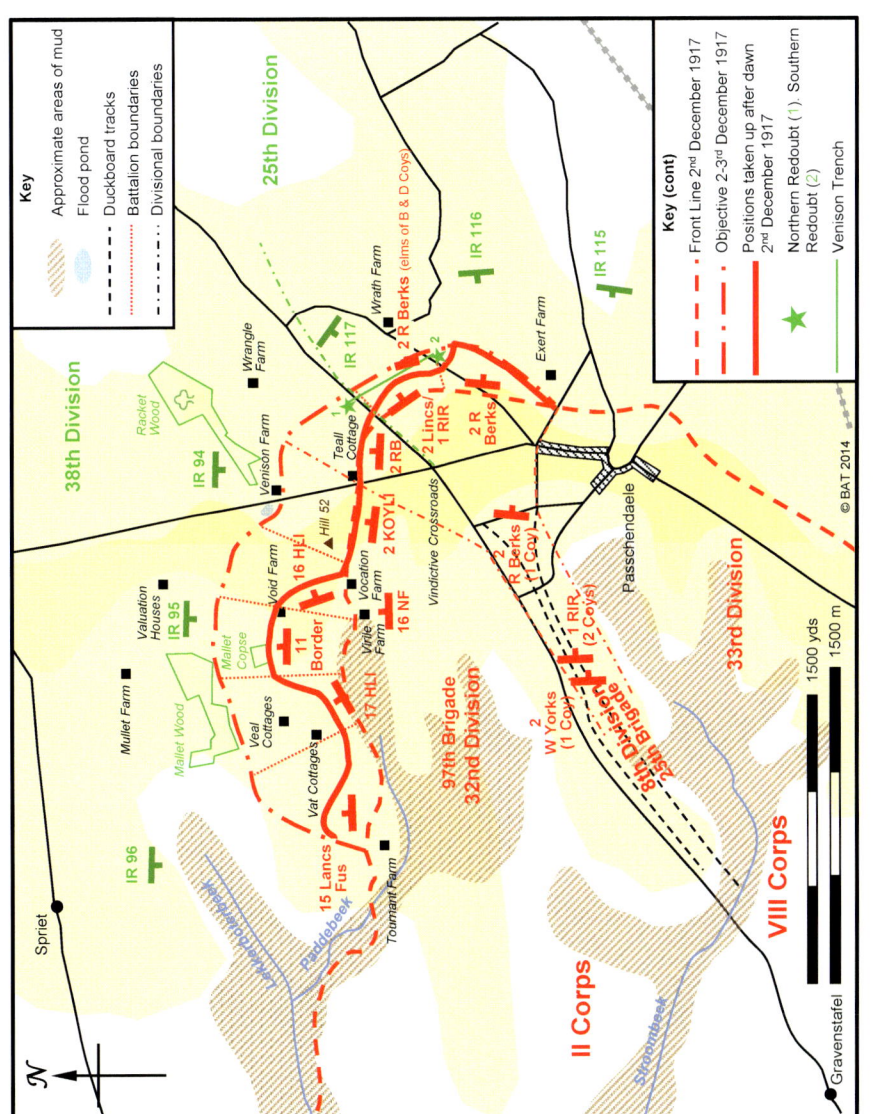

Positions taken up after dawn 2 December 1917

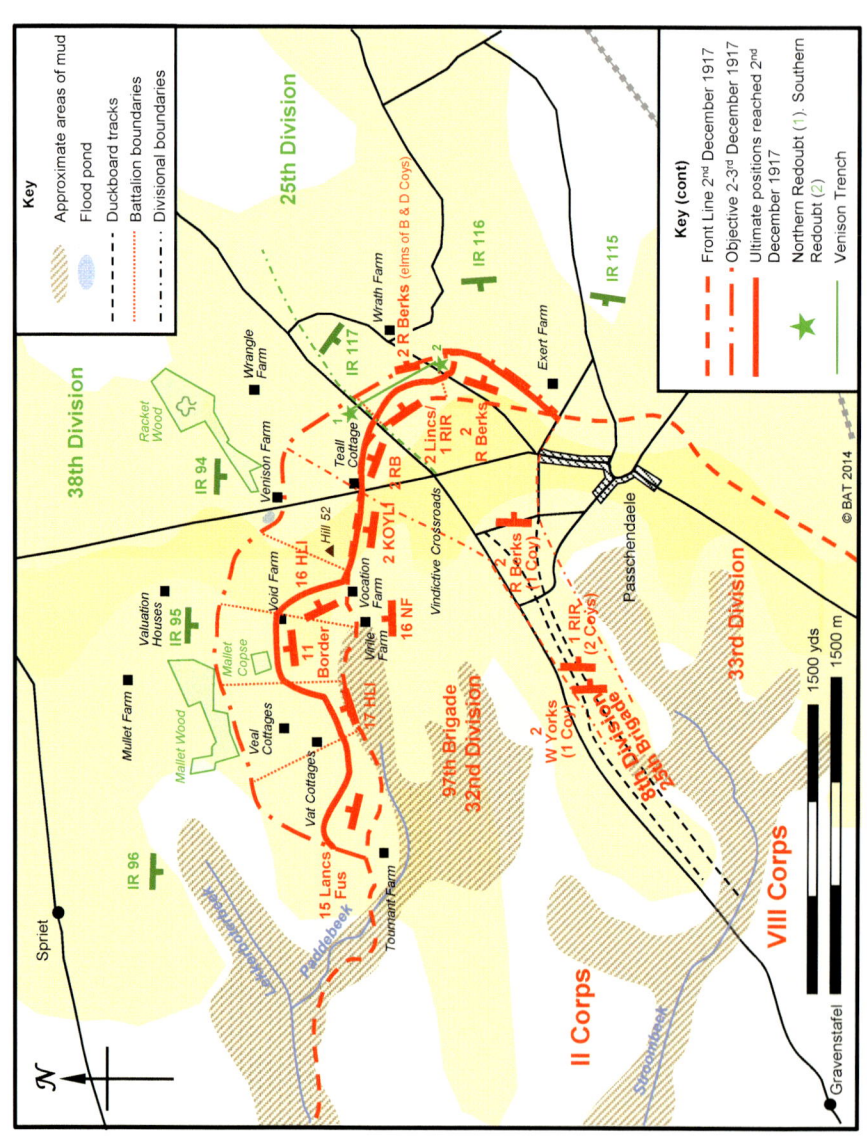

Ultimate positions reached 2 December 1917

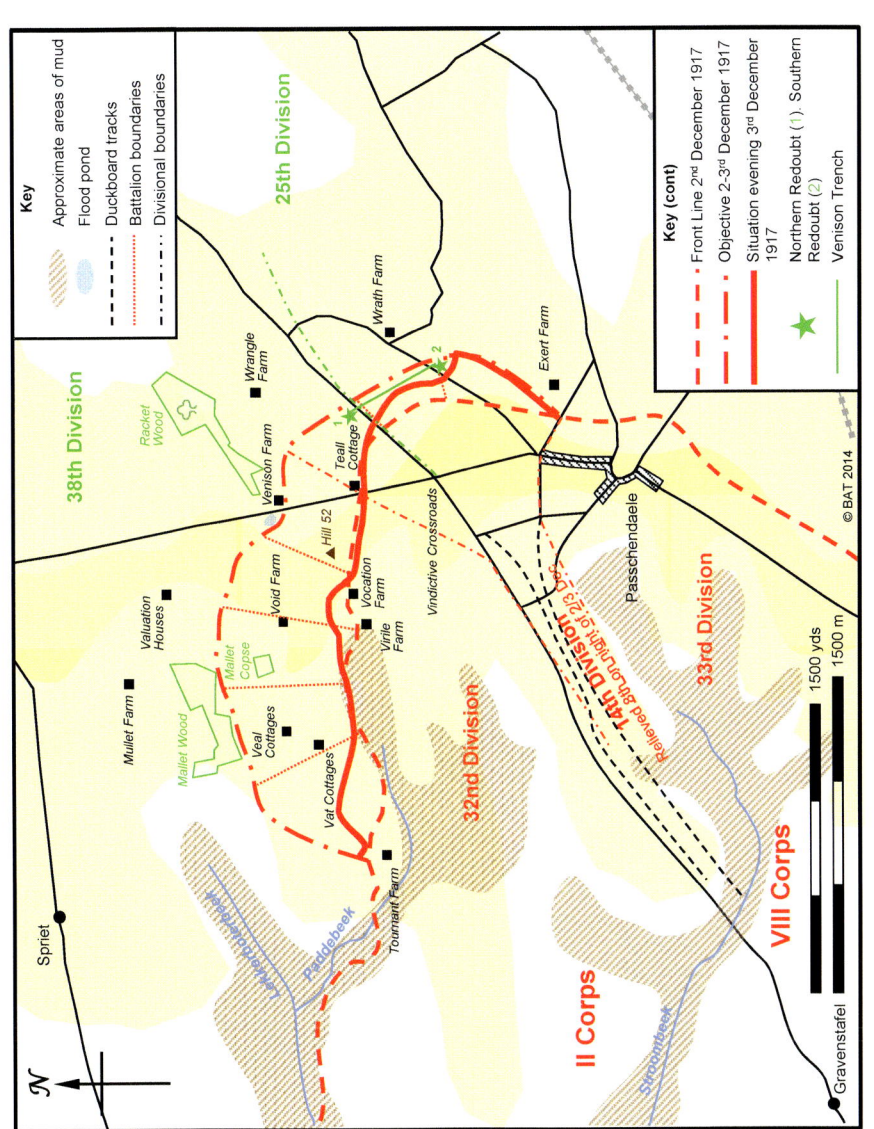

Situation evening 3 December 1917

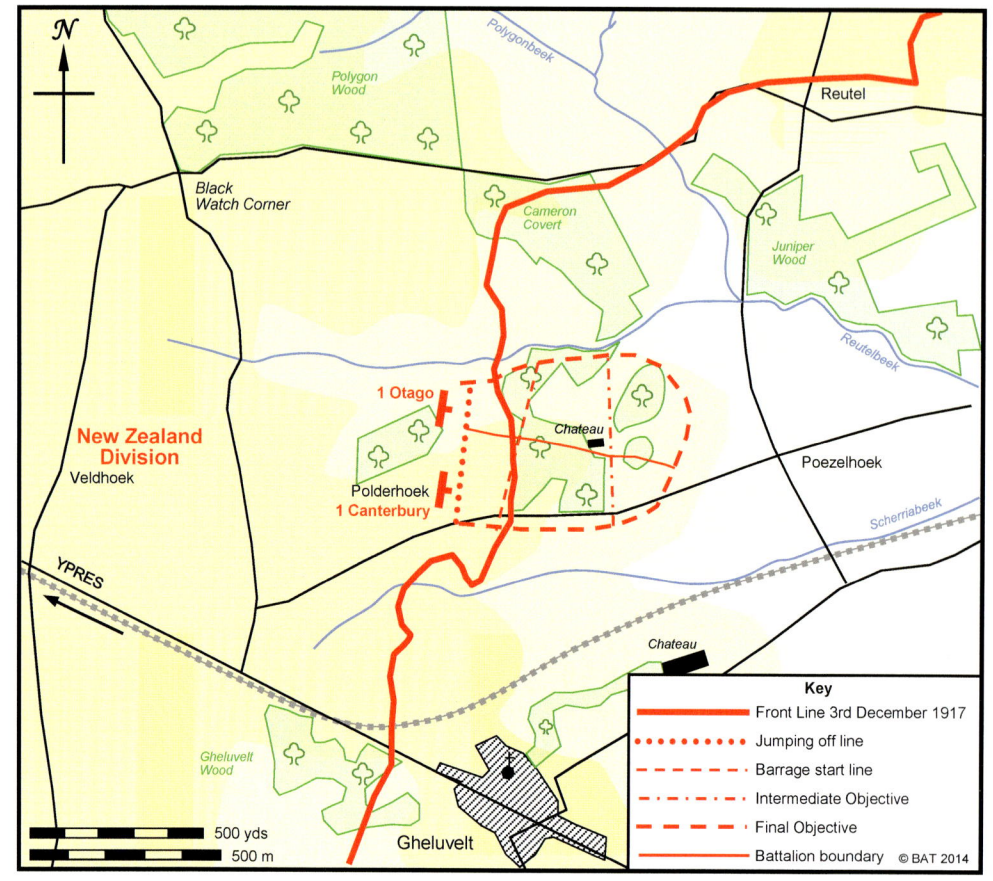

Polderhoek Chateau 3 December 1917

Private W. Hanson 2nd KOYLI
KIA 2 December 1917.
(Stephen Wilson)

mixed-up. He went forward with his few men until he reached two pillboxes. At this time he had three men of his platoon left, one being a Lewis Gunner, and he sent one man back for support but the man became a casualty. At this time he saw his company commander (Captain H.R. Forde MC) some distance off, when a Very Light went up and illuminated the surroundings. He was unable to reach him and never saw him again; this was some 250 yards in front of the tapeline. After this he got in touch with Number Thirteen Platoon, commanded by 2nd Lieutenant J.N. Ellis and they made an attempt to take the pillboxes but were unable to find an entrance. Here 2nd Lieutenant Ellis and his Platoon Sergeant were killed.[143] With the assistance of some men of the 16th Highland L.I., he worked round the pillboxes and, after going about 80 yards, he dug in.[144]

---

143 19-year-old 2nd Lieutenant J.N. Ellis is buried in Tyne Cot Cemetery.
144 TNA: WO/95/2402: 2nd KOYLI War Diary.

View north across present-day site of Hill 52. (Rob Thompson)

Consolidation of captured ground a further eighty yards beyond these concrete structures was carried out, under Sergeant Horne's direct supervision, by the mixed party of 2nd KOYLI and 16th HLI.[145]

'B' Company (CO Captain J. Hassell), following in the wake of 'C', found it necessary to carry out the second – "Support any of the leading companies should it become necessary to do so to enable these companies to reach their final objectives" – operational contingency assigned to it by 97 Brigade. 'D' Company, having sustained serious losses, had to be supported at all costs:

> 'B' Company, No. 4 or Support Company … recounted by the Company Commander Captain J. Hassell: 'B' Company started off the tape in correct order. Immediately the enemy illuminated the ground and opened machine-gun fire which did not impede his [Captain Hassell] progress or cause many casualties to his company, as it appeared to go overhead. He reached Hill 52 with Number 5 Platoon, the other three platoons being in front in positions

---

145 'D' Company officer casualties, in addition to Captain Forde and 2nd Lieutenant Ellis, were 2nd Lieutenant R.D. Abbiss DOW and 2nd Lieutenant J.S. Wilson (attached to 97 TMB) wounded. 30-year-old 2nd Lieutenant Reginald Donald Abbiss is buried in Mendinghem Military Cemetery.

from which the enemy had been driven out. The sappers [219th Field Company RE] who accompanied him immediately got to work and taped and sited the strongpoint and he set Number 5 Platoon to dig.[146] Whilst this was in progress, casualties of other companies reported to him and he set them to dig in. This trench was sited close to an old enemy trench, where he temporarily set up his company headquarters.

Thus 2nd KOYLI, disorganised and depleted of officers and men, dug in and expanded tenuous positions on Hill 52 with the assistance of the accompanying RE detachment.[147]

Three regiments (*IR94, IR95, IR96*) of *38th Division*[148] were responsible for *Gruppe Staden's Abschnitt B* since 1 December.[149] On the left, *IR94* (*Oberstleutnant* von Taysen) was tasked with defending the sector opposite 2nd Rifle Brigade and 2nd KOYLI. Its *Vorfeldzone* garrison was, regardless of a general state of alertness following the capture of the three prisoners in the waning hours of 1 December or the infliction of heavy losses on 2nd Rifle Brigade and 'A' and 'C' companies 2nd KOYLI, rapidly overwhelmed opposite the right and centre by elements of 'D' and 'B' companies.[150] *Höhenrücken – Passendale* (Hill 52) was lost, whilst isolated outposts continued to hold out against surrounding British forces. Reinforced companies of *IR94* prepared,

---

146 '[A] T-shaped strongpoint, with 4 fire bays and four traverses in each arm' was taped-out and dug with infantry assistance under the direction of Lieutenant Spottiswoode RE. 'Time spent on the job was 2 hours', after which the wounded Spottiswoode and his party departed for billets. See IWM 4723: 'Statement by OC [219th Field Company]', Brigadier-General T.S. Lambert Papers (Box 80/10/2).
147 TNA: WO/95/2400: '97 Brigade Operation Order No. 178', 27 November 1917, 97 Brigade War Diary and WO/95/2402: 2nd KOYLI War Diary.
148 The *38th* (Thüringian) *Division*, a pre-war formation attached to *XI Armeekorps*, sustained heavy losses during the opening phase of the Third Ypres campaign. Rest at Antwerp was followed by deployment south of the Scarpe in early September, after which it returned north to hold the line at Houthulst Forest from 19 to 25 November. Its 1917 intelligence 'value estimate' observed: 'As a rule it gave a good account of itself in the numerous battles in which it took part…' Its main objective on taking over *Abschnitt B* was 'to prevent the English from obtaining a foothold on the entire PASSCHENDAELE Ridge.' The divisional commander (*General-Leutnant* Hermann Schultheiss) was 'very emphatic on this point…' See Intelligence Section of the General Staff. American Expeditionary Forces, *Histories of Two Hundred and Fifty-One Divisions*, p. 431, TNA: WO/157/288: 'Annexe to II Corps Summary No. 34, Miscellaneous Information from a Prisoner of 94 I.R. (from Corps on Right), II Corps Summary of Information', 5 December 1917, II Corps Intelligence File and Appendix II for infantry orders of battle.
149 The dispositions of *38th Division's* regiments were, from right to left, roughly: *IR96*: Sector opposite Source Farm; *IR95*: Vicinity of Veal Cottages to *Osselstraat*; *IR94*: *Osselstraat* to Northern Redoubt (inclusive). See TNA: WO/157/288: 'Situation Map Showing Enemy Dispositions on 3/12/17', II Corps Intelligence File and Hartmann, *Das Infanterie Regiment Grossherzog von Sachsen (5. Thüringisches) Nr. 94 im Weltkrieg*, Skizze 32.
150 See Appendix XVI Part D (paras. 7 and 8).

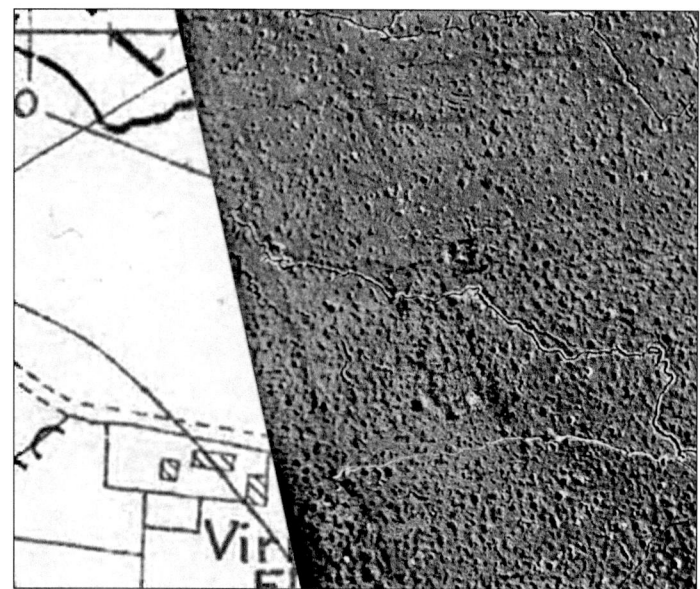

Vox and Vocation farms from the air. (Memorial Museum Passchendaele 1917)

throughout the remaining hours before dawn, to resist further enemy attacks beyond the *Hauptwiderstandslinie*, whilst embattled *Vorfeldzone* outposts hoped for imminent relief by counter-attack. Local commanders recognised the danger; immediate action was necessary if the British were to be denied a permanent hold on Hill 52 and its environs.

Increased distance to the red line required the two front companies of 16th HLI (acting CO Major W.D. Scott DSO MC)[151] to capture and consolidate a "dotted green" or "350 yard' line" halfway to the final objective. Following closely behind, the remaining two companies were to "leap frog on the dotted GREEN line and advance to the final objective and will be responsible for the capture of all occupied localities between the dotted GREEN line and their final objective."[152] Advancing roughly along two unusually close (present-day *Osselstraat* and *Haringstraat*) avenues the battalion would seize and consolidate Vox, Void, Veldt[153] and Volt farms respectively before halting on the red line south of Valuation Houses. The ground to be traversed consisted, in addition to four nearly indistinguishable farm sites, the usual expanse of

---

151 T/Major William Dishington Scott MC was awarded the DSO for gallantry at Nieuport on 10-11 July 1917.
152 TNA: WO/95/2400: '97 Brigade Operation Order No. 178', 27 November 1917, 97 Brigade War Diary.
153 Veldt Farm was situated astride the boundary between 16th HLI and 11th Border Regiment.

shell holes, dugouts and concrete shelters identified in the vicinity of Vox, Void and Volt farms. An anomaly to this standard *die Leer des Gefechtsfeldes* defensive arrangement was – having been previously identified as part of the *Hauptwiderstandlinie* defences south of the dotted green line – a continuous trench extending WNW across 16th HLI's front from the area allotted to the neighbouring 11th Border Regiment.[154]

"At Zero hour (1:55 a.m.)", 16th HLI's diarist recorded, "the battalion advanced." The weather was "bright moonlight, no wind, visibility good up to 300 yards, ground soft but quite practicable." Heavily encumbered men, organised into "worm" columns and line of sections, passed over the jumping-off tape and up the gentle slope into the illuminated void: "The fickle moon crept behind dark clouds as they attacked. Forward they drove in the black o' night, each man alone – robbed even of the comfort of human companionship in the face of eternity." Hopes of achieving complete surprise were almost immediately dashed by "intense enemy machine-gun fire from directions of MALLET COPSE, VOX FARM, VOID FARM and HILL 52." The attackers pressed forward: "Blundering on, sobbing for breath, they strove towards the vicious red flashes of the machine-guns that stabbed the gloom. These guns were densely packed in Mallet Copse, Vox Farm, Void Farm and Hill 52, strongholds that – with the weather – denied the British Army its coveted objective of Westroosebeke to the end." The low, mud-spattered pillbox and nearby trench sections at Vox Farm were "at once rushed and the garrison disposed of, 50 prisoners being sent to the rear." Concentrated fire nonetheless "seriously thinned" the battalion's ranks and was not checked until the opening of the barrage at Zero + 8. Further reduced by stragglers wandering into 2nd KOYLI's sector, 16th HLI, assisted by this timely suppressing shellfire, were able to establish a line running east and west "with the right flank refused toward Hill 52" through the SW corner of Void Farm by 2:40 a.m. On the immediate right, continued resistance by an outpost of the neighbouring German regiment isolated 16th HLI from 2nd KOYLI. On the left, touch with 11th Border Regiment was also lost in the confusion. Two officers (Captain G.L. Davidson and 2nd Lieutenant W.R. Bennie)[155] were subsequently killed "whilst endeavouring to locate this unit", by sniper fire from the direction of Mallet Copse. Efforts to rally and push on proved difficult in the period immediately after Zero. Lieutenant-Colonel Scully (CO 16th NF) recalled: "There was practically no artillery fire [,] a few shells only falling behind our original line. I consider the attack was sticky, anyhow just N[orth] of VIRILE FARM I personally found many men by VOCATION FARM and ordered them forward. This was about zero plus 10 minutes and there was very

---

154 TNA: WO/95/2400: 'Notes to Accompany Special Intelligence Maps of the Area V.15 – V.30' November 1917, 97 Brigade War Diary.
155 27-year-old Captain George Leslie Davidson (4th Battalion attached 16th Battalion HLI) and 22-year-old 2nd Lieutenant William Robertson Bennie (7th Battalion attached 16th Battalion HLI) have no known grave and are commemorated on the Tyne Cot Memorial to the Missing.

Captain G.L. Davidson. (George Heriot's School, *George Heriot's School Roll of Honour 1914-1919* (Edinburgh: War Memorial Committee, 1921))

little hostile fire. About 3 machine-guns were firing from about TEALL COTT., just N. of [HILL] 52 and MALLET COPSE."[156]

Remaining elements of 16th HLI, the anticipated area concentration barrage having momentarily suppressed the fierce German machine-gun fire, remained stalled just beyond the *Hauptwiderstandslinie* defences. Forced to dig in with exposed flanks east and west of Void Farm, its companies managed to overrun the *Vorfeldzone* during the 44 minutes after Zero:

> The remnants of the battalion then consolidated two positions on the line of our first [dotted green line] objective. One under Lieutenant J. Miller and Lieutenant J.W. Lumm with about 40 other o.r. from 'B' and 'D' companies was immediately in front of VOID FARM about V.23.d.9.4. facing N[orth]. The other under Captain J. Alexander, Lieutenant D.V. Charlton and Lieutenant R.B. Robertson with about 30 o.r. from 'A' and 'B' companies was about V.24.c.3.4 [east of Void Farm] facing NE.[157]

---

156 TNA: WO/95/2370: After-action report, 'Part III, Narrative of Events', 11 December 1917, 32nd Division War Diary, WO/95/2403: 16th HLI War Diary, IWM 4723: '32nd Div. No.G.S.1499/3/33', 5 December 1917, Brigadier-General T.S. Lambert Papers (Box 80/10/2), Chalmers (ed), *A Saga of Scotland*, p. 110 and Hartmann, *Das Infanterie Regiment Grossherzog von Sachsen (5. Thüringisches) No. 94* im *Weltkrieg*, p. 237. Lieutenant Kerr, CO RE party detailed to construct a strongpoint at Void Farm (see Chapter 2, p. 140), observed leaderless troops retiring from the front and right at about 2:30 a.m. Following this, he oversaw consolidation of Vox Farm by a mixed group of approximately 50 men from 2nd KOYLI, 16th HLI and 11th Border Regiment. See Lambert Papers: 'STATEMENT BY LIEUT. KERR R.E.'.
157 TNA: WO/95/2404: 16th HLI War Diary.

Shell holes and any other available cover were deepened and otherwise improved upon in the half-light whilst posted sentries fixed their gaze on front and flanks during the remaining hours before sunrise.

Colonel H.C. Wylly's history of the Border Regiment records that on 2 December 1917 the 11th Battalion took part in a "smart little action; moving up from Wurst Farm in the Westroosebeke area to the frontline" to carry out "a night attack on the German positions S[outh] of Westroosebeke in conjunction with other units of the 97th Brigade and two battalions of the 96th Infantry Brigade. The "Lonsdales" took their objectives and held them all through the day until the enemy launched a counter-attack at 4:30 p.m., when the battalion had to fall back to the old line."[158] This brief account – unavoidable due to limits of space when recounting the deeds of all sixteen Regular, Territorial and New Army battalions in one volume – only provides the barest outline of a tragic, but now forgotten feat of arms enacted on a low, wind-swept Flanders ridge in the immediate aftermath of a great campaign.

With two companies in front and two immediately behind, 11th Border Regiment awaited Zero along the 300-yard jumping-off tape. Silence was maintained as the battalion ascended the gentle incline toward the summit of Vat Cottages Ridge at 1:55 a.m. Confronting them was the anticipated collection of occupied shell hole outposts comprising the *Vorfeldzone*, the left-hand portion of linear trench facing 16th HLI and, beyond the *Hauptwiderstandslinie* and subsequent green line objective, the ramshackle agglomeration of dugouts, shelters and trenches situated approximately 200 yards south of the battalion's red line objective in Mallet Copse.[159]

The enemy remained quiescent as the four Lonsdale companies silently entered no man's land. Sporadic rifle bursts – immediately followed by a vicious fusillade and cascade of descending magnesium flares – put paid to any hoped for surprise. Resolute in the face of fierce machine-gun fire, the two front companies swept over the *Vorfeldzone* and, topping the ridge crest, seized the green line and Veldt Farm (a 16th HLI objective) just beyond 11th Border Regiment's right flank. The two succeeding companies, leap-frogging through the secured intermediate objective, rushed downhill to enter Mallet Copse at its southern end; bomb and bayonet made short work of occupants sheltering amongst the haphazard warren of mined dugouts, corrugated metal-roofed shrapnel shelters and narrow trench sections before the spinney was cleared and its northern edge reached. Any further advance from there through the muddy north valley to the red line was halted by machine-gun fire originating some

158 Colonel H.C. Wylly, *The Border Regiment in the Great War* (Aldershot: Gale & Polden, 1924), p. 173.
159 An aerial photograph, taken on 27 November, showed the 'area about old trench at V.23.d.00.45 and MALLET COPSE still dry. North of the [winding *Goudbergstraat*] road the ground is very wet except for the isolated shell holes which are dry probably because new. Pillbox can still be seen in southwest corner of MALLET WOOD. See TNA WO/157/287: 'Appendix to II Corps Summary No. 27, Preliminary Report on Photos Taken 27-11-17, II Corps Summary of Information', 28 November 1917, II Corps Intelligence File.

Captain A.F. Sandeman 11th Border Regiment KIA 2 December 1917. (University of Edinburgh, *University of Edinburgh Roll of Honour 1914-1919* (London: Oliver & Boyd, 1921))

2nd Lieutenant W.B. MacDuff 11th Border Regiment KIA 2 December 1917. (Andrew Arnold)

Watt Brothers: George right, John centre. (Colin Bardgett, *The Lonsdale Battalion 1914-1918* (Melksham: Cromwell Press, 1993))

200 yards distance from inundated Mallet Wood. Remnants of the leap-frogging companies, their position now rendered untenable by a shower of bullets, fell back to "the southern edge of the copse with their left flank refused."[160]

Stalled just 200 yards short of the final red line objective, 11th Border Regiment had driven some 500 yards into dispersed enemy defences north and south of the green line intermediate objective.[161] This epic action was, as with the other battalions of 25 and 97 brigades, underlined by hundreds of human tragedies now lost to time. One on record concerns two – George and John – of three serving Watt brothers. Hailing from the tiny Cumbria village of Skelton, George Watt was a ploughman whose first attempt at underage enlistment was thwarted by alert Penrith recruitment staff. Undeterred, he travelled to Carlisle where less vigilant or particular Lonsdale Battalion recruiters signed young George on for the duration. Severely wounded in both thighs on the opening day of the Somme campaign, the once underaged recruit was a seasoned veteran by the time of the impending "Passchendaele show". Waiting with George below the summit of Vat Cottages Ridge was his older brother John. Rifles held high at the port, they passed over the jumping-off tape at zero hour. John fell wounded not long afterwards. George, witnessing his brother's distress, dragged him into a nearby shell hole before moving on to be wounded a second time; John, left injured and alone in one of the many surrounding craters, was later posted as "missing" and never heard from again.[162]

Tasked with seizing the designated green and red lines respectively, 17th HLI formed up on a two company frontage with two companies behind; front companies to halt at the green line, rear companies passing through the former to secure a 500-yard red line objective overlooking low-lying ground in the vicinity of Mallet Wood and Double Copse:

> The intention was to advance on this front at zero hour and drive the enemy from positions occupied by him on the [Vat Cottages] Ridge. There were [as with 16th HLI and 11th Border Regiment] two objectives to be taken – a GREEN LINE,

---

160 See TNA: WO/95/2370: After-action report, 'Part III, Narrative of Events', 11 December 1917, 32nd Division War Diary.
161 Officer casualties for 11th Border Regiment were as follows: Killed: Captains I. Benson, A.F. Sandeman, P.M. Martin; 2nd Lieutenants R.C. Richardson, W.B. MacDuff; Missing: 2nd Lieutenant W.T. Ridgway; Wounded: Captain McConnan, 2nd Lieutenants Jamie, Fell, Hotchkiss, Malley Martin, Duff, Abbey. Thirty-four-year-old Captain Isaac Benson, 33-year-old Captain Albert Fitzroy Sandeman, 21-year-old Captain Peter Mcewan Martin, 2nd Lieutenant Robert Cecil Richardson (age unknown) and 24-year-old 2nd Lieutenant William Brown MacDuff have no known grave and are commemorated on the Tyne Cot Memorial to the Missing.
162 See Colin Bardgett, *The Lonsdale Battalion 1914-1918* (Melksham: Cromwell Press, 1993), pp. 43 and 129. 27-year-old 17322 Pte. John William Watt has no known grave and is commemorated on the Tyne Cot Memorial to the Missing. Pte. George Watt was evacuated after being wounded. He survived the war to return home and marry.

running approximately from VEAL COTTAGES on our battalion front, to a point right of No. 3 Company, No. 2 [16th HLI] Battalion, and a RED LINE running approximately from TOURNANT FARM to the [II] Corps boundary at a point opposite No. 1 Company, No. 5 [15th LF] Battalion. The 17th HLI were responsible for the capture of the first objective from a point V.23.d.06.32 (right of Mallet Copse) to V.23.c.19.09 (in front of and left of VEAL COTTAGES), and taking VAT COTTAGES. The Second objective or RED LINE was from V.23.c.04.91 to V.23.c.18.42. [northern slope of the Vat Cottages Ridge], the frontage on the final objective to be one of 500 yards.[163]

The post-war Battalion history observed: "There were two objectives to be taken, of which sections were detailed as the job of the 17th – a slice of which included two formidable 'pillboxes' known as the Vat and Veal Cottages."[164]

Aligned ('A' and 'B' companies in front; 'C' and 'D' in rear) before a start line extending east to west along the ascending southern slope of the Vat Cottages outcrop with Vat and Veal cottages lying beyond, 17th HLI crossed the jumping-off tape at Zero:

> The battalion assembled on a frontage of 400 yards and at zero hour (1:55 a.m.) moved forward to attack. Companies deployed from a two platoon frontage in snake formation – this method having been adopted owing to the shell torn nature of the ground – and advanced in four waves.[165] 'A' and 'B' companies were to capture the first objective, mopping up all occupied posts on the way, including the two pillboxes, while 'C' and 'D' were to "leap-frog" through them, carry the next objective and consolidate.[166]

---

163 TNA: WO/95/2400: '97 Brigade Operation Order No. 178', 27 November 1917, 97 Brigade War Diary and WO/95/2405: 17th HLI War Diary.
164 Arthur & Munro (eds), *The Seventeenth Highland Light Infantry*, p. 68. An aerial photograph taken on 27 November provided additional intelligence about German defences in the vicinity of Vat and Veal cottages: '7 B.13. V.23.c.d.29.a.b. Light good. Shows VAT and VEAL COTTAGES, MALLET COPSE and a considerable area north and south of the [*Goudbergsraat?*] road. There appears to be small posts still in the old trench running north from V.23.d. Probable MG position at about V.23.d.12.10 and numerous shell hole positions just east of this which appear comparatively dry and occupied. Area about VAT COTTAGES dry. Tracks lead along road southwest of this area. The location of the post reported here is apparently in two or three shell holes about V.29.a.65.80.' See 'Appendix to II Corps Summary No. 27, Preliminary Report on Photos Taken 27-11-17, II Corps Summary of Information', 28 November 1917, TNA WO/157/287, II Corps Intelligence File.
165 The distance between waves and companies was 20 yards and 40 yards respectively. See WO/95/2405: 17th HLI War Diary.
166 Arthur & Munro (eds), *The Seventeenth Highland Light Infantry*, p. 68.

A Moonlight Massacre   235

2nd Lieutenant P.N. Cunnigham 17th HLI KIA 2 December 1917. (Society of Telegraph Engineers, *The Roll of Honour of the Institution of Electrical Engineers* (London: W.A.J. O'Meara, 1924))

2nd Lieutenant R.H. Reid 17th HLI KIA 2 December 1917. (University of Glasgow Archives)

2nd Lieutenant J. Miller 17th HLI KIA 2 December 1917. (Bellahouston Academy, *Bellahouston War Memorial Volume August 4th 1914 – 28 June 1919* (Glasgow: J. Cossar, 1919))

2nd Lieutenant W. Morland 17th HLI KIA 2 December 1917. (Hillhead High School, *Hillhead High School War Memorial Volume* (Glasgow: William Hodge & Co., 1919))

Little opposition was encountered as the convergent snake columns pressed past or over scattered *Vorfeldzone* outposts. Hoped for complacency on the part of the enemy during the 8 minutes prior to barrage start time was, as elsewhere, instantly dispelled by almost ceaseless hostile fire: "Suddenly he opened heavy machine-gun fire upon the advancing companies, inflicting heavy casualties which, in the dark and over the difficult ground, had the effect of splitting up the sections and creating some confusion."[167] 'A' and 'B' companies, tasked with advancing "as far as the 'GREEN LINE' capturing and mopping up all occupied points on the way", encountered intense machine-gun fire before reaching the ridge crest. This, coupled with crippling losses from enfilade fire on both flanks, failed to deter survivors in their determination to get forward. Further efforts by dispersed elements of both companies were of little avail against merciless volleys from Vat Cottages; 'C' and 'D' companies, following close behind, failed to provide additional impetus. "Our men", the battalion diarist later wrote, "gallantly pressed on against these odds; but the enemy machine-gun and rifle fire became so intense that their advanced positions were rendered humanly untenable."[168] Shute recounted the outcome in his after-action report: "The 17th HLI … had been checked by machine-gun fire from VAT COTTAGES at a very early stage of the advance. Various efforts had been made to work round the flanks of this strongpoint but these attempts had resulted in the loss of many officers and NCOs and the advance had been definitely held up."[169] Vat and Veal cottages were discovered to be "heavily garrisoned" and, despite intelligence to the contrary, protected by barbed wire obstacles: "[S]trongpoints were found to be heavily garrisoned and wired and he was also found to be established in a strong line of trench also effectively wired." Battalion remnants, forced to retire in places, went to ground in the nearest shell holes and began the painful process of consolidation under fierce, continuous fire. Supporting artillery and machine-gun barrages, commencing at Zero + 8, failed to assist the stalled battalion; failure to breach the enemy's main line of resistance at any point made it unlikely that even the green line intermediary objective would be reached before daybreak.[170]

167 Ibid.
168 TNA: WO/95/2405: 17th HLI War Diary and Arthur & Munro (eds), *The Seventeenth Highland Light Infantry*, p. 68.
169 TNA: WO/95/2370: After-action report, 'Part III, Narrative of Events', 11 December 1917, 32nd Division War Diary. 17th HLI sustained heavy officer casualties: Killed: 2nd Lieutenants J. Osborne, P.N. Cunningham, R.H. Reid, M. Cameron, J. Miller, W. Morland; Wounded: Captain J.O. Westwater, 2nd Lieutenants R.D. Brown, G. Forsyth, G.T. M'Intosh, R.D.W. Nicholson, R. Smith. 24-year-old 2nd Lieutenant John Osborne, 2nd Lieutenant Peter Nesbit Cunningham (age unknown), 29-year-old 2nd Lieutenant Robert Hislop Reid, 24-year-old 2nd Lieutenant MacDonald Cameron and 22-year-old 2nd Lieutenant John Miller have no known grave and are commemorated on the Tyne Cot Memorial to the Missing. 21-year-old 2nd Lieutenant William Morland is buried in Poelcappelle British Cemetery. Lieutenant J.D. Brown DOW on 3 December. He is interred at Mendinghem Military Cemetery.
170 WO/95/2405: 17th HLI War Diary.

A Moonlight Massacre   237

Wallemolenstraat from Tournant Farm looking north: Approximate site of jumping-off line boundary between 17th HLI and 15th LF. (Rob Thompson)

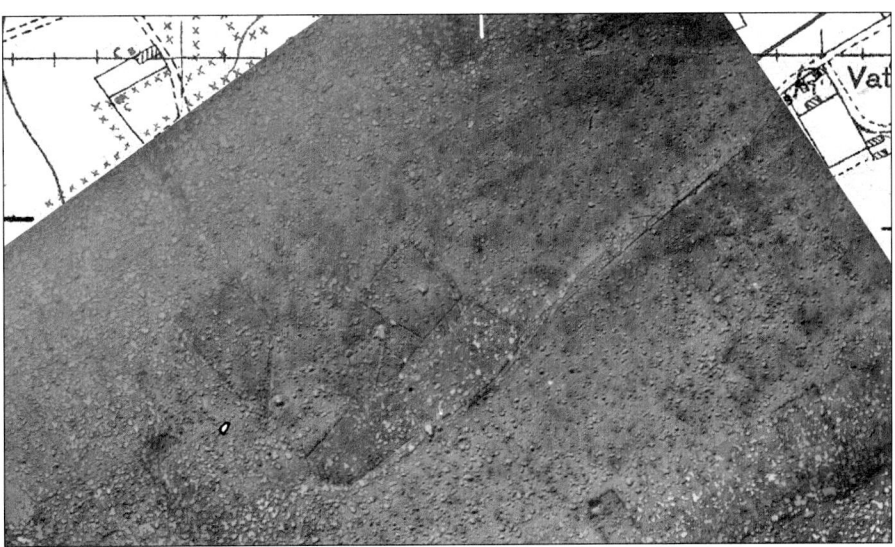

Tournant Farm from the air. (Memorial Museum Passchendaele 1917)

Four companies, organised along the same lines as 2nd KOYLI, of 15th LF (acting CO Major H.K Utterson DSO)[171] jumped-off without incident at 1:55 a.m. Tasked with forming a left flank guard, 'A', 'B' and 'C' companies were deployed on the right, centre and left respectively; 'D' Company remaining in support behind 'A': "Theirs was a difficult manoeuvre, a sort of echelon attack: the left company had to move only a short distance, while the right traversed over 500 yards."[172] Thus the entire battalion would, on gaining possession of the red line objective, establish a secure left flank for the remaining four battalions of 97 Brigade:

> The Battalion's frontage in the assembly area was four hundred and fifty yards, but as it had to pivot on its left and to link the original line with the position gained by the rest of the brigade, its holding on the [final] objective would measure seven hundred yards. The orders provided that 'A' (Lieutenant J.W. Brockman), 'B' (Captain R.F. Greenhill) and 'C' (Lieutenant D.H. Smith DCM) companies should advance to their allotted area in the objective, called the "red line", and 'D' Company (Captain L.C. Mandleberg) should move in rear of 'A' Company and be prepared to support any of the leading companies if they should need help to enable them to attain the objective. If its services were not used in that capacity, 'D' was to consolidate in depth when the "red line" was taken.[173]

The German defences opposite comprised, in addition to the usual shell hole outposts, pillboxes, dugouts and short trench sections, a previously identified circular strongpoint situated within the *Vorfeldzone* approximately 200 yards SW of Vat Cottages.[174]

'A' Company, deviating right to keep touch with 17th HLI, came under intense machine-gun fire six minutes after Zero; all officers and the CSM were killed or wounded whilst traversing the *Vorfeldzone*. "The survivors struggled on … only about twenty NCOs and men remaining in any organised form." Major Utterson later observed: "I have not yet been able to clearly grasp what happened as the men's accounts are conflicting. Considerable casualties were suffered from machine-gun fire

---

171 Major Henry Kelso Utterson. Commissioned Dorset Regiment 1897; Lieutenant 1899; South Africa 1900-02; West African Frontier Force 1904-09; Captain 1905; DSO and Major 1915; War Office 1916; Brigade Major January-September 1917; CO 15th LF 31 October.
172 IWM 4723: 'Narrative of Operations 2/3rd December 1917, 15th (S) Battalion Lancashire Fusiliers', 4 December 1917, Brigadier-General T.S. Lambert Papers (Box 80/10/2) and Cooke, *Historical Records of the 16th (Service) Battalion Northumberland Fusiliers*, p. 89.
173 Latter, *The History of the Lancashire Fusiliers in Two Volumes Vol. 1*, p. 276.
174 See surviving 97 Brigade intelligence 'mud map' (10 A), TNA: WO/95/2404: 16th HLI War Diary.

2nd Lieutenant J.S. Scrivener. (*De Ruvigny's Roll of Honour 1914-1918* (London: Naval & Military Press reprint of 1922 edition))

2nd Lieutenant Charles Buchan 15th LF KIA 2 December 1917. (Mabel Desborough Allardyce (ed), University of Aberdeen, *Roll of Service in the Great War 1914-1919* (Aberdeen: Aberdeen University Press, 1921))

and the company got rather scattered ..."[175] 'B' Company encountered little opposition from the startled German outposts before reaching its objective, while 'C', "joined up the original line at TOURNANT FARM on the left, to 'B' Company on the objective forming a defensive flank of about 250 yards. This they did very rapidly and great credit is due to their work and they suffered no casualties from the enemy's barrage."[176]

Unsuppressed enfilade fire from the right – where 17th HLI were pinned down – halted 'A' Company in its tracks. 2nd Lieutenant Scrivener, who had carefully taped-out the battalion's jumping-off position prior to Zero, and his batman Private H.R. Poole "showed the greatest gallantry; they attacked and captured a 'pillbox' containing a machine-gun." Scrivener was slain as he approached the objective shortly afterwards; Poole, his officer down, stalked and killed a nearby enemy machine-gunner, after which he brought in the many wounded lying about.[177] Survivors on the far right

175 IWM 4723: 'Narrative of Operations 2/3rd December 1917, 15th (S) Battalion Lancashire Fusiliers', 4 December 1917, Brigadier-General T.S. Lambert Papers (Box 80/10/2).
176 Ibid and Latter, *The History of the Lancashire Fusiliers in Two Volumes Vol. 1*, p. 276.
177 200969 Pte. H.R. Poole was subsequently awarded the MM for his heroism. 20-year-old 2nd Lieutenant John Sidney Scrivener has no known grave and is commemorated on the Tyne Cot Memorial to the Missing. 15th LF's only other officer fatality (29-year-old 2nd

attached themselves to 17th HLI, whilst the remainder, "finding their right flank unguarded", dug small posts to form a defensive flank. Observing a widening gap and desirous to get the attack going again, 'D' Company rushed a single platoon forward to support 'A': "Shortly after the advanced commenced the officers with the leading platoons saw that 'A' Company were bearing too much to their right, so 2ND LIEUT POLLITT took his platoon forward … As the gap widened 2ND LIEUT HURST also went forward but was enfiladed by fire from VAT COTTAGES and lost most of his platoon. 2ND LIEUT SCHOLES who was with the two rear platoons was wounded and the platoons halted and dug themselves in … 2ND LIEUT HURST having only three men left retired to the rear half of the company and as he feared that 'A' Company's flank was in the air, he sent a post forward to connect with them, and remained in support." Thus 'A' Company, assisted by two platoons from 'D', was halted halfway to the final objective.[178] On the left, 'B' Company and 'C' Company positions established on the red line offered a considerable view of low-lying territory west and NW of Vat Cottages Ridge where Lind Cottage, Hinton Farm, Cameron House and other fortified enclosures north of the Lekkerboterbeek remained, as part of adjacent defenses, in German hands.[179] Massed machine-guns from Major-General Franks' 35th Division (left sector of II Corps) expended thousands of rounds into this inundated area in support of 32nd Division's attack: "No undue retaliation was experienced, and the resultant disquietude of the enemy on the front enabled the 4/North Staffordshire to capture two prisoners."[180]

IR 95 (*Oberstleutnant* von Selle) faced four battalions as they stormed the centre sector of *38th Division*'s line.[181] Tenacious resistance promptly displaced the initial surprise and shock.[182] Supporting artillery, in reply to flares discharged by the hard-pressed infantry, put down a defensive barrage 3 or 4 minutes after the British bombardment

Lieutenant Charles Buchan) is buried at Ypres Reservoir Cemetery. See Latter, *The History of the Lancashire Fusiliers in Two Volumes Vol. 1*, p. 277 and Stedman, *Salford Pals*, p. 156
178 IWM 4223: 'Narrative of Operations 2/3rd December 1917, 15th (S) Battalion Lancashire Fusiliers', 4 December 1917, Brigadier-General T.S. Lambert Files (Box 80/10/2), Latter, *The History of the Lancashire Fusiliers in Two Volumes Vol. 1*, p. 277.
179 The MM was subsequently awarded to two company runners, 35736 Pte H. V. Atkinson. 39645 Cpl J.W. Horton was awarded the same decoration for carrying back a wounded officer and later organising a supply of rations. 23551 Signaller Pte A. Bradburn received the Belgian *Croix de Guerre* for repairing damaged wires whilst under fire.
180 Lieutenant-Colonel H.M. Davson, *The History of the 35th Division in the Great War* (London: Sifton & Praed, 1926), p. 176. The capture and retention of a particular 'point about V.22.d.2.4' by 15th LF, II Corps intelligence surmised, would probably force the enemy to evacuate all the ground south of the Lekkerboterbeek.' See TNA: WO/95/2370: 'Notes to Accompany Special Intelligence Maps of the Area V.15 – V.30' November 1917, 32nd Division Diary.
181 From right to left: 16th HLI, 11th Border Regiment, 17th HLI and 15th LF. *IR96*, occupying low ground on the immediate right, was not attacked, its front being beyond designated British objectives. See Appendix XVI, Part F (paras. 6 and 7).
182 See Appendix XVI Part E (paras. 8 to 11).

Panorama looking north from Vat Cottages Ridge. (Author)

Panorama of low-lying region NW of Vat Cottages Ridge. (Author)

opened "on and in front of a line 350 yards" in front of the jumping-off line: "It was not heavy and was on the line of the PADDEBEEK." At Zero + 14 British batteries "formed a barrage in front of the first objective and then moved forward at the rate of 100 yards in three minutes to the final [red line] objective." Heavy shelling of 97 Brigade's jumping-off positions did not commence until Zero + 25. The first British SOS rocket, bursting at its acme into three lingering spheres of red-green-red, was observed around 3:30 a.m.[183] Shute later summed up the troubling state of affairs, still unknown at his HQ, as follows:

> The situation in which each of the five battalions found themselves from about zero plus 8 onwards was an exceedingly difficult one. The enemy's machine-guns had gained complete fire superiority. The various local advances made by our troops after this period cost us heavily in our best officers and NCOs, who necessarily had to expose themselves in leading and organising attacks on the different strongpoints holding up their advance.[184]

Daylight would shortly reveal the extent of the British breakthrough to both sides. Time was running out for 32nd Division: Could 97 Brigade secure its entire red line objective before sunrise in the face of a solidifying German defence?

---

183 TNA: WO/95/643: 'II Corps Summary of Operations for Week Ending 6 December 1917', II Corps War Diary and WO/95/2370: After-action report, 'Appendix 'J', 32nd Division: Telephone and Telegraph Messages, 2 December 1917', 11 December 1917, 32nd Division War Diary.
184 TNA: WO/95/2370: After-action report, 'Part III, Narrative of Events', 11 December 1917, 32nd Division War Diary.

4

Dawn & Dénouement

For a dreamer is one who can only find his way by moonlight, and his punishment is that he sees the dawn before the rest of the world.[1]

4.1 Loss of Southern Redoubt and Hill 52

Previously established signal communications infrastructures kept HQ staffs informed on the progress, so far as could be ascertained, of the night attack. Reports from a variety of sources (flanking units, corps HQs, division observation officers, FOOs) supplied commanders with up-to-the-minute operational and tactical intelligence. VIII Corps received the earliest telegraph message – recorded by signals personnel on the ubiquitous C2121 pink message form – from 8th Division at 2:35 a.m.:

> Following from 25th Infantry Brigade. aaa At 2 a.m. enemy coloured lights seen [,] rifle and M.G. fire opened aaa 2.2 a.m. many lights and heavy musketry aaa Our barrage to time aaa Enemy's [barrage] opened 2.7 a.m. approx[imate] aaa 8th Corps repeated flank divisions.

A second message, arriving the same time as the first, was dispatched by the gunners: "8th Divisional artillery report that at 2.0 a.m. – Considerable rifle and MG fire heard. 2.5 a.m. – Very heavy rifle fire and MG fire heard [.] Several lights up. 2.7 a.m. – Enemy barrage came down."[2] These communiques were immediately passed on

---

1   Oscar Wilde, *The Critic as Artist* (1888).
2   BL: 48359: 'Report of Operations Carried Out by the VIII Army Corps on the Morning of 2nd December 1917, Official War Diaries with Appendices and Addenda, VIII Army Corps, Passchendaele Front, November 1917-April 1918', Vol. V, Hunter-Weston Papers.

to Brigadier-General Aspinall. Over three hours would expire before the BGGS VIII Corps received further information.

Reports also poured in on the left in II Corps' sector. A complete transcript of telephone and telegraph messages, received and despatched by 32nd Division HQ whilst the assault was in progress, sheds light on Shute's somewhat inconsistent command style. The document also "conveys very well", John Lee has observed following examination of a similar document, "the chaotic environment generated by modern battle, the problem of contradictory and erroneous messages and the desperate quest for up-to-date information on how the battle was developing at the front."[3] Given these circumstances, two hours would pass before Shute had a reasonably clear picture of the situation.[4] The first post-zero information, communicated over the telephone by an anonymous artillery major at 2:02 a.m., received by 32nd Division related the moment surprise was lost: "At 2 a.m. all quiet. No artillery fire: no machine-gun fire: two rifle shots: two yellow lights sent up." A second telephone message, from the CO Division signals observing near Shute's Canal Bank HQ, followed at 2:03 a.m.: "Two orange lights at Zero plus 3. At Zero plus 4 ½ first green light. More green lights followed at Zero plus 5 ½. Apparent flashes of a few Boche guns at Zero plus 7. Our own guns started off almost all together at Zero plus 8." The first telegraph report from 97 Brigade arrived at 2:22 a.m.: "HUNT started 1:55 a.m.[5] Rifle and machine-gun fire heavy before Zero plus 8. No Boche artillery fire before Zero plus 8." More messages followed before the situation was understood:

> Various reports[6] reached divisional headquarters between between Zero and 3:55 a.m., the general tenor of which was (a) That heavy machine-gun fire had

---

3   Lee, 'Command and Control in Battle' in Sheffield & Todman (eds), *Command and Control on the Western Front*, p. 137
4   'Once the battle had commenced there was little enough the individual general could do to influence its course and conduct. The friction of war and the fragility of most available means of communication made the overall situation complex and difficult and it was only by inculcating these standard procedures and battle drills that the British generals could commit their troops to battle with confidence.' Ibid. p. 139.
5   'HUNT' was the designated night operation code name. Application of a simple substitution code with alternative operational activity ('HUNT') and formation/unit (YAWL: II Corps, ELDER: 32nd Division, PRISM: 97 Brigade, PRINT: 2nd KOYLI, etc.) references prevented discovery of intent and unit identifications by German 'Moritz II' telephone listening sets and wireless intercept stations. For the development and use of listening apparatus and wireless interception technology by the British and German armies see Michael Occleshaw, *Armour Against Fate: British Military Intelligence in the First World War* (London: Columbus Books, 1989), pp. 113-14, 119-22, John Ferris, *The British Army and Signals Intelligence During the First World War* (Stroud: Allen Sutton & Army Records Society, 1992), pp. 13-16 and Beach, 'British Intelligence and the German Army, 1914-1918', pp. 80-86.
6   For example, 14 Brigade observers, situated on Bellevue Spur, reported in a telephone message timed 3:20 a.m.: 'Z[ero] plus 17 – All enemy lights going up further back …

been opened by the enemy at Zero plus 7. (b) That the enemy's artillery barrage had opened at Zero plus 12, but was not severe and was mostly behind our own frontline on the general line VINE COTTAGE – VALOUR FARM. At 3:30 a.m., an SOS was reported from the direction of Hill 52.[7]

Hostile machine-gun and trench mortar fire from the vicinity of Valuation Houses was a primary concern throughout this uncertain period, the divisional artillery receiving a specific request to engage the area: "The General wants you to ginger things up in Square 22 and would like a couple of 6 [inch] on it if it can be done."[8] News concerning the assault's actual progress remained scanty until 3:55 a.m. The situation by that time, Shute and his staff would shortly discover, had gone from bad to worse.[9]

On 25 Brigade's front, two platoons (one each from 'B' and 'D' companies) of 2nd Royal Berkshire carried on the fierce struggle to maintain a tenuous hold in Southern Redoubt. Hand grenades, flying to and fro in the darkness, detonated with sharp reports as small parties of bombers and riflemen, trampling the dead and dying as they moved through the oblong bastion's trough-like depressions, engaged in close quarter combat.[10] Lieutenant-Colonel C.R.H. Stirling (CO 2nd Royal Berkshire) wrote afterwards: "The enemy lost a great many casualties to bayonet and bomb, but we, unfortunately, also lost many men including the platoon [engaged in the redoubt] commander."[11] Sustained losses, coupled with lack of support from 2nd Lieutenant Upton's divergent platoon, resulted in remnants of both companies gradually giving way, under a deluge of hurled stick bombs, to increased pressure from elements of *IR116*. A final position was eventually established "close to the SW front of the redoubt where they dug in."[12] This retirement "exposed the left of 'D' company; but our troops there succeeded in maintaining themselves nonetheless and repelled minor attacks by which the enemy attempted to dislodge them."[13] Meanwhile, to the left of

---

Zero plus 18 – Enemy barrage increased and carried to our back area … Zero plus 22 – Light shelling of BELLEVUE Road and Ridge and GOUDBERG Valley … Zero plus 26 – Enemy barrage thickened'; 'Zero plus 28 – 'Enemy shelling MOSSELMARKT – MEETCHEELE and BELLEVUE Ridge … Zero plus 29 – Enemy searchlights playing from WESTROOSEBEKE.'

7   See TNA: WO/95/2370: After-action report, 'Part III, Narrative of Events', and 'Appendix J', 32nd Division: Telephone and Telegraph Messages 2 December 1917', 11 December 1917, 32nd Division War Diary.
8   Ibid. A barrage was subsequently placed on the designated SOS line.
9   The 3:55 a.m. report related that 17th HLI 'had not yet captured' the first objective. See IWM 4273: 'Summary of the Attack of the 97th Inf. Bde. and 2 Battalions of the 96th Inf. Bde. on December 2 [1917]', Brigadier-General T.S. Lambert Papers (Box 80/10/2).
10 See Appendix XVI Part B (para. 15).
11 TNA: WO/95/1929: 'Appendix B', 5 December 1917, 2nd Royal Berkshire War Diary.
12 Ibid.
13 TNA: WO/95/1677: 'Narrative of Operations Carried Out by the 8th Division on 1st/2nd December 1917', 13 December 1917, 8th Division War Diary.

Southern Redoubt, Upton's platoon had "captured a portion of the [Venison] Trench connecting the Northern and Southern redoubts [,] killing Germans and capturing three MGs." This portion of the objective, originally assigned to 2nd Lincolnshire, was held and consolidated despite the loss of Southern Redoubt.[14]

British inroads at the boundary between *IR116* and *IR117* brought forth the anticipated German response, as support troops deploying in the immediate rear encountered a hostile artillery bombardment starting at Zero + 8.[15] Sketchy reports, dispatched under the confused conditions of a surprise night attack, also gave local *Kampftruppenkommandeurs* (*KTK*) cause for concern. Positions of local tactical importance had, as far as it was known, been captured by an enemy whose exceptional ability to seize and hold limited objectives had been amply demonstrated since 20 September. The likely outcome, based on previous battle experience, could be as costly as offensive action: Staggered counter-attacks by supports and reserves, advancing through a morass of shell holes under a devastating barrage, would encounter steady machine-gun and rifle fire from newly entrenched British infantry. Moving uphill in the dark heightened the tactical difficulties; *IR117's* post-war history acknowledging that "Only two groups eventually reached the breach. Further resistance was hopeless; defence of the remaining ground was all that could be hoped for."[16]

Undergoing his first test as BGGS VIII Corps, Brigadier-General Aspinall received the first situation report at 2:07 a.m. The intervening hours must have seemed interminable to those awaiting the result at Hunter-Weston's HQ. Novelist Compton Mackenzie recalled a similar waiting period at Sir Ian Hamilton's MEF HQ on the night (6-7 August 1915) of the Suvla Bay landings. There he observed a pensive Aspinall "after giving moustaches and beards to all the ladies in the weekly illustrated papers was now drawing wooden lady after wooden lady of his own invention on sheets of foolscap."[17] A fairly inconclusive telegraph message, concerning the observed SOS signal near Goudberg and the slackening of enemy fire opposite 25 Brigade, from 8th Division arrived at VIII Corps at 4:22 a.m. Another message, telegraphed by the gunners, arrived eighteen minutes later: "Report from 8th Divisional Artillery – Message from BELLEVUE timed 3.5 a.m. – aaa "Attack progressing favourably." At 5:30 a.m. 8th Division reported: "Situation report aaa No definite news but attack believed to have made some progress aaa Liaison officer reports wounded state Southern Redoubt was captured and that hostile barrage fall at Zero + 9 on VINDICTIVE X Roads – PASSCHENDAELE Road afterwards shortening to Southern Redoubt." A fourth report was received from the same source at 6:50 a.m.: "Situation Report aaa Enemy artillery more active than usual [,] particularly

14   Ibid and Boraston & Bax, *The Eighth Division*, p. 166.
15   See Appendix XVI Part B (paras. 15 and 16) and Part C (paras. 12 and 13).
16   Hauptmann Kurt Offenbacher, *Die Geschichte des Infanterie-Leibregiments Grossherzogin (3. Grossherzoglich Hessisches) Nr. 117* (Oldenburg: Gerhard Stalling, 1931), p. 195.
17   Mackenzie, *Gallipoli Memories*, pp. 370-71.

on tracks aaa No definite information from left [32nd] Division on operations aaa State enemy barrage came down 9 minutes after zero and [97 Brigade] attack believed to have made progress." Sunrise was one hour and seventeen minutes away when II Corps telegraphed what was known about 32nd Division's situation: "Assembly for attack carried out satisfactorily with few casualties aaa Assault launched at 1:55 a.m. aaa Hostile M.G. fire opened 2.1 a.m. and artillery barrage about 2.7 a.m. aaa Attack held up in several places by M.G. fire but now apparently proceeding satisfactorily aaa Information still indefinite."[18]

Casualties amongst "officers and good NCOs", the GCO 97 Brigade later observed, "were severe." The leading wave was "very depleted, the men checking and taking up shell hole positions and firing. The rear companies consequently pushed through them, and when the furthest positions to which Battalions got to were reached, companies and platoons were very mixed and depleted and there were very few officers to conduct reorganisation and consolidation." A general summary of the assault's course from Zero to dawn was pieced together with a fair degree of accuracy in Blacklock's after-action report:

No. 1 Battalion [2nd KOYLI]
No. 1 Company failed to take TEAL[L] COTTAGE and eventually dug in with 2nd Rifle Brigade.
No. 2 Company overlapped No. 1 Company area and were also held up at TEAL COTTAGE.
No. 3 Company reached its objective after a good fight for pillboxes at V.24.c.5.1 suffering severely from enfilade fire from VENISON TRENCH.
No. 4 Company less one platoon sent to reinforce No.3 Company commanded to dig on HILL 52 on taped strongpoint.
This Battalion was counter-attacked at 3:25 a.m. from the northeast and fell back.

No. 2 Battalion [16th HLI]
Nos. 1 and 2 companies reached their objectives with very heavy loss.
The action of Nos. 3 and 4 companies is not at present clear, though it has been established that elements of all four companies dug in on the line VOID FARM inclusive with right refused towards HILL 52.

No. 3 Battalion [11th Border Regiment]
Met with little direct opposition but suffered severely from enfilade fire from both flanks.

18   BL: 48359: 'Report of Operations Carried Out by the VIII Army Corps on the Morning of 2nd December 1917, Official War Diaries with Appendices and Addenda, VIII Army Corps, Passchendaele Front, November 1917-April 1918', Vol. V, Hunter-Weston Papers.

No. 1 Company took VELDT FARM.
No. 2 Company reached its objective short of MALLET COPSE.
Nos. 3 and 4 companies leapfrogged Nos. 1 and 2, but were driven back by machine-gun fire from MALLET WOOD on to the line VOID FME – south of edge of MALLET COPSE with left refused, where they dug in, strength 100 men and 3 officers.

No. 4 Battalion [17th HLI]
Nos. 1 and 2 companies were held up almost at once by fire from VAT COT[TAGES] and a machine-gun about V.23.c.99.30 [vicinity of Veal Cottages].
No. 3 Company pushed through No.1 Company but was entirely held up by VEAL COT.
No. 4 Company pushed through No. 2 Company but was entirely held up by machine-gun fire from V.22.d.9.2 [west of Veal Cottages].

No. 5 Battalion [15th LF]
No. 5 Battalion advanced their left but were held up on the right with No. 4 Company of No. 4 Battalion by machine-gun fire from V.22.d.9.2.[19]

Lieutenant-Colonel Scully (CO No. 6 Battalion), in anticipation that 16th NF would be called upon to act in its "counter counter-attack" role, concentrated his four component companies in the vicinity of Virile Farm at "Zero plus 1 ½ hours … As the situation was obscure I ordered them to hold the original line and be ready to support the attacking troops."[20]

The first report concerning presumed progress by the infantry reached 32nd Division at 3:55 a.m.[21] The message, "timed 3:33 a.m. from 97th Infantry Brigade", imparted, "that the right of No. 4 Battalion (17th HLI) was held up by machine-gun fire and that the enemy was offering considerable resistance." At 4:00 a.m. a liaison officer with 14 Brigade reported a worrying German counter-attack on the left flank,

---

19 IWM 4723: 'Preliminary Report on Operations December 1st, 2nd and 3rd December', 4 December 1917, Brigadier-General T.S. Lambert Papers (Box 80/10/2).
20 Ibid: '32nd Div. No.G.S.1499/3/33', 4 December 1917.
21 Visual signalling efforts, Major Evelegh (CO 32nd Division Signal School) subsequently observed, 'worked very successfully both with RFA and battalions backward, but from companies to battalions apparently not attempted and it is believed that in cases the Lucas Lamps were left behind by the company signallers, although they were the only portable means to communicate except runners.' The latter organised on a 'relay system with relay posts and linesmen's posts coinciding as far as possible' proved 'extremely reliable if somewhat slow form of communication.' Few messages were dispatched by pigeon, but 'those that were arrived in good time, except in the case of some units which tried to fly them during the hours of darkness.' See TNA: WO/95/2370: After-action report: 'Appendix 'T': Communications', December 1917, 32nd Division War Diary.

"Otherwise all going well." This was immediately followed by a query from Shute to Brigadier-General J.A. Tyler (Division BGRA): "Above message read. Have you had that? They [batteries] have been asked by 97 Bde. to stop firing on the SOS lines on the left as counter-attack had been beaten off." Over a dozen more telephone and telegraph messages from various (FOO, RE, interviewed wounded, etc.) relating the attack's progress were exchanged during the next forty-six minutes. News of Hill 52 was confirmed at 4:59 a.m. when 97 Brigade telephoned to report the situation as related by a previously quoted eyewitness:

> Wounded RE officer [Lieutenant Spottiswoode] left HILL 52 between 2:30 a.m. and 3 a.m. after having planned a strongpoint there. He marked out trench for the strongpoint and left the [2nd] K.O.Y.L.I. at work on this trench and others [.] [They] had gone past towards their objective and as far as he could tell [,] thought they would get on it. He also came across some of the 16th HLI.

This heartening disclosure, based on the observations of an injured sapper almost three hours after Zero, would soon prove to be sadly out of date.[22]

Severe enfilade machine-gun fire hampered efforts by 2nd KOYLI to consolidate Hill 52, a continuous hail of bullets from the direction of Venison Trench raining down on to 'D' and 'B' companies and attached sappers of 219th Field Company RE. Captain J. Hassell (OC 'B' Company), in command of mixed remnants beyond the summit, did his best to ensure the position was secured against counter-attack from his newly-established trench HQ: "2nd Lieutenant Corcoran here joined him with the remains of his platoon, reporting that he had got to the objective, two pill-boxes (V.24.c.5.0 ½) and had been driven back by superior numbers." Hassell, fearing an imminent enemy riposte, placed all available elements from the three remaining companies under Corcoran and "ordered him to again advance and take the two pillboxes. In the meantime, consolidation was taking place at V.30.a.5.7. The Royal Engineer officer was wounded during the advance, but work was carried on by his men."[23]

2nd Lieutenant Corcoran's advance had not progressed far before colliding with the first local counter-attack at 3:30 a.m.[24] Files and blobs of *Feldgrau*-clad troops, wearing the distinctive "coal scuttle" steel helmet, were distinguished moving across the multitude of shell holes in the crepuscular half-light before dawn. This was too much for the exhausted and almost leaderless British infantry. Picks and shovels were

---

22 TNA: WO/95/2370: After-action report, 'Appendix 'J', 32nd Division: Telephone and Telegraph Messages 2 December 1917', 11 December 1917, 32nd Division War Diary. See Chapter 3, p. 227, fn. 146.
23 Ibid: After-action report, 'Part III, Narrative of Events', 11 December 1917, and TNA: WO/95/2402: 2nd KOYLI War Diary.
24 2nd Lieutenant Corcoran (age unknown) was killed sometime afterwards. He is buried in Duhallow ADS Cemetery.

downed as groups of overwrought men made their way to the rear. Captain Hassell did what he could to rally them, but the rot had set in:

> At this time a counter-attack on a large scale appeared to develop to his front with the result that the troops of the [2nd] Yorkshire Light Infantry and [16th] Highland Light Infantry and [11th] Border Regiment passed through his line of consolidation, carrying his own men with them. He was unable to rest the retirement until the "jumping-off" tape line was reached. He here re-organised the men and discovered they consisted of every battalion of the [97] Brigade except the 17th Highland L.I. He attempted to get them to advance again but, failing in this, he distributed the men along a line and consolidated … This line was held until daybreak.

Sergeant Horne ('D' Company) and his small party, still labouring to consolidate advanced positions 80 yards beyond the two resisting pillboxes, ordered a retirement during which they sustained several casualties. "He withdrew his party to a trench in rear where he found three officers and twenty other ranks of the [16th] High. L.I. …"[25]

Following this (5:25 a.m.), 97 Brigade reported that 11th Border Regiment had "occupied Mallet Copse and formed a defensive flank towards VEAL COTTAGES where the advance of 17th HLI had been checked by heavy machine-gun fire", while 15th LF had "secured their objective." Stokes mortars, it was also related, had been sent forward under the personal command of Lieutenant-Colonel J. Inglis "to deal with VEAL COTTAGES and to assist in the advance of 17th HLI." The situation at that time, as far as it was known at 32nd Division HQ, was as follows:

> The Right Battalion (2nd KOYLI) was in position on Hill 52 and consolidating.
>
> No. 3 Battalion (11th Border Regt.) and No. 5 Battalion (15th Lanc. Fusiliers) had secured their objectives.
>
> The advance of No. 4 Battalion (17th HLI), however, seemed to be definitely checked by machine-gun fire from VEAL COTTAGES.
>
> The situation of No. 2 Battalion (16th HLI) was unknown.

Shute, having been recently apprised of the situation and assured by the positive reports emanating from Hill 52, now fixed his gaze elsewhere. He quickly recognised that a dangerous gap – formed by the failure of 17th HLI to get forward – had opened

---

25 WO/95/2402: 2nd KOYLI War Diary. The attached sappers of 219th Field Company RE, their work complete, had already departed by the time of the German riposte. See Chapter 3, p. 227, fn. 146.

between 11th Border Regiment and 15th LF. A telegraph message, forwarded to 97 Brigade at 5:30 a.m., attempted to get the stalled attack of the centre left battalion moving again: "Instruct 11th Border Regt. and 15th LF to join hands on [final] objective of 17th HLI else garrison at VEAL COTTAGES will escape. Remaining companies of 17th HLI should also work around VEAL COTTAGES."[26]

A profusion of back and forth reports and queries continued to keep 32nd Division signals office busy in the hours following the dispatch of the 5:30 a.m. message to 97 Brigade. At 7:10 a.m., seventeen minutes before sunrise, 32nd Division discussed possible artillery targets and the general situation with 97 Brigade:

> Div. HQ: Are you being bothered from VALUATION HOUSES or MALLET WOOD? The Divisional Commander wants to know if Genl. BLACKLOCK would like an artillery concentration on either or both.
> 97 Brigade: Genl. BLACKLOCK would like to wait until he gets more news before he decides that question. 3 companies of 15th Lancs. Fus. are on their objective. 17th HLI held up at VEAL COTTAGES. Borders 100 yards other side of MALLET COPSE. No. 1 [2nd KOYLI] had got TEALL COTTAGE about Hill 52. Nothing known about No. 2 [16th HLI] Battalion. Up to 4:30 [a.m.] no message from them. You know they were 300 yards from their starting point.

A telegraph message from II Corps intelligence (codenamed "Mr MONTGOMERY") arrived while this telephone conversation was in progress: "4 prisoners 95 I.R. 5th Coy. captured in enemy frontline. Spot unknown but prisoner past to the east of VELDT FARM on the way to the trenches. Order of battle east to west 94, 95, 96 I.Rs. States attack was a surprise. Orders to hold frontline." One more message passed through the divisional signal office before daybreak: "Wire timed 7:15 a.m. from CRA. Situation normal."[27]

Shute's vaunted night attack scheme appeared, if received reports were accurate, to have achieved some success, his 32nd Division having secured most of the final red line objective. No doubt the planned pincer movement, to be carried out by 11th Border Regiment and 15th LF, would cut off and overwhelm strongpoints holding up 17th HLI. Nothing had been heard from 16th HLI, but 2nd KOYLI were, it was still believed, firmly established on Hill 52 at first light.

---

26   TNA: WO/95/2370: After-action report, 'Part III, Narrative of Events', and 'Appendix 'J', 32nd Division: Telephone and Telegraph Messages 2 December 1917', 11 December 1917, 32nd Division War Diary.
27   TNA: WO/95/2370: After-action report, 'Appendix 'J', 32nd Division: Telephone and Telegraph Messages 2 December 1917', 11 December 1917, 32nd Division War Diary.

4.2 Dawn

Sunday 2 December 7:27 a.m.: Sunrise heralded a fine winter day with strong 20 to 30 mph westerly and NW winds. Both RE 8 two-seater contact aircraft, scheduled to be airborne over the attack area by 7:30 a.m., remained grounded at the aerodromes of No. 7 and No. 21 corps squadrons because of the rough – "a strong gusty wind" – local atmospheric conditions.[28] A fighter pilot of No. 65 Squadron, struggling through a "perfectly shrieking wind" whilst on offensive patrol later that morning, encountered no enemy aircraft, "hardly any 'Archies' no MG – no signs of a push."[29] Visibility remained fair under a relatively clear sky. The weather continued to be "very cold throughout the day. A little snow fell in the early morning." An artillery officer, stationed west of the Steenbeek, noticed hard frost in the emerging forenoon light: "All the water in the crump holes was frozen over and a bitter north wind was blowing."[30] To the east, remnants of eight battalions remained alert to anticipated German counter-attacks whilst consolidating a ragged front. Heavy casualties amongst officers and NCOs deprived these units of leadership when it was most needed. Lieutenant A.B. Scott MC (32nd Division Artillery Reconnaissance Officer) encountered consequent muddle and uncertainty during a hazardous morning intelligence-gathering mission:

> I went up the line taking with me James of 168 Brigade RFA. By dawn we were well forward and observed the later barrages. We arrived at Colonel Scully's HQ (commanding [16th] Northumberland Fusiliers) and found the Colonel there. These headquarters had been established after the first assault: and were one of the posts of our old frontline – Vine [sic Virile] Farm. On our way there we were

---

28   TNA: WO/95/15: 'Weather Diary, December 1917', GHQ War Diary and BL: 48359: 'Report of Operations Carried Out by the VIII Army Corps on the Morning of 2nd December 1917, Official War Diaries with Appendices and Addenda, VIII Army Corps, Passchendaele Front, November 1917–April 1918', Vol. V, Hunter-Weston Papers. *Fourth Army's* weekly report observed that flying conditions remained unfavourable throughout 2 December. RFC losses that day amounted to (1) Spad 7, (1) Bristol F2b, (1) Nieuport 17 and (2) DH4s. See KA HKR 145: 'AOK 4 I/a MSO, AHQ 6.12.17, Fiendliche Luftstreitkräfte, Wochenzusammenstellung, Vom 29.11 bis 5.12.17, pp. 7-8 and Trevor Henshaw, *The Sky Their Battlefield: Air Fighting and the Complete List of Allied Air Casualties from Enemy Action in the First War: British, Commonwealth and United States Air Services 1914 to 1918* (London: Grub Street, 1995), pp. 259-60.

29   Christopher M. Burgess (ed), *The Diary and Letters of a World War I Fighter Pilot: 2nd Lieutenant Guy Mainwaring Knocker's accounts of his experiences in 1917-1918 while serving in the RFC/RAF* (Barnsley: Pen & Sword, 2008), p. 97.

30   BL: 48359: 'Report of Operations Carried Out by the VIII Army Corps on the Morning of 2nd December 1917, Official War Diaries with Appendices and Addenda, VIII Army Corps, Passchendaele Front, November 1917–April 1918', Vol. V, Hunter-Weston Papers and Lieutenant-Colonel H.M. Davson, *Memoirs of the Great War* (Aldershot: Gale & Polden, 1964), p. 113.

sniped at; several runners were lying dead along this path and we quickened our pace.

Colonel Scully explained the situation to me, and asked me to take back a dispatch to General Blacklock. I asked if I could first go forward to see if I could find out any further information. He said he would have the dispatch ready when I returned if I would call at his headquarters. James and I then went forward and saw first of all several dead Huns, one of whom was a cavalry officer. I took off his identification – while doing so I was again sniped at, and we lay low at the bottom of the shell hole.

I saw another Hun lying against a stump of a tree and yelling like blazes. He apparently was badly wounded, but lay either in No Man's Land or between the enemy's posts. After going forward to our most forward post we returned to Colonel Scully to receive his dispatch. He warned us again of the sniping at one particular point of the duck walk and we hurried on past it.[31]

The general view from new positions, relative to depth of advance, after dawn varied: a dreary, pockmarked expanse opposite Exert Farm; due east to the near edge of sloping dead ground from a captured portion of Venison Trench; north and NW into low-lying ground opposite Poelcappelle from the western extremity of Vat Cottages Ridge or, in comparison, more limited – the next shell hole, bomb stop, nearby trench, pillbox, gun pit or spinney – vistas in sectors where the surprise night attack failed to make significant headway; irregular rifle and machine-gun fire, along with desultory rifle grenade discharges and shell bursts, echoed across the raw shambolic wilderness. Seemingly random individual figures and remote groups or columns, taking belated advantage of the rapidly fading darkness, dashed from shell hole to shell hole or plodded along some distant skyline. Such activity brought forth an immediate response from snipers or artillery when within range. Other figures, torn, riddled and lying in heaps or half in and out of the numerous craters, added to the already desolate scene. A crimson-coloured film, tinting the surface of turbid shell hole waters, marked the fate of men lost from sight. Overall, a nauseating stench of rotting, sodden battle detritus, blood and poisoned earth combined with a sickly odour of cordite and high explosive pervaded the frigid atmosphere. *Fourth Army's* morning report (timed 8:45 a.m.) related what was known thus far: "Weather slightly stormy with bright moon. Enemy artillery fire still active in *Gruppe Staden's* sector, pattern of fire falling mainly about rear areas in planned shoots; fire on *Gruppe Ypern* lasting throughout the evening hours until 3:00 a.m. Shelling of increased intensity commencing in the Passchendaele area shortly afterwards; enemy infantry attacked in vicinity of the Passchendaele – Oostnieuwkerke and Passchendaele – Westroosebeke roads at approximately 4:00 a.m. [sic]. Attacks still in progress."[32]

31   Scott, Grice-Hutchison, et al, *Artillery & Trench Mortar Memories*, pp. 84-85.
32   KA HKR 99: Telegraph/wireless pro formas 2 December 1917.

4.3 25 Brigade

Four more (two telegraph and two telephone) situation reports were received at VIII Corps between 6:45 and 7:45 a.m.:

> 6:45 a.m. from I.O. 8th Division (Thro' 'I' 8th Corps). 4 prisoners 94th I.R. captured by left [32nd] Division aaa Relieved 357 [IR] last night aaa 3rd Battalion in line reinforced by 3 coys. 1st Bn.
>
> 6:55 a.m. from Second Army. Morning Report aaa 8th 19th 1st and 2nd ANZAC corps report situation unchanged aaa Our troops attacked north of PASSCHENDAELE this morning aaa Attack believed to be proceeding satisfactorily.
>
> 7:40 a.m. from 21st Squadron RFC (telephone). Too rough to get up at present. Will go out as soon as it is possible.
>
> 7:45 a.m. from 8th Division (telephone). No more information than that already sent in. Have told [25] Brigade to send in report on situation.

News, reasonably accurate as it turned out, of 25 Brigade's plight finally arrived at 8:00 and 8:20 a.m.:

> Following from 25th Inf. Bde. aaa Verbal message timed 6:20 a.m. One coy. left battalion held up in front of Vension Trench aaa Left of centre battalion believed to have been held up.
>
> 6:20 a.m. 8th Division (Telephone). Situation aaa We have probably got the Southern Redoubt and a little of the trench north of it. Line probably runs through practice trenches to our original line. 32nd Division off Hill 52 and 8th Division believes out of TEALL COTTAGES [sic]. This is all presumption.

A telegraph from the same source, also received at 8:20 a.m., cast some doubt on the accuracy, as far as 25 Brigade's situation was concerned, of the previous updates: "Report timed 7:10 a.m. states aaa Enemy artillery fire very much increased during last half hour aaa Have asked for counter-battery aaa Impression aaa Left and centre move obscure and nothing received from them aaa Centre possibly successful aaa Left probably not."[33]

The single platoon of 'D' Company 2nd Royal Berkshire was still in position just SE of Southern Redoubt at sunrise. Here they "found themselves without officers and with their left flank in the air." Groups of German infantry were observed entering

---

33 BL: 48359: 'Report of Operations Carried Out by the VIII Army Corps on the Morning of 2nd December 1917, Official War Diaries with Appendices and Addenda, VIII Army Corps, Passchendaele Front, November 1917–April 1918', Vol. V, Hunter-Weston Papers.

the adjacent earthwork from the left after which – "inflicting casualties on the enemy" – the hard-pressed platoon withdrew "to gain touch with the ['B' Company] troops SW of the redoubt..." *IR116* had reclaimed the lost bastion, its post-war regimental history observing: "Hard work was done and the line again in our possession at approximately 10:00 a.m. Enemy losses in dead and wounded were great with twenty prisoners remaining in our hands, but many good *Kameraden* were missed on our side."[34] 2nd Lieutenant Upton's platoon, still occupying a section of Venison Trench NW of Southern Redoubt, engaged the counter-attacking Hessians from the left. Galling fire from a strongpoint on their immediate left was "suppressed chiefly with rifle grenades." The threat to both flanks, reduced state of his platoon and continued isolation worried Upton. A hurriedly scribbled message, dispatched by runner to Battalion HQ, spelled out their perilous position.[35]

Lieutenant-Colonel Stirling (CO 2nd Royal Berkshire), taking advantage of the slackening bombardment on the Passchendaele – Westroosebeke Road, made his way to the Mosselmarkt HQ of Lieutenant-Colonel Irwin (CO 2nd Lincolnshire) at 8:00 a.m.:

> On my way I found a wounded orderly from 'B' Coy and got from him a message, timed 3:45 a.m., saying that 'B' Coy. was in position and all was well. This was the first report I had received from an officer. On reaching MOSSELMARKT, OC 2nd Lincolns told me that his Battalion and 2nd Rifle Brigade had not reached their objective. I therefore took advantage of the quietness [sic] then prevailing to go forward to try and ascertain the situation on my own front and got forward through an old outpost line to the trench joining the two redoubts where I saw some of our stretcher-bearers at work. On approaching the trench, however, I found it occupied by the enemy.

Returning to Battalion HQ around 10:00 a.m., he received a message which gave "the impression that the enemy was working round my right."[36] Stirling's response was immediate and decisive: "I, therefore, sent my support ['A'] coy, which had been much reduced by casualties from the heavy shellfire to work forward to cover my right at the same time warning the Lincolns and 1st R.I. Rifles of what I thought was going on." At this point three incidents occurred that ensured Southern Redoubt remained in enemy hands. First, the CO 'A' Company, Battalion HQ would discover sometime later, was wounded whilst leading his men to the right. Second, receipt of Upton's message made Stirling aware of the former's "isolated position & strength and that

---

34   Prof. Albert Hiss, *Infanterie-Regiment Kaiser Wilhelm (2. Grossherzoglich Hessisches) Nr. 116* (Oldenburg: Gerhard Stalling, 1924), p. 158.
35   TNA: WO/95/1677: 'Narrative of Operations Carried Out by the 8th Division on 1st/2nd December 1917', 13 December 1917, 8th Division War Diary and WO/95/1929: 'Appendix B', 5 December 1917, 2nd Royal Berkshire War Diary.
36   TNA: WO/95/1929: 'Appendix B', 5 December 1917, 2nd Royal Berkshire War Diary.

News from the firing line: A contemporary illustration. (*The War Illustrated*, 16 March 1918)

he was much worried from both flanks." Third, Captain Flint (CO 'C' Company), whom Stirling had sent for, arrived to report the right flank was "fairly established and in touch with 33rd Division." The last two updates, the CO 2nd Royal Berkshire instantly recognised, confirmed the support company had been ordered to the wrong part of the line.[37]

37 Ibid.

Lieutenant-Colonel N.M.S. Irwin MC (centre). (IWM 1100)

Irwin, for his part, remained equally uninformed after sunrise:

> Owing to officer casualties[38] the first report received by me was in reply to a message I had sent forward. This was received around 6:20 a.m. and said that our advance had gone through the outpost line and had dug in 30 yards from enemy main trench. At 8:00 a.m. I sent up an officer to reconnoitre who confirmed above report & stated that advanced line was successfully dug in with left post near road (on left of Battalion front) in touch with RIFLE BRIGADE [,] but the connection with Berkshire on our right was uncertain.

Thus he remained unaware that Upton's beleaguered Royal Berkshire platoon was consolidating a small section of 2nd Lincolnshire's assigned Venison Trench objective opposite his right flank. Informed at 10:00 a.m. "that all officers of assaulting

---

38 2nd Lincolnshire officer casualties: Lieutenant R.H. Parker wounded and missing; 2nd Lieutenant B.W. Griffin DOW; 2nd Lieutenants Eliot, Sowerby, Joyce, Groom, Green, Graves, Grant and Perkins wounded. 2nd Lieutenant Basil Walker Griffin (age unknown) has no known grave and is commemorated on the Tyne Cot Memorial to the Missing. See Simpson, *The History of the Lincolnshire Regiment 1914-1918*, p. 284.

companies were casualties", Irwin dispatched a reserve company junior officer "to take command and re-organise"; the unfortunate subaltern was killed by a sniper whilst attempting to carry out these duties.[39]

On the left, surviving elements of 'A', 'B' and 'C' companies 2nd Rifle Brigade clung to outposts consisting of three to six men each just 100 yards from the start line. The enemy's "attitude", battalion adjutant Lieutenant Anderson later observed, "was aggressive. Several attempts were made to raid our posts but these were driven off. There was also a considerable amount of bombing and rifle bombing from the enemy's forward posts."[40] Nettleton, having done all that he could to organise some sort of coherent line, returned to the crowded Meetcheele pillbox before daybreak:

> Back at Battalion HQ, however, we were out of sight of the enemy by eight o'clock. I was sent out to look for some more accommodation to relieve the congestion in and around our pillbox. I found another pillbox about two hundred yards down the road but it was choked with dead Germans. They must have been caught by the Canadians and bombed as they were trying to escape. We had to pull out more than a dozen corpses before we could get into it. However, when we got it cleared, it gave us room to sit down and have breakfast and, as there was nothing anyone could do outside, we passed the day in comparative peace.
>
> Only comparative though – there was shelling going on all the time and the Boche seemed to have got our pillbox taped. One shell hit the back wall of the pillbox and burst along the trench outside, causing several casualties. One man caught most of the blast and had one side of his body ripped to pieces. While the stretcher-bearers were trying to bandage him up, he was screaming and groaning, but not because of his terrible wounds. He had got a splinter in the foot away from the side that had been blasted and it appeared to have broken his toe and it was that he was groaning about. I suppose the side of his body that had been torn to bits was so numb that he did not realise what had happened. But it sounded odd to hear him crying, "Oh, my toe, oh my toe" when that was such a minor part of his injuries. Luckily we were able to evacuate him without having to wait for nightfall, but I don't think he can have survived.[41]

This horribly injured man, a victim of a waning but still deadly hostile bombardment, was one of the many wounded fortunate enough to be evacuated from the battlefield during what was an almost routine, albeit short-lived, period of joint co-operation between enemies.

---

39 TNA: WO/95/1730: 'Report on Action of Battn from 2:30 p.m. 1.12.17 – M.N. 2/3 .12. 17', 2nd Lincolnshire War Diary.
40 TNA: WO/95/1731: 'Report of the part played by the 2nd Battn. The Rifle Brigade in the Operations at Passchendaele', 6 December 1917, 2nd Rifle Brigade War Diary.
41 Nettleton, *The Anger of the Guns*, p. 118-19.

Published German regimental accounts often relate the mutually recognised *Sanitätspause* (cease-fire to allow the collecting of the dead and wounded) with their British opponents. A German officer wrote of an earlier arrangement the previous November: "Only between 9:00 a.m. and 10:00 a.m., the so-called "medical pause", could I get around the sector without difficulty. This was the time when both sides observed the unwritten rule that there would be no firing to permit the recovery of the wounded."[42] Identical activity commenced on 25 Brigade's front one half hour after dawn: "At about 8 a.m. stretcher parties of both sides were at work and the shelling, which had, up to that time, been heavy; slackened somewhat."[43] Red Cross flags and armbands, white handkerchiefs attached to sticks and other overt displays were sufficient to communicate the intentions of medical personnel and stretcher parties. The garrison of Teall Cottage, situated just beyond the left flank where the mutual succour of casualties was also under way on 97 Brigade's front, held their fire throughout the clearance process:

> The team working that machine-gun in Teall Cottage allowed wounded men to be brought in so long as stretcher-bearers did not get too near the post. At the same time they could see the encouraging spectacle of their own countrymen going through our lines as prisoners. The latter were in sad condition; their morale was gone: but the machine-gunners in Teall Cottage were in rare form![44]

Wounded were carried on litters to the nearest RAP, where they were treated and sent down the line as rapidly as possible under sporadic shellfire. One battalion medical officer (Captain A. Cowe of 2nd Lincolnshire Regiment) was killed while tending a wounded officer.[45]

42 Sheldon, *The German Army at Passchendaele*, p. 292.
43 TNA: WO/95/1677: 'Narrative of Operations Carried Out by the 8th Division on 1st/2nd December 1917', 13 December 1917, 8th Division War Diary.
44 Cooke, *Historical Records of the 16th (Service) Battalion Northumberland Fusiliers*, p. 89. *IR94's* regimental history states: 'English medical personnel arrived around 9:00 a.m. [German time]. Efforts to recover their dead and wounded were observed at many places before our line. *4th Company* removed the remaining enemy casualties from the *Vorfeldzone*. The sector of the neighbouring regiment was cleared of fallen English with the assistance of *4th Company* that afternoon.' See Hartmann, *Das Infanterie Regiment Grossherzog von Sachsen (5. Thüringisches) No. 94* im *Weltkrieg*, pp. 237-38.
45 Son of the late Archibald Cowe JP (a well-known Midlothian Liberal) and Sarah, née Murdoch, Cowe, 28-year-old A/Captain Archibald Cowe was educated at Penicuik Public School, George Watson's College and Edinburgh University where he qualified MB, ChB (Hons) in 1913. Graduation was followed by receipt of an Edward VII Anglo-German scholarship to study neurology and gynaecology at Freiberg University. Returning home after the outbreak of war in August 1914, Cowe held the prestigious post of house surgeon at King Edward VII Hospital Windsor for several months before accepting an RAMC commission in February 1915. Invalided home after 18 months active service, he returned to France in September 1917. Archibald Cowe has no known grave and is commemorated

Coffin was pessimistic about continuing the attack on the centre and left of 25 Brigade's front. This grim forecast, passed on to Heneker for consideration, was based on direct observation from Mosselmarkt and subsequent consultations with Irwin and acting CO 2nd Rifle Brigade Lieutenant Anderson. Northern Redoubt, the GOC 25 Brigade concluded, could only be attacked in conjunction with an assault on Teall Cottage. This "required fresh troops as those now engaged have had considerable losses particularly in officers." Forming up would "have to be at night", as the jumping-off positions were in full view of the enemy. A daylight attack, he also observed, would be a "difficult and hazardous" undertaking.[46]

Aware that his reserve company had been dispatched to the wrong place, Lieutenant-Colonel Stirling anxiously viewed the *Sanitätspause* still in progress: "At this time [10:00 a.m.] I sent out orders to all commanders to stop the enemy's stretcher-bearers from moving in the open, as they appeared to be taking advantage of their freedom to approach our line."[47] *IR117's* regimental history provides evidence that his suspicions were correct:

> The morning came and with it unbelievable behaviour by the English. Troops of *Sanitäts Komp.* 45 assisted with bandaging and cared for our own and the enemy wounded. English stretcher-bearers also provided succor. Our *Sanitäts* helpers discovered there were approximately 150 English in the vicinity of the breach, and altogether about 600 between and behind their own position. There was no reaction, despite considerable local superiority, when *Gef.* Speiz (*9th Company*) led eight prisoners away.[48]

The situation could not continue, Coffin noting the swift retribution that followed: "At one time the enemy, under cover of a Red Cross flag, sent a large body out to try and reconnoitre our positions. This effort was treated as it deserved to be."[49]

For the Germans, the situation at the breach had gone from seemingly "hopeless" to hopeful, as three companies of 2nd Lincolnshire Regiment, unaware of Upton's isolated platoon in front, remained stationary just 30 yards from Venison Trench. Fierce enemy resistance, consequent confusion and heavy losses amongst officers

---

on the Tyne Cot Memorial to the Missing. See RAMC in the Great War <http://www.ramcww1.com/profile.php?cPath=292_511_545&profile_id=10097&osCsid=7326968b669af351338a02e2ea3dc7c1>

46 BL: 48359: 'Report of Operations Carried Out by the VIII Army Corps on the Morning of 2nd December 1917, Official War Diaries with Appendices and Addenda, VIII Army Corps, Passchendaele Front, November 1917-April 1918', Vol. V, Hunter-Weston Papers.
47 TNA: WO/95/1929: 'Appendix B', 5 December 1917, 2nd Royal Berkshire War Diary.
48 Offenbacher, *Die Geschichte des Infanterie-Leibregiments Grossherzogin (3.Grossherzoglich Hessisches) Nr. 117*, p. 196.
49 TNA: WO/95/1677: 'Narrative of Operations Carried Out by the 8th Division on 1st/2nd December 1917', 13 December 1917, 8th Division War Diary.

Captain A. Cowe. (University of Edinburgh, *University of Edinburgh Roll of Honour 1914-1919* (London: Oliver & Boyd, 1921))

October 1917: *Hauptmann* von Arnim at the head of *III Battalion, IR117* during a regimental parade. (Hauptmann Kurt Offenbacher, *Die Geschichte des Infanterie-Leibregiments Grossherzogin (3. Grossherzoglich Hessisches) Nr. 117* (Oldenburg: Gerhard Stalling, 1931))

and NCOs contributed to collective weariness and inactivity – "unbelievable behaviour by the English" – despite their almost overwhelming local superiority. *IR117's Kampftruppenkommandeur* immediately recognised the opportunity to exploit British lassitude: "*Hauptmann* von Arnim realised he only had 80 to 90 rifles, 10 machine-guns, with limited supplies of ammunition, available. The enemy, however, lacked the will to continue the struggle. Leaving *Vzfw.* Woeste (*2nd Company*) in charge, he raced to the rear to organise a systematic counter-attack."[50] Woeste, observing *IR116's*

---

50 See Appendix XVI Part C (para. 15).

efforts to recapture Southern Redoubt, "seized this moment to order an all-out attack" at 12:00 p.m. (German time). "Taking prisoners as the English hurriedly withdrew, the *Hauptwiderstandslinie* was reached and contact made" with previously isolated elements of 9th *Company*.[51]

Stirling, certain his right flank was secure, gave orders to withdraw 2nd Royal Berkshire's misdirected support company and dispatched Captain Flint "to find out the situation on the left."[52] Irwin, in an attempt to clarify the situation on his right, "went round to the OC [2nd] Berkshires", who, having received 2nd Lieutenant Upton's written message, related that "he had a post reported in enemy trench in advance of my right one near road about W.25.c.2.3. This meant a gap of about 150 yards. This [,] however [,] was covered by the original [Lincolnshire] outpost in rear." Stirling's account of this meeting, which took place at approximately 11:30 a.m., noted: "OC 2nd Lincolns arrived at my HQ and informed me that he had definitely established that his Battalion was dug in close up to the German trench between the two redoubts. He [Irwin] awaited [sic] until Captain Flint returned about 12:30 p.m. with the report that the Lieutenant [Upton] was in command of elements of B, C & D coys. dug in near the southern and south-western edges of Southern redoubt." Stirling informed Irwin that he planned to withdraw Upton's isolated Venison Trench outpost after dark in order to "fill up the gap between our two battalions." Runners were dispatched with orders for the eventual retirement not long afterwards. Half past twelve also heralded an intensified bombardment by German batteries. Hostile shells pounded 2nd Royal Berkshire's pillbox HQ – situated along the Passchendaele – Wetroosebeke Road just north of Passchendaele village – for the next three hours and forty minutes. No information was received from the frontline during this time. Stirling, forced to remain under cover, recalled: "I was also unable to send out any further orders or reconnaissance farther."[53]

Meanwhile, wireless intercept stations dispatched their findings to Corps' 'I' sections, which passed the information on to VIII and II corps HQs. Some idea of

---

51   Ibid.
52   TNA: WO/95/1929: 'Appendix B', 5 December 1917, 2nd Royal Berkshire War Diary. Concern about the security of 2nd Royal Berkshire's right flank re-emerged in a message from Coffin to 8th Division HQ: 'Following from 25th Inf. Bde. Timed 11:38 a.m. aaa Enemy trying to work round right flank of 2nd R. Berks (right Battn) aaa Have asked for SOS [barrage] on zones U and V.' See BL: 48359: 'Report of Operations Carried Out by the VIII Army Corps on the Morning of 2nd December 1917, Official War Diaries with Appendices and Addenda, VIII Army Corps, Passchendaele Front, November 1917-April 1918', Vol. V, Hunter-Weston Papers.
53   TNA: WO/95/1929: 'Appendix B', 5 December 1917, 2nd Royal Berkshire War Diary and WO/95/1730: 'Report on Action of Battn from 2:30 p.m. 1.12.17 – M.N. 2/3 .12. 17', 2nd Lincolnshire War Diary. Two pigeon messages, relating the 12:30 p.m. heightening of the German bombardment, were sent off by the artillery liaison officer attached to 2nd Lincolnshire HQ. The pigeon loft recorded the dispatched bird's arrival at 3:40 p.m. See original message forms found in TNA: WO/95/1677: 8th Division War Diary.

the enemy's predicament was thus discerned, although the immediate value of this intelligence was, to a certain extent, of limited usefulness.[54] Three intercept transcripts reached Captain Eric Chaplin (ADC to Hunter-Weston) before noon. The enemy, their contents inferred, appeared to be undergoing a serious ordeal:

> 8:30 a.m. Second Army 'I' (Through 8th Corps I). Group 200 two messages from GC to NZ aaa First message reads aaa *Sofort reserve Kompagnie dem b verfurgung stellen* aaa German time of message 8:10 a.m. aaa Second message reads aaa *STAB 94 und dritte Kompagnie im marsch zum b* rest of message jammed out aaa German time of message 7:00 a.m.
> 10:30 a.m. WIO Bar (Thro' 8th Corps I). Group 200 sends *IN VORDERE LINIE MUNITION ERFORDERLICH.*
> 11:00 a.m. WIO BAR (Thro' 8th Corps I) Group 200 sends Coy. Commander 12th Coy. reports 5 wounded 9th Coy. not yet returned up to the present 7 wounded aaa Group 205 sends 2nd Coy. Commander wounded Bn. Commander wounded, present frontline Company Commander killed. Group 205 sends troop has advanced as far as line GH K F – 41.[55]

The more conventional telegraph and telephone messages – forwarded by neighbouring corps and division HQs, attached division HQs, corps subsections, observers, etc. between 9:00 and 11:00 a.m. – revealed, despite the grounding of aerial contact patrols, the general situation to Hunter-Weston's staff:

> 9:10 a.m. from 2nd Corps. Corps observers report a lot of movement is taking place around VALUATION HOUSES V.24.a.1.6 as if to meet an attack on Hill 50.
> 9:30 a.m. from 2nd Corps 'I' (Thro' 8th Corps I) 4 prisoners 94th I.R. captured near VOX FARM [,] 3 of the 3rd Coy. and 1 of the 12th Coy. state 12th Coy. 94th I.R. relieved 237th Regt. [*199th Division*] in frontline on 29th or 30th aaa They mention 133rd I.R. as being in ROULERS. This is not confirmed.
> 10:30 a.m. from 2nd Corps 'I' (Thro' 8th Corps I) Wind too puffy for contact patrols but situation appears to be that we hold [Southern] redoubt in W.25.c and about 100 yards of [Venison] trench running N.W. aaa Our

---

54 The primary drawback was due to the 'fact that the Germans normally used wireless only for communication of immediate, and therefore, perishable messages from Army headquarters downwards.' See Beach, 'British Intelligence and the German Army, 1914–1918', p. 87.
55 See BL: 48359: 'Report of Operations Carried Out by the VIII Army Corps on the Morning of 2nd December 1917, Official War Diaries with Appendices and Addenda, VIII Army Corps, Passchendaele Front, November 1917–April 1918', Vol. V, Hunter-Weston Papers.

> [8th Division] line apparently runs through practice trenches in V.30.b to original jumping-off line near Teall Cottages.
>
> 10:40 a.m. from 8th Division. Following from 25th Infantry Brigade aaa Line now runs all objectives on right to W.25.a.15.30. 150 yards approximately S.E. of Northern Redoubt thence Teall Cot. exclusive.[56]

At 11:00 a.m. 8th Division notified VIII Corps of Coffin's reservations about continuing the operation, Heneker adding that he concurred with this view. Another telegraph message (received at 11:15 a.m.) from II Corps recounted unsatisfactory news from the left:

> Situation appears that we [32nd Division] hold line from Teall Cott. to VOID FARM exclusive [,] southern edge of MALLET COPSE – VEAL COTTAGES exclusive – V.23.c.0.3 – V.22.d.8.0. [objective assigned to 15th LF] – to old frontline at V.28.b.5.4. aaa We captured Hill 52 but heavy enfilade fire from VENISON TRENCH and a counter-attack from NE drove us back aaa Measures are being taken to recapture Hill 52.

Eingreifdivisionen activity had gone undetected as of mid-morning: "Noon from [Second] Army Report Centre. No troop movement of parties larger than 10 seen in WESTROOSEBEKE area and 2 miles east of it. This message was dropped from an aeroplane, timed 10 a.m."[57] The German defenders, it could be reasonably surmised, were still relying on local reserves to contain the British attack.

4.4 97 Brigade

Thirty-five minutes (7:10 to 7:45 a.m.) passed before Shute received confirmation that Hill 52 was still in enemy hands. His immediate concern was the artillery's ability to engage Valuation Houses, "where considerable movement of the enemy was reported", and the troublesome centre of resistance at Mallet Wood:

> Div. HQ: 7:20 a.m. Verbal. To Div. Arty. What are the heavies doing now?
> Reply: They are doing harassing fire as usual.
> Div. HQ: What are the field artillery doing now?
> Reply: They are not firing at all.

---

56 Ibid.
57 Ibid. This aircraft had, before jettisoning the message over Second Army Report Centre, probably been on offensive patrol or flash-spotting duty, as specially designated RE 8 contact machines from both (No. 7 and 21) corps squadrons were still grounded by strong winds.

Div. HQ: The field artillery are to put a good heavy concentration on to VALUATION HOUSES and MALLET WOOD.

Div. HQ: 7:35 a.m. Verbal. To CRA. At 7:30 a.m. artillery ordered to have a heavy concentration on VALUATION HOUSES and MALLET WOOD.

Mallet Wood, the CRA replied one minute later, "is within [our] SOS lines." Shute, not willing to risk shelling his own men, ordered that Mallet Wood should be ignored, all field gun batteries to be directed on to Valuation Houses instead.[58]

Blacklock telephoned with unpalatable news at 7:45 a.m.: "GOC 97th Brigade telephones that they have been driven out of TEALL COTTAGE and VEAL [COTTAGES] and HILL 52. The attack appears to be considerably disorganised and they are trying to rectify this." Shute was unequivocal in his reply: "Absolutely necessary that TEALL COTTAGE and VEAL and HILL 52 should be regained.[59] Do this with your reserve Battalion assisted, if safety permits, by fire from your special battery[60] and Stokes mortars. Any more considerable barrage is impossible owing to your uncertainty as to the position of your troops." The first phase of 97 Brigade's attack had, except where the advance was held up at Teall Cottage and Vat Cottages, reached or moved beyond the "200 yard" or yellow line that roughly delineated the *Vorfeldzone's* northern boundary. This apparent half success could, Shute hoped, be followed up and the dire situation turned around by on-the-spot reorganisation of the five assault battalions and commitment of 16th NF (Blacklock's sole reserve or counter-counter-attack battalion) from positions situated on 97 Brigade's right front about Virile Farm.

Survivors of 2nd KOYLI, intermixed with stray elements of 16th HLI and 11th Border Regiment following the general retirement, remained in position along the original jump-off line until after sunrise. At dawn, 'A' Company's outposts, situated east of the Passchendaele – Westroosebeke Road, experienced heavy, sustained machine-gun fire from the direction of Venison Trench that was maintained throughout the day. Sergeant Hayward (*de facto* commander of 'C' Company) "could see no one near him and only having seven men with him" withdrew his isolated outpost to the left rear and dug in. Captain Hassell, the last unwounded company officer, only managed

---

58 See TNA: WO/95/2370: After-action report, 'Part III, Narrative of Events', and 'Appendix 'J', 32nd Division: Telephone and Telegraph Messages 2 December 1917', 11 December 1917, 32nd Division War Diary. At 7:45 a.m. II Corps MDS reported the arrival of 1 officer and 105 ORs wounded up to 7:00 a.m.; no German prisoners had been brought there up to that time.
59 Veal Cottages was, of course, not even temporarily seized on 2 December.
60 'Special battery' as per O.O. No. 138 (27 November 1917): 'The C.R.A. will detail an R.F.A battery commander to be attached to headquarters 97th Infantry Brigade. This officer's battery will, when required, be at the direct disposal of the G.O.C. 97th Infantry Brigade.' See TNA: WO/95/2370: '32nd Division Operation Order No. 138', 32nd Division War Diary.

to find twelve members of the Battalion.⁶¹ Lieutenant-Colonel Lamotte gathered in eleven more who were immediately placed, in addition to a sergeant and six men detached from Battalion HQ, under Hassell's command. Reorganisation commenced at 8:00 a.m., as the tireless Hassell "collected all the men of the Yorkshire Light Infantry in the area." These residual elements were organised into "three posts of ten in each under one Sergeant." Two of the three posts were armed with Lewis guns to form an advanced outpost line opposite Teall Cottage.⁶²

"Pitifully thinned" elements of 16th HLI still retained the small salient east and west of the tactically important Void Farm at daybreak.⁶³ Exposed flanks on left and right halted all movement beyond the dotted green line. Captain Alexander (CO 'C' Company), concerned by the exposed right flank, led what remained of 'A' and 'B' companies towards Teall Cottage where they dug in.⁶⁴ German reconnaissance aircraft were, as on 10 November, observed "flying low over our positions, but there was little enemy artillery activity." Five officers and seventy men – out of a pre-battle complement of twenty officers and 469 ORs – remained to defend the hard-won gains; word of their positions and plight remained unknown at Division and Brigade HQs.⁶⁵

---

61   Officer casualties sustained by Captain Hassell's 'B' Company, in addition to 2nd Lieutenant Corcoran, were 2nd Lieutenant A.W. Stark wounded and 2nd Lieutenant E. Cain missing. 2nd Lieutenant Edward Cain (age unknown) has no known grave and is commemorated on the Tyne Cot Memorial to the Missing.
62   Captain Hassell later observed: 'At the time it was thought that only the twenty-three men found at dawn were survivors, but from later knowledge it is quite clear that the other men of the battalion got mixed-up with and assisted other units of the Brigade to hold the line retired to. No report was received from any detached party, notwithstanding that the sending of reports had received special training and emphasis during training out of the line.' TNA: WO/95/2402: 2nd KOYLI War Diary.
63   Lieutenant Kerr 219th Field Company RE, unable to 'get in touch with anyone who could tell me the situation', left Vox for Void Farm sometime after 2:30 a.m. Proceeding due north he encountered 3 'Borders' and a 'Captain Maddison' (sic Captains Sandeman or Martin? See Chapter 3, p. 233, fn. 161.) who was killed before he could be queried. The nonplused sapper subaltern, finding the situation at Void Farm 'a bit muddled', returned to discover Vox Farm in good state of defence, the men, who 'wanted a bit of swearing', eventually digging 'right down 6' in the trench' before dawn. He also claimed to have set out for 16th HLI HQ 'about 1 hour after Zero', but made no mention of arrival until sometime after 6:00 a.m. when he 'reported to the Major [Scott] there, telling him exactly what I had done and asking him if he wanted anything further.' He subsequently reported to 97 Brigade HQ (Kronprinz Farm) at 12:15 p.m. The Brigade Major, he added, 'did not know at the time we had VOX FARM.' See IWM 4723: 'STATEMENT BY LIEUT. KERR R.E.' Brigadier-General T.S. Lambert Papers (Box 80/10/2).
64   This gallant officer subsequently vanished, 16th HLI's diarist noting: 'During this operation Captain Alexander was found to be missing. It is believed that he was caught by a shell while visiting the shell hole posts.' 37-year-old Captain James Alexander has no known grave and is commemorated on the Tyne Cot Memorial to the Missing.
65   See TNA: WO/95/2402: 2nd KOYLI War Diary, WO/95/2404: 16th HLI War Diary and Chalmers (ed), *A Saga of Scotland*, pp. 110-11.

Four depleted companies, two occupying the dotted green line intermediary objective and two (approximately 3 officers and 100 ORs) still clinging to the southern fringe of Mallet Copse, of 11th Border Regiment maintained their tenuous advanced positions throughout the night. It was just before sunrise when unrelenting enfilade machine-gun fire and hostile infantry probes supported by rifle and rifle grenade fusillades from the direction of Mallet Wood, forced back what was left of the leap-frogging companies. Worn survivors and walking wounded, retiring from the splintered, debris-strewn desolation of the copse, staggered back as far as the dotted green line where they dug in with the first wave companies.[66]

Intense machine-gun fire from the wired and heavily garrisoned strongpoints at Vat and Veal cottages continued to hold up the advance of 17th HLI. Subsequent attempts to outflank the two centres of resistance added to the already debilitating casualty list. "The Battalion hung on all night in its isolated positions, and orders were received that the attack would be resumed in the morning, but this order was afterwards cancelled." Dawn brought diminished shelling "but enemy machine-gunners and snipers kept up a harassing fire from their well-established posts against our men in their exposed and isolated positions."[67]

On the left, three companies ('A', 'B' 'C'), supported by two platoons from the reserve ('D') company, of 15th LF maintained a left flank guard from positions gained after Zero. "Things had not gone so well on the right. The 17th Highland Light Infantry had been held up by German machine-gun fire and there was a risk of a dangerous gap occurring between the 15th Lancashire Fusiliers and the 11th Border Regiment." Shute's 5:30 a.m. order for a pincer movement behind Vat and Veal cottages "proved to be impossible owing to continued machine-gun fire; and by 11:15 a.m., the 15th Battalion had to bend its right flank back somewhat, so as to establish touch with the Highland Light Infantry and thus prevent enemy penetration."[68] Major Utterson (CO 15th LF) attempted to retrieve the situation with his reserve element:

> About 8-0 a.m. I went forward to 'C' [left] Company and finding there was a gap between 'B' [centre] and 'D' [support] companies [,] brought up one of 'C' company's reserve platoons to reinforce 'B' Company and ordered OC 'B' Company to prolong his line to the right and to get in touch with the battalion [17th HLI] on his right and failing that with 'D' Company [,] with the object of preventing a counter-attack from Veal and Vat Cottages. I sent word to OC 'D' Company to detach two platoons to assist the 17th HLI in taking VEAL

---

66 TNA: WO/95/2403: 11th Border War Diary and IWM 4723: 'Preliminary Report on Operations, December 1st, 2nd and 3rd', 4 December 1917, Brigadier-General T.S. Lambert Papers (Box 80/10/2).
67 TNA: WO/95/2405: 17th HLI War Diary and Arthur & Munro (eds), *The Seventeenth Highland Light Infantry*, p. 68.
68 TNA: WO/95/2397: 15th LF War Diary and Latter, *The History of the Lancashire Fusiliers in Two Volumes Vol. 1*, p. 277.

Right: Captain J.A. Alexander. (University of Glasgow Archives)

Below: Site of Mallet Copse looking from southern to northern edge. (Rob Thompson)

COTTAGES. By the time the message reached him he had only two platoons left and the attack on VEAL COTTAGES appeared to have failed. He accordingly did not attack.[69]

Lieutenant-Colonel Scully (CO 16th NF), housed with his staff in a filthy, congested pillbox on the right of 97 Brigade front near Virile Farm, awaited notification of operational success or otherwise.[70] His battalion, detached from 96 Brigade as reserve or "counter counter-attack battalion" remained stationary until 3:00 a.m. when, not having received word, "sections closed in on their Coys. ready to advance if called upon." A message received from Lieutenant Ross (11th Border) at 3:15 a.m. reported "he was just E. of Mallet Copse." This was, despite the fact that Scully had "liasion officers with Nos. 1 [2nd KOYLI], 2 [16th HLI] and 3 [11th Border] Bns. of 97th Bde", the only intelligence received up to that time. At 5:30 a.m. Captain Gray (11th Border), who had gone forward at 3:30 p.m. to "try and get touch", reported "that the 11th Border Regt. were holding a line just S. of MALLET COPSE." Scully, on receipt of this message, "at once sent forward two patrols – one to the SE and one to the SW of MALLET COPSE to get touch." This "took some time", their reports not arriving until 8:00 a.m. "By morning it was known that the 11th Bn. Border Regt. was digging in [south of Mallet Copse] some 400 or 500 [yards] in front, but they were not in touch with the Bns. on their flanks." An existing gap, approximately 100 yards on their left, appeared to be occupied by elements of 17th HLI. On the right, 16th HLI "were holding a line of shell holes approx. VOX FM – VOID FM to SE corner of MALLET COPSE where they were in touch with 11th Border Regt." Scully's two left companies were alerted to stand by and "be ready to support this line" if necessary.[71]

Crews operating the 144 Vickers machine-guns (organised into close defence, barrage and area concentration batteries) were, despite "darkness, state of ground and hostile shelling", in place and ready by 5:00 p.m. on 1 December. At Zero + 8 minutes all guns fired on their previously assigned barrage lines. Opportunities for indirect concentration fire ensued and were acted upon: "At about 5:15 a.m.

---

69   IWM 4723: 'Narrative of Operations 2/3rd December 1917, 15th (S) Battalion Lancashire Fusiliers', 4 December 1917. Brigadier-General T.S. Lambert Papers (Box 80/10/2).
70   Major Evelegh (CO 32nd Division Signal School) subsequently remarked: 'A Power Buzzer and Amplifier Station was established at VIRILE FARM in the frontline, but the power being forward [with the assaulting infantry] to work back to it did not reach their objective and so this means was not used.' The amplifier, however, worked throughout the day, overheard every single telephone conversation and message that was sent to KRONPRINZ [FARM] or forward of it.' See TNA: WO/95/2370: After-action report: 'Appendix 'T': Communications', December 1917, 32nd Division War Diary.
71   TNA: WO/95/2398: 16th NF War Diary, IWM 4723: '32nd Div. No.G.S.1499/3/33', 5 December 1917, Brigadier-General T.S. Lambert Papers (Box 80/10/2) and Cooke, *Historical Records of the 16th (Service) Battalion Northumberland Fusiliers*, p. 88.

information was received that parties of the enemy were moving from the direction of WESTROOSEBEKE toward VALUATION HOUSES. K and L batteries were ordered by telephone to concentrate on the area about VALUATION HOUSES: the batteries opened fire at the rate of 100 rounds per minute at interval of three minutes." Hostile shelling was "fairly heavy, especially on 'A', 'B', 'C' batteries about the MEETCHEELE [BELLEVUE] SPUR. 'C' Battery at one time had six guns knocked out, but subsequently got four of them into action again, which was a very creditable performance."[72]

Shute, never one to sit idly by while battlefield events took their course, remarked to his post-war audience of senior officers: "Don't believe in commanders being able to see unless they also do their work in safety ... Better to drive from the box than sit on the necks of the leaders."[73] No doubt disappointed and concerned over the loss of Hill 52 and the holdup at Vat Cottages and Veal Cottages, he made every effort to monitor operational progress as messages were exchanged in rapid succession within the confines of 32nd Division's Canal Bank HQ:

> From CRA. 200 or 300 Boche seen moving from depot at Spriet toward VALUATION HOUSES (V.17.d.1.9.). Batteries are firing on them. The heavies have been told.
> To 97th Brigade. Verbal. Observers report party of enemy about 300 strong are moving from V.17.d.1.9. towards VALUATION HOUSES We are getting heavies on them and we have a concentration on VALUATION HOUSES now.

Blacklock's HQ telephoned (7:56 a.m.) with an ad hoc plan to get the attack going again:

> 97 Brigade: Situation is that 97th Brigade have been biffed out of TEALL COTTAGE and HILL 52. Situation of No. 2 Battalion (16th HLI) is uncertain. At 9:20 a.m. they are going to attack with reserve battalion and Nos. 1 and 2 battalions (2nd KOYLI and 16th HLI) and try to push forward.
> Div. HQ: The Divisional Commander wishes a strong counter-battery shoot to start at 9:15 a.m.

---

72 TNA: WO/95/2370: After-action Report, 'Appendix 'H': Action of Machine-guns During Operations near Passchendaele, 1st and 2nd December', 16 December 1917, 32nd Division War Diary.
73 JSCSC: Major-General A.H. Marindin Papers: 'Senior Officers' School: Lecture Delivered by Major-General Sir C.D. Shute, KCG, KCMG November 1920.

97 Brigade: General Blacklock is arranging what he can about a barrage [,] but owing to uncertainty of positions occupied by them, a general barrage is unlikely.[74]

Widespread disorganisation, along with the dearth of essential junior leadership at a critical juncture, were just two of the obstacles 97 Brigade had to contend with before sorting out its battalions for another effort. Nothing had been heard from 16th HLI and, more importantly, absence of a general artillery barrage would leave the infantry unprotected and exposed in broad daylight. Previous experience demonstrated that such attacks, when hurriedly organised and executed, almost certainly failed in the face of a forewarned and alert enemy. Nevertheless, the same "uncertainty" about 97 Brigade's new positions prevailed across no man's land, so German batteries, unable to determine their own infantry's whereabouts, had to resort to steady interdiction fire on the British rear area. This undoubted advantage, however, was likely to be moot if the attackers, in the absence of appropriate artillery assistance, were unable to reform and capture strongpoints like Vat and Veal cottages.

Participant accounts recounting the attack's limited progress and reports on the current state of overland communications were received by Shute's HQ at 8:00 a.m.:

> From Capt. Knox [stationed at the CMDS to interview incoming wounded]. Wounded 17th HLI man states his company (left) was held up at 3:30 a.m. and did not get to VAT COTTAGES. Right company also held up. No enemy artillery barrage worth speaking of but MGs from direction of VAT COTTAGES. 16th HLI have taken 1st objective and were going well and consolidating. 16th NF got most of the barrage but they say barrage was not heavy.
>
> From CRE [Lieutenant-Colonel Pollard]. Following telephone message from OC 206th Field Coy. timed 7:30 a.m. begins. No. 6 track is in good condition up to VIRILE FARM with 4 exceptions between VINE COTTAGE and VIRILE FARM [,] which are being repaired at 6:20 a.m. Casualties up to 6:30 a.m. – NIL. No. 6 track only little shelled since Zero. Situation at 6:50 a.m., fairly quiet, though heavy shelling was seen near VAPOUR FARM at 6 a.m.
>
> From CRE. Following telephone message received from OC 218th Field Company RE at 7:25 a.m. Condition of KRONPRINZ TRACK at 6:15 a.m. 2/12/17. In good order up to 200 yards beyond MURRAY SWITCH D.4.a.3.1 at 6:15 a.m. Far end of the track just south of VAPOUR FARM was being heavily shelled. Maintenance party ordered to proceed to VAPOUR FARM 6:20 a.m. Casualties 6 a.m. – NIL. Situation fairly quiet.

---

74 TNA: WO/95/2370: After-action report, 'Appendix 'J', 32nd Division: Telephone and Telegraph Messages 2 December 1917', 11 December 1917, 32nd Division War Diary.

Panorama looking east to north towards Vat Cottages and Veal Cottages. (Rob Thompson)

8th Division was informed about the uncertain state of affairs at 8:10 a.m.: "We believe, but are not quite sure, been biffed out of HILL 52 and TEALL COTTAGES." 97 Brigade fielded a verbal query for more news at the same time: [Div. HQ] "Do you know sufficiently well where your No. 1 and No. 2 battalions (2nd KOYLI and 16th HLI) are for us to safely put a barrage on the final objective for your attack at 9:20 a.m.?" [97 Bde] "Put it just clear of the final objective except possibly in the case of VOID FARM, we may be there."[75] [Div. HQ] "The Divisional Commander thinks Stokes Mortar barrage would be a good thing." 97 Brigade confirmed this was being arranged for adding that no news had arrived from the left flank.[76]

Shute made a lengthy telephone call to II Corps at 8:30 a.m. Circumstances and events, placed in the best possible light, preceded a synopsis of rushed plans to resume the attack:

> We are not so successful as we hoped. We had a good deal of fighting – hand to hand. The Bosch artillery barrage has never been bad. That is proved by the fact that the troops working on the tracks had no casualties. We got up to our 8 minutes without any artillery barrage and inconsiderable machine-gun fire. After that the

75 16th HLI had indeed reached Void Farm before dawn.
76 TNA: WO/95/2370: After-action report, 'Appendix J', 32nd Division: Telephone and Telegraph Messages 2 December 1917', 11 December 1917, 32nd Division War Diary.

machine-gun fire seems to have got worse. We [15th LF] are well up on the left and seem to have got on our objective. The next Battalion [17th HLI] got hung up about its intermediate objective. No. 3 Battalion [11th Border Regiment] got right up to its objective. No. 2 Battalion [16th HLI] only got about halfway we gather, and I am not very sure they are even about that. The right Battalion [2nd KOYLI] got HILL 52 but early this morning got pushed off it. I also hear that the [2nd] Rifle Brigade have not got on (this from the 8th Divn.) but no one is quite sure. We have ordered a further attack to be made all along the line at 9:20 a.m. and we have asked the counter-battery people to bring down their fire at 9:15 a.m. We are getting our own artillery fire also on the old objective line. The [enemy] artillery fire has not been bad all through. I think it has been a fight for a series of machine-gun emplacements. I propose tonight to relieve the right sector by two battalions of the 14th Bde. [,] which will attack through them tonight. Genl. Blacklock will then hold the left half of the divisional front with his brigade, pushing on again to his final objective where he is not on it – the 2 Bns of 96 Brigade [15th LF and 16th NF] will be relieved and sent back to CANAL BANK. Nothing of this is certain. Our lines are holding to Bde. HQ, but forward of that it is very difficult.[77]

Five minutes later (8:35 a.m.) 97 Brigade was verbally informed that the new barrage would be brought down "150 yards outside the original final objective" of 2nd KOYLI and 16th HLI. Counter-battery fire, it was also related, had been scheduled to commence five minutes before Zero. "The infantry will start at 9:20 and the artillery at 9:15 [a.m.]. Blacklock replied that he was "quite satisfied" with these arrangements.[78]

Six telegraph messages were received or dispatched during the eleven minutes between 8:39 and 8:50 a.m.: First, "From 8th Divn. Following from 25th Inf. Bde. Verbal message timed 6:20 a.m. One Coy. left Bn. [2nd Rifle Brigade] held up in front of VENISON TRENCH. Left of centre Bn. [2nd Lincolnshire] believed to have been held up." Second, "To 97th Bde. RA reports 7:45 a.m. 200 hundred to 300 infantry were seen by an artillery officer at HUBNER FARM to be moving from the depot at V.17.d.1.9. [Spriet] towards VALUATION HOUSES. An 18-pdr battery at once fired on them and the HA were informed." The third shared intelligence gathered from the four prisoners captured near Vox Farm with II Corps HQ. The fourth, received from the divisional artillery at 8:40 a.m., confirmed that the Germans were on Hill 52: "Enemy seen moving on the crest towards VALUATION HOUSES, VOLT FARM and VOID FARM. These were fired on by our 18-pdr with direct observation and scattered." The fifth, again from 8th Division, reported an increase in enemy shelling with counter-battery fire solicited for in response and general impressions – "Right probably successful. Left and centre more obscure and nothing received from them. Centre possibly successful. Left probably not" – of 25 brigade's position.

77   Ibid.
78   Ibid.

The sixth, a general situation report, was telegraphed to II Corps and the neighbouring 35th Division at 8:50 a.m.:

> Situation 8:30 a.m. as far as known. No. 1 Bn. [2nd KOYLI] took TEALL COTTAGE and HILL 52 but has been driven back again. No. 2 Bn. [16th HLI] uncertain but probably on line short of VOID FARM. No. 3 Bn. [11th Border Regiment] on objective. No. 4 Bn. [17th HLI] held up in front of VEAL COTTAGES. Resistance mainly machine-gun fire. Artillery fire not very heavy. Attack to retake HILL 52 and final objective of No. 1 and No. 2 Bn. will be launched at 9:20 a.m. No. 3 and No. 5 [15th LF] battalions [will] work round VEAL COTTAGES.

Shute had done everything possible to salvage 97 Brigade's stalled attack. This intervention was in keeping with his seemingly inconsistent leadership style. A commander acting as rapidly as possible under prevailing circumstances, he later observed, could surmount his remoteness from the sharp end and inherent chaos of the distant battle by taking decisive action:

> Any fool can solve a military problem in several days or hours. It will then be too late. [It] must be decided at once. Then, if only nearly right, if carried through with determination overcoming all obstacles, all will be well. "Look before you leap but if you're going to leap don't look too long" … Here is where a bad commander fails. All right as long as all goes "according to plan". But if his attack or a neighbouring attack fails or succeeds more than was anticipated, or if he is confronted with some other unexpected situation, he does not know what to do. He does nothing. The golden chance is fleeting. He is done. Every possible quality of a commander is contained in this: "Act according to circumstances."[79]

The attackers, exhausted and disorganised from previous exertions, required immediate reorganisation and ruthless persuasion to push on: "Don't admit your men are tired. When the enemy is beat all must go on until they drop."[80] Stamina permitting and acting on the assumption that 11th Border Regiment and 15th LF were ideally placed to outflank Vat and Veal cottages, 97 Brigade stood a good chance of securing

---

79 JSCSC: Major-General A.H. Marindin Papers: 'Senior Officers' School: Lecture Delivered by Major-General Sir C.D. Shute, KCB, KCMG November 1920.'
80 Ibid. This uncompromising perspective was demonstrated five months earlier near Nieuport on 10 July when Shute had to be restrained by the GOC XV Corps from pushing on with a hasty follow-up night attack on Lombartzyde. Further operations to capture the seaside village were contemplated but not sanctioned for early August, as the GOC 32nd Division 'to whom the events of July 10 – and notably, the first loss of trenches ever admitted by the division – were not palatable.' See CAC: RWLN 1/9: Rawlinson Diary, 11 July 1917 and Chalmers (ed) *A Saga of Scotland*, pp. 104-05.

Teall Cottage and Hill 52. If not, a contingency plan, whereby two fresh battalions of Brigadier-General Lumsden's 14 Brigade attacked through 97 Brigade's right in conjunction with a resumed advance on the latter's left, would occur after dusk in order to exploit the relative darkness of another moonlit night. Placed on alert, 14 Brigade HQ received copious dictated instructions by telephone from Shute at 9:10 a.m.:

> You know what the situation is. As far as I can gather the right of the 97th Brigade have been biffed back to their frontline; on the left they are somewhere near their objective. They are going to re-attack at 9:20 a.m. They may or may not in the course of the day improve their position. I will read you a draft order, which will be going out:
>
> Para. 1. The following moves will take place tonight 2/3rd December:
> 1. Two battalions of 14th Brigade now at BELLEVUE and WURST will form up by 10 p.m. in rear of the sector held by the 2 right Battns of the 97th Bde viz., from TEALL COTTAGE – V.29.b.60.55. These two battalions will attack at 10:30 p.m. through the 2 right battalions of 97th Brigade, and will capture and consolidate a fresh objective from V.24.d.6.2. to the crossroads V.24.a.75.15. to V.23.d.85.95.
> 2. 2nd KOYLI and 16th HLI will remain in their then positions until this objective is gained and will then concentrate in our old frontline.
> 3. From 10 p.m. the 2nd KOYLI and 16th HLI will pass to the command of GOC 14th Infantry Brigade until they are concentrated in our frontline as mentioned in para. 2.
> 4. As soon as the 2nd KOYLI and 16th HLI are back in our old frontline, they will, under the orders of the 97th Brigade, relieve the 15th Lancs. Fus. and 16th North'd. Fus., which two battalions will move back to a camp in the neighbourhood of IRISH FARM.
> 5. The battalions of the 14th Brigade now at WURST & BELLEVUE will be replaced at these places by the remaining two battalions of the 14th Brigade.
> 6. At 10 p.m. tonight the GOC 14th Brigade, with headquarters at KANSAS (Adv. HQ at VIRILE FARM) will be in command of the right sector from TEALL COTTAGE to V.29.b.6.55. GOC 97th Brigade, with headquarters at KRONPRINZ [FARM] will be in command of the left sector.
>
> I want you to think over that and let me know your ideas. You have got to relieve and it is better to attack straight through them than to relieve and attack again.

What it is necessary to know is whether you consider the task too difficult for you to carry on.[81]

Blacklock telephoned Division ten minutes later (9:20 a.m.); rampant disorganisation and officer casualties had proved too debilitating to recommence the assault: "Message from 97 Brigade to the effect that they could not assemble their two right battalions for the attack and they want the barrage to cease.[82] Their Nos. 1 & 2 (2nd KOYLI and 16th HLI) are too disorganised to assemble for the attack, therefore the barrage has been stopped for ten minutes." Shute's growing impatience and obvious displeasure are evident in the subsequent verbal exchange with the GOC 97 Brigade:

> Shute: Will you be ready in ten minutes?
> Blacklock: At present it cannot be said when they will be ready to attack.
> Shute: Will you be able to fix an hour for the attack? Do you know where they are?
> Blacklock: Line runs from VOX FARM S.W. corner of VOID FARM to S.W. corner of MALLET COPSE.[83]
> Shute: Then you haven't got anywhere near VEAL and VOX?[84] Well you have got to get on today on your right and I will probably want you to hand over command of the right sector to the 14th Infantry Brigade. You will move your Brigade into the left sector and let the 15th Lancs. Fus. and 16th North'd Fus. march away tonight. You will have your Brigade to hold the left sector and to get on to your objective. All these valuable hours of darkness between 2 a.m. and 6 a.m. have been wasted by your Battalion Commanders not getting their battalions on.[85]

81 These verbal orders, subsequently communicated to II Corps at 9:28 a.m., were in keeping with '32nd Division Instructions No. 11, Special Instructions to GOC Brigade in Divisional Support [14th Infantry Brigade] and GOC Brigade in Divisional Reserve [96th] Infantry Brigade' of 30 November. See Appendix VIII a & b.
82 The 32nd Division DMGO's after-action report noted: 'At 9 a.m. orders were received from GOC 97th Infantry Brigade to fire on barrage lines from 9-20 a.m. to 9-45 a.m. in order to support a fresh attack. This order was cancelled at 9:15 a.m.' See TNA: WO/95/2370: After-action Report, 'Appendix 'H': Action of Machine-guns During Operations near Passchendaele, 1st and 2nd December', 16 December 1917, 32nd Division War Diary.
83 11th Border Regiment's retirement from Mallet Copse was still unknown at this time.
84 Reproduced from original transcript. Vox Farm, as related by Blacklock in the previous exchange, had been secured. Shute may have meant Vat instead of Vox or his recorded reference to the latter was the result of a clerical error during transcription or subsequent 'Telephone and Telegraph Messages' appendix compilation.
85 Shute's account of this episode (related in his after-action report of 11 December) differs from surviving telephone and telegraph transcripts: 'On receipt of this information' i.e., the cancellation of the 9:20 a.m. attack, 'the Divisional Commander informed the GOC 97th Infantry Brigade that he must fix an hour in the afternoon to resume his attack and pointed out it was of special importance to capture HILL 52 and the high ground about

A chastened Blacklock then enquired if it was possible to resume operations in the afternoon to which Shute readily replied that he could.[86] The GOC 32nd Division's hastily improvised contingency plan, to be put in motion if 97 Brigade failed to press on during the afternoon, was somewhat intricate and ambitious given prevailing circumstances. Two battalions of the support brigade were, after nightfall, to pass through two stalled and disorganised assault battalions, reeling from heavy casualties, on the right of the attacking brigade and seize a newly designated objective line. The relieved battalions would, following the capture of their former objectives by the support battalions, then shift from the old frontline – one to the left and one to immediate reserve about Virile Farm –to relieve two battalions previously loaned by the reserve brigade, which, in turn, were to march back to reserve positions west of the Zonnebeke – Langemarck road. All of this, it should also be noted, was to occur under the bright light of a waning gibbous moon whilst in close proximity to an agitated and watchful foe.

The observed threat from supporting German infantry, still massing in the vicinity of Valuation Houses, opposite the right centre of 97 Brigade worried 32nd Division during a brief span of minutes between 9:25 and 9:28 a.m.; the gunners, as related in subsequent telephone and telegraph reports, appeared to have engaged this menace with desired effect:

> Division HQ to II Corps: "Much movement around VALUATION HOUSES. Are the heavies on to it?
> II Corps: Corps have told the gunners.
> To CRA: Corps observers report great deal of movement around VALUATION HOUSES at 9:10 a.m.
> From CRA: FOO No. 4 Group reports that he scattered Germans moving from depot towards VALUATION HOUSES. FOOS Nos 3 & 4 groups have engaged enemy moving from direction of VALUATION HOUSES to V.24.a.4.2.
> From CRA: Officer of No. 4 Group at HUBNER FARM has seen parties of men moving along the road from VALUATION HOUSES to VOLT FARM, behind which they appear to be collecting. Two 18-pdr batteries have engaged them with direct observation.[87]

32nd Division telegraphed II Corps, 8th Division and 35th Division about the delay to 97 Brigade's renewed attack at 9:45 a.m.: "Attack on HILL 52 postponed from 9:20

VOID FARM.' See TNA: WO/95/2370: After-action report, 'Part III, Narrative of Events', 11 December 1917, 32nd Division War Diary.
86 Ibid: After-action report, 'Appendix 'J', 32nd Division: Telephone and Telegraph Messages 2 December 1917', 11 December 1917, 32nd Division War Diary.
87 Ibid.

German infantrymen Flanders December 1917. (Author)

a.m. to a later hour." Captain Knox telephoned fifteen minutes later (10:00 a.m.) with additional eyewitness accounts from the wounded: "It is reported that the 16th HLI have had to retire and they were last seen in the old Bosche frontline consolidating. They had gained their first objective [dotted green line], but were too weak to hold it.[88] An officer says the Bosche never waited for them. Whenever they got near they took up their guns and ran.[89] I cannot get any information about the 17th HLI."[90] 97 Brigade telegraphed probable losses sustained by their right centre battalion shortly after Knox's report: "11/Borders report timed 8:35 a.m. Casualties estimated at 10 [officers] and 150 [ORs]." This was followed by a lengthy telephone situation report communicated (10:05 a.m.) by one of Blacklock's staff officers:

> Situation on the right of 25th Brigade – Attack commenced quite satisfactorily. They had a very bad time before our artillery barrage opened and they had a good many casualties chiefly by machine-guns in VENISON TRENCH,

88 Parties of 16th HLI were still established about the dotted green line east and west of Void Farm at this time. See below.
89 The perceived German retirement was, according to *OHL's* recently introduced 'elastic arrangement', the desired response of a hard-pressed *Vorfeldzone* garrison. See Chapter 1, pp. 65-68.
90 TNA: WO/95/2370: After-action report, 'Appendix 'J', 32nd Division: Telephone and Telegraph Messages 2 December 1917', 11 December 1917, 32nd Division War Diary.

which enfiladed the left company of the centre [sic] [2nd Rifle Brigade] battalion and our right [2nd KOYLI] battalion. Our right held on to HILL 52 for a good time and apparently the left of the 25th Brigade held on fairly well everywhere, but when the Germans counter-attacked, they were not strong enough, owing to casualties by machine-gun fire, to hold their ground. They both fell back and the line at present, taking it from the 25th Brigade – W.25.a.3.1. – line runs due west to south of TEALL COTTAGE where they are in touch with the 16th North'd Fus. The 16th North'd Fus. have one company pretty badly knocked about and three companies moderately knocked about. 2nd KOYLI can only muster 2 officers and 20 OR and are somewhere south of the first O in VOCATION FARM. The situation on the left of 2nd KOYLI is being ascertained. Battalion commanders have been sent to find out the situation. They are sending out patrols to try and get the line established in VOCATION and VOID farms. They are just in MALLET COPSE with left refused, and on the left some of the 17th HLI are due east of VEAL COTTAGE. It is thought that No. 5 [15th LF] battalion are on their objective still, and that they have pushed out patrols and joined hands north of VEAL COTTAGE with the 17th HLI. The right of the 17th HLI has pushed forward level with VEAL COTTAGE, but fell back southwestwards and are not now level with VEAL COTTAGE.[91]

Divisional HQ, unclear about particular points not related in this update, pressed for more details: "It is not understood where 17th HLI are. Have we got VAT COTTAGES? Can we put artillery on VEAL COTTAGES? Can you get Stokes Mortars on to them?" Brigade replied that attempts had been made to register these supporting assets on both objectives. Further queries followed: "Can you tell me how far the 15th LF have got? You think they have got the southern edge of DOUBLE COPSE. They are not in MALLET COPSE."[92] The last part of this exchange confirmed that 11th Border Regiment, unable to secure Mallet Copse in its entirety, was still holding on just inside its southern fringe.

Blacklock, forsaking the security of his pillbox HQ at Kronprinz Farm, had previously gone forward to discover the whereabouts of the current frontline. It was during this absence that 32nd Division HQ, in an attempt to subdue enemy resistance at Veal Cottages and Mallet Copse, telephoned a new artillery support scheme to 97 Brigade at 10:30 a.m.: "We are going to help you with artillery on to MALLET COPSE and possibly on to VEAL COTTAGES if you are not too close. We must wait until Genl. Blacklock comes back and tells us where you are exactly. We will put

---

91 Ibid. Blacklock ordered battalion commanders to 'clear up the situation' at 8:00 a.m. Daylight made the task of going forward almost impossible. See IWM 4732: 'Summary of the Attack of the 97th Inf. Bde. with 2 Battalions of the 96th Inf. Bde. on December 2 [1917]', Brigadier-General T.S. Lambert Papers (Box 10/80/2).
92 Ibid.

artillery concentrations (Howitzers) on to anything you like. If you are being stopped by sniping from machine-guns then you must get on and blow them out."⁹³

Shute updated II Corps about the general situation of 97 Brigade by telephone at 10:35 a.m.: "I can tell you roughly our line. From TEALL COTTAGE (exclusive) VOX FARM (inclusive) southern edge of MALLET COPSE [and] VEALL COTTAGES (exclusive) then up to the edge of DOUBLE COPSE. A tremendous lot of MG fire from VENISON trench enfiladed the KOYLI on HILL 52." Another verbal exchange with 14 Brigade, during which the proposed contingency plan along with 97 Brigade's current status was discussed, occurred ten minutes later:

> 14 Brigade: As far as he [Blacklock] knows, the position of 97th is – His two right battalions [2nd KOYLI and 16th HLI] are back on their original frontline. No. 3 Battalion [11th Border] is 200 yards south of MALLET COPSE. No. 4 Battalion [17th HLI] is 200 yards south of VEAL COTTAGES. No. 5 Battalion [15th LF] is on its final objective he thinks. You assume that your proposed attack will be carried out with his attack.
>
> Div. HQ: The Divisional commander says "YES" if Genl. Blacklock can do it, but his plans are very uncertain until the position of the 97th is cleared up. There is another possibility. It may turn out more advisable for you to attack on the front of Nos. 2 [16th HLI] & 3 Bns instead of Nos. 1 [2nd KOYLI] & 2 and go right through to the final objective.⁹⁴ To carry out the attack it is essential for the 97th to attack on your left. That is the original proposal if you were to attack on the front of the other two battalions. It may not be so essential now, but you would want your right covered.
>
> 14 Brigade: We are waiting for Genl. Blacklock to come back to find out what his dispositions are.
>
> Div. HQ: Do you consider it more advisable to relieve and then attack or form up behind the troops who are there and go through them?
>
> 14 Brigade: The point is that they will be better organised tomorrow night. What he [Lumsden] would like to do is to relieve the line tonight and attack tomorrow night. He would rather takeover the line one night and attack another, but in the event of having to do both on one night, he would rather attack through them.⁹⁵

---

93 Ibid.
94 This 'more advisable' second option would, if pressed on through 16th HLI and 11th Border Regiment, place 14th Brigade's battalions to the NW of German occupied Hill 52. Shute, as we shall see, appears to have entertained hopes that the hill would be regained prior to this stage of the renewed assault.
95 TNA: WO/95/2370: After-action report, 'Appendix 'J', 32nd Division: Telephone and Telegraph Messages 2 December 1917', 11 December 1917, 32nd Division War Diary.

Lumsden's operational preferences were now clear to Division HQ; the final decision to resume the attack on the nights of 2/3 or 3/4 December remained pending, as 97 Brigade attempted to sort out its battalions before the proposed afternoon assault.

Lieutenant-Colonel Pollard (CRE) telegraphed (10:42 a.m.) further updates in regard to the condition of duckboard tracks: "Following message by orderly from 219th Field Coy. timed 9:40 a.m. today begins. MOUSETRAP TRACK in good order. All breaks forward of WALLEMOLEN repaired by 3 a.m. No breaks to rear of WALLEMOLEN at 8:30 a.m." The desire to press on after dark was related to Brigadier-General Wilson (BGGS II Corps) by a 32nd Division staff officer at 10:58 a.m.: "My General feels he must do something tonight because the enemy is so disorganised that he thinks tonight is the time to do it. The [Second] Army think it is very important to get hold of HILL 52 tonight. My General thinks so also. VENISON TRENCH ought to be hammered [by artillery] today: we got beyond HILL 52 today but then got badly done in by machine-guns from there." A ninth report from Captain Knox (11:00 a.m.)[96] was succeeded by a telegraphed situation report[97] from VIII Corps at 11:02 a.m.[98]

Sometime before 11:00 a.m., a mud-spattered Blacklock returned hot-footed to Kronprinz Farm from his reconnaissance of 97 Brigade's muddled frontline. A Brigade staff officer (Captain H. Wailes) fielded a call from 32nd Division five minutes later. The latter enquired whether or not the doughty brigadier had been made aware of the new barrage arrangements:

> Div. HQ: Did you give Genl. Blacklock the Divisional Commander's message?
> Captain Wailes: With regard to Howitzers he said he did not want them, but would do it with Stokes. He thinks he is in VOID FARM and VELDT FARM, V.23.d.7.6.,[99] and at southern edge of MALLET COPSE.[100] We had not got VAT COTTAGES or VEAL COTTAGES. He would like to see Scott [CO 16th HLI] before he decides. He feels sure he cannot use Howitzers. He had a lot of casualties to trench mortar personnel and finds it difficult to collect them.[101] The Bosche is holding VAT COTTAGES.

---

96 'There are two wounded Germans here [CMDS]. (1) belongs to 3 Coy. 1st Bn. 94th I.R. 38th Division. He has been two days in the line and fourteen days in Flanders: he came to here from before ARRAS. *The attack this morning was unexpected* [My emphasis]. He has not heard of any attack against us. He is 21 years of age and seems quite willing to answer any questions. (2) 5 Coy. 2nd Bn. 95th I.R. 38th Division.'
97 Originally telegraphed by '2nd Corps 'I' (Thro' 8th Corps I)' at 10:30 a.m. See above.
98 TNA: WO/95/2370: After-action report, 'Appendix 'J', 32nd Division: Telephone and Telegraph Messages 2 December 1917', 11 December 1917, 32nd Division War Diary.
99 Veldt Farm and vicinity, situated on the boundary between 16th HLI and 11th Border Regiment, was still in enemy hands.
100 Blacklock was, despite his recent reconnaissance, still unaware of 11th Border Regiment's pre-dawn withdrawal from the southern edge of Mallet Copse.
101 *Fourth Army's* midday report for 3 December observed that 'the centre of *38.I.D.* suffered mortar fire for the first time' thus confirming heavy losses sustained by Stokes

> Div. HQ: You mean you are to the south of VAT COTTAGES? You had a message timed 8:40 from 2nd KOYLI saying 12 officers and 300 OR casualties.[102]

Shute later observed that the frontline, based on information received at the time, appeared to run from "about 200 yards south of TEALL COTTAGES to VOX FARM inclusive thence to VOID and VELDT farms thence to southern edge of MALLET COPSE where it turned south and ran almost to our old frontline where it turned west and ran to the south of VAT COTTAGES then turning north again to about point [opposite Double Copse] V.22.d.8.2."[103] Another telegraph (11:15 a.m.) from Pollard informed Division HQ that the "GENOA – STROOMBEEK" beech slab corduroy road had been kept open all morning by 14th Worcester. At 11:20 a.m. the 32nd Division DMGO was ordered to "put down from 12 noon to 12:30 p.m." a machine-gun barrage "to catch any enemy who might be assembling for a counter-attack" Three more messages, concerning 8th Division's relief after nightfall, current disposition of 25 Brigade's frontline and Coffin's dim forecast for the continuance of operations, followed between 11:20 and 11:25 a.m.[104]

A note, collated and dispatched by the ADMS, listing casualties (20 officers and 288 ORs) received at the ADS up to 10:25 a.m., was delivered to 32nd Division at 11:40 a.m. Another situation report, relating German attempts to work round the right of 25 Brigade, arrived from 8th Division 25 minutes later at 12:05 p.m. Meanwhile, 14 Brigade's projected deployment remained an uncertainty, Lumsden's HQ receiving the following verbal message (12:05 p.m.) from Division HQ: "The probability is that you won't relieve or attack tonight, but you will have to be ready. At any rate, your officers will have to go up and reconnoitre tonight." 97 Brigade telephoned with a general situation report at 12:15 p.m. This information, recorded at the receiving end during real-time transcription, raised expectations that the attack would be continued: "You think you can get on to your line. You are going to use Stokes guns. As regards the situation at VOID FARM you are on one outskirt and the Boche the other. You are going to include VOID FARM in your line. You are in rather a difficulty about No. 2 Battalion (16th HLI). They have no officers left except one subaltern." Shute, convinced that 97 Brigade was capable of one more effort, replied: "I think I am going to leave you in tonight, so would you rather attack

  mortar personnel the previous day. See KA HKR 99: Telegraph/wireless pro forma, 3 December 1917.
102 The puzzling non sequitur found in the last exchange is reproduced from the original telegraph and telephone transcripts. See TNA: WO/95/2370: After-action report, 'Appendix 'J', 32nd Division: Telephone and Telegraph Messages 2 December 1917', 11 December 1917, 32nd Division War Diary.
103 Ibid: After-action report, 'Part III, Narrative of Events', 11 December 1917.
104 Ibid and 'Appendix 'J', 32nd Division: Telephone and Telegraph Messages 2 December 1917', 11 December 1917.

in the afternoon or at night?" [97 Brigade] "General Blacklock said he would rather do it at night." [Shute] "Very well then. Arrange to do it at night. Would it be any good to you to see me either at your headquarters or for you to come and meet me at General Lumsden's Headquarters?" Blacklock replied that he preferred 14 Brigade HQ for the proposed conference. "Very well then", Shute concluded, "I will come up there now. I can get to KANSAS at about 1:15 p.m." Word of this meeting was communicated to 14 Brigade five minutes later at 12:20 p.m.[105]

Fourth Army's midday report identified, based on prisoner interrogations, 32nd Division and 8th Division as the attacking British formations. Incoming communiques appeared to confirm the night assault's primary focus was opposite *25th Division's* right and *38th Division's* centre and left. The former, having successfully defended its right flank, had been thrown back approximately 100 metres on the left. The latter, following fierce fighting opposite the *Hauptwiderstandslinie*, was in possession of almost all its *Vorfeldzone*. Hostile artillery fire, the report continued, died away around 10:00 a.m. Preparations to retake lost territory were, it was confidently asserted, now in hand. *Heeresgruppe Kronprinz Rupprecht*, assured this latest enemy offensive had been contained, cautiously observed: "An attack against the heights Westroosebeke – Droogenbroodhoek may still have to be reckoned with."[106]

4.5 Dénouement

Both 8th and 32nd divisional staffs had formulated, regardless of the grounding of designated contact aircraft, a fairly accurate picture of the general situation by 12:30 p.m. Brigadier-General Coffin, taking into account heavy losses amongst regimental officers and NCOs, made it clear that the continuance of operations against Venison Trench and its redoubts was dependent on fresh troops and seizure of Teall Cottage. Nevertheless, any success by day or night was, he concluded, highly improbable. Heneker backed the GOC 25 Brigade's on-the-spot judgement in a report to VIII Corps at 11:00 a.m.[107] Shute thought otherwise. The controversial operational approach had been his brainchild from the start. Confidence of impending success – unabashedly declared to Sir Henry Rawlinson amongst others before the assault – and consequent recognition that such boasts may have been ill-founded, reveal, in subsequent actions and words, an overriding personal stake in a successful outcome after the crucial surprise element of the plan had been lost.[108]

---

105 Ibid.
106 KA HKR 99: Telegraph/wireless pro forma 2 December 1917 and 71 'Lagge am 2.12.17 mittag'.
107 BL: 48359: 'Report of Operations Carried Out by the VIII Army Corps on the Morning of 2nd December 1917, Official War Diaries with Appendices and Addenda, VIII Army Corps, Passchendaele Front, November 1917-April 1918', Vol. V, Hunter-Weston Papers.
108 See CAC: RWLN 1/9: Rawlinson Diary, 19 November 1917 and IWM: P363: Strickland Diary, 21 November 1917.

German map abstract of the Passchendaele – Westroosebeke sector.
(Memorial Museum Passchendaele 1917)

25 Brigade struggled to retain its small territorial gains throughout the afternoon. German forays, covered by bombs and rifle grenades, against the left flank "were all repulsed without difficulty" and touch maintained with 2nd KOYLI. Lieutenant-Colonel Stirling, still confined to his HQ by the hostile bombardment, remained out of touch with companies of 2nd Royal Berkshire. 2nd Lieutenant Upton and his detached party, isolated in their short stretch of Venison Trench, received word by runner of their impending withdrawal after dark. Along the centre and left, advanced companies of 2nd Lincolnshire and 2nd Rifle Brigade remained stationary under relentless shellfire while losses steadily mounted. Lieutenant Anderson recalled: "Except for a few hours during the morning, it was practically impossible, owing to the accurate sniping, to get from post to post."[109]

8th Division's IO reported the current haul (3 officers, 16 NCOs, 32 men) of prisoners and identified ("N to S, 96, 95, 94, 117, 116, 115") German order of battle to VIII Corps at 1:00 p.m. "Evidence as to the enemy's intention", he added, "varies too much to form an opinion." Second Army Report Centre telegraphed a general situation report concerning what was known of 32nd Division's forward positions at 1:50

---

109 TNA: WO/95/1677: 'Narrative of Operations Carried Out by the 8th Division on 1st/2nd December 1917', 13 December 1917, 8th Division War Diary, TNA: WO/95/1929: 'Appendix B', 5 December 1917, 2nd Royal Berkshire War Diary and TNA: WO/95/1731: 'Report of the part played by the 2nd Battn. The Rifle Brigade in the Operations at Passchendaele', 6 December 1917, 2nd Rifle Brigade War Diary.

Brigadier-General Frederick William Lumsden VC. (Author)

p.m. Two more messages, passing on intelligence culled from the captured *Feldwebel* of *IR94*[110] and 2nd Rifle Brigade's estimated (approximately 200 men) losses, crossed Captain Chaplin's desk at 1:50 and 2:30 p.m. The situation remained, VIII Corps receiving no additional reports until 4:30 p.m., somewhat obscure after this.[111]

Shute, having made his way due east through St Jean and Wieltje along designated corps/divisional roads and tracks, arrived amidst the ubiquitous supply dumps and steady, two-way traffic of Kansas Cross at 1:15 p.m. Joining Blacklock and Lumsden in the latter's pillbox HQ, he wasted no time in issuing instructions "as to the action to be taken" by 97 and 14 brigades: The former was "to establish itself on the line TEALL COTTAGES inclusive – HILL 52 inclusive – VOID FARM and MALLET COPSE inclusive – V.23.c.2.4. after darkness and to push on thence, if possible, to the line of its final [red line] objective."[112] The latter was now detailed "to attack through the 97th Infantry Brigade on the night of December 3/4 and to capture any portions of the final objective which the 97 Infantry Brigade might have failed to secure on the previous night." Shute noted in his subsequent after-action report that "no definite orders as to the scope of these operations could be given to the 14th Infantry Brigade until the result of the operations to be undertaken by the 97th Brigade was known, but GOC 14th Infantry Brigade was directed to send officers up

---

110 See Chapter 3, p. 202.
111 BL: 48359: 'Report of Operations Carried Out by the VIII Army Corps on the Morning of 2nd December 1917, Official War Diaries with Appendices and Addenda, VIII Army Corps, Passchendaele Front, November 1917-April 1918', Vol. V, Hunter-Weston Papers.
112 See Appendix X for 97 Brigade O.O. 181 issued later that afternoon at 3:50 p.m.

to reconnoitre the line and be prepared to carry out an operation on the line indicated as soon as the situation of the 97th Infantry Brigade was known."[113] Matters having been settled for the time being, the GOC 32nd Division departed for the return journey to his Canal Bank HQ.[114]

One written note and two telephone messages were received at 32nd Division HQ during Shute's absence. The note, eighth in a series dispatched by Captain Knox, further demonstrates the often dilatory and, given passage of time and understandably limited combatant perspectives, inaccurate nature of information gleaned from interviews of the recently accessible wounded: "A CSM 16th HLI states that they had reached their first objective early this morning, but were heavily counter-attacked and had to fall back. A man of the Borders says the Borders were being counter-attacked from all sides at 9 a.m. this morning, but were holding all they had gained. He said they had reached their final objective…" The contents of two wireless intercepts, telephoned by II Corps at 1:56 p.m., further emphasised the imminent threat of counter-attack: "German wireless message received orders forward zone to be taken at once and the line to be straightened out. Second message calls for more ammunition." The danger was further stressed by the same source at 2:18 and 2:33 p.m.: "Corps observers report several parties of about 100 all told at VALUATION HOUSES going toward line at 1:40 p.m. The Corps have told the artillery" and "XIX Corps report there is a large concentration at V.24.a.0.5. [vicinity of Valuation Houses]."[115]

Shute, having returned to his HQ by 2:40 p.m., was immediately brought up to date about the contents of a telegraph (received at 2:00 p.m.) from 97 Brigade:

> Situation appears to be as follows: We hold the line from S[outh] of TEALL COTTAGES along old frontline to VOCATION and VOX [farms] both inclusive along western edge of VOID [FARM] to 50 yards S[outh] of MALLET COPSE, thence south of VAT COTTAGES through fork roads to enclosure at V.22.d.5.2. inclusive, then SSW along objective to TOURNANT FARM. Possession of TEALL COTTAGE doubtful.

A second situation report, related by telephone, was communicated by 97 Brigade at 2:35 p.m.: "97th Brigade reports – In occupation of VOX, VOCATION and VOID farms: continuous line running south of MALLET COPSE to the left in touch all the way. Also in possession of VEAL COTTAGES." The overall situation, as it now appeared to the GOC 32nd Division, was that 97 Brigade had managed to secure and

---

113 14 Brigade telephoned (12:58 p.m.) 32nd Division HQ with the following query: 'In view of what is coming off, are we to provide 50 men from the [1st] Dorsets as carrying party asked for by ADMS?' The 50 in question were duly detached from 96 Brigade.
114 TNA: WO/95/2370: After-action report, 'Part III, Narrative of Events', 11 December 1917, 32nd Division War Diary.
115 Ibid: After-action report, 'Appendix 'J', 32nd Division: Telephone and Telegraph Messages 2 December 1917', 11 December 1917.

hold – with the exception of Hill 52 and Vat Cottages – objectives south of the dotted green line.[116] II Corps received another lengthy telephone update minutes after Shute digested the contents of 97 Brigade's report:

> I don't think General Blacklock will be able to attack till 3 or 4 in the morning because he has to collect his fellows. Tomorrow night [forthcoming attack by 14 Brigade] we may be a bit earlier. He cannot be earlier than 3 or 4. He won't attack before ½ past 2. I rather want him to attack before they attack him. If they do relieve they had better finish it by 2 p.m. We hope to get on the line of VEAL, VOID and down on to HILL 52. The thing is there is such a lot of machine-guns. It is almost impossible to get a sufficient amount of artillery fire to knock-out the machine-guns. There has been very little fire (artillery). It's been the machine-guns that are the trouble. Tomorrow night we shall finish the show with the 14th Bde.

Following a short verbal update to his CRA,[117] Shute telephoned (2:57 p.m.) Blacklock next with a query as to who actually held Veal Cottages: [Shute] "We have this message [received at 2:35 p.m.] from the 97th Brigade. Is that right?" [Blacklock] "It is not VEAL COTTAGES but it is TEALL COTTAGE. 40 prisoners taken there." Teall Cottage, contrary to this claim, still remained in German hands. The origin of the report concerning its capture, difficult to trace after passage of time, certainly conveyed a false impression of mounting success at 32nd Division HQ.[118] Shute, no doubt pleased by what appeared to be an improvement of the general situation, telephoned II Corps (2:59 p.m.) to relate the news: "We are in occupation of VOID FARM and have a continuous line from there running westwards south of MALLET COPSE. We are in touch all the way. Have just taken TEALL COTTAGE and 40 prisoners."[119]

Diligent Captain Knox had in the meantime dispatched a ninth note (received by 32nd Division at 2:50 p.m.) relating further battlefield impressions of the wounded:

---

116 Ibid.
117 'We are said to be in possession of VEAL COTTAGES and VOID FARM. It is not confirmed yet.'
118 It is possible that the report confirming the capture of Teall Cottage was directly related to the right flanking movement by remnants of 'A' and 'B' companies 16th HLI. A third company (as per Shute's 7:45 a.m. verbal order to 97 Brigade) was also sent forward to support vain efforts to seize the troublesome strongpoint.
119 TNA: WO/95/2370: After-action report, 'Appendix J', 32nd Division: Telephone and Telegraph Messages 2 December 1917', 11 December 1917, 32nd Division War Diary. Further confirmation of 97 Brigade's reported frontline was telegraphed by 32nd Division to II Corps, 8th Division, 35th Division, 14 Brigade and 96 Brigade respectively at 3:45 p.m.

An officer of the 16th HLI states that as far as he knew, the situation was as follows: At 9 a.m. KOYLI south side of HILL 52. 16th HLI at first objective. Borders on final objective. He thinks direction kept was bad: the KOYLI went too far to the right and one Coy. of 16th HLI was reported at TEALL COTTAGE. Estimates casualties in his Battalion at 200. He states the Bosche put up no fight, whenever they got near him he ran. A man of the Borders states that at 9 a.m. Borders on final objective and were digging. They had beat-off several counter-attacks.

The growing mass of German counter-attack troops, congregating between Valuation Houses and Mallet Copse, became a serious source of concern to Shute and his staff following receipt (3:20 p.m.) of a telegraph report originating from divisional artillery observers. Parties of enemy infantry could be discerned "doubling down from VALUATION HOUSES to VOLT FARM and thence into valley to east of VOLT FARM."[120] Three 18-pdr batteries were in the process of engaging the area of this dangerous build-up when the GOC 32nd Division ordered additional fire support by machine-gun batteries and heavy guns to commence at 3:50 p.m.[121] Lieutenant-Colonel Scully, awaiting further word of the attack's progress, recollected: "The situation was quiet all morning up to 4 p.m. I ordered two platoons to move forward as soon as it was dark to support the 11th Border Regt. and sent a message to this effect to the 11th Border officer at MALLET COPSE. At 3:30 p.m. my right company reported that they had seen about 100 enemy moving to the north edge of MALLET COPSE. This I reported to the GOC 97th Brigade by telephone."[122]

4:10 p.m.: darkness (sunset was at 3:46 p.m.) began to cloak the battlefield when Shute received welcome news from 97 Brigade: "Col. Scully [CO 16th NF] reports that he has got HILL 52 with one company."[123] The GOC 32nd Division – convinced

---

120 News of the mounting threat was telegraphed to 97 Brigade, 8th Division, 14 Brigade and II Corps respectively at 3:45 p.m.
121 TNA: WO/95/2370: After-action report, 'Part III, Narrative of Events', and 'Appendix 'J', 32nd Division: Telephone and Telegraph Messages 2 December 1917', 11 December 1917, 32nd Division War Diary. Machine-gun companies tasked with indirect fire support had (acting on information received at 2:30 p.m.) previously strafed the German build-up: '[I]information was received that enemy were concentrating in the vicinity of VALUATION HOUSES. E, F, G and H batteries were ordered to engage this target, the batteries opening fire at 3-5 p.m. at the rate of 100 rounds per minute for five minutes and afterwards for 1 minute at intervals of 3 minutes.' See Ibid: After-action Report, 'Appendix 'H': Action of Machine-guns during Operations near Passchendaele, 1st and 2nd December', 16 December 1917.
122 IWM 4723: '32nd Div. No.G.S.1499/3/33', 5 December 1917, Brigadier-General T.S. Lambert Papers (Box 80/10/2).
123 16th NF's war diary, Scully's after-action report and the post-war battalion history make no mention of the temporary seizure of Hill 52. Shute's earlier (7:45 a.m.) verbal order – 'Absolutely necessary that TEALL COTTAGE and VEAL and HILL 52 should be regained. Do this with your reserve Battalion assisted, if safety permits, by fire from your

his right flank was now secure – readily commended the apparent "good work" and ordered close support for Scully to be arranged. He subsequently observed: "The situation then at 4:10 p.m., as far as known at Divisional HQ, seemed to be rapidly improving. Although the situation of the 17th HLI in front of VAT COTTAGES remained unsatisfactory, it was considered that with HILL 52, VOID FARM and MALLET COPSE[124] in our possession, the ultimate capture of VEAL and VAT COTTAGES would be accomplished."[125]

The now obvious German build-up for counter-attack (*Gegenangriff*) still relied on units organic to both the *25th* and *38th* divisions; assistance (*Gegenstoss*) from nearby *Eingreifdivisionen* had been unnecessary. Large bodies of infantry from the support and reserve, directed by *Kampftruppenkommandeur* of *IR116* and *IR117*, deployed in the area east of Southern Redoubt for an all-out assault against 25 Brigade. Reported activity in the vicinity of the large shelters at Valuation Houses resulted from an order issued by *IR95's* regimental commander that morning:

> *Oberstleutnant* von Selle (HQ in Westroosebeke) recognised the critical situation at the *Feldherrnhügel*. At 8:30 a.m. [German time] he ordered *Leutnant* d.R. Martini – the most senior officer present – to attack from the left wing near *Nordhof* [Void Farm] and force back the enemy breakthrough. This order proved extremely difficult to execute owing to the fact that the enemy could observe all daylight movement. The task was accomplished by having men crawl forward a

---

special battery and Stokes mortars' – to 97 Brigade was succeeded by orders for a second assault on the key promontory. Scully, his companies concentrated about Virile Farm until the afternoon German counter-attack, did not order a company to Hill 52 until after dusk. The actual course of events is tersely outlined in the 2nd KOYLI war diary: 'At about 10:30 a.m. on the 2nd, he [Captain Hassell] received instructions to recapture HILL 52 with the assistance of one company of the 16th Northumberland Fusiliers. This company failed to materialise, but he advanced his line by the process of dribbling some 200 yards.' Shute later observed: 'We were never in possession of HILL 52 after we had been driven off it by the enemy's big counter-attack at 3:30 a.m.' The origin of the false report remains unexplained. See TNA: WO/95/2398: 16th NF War Diary, WO/95/2370: After-action report, 'Part IV, Narrative Dealing with the Retirement of the 97th Infantry Brigade', 'Appendix 'J', 32nd Division: Telephone and Telegraph Messages 2 December 1917', 11 December 1917, 32nd Division War Diary, WO/95/2402: 2nd KOYLI War Diary, IWM 4723: '32nd Div. No.G.S.1.1499/3/33', 5 December 1917, Brigadier-General T.S. Lambert Papers (Box 80/10/2) and Cooke, *Historical Records of the 16*th *(Service) Battalion Northumberland Fusiliers*, p. 89.

124 The southern edge of Mallet Copse was, as related above, already lost by this time, survivors of both 11th Border Regiment companies having retired to the dotted green line just before daybreak.

125 See TNA: WO/157/288: 'Calendar for December 1917: Times Calculated for Second Army Front and Greenwich Mean Time', II Corps Intelligence File, WO/95/2370: After-action report, 'Part III, Narrative of Events', and 'Appendix 'J', 32nd Division: Telephone and Telegraph Messages 2 December 1917', 11 December 1917, 32nd Division War Diary.

290 A Moonlight Massacre

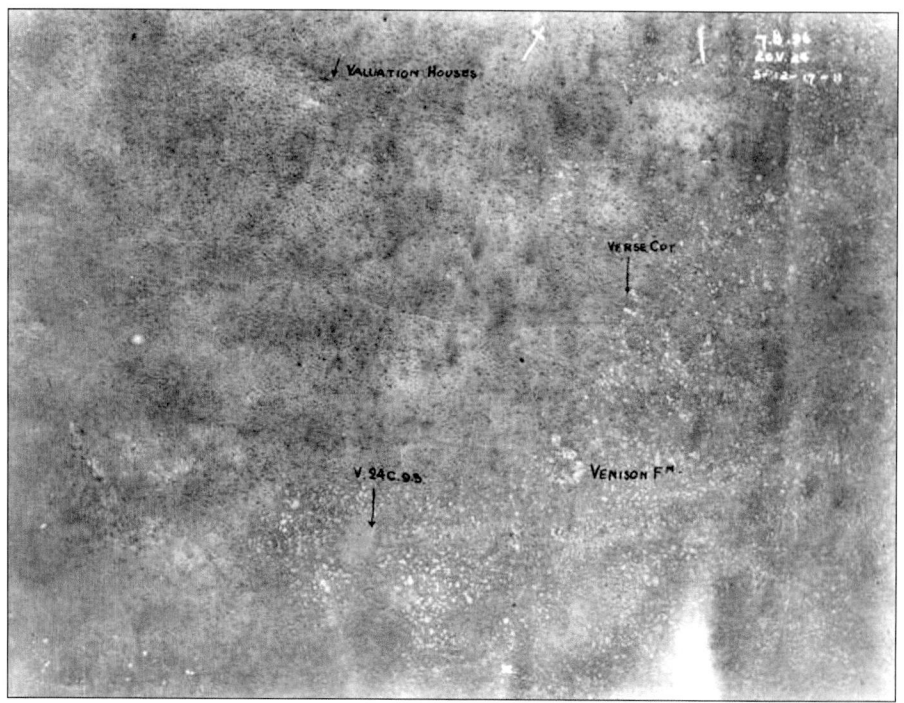

Valuation Houses and vicinity from the air December 1917. (McMaster University)

Passchendaele battlefield late November 1917. (Eleonore von Bojanowski, et al, *Thüringen im Weltkrieg: Vaterländisches Kriegsgedenkbuch im Wort und Bild für die Thüringischen Staaten Vol. 2* (Leipzig: Verlag der Literatur "Minerva" R. Max Lippold, 1919))

few at a time. Martini, although delayed until the afternoon, managed to carry out this deployment. The enemy, unwilling to surrender his gains, proceeded to strengthen the newly captured positions.[126]

Embattled survivors of 16th HLI, defending the salient east and west of Void Farm, began to feel the pressure as early as 1:00 p.m. when Martini, "with *Leutnant* d.R. Klopple and *12th Company*, counter-attacked the enemy" as a necessary preliminary to the counter-stroke scheduled for 4:15 p.m. British time. "Step by step, with intense hand grenade fighting, they slowly but surely, as planned" secured the left flank NW of Hill 52.[127] Captain Hassell's depleted command bore the brunt of this concerted preliminary effort: "At 3:30 p.m. on the 2nd, the enemy counter-attacked and drove his advanced posts back to their original position, approximately the assembly tape."[128]

German troops braced themselves under a fierce barrage (starting at 3:50 p.m.) of artillery and indirect machine-gun fire as the minutes leading up to the localized *Gegenangriff* ticked by. Some were dismayed at the prospect of leaving existing cover to advance in the fading light.[129] Their commanders, unwilling to sanction the loss of further territory, had once again demonstrated a steely determination to retain the northern portion of Passchendaele Ridge at all costs. *IR95's* post-war historian baldly articulated contemporary perceptions of the contested high ground's crucial importance: "The enemy could redeem past failures if he captured the *Höhenrücken* of the *Feldherrnhügel*. Yes. If not for the damned Germans – the Huns; they forgot that we fight for the safety of our home and country."[130] Coffin, discerning the renewed clamour of the enemy preparatory barrage, later observed: "At 4:10 p.m., the enemy's shellfire became intense and the SOS signal was sent up by the [32nd] Division on our left at 4:15 p.m."[131]

---

126 Buttmann, *Kriegsgeschichte des Koninglich Preusischen 6. Thüringischen Infanterie Regiment Nr. 95*, p. 253.
127 Ibid.
128 TNA: WO/95/2402: 2nd KOYLI War Diary.
129 TNA: WO/157/120: 'Annexe to Second Army Summary Dated 19th Decr. 1917: Translation of the closing pages of a diary taken from a dead German (probably a warrant officer of the 3rd Coy. 95th Inf. Regt., 38th Division) who was shot in V.29.b. in the early morning of the 15th inst.', Second Army Intelligence Files. For the intelligence value of captured documents, letters and diaries see Beach, 'British Intelligence and the German Army, 1914-1918', pp. 36-40.
130 Buttmann, *Kriegsgeschichte des Koninglich Preusischen 6. Thüringischen Infanterie Regiment Nr. 95*, p. 253.
131 TNA: WO/95/1727: 'Report on Operations', 7 December 1917, 25 Brigade War Diary. Blacklock subsequently remarked that this 'was the only really severe shelling encountered by the attacking troops.' See IWM 4723: 'Preliminary Report on Operations, December 1st, 2nd and 3rd, 4 December 1917, Brigadier-General T.S. Lambert Papers (Box 80/10/2).

5

Counterblow & Aftermath

It is an easy thing for one whose foot is on the outside of calamity to give advice and to rebuke the sufferer.[1]

5.1 Counterblow

Massed German batteries commenced a roaring counter-attack preparatory deluge of projectiles on to British positions NE and NW of Passchendaele at 4:10 p.m. on 2 December. Drifting banks of acrid, cordite-tinged smoke from the steady bombardment obscured the blighted region of unending shell craters, choked watercourses, shivered coppices and dispersed concrete pillboxes. Almost leaderless companies, platoons and sections, exhausted, wet-through and cowering under the ceaseless rain of hostile shells, steadied themselves for the expected counter-attack. One high-velocity missile detonated inside the pillbox HQ of 16th HLI with a particularly horrifying effect: "A shell passed through the slot, killed several men seated in a row on a form in its path, and finally exploded in an emplacement, rendering all the occupants in a greater or lesser degree casualties."[2] Nine men, including two officers (2nd Lieutenant J. Ferris and FOO 2nd Lieutenant V.J. Horton), were killed and 10 ORs wounded.[3] Major Scott (acting CO), Lieutenant J. McLellan MC and another TMB officer were among the injured. "It is amazing the HQ was not entirely wiped out."[4]

---

1 Aeschylus, *Prometheus Bound* (Unsourced quotation variant).
2 Chalmers (ed), *A Saga of Scotland*, p. 111.
3 29-year-old 2nd Lieutenant James Ferris 16th HLI (attached 97 TMB) has no known grave and is commemorated on the Tyne Cot Memorial to the Missing. 2nd Lieutenant V.J. Horton (age unknown) of 'D' Battery, 161 Brigade RFA is buried in Duhallow Cemetery.
4 Chalmers (ed), *A Saga of Scotland*, p. 111.

This truly devastating barrage, fired with effect by hundreds of field and heavy guns ringing the Passchendaele Salient, had little impact on the ability of 25 Brigade's supporting gunners to respond in kind. The situation had occurred dozens of times since Sir Herbert Plumer's first push on 20 September: Strictly limited objectives, captured and consolidated by the infantry, remained suitably protected by batteries deployed and ready to engage any counter-stroke. Lieutenant-Colonel Stirling (CO 2nd Royal Berkshire) ordered an SOS signal to be discharged in succession to the one discharged at 4:15 p.m. by 32nd Division. The evolving counter-attack, he learned afterwards, appeared to be primarily directed against the vicinity of Southern Redoubt, where 2nd Lieutenant Upton's platoon still held a section of Venison Trench 50 yards north of the lost earthwork. In the centre, Lieutenant-Colonel Irwin (CO 2nd Lincolnshire Regiment) recalled "an intense barrage was put down. SOS went up on 32nd Div. front and on Berkshire front, but no infantry action developed on my front." Hundreds of high explosive shells, fired at once in response to Stirling's flare, blanketed predetermined SOS lines along with an accompanying indirect machine-gun barrage before the German infantry could fan out into any sort of assault formation. Survivors went to ground or fled to the rear. Coffin subsequently observed: "Although no action followed on the part of the enemy's infantry, it is believed that they were forming up in considerable strength opposite our front and that they were scattered by our artillery fire. The wide front over which the lights were sent up led me to believe that the enemy was about to carry out an attack on a large scale." *25th Division's* local *Gegenangriff* appeared, as far as 8th Division was concerned, to be over before it could unfold: "By 5 o'clock the enemy's barrage was dying down and unusual quietness prevailed."[5]

On 97 Brigade's front, reduced elements of 11th Border Regiment, clinging to green line positions south of Mallet Copse and 16th HLI, defending a small salient east and west of Void Farm, faced the full force of the developing German counter-attack. 2nd KOYLI had been driven off Hill 52 and 17th HLI stopped dead in front of Vat Cottages on their right and left respectively. The equally hard-pressed *IR95*, having lost all of its *Vorfeldzone* and a considerable portion of the *Hauptwiderstandslinie*, was ordered to "straighten out the line" by forcing the beset 16th HLI and 11th Border Regiment back to the *Vorfeldzone's* forward edge.[6] *Leutnant* Martini, his left flank

---

5   TNA: WO/95/1929: 'Appendix B', 5 December 1917, 2nd Royal Berkshire War Diary, WO/95/1730: 'Report on Action of Battn from 2:30 p.m. 1.12.17 – M.N. 2/3 .12. 17', 2nd Lincolnshire War Diary, WO/95/1727: 'Report on Operations', 7 December 1917, 25 Brigade War Diary and Lieutenant-Colonel Boraston & Bax, *The Eighth Division: 1914-1918*, p. 166. Reference to the attempted riposte in consulted German regimental histories is sparse. Mention is made of *Hauptmann* von Arnim's morning rush to the rear to 'organise a systematic counter-attack' prior to the recapture of Southern Redoubt. The narrative then claims that 'Heavy fighting started again at 5:00 p.m.' but provides no specific details of a localised counter-attack. See Offenbacher, *Die Geschichte des Infanterie-Leibregiments Grossherzogin (3.Grossherzoglich Hessisches) Nr. 117*, p. 196.
6   Counter-attack orders (forwarded by wireless) to regain the line as far as the *Vorfeldzone* had been intercepted during the afternoon; this information was passed on by II Corps

Panorama looking south from site of Mullet Farm towards Vat Cottages Ridge.
(Rob Thompson)

secure since the 2:00 p.m. preliminary attack, ordered his men forward from the vicinity of Volt Farm: "The [main] counter-attack began in broad daylight at 5:15 p.m. [German time] when *11th* and *12th* companies with two *Truppen* of *9th Company* attacked the enemy. At the same time, annihilation fire was requested and fixed on the right positions simultaneously."[7]

16th HLI, its forward posts overrun by the enemy, put up a stout resistance: "About 4 p.m. the enemy infantry were observed to be concentrating on N side of Mallet Copse and about V.24 central. Our SOS was fired by Lieut. Charlton, and our barrage was probably put down. The enemy infantry attacked our positions about 4:30 p.m., but were driven off by Lewis guns and rifle fire with the assistance of one Vickers gun, which had been brought up."[8] On the left, *Leutnant* Martini's counter-attack drove 11th Border Regiment to its original jumping-off line; "About 18 men came back."[9] Shute, although dubious about calculated German strength, readily confirmed the

at 1:56 p.m. See TNA: WO/95/2370: After-action report, 'Appendix 'J', 32nd Division: Telephone and Telegraph Messages 2 December 1917', 11 December 1917, 32nd Division War Diary.
7   Buttmann, *Kriegsgeschichte des Koninglich Preusischen 6. Thüringischen Infanterie Regiment Nr. 95*, p. 254.
8   TNA: WO/95/2404: 16th HLI War Diary.
9   See Appendix XVI Part E (para. 13) and IWM 4723: 'Preliminary Report on Operations December 1st, 2nd and 3rd December', 4 December 1917, Brigadier-General T.S. Lambert Papers (Box 80/10/2).

punishing ordeal that proceeded the Lonsdales' general retirement in his subsequent after-action report:

> The enemy's counter-attack was made through MALLET COPSE against 11th Border Regt. who estimate the probable strength of the enemy who attacked at 300. This number is probably exaggerated, but the enemy had undoubtedly been collecting in some numbers in the vicinity of MALLET COPSE all day. The 11th Border Regiment had done well in the early morning fighting … The losses of this Battalion were considerable, especially in officers and NCOs and by 4:10 p.m. 15 of the officers and most of the NCOs had been hit and the men were practically without leaders. At 4:10 p.m. the enemy put a barrage well in rear of 11th Border Regt. and counter-attacked under cover of rifle and rifle grenade fire. Our men fell back in front of this attack to our old frontline.[10]

Hostile movement was also discerned opposite the left centre: "At 4:15 p.m. 2 companies of the enemy … about 200 men [,] advanced on Veal Cottage and thence to Vat Cottages."[11] 16th HLI, its flanks exposed by 2nd KOYLI's earlier repulse on the right and the withdrawal of 11th Border Regiment on the left, stubbornly clung to positions around Void Farm. Situated beyond the established *Hauptwiderstandslinie* defences, further efforts to eliminate this troublesome *Engländernest* met with furious rifle, rifle bomb and machine-gun fire.[12]

Lieutenant-Colonel Scully (CO 16th NF) received word of Lieutenant Charlton's SOS signal at 4:15 p.m. About 200 stragglers, many of them wounded, were then observed "returning in numbers" towards Virile Farm. Scully immediately dispatched his two remaining companies forward with instructions "to take with them every man of any regiment. He set the example; he brought out every available man of headquarters and led the way. It was an advance into the unknown, for no information had been received all day…"[13] Pondering a "sea of mud and the leaden sleet of bullets from the pill-boxes" in the ascending afternoon twilight:

---

10 TNA: WO/95/2370: After-action report, 'Part IV, Narrative Dealing with the Retirement of the 97th Infantry Brigade', 11 December 1917, 32nd Division War Diary. Shute's disbelief of enemy numbers was likely based on the CO 16th NF's subsequent after-action report.' See p. 347 below.
11 IWM 4723: 'Summary of the Attack of the 97th Inf. Bde with 2 Battalions of the 96th Inf. Bde. on December 2 [1917]', Brigadier-General T.S. Lambert Papers (Box 80/10/2).
12 *Engländernest*: An improvised but strong defensive position dug by infiltrating British troops. A Bavarian regiment noted the previous year: 'Once they had established themselves the British could prove very hard to dislodge, for they might have their Lewis guns and trench mortars with them, and they were astonishingly speedy diggers.' See Duffy, *Through German Eyes*, p. 274.
13 Cooke, *Historical Records of the 16th (Service) Battalion Northumberland Fusiliers*, p. 89 and IWM 4723: '32nd Div. No.G.S.1499/3/33', 5 December 1917, Brigadier-General T.S. Lambert Papers (Box 80/10/2).

Lieut. Col. Scully at once ordered 'C' and 'D' Coys, which were in the vicinity of Bn. HQ, to advance; the men got out of their trenches and moved forward keeping a good line under fairly heavy machine-gun fire. Runners and signallers of Bn. HQ details were sent forward with them. They advanced about 300 [yards] in front of VIRILE FARM and dug themselves in. The line thus forward ran from VOX FARM on the right to about V.29.b.40.70. when it bent back to the original line. The enemy attack did not get through our barrage.[14]

The enemy, Scully later observed, "did not follow up" the retreating troops, nor did he observe any Germans. His primary concern whilst leading his men forward into the void was for his companies' vulnerable flanks: "In view of the fact that the enemy were in possession of HILL 52 and that there were no organised troops to hold our frontline, the OC 16th North'd Fusiliers decided that any further advance of his Battalion would expose our line to attack from the direction of Hill 52 and that, moreover, both his own flanks would be exposed as he advanced."[15] *IR94's* post-war historian, writing of Scully's forlorn progress, remarked: "At 5:00 p.m. [German time] the English, attacking again in many waves, attempted to capture the area on the right flank. Rifle and machine-gun fire prevented this."[16] The new position, a shallow bight of ground on a line "250 to 300 yards in advance" of the original line, was rapidly consolidated in the growing darkness. "My No. 3 Company", Scully recollected, "dropped back a defensive flank to VOCATION FARM to keep in touch with my No. 2 Company. My No. 4 Company dropped back a defensive flank to cover the left of the Battalion."[17]

Forced back to its jumping-off line at 3:30 p.m., 2nd KOYLI did not experience any further attacks after 4:15 p.m.[18] The Germans, satisfied with reclaiming the *Vorfeldzone* below Hill 52, focused their efforts on strengthening shell hole outposts and sections of trenchline. 17th HLI, still stalled in front of Vat Cottages, failed to maintain the small gains beneath the dominant strongpoint:

> It was obvious that a hostile counter-attack might be expected and this took place about 4 p.m. on the afternoon of the 2nd, preceded by an intense artillery barrage. What exactly happened is not very definite, but it is clear that the line [came] under the enemy barrage, and owing to difficulties of communication and the heavy casualties amongst officers and NCOs, was found farther back toward our original position. It appears that, following the barrage, the enemy attacked

---

14 Ibid, Stedman, *Salford Pals*, p. 156 and TNA: WO/95/2398: 16th NF War Diary.
15 TNA: WO/95/2370: After-action report, 'Part IV, Narrative Dealing with the Retirement of the 97th Infantry Brigade', 11 December 1917, 32nd Division War Diary.
16 Hartmann, *Das Infanterie Regiment Grossherzog von Sachsen (5. Thüringisches) No. 94 im Weltkrieg*, p. 238.
17 IWM 4723: '32d Div. No.G.S.1499/3/33', 5 December 1917, Brigadier-General T.S. Lambert Papers (Box 80/10/2).
18 TNA: WO/95/2402: 2nd KOYLI War Diary.

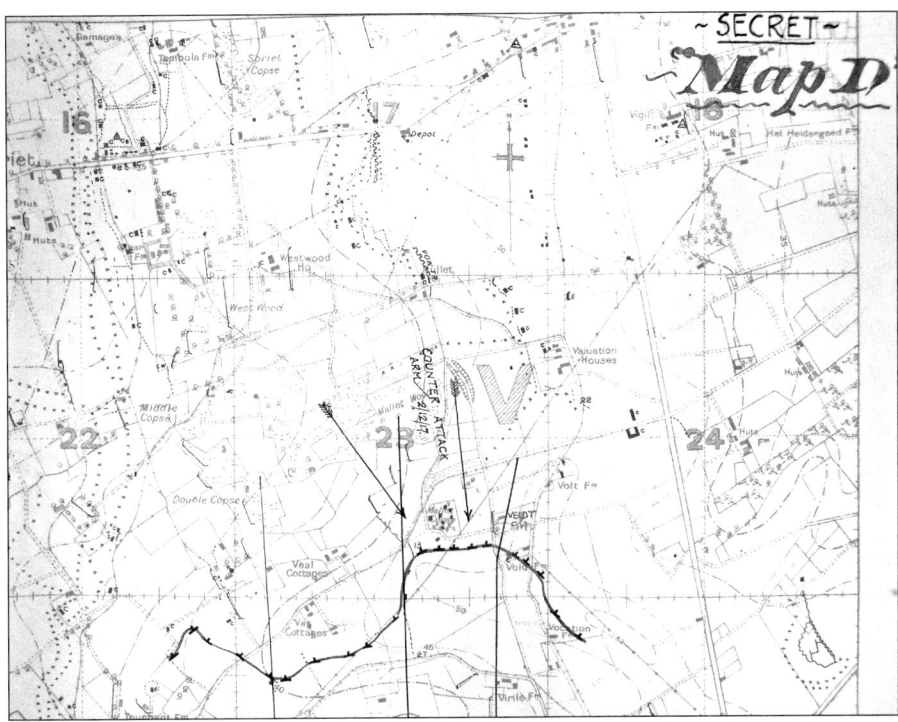

Map showing direction of the 4:15 p.m. German counter-attack. (TNA: WO/95/2370: 32nd Division War Diary)

Lieutenant-Colonel A.J. Scully MC. (Captain C.H. Cooke, *Historical Records of the 16th (Service) Battalion Northumberland Fusiliers* (Newcastle-upon-Tyne: Council of the Newcastle and Gateshead Incorporated Chamber of Commerce, 1923))

with one battalion, which considerably cut-up by our counter-fire, came within a certain distance of our positions and then broke and retired. The attack and counter-attack, therefore, though not exactly a failure had on account of unexpected difficulties, only partially succeeded."[19]

17th HLI's retirement to the jumping-off line, its post-war historians notes, was "almost general", some outposts "still hanging on to the advanced positions on the 3rd."[20] On the far left, 15th LF repelled vigorous attacks against a refused right flank extended during the late morning to connect with 17th HLI.[21] Counter-attacks originating north and NW of the Battalion's established positions failed, as predicted, to materialise due to impassable ground conditions.[22]

VIII Corps first received notice that something was afoot at 4:20 p.m.: "From II Corps. SOS went up on right of II Corps 4:10 p.m." 8th Division followed with another report ten minutes later: "SOS up on our front at 4.3 p.m."[23] II Corps telegraphed a second message the contents of which confirmed plans to resume operations during the early hours of 3 December, at 4:40 p.m.:

> 32nd Division will consolidate the line now held between TEALL COT (V.30.b.15.50.) and TOURNANT FARM in V.28.b.4.1. aaa The 32nd Division will [,] on the night of 2/3 December [,] carry out a minor operation with a view to capturing VEAL COT. and HILL 52 and improving the siting of the line held in the vicinity of these places aaa The zero hour for this operation will be settled by the GOC 32nd Division, but will not be before 3:30 a.m. on the morning of 3 Dec. aaa as soon as the exact hours is decided [,] the 32nd Div. will inform II Corps HQ, II Corps HA, and 8th, 14th and 35th div. direct aaa 7 Sqd. RFC will arrange for a contact aeroplane to fly over the front in question at 7:30 a.m. on 3rd Dec. and call for flares [,] and also arrange for an aeroplane to be in the air from dawn 3rd Dec. to give warning of counter-attacks and to receive messages from Bn HQ.[24]

Three more reports from the CHA, "Counter-batteries carried out 4 concentrations and intense neutralization throughout the day aaa SOS calls 4.3 and 4:27 p.m.

---

19 TNA: WO/95/2405: 17th HLI War Diary.
20 Arthur & Munro (eds), *The Seventeenth Highland Light Infantry*, p. 69.
21 Latter, *The History of the Lancashire Fusiliers in Two Volumes Vol.1*, p. 277.
22 See TNA: WO/95/2400: 'Notes to Accompany Special Intelligence Maps of the Area V.15 – V.30' November 1917, 97 Brigade War Diary.
23 BL: 48359: 'Report of Operations Carried Out by the VIII Army Corps on the Morning of 2nd December 1917, Official War Diaries with Appendices and Addenda, VIII Army Corps, Passchendaele Front, November 1917-April 1918', Vol. V, Hunter-Weston Papers.
24 Ibid and TNA: WO/95/643: 'Secret Priority G.520', 2 December 1917, II Corps War Diary.

were answered"; 33rd Division: "Intermittent shelling of Passchendaele all day aaa Heavy shelling of D.15 at 2:30 p.m. aaa Wind NW aaa SOS left of Passchendaele at 4.3 p.m. aaa Prisoners total 2" and II Corps: "32nd Div. report time 3:45 p.m. aaa TEALL COTTAGE recaptured with 40 prisoners aaa Line now reported to run TEALL COT. inclusive VOCATION and VOX FARMS both inclusive [,] VOID inclusive thence along southern edge of MALLET COPSE, south of VAT COTTAGES to about V.23.c.0.2. aaa VAT COT. held by M.G.s and wired", followed in succession before news of the German counter-attack arrived from 8th Division at 5:05 p.m.: "25th Brigade report enemy attacking believed in some force aaa Report time 4:20 p.m.."[25]

Shute, certain that Hill 52, Void Farm and Mallet Copse were in British hands, still anticipated the eventual capture of Vat and Veal cottages when an SOS signal was reported (4:07 p.m.) from the direction of Mallet Copse.[26] A telephone message to Brigadier-General Tyler (BGRA 32nd Division) followed three minutes later: "SOS on 97th Brigade front at MALLET WOOD. They are coming through MALLET WOOD. We occupy HILL 52." This report, its sender obviously unaware of the dire circumstances, appears to relate the earlier observed trickling of enemy troops from the direction of the inundated weald, so no word of the developing counter-attack reached Division HQ during this time. Indeed, the usual reports, orders and queries continued to flow as *38th Division's* riposte developed: Captain Knox forwarded the most recent interview results – reasonably accurate as it turned out – gathered from wounded survivors at 4:00 p.m.: "A man of 16th HLI states that his Battalion are holding VOID FARM. A man of the Borders states his Battalion is holding VELDT FARM. A man of 17th HLI states his Battalion holds approximately the line of 1st objective. A man of 15th Lancs. Fus. states they hold final objective. Very few give any idea of time." Concerns about the timing of 97 Brigade's resumption of operations were expressed during a telephone conversation at 4:20 p.m.: "Attack is not to be before 3:30 a.m. – Order from the [II] Corps – on account of something else on the right.[27] We have got to tell them exact. Will you let us know as soon as you know?" Previous anxiety over retention of objectives was exacerbated by a telegraph

25 BL: 48359: 'Report of Operations Carried Out by the VIII Army Corps on the Morning of 2nd December 1917, Official War Diaries with Appendices and Addenda, VIII Army Corps, Passchendaele Front, November 1917-April 1918', Vol. V, Hunter-Weston Papers.
26 32nd Division's DMGO wrote afterwards: 'At 4-06 p.m. [sic] all [barrage machine-] guns replied to the SOS, 'fire being opened within 30 seconds.' See TNA: WO/95/2370: After-action Report: 'Appendix 'H': Action of Machine-guns During Operations Near Passchendaele, 1st and 2nd December 1917', 16 December 1917, 32nd Division War Diary.
27 '[S]omething else on the right': A possible reference to renewed activity contemplated by 8th Division.

message received three minutes later: "Wire timed 4:23 p.m. From 97th Brigade. SOS 4:23 p.m."[28]

The exchange of messages continued as before, 14 Brigade, in the process of preparing to attack through 97 Brigade on the night of 3/4 December, being queried by telephone about recent troop movements at 4:30 p.m.: [Div. HQ] "Which of your battalions are moving up tonight?" [14 Bde] "2 companies of 15th HLI have moved to Meetcheele at request of 97th Bde." [Div. HQ] "What is this about do you know? Nothing is going wrong?" [14 Bde] "Latest report from 97th Brigade is that they are on HILL 52. They have also got TEALL COTTAGE and 40 prisoners and they have also VOID FARM. That was before the SOS sent up." A final note from Captain Knox was delivered at 4:49 p.m.: "A Captain of the 17th HLI states that the situation on the left was as follows at 12 noon: 15th LF in original front line.[29] Left Coy. of 17th HLI in original line. Right Coy. 17th HLI slightly advanced on line approximately of VAT COTTAGES, but he does not know situation on right."[30]

Lack of any available intelligence following the observed SOS signal led, at Blacklock's request, 32nd Division to order batteries (engaging enemy movements since 3:20 p.m.) to reduce rates of fire: "To CRA. General Blacklock thinks you should go back to normal rates. You should search all around VALUATION HOUSES, etc." A telegraph (5:05 p.m.) reporting the SOS signal on 8th Division's front preceded an inconclusive telephone conversation – copied down at the receiving end during real-time transcription – between Shute and Blacklock at 5:10 p.m.:

> I have just wired to you that the SOS has gone up on the 8th Division front. You have heard from the wounded that certain parts of your front have had to give way. You think it is the front of the 17th HLI. Have you heard anything about the Borders? What time did this [counter-] attack take place? You have stopped firing on SOS lines: fairly quiet now. A certain amount of machine-gun fire from VALUATION HOUSES, artillery fire has died down. Do you know what is happening on the right? You have sent out patrols to VINDICTIVE CROSSROADS and to VIRILE FARM for information to try and find out your right and what is going on your front.[31]

Shute later observed: "This information was regarded as unreliable by the 97th Infantry Brigade who thought that the attack was on the front of the 17th HLI." The

---

28 TNA: WO/95/2370: After-action report, 'Part III, Narrative of Events', and 'Appendix 'J', 32nd Division: Telephone and Telegraph Messages 2 December 1917', 11 December 1917, 32nd Division War Diary.
29 The informant's statement was probably based on his earlier proximity to 15th LF's refused right flank.
30 TNA: WO/95/2370: After-action report, 'Appendix 'J', 32nd Division: Telephone and Telegraph Messages 2 December 1917', 11 December 1917, 32nd Division War Diary.
31 Ibid.

somewhat mollified GOC 32nd Division's focus now shifted to where his line joined Coffin's 25 Brigade. He telephoned (5:19 p.m) 8th Division to discover the situation of its left (2nd Rifle Brigade) battalion opposite Northern Redoubt. Blacklock was rung up a second time (5:32 p.m.) after a brief conversation with Heneker's HQ:

> Shute: The information from the 8th Division is that their line runs D.6.b.9.1. – E.1.a.2.8. – W.25.c.3.1., W.25.c.2.4. – W.25.c.1.9. – V.30.b.7.3. – V.30.b.1.4., which is practically TEALL COTTAGE with a post at V.30.b.8.5.[32]
> Blacklock: The five commanding officers are now with their Bns. Officers are trying to find out the situation. 16 MGs of 96th Bde are at VIRILE FARM: 8 of them are going to be employed for the close defence of the line.[33] [I am going] to get in touch with Colonel Scully.
> Shute: He has got on to HILL 52 hasn't he? Have you found any of the KOYLI yet?
> Blacklock: Not any more yet.
> Shute: When do you think we will get news of what did happen?

Blacklock's reply is not recorded in the consulted telephone and telegraph transcript.[34]

Two reports detailing the latest available intelligence were telegraphed to 32nd Division by 8th Division HQ: "25th Brigade report enemy attacking believed in some force. Report timed 4:20 p.m." and "Hostile artillery fairly quiet till 11:40 a.m. then heavy barrage round KOREK – GRAVENSTAFEL area. SOS went up at 4:10 p.m. Situation now reported quieter. Prisoners captured now 3 officers and 52 ORs." The latter was "repeated by wire" to Second Army Report Centre and II Corps."[35] Twenty-five minutes passed before Shute fielded (6:15 p.m.) a telephone report from 97 Brigade:

---

32 The original report, received by VIII Corps at 5:35 p.m., began: 'SOUTHERN REDOUBT now reported held by enemy…' See BL: 48359: 'Report of Operations Carried Out by the VIII Army Corps on the Morning of 2nd December 1917, Official War Diaries with Appendices and Addenda, VIII Army Corps, Passchendaele Front, November 1917-April 1918', Vol. V, Hunter-Weston Papers.
33 Sixteen Vickers guns of 96 Company MGC were deployed near Virile Farm to provide indirect fire support. See Chapter 2, p. 153.
34 TNA: WO/95/2370: After-action report, 'Part III, Narrative of Events', and 'Appendix 'J', 32nd Division: Telephone and Telegraph Messages 2 December 1917', 11 December 1917, 32nd Division War Diary.
35 Ibid and BL: 48359: 'Report of Operations Carried Out by the VIII Army Corps on the Morning of 2nd December 1917, Official War Diaries with Appendices and Addenda, VIII Army Corps, Passchendaele Front, November 1917-April 1918', Vol. V, Hunter-Weston Papers.

Situation as follows: When [counter-] attack started Colonel Scully sent two platoons to HILL 52, where he had already one company.[36] He is up there now, no reports received from him, but I think it is fairly alright there. 2 more platoons [were sent] to the Borders, who are well forward in MALLET COPSE and probably suffered a good deal, but wherever they are they are probably very thin. 17th HLI men doubtful part of the line. I have not been able to get any news of them. It seems that their line may be anywhere. The 15th [LF] on the left report their left company is on objective and possibly their other two companies are there. It is possible that the people on their right [17th HLI] brought them back. Otherwise all clear.

Major Scott 16th HLI and McLellan 2nd in command have been wounded, which only leaves the Adjutant with the Battalion. All battalions have suffered heavy casualties in officers. The General [Blacklock] thinks this operation would be very difficult to carry out, as he has not got officers to collect the men. With the help of his MGs he can take on holding the line, but might like an extra two companies sent to him in case he wants them on the left. He won't ask for them unless he cannot possibly help it. Left company of 15th [LF] has two machine-guns with it. Major Scott, who was taking orders to Col. Scully from him has been wounded. TM Battery commander killed. Genl. Blacklock will push out where he can but cannot take on minor operation.[37]

The situation was more serious than this report made out: Hill 52 had been lost before dawn; 16th HLI was holding on to an exposed salient around Void Farm; remnants of 11th Border Regiment and 17th HLI were, with the exception of a few outposts, back on their original jumping-off line. 15th LF had been forced to extend a refused right flank to 17th HLI, whilst 16th NF's afternoon advance came nowhere near Hill 52 or Mallet Copse. 97 Brigade's ignorance of the true state of affairs is explicable when one considers the often fragmentary and contradictory nature of incoming reports. Blacklock, nonetheless, recognised his shattered battalions could do no more; the proposed pre-dawn operation to secure what remained of the red line objective was beyond their capabilities.

A more reassuring telegraph was transmitted (6:30 p.m.) by 14 Brigade to 32nd Division: "15th HLI reports 5:50 p.m. Situation apparently normal. The 2 companies have not been sent to MEETCHEELE. Apparently calm all along the front." 8th Division followed with a telegraph reiterating previously confirmed (by telephone at 5:19 p.m.) map reference coordinates of 25 Brigade's current line.[38] Hill 52, overlooking the Paddebeek valley south of Vat Cottages Ridge, remained the key feature

36 See Chapter 4, p. 288, fn. 123.
37 TNA: WO/95/2370: After-action report, 'Appendix 'J', 32nd Division: Telephone and Telegraph Messages 2 December 1917', 11 December 1917, 32nd Division War Diary.
38 Ibid.

north of Passchendaele. The tactically important hillock and its environs, so Blacklock believed, had been secured despite the recent German counter-attack. Subsequent post-dusk discussions between 32nd Division and 97 Brigade were based on this misconception:

> 6:55 p.m. Verbal. [Div. HQ] To 97th Bde. 97th Brigade will establish itself tonight on the line TEALL COTTAGE (inclusive) HILL 52 (inclusive) VOID FARM (inclusive) MALLET COPSE – VEAL COTTAGES (inclusive) – V.23.c.2.4. This line to be strongly consolidated. Battalions and companies to be re-organised. Guides to learn position of their units so as to be able to lead up reliefs tomorrow night. Two companies cannot be placed at your [Blacklock's] disposal in view of tomorrow's relief. If you require more troops you should keep KOYLI in reserve behind the left about TOURNANT FARM. Machine-guns to be moved up to defensive positions in the line indicated. Corps has been informed that 3:30 a.m. is the time the VEAL COTTAGE thing will be done. The General [Blacklock] has had that?
>
> 97 Bde: Genl. Blacklock spoke to Major Turner about it.[39]

Blacklock, armed with new information concerning the state of his Brigade and clearly apprehensive about the security of the frontline, took up the receiver and, with characteristic directness, spelled out the unpleasant operational particulars (the first part copied down at the receiving end during transcription) to his superiors:

> Div. HQ: Genl. Blacklock speaking now: You are afraid of the responsibility of the line: You are very weak on your left and very disorganised. Major Scott [CO 16th HLI] and other Colonel[40] who were running the show have been knocked out. Borders back in our frontline. Do you mean to say you are back on your frontline everywhere? I never heard that before.
>
> Blacklock: They [Germans] came right through down to our old frontline. VOID FARM has gone back to VOCATION [FARM].[41]
>
> Div. HQ: Is the Boche in our frontline?
>
> Blacklock: He is back in his forward zone in the areas of No. 3 [11th Border Regiment] and No. 4 [17th HLI] battalions.

---

39 I have been unable to ascertain Major Turner's unit affiliation.
40 Consulted war diaries and regimental histories shed no light on the identity of the 'other Colonel' referred to.
41 16th HLI, contrary to Blacklock's belief that a withdrawal to Vocation Farm had occurred, still maintained posts around Void Farm after dusk.

Div. HQ: Are we behind our old frontline do you know? You cannot get on to the old [red line] objective. Are you sure you have any line of defence at all now?[42]

Shute, finally acquiescing to Blacklock's on-the-spot estimation, concluded it was "impracticable to resume the offensive with the 97th Infantry Brigade." A rash scheme to carry on with Lumsden's 14 Brigade was pondered shortly afterwards: "The question of moving the 14th Infantry Brigade forward at once and attacking with them through 97th Infantry Brigade was considered, but this course was rejected, as it was considered that the assembly of the Brigade and the delivery of an attack in the dark without adequate reconnaissance was an operation not offering the necessary chances of success."[43]

Shute telephoned II Corps at 7:08 p.m.; nothing else remained but to inform his superiors about the retirement:

> I have bad news for you. We were counter-attacked and except for holding HILL 52, where we have got a couple companies, we are back on our frontline. I had sent out my orders when I had got this news through, but I'm afraid it is no good trying to carry out your orders.[44] I do not think we can do anything until tomorrow. I think we can do it then with another brigade on the line where we started from except on HILL 52. The Bosche is very close up to our old line. If I had known this earlier, I would have relieved tonight. I do not think we are at VOX [FARM].[45] This is the first news I have had: I presume it was that SOS. What I can do tonight is to push that line forward a little if I can.[46]

The doleful situation, Shute was fairly certain, could be turned around by another effort the following night: "The Divisional commander, therefore, decided to attack with 14th Infantry Brigade and two battalions of the 96th Infantry Brigade on the night December 3/4." Orders "indicating the situation which had arisen on the front of 97th Infantry Brigade and the operation to be undertaken" were subsequently issued to Brigadier-General Lumsden who was asked to "submit his plans at once…"[47]

Hours had passed since the start of the German counter-attack. Earlier reports, based on sketchy information and erroneous conclusions, concerning the extent and

---

42 TNA: WO/95/2370: After-action report, 'Appendix 'J', 32nd Division: Telephone and Telegraph Messages 2 December 1917', 11 December 1917, 32nd Division War Diary.
43 Ibid: After-action report, 'Part III, Narrative of Events', 11 December 1917.
44 Telegraphed by II Corps at 4:40 p.m. See above.
45 Vox Farm remained in British hands. It was temporaily abandoned and reoccupied sometime during the night. See below.
46 TNA: WO/95/2370: After-action report, 'Appendix 'J', 32nd Division: Telephone and Telegraph Messages 2 December 1917', 11 December 1917, 32nd Division War Diary.
47 Ibid: After-action report, 'Part III, Narrative of Events', 11 December 1917.

consequences of the recently reported withdrawal resulted in a heated telephone exchange (7:20 p.m.) between Shute and Blacklock:

> Shute: Why did you not report that you had been biffed back by that counter-attack? No message came through to us. No. It was not reported to Col. MacNamara [sic][48] nor to me. Are you in TEALL COTTAGE? Are you holding HILL 52? Is it to be understood that you have not got VOX FARM? On the left are you beaten back behind our old frontline? On their old frontline. What attacked you and at what time? Why did they have to come back then? Had you no MGs or Lewis Guns or Stokes Mortars? Well why didn't they fire?[49]

Blacklock's replies to this relentless cross-examination are not recorded in the telephone and telegraph transcripts, but it is easy, given the heavy casualties, ensuing disorganisation and how much still remained unknown in the chaotic aftermath of the German counter-thrust, to commiserate with the censured Brigadier.[50] Shute, his ire aroused by what appeared to be an avoidable setback and – taking into account the local dominance of enemy machine-guns – wanting to husband 14 Brigade for the next effort, then informed Blacklock of his intention to keep the worn-out 97 Brigade in the line for two more nights:

> Well then, the only possible way of facing the situation is that you have to improve your position as you can during the night. It is impossible to relieve you and it is impossible to reinforce you. You are practically right back into your old line. That's what it comes to. There is nothing more to say except that you must hold on to what you have got. They [battalions] had evidently not consolidated their line, MGs were not in position and Stokes mortars were not firing and, of course, as a result they simply came straight back as soon as they were attacked. The only thing to do is improve your line and get it thoroughly organised. You are to try and get VAT COTTAGES if you can and Lumsden will have to make the same attack tomorrow.

The discussion concluded with a query as to where the GOC 97 Brigade would like his SOS lines placed. Shute closed with a terse statement of expectations: "You

---

48 Lieutenant-Colonel A.E. McNamara (GSO 1).
49 TNA: WO/95/2370: After-action report, 'Appendix 'J', 32nd Division: Telephone and Telegraph Messages 2 December 1917', 11 December 1917, 32nd Division War Diary.
50 'The ramifications of casualties are great. Strength, equipment and leaders are lost. Apart from its physical impact, [hostile] fire contributes to the dispersion and dislocation of surviving troops. In concert with terrain, reduced visibilty and noise it creates a chaotic environment.' See Roger Noble, 'Raising the White Flag: The Surrender of Australian Soldiers on the Western Front', *Revue Internationale d'Histoire Militaire*, No. 72 (1990), p. 57.

will have to hold your line throughout tomorrow and I will order Lumsden to attack through you tomorrow night."[51]

Efforts to form a "continuous and connected" line proceeded after dusk on 25 Brigade's front. Moonrise was at 7:28 p.m., so several hours of darkness remained to organise and improve positions just opposite Venison trench and the redoubts.[52] Coffin, "Knowing that his line was but thinly held, owing to casualties which had been sustained, decided to order the 3 remaining companies of the 2nd West Yorkshire Regt. to move up to BELLEVUE.[53] At the same time, the 41st Infantry Brigade [14th Division] were informed of the situation and warned to be ready to reinforce if required." A consequence of the German counter-attack, these precautions proved unnecessary: "At 5 p.m. the enemy's barrage began to die down ... Information was also received that our line was intact and at 5:20 p.m. a message was sent informing the 2nd West Yorkshire Regt. that the 3 companies were not now required."[54]

Sporadic flare-ups continued as the enemy, alarmed by the close proximity of the new British frontline to the *Vorfeldzone*, engaged any signs of activity with rifle and machine-gun fire: "Heavy fighting started again at 5:00 pm. [German time]. It was especially severe for *12th Company*. By sheer luck this unit had been issued new hand grenades and was thus well equipped to resist. Arrival of darkness also assisted the beleaguered men."[55] 25 Brigade's situation remained, regardless of enemy efforts, relatively secure following the attempted counter-attack. Battalion commanders, anticipating the promised relief by 41 Brigade (7th King's Royal Rifle Corps, 8th King's Royal Rifle Corps [KRRC], 7th Rifle Brigade, 8th Rifle Brigade) eagerly awaited the appearance of advanced parties from the incoming battalions.[56] Lieutenant-Colonel Stirling recalled: "All guides for the relief who tried to reach Bn. HQ up to date having been casualties, I sent down Lieutenant Burne (Signal Officer) with guides

---

51 TNA: WO/95/2370: After-action report, 'Appendix 'J', 32nd Division: Telephone and Telegraph Messages 2 December 1917', 11 December 1917, 32nd Division War Diary. A subsequent complaint concerning the perceived failure of 14 Brigade's Stokes mortars to deploy near Tournant Farm (see Chapter 2, p. 153) was submitted by the CO 15th LF. Brigadier-General Lumsden replied that the battery was in place by zero + 2 hours, the officer in charge testifying that he reported to Major Utterson at 4:30 a.m. Shute, based on Lumsden's response, rejected Utterson's claim. See IWM 4723: '32nd Div. No.G.S.1.1499/20/1' 5 December 1917 and '14th Inf. Bde. G.230/0/5', 10 December 1917, Brigadier-General T.S. Lambert Papers (Box 80/10/2) and Appendix VIII.
52 Boraston & Bax, *The Eighth Division*, p. 167 and TNA: WO/157/288: 'Calendar for December 1917: Times Calculated for Second Army Front and Greenwich Mean Time', II Corps Intelligence File.
53 2nd West Yorkshire's remaining company was still in 25 Brigade reserve. See Chapter 3, p 181.
54 TNA: WO/95/1727: 'Report on Operations', 7 December 1917, 25 Brigade War Diary.
55 Offenbacher, *Die Geschichte des Infanterie-Leibregiments Grossherzogin (3. Grossherzoglich Hessisches) Nr. 117*, p. 196.
56 See TNA: WO/95/1677: '8th Division Instructions No. 2', 25 November 1917, 8th Division War Diary.

from HQ details at about 6:45 p.m. to meet incoming unit, at the same time collecting more guides from coys. [to] take the 8th Bn. KRRC forward from Bn. HQ." 2nd Lieutenant Upton had not reported in yet, but hopes he would be able to extricate his small party from Venison Trench before 2nd Royal Berkshire's relief was complete were still entertained.[57]

At Volgeltje Chateau, Brigadier-General Aspinall (BGGS VIII Corps) – still awaiting word about the general situation after nightfall – received two telegraphed situation reports from 8th Division at 5:55 and 6:40 p.m respectively: "Following from 25th Infantry Brigade. Timed 5:10 p.m. aaa Situation appears to be quietening down aaa Another wire timed 5:35 p.m. reads aaa Situation quiet but still obscure"; "Reference Corps Commander's enquiry: Heavy MG fire, which opened at Zero in bright moonlight appear to be cause of failure left battalion." Another telegraph, this time from II Corps reported, "No change in the situation in Goudberg sector." Relative peace, readily discerned by a measurable decline in artillery and small arms fire, seemed to reign on 8th Division's front when the neighbouring 33rd Division telegraphed, "Front now reported quiet" at 7:00 p.m.[58] Additional confirmation of what was already known at 32nd Division HQ was telegraphed by its supporting gunners twenty minutes later: "No. 2 FOO Group reports situation approximately back in old frontline from VIRILE FARM to V.29.a.5.3. Situation on the left [vicinity of Hill 52] not clear. Front quiet. Timed 7 p.m."[59]

Advanced companies of Brigadier-General P.C.B. Skinner's 41 Brigade "reached WATERLOO about 8:30 p.m." and the expected relief of 25 Brigade "was carried out by small parties and was completed without any great difficulty..."[60] On the right, Lieutenant-Colonel Stirling, overseeing the relief of 2nd Royal Berkshire recalled: "At about 9 p.m. or 9:30 p.m. 2nd Lt. Upton reported with his party at Bn. HQ having succeeded in extricating himself. I sent him forward to a position [gap between 2nd Royal Berkshire and 2nd Lincolnshire] where he later reported himself to be." Upton and his men, gaunt, muddy and bloodstained, had held on to their short section of Venison Trench for almost twenty hours. Heavy losses amongst officers and men left Stirling with no choice but to order them back as reinforcements for the "continuous and connected line" occupied prior to the arrival of 8th KRRC.

57 TNA: WO/95/1929: 'Appendix B', 5 December 1917, 2nd Royal Berkshire War Diary.
58 BL: 48359: 'Report of Operations Carried Out by the VIII Army Corps on the Morning of 2nd December 1917, Official War Diaries with Appendices and Addenda, VIII Army Corps, Passchendaele Front, November 1917-April 1918', Vol. V, Hunter-Weston Papers.
59 TNA: WO/95/2370: After-action report, 'Appendix J', 32nd Division: Telephone and Telegraph Messages 2 December 1917', 11 December 1917, 32nd Division War Diary.
60 TNA: WO/95/1677: 'Narrative of Operations Carried Out by the 8th Division on 1st/2nd December 1917', 13 December 1917, 8th Division War Diary. Relieving troops of 41 Brigade remained under Heneker's command until 12:00 p.m. on 3 December. See TNA: WO/95/1873: 'VIII Corps G. 2236', 29 November 1917, 14th Division War Diary.

"The relief occurred without further incident."[61] In the centre, 2nd Lincolnshire was, like 2nd Royal Berkshire, able to disengage unmolested. Lieutenant-Colonel Irwin observed: "Two companies of 8th R[ifle] B[rigade] relieved the Battalion that night. One company taking over the advanced outpost line, the other company relieving my reserve coy. The relief was complete between 10 p.m. and 11 p.m."[62] On the left, posts occupied by elements of 2nd Rifle Brigade were also taken over by 8th Rifle Brigade. "Relief was carried out individually by small bodies of men and few casualties were sustained." 1st RIR, in immediate support since the night of 1/2 December, remained in position until replaced by an incoming battalion of 41 Brigade.[63]

Shute's determination to resume the attack on the night of 3/4 December was almost certainly influenced by the mistaken belief that Hill 52, notwithstanding reported reverses on the right and left, was still held by "a couple of companies." Retention of its tactically valuable false crest and NE slope would, it appeared, facilitate another attempt to gain Vat Cottages Ridge. A telephoned brief (7:55 p.m.) to 14 Brigade revealed, regardless of prevailing uncertainties, the GOC 32nd Division's intent:

> Shute: You have just heard the news [retirement of 97 Brigade]. We have just heard it also. Yes. It will be another scheme and it will be more troops. Yes. It is the whole thing over again. That is how it stands at the moment. We have only just got this news, so it is rather hard to answer now. You know the orders for the battalion [15th HLI] at BELLEVUE occupying MEETCHEELE – MOSSELMARKT Spur.[64] Well it is to be ready and alert as the whole of that front is pretty rocky. You will have two battalions up there tonight.[65]

Meanwhile, in response to Blacklock's request, "artillery and machine-guns were ordered to bring SOS lines back to cover the positions now held by 97th Infantry

---

61 TNA: WO/95/1929: 'Appendix B', 5 December 1917, 2nd Royal Berkshire War Diary and Boraston & Bax, *The Eighth Division*, pp. 166-67. The relief was confirmed in *Fourth Army's* evening report for 3 December: 'A prisoner from the British 14th Division has been brought in by troops on the right flank of *25.I.D*. He is reported to have told his captors that his unit had replaced 8th Division the previous night.' See KA HKR 99: Telegraph/wireless pro forma.
62 TNA: WO/95/1730: 'Report on Action of Battn from 2:30 p.m. 1.12.17 – M.N. 2/3 .12. 17', 2nd Lincolnshire War Diary.
63 TNA: WO/95/1731: 'Report of the part played by the 2nd Battn. The Rifle Brigade in the Operations at Passchendaele', 6 December 1917, 2nd Rifle Brigade War Diary and Taylor, *The 1st Royal Irish Rifles in the Great War*, p. 119.
64 14 Brigade's battalions were deployed from west to east at Irish Farm, Hilltop, Wurst Farm and Bellevue. See TNA: WO/95/2370: '32nd Division Offensive Instructions No. 11: Special Instructions to G.O.C., Brigade in Divisional Support (14th Infantry Brigade) and G.O.C., Brigade in Divisional Reserve (96th Infantry Brigade)', 30 November 1917, 32nd Division War Diary.
65 Ibid: After-action report, 'Appendix 'J', 32nd Division: Telephone and Telegraph Messages 2 December 1917', 11 December 1917.

Brigade." Reorganisation and reliefs duly commenced in close proximity to the enemy, while Lumsden and his staff, still situated at Kansas Cross, drew up plans for the proposed operation. Shute and his GSO 1 Lieutenant-Colonel McNamara simultaneously prepared their own yet to be sanctioned proposal for the continuance of operations. Preparations to resume operations the following night would therefore progress in anticipation of the hoped-for assent from II Corps.[66]

Erratic machine-gun and rifle fire exchanges erupted under the momentary glow of descending flares as inter-battalion reliefs and adjustments were carried out along 97 Brigade's indiscriminate frontline.[67] Ration carrying parties for units tasked to remain in that line, well under way before the onset of darkness, were overseen by dedicated transport officers and quartermaster sergeants [QMS]: "Up the long, perilously exposed tracks hot meals were carried: the fatigue of the carry alone was enough for normal men." The hazards of negotiating winding, broken duckboard paths leading to and from the forward zone were further demonstrated by the fate of those directly responsible for delivering rations to 16th NF: "Tragedy hovered over the trip. On the night of 2nd December, Second-Lieutenant Collings, the Transport Officer, accompanied by QMS Hood, reached Battalion HQ [at Virile Farm] in fulfilment of their duty. They left, were guided on to the track, but were never seen again."[68] Withdrawn into their respective units, the men were reorganised as far as possible during the hours after sundown. No amount of reorganisation and adjustment could make up for the severe losses sustained by 2nd KOYLI; surviving elements were withdrawn, their positions between Teall Cottage and Hill 52 taken over by the previously dispatched companies of 16th NF, to Irish Farm before dawn on the 3rd.[69] 16th HLI still resolutely clung to the salient about Void Farm. Its injured commander (Major Scott), seriously wounded by an enemy shell, "reported at Brigade HQ and command of the Battalion was transferred to OC 16th Northumberland Fusiliers…"[70] Lieutenant-

---

66 Ibid: After-action report, 'Part III, Narrative of Events', 11 December 1917.
67 See Appendix XI for '97 Brigade Order No. 182' issued at 9:30 pm on 2 December. One officer and 12 men of 219th Field Company RE reported to 97 Brigade HQ after 7:00 p.m. 'for any work that might require to be done in way of consolidation. They were ordered by the Brigadier to proceed with shovels, rations & water, for the [16th] Northd Fus., to report to Battalion HQ at VALOUR FARM [Virile Farm?] & keep with any entrenching that might be required & bring back report as to position of the line in that neighbourhood. Three boxes of rations and 8 tins of water were carried up. NO RE assistance was required and party returned to Bde. HQ at 5 a.m. on the 3rd & reported position of line to Brigadier.' See TNA: WO/95/2384: 219th Field Company RE War Diary, 2 December 1917.
68 Cooke, *Historical Records of the 16th (Service) Battalion Northumberland Fusiliers*, p. 89. 17-year-old 2nd Lieutenant Frank Reginald Collings and 33-year-old QMS Thomas Hood have no known grave and are commemorated on the Tyne Cot Memorial to the Missing.
69 TNA: WO/95/2402: 2nd KOYLI War Diary.
70 TNA: WO/95/2404: 16th HLI War Diary.

Colonel Scully's responsibilities were now two-fold: Take both (16th HLI and 16th NF) battalions in hand to consolidate all territorial gains before sunrise: "At about 8 p.m. Capt. Gray, 11th Borders reported to us and collected all available men of the 11th Borders and 16th HLI and manned our original frontline with its right on VIRILE FARM and its left in touch with the 17th HLI. This line was handed over on relief."[71] Remnants of 11th Border Regiment, now reformed on the jumping-off line, fortified positions from the left of Virile Farm to the boundary with 17th HLI. Scully's "No. 3 Company reported VOX FARM unheld and pushed a Lewis Gun section up on to it, the main line being about 50 yards short" of the former. On the left and far left, 17th HLI, uncertain of the location of advanced posts still holding out beyond the old frontline "dug in and consolidated on its objective" to preserve a connected line. 15th LF's final dispositions were, as reported by Major Utterson, "'C' and 'B' companies established on their objectives, a chain of posts of 'A' and 'D' companies men from right of 'B' Company … The latter were in touch with the 17th HLI who prolonged the right flank."[72]

Fourth Army's evening report for 2 December confidently asserted the defeat of the enemy's latest offensive: "British incursions on the left flank of the line east of Passchendaele have been neutralised. British artillery fire increased in intensity between 5 p.m. and 5:45 p.m.; our artillery replied. Up to date reports are still lacking. From midday until around 5 p.m. the strongest British artillery fire was upon *Gruppe Ypern*. Weather continued with strong winds and variable cloud cover." *Heeresgruppe Kronprinz Rupprecht* evaluated the day's activity as follows: "Localised attacks by about two British brigades in the direction of Westroosebeke were repelled. Tactical – operational measures: *4.Armee* – An attack along a wider front is not to be reckoned upon, however an assault on Westroosebeke is still possible. [The] British can maintain a large number of reserves in this sector and have strong enough artillery to undertake such an attack."[73]

Sir Henry Rawlinson expressed dismay about the unsatisfactory operational outcome in his diary that evening:

> The 32 and 8 Div. attacked at 1:55 AM this morning with limited objectives and though they won some ground [,] they did not get very far forward – In the afternoon at 4:15 PM [,] the Bosch put in a strong counter-attack and drove us back to our original line [,] which is very disappointing – We cannot [,] I fear [,]

---

71 IWM 4723: '32nd Div. No.G.S.1499/3/33', 5 December 1917, Brigadier-General T.S. Lambert Papers (Box 80/10/2).
72 TNA: WO/95/2405 17th HLI War Diary, WO/95/2397 15th LF War Diary and IWM 4723: 'Narrative of Operations 2/3rd December 1917, 15th (S) Battalion Lancashire Fusiliers', 4 December 1917 and 32nd Div. No.G.S.1499/3/33', 5 December 1917, Brigadier-General T.S. Lambert Papers (Box 80/10/2).
73 KA HKR 3: 'Tagesverlauf and der front Taktisch – operative – massnahmen' 1-2 December 1917 and HKR 99: Telegraph/wireless pro forma 2 December 1917.

continue the offensive [,] as we have no fresh div. and reinforcements are coming in but [unintelligible] so I have told corps to consolidate the line they are now on with a view of making it quite secure against attack.[74]

Sir Douglas Haig's first impressions – no doubt based on early reports – was one of conditional success: "Second Army carried out an operation on north end of the Passchendaele ridge in the moonlight on a front of about 4000 yards [sic] by the 8th and 32nd divisions. The object was to obtain certain points, which gave the enemy observation westwards onto our communications. All were captured except one and our troops are now within a hundred yards of it."[75] Shute's request to resume the attack on the night of 3/4 December had been passed on to II Corps, which in turn asked Second Army for sanction. The final decision was out of Rawlinson's hands; it was now up to Haig – apprised of the actual situation by the morning of the 3rd – to determine whether or not further efforts and consequent losses would produce tangible attainment of objectives.

5.2 Aftermath

Hunter-Weston motored to II Corps' HQ at Lovie Chateau on the morning of 2 December. Lunch with Heneker at his Canal Bank dugout followed before attending a 3:00 p.m. conference with Rawlinson at the previous venue. Meanwhile, mixed reports, received by VIII Corps between 2:35 a.m. and 4:00 p.m., told of hold-ups at some points and objectives gained at others. "The situation remained obscure until 4:30 p.m. at which hour reports had been received that the SOS had been sent up on the entire front of the attack, and, shortly afterwards, a report was received from II Corps that they had re-captured TEALL COTTAGE with 40 prisoners at 3:45 p.m. but that VAT COTTAGES were held by the enemy with machine-guns." 8th Division telephoned (5:30 p.m.) the latest map coordinates of 25 Brigade's frontline along with intelligence confirming the loss of Southern Redoubt. Another report, telegraphed by II Corps at 7:45 p.m., divulged the regrettable news that 97 Brigade had been driven back to the jumping-off line, "with the possible exception of two companies holding the near lip of HILL 52, and some little ground on the extreme left." At 8:30 p.m. II Corps reported "the enemy had delivered a heavy counter-attack against the left and centre [of 32nd Division], which had succeeded in driving the attacking troops back to the original frontline. It was, however, thought that TEALL COTTAGE and HILL 52 were in our hands and the ground had been gained on the left of the attack."

---

74 CAC: RWLN 1/9: Rawlinson Diary, 2 December 1917.
75 Haig diary entry 2 December 1917 in 'The First World War Political, Social and Military Manuscript Sources: Series One: The Haig Papers from the National Library of Scotland, Part I Haig's Autograph Great War Diary', Reel 5 and Sheffield & Bourne (eds), *Douglas Haig*, pp. 354-55.

Heneker, never hesitant about expressing unwelcome viewpoints to superiors, had already passed on Coffin's morning pronouncement that "Northern Redoubt could only be attacked in conjunction with an attack on TEALL COTTAGE and HILL 52." Available documentary evidence fails to confirm whether or not VIII Corps, now that both neighbouring objectives were reported secure, contemplated or approached Second Army about renewing operations with fresh troops the following night: such a proposal, if actually put forward, was likely dependent on authorisation of Shute's earlier attack recommendation.[76]

The disastrous operational outcome, predicted by Heneker during the course of planning discussions in mid-November, led to a thinly veiled recrimination in the guise of a verbal report: "In the evening, following on a telephone conversation with the Corps Commander, [the] GOC 8th Division reported he considered that heavy machine-gun fire, which opened at zero hour, in bright moonlight, had hindered the advance on his left flank."[77] Hunter-Weston, who had backed Shute's controversial attack scheme, could hardly have failed to miss his subordinate's point. Heneker's subsequent diary entry reveals outrage and disgust over the perceived waste and futility: "Attacked at 1:55 a.m. 32nd Division got nowhere and are back on original frontline owing to heavy casualties from M.G. fire. I took a bit of ground but not all my objectives. Just as I said. Damnable operation. Lost 600 officers and men and did little. Tillett, commanding 2nd Devons, mortally wounded.[78] Brand, 2nd Rifle Brigade, badly wounded but I hope he will recover."[79]

II Corps reported the situation, based on information received up to 10:00 p.m., of the current frontline as "still obscure but it is probable we still hold the line from HILL 52 to TEALL COTT. inclusive."[80] Further intelligence dispatched from the forward zone or, weather permitting, resulting from the early morning flyover by the designated contact aircraft from No. 7 Squadron, was expected to clear up indefinite aspects of earlier reports. Major Nosworthy (GSO Intelligence) advised those authorised to review his evening summaries that a "map would be issued with tomorrow's summary showing our new frontline and the dispositions of the enemy's troops opposed to us." A recently acquired German map, he added, "captured by the [VIII]

---

76 BL: 48366: Hunter-Weston Diary, 2 December 1917, Vol. XII and 48359: 'Report of Operations Carried Out by the VIII Army Corps on the Morning of 2nd December 1917', Official War Diaries with Appendices and Addenda, VIII Army Corps, Passchendaele Front, November 1917-April 1918', Vol. V, Hunter-Weston Papers.
77 Ibid.
78 25-year-old Lieutenant-Colonel Alexander Tillett MC (CO 2nd Devonshire): Wounded by shellfire 29 November; DOW 3 December; awarded a posthumous DSO. The regimental history incorrectly states that he was wounded during the German riposte on 30 November. See TNA: WO/95/1712: 2nd Devonshire War Diary and Atkinson, *The Devonshire Regiment 1914-1918*, p. 319.
79 IWM: 66/541/1: Heneker Diary, 2 December 1917.
80 TNA: WO/157/288: 'II Corps Summary of Information', 2 December 1917, II Corps Intelligence File.

Map showing 8th Division final positions prior to relief by 14th Division.
(TNA: WO/95/1677: 8th Division War Diary)

Corps on our right shows the positions of various headquarters of the division in reserve to the WESTROOSEBEKE – PASSCHENDAELE sector and the actual and proposed positions of readiness of the battalions. Copies of this map will be issued to all concerned."[81]

41 Brigade completed its relief of 25 Brigade by 2:40 a.m. on 3 December. Casualties were reported as "slight" despite the loss of popular Major and acting Lieutenant-Colonel John Maxwell (CO 8th KRRC) who was mortally wounded whilst making his way up the Gravenstafel – Bellevue Road.[82] On 97 Brigade's front, Lieutenant-

81 Ibid.
82 7th Rifle Brigade, 8th Rifle Brigade and 8th KRRC had twelve men killed during the relief; 36-year-old Major John Maxwell MC DOW on 4 December. He is buried in Ypres

Private W. Gilmour. (George Gilmour).

Colonel Scully, uneasy about the vulnerable salient around Void Farm, ordered 16th HLI to retire before sunrise: "Next morning at 5 o'clock the survivors of 16th HLI were ordered to withdraw from their isolated posts at Void Farm and, under Captain A. Fraser, came into the line with the other divisional units. Although sorely beset, they had obeyed orders and clung to their shell holes for 28 hours." The exhausted survivors took their place on the original jumping-off line by 6:00 a.m. Others, cut off or too far forward, were unable to make their way back before daylight.[83] Twenty-year-old 40717 Private William Gilmour of 'C' Company and several companions received no word of the withdrawal in their shell hole outpost. The coming of dawn and rifles rendered useless by glutinous mud left no alternative but surrender to cautiously advancing German infantry. Disarmed without incident, they were marched off to distant Roulers.[84]

Monday 3 December: The sun rose at 7:29 a.m. to impart a clear, cold day with strong winds.[85] *Fourth Army* HQ's morning report confirmed a stabilized front near Passchendaele and recently obtained disclosure of the enemy's limited attack objectives:

Reservoir Cemetery. See Geoff's CWGC 1914-21 Search Engine <http://www.hut-six.co.uk/cgi-bin/search14-21.php>
83   TNA: WO/95/2404: 16th HLI War Diary and Chalmers (ed), *A Saga of Scotland*, p. 111.
84   Reported missing presumed killed before official confirmation of his prisoner status, Gilmour spent the remainder of the war as a POW farm labourer. It was during this time that he became a proficient German speaker. Repatriated in 1919, he went on to lecture in foreign languages. Email correspondence with Dr George Gilmour (Pte. Gilmour's son) 6 October 2008.
85   TNA: WO/157/288: 'Calendar for December 1917, Times Calculated for Second Army Front and Greenwich Mean Time', II Corps Intelligence File and LHCMA: Second Army War Diary, Montgomery-Massingberd Papers, File 7/16, King's College, London.

"Lively hostile artillery fire reported late yesterday afternoon did not herald further infantry attacks. In the course of the night elements of *25.I.D.* pushed forward posts into no man's land. Further reports are lacking in regard to their progress. The British objective was a line approximately 600 metres behind our front. This has been verified by a captured order. The successful defence is thanks to Thüringian and Hessian troops. British casualties are reported to be extremely heavy and 60 prisoners have been taken. At 6:00 a.m. there was heavy harassing fire upon the *25.I.D.* sector."[86]

British anxiety for the frontline opposite Venison Trench diminished – "Intermittent shelling of Passchendaele and surrounding areas" was reported by 33rd Division, while 8th Division noted "situation quiet" – as the hours before dawn passed without serious disturbance in VIII Corps' sector.[87] II Corps HQ, still in the dark about 97 Brigade's frontline, reported: "Situation quiet on left [35th] divisional sector aaa Report from right [32nd] Division sector is not yet received" at 5:50 a.m.[88] Previously grounded contact aircraft were skyward not long after first light: "High wind interfered with work, though contact patrols and a certain amount of artillery and photographic work was carried out" by corps squadrons. "Vertical photographs over the enemy area were unsuccessful…"[89] Reports that Hill 52 and Teall Cottage remained in enemy hands were confirmed by II Corps sometime before 10:00 a.m.: "Line runs from point 150 yards south of Teall Cot. along original frontline to VOX FARM inclusive."[90] The crew of the low-flying RE 8 contact aircraft of No. 21 Squadron, discharging a fuselage-mounted Klaxon Horn whilst sweeping over Venison Trench and its redoubts at 9:40 a.m., observed a pell-mell collection of outposts close up or inside the *Hauptwiderstandslinie*:

> Contact plane reports our troops seen in whole of Southern Redoubt in W.25.c. and in trench connecting same to Northern Redoubt in V.30.b. aaa Our troops also located in southern portion of Northern Redoubt and in a newly dug post

---

86 KA HKR 99: Telegraph/wireless pro forma 3 December 1917.
87 Two prisoners from *IR117* gave themselves up to the right battalion of 33rd Division before dawn. They claimed to be Belgian nationals from Liege who 'only came into the line last night.'
88 BL: 48359: 'Report of Operations Carried Out by the VIII Army Corps on the Morning of 2nd December 1917, Official War Diaries with Appendices and Addenda, VIII Army Corps, Passchendaele Front, November 1917-April 1918', Vol. V, Hunter-Weston Papers.
89 TNA: WO/157/288: 'II Corps Summary of Information', 3 December 1917, II Corps Intelligence File.
90 How this was discovered remains unclear. Major Evelegh (CO 32nd Division Signal School) subsequently remarked: 'Neither contact planes nor counter-attack planes dropped any messages throughout the operations.' See BL: 48359: 'Report of Operations Carried Out by the VIII Army Corps on the Morning of 2nd December 1917, Official War Diaries with Appendices and Addenda, VIII Army Corps, Passchendaele Front, November 1917-April 1918', Vol. V, Hunter-Weston Papers and TNA: WO/95/2370: After-action report: 'Appendix 'I': Communications', December 1917, 32nd Division War Diary.

[at] V.30.b.55.55. aaa Northern portion of Northern Redoubt contains several bombing blocks and all of this portion appears to be occupied by Germans aaa Observer has no doubt as to corrections of his observations. Colours of uniform were clearly distinguishable aaa There was no khaki visible in the northern portion of Northern Redoubt and no field grey in line occupied by British aaa Inference therefore is that all troops seen were alive but they lighted no flares and made no signs to aeroplane.[91]

Failure to discern lit flares or manipulated Watson Fans combined with high speeds, hostile ground fire and consequent fleeting opportunities for direct observation made accurate assessments difficult even at low altitudes. Southern Redoubt had been recaptured by *IR116* during the late morning of 2 December, so it must be surmised that any observed khaki clad only the dead and wounded left behind in its environs. Infantry outside the redoubt, reluctant to expose new positions to the enemy, shrank from making their presence known to designate aircraft.[92] Who actually held the bastion did not become known with certainty until the morning of 4 December.[93]

Projected manpower shortages, coupled with the slim possibility of any favourable outcome, gave GHQ pause when considering Shute's request to resume operations. Brigadier-General Davidson (DMO GHQ) conveyed Sir Douglas Haig's final decision to Second Army during a brief morning telephone exchange:

> Sir H. Rawlinson rang up [at] 10:45 a.m. & stated that the enemy attacked last night & drove most of our troops back to where they had started from on the

---

91 TNA: WO/157/288: 'II Corps Summary of Information', 3 December 1917, II Corps Intelligence File.
92 The reluctance of infantry to signal overhead contact aircraft was a perennial problem throughout 1915-17. David Jordan, in an analysis of air/ground communication efforts during the Battle of Arras, observed that climate "was not the chief culprit: the lack of flares was the main failing." Sir Edmund Allenby (GOC Third Army) "noted that the pilots had attempted direct observation but that this was ineffective. On 23 April he sent a succinct order to his officers making clear his views on the matter: 'RFC report flares hardly used by infantry again today. This makes effective artillery support almost impossible. Attention of all ranks is to be called to the importance of lighting flares when called for." No other Army Commander appears to have followed Allenby's lead: it is tempting to speculate that the success of contact patrols would have been less erratic had others done so. See Jordan, 'The Army Co-operation Missions of the Royal Flying Corps/Royal Air Force 1914-1918', p. 101.
93 8th Division telegraphed VIII Corps at 10:10 a.m.: 'Aeroplane reconnaissance carried out at 9:40 a.m. this morning shows our line as follows aaa D.6.b.9.1. – W.25.c.4.3. (from bottom grid) *Southern Redoubt inclusive* [My emphasis] – V.30.b.80.10. – TEALL COTTAGES exclusive.' See BL: 48359: 'Report of Operations Carried Out by the VIII Army Corps on the Morning of 2nd December 1917, Official War Diaries with Appendices and Addenda, VIII Army Corps, Passchendaele Front, November 1917-April 1918', Vol. V, Hunter-Weston Papers.

previous night. Shute wanted to resume the attack again tomorrow. I said that the C in C wished to economise troops & did not want to get involved in anymore unnecessary fighting. Sir HR said he would stop anything further being done. It was also his opinion – The N. Zealanders are going for Polderhoek Chateau today between 12 & 1 pm.[94]

The British Field Marshal's choice, primarily influenced by an overriding concern for deficits in the BEF's potential reinforcement pool, was based on recent disturbing developments at home and abroad. The effective distribution of available manpower to meet the military and industrial demands of Great Britain's war effort had become a significant point of civil-military contention by the close of the year. "Indeed in December 1917 a manpower crisis was identified, and, for the first time, the War Cabinet became actively involved in relating manpower provision to priority areas of the war effort."[95] A highly critical public speech on 4 November followed by an equally contentious opening address to the recently convened Supreme War Council[96] on 1 December, made clear Prime Minister David Lloyd George's resolve to husband manpower resources whilst diminishing perceived prodigality of British lives on the Western Front.[97] On 27 November Haig told Adjutant General of the Forces Lieutenant-General Sir Nevil Macready that by "31 March British infantry units would be 250,000 men or approximately forty per cent below establishment, unless reinforcements were sent to rectify this situation." Secretary of State for War Lord Derby followed his lead at a Cabinet meeting on 3 December by demanding to know when the BEF could expect substantial reinforcements.[98] Such appeals, following on

---

94 Brigadier-General J.H. Davidson hand-written note (3 December 1917), TNA: WO/158/209: Second Army Operations File.
95 Keith Grieves, *The Politics of Manpower 1914-18* (Manchester: Manchester University Press, 1988), p. 175.
96 John Grigg, *Lloyd George: War Leader 1916-1918* (London: Penguin Books, 2003), pp. 283 and 288. Lloyd George's controversial November speech was delivered in Paris after attending (6-7 November) the Rapallo Conference on the Ligurian coast east of Genoa. This summit of French, British and Italian leaders, ostensibly convened to address the dire situation after Caporetto, was the vehicle by which the British prime minister successfully advocated for a Supreme War Council to facilitate the Entente's war effort.
97 It is beyond the scope of this study to examine in detail the political/strategic ramifications of the Flanders offensive. For interpretations of the British government's deliberations and decisions before, during and after the Third Battle of Ypres see David Woodward, *Lloyd George and the Generals* (East Brunswick NJ: Associated University Presses, 1983), chapters 8-10, David French, *The Strategy of the Lloyd George Coalition 1916-1918* (Oxford: Clarendon, 1995), chapters 4-6, Prior & Wilson, *Passchendaele*, chapters 14 and 18, John Turner, 'Lloyd George, the War Cabinet and High Politics' in Liddle (ed) *Passchendaele in Perspective*, pp. 14-44, Grigg, *Lloyd George*, chapters 13-16 and Brock Millman, *Pessimism and British War Policy 1916-1918* (London: Frank Cass, 2001), pp. 92-108.
98 Grieves, *Politics of Manpower*, pp. 157, 166. Lord Derby subsequently informed the War Cabinet on 6 December that the BEF was short an estimated 100,000 men. See Prior

the costly and seemingly inconclusive Flanders campaign and subsequent Cambrai debacle, would make little headway with an increasingly disenchanted War Cabinet. Governmental concerns appeared to be further substantiated when, after Derby's outburst, Director of National Service Sir Auckland Geddes "submitted a memorandum which indicated how close the nation was to the limit of its manpower." The "stark reality" behind this report was that "future quotas of fit men for military service would necessitate the automatic reduction of either the shipbuilding, food-production or munitions programmes."[99] 3 December was also the date armistice negotiations commenced between the new Bolshevik regime and Imperial Germany. That same day, Haig – in recognition of the grand strategic implications of a Russian cease-fire – instructed his four Army commanders to prepare for the imminent, albeit short-term, loss of the strategic initiative:

> [T]he general situation on the Russian and Italian fronts, combined with the paucity of reinforcements which we are likely to receive, will in all probability necessitate our adopting a defensive attitude for the next few months. We must be prepared to meet a strong and sustained hostile offensive. It is therefore of the first importance that Army commanders should give their immediate and personal attention to the organisation of the zones for defensive purposes and to the rest and training of their troops.[100]

GHQ's desire to gain more ground in the vicinity of Passchendaele and Westroosebeke would, given prevailing circumstances, have to be set aside while larger issues of manpower and strategy were debated in London and Versailles. Shute subsequently observed: "The proposal to attack with the 14th Infantry Brigade on the night of 3/4th December was submitted to the [II] Corps but was not approved and orders were received that no further active operations were to be undertaken."[101] The projected two-battalion attack against Polderhoek Chateau by the New Zealand Division would, nonetheless, be allowed to proceed. Zero hour was scheduled for 12:00 p.m. on the 3rd.

The morning of 3 December, 41 Brigade's diarist noted, was "fairly quiet" in the sector opposite Venison Trench. 14th Division's GSO 3, acting on direct orders from

      & Wilson, *Passchendaele*, p. 190 and Keith Grieves, The 'Recruiting Margin' in Britain: Debates on Manpower during the Third Battle of Ypres' in Liddle (ed), *Passchendaele in Perspective*, pp. 390-405.
99 Grieves, *Politics of Manpower*, pp. 166-67.
100 Sir J.E. Edmonds, *Military Operations: France and Belgium 1918 Vol. 1* (London: Macmillan, 1935), p. 37. GHQ, Edmonds also observed, brought the lengthy 1917 campaign season to an 'official' end on 3 December with the termination of the Battle of Cambrai.
101 TNA: WO/95/2370: After-action report, 'Part III, Narrative of Events', 32nd Division War Diary.

VIII Corps, was sent forward to reconnoitre and pinpoint advanced posts: "Owing to lack of guides he did not go beyond Battalion HQ, and obtained dispositions as far as could be ascertained from the Battalion intelligence officer of the 8th Rifle Brigade." It would be several days before the general course of the outpost line was plotted out with a degree of accuracy.[102] 32nd Division's diarist recorded more activity in the sector opposite Hill 52 and Vat Cottages Ridge: "Enemy artillery fairly active on roads and tracks throughout the day. His snipers were active particularly near Vat Cottages." Fire by the latter eventually subsided as repeated efforts to retrieve casualties were observed:

> Many wounded were lying out, suffering the most appalling rigours of war and the Battalion stretcher-bearers displayed great devotion to duty in ignoring the heavy fire while bringing them to comparative shelter. The work at first was extremely dangerous, but later on in the day a lull occurred when it was possible to carry on this labour of mercy under less trying conditions. And it must be recorded, as far as this battle is concerned, that from this point onward the German reversed his frequent policy and shewed respect for the Red Cross flag, only one instance of sniping taking place when one of the Battalion stretcher-bearers was shot dead while bending over a wounded comrade. Enemy stretcher-bearers were also at work and in some instances they reciprocated attentions given to their wounded by dressing and carrying our casualties. In this way all the wounded were got in before the [97] Brigade was relieved that night.[103]

The Reverend R.E. Grice-Hutchison (Chaplain to 32nd Division's attached 161 Field Artillery Brigade) first heard news of "a fairly extensive attack which our infantry made last night from Passchendaele" on 2 December following the usual Sunday services. Word of 2nd Lieutenant V.J. Horton's (FOO attached to 16th HLI) death was received early on the 3rd. Grice-Hutchison, distressed by the loss of this officer, resolved to retrieve his remains from the forward area:

> I went in the morning to D.161 waggon-lines to see about poor Horton. I found he had been killed on liaison with the infantry at Bellevue some little way behind the line. Buckley and I first went back to CRA, where we telephoned through to the place to make sure his body was there before going up. We left about 11:30 with four volunteers, and walked the whole way to Bellevue. Never have I been through or pictured such a scene of desolation – mile after mile of shell holes and wreckage. We found poor Horton lying just outside the pillbox where he was killed together with another officer and seven men. The shell went clean through the door and burst inside. The pillbox (there are two) stands on the top of a kind

---

102 TNA: WO/95/1894: 41Brigade and WO/95/1873: 14th Division war diaries.
103 Arthur & Munro (eds), *The Seventeenth Highland Light Infantry*, p. 69.

of knoll with a fine view in every direction, particularly of Westroosebeke and the ridge. We had a very long and heavy carry along the duckboards for some four miles to Cheddar Villa, where we put him on a light railway which runs close to the waggon-lines. What shelling there was was always where we had been. So back home.[104]

Across no man's land a young German *Offizier-Aspirant* (candidate for commission) attached to *IR95* experienced for the first time the same grim conditions encountered by the imperturbable Grice-Hutchison. His introduction to the Passchendaele – Westroosebeke sector had been a gradual initiation into miserable surroundings:

> On 1st Decr. we paraded before the Battalion Commander (GOFLER) who kept us in the bitter cold for an hour to listen to his babbling. In the afternoon we went forward. As we knew, we were destined for the most contested bit of all FLANDERS, PASSCHENDAELE, a peculiar mood seized hold of us – some of us tipsy from the tea-with-alcohol, some full of the fear of death. To OOSTNIEUWKERKE, the billet was occupied, and before we could bivouac, the order came back to pack up and back we went to ROULERS. Here we were put into an out of the way farmhouse, the wealthy owner of which had apparently left in great haste.
>
> 2 December. The next morning we had made ourselves quite comfortable. F… came, and we drank and read together. Again came orders to "get ready" and a quarter of an hour later "corpses" marched off past us. Half an hour later we all got orders to go further forward; since then I have never seen F… again. To COLLIEROLENHOEK. Once more into ruined barns in the bitter cold … En route we met wounded of the [25th] Division on the left, the 116th and 117th, who told us that the English had attacked their Rosbautz (?) Bn., had advanced in some places and been driven back with loss in others. In the morning, therefore, we were alarmed and shuddered. At 6 o'clock in the evening the barrage began; at 7 we were warned by telephone that a counter-attack without artillery preparation would be made at 10:32. At 11 p.m. I was called by the Coy. Commander and told I must go forward into support as advanced party. HEIDENGOED at 8 o'clock next morning.

The long trek to the mined dugouts at Heidengoed Farm (SE of Westroosebeke) began just before sunrise on 3 December:

> Next day I went forward. I wanted to go by the map but N… begged me to go his way. The further we went the more miserable it became. Got to

---

104 Scott, Grice-Hutchison, et al, *Artillery & Trench Mortar Memories*, pp. 282-83.

HEIDENGOED near WESTROOSEBEKE. Quarrelled with the 4th Coy. regarding accommodation. The night previous a dugout had been hit and 1 officer and 8 men killed. The CSM of the coy. in support was filled with horror; his coy. had to counter-attack in full daylight. To settle the quarrel, went to the KTK. Heard our Bn. is to go into frontline tonight. I went in daylight to NORDHOF (VOID FARM). 12 dead lying there from yesterday and a wounded Tommy. I heard from Lieut. X that the 5th Coy. was in front, 14 men all told, supported by the 3rd Bn. The English had broken in on the front of the 94th and got behind the 5th Coy. ... they had got to within 50 yards of the NORDHOF.[105]

25th Division reinforced and consolidated threatened portions of its *Hauptwiderstandslinie* throughout the night of 2/3 December. *IR115*, responsible for the defences opposite Passchendaele, dispatched its reserve battalion to the embattled centre where, after bolstering *IR116*'s front battalion, it "eked out two full days in the forward-most lines of the adjacent right sector."[106] Hard-bitten, heavily armed *Stosstruppen* of *25th Sturmabteilung*,[107] appearing in *IR117*'s advanced positions sometime after midnight, immediately went forward and "cleared the *Sicherungslinie* area without further loss."[108] Observers in *Luftstreitkräfte* (German Army Air Service) two-seater reconnaissance and artillery spotting aircraft, communicating with *25th Division* HQ by wireless or lamp signalling apparatus, reported the "enemy line to be heavily occupied" after daybreak on the 3rd, "although the anticipated attack failed to materialise."[109]

---

105 TNA: WO/157/120: 'Annexe to Second Army Summary Dated 19th Decr. 1917: Translation of the closing pages of a diary taken from a dead German (probably a warrant officer of the 3rd Coy. 95th Inf. Regt., 38th Division) who was shot in V.29.b. in the early morning of the 15th inst.', Second Army Intelligence Files.
106 Frankenberg und Ludwigsdorff, *Das Leibgarde Infanterie Regiment (1. Grossherzoglich Hessisches Nr. 115) im Weltkrieg 1914-1918*, p. 162.
107 Two members of this elite divisional asset were captured east of Passchendaele on 2/3 December. They 'had been completing their course of instruction (commenced in July) at ZILVERBERG under the direction of the OC 25th Sturmabteilung (Lt. von der Bense). Organic *Stosstruppe* companies had been established in most, but by no means all, German divisions at the close of 1916; *38th Division* had 'no trained storm troops.' See TNA: WO/157/121: 'Annexe to Second Army Summary Dated 3rd December 1917: Information Obtained from Prisoners', 'Annexe to Second Army Summary Dated 4th December 1917: Information Obtained from Prisoners', Second Army Intelligence File and D.B. Nash, *Imperial German Army Handbook 1914-1918* (London: Ian Allen, 1980), p. 46
108 Offenbacher, *Die Geschichte des Infanterie-Leibregiments Grossherzogin (3.Grossherzoglich Hessisches) Nr. 117*, p. 196.
109 Hiss, *Infanterie-Regiment Kaiser Wilhelm (2. Grossherzoglich Hessisches) Nr. 116*, p. 159. Reconnaissance Flights 'A' [artillery spotting] were 'under the command of the division for reconnaissance and for observation of artillery and Minenwerfer fire. Its wireless transmissions were received at the aerodrome by the divisional ARKO [Artillery

Battalion stretcher-bearers and RAPs carried out removal and initial succour of the wounded with reasonable efficiency during 2-3 December. Devoted RAMC personnel of the 25th, 90th, 91st and 92nd field ambulances, supported by attached parties of infantry, continued the tortuous evacuation by "hand carriage" from RAP to ADS under intensive shellfire on roads and tracks. Colonel G. St. C. Thom (ADMS 32nd Division) recorded that by 6:00 a.m. on the 2nd: "2 officers and 74 other ranks, all walking cases, had passed through" the ADS. These were transported by light railway to the CMDS. Stretcher cases, he added, began to arrive at the ADS shortly after 6:00 a.m. "Owing to enemy shellfire it was decided that, as the light railway was about to be destroyed, lying cases should all be evacuated by ambulance cars and the railway used for walking and sitting cases only." A section of light railway track was subsequently interdicted by shellfire near Bridge House on the Kansas Cross – Wieltje Road at 11:00 a.m. "This, however, did not delay evacuation as Red Cross lorries were available to take walking wounded from BRIDGE HOUSE. A train happened to be on the line between the Advanced Dressing Station and the destroyed part, consequently sitting cases were sent by train from the Advanced Dressing Station as far as the destroyed part of the line", where they "detrained and entrained again on the farther side of the destroyed part." The evacuation, nonetheless, "went on smoothly" following track repairs by 2:00 p.m. "After fighting had ceased both our and the enemy bearers collected wounded in the open. The bearers carried small Red Cross flags and were not fired upon." Additional support provided by 14 Brigade (one officer and fifty men) was sent forward at 11:00 p.m. "to assist the stretcher-bearers of 92nd Field Ambulance who were getting quite done up." All RAPs, Thom concluded, were "reported clear by 3 a.m. on the 3rd December." The entire line was clear of any remaining wounded as far as the ADS by 5:00 a.m. A total of 31 officers and 552 ORs were admitted to the MDS between midnight on 1/2 December and 12:00 p.m. on 3 December. On 4 December – a fair, cloudy day interspersed with sudden snow storms – British observers reported considerable movement of small German parties "throughout the day on the WESTROOSEBEKE – PASSCHENDAELE Ridge and collection of the wounded is apparently still in progress."[110]

> Commander] and his subordinate groups. Since, against the repeated wishes of the troops, special flights could not be made available for infantry aircraft service, so the Reconnaissance Flights A had to take over that service. For that purpose the number of their aircraft was increased from 6 to 9. The infantry aircraft, called 'jfl', monitored the battlefield. Both in attack and defence they offered the quickest and most reliable transmission to the command posts of events and progress, on the most advanced front, at any given time.' See Hermann Cron, *Imperial German Army 1914-18*, p. 184.
> 110 See TNA: WO/95/1677: '8th Division Instructions No. 2', 25 November 1917, 8th Division War Diary, WO/95/2370: 'Report on Medical Arrangements During the Recent Operations: Night 1/2nd December 1917', 15 December 1917, 32nd Division War Diary, WO/157/288: 'II Corps Summary of Information', 4 December 1917, II Corps Intelligence File and LHCMA: Second Army War Diary, Montgomery-Massingberd Papers, File 7/16, King's College, London.

Little notice was probably taken by the average *Times* reader, the majority no doubt enjoying the meagre fare of a home front breakfast, of recent developments in Flanders. Headlines above the usual column of despatches (telegraphed daily by GHQ for domestic consumption) on 3 December read:

BATTLES FOR CAMBRAI

ENEMY'S BIG PLAN FAILS

MORE LOST GROUND WON BACK

The following communiqués primarily dealt with Third Army's dogged defence against counter-attacking German "hordes" during 2 December. A comparatively unremarkable report – inserted by time of receipt amongst more newsworthy items – recounted further territorial gains on the Passchendaele Ridge with a brief summation of the basic facts:

> 10:14 p.m. – A minor operation was undertaken early this morning by Rifle, North Country and Home County battalions north-east of Ypres. Some fortified buildings and strongpoints on the main ridge north of Passchendaele were captured and our troops have taken a number of prisoners.[111]

---

111 Achiel Van Wallenghem, *1917. The Passchendaele Year: The British Army in Flanders* (Brighton: EER, 2017), p. 271 and *The Times*, Monday 3 December 1917, p. 9. A subsequent despatch, appearing in print the following day, stated: 'In a minor operation carried out yesterday north of Passchendaele 129 prisoners and a few machine-guns were taken by us.' A contemporary French newspaper account provided additional operational detail followed by a false pronouncement of complete success: 'BRITISH CAPTURE 45 STRONGPOINTS NORTH OF PASSCHENDAELE: The British wanted to demonstrate that the violent offensive directed by the Germans on their Cambrai front did not impinge their freedom of action in Flanders at all. That is why yesterday morning they contrived to advance north of Passchendaele along the road which connects with the town of Westroosebeke. The operation, rapidly executed, was a complete success. We know that during the last knock-down blow in this sector our allies, on taking over Passchendaele, had reported their advanced lines to the north along the entirety of the aforementioned road to Goudberg. Beyond the line to Westroosebeke, the field, which consists of small undulations, is dotted with farms and isolated spinneys that the enemy had organised defensively into authentic fortresses. It was against these tiny strongpoints that the British launched the moonlight assault before dawn. The attack was so dashingly executed that all objectives were reached by the first hour of daylight. Our allies occupied no less than 45 strongpoints. The success had the effect of enabling the British to capture the last observation posts the Germans possessed north of Goudberg.' See *Le Petit Journal*, 3 December 1917.

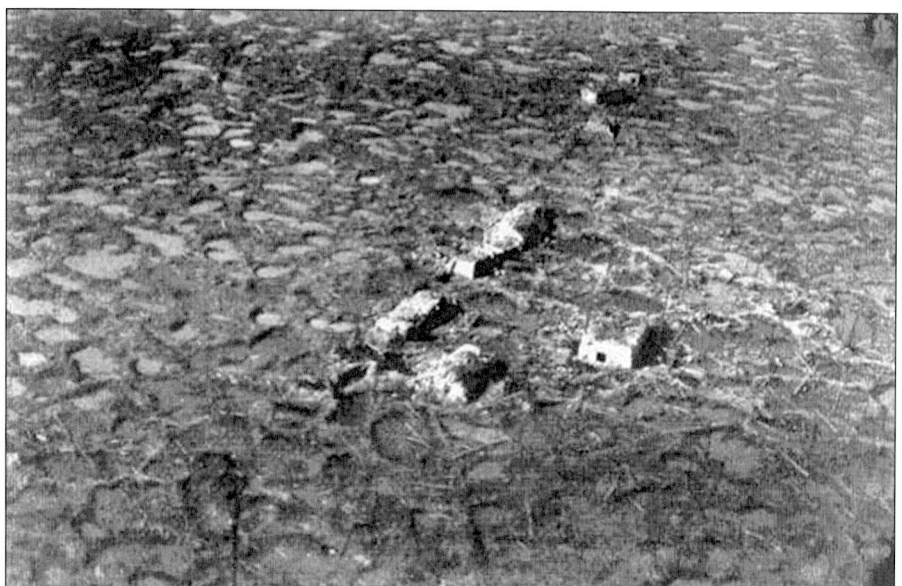

Polderhoek Chateau grounds from the air. (Author)

A concise synopsis of another "minor operation", launched some 7,000 yards SW of Passchendaele village on 3 December, would further remind those perusing next day's despatch column that the Flanders fighting was far from over.

The New Zealand Division (temporary GOC Brigadier-General W.G. Braithwaite)[112] took over the frontline opposite Polderhoek Chateau on the night of 25 November. Its scheduled attack against the worrying German strongpoint was fraught with difficulties.[113] The flooded Reutelbeek and Scherriabeek streams bound the spur on which the chateau and its outlying defences were situated to the north and south respectively. "Two alternative lines of attack offered themselves. The chateau might be carried from the flank and rear by troops advancing from the [II] ANZAC [Corps] positions across the Reutelbeek, or, secondly, a frontal assault could be delivered straight down the spur from the IX Corps position on the [Gheluvelt] plateau." Deadly enfilade fire from the east, supporting artillery barrage issues,[114] lack of satisfactory assembly positions and a virtually impassable Reutelbeek valley[115] ruled out

---

112 Major-General A. Russell had been invalided back to Great Britain with bronchitis. See Glyn Harper, *Massacre at Passchendaele: The New Zealand Story* (Auckland: Harper Collins, 2000), p. 99.
113 See Chapter 1, pp. 104–05 for the genesis of the Polderhoek Chateau operation.
114 Batteries situated to the north would have to fire in enfilade.
115 The Reutlebeek was by this time an unfordable mass of continuous shell holes 20 to 30 feet wide. From its left bank extended an 'impenetrable black morass of soft mud, into

any possible advance from the north. "For these reasons recourse was had for the second alternative, which offered several advantages. Assembly trenches were available directly opposite and in close proximity to the chateau. A frontal barrage could be obtained. The IX Corps heavies could carry out a preparatory bombardment, and the tell-tale registration by a large number of new guns could be avoided."[116]

Two battalions (1st Canterbury and 1st Otago) of 2 New Zealand Brigade jumped off from the support line at 12:00 p.m. on 3 December. Preliminary forenoon bombardments, a ruse devised to keep the defenders below ground at the time of assault, on 28 and 30 November failed to cow an alert enemy ensconced in pillboxes and ruin cellars: "The garrison of the chateau was confidently aggressive. Both on the 26th and 30th they attempted small raids which were completely repulsed. They had, however, no suspicion of the impending attack and exposed themselves injudiciously about the spur to our snipers." The attack plan was conceived as a pincer movement to envelope the enemy defences: "It would be made by 2 companies in each battalion advancing abreast in 2 waves. The first wave would carry the line to an intermediate objective beyond the chateau, and the second, following 50 yards behind, would then "leap frog" through, and push on to a final objective some 300 yards further, sufficiently far down the eastern slope to give observation of the flats" beyond. Companies of select personnel, recently reinforced by a large proportion of inexperienced drafts, had been reduced for this operation to an acceptable fighting strength of 100 all ranks.[117] Hopes of catching the enemy off guard were immediately frustrated when, maintaining vigilance throughout the now customary forenoon bombardment, *IR163* (*17th Reserve Division*) opened fire with machine-guns from pillboxes situated about the chateau grounds and from the south at Gheluvelt.[118] "Undismayed, however, the first wave pushed on, crossed our frontline, and were rapidly among the wilderness of tree stumps where the wire was found demolished." Protective smoke barrages, discharged to cover the exposed left and right flanks from enfilading machine-guns, were dissipated by strong winds and casualties began to mount. 1st Canterbury, "faced with a series of strong pillboxes, including those at the stables and at the Manager's House" was, nevertheless, able to secure, after fierce fighting, the right flank along slopes overlooking the mired Scherriabeek valley to a point 150 yards short of the first objective. 1st Otago, tasked with capturing Polderhoek Chateau, made good initial progress until an "overwhelming barrage of machine-gun fire" forced survivors to seek

---

which patrols sank to their knees within 100 yards of advanced posts…'
116 Stewart, *The New Zealand Division 1916-1919*, pp. 305-06.
117 Ibid, pp. 307-09. 'Reinforcements received during November were particularly poor, lacking even in elementary training.' See TNA: WO/95/3659: 'Operations of the New Zealand Division: Period November 1st–December 1st 1917', New Zealand Division War Diary.
118 Close proximity of the opposing lines prevented German batteries from engaging the attackers after Zero. Identical circumstances compelled British gunners to abandon a preliminary heavy bombardment.

cover opposite the first objective.[119] "The enemy's pillboxes", II ANZAC Corps' diarist later observed, "undamaged and strongly garrisoned with troops and MGs, proved so formidable an obstacle that our attacking troops were held up and were compelled to consolidate a line about 150 yards east of the CHATEAU grounds, but west of the CHATEAU itself."[120] Loss of half the assault battalions' effectives hindered fresh attempts to push on. Braithwaite "urged a further effort after dark and suggested an enveloping movement from the Reutelbeek slopes", but arrival of German reinforcements, "together with the continued alertness of the enemy and the continued activity of his machine-guns did not favour surprise."[121] A brief assessment of the unsuccessful two-battalion assault appeared in *Fourth Army's* midday report the following day: "Around midday yesterday enemy fire in the sector Poezelhoek – Gheluvelt rose in intensity, and the British attacked on a front of 400 metres north of the Menin – Ypres road. Apart from some small *Engländernest*, it was thrown back."[122]

Heeresgruppe Kronprinz Rupprecht's midday report for 3 December observed: "The British attack carried out early yesterday in the Passchendaele area was conducted by a brigade each from the 32nd and 8th Divisions, and reached territory approximately 600 metres behind our frontline. By midday the vast majority of captured positions were back in our hands, the remainder recaptured the following evening ..."[123] 97 Brigade's situation remained unchanged throughout the day. Hours of tedium punctuated by incidents of sudden terror passed, as the somewhat irregular frontline was reinforced and strengthened under active sniping and desultory machine-gun fire. Brigade HQ issued orders for the anticipated relief at 2:00 p.m.[124] The prospect of

119 Stewart, *The New Zealand Division 1916-1919*, pp. 309-10 and 312. Private Henry James Nicholas MM (Nelson Company, 1st Battalion Canterbury Regiment) was awarded the Victoria Cross for destroying a machine-gun position during the advance.
120 TNA: WO/157/593: II ANZAC Corps Intelligence File.
121 Stewart, *The New Zealand Division 1916-1919*, p 313. 2 NZ Brigade's after-action report observed the primary cause of the failure was 'inadequacy' of training: 'Though several days (November 27th to 30th, both inclusive) were devoted to practice over ground especially marked out for the purpose, all reports go to show that the men were not 'intensively' trained to the necessary standard. They started off with considerable *élan*, and there was no lack of natural courage and grit once a line was formed and the course of action obvious. But a large proportion of officers and men were reinforcement drafts quite unfamiliar with hostile shelling or our own barrage fire. When the experienced officers and other ranks became casualties, many falling in the most gallant efforts to push forward, the new hands ... were at a loss and failed to show the necessary qualities of dash, determination, and readiness for self-sacrifice which were indispensable factors for success in this operation ... All competent observers lay stress on this lack of training, and there is no question but that this is the main reason for the failure.' See Captain David Ferguson MC, *The History of the Canterbury Regiment NZEF 1914-1919* (Auckland: Whitcombe & Tombs, 1921), pp. 217-18.
122 KA HKR 69: 'Lage am 4.12.1917 mittags'.
123 KA HKR 71: 'Lage am 3.12.1917 mittags'.
124 See Appendix XII.

impending escape from the frightful Goudberg sector cheered weary men whose units had been in close contact with the enemy for over forty-eight hours. The 5/6th Royal Scots, 1st Dorsetshire Regiment and 2nd Manchester Regiment (14 Brigade) began to relieve the depleted battalions of 97 Brigade after nightfall:

> On arrival here early on the 3rd it was learnt that the situation was very bad and the Battalion was placed under orders to be ready to move at a moment's notice: while waiting orders, however, the enemy shelled Bellevue heavily, killing 2 and wounding 4 men. At 10:30 p.m., the Manchesters moved up to the left sub-sector and relieved the 15th Battalion Lancashire Fusiliers, the front held being an organised system of shell holes, and Battalion headquarters being at Pillbox 88.[125]

Brigadier-General Lumsden observed after a thorough personal reconnaissance that the "Dorset line was in all respects that reported by the OC NORTHUMBERLAND FUSILIERS ... VOX FARM was unoccupied, but a post was established there by the Dorsets on the following night ... Royal Scots line ran from VIRILE FARM along the taped assembly line ... right company of Manchesters also ran along assembly line ... The tape and forming-up discs did not run up to Copse [east of Tournant Farm] ... but I checked the continuation of the line by compass bearing, with the portion that was taped.[126] All the above units were digging in advanced posts from 40 to 50 yards in advance of this line, in accordance with instructions previously issued."[127] Security of the rambling frontage was almost compromised when a portion of territory constituting 15th LF's refused right flank was unintentionally abandoned during the confusion of the Manchester's relief.[128] Harassing fire, maintained by supporting artillery

---

125 TNA: WO/95/2370: 32nd Division War Diary and Colonel H.C. Wylly, *History of the Manchester Regiment (Late 63rd and 96th Foot) Vol. 2* (London: Foster Groom & Co., 1925), p. 169.
126 Major Utterson (A/CO 15th LF) later explained: 'OC 'C' Company informed me on the morning of the 3rd inst that he had pulled up the tape line and used it as a guide to his posts on the ridge. Possibly this is what the GOC 14 Brigade saw.' See IWM 4723: 'Sender No. V.B.84.A', 5 December 1917, Brigadier-General T.S. Lambert Papers (Box 80/10/2).
127 See IWM 4723: '32nd Div. No.G.S.1499/20/2', 'Sender No. V.B.84.A', 5 December 1917 and 'G.230/0/4', 8 December 1917, Brigadier-General T.S. Lambert Papers (Box 80/10/2).
128 The reason for this apparent oversight, as ascertained by a subsequent brigade-level investigation, was 'the left centre company of the [15th] Lancs. Fus. was relieved, but not as handed over, as the right was refused, leaving the Mebus [pillboxes] at V.28.b.5.8 outside our lines. The right centre company of the Lancs. Fus. was not on the ground, and any positions previously occupied by this company were not handed over. OC [2nd] Manchesters therefore, covered the gap which existed from right of left centre company to left of right company by a line of scouts, and dug in a series of posts behind the scouts.' Explanations put forward by the relieving Manchester company were pronounced

and machine-guns throughout the day, continued into the night. The historian of 309th Honourable Artillery Company Siege Battery, situated in advanced positions just south of the Lekkerboterbeek, recalled:

> As for our own shooting, we had taken up so advanced a position at Hannixbeek in anticipation of an attack to be made on the night of December 1st – 2nd. This was duly made, and we fired in it, but unfortunately it met with but little success. We retained the position, however, and fired (but not too frequently, as we could often be observed) on batteries, and at night on roads, our "arc of fire" extending from Stadenreef almost to Passchendaele itself, but our chief activity centring round Westroosebeke.[129]

Reconnaissance patrols were active in the semi-darkness, as relieving infantry attempted to discover the enemy's whereabouts. Several of these enterprises came under direct fire when approaching hostile, heavily manned outposts, one particularly active sniper near Vat Cottages easily engaging targets under the bright moonlight. Losses, nevertheless, had been surprisingly light by the time 14 Brigade telegraphed "HOLES" or relief complete before dawn on 4 December.[130] The weather remained "damp and frightfully cold" as the desolate landscape came into view after sunrise: "It is almost impossible to describe the barrenness of the country in that locality. There was not a shrub or a tree of any kind and the whole place was mud, ploughed up by continuous shellfire. We were occupying ground that had been fought for every inch, and the only features in the landscape behind our lines were badly battered pillboxes and derelict tanks."[131] Morning, with all its apocalyptic-like revelations, also found the young *Offizier-Aspirant* still trying to locate his company:

> 4 December. The position is better than the HOUTHULST FOREST one, drier, just as sinister; it reeks of battle and blood. Only the dead of yesterday and

'inadequate … the failure to take over all portions of the line as held by the out-going battalion might have led to serious results.' See TNA: WO/95/2370: 32nd Division War Diary, IWM 4723: 'C2121 Message and Signals' form and accompanying message map 4 December 1917, '32nd Div. No.G.S.1499/20/2' 5 December 1917, Sender No. V.B.84.A', 5 December 1917 and 'G.230/0/4', 8 December 1917, Brigadier-General T.S. Lambert Papers (Box 80/10/2).
129 Kingham, *London Gunners*, pp. 78-79.
130 Total fatalities for 1st Dorsetshire, 2nd Manchester and 15th HLI (in immediate support) were 8 ORs. See TNA: WO/95/2370: 32nd Division War Diary, WO/95/2400: '97th Inf. Bde. Operation Order No. 183', 3 December 1917', 97 Brigade War Diary and Geoff's CWGC 1914-21 Search Engine <http://www.hut-six.co.uk/cgi-bin/search14-21.php>
131 Major H.D. Thwaytes *op.cit.* in Regimental History Committee, *History of the Dorsetshire Regiment 1914-1919 Vol. 1* (London: Henry Ling, 1932), p. 111.

the day before around, bootless and sockless …¹³² There is more firing here than in the HOUTHULST FOREST sector and less protection. Relief is to come on the 5th at midnight … Well, I went to the KTK for the second time and learned that our Coy. had gone over to Tommy. I went, therefore, to HEIDENGOED and reported to POHLENER, who was quite disheartened.¹³³

Sir Henry Rawlinson, unhappy although not wholly disheartened about the outcome of the Passchendaele and Polderhoek operations, confided sentiments in his diary the previous evening that were sadly reminiscent of the 10 November entry: "The New Zealanders attacked at Polderhoek Chateau today but [,] after severe fighting [,] failed to take it chiefly on account of the pillboxes on the south of it and a trench in the rear [,] which commanded the entrance to the concrete shelter in the chateau – It is very disappointing that both the attack n[orth] of Passchendaele and on Polderhoek should have failed."¹³⁴ Sir Douglas Haig's 3 December instructions on projected manpower deficiencies and adoption of a short-term defensive policy had been the primary reason for halting further attacks north of Passchendaele. GHQ's additional demands for reinforcements would stretch Rawlinson's available reserves for attack or defence to the limit: "News from Cambrai area is that the Bosches are persisting in their assaults in spite of very heavy casualties – Tonight Tavish [Davidson DMO GHQ] rang up to say they wanted nine div. down south [,] so I have to send away the 63 Naval Div. which is well up to strength and the 19 Div. which is well rested and I had hoped to put in the line to relieve tired ones. The Cambrai battle is going to make us very short of troops I fear…"¹³⁵

Fourth Army HQ, having sifted through all available intelligence and after-action reports, dismissed the most recent British effort in its weekly operations report:

> As a result of the hitherto fruitless efforts to improve their positions north and east of Passchendaele by gaining complete possession of the heights, the enemy launched, as was freely admitted by prisoners, a new attack in the early morning of 2.12. At 3:00 a.m. extremely strong hostile fire began abruptly, falling on the left flank division of *Gruppe Staden* and the two northern divisional sectors of

---

132 Shortage of materials to manufacture quality issue footwear for the German Army often led to the appropriation of boots and socks from the British dead.
133 TNA: WO/157/120: 'Annexe to Second Army Summary Dated 19th Decr. 1917: Translation of the closing pages of a diary taken from a dead German (probably a warrant officer of the 3rd Coy. 95th Inf. Regt., 38th Division) who was shot in V.29.b. in the early morning of the 15th inst.', Second Army Intelligence Files.
134 CAC: RWLN 1/9: Rawlinson Diary, 3 December 1917.
135 Ibid. Second Army related the decision to 'consolidate the line at present held and discontinue further offensive operations for the present' in a general order the following day. See LHCMA: '1/7 (G)', 4 December 1917, Second Army War Diary, Montgomery-Massingberd Papers, File 7/16, King's College, London.

330 A Moonlight Massacre

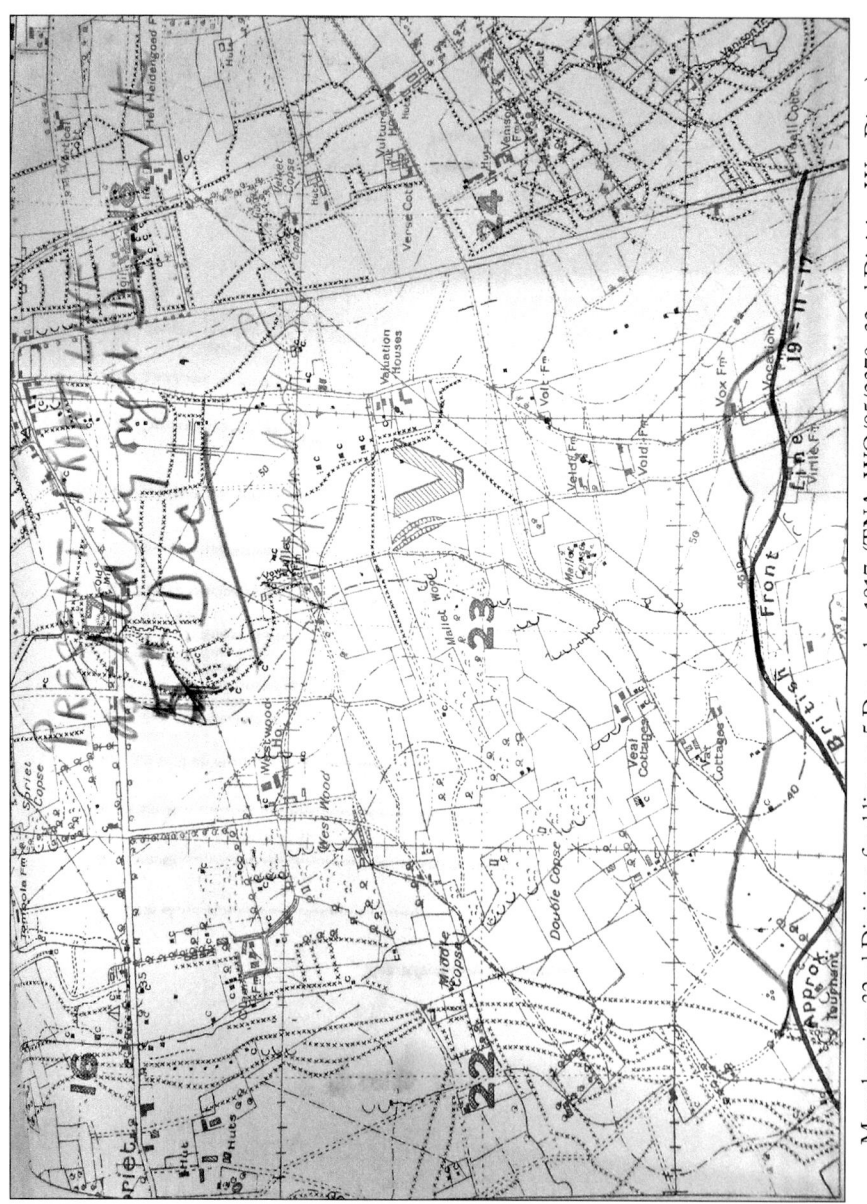

Map showing 32nd Division final line on 5 December 1917. (TNA: WO/95/2370: 32nd Division War Diary)

Gruppe Ypern. Shortly thereafter, a strong British attack was launched against the left flank regiment (*I.R. 94 of 38 I.D.*) of *Gruppe Staden* and against the right flank (*I.R.116* and *117 of 25 I.D.*) of *Gruppe Ypern* as far as the *Kolonnenhof* [Exert Farm] east of Passchendaele. North of the Passchendaele – Oostnieuwkerke Road formed the *Hauptwiderstandslinie*, parts of the *Vorfeld* were occupied; south of here, as far as the marshy land to the *Kolonnenhof* [where] the enemy succeeded in slightly piercing the *Hauptwiderstandslinie*. Further south, apart from an unsuccessful patrol-strength attack against *I.R.115*, there were no enemy attacks against the left flank of *25. I.D.* or *I.R.51* on the right flank of *12. R.D.*[136] At 5:00 a.m. a new enemy attack commenced against the left flanking (*I.R.95* and *94*) regiments of *Gruppe Staden*, but both collapsed.[137] By 11:46 a.m., on the right flank of *Gruppe Ypern*, our *Hauptwiderstandslinie* and, in due course along the whole front of the attack, nearly the entire *Vorfeld* was retaken. The British assault, which had been carried out by the 8th and 32nd divisions, had – per a captured order – as its objective an approximate line of 600 metres behind our foremost trenches. Apart from heavy casualties, the enemy also left 60 prisoners in our hands.[138]

Heeresgruppe Kronprinz Rupprecht, as related in its daily situation report, harboured no further anxieties about the Passchendaele Ridge defences: "Tactical – operational measures: *4.Armee* – Our forces have sufficient power to defend against any possible attacks on the high ground in the Westroosebeke sector."[139] Crown Prince Rupprecht, in a diary entry for 3 December, briefly remarked: "Yesterday the 4th Army halted attacks by two English divisions near and north of Passchendaele."[140] Extraordinarily hard fighting succeeded by conspicuous enemy failure, contributed to the reservedly triumphalist tone of the daily German *Heeresbericht* (Army Bulletin):

> Front of Crown Prince Rupprecht: – Early yesterday, after violent drumfire during a moonlight night, the English with strong forces attacked our positions at and north of Passchendaele. Thüringian and Hessian troops threw back the enemy in a sharp counter-attack and made 60 prisoners. After the attack had

---

136 The 'patrol-strength attack' no doubt refers to 100 Brigade's right flank diversion.
137 The erroneous view that the attack was renewed at 4:00 a.m. British time may have origins in sporadic battalion efforts to move forward in the 3½ hour period before dawn.
138 KA HKR 145: 'AOK 4 I/a MSO, AHQ 6.12.17, Feindliche Infanterietätigkeit, Wochenzusammenstellung, Vom 29.11 bis 5.12.17', pp. 2-3.
139 KA HKR 3: 'Tagesverlauf und der front Taktisch – operative – massnahmen', 3 December 1917.
140 See Kronprinz Rupprecht von Bayern, *In Treue Fest – Mein Kriegstagebuch Vol. 2* (Munich: Deutscher National Verlag, 1929), p. 300. Rupprecht's 3 December diary entry reveals that the Germans had, based on prisoner interrogations (see Appendix XVIII), already identified the attacking British divisions and brigades, their objectives and plan to "assault without any artillery preparation." GHA: Kronprinz Rupprecht Manuscript Diary 707, p. 3276.

been beaten off the firing died down. It increased again at times during the evening to considerable violence.[141]

There was, nevertheless, a great deal to be congratulatory about. The enemy's latest attempt to seize the northern heights had been repelled with heavy losses:

> The English gained not an inch of ground. They were thrown back to their position in the *sumpf* [mud]. The commanding heights remained in our hands. Maps discovered on the bodies of the English dead revealed the enemy had attacked with five battalions; very few of these poor souls returned. Hundreds of English dead lay about the *Vorfeldzone*. Our losses, however, were not few but, thank God, more were wounded than dead. Captured booty consisted of 14 prisoners and eight Lewis Guns. On 2 December 1917 the Regiment again demonstrated, despite lack of rest for months, great heroism. Through all this fighting it retained its reputation with the high command.[142]

IR95's post-war historian also grasped, with some exaggeration, the strategic stakes involved: "Captured maps divulged it was was vital for the English to reach the commanding heights overlooking U-boat bases situated in the Brugge basin. The eastern slopes of the *Feldherrnhügel* protected the entire light and heavy artillery. It would have been a tremendous victory had the enemy succeeded. Such a success might have led to an early end of the war."[143] The German official history of the desperate series of defensive battles conducted by *Fourth Army* from late July to early December 1917 summed up the final result of this last (in their eyes) major British assault with exceptional accuracy: "On 2 December, after a long pause in the struggle, there roared again over Flanders terrain transformed into mud fields, a powerful storm of intense bombardment. But the attacks undertaken on a narrow front by two English brigades against the front divisions of *Gruppes Staden* (38. Inf. Div.) and *Ypern* (25. Inf. Div.) were, after initial partial success, driven back and proof restored to the English that there was no other outcome."[144] The "major battle in Flanders" was officially declared over by *Heeresgruppe Kronprinz Rupprecht* on 5 December.[145] *Fourth Army*, in consequence of heavy losses sustained by the relieved *25th Division*, requested a fresh

---

141 Hartmann, *Das Infanterie Regiment Grossherzog von Sachsen (5. Thüringisches) No. 94 im Weltkrieg*, p. 238 and *The Times*, Tuesday, 4 December 1917, p. 9.
142 Buttmann, *Kriegsgeschichte des Koninglich Preusischen 6. Thüringischen Infanterie Regiment Nr. 95*, pp. 253-54.
143 Ibid., p. 254.
144 Beumelburg, *Flandern 1917*, p. 167.
145 See KA HKR 28: 'Heeresgruppe Kronprinz Rupprecht Oberkommando, Ia Nr. 4716 geh., Betrifft: Die Schlacht in Flandern, Heeresbefehl', 5 December 1917 and Sheldon, *The German Army at Passchendaele*, pp. 312-13.

division to take up position behind *Gruppe Ypern's* right flank; an additional division was requested to take position behind *Gruppe Staden*.[146]

5.3 Tactical Debrief

The 8th Division moved to the Wizernes area SW of St Omer following its relief by 14th Division. Heneker, remarking in his diary with some satisfaction, wrote: "Nice comfortable chateau and good training area."[147] Briefly housed in depressing hutted camps about St Jean, 25 Brigade travelled by light railway to equally agreeable billets on 3 December, 2nd Royal Berkshire, 2nd Lincolnshire, 2nd Rifle Brigade and 1st RIR settling in for a much needed clean-up, reorganisation and training at Wizernes and the outlying hamlets of Boisdinghem, Noir Carme and Zudausque. Lieutenant Nettleton recalled on reaching the final destination that 2nd Rifle Brigade "looked more like a weak company than a proper battalion and everybody felt extremely low."[148] 32nd Division remaining responsible for the Goudberg sector following the relief of 97 Brigade, the five battle-worn assault battalions returned to camps in divisional reserve and support north and NE of St Jean and near Vlamertinghe respectively. 2nd KOYLI, departing from positions opposite Hill 52 on the night of 2/3rd December, made its way to Irish Farm before transportation by bus to Dambre Camp on the 3rd. 16th HLI, 11th Border Regiment and 17th HLI spent a short time at Hilltop and Irish farms before entraining at St Jean station for Brake and Hospital camps.[149] 15th LF and 16th NF, now back with 96 Brigade, settled in as best they could inside "Nissen huts floating in the mud" that made up the austere, unsalutary enclosures around Irish Farm. Battalion roll calls, one of the first orders of business in the immediate aftermath of an attack, were particularly poignant in the most hard-hit battalions: "At Brake Camp the roll-call was one of the saddest since 1915. Twenty officers and 469 other ranks went forward on Passchendaele [sic]. Eight officers and 204 other ranks

---

146 KA HKR 28: Telegraph/wireless pro forma, 5 December 1917.
147 IWM: 66/541/1: Heneker Diary, 4 December 1917. Lieutenant-Colonel Beddington (BGGS) departed from 8th Division the previous day to take up the post of GSO 1 (Operations) Fifth Army: 'Thus ended one of the happiest years of my life.' See Beddington, 'My Life', p. 119.
148 Boraston & Bax, *The Eighth Division*, p. 167, Loraine Petre, *The Royal Berkshire Regiment Vol. 2*, p. 97, TNA: WO/95/1730: 2nd Lincolnshire War Diary, Seymour, *The History of the Rifle Brigade in the War of 1914-1918 Vol. 2*, p. 166, Taylor, *The 1st Royal Irish Rifles in the Great War*, p. 119 and Nettleton, *The Anger of the Guns*, p. 119.
149 Celebrated Scottish war artist Fred A. Farrell (1882-1935), in Flanders on a roving commission for the Corporation of Glasgow, visited 15th, 16th and 17th HLI to render drawings of the Glasgow battalions and the places in which they were operating during this period. See Joanna Meacock, et al, *Fred A. Farrell: Glasgow's War Artist* (Glasgow: I.B. Tauris & Co. LTD, 2014), pp. 20-21.

334   A Moonlight Massacre

17th HLI church parade: Hill Top Farm 16 December 1917. Watercolour by Fred Farrell. (Glasgow Life Photo Library)

"Graves"; "In memory of Officers, NCOs, 16th Bn. HLI killed in action on Passchendaele Ridge 2nd/12/17"; "Not in Vain"; "Sgt Colin Turner", 19 December 1917. Watercolour by Fred Farrell. (Glasgow Life Photo Library)

now answered their names. More than half of the Battalion were casualties ... "¹⁵⁰ Among those unaccounted for were former tank gunner Private Fred Wakely, late Oxford undergraduate Lieutenant Rupert Hardy Parker, old soldier Private Albert Cooksey, underage enlistee Private Hugh Cairns and ex-sports journalist and popular former RAMC NCO 2nd Lieutenant Will Ridgway.¹⁵¹

"An important but often overlooked feature of [British] GHQ's thrust to improve standard tactics", Paddy Griffith has observed, "consisted of extensive debriefs and questionnaires that were often completed immediately after combat. On some occasions this was done to in an attempt to identify scapegoats and incompetents ... On other occasions a very different motive came into play, as some particular organisation or HQ attempted to establish and document its own credentials in order to impress its rivals."¹⁵² Some tactical debriefs "were mounted so quickly after the event that they should be classified more as "immediate situation reports" than as detached historical investigations."¹⁵³ Commanders and staffs, nevertheless, "really did often want to know the full detail of what was going on in mudfields ahead of them, and they were avid to interrogate absolutely every individual who emerged from that zone." Overall, the primary motivation for "collecting post-combat impressions was purely and simply an interest in genuine tactical science."¹⁵⁴ This empirical (bottom-up by necessity) approach is evident in the immediate aftermath of the night operation, as battalion commanders, having queried surviving subordinates, passed reports and questionnaires to brigade who, in turn, passed on their own reports compiled from battalion commentary to division. Division commanders and staffs, more often than not conducting their own enquiries and face-to-face interviews, were then expected to write up, based on total collected evidence provided by subordinate units, a final after-action report for the edification of Corps and Army HQs.¹⁵⁵

25 Brigade HQ initiated the formal process of gathering post-combat impressions by forwarding a questionnaire to its three assault battalion commanders who, in addition to supplying the routine after-action reports, were directed to comment on five distinct operational aspects (barrage, assembly, enemy fire, forming-up and equipment). Lieutenant-Colonel Stirling (CO 2nd Royal Berkshire) noted that the

---

150 Bond, *The King's Own Yorkshire Light Infantry in the Great War Vol. 3*, p. 912, TNA: WO/95/2404: 16th HLI, WO/95/2403: 11th Border Regiment, WO/95/2405: 17th HLI, WO/95/2397: 15th LF war diaries, Cooke, *Historical Records of the 16th (Service) Battalion Northumberland Fusiliers*, p. 89 and Chalmers (ed), *A Saga of Scotland*, p. 111.
151 See Appendix XVII.
152 Griffith, *Battle Tactics on the Western Front*, pp. 186-87.
153 Ibid.
154 Ibid.
155 'All divisions produced a narrative of operations after major actions and many specifically studied the lessons to be learned. The quality and thoroughness of these reports are a valuable source of study when asserting the performance of individual divisions and the evolution of the BEF in general.' See Lee, 'Command and Control in Battle' in Sheffield & Todman (eds) *Command and Control on the Western Front*, endnote 8, p. 139.

supporting barrage "was effective, although there "were many shorts." Battalion officers, he added, "state that the barrage seemed to lift too quickly after the original beginning. All agree that the defensive barrage of artillery … was excellent."[156] 2nd Royal Berkshire's assembly, Stirling also observed, was almost compromised by poor overland communications: "The duckboards were raised too high above ground, so when the men got off where there were gaps, it was difficult to get on again. A new tape should have been laid from the head of the duckboards, as the old one was hardly discoverable." Observations about enemy fire focused on the hostile barrage, which "came down from our old frontline back to behind the PASSCHENDAELE – VINDICTIVE X roads." Forming-up along the jumping-off line, regardless of the exhausting march forward, was expedited by accurate layout of direction tapes, although "some of them were not securely fastened and had moved in the wind." No shortage of equipment was experienced and overloading was not a serious problem "except in the mud and on the duckboards, but the carrying of spare stores by the 3rd wave was a mistake", as the use of these battle supplies "never eventuated." This designated 3rd wave "carrying platoon" would, in Stirling's opinion, have been "invaluable as a support but got it into its head that it was there to carry. I consider a totally separate carrying party to go up when the barrage had moderated would be better." Stirling concluded by attributing absence of "complete success to lack of depth on my centre due to the easing off of to keep touch with the left … I consider that the forming-up could only have been done in moonlight, but the attack would have gone better if it had been darker, as the Germans could not have located where our men were and I think, in this case, we could have held on to the [Southern] redoubt."[157]

2nd Lincolnshire Regiment's adjutant, in reply to the Brigade questionnaire on Lieutenant-Colonel Irwin's behalf, noted the barrage was "efficient", despite some unwelcome howitzer "shorts." Hostile machine-gun fire and the subsequent hold-up made it impossible to determine if the barrage pace was satisfactory or not. The march to assembly astride Track No. 5 South proved a very taxing ordeal: "There was not more than 20 yards length continuous + track was laid too high off the ground … Owing to the condition of the track, my battalion and the Berkshires were a little mixed up by the head of the track, otherwise the assembly was not worried much. Hostile fire caused an average of 10-15 casualties a company before assembly." The enemy's barrage fire was observed "about Zero + 9. It was his MG and rifle fire (rifle

---

156 For an account of the direct tactical support (bombardment of roads and support areas) provided by 62nd HAG see TNA: WO/95/1677: 'Action of Heavy Artillery', 8th Division War Diary. The accompanying map legend outlined the barrage scheme as follows: 'Searching roads in depth; commence firing at Zero + 8: 6-in. 5 batteries, 9.2-in. 3 batteries, Southern Group 3 batteries. Assembly areas and areas occupied by supports: 1 long range battery on each area commence fire at Zero + 15: 6-in. 2 batteries. 8-in. 1 battery, Southern Group: 2 batteries.'
157 TNA: WO/95/1929: 'Appendix B', 5 December 1917, 2nd Royal Berkshire War Diary. See Appendix XIII for complete transcript.

fire negligible), which stopped the advance. His MGs opened at Zero + 3 minutes." Forming-up was, as with 2nd Royal Berkshire, ably assisted by accurate placement of direction tapes which proved "undoubtedly useful." Equipment concerns were, for the most part, minimal, overloading and the abysmal state of No. 5 Track regarded as the chief causes of fatigue prior to Zero. Spare Lewis Gun magazines, however, were in short supply and it was recommended that these be distributed "throughout the assaulting troops" in the future.[158]

Lieutenant Anderson, adjutant and acting CO 2nd Rifle Brigade following Lieutenant-Colonel Brand's wounding on the jumping-off tape, also found the supporting barrage to be efficient with an acceptable pace and "not many shorts." Assembly had been "carried out with only slight interference from the enemy, although, from their subsequent action, the forming-up on the tapes was apparently observed by them." Hostile batteries maintained "searching fire from about Zero + 5 in rear of support line. Machine-gun fire [was] particularly deadly. Machine-guns firing low – about 2 feet from the ground." Forming-up along the direction tapes was, despite the enemy's close proximity in Teall Cottage, "all that could be desired." The men were not overloaded with equipment and there were no shortages "except for very lights." German losses, Anderson concluded, appeared equally severe: "From our new line the ground slopes very slightly to the Northern Redoubt and thence steeply to the NE. This has a considerable number of enemy dead between our advanced posts and the Northern Redoubt."[159]

All three battalion commanders, therefore, appear to have been in general agreement on the relative effectiveness of the supporting barrage, procedural soundness (notwithstanding the condition of Track No. 5) during assembly and forming-up, lethal efficiency of the German machine-gun fire and satisfactory quality and quantity of issue equipment. Two (Stirling and Anderson) believed the primary cause of the reverse was increased visibility resulting from the bright moonlight. The former, although acknowledging "forming-up could only have been done in moonlight", also opined it could have been darker whilst the latter noted "Visibility in the moonlight was

158 TNA: WO/95/1730: 'Report on Action of the Battn. from 2:30 p.m. 1-12-17 – M.N. 2/3-12-17', 6 December 1917, 2nd Lincolnshire War Diary. See Appendix 13 for complete transcript. Lieutenant-Colonel Irwin went on to a distinguished military career before retiring as a Lieutenant-General in 1948. He is best remembered for his controversial dismissal following the Arakan offensive in 1942.
159 TNA: WO/95/1731: 'Report of the Part Played by the 2nd Battn. The Rifle Brigade in the Recent Operations at Passchendaele', 6 December 1917, 2nd Rifle Brigade War Diary. See Appendix XIII for complete transcript. Heneker subsequently observed that the field artillery barrage could have remained on Venison Trench beyond the fixed (1 minute) part of the timetable: 'I did not like to leave it on this trench for a longer period for fear of catching my own infantry should they be sweeping successfully. As it happens [,] the 2/Rifle Brigade noted this barrage and say it did not stay on this line long enough.' WO/95/1677: 'Narrative of Operations Carried Out by the 8th Division on 1st/2nd December 1917', 13 December 1917, 8th Division War Diary.

up to 500 yards. The moon was behind us. It seems obvious that the enemy observed our forming-up…" Irwin's judgement that machine-guns "stopped the advance" of 2nd Lincolnshire appears by implication to have further substantiated Stirling and Anderson's perspective even though he failed to specifically endorse moonlight as the principal tactical handicap in his after-action report.[160]

Having predicted the negative impact of a full moon and unsubdued machine-guns, Heneker (whose contingency plans had been overruled) wholly agreed with his battalion commanders about the principal cause for the failure.[161] Bearing the signature of Brigadier-General Coffin, 8th Division's subsequent after-action report appears to have been the collaborative effort of Heneker and the like-minded GOC 25 Brigade.[162] A forthright narrative document, it closed with a damning indictment of the entire operational scheme:

> To attempt a surprise on a bright moonlight [sic] night when bodies of men can be seen easily on the move at a distance of 300 yards is not sound. Directly the right of 32nd Division and left of 2nd Rifle Brigade rose at Zero hour in order to advance, the machine-guns in TEALL COTTAGE opened and others N. W, and E of them took it up almost at once. I have heard it said that when snow is on the ground, and when the night is bright with the moon full, bodies of men at 200 yards cannot be seen. This is not my experience.
>
> To expect infantry to advance some 200 yards over an area cut-up by shell-fire in the face of accurate machine-gun fire, and without the protection of an artillery barrage, is to expect too much … I lost two very valuable commanding officers and a great many junior officers. As usual, the men were splendid …[163]

---

160 TNA: WO/95/1929: 'Appendix B', 5 December 1917, 2nd Royal Berkshire War Diary, WO/95/1731: 'Report of the Part Played by the 2nd Battn. The Rifle Brigade in the Recent Operations at Passchendaele', 6 December 1917, 2nd Rifle Brigade War Diary and WO/95/1730: 'Report on Action of the Battn. from 2:30 p.m. 1-12-17 – M.N. 2/3-12-17', 6 December 1917, 2nd Lincolnshire War Diary.
161 See Chapter 2, pp. 100–101.
162 Coffin's earlier after-action report was written without critical commentary in pure narrative style. His views on the failure to retain Southern Redoubt, however, are discernable in the 8th Division after-action report of 13 December: 'Owing to casualties to runners, and to the fact that a verbal message was delivered wrongly, the reserve ['A'] company of the right Battalion was sent to the extreme right where it was not needed. Had it been sent to help the situation in the SOUTHERN REDOUBT, there can be no doubt but that the objectives there would have been held.' This criticism is challenged by evidence that 'A' Company was dispatched to the right *after* 2nd Royal Berkshire was ejected from Southern Redoubt. See TNA: WO/95/1727: 'Report on Operations', 7 December 1917, 25 Brigade War Diary, WO/95/1677: 'Narrative of Operations Carried Out by the 8th Division on 1st/2nd December 1917', 13 December 1917, 8th Division War Diary.
163 TNA: WO/95/1677: 'Narrative of Operations Carried Out by the 8th Division on 1st/2nd December 1917', 13 December 1917, 8th Division War Diary. The two battalion

The night operation, 8th Division's post-war historians observed, could "only be regarded, at best, as a qualified success."[164] This surprising assessment must, however, be viewed in context; 8th Division had a gruelling and somewhat unlucky war experience and it is likely its "establishment" chroniclers moderated their judgment with targeted veteran readership in mind.[165] It is also certain, based on Heneker's diary entries and the divisional after-action report that post-operational impressions of any sort of "success", qualified or otherwise, amongst Division and Brigade leadership were without foundation. Boraston and Bax, nevertheless, adequately elucidated the lamentable tactical circumstances and melancholy results with contemporaneous clarity:

> [A]lthough about 150 prisoners[166] and 4 machine-guns had been captured and a certain amount of ground had been gained, the main purpose of this attack – the capture of the two redoubts and the gaining of observations down the valleys they commanded – had not been accomplished. The noise inseparable from forming-up for the attack among such trying conditions of mud and water had put the enemy on his guard; thereafter the brightness of the moonlight and the absence of a protecting barrage during the first crucial eight minutes were responsible for all that followed. It was evidently possible for the enemy to see our men, moving forward in bodies, at a distance of 200 yards. Assuming that he could do that and that he made proper use of his opportunities, failure was inevitable.[167]

commanders referred to were Lieutenant-Colonel R. Brand (CO 2nd Rifle Brigade) wounded just prior to Zero on 2 December and Lieutenant-Colonel A. Tillett (CO 2nd Devonshire) mortally wounded on 29 November.

164 The divisional history's foreword, signed by Haig but actually penned by Boraston in his capacity as private secretary to the former, observed: 'In the major offensives in which it took a direct part the 8th Division, despite unfailing gallantry, was signally unfortunate.' See Boraston & Bax, *The Eighth Division*, pp. viii and 167.

165 Boraston had previously edited (1919) the omnibus edition of the British Field Marshal's wartime despatches and co-authored, along with popular outdoor writer (*The Book of the Dry Fly 1897, South Country Streams* 1899, etc.), official war correspondent and editor (*Saturday Review* 1914-17 and *The Nineteenth Century* 1919-25) G.A.B. Dewar, the controversial two-volume *Sir Douglas Haig's Command 1915-1918* in 1922. In their preface (pp. ix-x) for the 1926 divisional history, the authors (Boraston & Bax) speculated the narrative would be of 'special interest to the junior officers and rank and file of the of the division, who, it is common experience, had neither the time nor the opportunity during the war itself to give much thought to what was happening outside their own battery or battalion. It is hoped that this history will be the means to enable them in retrospect to take a broader view of the memorable events in which they took so worthy a part...'

166 This figure is contradicted by contemporary reports. See pp. 374-75 below.

167 Boraston & Bax, *The Eighth Division*, p. 167.

Observation denied: site of Venison Trench looking east from new British outpost line. (Rob Thompson)

Lieutenant-Colonel Beddington (GSO 1) concurred in an unpublished memoir forty-three years later when he recollected that 8th Division had "gained two thirds of the ground we set out to capture, but did not succeed in gaining the crest of the hill and, with it, the observation north-eastwards that we wanted."[168]

Lieutenant Scott (32nd Division Artillery Reconnaissance Officer) briefly summed up the operation in his diary as follows: "The result of the attack was a failure. A few prisoners had been captured and one or two enemy posts. The ground was far too heavy for the infantry to have much of a chance. This was the last effort of the winter campaign to capture the ridge from Passchendaele to Westroosebeke."[169] That being the case, what sort of conclusions did the GOC 32nd Division arrive at in his nineteen-page after-action report? As with 8th Division, a deliberate bureaucratic method

168 Beddington, 'My Life', p. 119. An annotated Second Army operations map states the attack was 'partially successful.' Capture and retention of a further 'two-thirds' of the *Vorfeldzone* directly opposite the objective may have contributed to the official view of qualified operational success. See TNA: WO/153/267: 'German Artillery Groupings & Raids (British & German) Nov. to Dec. 1917' Confidential [Map] 1st-31st December 1917, Press 16, Drawer 3, YPRES 1917'.
169 Scott, Grice-Hutchison, et al., *Artillery & Trench Mortar Memories*, p. 85.

of obtaining facts from subordinate units existed within 32nd Division, although no evidence of a 97 Brigade questionnaire has come to light.[170] Thus an almost identical bottom-up enquiry process based on a routine combination of submitted written accounts, enquiries and personal interviews was applied during the subsequent tactical debrief.[171] Heavy casualties amongst the junior leadership would nonetheless contribute to some debatable conclusions whilst leaving a number of pertinent questions unanswered.

Only two (15th LF and 16th NF) of six battalion after-action reports were available for this study. The former focused on the adverse consequences of the battalion's exposed right flank; the latter, besides reiterating Lieutenant-Colonel Scully's contentious assertion that the enemy's defensive fire "was not heavy enough to stop the attack" had nothing further to add about the assault's initial phase.[172] Two (2nd KOYLI and 17th HLI) of six battalion war diary accounts attribute the failure to enemy foreknowledge of the attack, lethal defensive machine-gun fire and consequent heavy losses among officers and NCOs.[173] The remaining four (16th HLI, 11th Border Regiment, 15th LF, 16th NF) are perfunctory narratives with no real attempt at post-operational analysis, although most of the factors related by 2nd KOYLI and 17th HLI are referred to at one time or another. One post-war (2nd KOYLI) regimental history subsequently observed, "movement of troops before "Zero" hour had been only too easily observed" while another (16th HLI) remarked that the enemy had "a free hand for five minutes on a target that looked grotesquely big against the bright moon." The author of a third (16th NF) noted: "The night was clear and moonlit. At once the

---

170 A series of terse replies to questionnaire/interview queries (not reproduced in document) were attached to Major Utterson's after-action report: '(a) Yes. On reaching objectives (b) I do not know the strength. The direction of the attack was from the northeast (c) About 8-0 am (d) Lewis guns put in advance of the line to enfilade counter-attacks, and a proportion kept with the support platoons (e) My battalion did not come back.' The report also contains hand-written queries concerning action of 14 Brigade trench mortars, troop fatigue prior to the German counter-attack and activities of 97 Brigade machine-guns. See IWM 4723: 'Narrative of Operations 2/3rd December 1917, 15th (S) Battalion Lancashire Fusiliers', 4 December 1917, Brigadier-General T.S. Lambert Papers (Box 80/10/2).
171 A window into the process adopted by 32nd Division is available in IWM 4723 Brigadier-General T.S. Lambert papers (Box 80/10/2), which contains 'correspondence relating to the attack carried out by the Division on the 2nd December 1917…' not archived in corresponding TNA files. Standard subordinate (brigade, battalion, MG and RE companies) unit after-action reports are also accompanied by a series of memos, divisional enquiries and typescript/hand-written statements.
172 See IWM 4723: 'Narrative of Operations 2/3rd December 1917, 15th (S) Battalion Lancashire Fusiliers', 4 December 1917 and '32nd. Div. No.G.S.1499/3/33', 5 December 1917, Brigadier-General T.S. Lambert Papers (Box 80/10/2). Both reports contain terse, hand-written marginalia comments by Shute.
173 TNA: WO/95/2402: 2nd KOYLI and WO/95/2405 17th HLI war diaries.

advance was seen…"[174] These published inter-war impressions, however, still conform to contemporary war diary entries which, by manifest inference (passing mention of a bright moon when relating prevailing weather conditions, perceived enemy awareness of impending attack and almost instantaneous opening up of hostile machine-guns) indirectly emphasise the adverse effect of moonlight.[175]

Blacklock attributed the reverse to enemy foreknowledge, "therefore the element of surprise failed and the assault became movement without supporting fire of any description"; subsequent "heavy casualties and initial disorganisation were never overcome." Failure to retain objectives was, in his considered opinion, due to three primary factors: Loss of touch between units "in the dark and over bad going"; severe losses amongst junior officers that ensured "there was nobody on the spot to reorganise and supervise the consolidation" and the almost complete absence of timely reports deemed essential for ascertaining "a sufficiently clear situation to act upon."[176] A handwritten summary identified specific battalion-level command and control failures and a perceived absence of fortitude by the infantry:

(1) It was calculated that the 97th Bde would reach its objective at Zero + 32 or 2:27 a.m. At this time then [,] commanding officers should have moved up to supervise consolidation. Commanding officers had not visited their battalions even by 3 a.m. by which time daylight made moves difficult if not impossible. Had commanding officers gone up to their battalions any time before 3 a.m. & 5 a.m. [,] they would have been able to see the situation and push on the advance b[y] a series of encircling moves as taught.
(2) Report of a German prisoner says our men lay down when fired at. In any case [,] encircling movements were not made nor were the enemy strongpoints rushed. Casualties were thus largely increased & our men pinned to the ground & lost our barrage.
(3) Company officers and platoon commanders sent back no reports of the situation.
(4) Although the failure of the 17th HLI to advance was early known at Brigade HQ [,] the danger of this gap in our line, through which the final weak counter-attack eventually came, was not grasped, nor were orders sent out to move round Veal Cottages.
(5) Men scattered & hid in shell holes or moved to the rear as casualties when unfit. Thus very heavy casualties were reported when these had, in truth, not occurred.

174 See Bond, *The King's Own Yorkshire Light Infantry in the Great War Vol. 3*, p. 911, Chalmers (ed), *A Saga of Scotland*, pp. 109-10 and Cooke, *Historical Records of the 16th (Service) Battalion Northumberland Fusiliers*, p. 88.
175 See TNA: WO/95/2402: 2nd KOYLI, WO/95/2404: 16th HLI, WO/95/2403: 11th Border Regiment, WO/95/2405: 17th HLI, WO/95/2397: 15th LF and WO/95/2398: 16th NF war diaries.
176 IWM 4723: Typescript 'Preliminary Report on Operations, December 1st, 2nd and 3rd', 4 December 1917, Brigadier-General T.S. Lambert Papers (Box 80/10/2).

(6) The final counter-attack [,] which drove back the 17th HLI, 11th Border Rgt, & part of the 15th Lancs. Fus. only consisted of 200 men. Stokes mortars at Tournant Farm & south of Vat Cottages did not open fire upon them. No attempt was made to unit[e] & 2 ½ batt. moved rapidly to the rear [,] 50 odd men of them not stopping until caught by straggler points.
(7) Little or no effort was made to dig in or place Lewis guns or machine-guns in position.[177]

Battalion, company and platoon leadership was therefore, in Blacklock's estimation, the weakest link within the chain of command and a major contributory cause of the reverse. The tendency for men to seek cover instead of pressing forward, failures to take the initiative and encircle Vat Cottages or repel a perceived half-hearted enemy counter-attack thus had its roots in the command and control shortcomings of subordinates. These proscriptive conclusions, however, appear to disregard the aforementioned consequence of "severe losses amongst junior officers" and the detrimental impact of the often contradictory and erroneous messages which perpetuated transitory illusions that Hill 52 had been consolidated or Vat Cottages could be threatened by envelopment. Criticism directed at battalion commanders for not going forward to supervise consolidation appears, when considering tactical best practice as articulated in *S.S. 135 Instructions for the Training of Divisions for Offensive Action*, at face value to have some validity.[178] Nevertheless, expectations that they would move forward and establish headquarters in the vicinity of the captured objective was, according to historian Aimée Fox, "correct in principal; however, its applicability in operations was often unfeasible. Local control may have been achieved through battalion commanders going forward but, with poor communications within the battalion in battle, it is unlikely this would have been effective in the long term." This unavoidable disconnect was heightened by heavy casualties and a consequent debilitating vaccum of junior leadership initiative that left battalion commanders increasingly uninformed and isolated. Communication breakdowns encountered at battalion level and below were in marked contrast to the relatively secure telephonic/telegraph arrangements between 97 Brigade and 32nd Division headquarters. The unsatisfactory state of affairs beyond brigade is substantiated by the trackside corpses of fallen runners encountered by Lieutenant Scott during his perilous journey to Virile Farm on the morning of 2 December and the censorious Blacklock who revealingly remarked two days later: "Communications forward of Brigade Headquarters were intermittent [;] heavily shelled throughout."[179]

---

177 Ibid: 'Summary of the Attack of the 97th Inf. Bde. with 2 battalions of the 96th Inf. Bde. on December 2 [1917]'.
178 General Staff, *S.S. 135 Instructions for the Training of Divisions for Offensive Action* (December 1916), p. 41.
179 Aimée Fox, "'The word 'retire' is never to be used": The performance of the 9th Brigade, AIF, at First Passchendaele, 1917', Australian War Memorial Summer Vacation

Shute concluded his after-action report with a narrative of 97 Brigade's retirement followed by a general analytic précis – "Reasons for the Failure of the Operation". Losses among officers and NCOs, he observed at the head of the former, made it "difficult to collect reliable details as to the reason of [sic] the withdrawal …" Recent reports – based on "best information available" – debunking the belief that certain key objectives were captured or retained for any lengthy period had, nonetheless, finally been verified: "During no period of the day were we in possession of TEALL COTTAGE. We were never in possession of HILL 52 after we had been driven off it by the enemy's counter-attack at 5:30 a.m."[180]

Having advanced the greatest distance, 11th Border Regiment was the subject of a great deal of official disapprobation for retiring in the face of the 4:10 p.m. counter-attack. "There is nothing", Shute remarked, "to indicate that the strength of the attack or the artillery fire employed by the enemy in the slightest degree justified this withdrawal."[181] The Lonsdales' retreat, while highly questionable in his eyes, was somewhat mitigated by the Battalion's isolated position and enemy resourcefulness: "The German seems throughout to have shewn a good deal of enterprise and to have persistently tried to work round the flanks of 11th Border Regiment." Shute also recognised, unlike Blacklock, that the hard-pressed men were "without leaders, had been fighting all day and their stamina was probably nearly exhausted. This explanation", he nevertheless observed, "cannot be accepted and all that can be said is that the 11th Border Regt., who are normally fine fighters, failed on this occasion."[182]

This criticism was too much for overtaxed 11th Border Regiment CO Lieutenant-Colonel Tweed. A short note to the Battalion medical officer on 13 December summarised his deteriorating mental condition:

> I would be glad if you would come to see me as early as possible. I have not felt well for some time past – internal worries & shortage of experienced officers in my battalion have made it necessary for me to work day & night with the result that I am on the verge of a breakdown brought on by lack of sleep through nervousness & accompanied frequently by neuralgia & headache. This is periodical & I am not ill in any physical sense, but the present bad luck my Bn. has had on active operations & resultant criticism has created a state of depression & low spirits which prevent me from doing justice to my command. I feel most urgently

---

Scholarship Scheme Research Paper (Canberra: AWM, 2011), p. 19 <https://www.awm.gov.au/research/grants/summer_scholarship/papers/> Scott, Grice-Hutchison, et al, *Artillery & Trench Mortar Memories*, p. 84 and IWM 4723: 'Preliminary Report on Operations December 1st, 2nd and 3rd December', 4 December 1917, Brigadier-General T.S. Lambert Papers (Box 80/10/2).
180 TNA: WO/95/2370: After-action report, 'Part IV, Narrative Dealing with the Retirement of the 97th Infantry Brigade', 11 December 1917, 32nd Division War Diary.
181 Ibid.
182 Ibid.

the need for a long rest from worry & responsibility, the first I have asked for in over two years continual fighting at the front. I would like your opinion.[183]

The MO, on finding "no evidence of distinct physical ailment", deemed his commanding officer's psychological state serious enough to warrant "a complete change and absolute rest for an indefinite period" in hospital where he could "be properly cared for."[184] Tweed's nervous collapse appears to have been triggered by knowledge of an adverse report submitted by Blacklock on 9 December:

> During the operations of the Brigade under my command on Decr. 1st, 2nd and 3rd 1917, his Bn. failed to hold a position south of MALLET COPSE, which they had taken during the assault, and subsequently retired on to their original position … I consider that Lieut.-Col. TWEED showed a lack of experience, judgement and leadership in dealing with this situation … The Bn. now has very few trained officers and NCOs, and I do not consider that Lieut.-Col. TWEED has displayed during the period he has commanded his Bn. a sufficient power of leadership and a sufficient knowledge of soldiering necessary to bring the Bn. up to a proper state of efficiency … I therefore request that Lieut.-Col. TWEED be removed from command of the 11th Border Regt., and an experienced officer appointed in his place.[185]

Shute concurred solicitously adding that "My opinion is that Lieut.-Col. TWEED is an excellent man, keen and anxious to do well, but that with all the will in the world he is not capable of handling a battalion. This need be no slur on Lieut.-Col. TWEED. He is not a regular officer, and is doing, and has done his best."[186] Tweed was convalescing at a base hospital on the coast as Blacklock's request made its way up the chain of command from II Corps to Fourth Army to its final destination at GHQ where, in a correspondence to the War Office, his removal "from the permanent command of the 11th Battalion, the Border Regiment, and that he may not be sent out again to command a battalion in the field" was solicited.[187] Evacuated to Great Britain on 12 January 1918, Tweed spent the early months of his convalescence vainly petitioning the War Office for assignment to the army's home establishment.[188]

183 TNA: WO/339/21553: Tweed, hand-written note to Battalion medical officer 13 December 1917, Lieutenant-Colonel Thomas Frederic TWEED. The Lancashire Fusiliers.
184 Ibid: 11th Border Regiment MO to ADMS 32nd Division, 13 December 1917.
185 Ibid: Blacklock to 32nd Division HQ, 9 December 1917.
186 Ibid: Shute to II Corps HQ, 12 December 1917.
187 Ibid: II Corps HQ to Fourth Army, 20 December 1917, Fourth Army HQ to AMS GHQ, 25 December 1917 and AMS GHQ to MS War Office, 31 December 1917.
188 See Appendix XIX.

Denied further postings, he resigned his commission whilst retaining the rank of honorary lieutenant-colonel the following March.[189]

Shute also cast a critical eye on 16th HLI, remarking that the afternoon counter-attack extending as far as the Battalion's left brought about a corresponding withdrawal with 11th Border Regiment. Fatigue and losses amongst the junior leadership were, as with the neighbouring Lonsdales, taken into account: "This Battalion had also had very heavy fighting all day and had had heavy casualties in officers and NCOs, the commanding officer being amongst the officers hit." Shute, while not indifferent to these circumstances, nonetheless dryly observed that 16th HLI's "action in withdrawing is not explained and there seems little excuse beyond the extreme strain imposed on the men in their leaderless condition."[190] This conclusion, despite contrary evidence in the relevant Battalion war diary, is puzzling; 16th HLI, having repelled the enemy, did not withdraw from positions around Void Farm until ordered to do so before dawn on 3 December. Perhaps Blacklock's earlier remark that it had retired to Vocation Farm following the enemy's late afternoon thrust combined with the wounding and evacuation of Major Scott had a negative impact on the quality of information related by the latter's appointed successor, Lieutenant-Colonel Scully.[191]

The precipitate action taken by 16th NF in the wake of the afternoon counter-attack, Shute commented, "requires explanation." The designate "Counter counter-attack" battalion's advance from the vicinity of Virile Farm resulted in a minimal gain

189 TNA: WO/339/21553: Tweed to MS War Office, 26 March 1918, Lieutenant-Colonel Thomas Frederic TWEED. The Lancashire Fusiliers. Tweed went on to a distinguished political career as Secretary Manchester Liberal Federation 1918-26, co-founder of the innovative 'Liberal Summer Schools' movement (1921) and chief political advisor to David Lloyd George from 1926 until his untimely death at the age of 52 in 1940. Literary fame was also achieved as the celebrated author of three popular, but now almost forgotten novels (*Rinehard: A Melodrama of the Nineteen-Thirties* or, alternatively in the USA, *Gabriel Over the White House, Blind Mouths and Destiny's Man*), the first of which was made into a major motion picture by American press baron William Randolph Hearst's 'Cosmopolitan Productions' in 1933. Evidence has recently come to light that Tweed may have fathered the only child (Jennifer Longford 1929-2012) of the former prime minister and his long-time mistress and subsequent second wife Frances Stevenson. See John Campbell, *If Love Were All: The Story of Frances Stevenson and David Lloyd George* (London: Jonathan Cape, 2006) for an account of the five-year affair between Tweed and Stevenson and Longford's *The Times* obituary (24 March 2012).
190 TNA: WO/95/2370: After-action report, 'Part IV, Narrative Dealing with the Retirement of the 97th Infantry Brigade', 11 December 1917, 32nd Division War Diary. This assertion was based on the after-action report submitted by Blacklock. See IWM 4723: 'Preliminary Report on Operations, December 1st, 2nd and 3rd', 4 December 1917 and 'Summary of the Attack of the 97th Inf. Bde. with 2 Battalions of the 96th Inf. Bde. on December 2nd 1917', Brigadier-General T.S. Lambert Papers (Box 80/10/2).
191 Scully made no mention of the pre-dawn (5:00 a.m. 3 December) order for 16th HLI to withdraw posts from Void Farm in his subsequent after-action report. See IWM 4732:'32nd Div. No.G.S.1499/3/33', 4 December 1917, Brigadier-General T.S. Lambert Papers (Box 80/10/2).

of 300 yards from the original jumping-off line with both flanks refused. This circumscribed forward movement, made regardless of the fact that "the enemy did not follow up our retiring troops and the OC 16th North'd Fusiliers did not see any Germans advancing", was justified – during the course of an interview with Scully – by the claim that no organised troops remained to defend the old frontline as the Battalion entered the void. Scully's replies to a series of questions (not found) from Division HQ further illuminate his decision to halt the advance:

> Ref. Questions
> (a) My No. 3 and 4 companies dug in on the line they advanced to i.e. about 250 yards ahead of our line. They started digging in about 4:30.
> (b) No counter-attack was seen by any of my battalion but it was reported from the direction of MALLET COPSE.
> (c) I visited the advanced line (Nos. 2 and 3 companies) at 6 p.m. By that time they were reorganised and were already dug in (about 4 to 5 feet deep) they had established touch and put out defensive flanks.
> (d) I never saw any trench mortars. My Lewis guns were used to engage hostile machine-guns and to fire on any bodies of hostile infantry. Very few, however, were seen.
> (e) My Battalion was detailed as the forward body for CCA [counter counter-attack] My Battalion did not retire but pushed forward as soon as the troops in front were seen to be retiring.[192]

Concern for exposed flanks also contributed to the perceived untimely halt. Shute remained unconvinced: "I am of the opinion that the OC 16th Northumberland Fus. was wrong in the decision he came to and that he should have advanced at once to VOID FARM and attacked the enemy he encountered. The situation in which he found himself, however, was a difficult one, and the reasons he gives for his action are reasonable."[193]

The last section ("Reasons for the Failure of the Operation") of Shute's after-action report is of particular interest for what is not – the detrimental impact of moonlight – directly addressed in the document. This is not surprising given his past advocacy of night attacks under similar atmospheric conditions. Moreover, three pre-disposed tactical viewpoints likely influenced Shute's overall assessment of the disappointing

---

192 Ibid.
193 TNA: WO/95/2370: After-action report, 'Part IV, Narrative Dealing with the Retirement of the 97th Infantry Brigade', 11 December 1917, 32nd Division War Diary. Scully's post-war military career was marred by a tragic motorcycle accident in which he lost a leg. The succeeding years were spent unsuccessfully petitioning the War Office for compensation. He died whilst undergoing surgery for a war-related head injury in 1937. See TNA: WO/339/7031: Lieutenant Colonel Arthur John SCULLY. The Manchester Regiment.

results. First, the importance of units maintaining direction and cohesion by moonlight; second, a ready acceptance of the need for operational risk-taking; third, clear recognition that the enemy had successfully adapted to British offensive tactics, hence the unusual hybrid scheme that dispensed with the barrage for 8 minutes after Zero. It is also fair to point out that the unfortunate tactical situation confronting 32nd Division left few alternatives once Second Army ordered the attack. Thus Shute, always the confident and aggressive soldier, made the best of a bad job by introducing surprise as a crucial element in the first phase of the asault. Perceived errors had occurred at subordinate levels. The novel attack plan – the best that could be devised given the circumstances – was, in his view, not at fault.

The primary factor "which directly conduced to the failure of this operation", the GOC 32nd Division observed, "was the fact that machine-guns were all alive and in action from Zero plus 7 onwards." The enemy's establishment of complete "fire superiority" forced the attackers to seek cover in scattered shell holes. "Local advances were attempted and carried out after this period, but all movement cost us dearly in leaders, who had to expose themselves in organising and leading these advances." The majority of units, therefore, "were practically without leaders and when the time of stress [afternoon counter-attack] came, the men, being deprived of their usual commanders and a good deal disorganised by the day's fighting, failed to deal with the situation." The "indirect cause", Shute continued, was the "firing from west to east, while the attack was being delivered from south to north" of the supporting artillery. This made it "impossible to organise an effective creeping barrage to cover the infantry advance." Had it been possible to place batteries directly behind 97 Brigade, he concluded, "the enemy machine-guns might have been kept under until captured." The "contributory cause", Shute added in perhaps the most controversial section of "Reasons for the Failure of the Operation" was disorganisation resulting from an "attack delivered in darkness … accentuated by the loss of officers." Thus command and control broke down, as surviving ORs (lacking prerequisite training and initiative) proved unwilling or unable to act as substitutes for fallen commissioned leadership: "Although night attacks have been carried out with complete success, it must be realised that we are now dealing with only partially trained troops, whose training and discipline may not be sufficiently good to enable them to surmount the difficulties of control entailed by an attack in the darkness."[194]

---

194 TNA: WO/95/2370: After-action report, 'Part IV, Narrative Dealing with the Retirement of the 97th Infantry Brigade', 11 December 1917, 32nd Division War Diary. Severe losses amongst junior leadership would often decide the fate of an attack: "There is much to be said for the view that by summer 1917 the 'war was becoming more than ever a platoon commander's war, for it would be on their initiative and determination that success would depend." Nevertheless, prevailing operational circumstances appear to have been beyond the leadership capabilities of some commissioned ranks, Lieutenant Kerr RE (see Chapter 3, p. 230, fn. 156) subsequently claiming that two officers encountered near Void Farm did nothing and had no knowledge of their whereabouts. See A.M. McGilchrist

Shute prefaced his closing summary by observing "that an intercepted German message shews [sic] that an attack by us was expected by the enemy on the night of 1/2nd [December], and that although his frontline of posts had not been manned, his main line of defence had been reinforced, and his machine-guns were ready for our men." Enemy anticipation and consequent augmented vigilance, as opposed to bright moonlight was, therefore, the reason why his machine-guns achieved fire superiority shortly after Zero. "Our attack, therefore, although generally successful in surprising his posts, failed in coming as a surprise to his troops in the main line of defence and this fact made the operation more difficult." The reason for the afternoon retirement "in the face of a not very considerable enemy attack" by such "staunch fighters" as 11th Border Regiment was, Shute remarked, difficult to explain:

> The loss of officers was no doubt a direct cause of their failure. A contributory cause may be that conditions at this time of year are very trying on a man's vitality and that after some hours of fighting in the wet and muddy ground his stamina and powers of resistance are worn out and unless resolute leadership is present he is no condition to withstand further high tests on his endurance.

The remedy for this, he concluded, "is not easy to discover. It may be desirable to relieve the attacking troops a few hours after Zero by fresh troops moving through them. On this occasion this would have been difficult owing to the machine-gun fire. In most operations it would be equally difficult to accomplish owing to the enemy's barrage."[195]

No doubt influenced to some degree by Blacklock's highly critical after-action reports, the GOC 32nd Division's general and specific criticism of collective and individual actions by battalions and battalion commanders appears tainted with censure engendered by a personal stake in the success of the night operation.[196] These controversial views, echoed by the contentious verdict of the subsequent Cambrai enquiry, were also expressed in an existing atmosphere of personal and professional anxiety amongst responsible mid-level commanders over future employment in the aftermath of recent successful German counter-attacks.[197] Shute's observations in regard to

---

op.cit. in Gary Sheffield, 'The Indispensable Factor: The Performance of British Troops in 1918' in Dennis & Grey (eds), *1918*, p. 89 and IWM 4723: 'STATEMENT BY LIEUT. KERR R.E.', Brigadier-General T.S. Lambert Papers (Box 80/10/2).

195 TNA: WO/95/2370: After-action report, 'Part IV, Narrative Dealing with the Retirement of the 97th Infantry Brigade', 11 December 1917, 32nd Division War Diary.

196 See Chapter 4, p. 283.

197 A court of enquiry to investigate German success during the Cambrai counter-attack was convened (Lieutenant-General A. Hamilton Gordon GOC IX Corps presiding) at Hesdin by order of Sir Douglas Haig on 21 January 1918. "In its finding the court was careful to refrain from criticism of the 'higher commanders' and was mainly concerned with reasons why the British forward positions were taken by surprise and why resistance broke down. Whilst displaying some appreciation of their difficulties the tendency was

perceived infantry shortcomings appear to be founded on contemporary concerns about reinforcement training levels.[198] Absorption of new drafts similar to the hapless party of 4 officers and 65 ORs dispatched to 16th HLI on the eve of the Passchendaele night attack or, for that matter, a large reinforcement draft to 2 New Zealand Brigade prior to the Polderhoek Chateau operation,[199] were a constant source of concern throughout 1917, one infantry brigade HQ noting at the height of Third Ypres that 50 percent of brigade commanders had to rely on "short intensive training" to turn new men "into soldiers, as apart from brave men dressed in khaki."[200] New research into the origin, motivations and veracity of these doubts points to senior officer prejudice and a somewhat commonplace propensity for convenient scapegoating when things went awry, compounded by a late 1916 policy whereby drafts were dispatched to the continent for completion of military instruction at base or front. Shute's corollary claim that "little was left undone to ensure each man knowing his part", whilst contradictory in light of his remarks on the behaviour of "untrained troops", may imply adherence to a general policy implemented by Second Army that emphasised "it was more and more evident that greater stress must be laid on training in open warfare to encourage initiative and power of leading in the ranks of junior NCOs and privates, which are so necessary

      still to lay blame on the troops", whose level of training was perceived to be unsatisfactory. Nevertheless, three corps commanders (one by his own volition) went home as a result of Cambrai. Division and brigade commanders of the most affected infantry divisions remained in place. See Miles, *Military Operations: France and Belgium 1917 Vol. 3*, p. 297 and Jeffery Williams, *Byng of Vimy: General and Governor General* (London: Leo Cooper, 1983), pp. 204-08. Special thanks to Andy Lonergan for clarifying the circumstances by which Lieutenant-General Sir Thomas D'Oyly Snow (GOC VII Corps) departed from his post.

198 Lieutenant-Colonel C.G. Fuller (GSO 1 29th Division 1915-17; BGGS III Corps 1917-18), expressing a jaundiced Regular soldier's viewpoint, subsequently observed in a 1938 correspondence with official historian Cyril Falls that the 'British fought the war after 1914 (or say 1915) with almost untrained men, and whenever we had to move, in 1917, and especially in 1918, the troops did not know how to do it, nor did the artillery know how to support them' and as a result there was 'unnecessary slaughter, and non-attainment of objectives.' See Fuller *op.cit.* in Robbins, *British Generalship on the Western Front 1914-1918*, p. 85.

199 See Chapter 3, p. 192, p. 326, fn. 121 below and Fox, "The word 'retire' is never to be used: The performance of the 9th Brigade, AIF, at First Passchendaele, 1917", Australian War Memorial Summer Vacation Scholarship Scheme Research Paper (Canberra: AWM, 2011), p. 9 for similar conclusions in regard to the perceived inexperience of reinforcements.

200 TNA: WO/95/2404: 16th HLI War Diary and '74th Infantry Brigade, Operations 10th, 11th August 1917' quoted in Robbins, *British Generalship on the Western Front 1914-1918*, p. 89.

when officers become casualties."[201] Realisation of such lofty goals would prove almost unattainable with the time available and leadership material provided.[202]

Shute's observation in regard to ineffectual artillery as an "indirect cause" appears valid inasmuch as batteries firing west to east in support of an attack from south to north failed to provide adequate assistance during the afternoon counter-attack.[203] This handicap, engendered by the dearth of available battery sites within the restricted confines of the Passchendaele Salient, curbed gunner capabilities.[204] Alternative heavy and field battery positions due west of Westroosebeke proved, regardless of Herculean efforts to shift guns and supplies east of the Langemarck – Winnipeg Road, inadequate fire support bases from which to engage targeted strongpoints, pillboxes and troop concentrations with sufficient accuracy. Maintaining a steady indirect fire of 50 rounds per minute without overheating, the 128 Vickers machine-guns tasked with carrying out protective barrage and area concentration duties were also found wanting in their nominal role as an effective artillery substitute and force multiplier.[205]

The GOC 32nd Division, it will be recalled, praised RE efforts to improve and extend inadequate overland communications prior to the attack. Lieutenant-Colonel Pollard (CRE) summed up experience gained from an "R.E. POINT OF VIEW" in

---

201 TNA: WO/95/2370: After-action report, 'Part II, Plan of Operations, Section III, Preliminary Measures', 11 December 1917, 32nd Division War Diary, and 'Major-General C.H. Harington, Comments on Operations, 20th Sept. 1917, Second Army', 28 September 1917 quoted in Robbins, *British Generalship on the Western Front 1914-1918*, p. 93.

202 See Appendix XXI for a fresh analysis of the draft training and junior leadership controversies specially prepared for this volume by University of Birmingham colleague Dr Alison Hine.

203 Major Evelegh (CO 32nd Division Signal School) subsequently observed: 'The absence of any continuous wave wireless sets inside of RA OP's made itself seriously felt.' See TNA: WO/95/2370: After-action report: 'Appendix 'I': Communications', December 1917, 32nd Division War Diary.

204 *Fourth Army's* weekly summary observed: 'On the morning of 2.12 strong attacks were launched against the inner flanks of the *Gruppen* accompanied by intense bombardment of about an hour's duration. *Gruppe Staden's* left flank experienced extremely strong destructive fire for a longer period of time … The combat capability of [our?] artillery remains strong. *Gruppe Staden* reported 21 destructive shoots; *Gruppe Ypern* 40. The artillery zone of both *gruppes* was, especially on the inner flanks, under frequent heavy artillery fire, sometimes from heavy calibre weapons. The waves of enemy bombardment came over as strong destructive fire battery positions inclusive…' See KA HKR 145: 'AOK 4 I/a MSO, AHQ 6.12.17, Fiendliche Artillerietätigkeit, Wochenzusammenstellung, Vom 29.11 bis 5.12.17', p. 4.

205 Sixteen designate 'close defence' guns have been deducted from the 144 available. See TNA: WO/95/2370: After-action report: 'Appendix 'H': Action of Machine-guns During Operations near Passchendaele 1st and 2nd December', 32nd Division War Diary and IWM 4723: 'G.188/4/1', 14 December 1917, 'Action December 2, 1917', Brigadier-General T.S. Lambert Papers (Box 80/10/2) for general comments and detailed narrative by Major H.W. Bolton (DMGO 32nd Division), 14th and 188th MG companies respectively.

his lengthy "Report after Operations": Extension of duckboard tracks to the frontline was essential. "If for want of materials this cannot be done [,] tapes or wires should be carried on from the track-heads." RE dumps should be "placed as far forward as possible as long as they are not under direct observation." Pollard concluded by noting the usefulness of tramways for the transport of RE and infantry stores to the forward area. "This line should if possible be kept free of RFA traffic. [A] tramway for RFA to serve as many batteries as possible is of greatest service."[206]

Official historian Sir James Edmonds, commenting on their inherent efficacy, remarked that night attacks are "at least as old" as Gideon's assault on the Midianite encampment.[207] Shute, confronted by seemingly insurmountable tactical circumstances (inability to form up in daylight and a potentially devastating enemy counter-barrage) decided to revert to this age-old method of warfare, "as so many recent attacks had been made at dawn it was decided to risk the inherent dangers of a night attack on a big scale..."[208] Indeed, the Kirke Committee (established in 1932 to examine the lessons of the Great War)[209] subsequently observed that night operations often ensured that elusive tactical surprise was achieved on the far-flung battlefields of 1914-18:

> [T]he increasing use of darkness to cover preliminary movements was a noteworthy feature of all campaigns, whether in trench or open warfare. These were carried out on a large scale and over considerable distances in our eastern campaigns, favoured no doubt by conditions of comparatively good visibility. These same conditions also favoured the attacks by night on difficult objectives, which were a marked characteristic of the latter operations in Palestine and Syria. But the fact that night operations were eventually common to all theatres shows their great importance. And this is natural since without a doubt the automatic small-arm weapon forms the great strength of the modern defensive, and anything that tends to blind it must be to the advantage of the attacker if he is suitably trained. The conclusion is that movements by night may often be the only way of obtaining a tactical surprise, and attack by night the most economical way of crowning it by tactical victory.[210]

---

206 See Chapter 2, pp. 162–63 and IWM 4723: 'A.4/2', 6 December 1917, Brigadier-General T.S. Lambert Papers (Box 80/10/2).
207 Sir J.E. Edmonds, *Military Operations: France and Belgium 1918 Vol. 5* (London: HMSO, 1947), p. 586.
208 TNA: WO/95/2370: After-action report, 'Part II, Plan of Operations, Section I, General', 11 December 1917, 32nd Division War Diary.
209 One of the Kirke Committee's principal members was Major-General and former BGGS 32nd Division A.E. McNamara.
210 Great War Committee, 'Report of the Committee on the Lessons of the Great War (The Kirke Report)', *The British Army Review Special Edition* (April 2001), p. 11. 'In 1933', David French has observed, 'at least three officers who were to rise to very senior command in the Second World War took part in training exercises involving night attacks in which real effort was made to learn the lessons Kirke and his colleagues had

A need for "comparatively good visibility" was almost certainly taken into account when Shute proposed to attack under conditions of bright moonlight. Conditions of total darkness as opposed to optimal half-light would, based on Shute's previous experience, prevent assaulting troops from maintaining desired direction and cohesion whilst traversing the featureless, "cut-up" terrain. Similar demonstrations of this viable operational technique continued well into 1918 when Shute as GOC V Corps oversaw, along with other corps commander counterparts, steady advances during the final "Hundred Days", although these operations, according to Prior and Wilson, were often "continuous and small in scale. Plans were improvised by divisional generals or brigadiers as the situation demanded. Often there was no time to refer these plans to corps commanders, let alone army commanders."[211] The successful application of searchlights ("Monty's Moonlight") to duplicate artificial moonbeams during 1944-45 also attests to the advantage of attacking in semi-darkness provided, as we shall see, corresponding circumstances of atmosphere and terrain are scrutinized. Perhaps Shute, having readily embraced a difficult and dangerous task, should have considered Heneker's recommended contingencies to deal with potential hostile machine-gun fire before Zero + 8. Support for the original scheme without alteration by Jacob and Hunter-Weston further militated against adoption of these reasonable precautions.[212]

"Context and circumstance", Stuart Mitchell notes, played a "big part in Shute's seemingly inconsistent command style."[213] This generally effective but flawed combination of delegation of authority and direct intervention is clearly evident throughout what was 32nd Division's first, as opposed to the open and semi-open operations of the previous spring, set-piece attack under his aegis. Subsequent personal interven-

discovered. In Northern Command, Colonel H.R. Alexander drafted the Command's training instructions and took the report as his keynote. In the Aldershot Command, Brigadier A.P. Wavell's 6 Infantry Brigade practiced night attacks. Whilst in Egypt, Brigadier Frederick Pile and one of his battalion commanders, Lieutenant-Colonel Bernard Montgomery, practiced night operations around the Canal Zone. Perhaps it is not too fanciful to suggest that one of the seeds which was to germinate into the successful Second Battle of Alamein in 1942 was sowed by [Sir J.E.] Edmonds and fertilized by the Kirke Report.' See Edmonds, *Military Operations: France and Belgium 1918 Vol. 5*, p. 586 and David French, '"Official but not History"? Sir James Edmonds and the Official History of the Great War', *RUSI: Royal United Services Institute for Defence Studies Journal*, 131:1 (March 1986), p. 62.

211 Prior & Wilson, *Command on the Western Front*, p. 342. The highly successful night attacks by 64 Brigade (21st Division) on 24 August and V Corps on 23 October 1918 were conducted under Shute's aegis. See Edmonds, *Military Operations: France and Belgium 1918 Vols. 4 & 5*, pp. 242-47 and 362-64 and Peter Simkins, 'Somme Reprise: Reflections on the Fighting for Albert and Bapaume, August 1918' in Bond, et al, *'Look to Your Front'*, pp. 147-62.
212 See Chapter 1, p. 101.
213 Mitchell, 'An Inter-disciplinary Study of Learning in the 32nd Division on the Western Front 1916-18', p. 214.

tions, more often than not based on contradictory and erroneous intelligence gathered while fighting was still in progress, in regard to the situations at Hill 52, Vat Cottages and the proposed counter-attack by 14 Brigade can be interpreted as evidence of "an over-bearing commander who imposed impractical orders upon his subordinates. But this overlooks the context of his interventions and the consultative aspects of his command style; he did pass down direct orders but he also invited criticism, encouraged discussion and modified and shelved plans accordingly."[214] To this insightful analysis must be added the laudable – from a purely military standpoint – determination of a confident and aggressive commander to achieve the task set before him. Failure relative to personal[215] and/or divisional reputation[216] also appears to have been a contributing factor to sporadic GOC interventions associated with the tragic operation that from Mitchell's perspective is the sole "black spot" on the Division record from spring 1917.[217]

Shute's erroneous conclusion that the Passchendaele night operation was compromised prior to Zero was ultimately based on a flawed interpretation of an intercepted wireless message.[218] Thus the attackers, whose intentions and/or movements remained undetected during forming-up, were almost immediately observed whilst advancing into no man's land. That bright moonlight was subsequently recognised as a potential disadvantage to assembling assault troops is clearly demonstrated in a 32nd Division after-action report, which, in summarizing the planning phase of a large-scale raid launched in late February 1918, tellingly observed: "Moonrise on the night of the 27th was at 7:30 p.m. and this gave at least one hour of darkness for the assembling of troops. After 7:30, with the prevailing conditions, it was reasonable to suppose that towards 8 o'clock the light would improve. Zero hour was therefore fixed at 7:52."[219]

---

214 Ibid, p. 216.
215 This speculation appears to be confirmed by the following passage from Shute's regimental obituary: 'During his period in command of 32nd Division, it took part in the following operations: (a) The advance to the Hindenburg Line in the spring of 1917 (b) The operations at Nieuport in the summer of 1917, including the German attack on 10 July (c) The Passchendaele offensive at Ypres in December 1917 (d) The stemming of the German advance, south of Arras, in April 1918. *Every operation (with the exception of Passchendaele in December 1917) undertaken by the 32nd Division during his period of command was successful*' (My emphasis). See Parkyn (ed), *The Rifle Brigade Chronicle for 1936*, pp. 331-32.
216 Lieutenant-Colonel Tweed (late CO 11th Border Regiment) subsequently observed that 'this [32nd] Division has a very high reputation in France …' See TNA: WO/339/21553: Tweed to Military Secretary 27 February 1918, Lieutenant-Colonel Thomas Frederic TWEED. The Lancashire Fusiliers.
217 Mitchell, 'An Inter-disciplinary Study of Learning in the 32nd Division on the Western Front 1916-18', p. 265.
218 See Chapter 3, pp. 203-204, 206, fn. 85.
219 TNA: WO/95/2371: 'Report on Raids South of Houthulst Forest carried out by 32nd Division February 27/28th 1918, Section II: Plan', 32nd Division War Diary. Precautions for dealing with the anticipated full moon were moot, 'as it turned out the weather conditions were unfavourable; the night was cloudy and dark for 2 hours after moonrise

Such precautions, when one considers Heneker's scathing remark concerning the perceived fatal combination of snow, moon and unsuppressed machine-guns on the night of 1/2 December, were taken without due consideration of snow-covered ground as one of three critical foils to achieving surprise. Brigadier-General Aspinall noted on 21 November that the "actual time of Zero will be decided on after trials of the time required for forming-up have been carried out by the divisions concerned."[220] Visibility trials to assess Shute's disputable views on snowfall, bright moonlight and the conspicuousness of advancing infantry at 200 yards distance were, even if feasible, not contemplated in the days leading up to the attack. As former *Wehrmacht* Brigadier-General Alfred Toppe (reflecting on his extensive Second World War experience) astutely observed: "The effect of events taking place at night increases or decreases in proportion to the degree of darkness. Operations taking place during moonlight and starlit nights, especially across snow-covered terrain, may approximate daytime conditions."[221]

Pillbox, winter 1917-18. (*The Outpost*, January 1918)

and a drizzling rain made the going slippery.' The operation, carried out behind a creeping barrage on a two brigade (14 and 96) frontage, was, nevertheless deemed a great success. See Regimental History Committee, *History of the Dorsetshire Regiment 1914-1919 Vol.1*, pp. 114-17 and Major John Ewing MC, *The Royal Scots 1914-1919 Vol. 2* (Edinburgh: Oliver & Boyd, 1925), pp. 550-51.
220 See Chapter 1, p. 96, fn. 196.
221 Brigadier-General Alfred Toppe, *CMH Pub 104-3 Historical Study: Night Combat* (Washington DC: Center of Military History United States Army, 1986), p. 4.

6

Conclusion

6.1 Operational, Strategic & Political Consequences

Post-operation prisoner interrogations and examination of captured documents provided a ready source of intelligence concerning enemy defences, tactics, equipment, organisation, strength, morale and, most importantly to both sides, orders of battle. Information obtained from captive British ORs was often of limited tactical value, as they were purposely kept in "deliberate ignorance about the make-up of their formations, the names of their leaders and military affairs in general."[1] The German private soldier, a GHQ intelligence officer later observed, "knew remarkably little about anything except his own unit in the frontline and rarely had any information about reserve troops in their rear, so it was all very localized information we got from captured prisoners."[2] Nevertheless, "from at least the end of 1915 they [British intelligence officers] sought those that were 'intelligent' and willing to talk … In this respect officers were considered a waste of time because, although intelligent, they would be reluctant to talk. It was felt that the best results came from smart young NCO[s] and intelligent soldiers", who sometimes provided "direct insight into matters

---

1   This was not always the case. For example, *Fourth Army's* weekly report for the period 29 November–5 December observed: 'From a credible statement by a captured British sergeant from 8th Division one will find in and around St Jean (NE Ypres) numerous ammunition dumps …' See Duffy, *Through German Eyes*, p. 42, KA HKR 145: 'AOK 4 I/a MSO, AHQ 6.12.17, Wesentliche Erkungdungsergebnisse, Wochenzusammenstellung, Vom 29.11 bis 5.12.17, p 9 and Appendix XVIII. Examples of British POW interrogation reports during Third Ypres and types of intelligence conveyed by captive officers and ORs are available in BA-MA PH 3/585 and 586: Vernehmungsprotokolle französischer & englischer Kriegsgefangener im Bereich des AOK 4, Bd. 3 Aug.-Sept. and Oct.-Dez. [1917].
2   General James Marshall-Cornwall *op.cit.* in Occelshaw, *Armour Against Fate*, p. 100. Second Army, nevertheless, reckoned in 1917 that POWs were the 'most important of all sources.' See Beach, 'British Intelligence and the German Army, 1914-1918', p. 33.

of strategic importance."³ As probably anticipated, the three German officers captured on 2-3 December appear to have held their tongues. This was not the case with certain astute other ranks like the previously quoted *Feldwebel* of *IR 94*,⁴ who, besides providing a wealth of local intelligence, speculated on future offensives to eliminate the Passchendaele Salient: "There is no talk of any attack developing in this area from the enemy, and it is common rumour that the Battle of Flanders will be forced to die down on account of the condition of the ground … He did not think the enemy would attack, but we (the English) are not to be allowed to advance further along the ridge. There are many troops in the villages and especially in ROULERS for counter-attacking if necessary. All shoulder-straps are covered up, and it is impossible to say what units are seen." A *Gefreiter* of the same regiment corroborated this evidence: "The prisoner knew nothing of an intended attack on a large scale. OSTEND, BRUGES and GHENT are swarming with troops, and it is rumoured that many divisions have been transferred from RUSSIA to the Western Front, but it is not known how many have been transferred to RUSSIA." He also remarked that the general policy was to "advance the present outpost line about 400 metres", while the talkative *Feldwebel* observed: "Trenches near ROULERS [are] being worked on.⁵ They are not deep and wire is not very strong."⁶ Such revelations, when taking the local salient's extreme vulnerability and recent German counter-attacks near Cambrai into consideration, failed to allay the anxieties – expressed along with rapturous terms of endearment to his wife – of Lieutenant-General Hunter-Weston:

> The Army commander has given over the defences of the whole Passchendaele Salient to me. An honour, but a perfectly damnable position to hold. If the Germans think it worthwhile to put in an attack in force on this silly salient, we are, I fear, certain to lose it. However, I'll do my little bit to get the horrid place in the best order possible to safeguard it. I have & have had, many damnable & difficult jobs, and, as someone has to do them, it is just as well it should be me, for I am so happy that if the whole world tumbled about my head & everything

---

3   Beach, 'British Intelligence and the German Army, 1914-1918', pp. 29-30 and 33.
4   See Chapter 3, p. 202.
5   Aerial photographs taken in late November revealed 'a projected line of [German] trenches southwest of Roulers, halfway between the Roulers line and Roulers.' See TNA: WO/157/287: II Corps War Diary and WO/95/643, 'II Corps Summary of Information, 28 November 1917' and 'II Corps Summary of Information, 29 November 1917', II Corps Intelligence File.
6   TNA: WO/157/121 'Annexe to Second Army Summary … Information Obtained from Prisoners', 3 and 5 December 1917, Second Army Intelligence File and WO/157/288: 'II Corps Summary of Information' and attached annexes, 2-5 December 1917, II Corps Intelligence File. VIII Corps summaries for this period are incomplete, although snippets of their contents were duplicated in Second Army and II Corps intelligence reports.

went wrong (which, by God's help, it shall not do here) I shall still be a happy and contented man in the possession of your wonderous [sic] love… [7]

Sir Douglas Haig convened an army commanders' conference at Doullens on 7 December. "The main topic was the organisation of our defensive lines in view of the Russians having dropped out of the war. This will allow the Germans to employ some 30 more divisions on this front. These can be brought here at a rate of 8 to 10 per month if the Enemy so will it."[8] Sir Henry Rawlinson remarked on the potential threat of these substantial enemy reinforcements the following day: "Things are pretty quiet now here in Flanders but at Cambrai it looks as if there were going to be trouble for the Bosch has 34 div. concentrated there – and may try Passchendaele simultaneously – I think he means to have a jolly good go at us somewhere and I am anxious about this P[asschendaele] salient."[9] That the worrying strategic situation also put paid to any further discussion of a Flanders spring offensive was made clear during a Second Army conference on 9 December:

> The collapse of Russia would enable Germany to withdraw divisions from the Eastern Front. No large movement has so far commenced but there were indications that it might begin shortly. The rate of withdrawal can be calculated at from 8 to 10 divisions per month, so that, at this rate, the enemy will be able to increase his force on the Western Front up to the end of March 1918 by some 30 to 40 divisions. In view of the above facts, and taking into consideration the question of manpower, which at present is unsatisfactory, and the probability that America will not be able to put large forces into the field in the near future, there must be a period of five or six months when the enemy will be in preponderance

---

7   BL: 48366: Letter facsimile to Lady Hunter-Weston, Hunter-Weston Diary, 3 December 1917, Vol. XII. Hunter-Weston, unhappy about the burden of sole responsibility for the salient, contemplated resignation before receiving a certain amount of verbal support from a seemingly sympathetic Rawlinson. A subsequent meeting with Sir Douglas Haig provided the opportunity for the anxious GOC VIII Corps to state his case. He would later preside over the abandonment – a collateral consequence of the on-going Battle of the Lys (9-29 April 1918) – of the Passchendaele Salient. See Hunter-Weston Diary, 18 December 1917, Haig diary entry 19 December 1917 in 'The First World War Political, Social and Military Manuscript Sources: Series One: The Haig Papers from the National Library of Scotland, Part I Haig's Autograph Great War Diary', Reel 5 and Sheffield & Bourne (eds), *Douglas Haig*, p. 361. For Hunter-Weston's characteristically egocentric account of this episode see Appendix XV.
8   Haig diary entry 7 December 1917 in 'The First World War Political, Social and Military Manuscript Sources: Series One: The Haig Papers from the National Library of Scotland, Part I Haig's Autograph Great War Diary', Reel 5 and Sheffield & Bourne (eds), *Douglas Haig*, p. 358. *Sixteen* German divisions were transferred from east to west during December 1917. See John Hussey, 'The Movement of German Divisions to the Western Front, Winter 1917-1918', *War in Society*, Volume 4, Number 2 (April 1997) p. 219.
9   CAC: RWLN 1/9: Rawlinson Diary, 8 December 1917.

on the Western Front. Therefore, we must look, during this period, to a defensive rather than an offensive policy. Consequently, although the basis of the policy adopted heretofore on the Army front has been the resumption of the offensive in the spring, it is now clear such an offensive is not feasible.[10]

All of this begs the question, was it necessary to launch another operation from the dangerously exposed salient?[11] The apparent lack of any tangible gain caused one regimental historian to observe: "It has been difficult to find any reason why the operation about to be described ever took place."[12] The few recent historians who comment on this episode have been equally dismissive of a seemingly "futile" two-division attack on "meaningless fragments of trench, barbed wire and pillboxes..."[13] Such retrospective judgments, whatever their merit, fail to recognise the larger complex interaction of pressing (dire need for adequate observation facilities and overall tenability of the Passchendaele Salient) strategic/operational determinants, contemporary tactical methodologies, technological capabilities and on-going manpower deficiencies *vis à vis* their relation to the totality of Third Ypres and its uncertain military and political aftermath.

The formation of a salient is never desirable, "as there is too much of a threat that the other side will find a way to pinch it off. Additionally, the enemy can concentrate

---

10   LHCMA: 'Proceedings of a Conference held at Second Army Headquarters at 11 a.m., 9 December 1917', Montgomery-Massingberd Papers, File 7/16, King's College, London.
11   Second Army's subsequent war diary entry briefly summarised the night operation as follows: 'At an early hour our troops attacked north of PASSCHENDAELE. As a result of the fighting a small advance was made north of GOUDBERG COPSE and east of VINDICTIVE CROSSROADS. At one time our troops were reported to have advanced up to the southern end of VEAL COTTAGES – MALLET COPSE – VOID FARM, and to have held HILL 52, TEALL COTTAGE and the SOUTHERN REDOUBT in W.25.c. Counter-attacks, however, forced our troops back to certain points with the result that the line runs approximately – TOURNANT FARM – V.28.b.6.7. – V.29.a.0.7. – V.29.a.6.5. – north of VOX FARM – south of HILL 52 – south of TEALL COTTAGE – V.30.b.6.2. – V.30.b.9.0. – W.25.c.1.5. – W.25.c.3.2. – to original frontline. During these operations 3 officers, 126 other ranks and 3 machine-guns were captured. The reply to our barrage came down eight minutes after zero and was heavy on our front and support lines. Further hostile barrages were put down at 5:20 a.m. and 6:55 a.m. There was a heavy concentration against PASSCHENDAELE from 8:20 to 9:30 a.m. Hostile fire became intense during the afternoon in the area of operations in support of counter-attacks and throughout the day our battery positions near LANGEMARCK, in the STEENBEEK VALLEY and around KANSAS CROSSROADS were intermittently shelled.' See LHCMA: Second Army War Diary, Montgomery-Massingberd Papers, File 7/16, King's College, London. Similar operational summaries by VIII and II corps HQs exist in BL: 48359: 'VIII Corps Official War Diary with Appendices and Addenda', Hunter-Weston Papers, Vol. V and TNA: WO/95/643: II Corps War Diary.
12   Latter, *The History of the Lancashire Fusiliers in Two Volumes Vol. 1*, p. 275.
13   Prior & Wilson, *Command on the Western Front*, p. 273, Stedman, *Salford Pals*, p. 156 and Moore, *See How They Ran*, p. 31.

fire in the area of the salient at will."¹⁴ From 4 October, Second Army attempted a strategic breakthrough that devolved into a series of post-strategic assaults aimed at securing the northern portion of Passchendaele Ridge before winter set in. These successive drives, culminating in the attack on 10 November, resulted in a lamentably exposed bulge that was to worry the British high command throughout the first quarter of 1918. All thoughts of further local offensives put on hold following the Polderhoek Chateau operation,¹⁵ British GHQ issued (13 December) special instructions – "one of the most remarkable documents which ever emanated from a victorious staff" a cynical Lloyd George would later observe – ¹⁶ outlining measures to be taken by Second and Third armies for the defence of the Passchendaele and Flesquières¹⁷ salients: "Here it was decided that the front of the Battle Zone should be approximately the base of the salient, leaving all in front of it in the Forward Zone", which, in the event of a serious German attack, would be held chiefly by machine-guns protected by supporting artillery and ample placement of barbed

---

14   Brown, *British Logistics on the Western Front 1914-1919*, p. 172. Pre-war FSR stated: 'Salients and advanced posts which are held to deny ground to the enemy, and not merely as a screen to the main position, are a weakness if they are exposed to artillery fire which cannot be answered, and if they cannot be supported by effective infantry fire. As a general rule such positions had better be left unoccupied, and the ground between them and the main position be defended either by bringing a crossfire on to it from other parts of the position or by strong entrenchments, which are within supporting distance.' See War Office, *Field Service Regulations Part I*, p. 145.
15   IX Corps reclaimed the Polderhoek Chateau sector from II ANZAC Corps on 4 December. Though of 'distinct advantage' to the local garrison, New Zealand gains 150 yards east of the chateau grounds failed to 'effect an appreciable improvement with regard to the exposed slopes of Cameron Covert, Reutel and Polygon Wood, where protection from the Polderhoek fire would have to be won by the labour of the spade.' Nine days later (14 December), *IR162* of *17th Reserve Division* recaptured the territory overlooking the Scherriabeek valley. Rawlinson wrote afterwards: 'This morning at 5:45 a.m. the Bosch attacked our position at Polderhoek Chateau with a batt. and succeeded in driving some of the 30th Div. from the southern part of our frontline. Our left company held on well and drove off the enemy with loss but the two co [mpanies] on the right were forced back to the support line 100 yards in rear – It is possible the Bosch may press his attack further so as to gain observation.' Stewart, *The New Zealand Division 1914-1919*, p. 314 and CAC: RWLN 1/9: Rawlinson Diary, 14 December 1917. A scheme to regain the lost territory after Christmas was subsequently cancelled. See Brigadier-General F.C. Stanley, *The History of the 89th Brigade 1914-1918* (Liverpool: 'Daily Post' Printers, 1919), pp. 241-42.
16   David Lloyd George, *War Memoirs Vol. 2* (London: Odhams Press abridged edition, 1937), p. 1325. The ex-Prime Minister also remarked in a further display of accusatory excoriation, 'I need hardly say that this document was withheld from the War Cabinet', although contemporary maps illustrating positions at Passchendaele or Flesquières were certainly available to an enquiring chief executive and his government colleagues.
17   The development of the equally exposed Flesquières Salient was one of the melancholy consequences of the Battle of Cambrai. See Miles, *Military Operations: France and Belgium 1917 Vol. 3*, pp. 267-68.

wire obstacles.[18] This reasoned response to the appalling tactical circumstances was ultimately based on hardheaded consideration of the key (general withdrawal to a more defensible line) issue raised in Aspinall's "Appreciation" of November 1917. Lieutenant-General Kiggell (CGS GHQ) subsequently observed in an order dated 10 January 1918:

1. The policy as regards the defence of the PASSCHENDAELE Salient in the event of a hostile offensive in that neighborhood has been described in O.A.D. 291/29 dated 13 December 1917.[19] The question of shortening our line by a voluntary withdrawal north-east of Ypres, which under exceptional circumstances may become advisable, should also be considered and the necessary plans for such an operation worked out.
2. In this connection it is necessary to bear in mind that there are strong moral and political, as well as military objections to a voluntary withdrawal from Passchendaele. Such a move could, therefore, by the general situation necessitating the strongest possible reinforcement on some other part of the front, in which case the order for withdrawal would be issued from GHQ.[20]

Attention to aforementioned pressing operational determinants and the resultant night attack appear, with the benefit of hindsight, to have been irrelevant in light of subsequently adopted defensive policy. Nevertheless, the capture and retention of Venison Trench, Hill 52 and Vat Cottages Ridge could have resulted in a serious local setback for the German defenders. Loss of the former position and its conjoined redoubts would have provided Second Army with an extended panoramic view (from Broodseinde to NE of Passchendaele village) of the enemy-occupied hinterland west of Roulers, while the seizure of Hill 52 (which dominated the triangle Westroosebeke – Vindictive Crossroads – Oostnieuwkerke and nearby hostile battery positions) and Vat Cottages Ridge (overlooking low-lying enemy positions to the north and NW) would have secured the northern shoulder of the salient. Rawlinson acutely articulated his disappointment over the failure to even achieve these limited objectives, thereby emphasising the perceived importance of the night attack as a carefully considered attempt to improve a "defective, not to say dangerous" position following the post-strategic phase that officially ended with the Second Battle of Passchendaele,

---

18 Edmonds, *Military Operations: France and Belgium 1918 Vol. 1*, pp. 41-43. The 'Forward Zone' coincided with the existing front system, while the 'Battle Zone' (two or three miles behind) was sited on the best ground available to give battle. A 'Rear Zone' (two to eight miles in rear of the Battle Zone) was to be constructed as additional labour became available. See C.E.W. Bean, *The Australian Imperial Force in France 1918 Vol. V.* (Sydney: Angus & Robertson, 1943), pp. 35-36.
19 See Appendix XIV.
20 TNA: WO/158/210: 'OAD 745', 10 January 1918, Fourth Army Operations File. Second Army became 'Fourth Army' on 20 December 1917.

in a memorandum dated 10 December: "Nothing we can hope to do can make the line now held a really satisfactory defensive position. We must therefore be prepared to withdraw from it, if the Germans show signs of a serious and sustained offensive on this front, or if an attack elsewhere necessitates the withdrawal of more troops from the front of Second Army."[21]

No doubt perceived by contemporaries as a "dud" or "bad show", the night operation on the Passchendaele Ridge can also be viewed, irrespective of apparent failure, as indicative of a bite and hold "style of attack" (adopted from September 1917) where "army merely passed to corps an outline of what it had to do, and corps organised the whole operation, delegating to divisions as necessary."[22] Pre-assault tactical preparations and organisation prior to this last – albeit unofficial – large-scale formulaic attack of the campaign were further expedited by general adherence to relevant sections of *S.S. 135 Instructions for the Training of Divisions for Offensive Action*.[23] This was especially true in regard to the all-important logistical arrangements: Light railways, corduroy roads and duckboard tracks were maintained and extended with satisfactory results. Supply dumps along with vital artillery assets, moved forward regardless of almost unimaginable battlefield conditions, were also in place before zero hour on 2 December. Counter-battery work by HAGs (a corps artillery asset), according to a II Corps intelligence summary, was "exceptionally successful."[24] The accuracy of this conclusion is, when considering aerial observation was "impossible owing to the high winds", prevailing poor visibility and mist, on-going sound ranging and flash spotting complications, frequent shifting of hostile guns, manipulation by the enemy of dummy batteries and the subsequent intense preparatory bombardment experienced before the 4:15 p.m. counter-attack, difficult to substantiate. Perhaps a general comparative perception that the "enemy's artillery activity was not intense, and it was certainly far less heavy than on our attack of the 10th November",[25] appeared to confirm the overall effectiveness of the recently adopted pre-assault artillery programme (Second Army Artillery Instructions No. 28) notwithstanding acute absence of the usual

21 Prior & Wilson, *Command on the Western Front*, pp. 273-74.
22 Andy Simpson, 'British Corps Command on the Western Front, 1914-1918' in Sheffield & Todman (eds), *Command and Control on the Western Front*, p. 115.
23 'Large-scale' when compared with the number of battalions participating in post-strategic Anglo-Canadian operations from 26 October to 10 November: 26 October (34 battalions); 30 October (12¼ battalions); 6 November (10 battalions); 10 November (11 battalions), 2 December (10 battalions). The Polderhoek Chateau attack (3 December) was carried out by two battalions. See General Staff, *S.S. 135 Instructions for the Training of Divisions for Offensive Action* (December 1916) and Chris McCarthy, *Passchendaele: The Day-by-Day Account* (London: Arms & Armour Press, 1996), pp. 125-39.
24 TNA: WO/157/288: 'II Corps Summary of Information', 2 December 1917, II Corps Intelligence File.
25 Ibid and TNA: WO/95/643: 'Daily Artillery Report: From Noon 1/12/17 to Noon 2/12/17', II Corps War Diary

battle-proven air-artillery co-operation component.²⁶ Nevertheless, these relatively positive developments must be considered along with elements (attacking on a narrow front and problematic division of corps-level authority) of what appear to be operational and administrative bad practice.

Adoption of a narrow attack frontage astride firmer ground within the Passchendaele Salient was, given prevailing swampy conditions west of the main ridge opposite Poelcappelle and its environs, clearly unavoidable in early December 1917. Formation of the salient during Plumer's successive attacks in October and November was a deplorable operational outcome inherited by Rawlinson and his staff. The new GOC Second Army, lacking final authority to withdraw from strategically valuable high ground, deemed one more attack necessary in order to improve an unsatisfactory local situation. Having duly sanctioned the hybrid assault scheme, designated objectives lying between 100 and 700 yards beyond the jumping-off line were not considered at army or corps level to be beyond the attacker's capabilities when compared with measurable Canadian success (two bounds of 500 yards on similarly restricted frontages)²⁷ against more formidable German defences on 6 and 10 November.²⁸ With a fortnight (18 November–1 December) available for planning and preparation, the expectation was not considered unreasonable. Division of corps responsibilities inside the limited confines of the salient resulted from the maintenance (with some minor adjustments before 2 December) of previously established Second Battle of Passchendaele formation boundaries.²⁹ Perhaps, when taking into account subsequent relegation of responsibility to VIII Corps, Second Army should have contemplated turning over the entire salient to II Corps (tasked with overseeing the most difficult part of the operation) prior to the attack. Administrative and organisational aspects would, no doubt, have been rendered more efficiently by having one corps provide operational oversight instead of two.³⁰

26   VIII and II corps carried out 5 and 2 specified counter-battery programmes respectively during the period 22 November-1 December. RFC counter-battery work was highly rated throughout Third Ypres. During the summer Battle of Langemarck (16-18 August), 67% of missions were classified as 'faultless', while 33% varied from 'adequate to poor. Although such percentages would vary from area to area, depending on local factors (strength of enemy opposition, weather conditions while observing), it is still fair to say that the variations would not be great between brigades.' See BL: 48359: 'VIII Corps Official War Diary with Appendices and Addenda', Hunter-Weston Papers, Vol. V, TNA: WO/95/643: II Corps War Diary and Jordan, 'The Army Co-operation Missions of the Royal Flying Corps/Royal Air Force 1914-1918', p. 200.
27   Flank attacks on neighbouring Fifth Army's front were discontinued after 30 October. See Prior & Wilson, *Passchendaele*, p. 177.
28   A dearth of available concrete pillboxes remained a significant drawback to German defenders following the breach of in-depth positions (where *Flandern I* and *Flandern II* lines intersected) during October-November 1917. See Appendix XVI Part A (paras. 13 and 31), Part B (para. 5), Part C (para. 5) and Part F (para. 6).
29   See TNA: WO/95/643: II Corps and WO/95/821: VIII Corps war diaries.
30   Captain Guy Chapman, writing of a vulnerable salient held by his division near Bucquoy in April 1918, observed: 'In defiance of all the rules laid down by FSR, and other

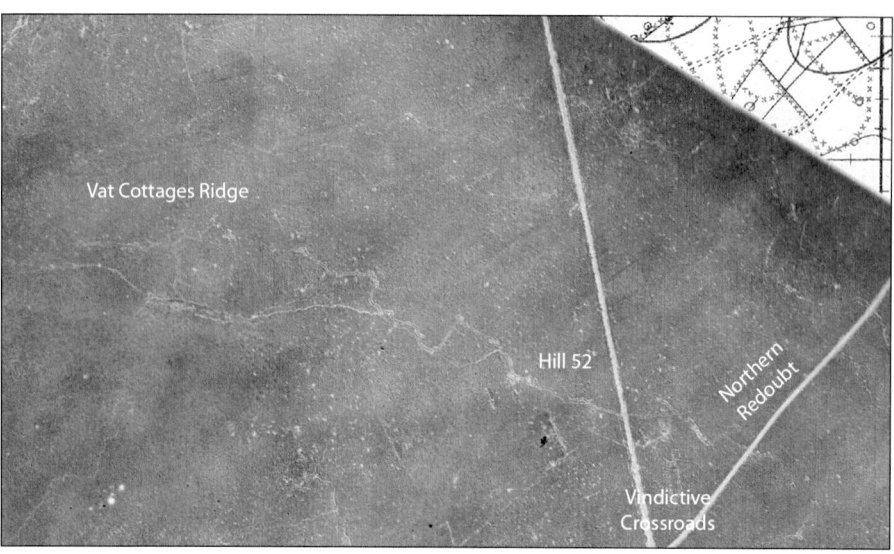

Area north and NW of Passchendaele January 1918.
(Memorial Museum Passchendaele 1917)

Sir Douglas Haig's overall position had, by the winter of 1917-18, eroded considerably as growing pessimism amongst Great Britain's policy-making elite appeared to be confirmed by the inconclusive results of Third Ypres and Cambrai. Preparations for the former offensive had been "accompanied by fierce struggles in Whitehall between the War Office and civil departments" over manpower resources, "which grew in intensity as the phases of the offensive unfolded. In effect the character of the British war effort underwent a transformation in which the military dimension became part of a more integrated and, eventually, transnational [i.e. establishment of a Supreme War Council] war effort." This state of affairs, hastened by a "political response to the final phase and immediate aftermath of Passchendaele", manifested itself in virulent partisan press campaigns, acrimonious Parliamentary debate and bitter civil-military contention that left Haig at a distinct disadvantage in the months leading up to the anticipated German

> authorities that a salient should be held all around by one unit, the apex of this one was the dividing line between battalions, brigades, divisions and, for all I know, corps. In the agitation of the [March] retreat, the higher command appeared to have abandoned even the most rudimentary principles.' Perusal of contemporary FSR reveals the following axiom: 'When a position is extensive it should be divided into sections, each of which should be *assigned to a distinct unit* (My emphasis).' Chapman's interpretation, when one considers the Passchendaele Salient as a distinct part of Second Army's 29,000-yard front, is, as intimated, likely further substantiated by contemporary authoritative sources or generally accepted practice. See Chapman, *A Passionate Prodigality*, p. 240 and War Office, *Field Service Regulations Part I*, p. 142.

spring offensive.³¹ It is in this context of political doubt and despondency, recognised dwindling manpower assets and consequences of conducting simultaneous operations at Cambrai and Passchendaele that the night attack will now be evaluated.

The desire to clear the Belgian coast in spring 1918 remained Sir Douglas Haig's chief strategic priority as 1917 drew to a close. Indeed, as late as 7 January – during a War Cabinet meeting ostensibly convened to discuss the current state of BEF defences and French demands to take responsibility for forty miles of front south of the Somme – he expostulated that the next four months would be the "critical period of the war" and that the "best defence" in anticipation of a major enemy offensive "would be to continue our offensive in Flanders, because we would retain the initiative and attract German reserves against us."³² Two and a half months earlier, on 13 October 1917, "when it was evident that no visible success would soon come to British arms in Flanders, the Field Marshal approved preliminary preparations for an operation designed to restore British prestige and strike a theatrical blow against Germany before the winter set in."³³ This often overlooked aspect of the "first great tank battle" implies political motive for some sort of tangible Western Front victory, albeit without the glittering strategic prospects offered farther north, as an obvious foil to alternative strategic options then under consideration by the Lloyd George government. In the meantime, Second Army prepared to carry out phase one of a projected "advance north of PASSCHENDAELE to include HILL 52 and SPRIET to north of POELCAPPELLE", which would, along with other contemplated attacks, "facilitate the initial stages of a possible general offensive operation in the spring."³⁴ Thus Haig, with one strategic eye still fixed on Flanders, oversaw Third Army's preparations for the Cambrai battle. One suspects that the Passchendaele night operation would, considering the close downhill proximity of Roulers and embryonic state of its western defences,³⁵ have received more support

31 Millman, *Pessimism and British War Policy 1916-1918*, pp. 92-108, Keith Grieves, 'The "Recruiting Margin" in Britain: Debates on Manpower during the Third Battle of Ypres' in Liddle (ed), *Passchendaele in Perspective*, p. 24, J. Lee Thompson, *Northcliffe: Press Baron in Politics 1865-1922* (London: John Murray, 2000), p. 294 and House of Commons, *The Parliamentary Debates: Official Report, Fifth Series – Volume 101* (London: HMSO, 1918), columns 2247-2251 for Commander Josiah Wedgwood's (MP Newcastle-under-Lyme) spirited criticism of the recent Flanders offensive.
32 Haig diary entry 7 January 1918 in 'The First World War Political, Social and Military Manuscript Sources: Series One: The Haig Papers from the National Library of Scotland, Part I Haig's Autograph Great War Diary', Reel 6 and Robert Blake (ed), *The Private Papers of Douglas Haig 1914-1919* (London: Eyre & Spottiswoode, 1952), pp. 277-78.
33 Paul Guinn, *British Strategy and Politics 1914 to 1918* (Oxford: Clarendon Press, 1965), pp. 271-72.
34 LHCMA: 'Second Army No. 57 (G), Organisation of Army Front During Winter of 1917-18', 18 November 1917, Montgomery-Massingberd Papers, File 7/15, King's College, London. See Chapter 1, pp. 61-62.
35 See TNA: WO/157/287: II Corps War Diary and WO/95/643, 'II Corps Summary of Information, 28 November 1917' and 'II Corps Summary of Information, 29 November 1917', II Corps Intelligence File

German cartoon: The British Lion "After sixteen Flanders battles, At least they have left me my growl." (*Simplicissimus*, 1 January 1918)

but for GHQ's commitment to a triumphal prestige offensive before 1917 reached its indeterminate and bloody conclusion. Haig's subsequent insistence that costly Cambrai attacks be maintained after all prospects of success vanished need only concern us in relation to recognised manpower deficits, expectations that the BEF would, in addition to dispatching 5 of 62 infantry divisions to Italy, take over a sizeable portion of French line as far as the Oise and such extraneous operational schemes contrived to improve the overall position in Flanders before year's end.

Manpower shortages became a major cause for concern at GHQ as Third Ypres progressed into its first full month, Sir Douglas Haig informing his senior staff in late August that in order to maintain the flow of drafts it would be "necessary that every service and department should immediately give up every man who is in any way likely, by training, to become fit for service in the ranks of the infantry" if final victory were to be achieved by December.³⁶ The reinforcement outlook did not improve, as Whitehall's commitment, Keith Grieves has observed, to a "frontline 62 division force in France, comprising 680,861 rifles, was thoroughly undermined by news of the battles in the second phase of the offensive which started on 28 August and continued through Menin Road Ridge, Polygon Wood and Broodseinde into the first week of October." The last appalling phase, which Lloyd George and his cabinet colleagues all but sanctioned despite extreme doubts of a favourable outcome,³⁷ culminating in the capture of Passchendaele, also "marked the end of the government's commitment to the "large army first" principle as its confidence in Haig's purpose in the Ypres salient was progressively undermined." War Cabinet fears that a "resilient, stoical home front might not withstand the costly and disillusioning outcomes of these continuous battles became of more urgent concern." By December, the same month that manpower allocation was formally referred to in Cabinet committee, replacement drafts were arriving on the continent at a rate of just 180 men per day.³⁸

---

36 Haig diary entry 19 August 1917 in 'The First World War Political, Social and Military Manuscript Sources: Series One: The Haig Papers from the National Library of Scotland, Part I Haig's Autograph Great War Diary', Reel 5 and Sheffield & Bourne (eds), *Douglas Haig*, p. 319. Comb-outs of rear echelon service personnel had mixed results. An officer of the 6th Cameron Highlanders subsequently recollected the poor performance of dispatched base and lines of communication details, along with disparate elements from other regiments, during an assault near Frezenberg in late August: 'The attack on 23 August [sic 22 August] in many places was a complete fiasco. Some men flatly refused to go over the top, saying they were not going to fight under officers they'd never seen, and in strange units; that their commanders were deceiving them and that no breakthrough was possible. Some men lay down and refused to move, others arranged with their pals to shoot each other in cushy parts in the first shell hole. The troops had been bluffed and they knew it.' See Colonel A.F.P. Christison *op.cit.* in Peter Scott, 'Law and Order: Discipline and Morale in the British Armies in France, 1917' in Liddle (ed), *Passchendaele in Perspective*, pp. 357-58.
37 See Prior & Wilson, *Passchendaele*, pp. 151-155 and 185-89 for War Cabinet 'inaction' and the final phase of Third Ypres.
38 Grieves, The 'Recruiting Margin' in Britain: Debates on Manpower during the Third Battle of Ypres' in Liddle (ed), *Passchendaele in Perspective*, p. 395 and Edmonds, *Military Operations: France and Belgium 1918 Vol. I*, p. 50. The controversy over manpower is further complicated by Lloyd George's later assertion that the War Office 'decided whether or not to allocate men to machine-gun units, the tank corps, etc., rather than the infantry…' David Woodward, nonetheless, concludes that 'throughout 1917 Lloyd George had resisted giving the army all the recruits it requested. To a considerable degree his motive had been to force Haig, albeit unsuccessfully, to economise his losses.' Moreover, a 'structural manpower problem', unrecognised by Lloyd George and Sir Douglas Haig, had an overall negative impact on 'Logistico-Engineering' efforts throughout Third Ypres: 'The former was interested in cutting infantry establishments based on manipulation of manpower figures, whilst the latter still thought in terms of combat infantry.' See Woodward, *Lloyd George and the Generals*, p. 290 and Thompson, 'Mud, Blood and Wood' in Doyle & Bennett (eds), *Fields of Battle*, p. 252.

Was Sir Douglas Haig wise to sanction the night operation given prevailing strategic and political circumstances? Over three-quarters of the Passchendaele Ridge had been secured during three and a half months campaigning. The prospect of a relatively modest offensive toward Roulers in spring 1918 offered an enticingly close strategic prize just beyond reach. Overall feasibility of this paper scheme, of which the hybrid two-division attack on 2 December was a notable preliminary, is debatable. The highly unsatisfactory supply and overland communications infrastructure – unrelentingly harassed by German artillery – east of Ypres may or may not have been sufficiently developed in time for another offensive, but that is by the way when considering consequent political backlash and husbanding of Great Britain's vital manpower resources.[39] The writing, insofar as manpower appropriation and GHQ's future Western Front strategy are concerned, was already on the wall by the autumn of 1917 if not earlier. Determined that his strategic vision for 1918 would ultimately prevail, one has to consider in hindsight the British field marshal's wisdom in ordering a large-scale subsidiary night attack that was, to "economise troops" and avoid getting "involved in anymore unnecessary fighting", terminated within ten hours of Zero.[40] The 1,689 combined casualties sustained by 8th and 32nd divisions may seem a drop in the bucket when compared with 733,308 total estimated killed, wounded and missing from 9 April to 31 December.[41] It remains nonetheless, in light of the political fallout engendered by the BEF's staggering losses and subsequent unpropitious strategic circumstances as 1917 drew to a close, questionable that two relatively

---

39 Prevailing supply and communication difficulties were, given the poor state of the battlefield and almost continuous hostile bombardments, often overcome with remarkable results: 'The perfecting of these [corduroy roads and duckboard tracks] communications was jealously guarded by Lieutenant-General Hunter-Weston, KCB, DSO, the [VIII] Corps Commander, himself an officer of the Royal Engineers. Under enormous difficulties he succeeded in establishing a "Decauville Track" from Ypres to Crest Farm, upon which ran an almost regular service of trains consisting of six to eight open trucks driven by a miniature motor engine. Undoubtedly this railway not only saved many lives, but owing to the stealth with which it moved, and the "shell-craft", which is indeed a science, of the drivers, the little trains completed their daily journeys almost without mishap. In fact, the relief train became [sic] to be known as the "Passchendaele Express".' Whether or not such achievements would have constituted the logistical basis for a resumed Flanders offensive remains questionable. See Hutchison, *The Thirty-Third Division in France and Flanders 1915-1919*, p. 77.
40 TNA: WO/158/209: Brigadier-General J.H. Davidson hand-written note (3 December 1917), Second Army Operations File.
41 BEF casualties (killed, wounded and missing) for the April to December 1917 period covering Arras, Messines, Third Ypres and Cambrai were: 9 April-6 June: 178,416; 7 June-30 July: 103,505; 31 July-19 September: 129,706; 20 September-31 December (losses sustained during the Passchendaele night operation inclusive): 250,296; 20 November-31 December (Battle of Cambrai): 71,385 or 733,308 total. See War Office, *Statistics of the Military Effort of the British Empire During the Great War 1914-1920* (London: HMSO, 1922), pp. 325-27.

full-strength and rested infantry divisions should have been employed in a somewhat risky and ultimately barren "local operation" as the crisis of the war fast approached.[42]

The near fatal consequences of all this would be amply demonstrated during the coming year. In the meantime, life in the squalid and dangerous Passchendaele Salient continued along the same lines as before. Gazing across no man's land at dawn on 1 January 1918, Captain Hubert Essame (2nd Northamptonshire Regiment) poignantly recollected a stricken winter prospect littered with unburied dead and discarded equipment opposite enemy-occupied Venison Trench:

> Shell hole intersected shell hole, often containing the ghastly remains of a soldier fallen in the attacks of late November and early December. Around here their shoulder patches showed them to be mainly Royal Berkshires, Lincolns and Rifle Brigade. Defiled with mud and slime they lay huddled on their faces, their equipment still on their backs, their rifles with bayonet fixed still in their hands, their faces almost as if they were asleep. British and German steel helmets, petrol tins, sandbags of jettisoned rations and coke, mingled with the abandoned equipment of the wounded, littered the landscape particularly along the dirty white tapes laid out to show the way to the frontline.[43]

6.2 Costs

Subsequent battalion and company roll-calls, supported by eyewitness accounts and enquiries, established approximate first casualty returns for both divisions. 8th Division's losses for 2-3 December were estimated at 40 officers and 584 ORs, 2nd Royal Berkshire Regiment suffering the most with 154 killed, wounded and missing. 2nd Lincolnshire Regiment and 2nd Rifle Brigade trailed slightly behind with 130 casualties each. 1st RIR lost 91 men, whilst 25 Brigade's supporting machine-gun company and TM battery lost 16 and 12 respectively. Additional losses, besides 1 officer attached to 25 Brigade HQ: 23 Brigade (21), 24 Brigade (37) and component RFA, MGC and RAMC units (32) increased total reported casualties to 624 officers and men.[44] Added to the number

---

42 The British Empire was, in the long run, capable of absorbing its excessive manpower losses better than Imperial Germany, although this was not evident at the time. It could be argued that Haig's 1917 strategy was partially based on the BEF's staying power *vis à vis* the *Westheer* in that a failed risk (i.e., heavy casualties without achieving final victory) as opposed to an outright gamble with the Empire's reinforcement pool, could be followed by sustainable recovery. Conversely, 'the German citizen army, the reservists and wartime conscripts, was eviscerated at Passchendaele.' Lloyd George and the War Cabinet would, of course, arrive at a different conclusion in the immediate aftermath of Third Ypres and Cambrai. See Dennis Showalter, 'Passchendaele' in Dennis Showalter (ed), *History in Dispute Volume 8: World War I* (Detroit: St James Press, 2004), p. 224.
43 H. Essame, *The Battle for Europe 1918* (London: B.T. Batsford, 1972), pp. 5-6.
44 Boraston & Bax, *The Eighth Division*, p. 167.

Passchendaele Ridge late December 1917: 2nd East Lancashire Regiment officers in the salient. (Lancashire Infantry Museum)

of verified deaths for 2nd Royal Berkshire Regiment (36), 2nd Lincolnshire Regiment (18), 2nd Rifle Brigade (25) and 1st RIR (6) were 141 infantrymen recorded as missing.

Table A[45]

	Killed		Wounded		Missing		Total
	Officers	Other ranks	Officers	Other ranks	Officers	Other ranks	
8th DIVISION							
25 Brigade							
Bde HQ			1(b)				1
2 Lincs	1	17	11	56		45	130
2 R Berks	1	35	3	73	2	40	154
1 RIR		6	3	55	1(c)	26	91
2 RB	3	22	7	71		27	130
MGC		4	2	10			16
TM Batt.		5		7			12
24 Brigade							
1 Worcs				2		1	3
2 E.Lancs		1		2			3
2 Northants		1					1
MGC		6	3	21			30
23 Brigade							
MGC		6		15(a)			21
RFA			1	5			6
MGC		7	1	8(d)			16
FA RAMC		2		8(e)			10
Total	5	112	32	333	3	139	624

Note: (a) 2 ORs at duty (b) At duty (c) Wounded and missing (d) 1 OR at duty (e) 5 ORs at duty.

Their ultimate fate can be deduced by examination of available CWGC data, which lists 173 gravesites and commemorations for the four battalions of 25 Brigade during the period 30 November-3 December as follows: 2nd Royal Berkshire Regiment (49), 2nd Lincolnshire Regiment (52), 2nd Rifle Brigade (44) and 1st RIR (28). To this figure should be added 12 men from attached MGC and RAMC units and 12 infantry who died of wounds (3 in captivity) seven days after 3 December.[46] Thus 8th Division's losses amounted, by adding the combined adjusted figure of 197 men killed/missing/DOW with the reported 365 wounded minus 10 (9 infantry[47] and 1 RAMC) men

---

45 TNA: WO/95/1677: 'Appendix 'J' 8th Division: Casualties – 2nd/3rd December 1917, Narrative of Operations Carried Out by the 8th Division on 1st/2nd December 1917', 13 December 1917, 8th Division War Diary.
46 See Appendix XVII.
47 Three infantrymen (10359 Pte. G.W. Hodgson, 2nd Royal Berkshire, Z/738 Rifleman P. Higginbottom and S/10061 Rifleman R.W.G. Shepherd, 2nd Rifle Brigade) who DOW in captivity have been deducted from the aforementioned CWGC total of 12 infantry

known to have expired at CCS and base hospitals during 4-10 December, to approximately 552 officers and men.[48]

"It only remains to add", Boraston and Bax observed, "that the 32nd Division had been even more unfortunate; for though some ground was won at the opening of the assault, all its gains were lost in the afternoon counter-attack…"[49] Casualties incurred by 97 Brigade were estimated at 66 officers and 1,036 ORs (1,102), 16th HLI sustaining the heaviest losses with 245 killed, wounded and missing. 11th Border Regiment and 17th HLI suffered almost as heavily with 242 and 181 respectively. Submitted casualty returns for the remaining three assault battalions and component machine-gun company were 2nd KOYLI (178), 16th NF (97), 15th LF (93) and 97 MGC (27). Verifiable deaths reported by these units amounted to 167. The 188 recorded missing must, as with 8th Division returns, be compared with available CWGC data for the period 30 November-3 December, the breakdown of which is as follows: 16th HLI (65), 11th Border Regiment (99), 17th HLI (62), 2nd KOYLI (60), 16th NF (27), 15th LF (29) and 97 MGC (7) or 349 total identified gravesites and commemorations. To this figure should be added a further 17 men from attached RFA[50] and MGC units[51], along with 28 additional infantrymen who died of wounds (one in captivity) between 4-10 December.[52] Total casualties for 32nd Division, when adding 394 killed/missing/DOW with 774 recorded wounded (minus 27 infantry[53]

DOW during the period 4-10 December, as they would have been originally recorded 'missing.' See Appendix XVII.
48   Comparisons of contemporary casualty returns with on-line sources produced the inevitable number of minor anomalies. For instance, 1st Worcestershire, 2nd East Lancashire and 2nd Northamptonshire of 24 Brigade are recorded as having lost a combined total of 3 men (1 missing) during 2/3 December, although no matching fatalities have been identified using CWGC data. Twenty-four total fatalities were also reported for 8th Division's component 23rd, 24th, 25th and 218th machine-gun companies as compared with 11 listed deaths (none from 23rd or 24th companies) obtained from the same source. It is also recognisedthat that some casualties may have DOW in the weeks and months following 4-10 December. This was addressed by examination of the seven days after 3 December which were chosen as a seemingly appropriate cut-off point. See Boraston & Bax, *The Eighth Division*, p. 167, Geoff's CWGC 1914-21 Search Engine <http://www.hut-six.co.uk/cgi-bin/search14-21.php> and Appendix XVII.
49   Boraston & Bax, *The Eighth Division*, p. 167.
50   Two of three fatalities (116739 Gunner Nigel Edmondson and 152893 Gunner William Edward Healer) sustained by the component 161 RFA Brigade are inexplicably commemorated on the Louverval Memorial to the Missing near Cambrai. See Commonwealth War Graves Commission. <http://www.cwgc.org>
51   14th, 96th, 219th MG companies and 161 and 168 field artillery brigades. See Appendix XVII.
52   See Appendix XVII.
53   One infantryman (260268 Pte. Frederick F. Bent, 11th Border Regiment) who DOW in captivity has been deducted from the aforementioned CWGC total of 28 infantry

and 4 machine-gunners known to have expired at CCS and base hospitals), amounted to approximately 1,137 officers and men.[54]

Table B[55]

	Killed		Wounded		Missing		Total	
	Officers	Other ranks	Officers	Other ranks	Officers	Other ranks	Officers	Other ranks
32nd DIVISION								
97 Brigade								
16 NF		24	4	65	1	8	5	97
15 LF	2	15	5	63		17	7	93
11 Border	5	32	9	159	1	51	15	242
2 KOYLI	4	21	8	116	2	41	14	178
16 HLI	3	17	9	179	1	4	13	245
17 HLI	6	37	5	131		13	11	181
MGC		3	1	20		4	1	27
Totals	**20**	**147**	**41**	**733**	**5**	**183**	**66**	**1036**

German casualties, based on examination of published post-war regimental histories, can only be surmised; *IR117* (239) and *IR94* (211) suffering a combined total of 450 killed, wounded and missing.[56] The former unit, however, combined losses – the bulk of which were likely sustained during 2-3 December – experienced over a period of six days i.e., after *25th Division's* takeover of *Abschnitt A* on 26 November.[57] The histories of *IR116* and *IR95*, whilst acknowledging severe (more wounded than dead in the latter's case) losses provide no concrete numbers to work with.[58] Best estimates,

DOW during the period 4-10 December, as he would have been recorded 'missing'. See Appendix XVII.
54 See Geoff's CWGC 1914-21 Search Engine <http://www.hut-six.co.uk/cgi-bin/search14-21.php> and TNA: WO/95/2370: After-action report, 'Part III, Narrative of Events', 11 December 1917, 32nd Division War Diary.
55 TNA: WO/95/2370: After-action report, 'Part III, Narrative of Events', 11 December 1917, 32nd Division War Diary.
56 Some of the reported missing would have been captured. See below.
57 Casualties for the period 21-30 November: *25th Division* (from 21 November) – 6 officers and 247 men; *38th Division* (from 27 November) – 100 men. Figures for December were unavailable. See KA HKR 189: 'Verlust-Meldung: Kämpfe in Flandern', 5 December 1917.
58 See Offenbacher, *Die Geschichte des Infanterie-Leibregiments Grossherzogin (3. Grossherzoglich Hessisches) Nr. 117*, p.196, Hartmann, *Das Infanterie Regiment Grossherzog von Sachsen (5. Thüringisches) No. 94 im Weltkrieg*, p. 238, Hiss, *Infanterie-Regiment Kaiser Wilhelm (2. Grossherzoglich Hessisches) Nr. 116*, p. 158 and Buttmann, *Kriegsgeschichte des Koninglich Preusischen 6. Thüringischen Infanterie Regiment Nr. 95*, p. 254.

Passchendaele 2 December 1917: British prisoners pose with their German captors. (Eleonore von Bojanowski, et al, *Thüringen im Weltkrieg: Vaterländisches Kriegsgedenkbuch im Wort und Bild für die Thüringischen Staaten Vol. 2* (Leipzig: Verlag der Literatur "Minerva" R. Max Lippold, 1919))

when considering available casualty figures of just over 200 men each for *IR117* and *IR94*, could reasonably be presumed to have totalled around 800 officers and men.[59]

The exact number of British prisoners, included as part of aforementioned contemporary figures for the missing, taken during the night operation is contradictory.[60] Sixty POWs, according to the daily *Heeresbericht*, remained in German hands at the close of the attack, but this was probably a general estimate based on early returns.[61] Combined (*IR116* (20), *IR94* (46), *IR95* (14) figures obtained from three of four consulted regimental histories allow for a collective headcount of 80 prisoners.[62] *IR117's* narrative account is, unfortunately, vague in regard to numbers; the only figure provided being a reference to eight compliant prisoners led away in broad daylight by *Gefreiter* Speiz on the morning of 2 December.[63] *Fourth Army's* daily prisoner and captured equipment reports provide the most accurate estimates, a combined total of 67 ORs recorded for the period 2-3 December.[64] Conversely, Second Army recorded, based on reports received up to nightfall 2 December, a combined total of "3 officers, 126 other ranks and 3 machine-guns" captured by 8th and 32nd divisions.

59 Casualties, if any, sustained by *I Battalion, IR115* (dispatched from reserve to assist the beleaguered *IR116* and *IR117*) could not be ascertained.
60 No British officers were taken prisoner during the attack. See Messrs. Cox & Co., *List of Officers taken prisoner in the Various Theaters of War between August 1914, and November 1918* (London: London Stamp Exchange, 1988 reprint of 1919 edition).
61 Hartmann, *Das Infanterie Regiment Grossherzog von Sachsen (5. Thüringisches) No. 94 im Weltkrieg*, p. 238 and *The Times*, Tuesday, 4 December 1917.
62 See Hiss, *Infanterie-Regiment Kaiser Wilhelm (2. Grossherzoglich Hessisches) Nr. 116*, p. 158, Hartmann, *Das Infanterie Regiment Grossherzog von Sachsen (5. Thüringisches) No. 94* im *Weltkrieg*, p. 238 and Buttmann, *Kriegsgeschichte des Koninglich Preusischen 6. Thüringischen Infanterie Regiment Nr. 95*, p. 254.
63 The narrative implies that additional prisoners were taken before and after this incident. See Appendix XVI Part C (paras. 14-16).
64 2.12.1917: *Gruppe Staden* 14 POWs; *Gruppe Ypern* 1 POW; 3.12.17: *Gruppe Ypern*: 52 POWs. See KA HKR 313: Telegraph/wireless pro formas.

Subsequent figures tabulated by VIII Corps (2 officers and 52 ORs) and II Corps (1 officer and 42 ORs of which 15 were wounded) amounted to 96 captives assembled at divisional prison cages or CCS by dusk on the 3rd.[65]

6.3 Epilogue

Perceived historical inconsequence does not render insignificant the human tragedy befalling hundreds of bereaved families like those of Private Frederick Wakely, Lieutenant Rupert Hardy Parker, Captain Henry Rawson Forde, Private Albert Cooksey, Private Hugh Cairns and 2nd Lieutenant William Ridgway, all of whom – with the sole exception of Forde – were reported missing prior to presumption of death by the War Office. Fred Wakely's remains were discovered with those of another (17129 Private F. Knott) 2nd Royal Berkshire comrade, SE of Exert Farm by an "Exhumation Company"[66] in 1921. The location of the bodies confirms both were shot down after mistakenly advancing beyond the final right flank objective.[67]

A War Office enquiry into the status of Lieutenant R.H. Parker (reportedly wounded on 2 December) was dispatched to continental base authorities on 15 December. Three days later (18 December), in response to a telegram from Parker's distraught mother, the military secretary replied that "no further word" had been received of her only son. A "special enquiry", however, had been "made to the base in France to ascertain his condition and location, and when a reply is received Mrs. Parker" could no doubt "rest assured that she will at once be informed." Two more days passed before an inconclusive official telegram was delivered to the affluent Grimsby address where Parker senior – a captain in 3rd Battalion Lincolnshire Regiment – resided with his wife: "Regret to inform you Lieut. R.H. PARKER Lincolnshire

---

65 For data relating to numbers of German prisoners taken during 2-3 December see LHCMA: Second Army War Diary, Montgomery-Massingberd Papers, File 7/16, King's College, London, TNA: WO/157/120: 'Second Army: 868th Intelligence Summary, Part 1', 3 December 1917, Second Army Intelligence File, BL: 48359: 'Report of Operations Carried Out by the VIII Army Corps on the Morning of 2nd December 1917, Official War Diaries with Appendices and Addenda, VIII Army Corps, Passchendaele Front, November 1917-April 1918', Vol. V, Hunter-Weston Papers, TNA: WO/157/288: 'II Corps Summary of Information', 2 and 3 December 1917, II Corps Intelligence File and Boraston & Bax, *The Eighth Division*, p. 167. The latter source, given its nebulous contradictory figure of 'about 150 prisoners', is probably a rough estimate of total captures obtained by 8th and 32nd divisions.

66 For the organisation and work of post-war exhumation units see Franky Bostyn, et al, *Passchendaele 1917: The Story of the Fallen at Tyne Cot Cemetery* (West-Vlaanderen: Roularta Books, 2007), pp. 224-30.

67 Privates Wakely and Knott are buried in Tyne Cot Cemetery. Their CWGC recorded death date (1 December) is, when taking into account where their remains were unearthed, open to question. Special thanks to Jan Van der Fraenen for providing additional details on discovery of the bodies at E.1.d.2.4., 'Passchendaele Sheet 28' (1:10,000 scale) map reference.

Regiment previously reported wounded was reported wounded & missing December second. Any further news sent when received."⁶⁸ The remainder of the month passed without confirmation of the missing subaltern's whereabouts. Subsequent enquires, including one through the Netherlands legation, produced no result. It was not until June 1918 that the anxious parents were notified "in view of the lapse of time … the Army Council are now regretfully constrained to conclude that Lieutenant Parker died on or since the 2nd December 1917…"⁶⁹ Rupert Hardy Parker has no known grave and is, in addition to an inscription on the Tyne Cot Memorial to the Missing, commemorated on St Wulfrum's Church Grantham, Wellington College and Christ Church College Oxford war memorials.

Six days expired before a telegram arrived (8 December) at 'Manor of St John' Waterford, the Forde family's redbrick 19th century gothic residence: "Deeply regret to inform you Captain H.R. Forde MC King's Own Yorkshire Light Infantry was killed in action December second. The Army Council offers their sympathy." The official (Army Form R 250/1676) report recording place of death: "In the Field, France"; cause of death: "Killed in Action" and burial place: "Not known" was forwarded to the War Office by base authorities on 10 December. Forde's salvaged personal effects – "1 wrist watch with strap & guard (glass deficient)"; "1 wrist watch (smashed)"; "1 counterfoil advance book" and "80 centimes (souvenir)" – were posted to Messrs. Cox & Co for return to next of kin and his military file officially closed.⁷⁰ Forde's post-war *De Ruvigny's* entry offers more moving testimony to the esteem in which the young officer who made good was held: "Buried where he fell. A brother officer wrote: "It's an awful blow to us all … for he was looked upon by everyone as a true friend. He is a great loss to the battalion" and another: "A brave and gallant officer has been taken by God, but he did his work, and he was a man among men when danger lurked about." An officer of another regiment wrote: "All his company officers had been killed, and he was rallying his men, when a German sniper hit him in the head and, poor lad, he was killed at once."⁷¹ Forde's remains were identified and interred (Plot IX E.23) at Tyne Cot Cemetery after the war. The prospect of a divine afterlife is expressed in the biblical passage (Matthew 28:9) inscribed on his CWGC headstone: "JESUS MET THEM SAYING ALL HAIL."

Albert Cooksey disappeared sometime after crossing the jumping-off line opposite Hill 52 and Teall Cottage. Officially declared missing presumed killed, his mother, father John Cooksey dying of natural causes in July 1918, became the beneficiary

---

68 Telegrams were sent to an officer's next of kin. Form 'B104-82' filled out with a casualty's particulars was posted to the families of ORs.
69 TNA: WO/339/24923: Telegrams and correspondence December 1917-June 1918, Lieutenant Rupert Hardy PARKER. The Lincolnshire Regiment.
70 TNA: WO/339/1191: Captain Henry Rawson FORDE. The King's Own (Yorkshire Light Infantry).
71 Marquis De Ruvigny, *De Ruvigny's Roll of Honour 1914-1918 Vol IV* (London: Naval & Military Press reprint of 1922 edition), p. 58.

Tyne Cot Cemetery: Gravesite of Captain Henry Rawson Forde MC. (Rob Thompson)

of a welcome military "Dependants Pension" of 13 shillings per month which was collected until her death in 1932. Little documentation remains – Albert's service record having been lost along with thousands of others during an air raid in 1940 – to chronicle the old soldier's army career. Victorian/Edwardian census data, "Pip, Squeak and Wilfred" campaign medals, snuff box, cigarette case bearing the inscription "Long Live Taiwan" and a recently discovered wartime photograph depicting Albert "in all his muddy-booted, creased and crumpled glory" constitute the sum total of tangible familial evidence pertaining to a long lost relative; sole commemoration is represented by inscriptions on the Tyne Cot and Royston memorials.[72]

Hugh Cairns' parents received no further word about the fate of their next-to-youngest son who vanished without a trace somewhere in the vicinity of Void Farm. A condolence letter, composed by Lieutenant-Colonel Tweed, was received at the Ridgway family home on Buckingham Road, Tingewick:

> It is with a heavy heart that I have to inform you that your son is wounded and missing after the fight at Ypres. He gallantly led his platoon in the attack and was seen to fall at the moment of success. The enemy counter-attacked and retook the advanced position and it was not possible to get to your son. It is just possible that the Germans may have attended to him, and that he is now in a German hospital, I pray it is so. Your boy was always a fearless and gallant soldier, loved by everyone who knew him and your great anxiety is shared by all of us.[73]

---

72 Jon Cooksey, 'Visiting the Western Front 2: Slaughter by Moonlight: The Passendale – Westrozebeke Road north of Passendale, Belgium', *Britain at War*, November 2012 and *Stand To!* No. 98, September 2013.
73 Pat Swinburne, et al, *Tingewick's Fallen Soldiers of the Great War* (Tingewick: Tingewick Historical Society, 2014), p. 19.

The Ridgway family remembers: Tyne Cot Memorial to the Missing 2003. (Author)

Official confirmation of Will's death arrived shortly afterwards. Fred Ridgway recalled, "My parents received received a telegram informing them that Will was missing. Another telegram told them he was dead. Like many thousands of other soldiers Will has no marked grave but his name is on the memorial at Tyne Cot Cemetery near Passchendaele..."[74] Such anonymity in death has been overcome by official memorialisation and lingering memories of lost loved ones like Will Ridgway, whose 90-year-old brother paid a final remembrance tribute during a visit to West Flanders shortly before his own passing in late 2000.[75]

Venison Trench, Southern and Northern redoubts, Teall Cottage, Mallet Copse and Mallet Wood have long since vanished. The backwater West Flanders setting, now interspersed with prosperous farms, gigantic greenhouses and some light industry, for the long-ago night operation has no draw for battlefield tourists seeking more appreciable sites of commemoration and memorialisation. Little evidence, beyond pertinent gravesites primarily distributed about nearby Tyne Cot and Passchendaele New cemeteries or names listed by regiment on the former's immense memorial to missing United Kingdom and New Zealand servicemen, of the almost forgotten incident

---

74 Telephone interview with Dr Joanne Coyle 29 May 2010 and Angela Foster, 'Fred Paid His Final Tribute', *Buckinghamshire Advertiser* (November 2000).
75 Foster, 'Fred Paid His Final Tribute'.

Junction of *Haringstraat* and *Goudbergstraat* 11 August 2004: A hazel sapling commemorating Private Hugh Cairns is ceremonially planted by niece Joanne Coyle. (Author & Wereldoorlog 1 in de Westhoek <www.wol.be>)

remains. One tangible piece of period material culture (currently on display at Tyne Cot Visitor's Centre) connected with the remote events of early December 1917 is a fine sepia military portrait of Fred Wakely bordered by the moving inscription:

> 'I have fought the good fight, I have finished my course'.
> In Loving Memory of
> Gunner FREDERICK JOHN WAKELY
> Dearly Beloved Son of Mr and Mrs F.J. Wakely
> Killed in Action December 1st 1917[76]
> While Serving His King and Country
> Aged 21 Years
> Too Dearly Loved to be Forgotten

Most recently, on a warm sunny day in August 2004, a hazel sapling was ceremonially planted not far from where the *Goudbergstraat* and *Haringstraat* (just opposite the present-day site of Virile Farm) intersect to commemorate 20-year-old Private Hugh Cairns' short life. An all-weather plaque placed beneath read:

> In loving memory of
> Pte Hugh Cairns
> of 16th Bn Highland Light Infantry
> who died near this place on Dec 2nd 1917
> and who has no known grave
> REST IN PEACE

This modest tribute, a final act of remembrance by Joanne Coyle of Tayport Fife for the maternal uncle neither she nor her mother (born 1922) ever knew, constitutes the only existing memorial directly related to an arcane First World War military operation in which 1,689 British officers and men were killed or wounded.[77] Subsequent familial memorialization some eighty-seven years on originated with a dedicated niece's fervent desire to do something meaningful and permanent, for young Hugh, as intimated by relatives, was someone "well-loved and precious." The now burgeoning hazel tree is thus symbolic of potential maturity unrealised.[78]

---

76   See fn. 67 above.
77   An author-funded memorial to the Passchendaele night operation was dedicated near Westrozebeke (Tganzengoed Staden, Wallemolenstraat 10, 8840 Staden)100 years to the day on 2 December 2017.
78   Telephone interview with Dr Joanne Coyle 29 May 2010.

Appendix I

Second Army Infantry Orders of Battle
Divisions: II Corps & VIII Corps
November/December 1917[1]

1st Division (Regular): Major-General E.P. Strickland

1st Brigade: Brigadier-General C.J.C. Grant
1st Black Watch   1st Cameron Highlanders
10th Gloucester Regiment   8th Royal Berkshire Regiment

2nd Brigade: Brigadier-General G.C. Kemp
2nd Royal Sussex Regiment   1st LNL
1st Northamptonshire Regiment   2nd KRRC

3rd Brigade: Brigadier-General R.C.A. McCalmont
1st South Wales Borderers   1st Gloucestershire Regiment
2nd Welsh Regiment   2nd Royal Munster Fusiliers
Pioneers: 6th Welsh Regiment

8th Division (Regular): Major-General W.C.G. Heneker

23rd Brigade: Brigadier-General G.W. St. G. Grogan
2nd Devonshire Regiment   2nd West Yorkshire Regiment
2nd Cameronians   2nd Middlesex Regiment

---

1   As relevant to the narrative.

24th Brigade: Lieutenant-Colonel H.R.C Stirling (Acting GOC 7 to 21 November)
Brigadier-General R. Haig (from 21 November)
1st Worcestershire Regiment   2nd East Lancashire Regiment
1st Sherwood Foresters   2nd Northamptonshire Regiment

25th Brigade: Brigadier-General C. Coffin VC
2nd Lincolnshire Regiment   2nd Royal Berkshire Regiment
1st Royal Irish Rifles   2nd Rifle Brigade
Pioneers: 22nd DLI

14th (Light) Division (New Army): Major-General V.A. Couper

41st Brigade: Brigadier-General P.C.B. Skinner
7th KRRC   7th Rifle Brigade
8th KRRC   8th Rifle Brigade

42nd Brigade: Brigadier-General G.N.B. Forster
5th Oxford & Bucks Light Infantry   5th KSLI
9th KRRC   9th Rifle Brigade

43rd Brigade: Brigadier-General R.S. Tempest
6th Somerset Light Infantry   6th DCLI
6th KOYI   10th DLI
Pioneers: 11th King's (Liverpool Regiment)

32nd Division (New Army): Major-General C.D. Shute

14th Brigade: Brigadier-General F.W. Lumsden VC
5/6th Royal Scots   1st Dorsetshire Regiment
2nd Manchester Regiment   15th HLI

96th Brigade: Brigadier-General A.C. Girdwood
2nd Royal Inniskilling Fusiliers   15th Lancashire Fusiliers
16th Lancashire Fusiliers   16th Northumberland Fusiliers

97th Brigade: Brigadier-General C.A. Blacklock
2nd KOYLI   11th Border Regiment
16th HLI   17th HLI
Pioneers: 17th Northumberland Fusiliers[2]

2   Reassigned GHQ Railway Construction troops on 15 November 1917.

33rd Division (New Army):
  Major-General P.R. Wood (to 28 November)
  Major-General R.J. Pinney (from 28 November)

19th Brigade: Brigadier-General C.R.G. Mayne
2nd Royal Welsh Fusiliers   20th Royal Fusiliers
1st Cameronians   5/6th Cameronians

98th Brigade: Brigadier-General J.D. Heriot-Maitland
1/4th King's (Liverpool Regiment)   1/4th Suffolk Regiment
1st Middlesex Regiment   2nd A&SH

100th Brigade: Brigadier-General A.W.F. Baird
1st Queens (Royal West Surrey) Regiment   2nd Worcestershire Regiment
16th KRRC   1/9th HLI
Pioneers: 18th Middlesex Regiment

35th (Bantam) Division (New Army): Major-General G. Franks

104th Brigade: Brigadier-General A.W. Sandilands
17th Lancashire Fusiliers   18th Lancashire Fusiliers
20th Lancashire Fusiliers   23rd Manchester Regiment

105th Brigade: Brigadier-General A.H. Marindin
15th Cheshire Regiment   16th Cheshire Regiment
14th Gloucestershire Regiment   15th Sherwood Foresters

106th Brigade: Brigadier-General J.H.W. Pollard
17th Royal Scots   18th HLI
19th DLI   4th North Staffordshire Regiment[3]
Pioneers: 19th Northumberland Fusiliers

---

3   Replaced 17th West Yorkshire on 15 November 1917.

Appendix II

Infantry Orders of Battle: 25th Division & 38th Division

25th Division: 49 Infanterie-Brigade
Leibgarde Infanterie-Regiment (1.Grossherzoglich Hessisches) Nr. 115
Infanterie-Regiment Kaiser Wilhelm (2.Grossherzoglich Hessisches) Nr. 116
Infanterie-Leibregiment (3.Grossherzoglich Hessisches) Nr. 117

38th Division: 83 Infanterie-Brigade
Infanterie-Regiment Grossherzog von Sachsen (5. Thüringisches) Nr. 94
6. Thüringisches Infanterie-Regiment Nr. 95
7. Thüringisches Infanterie-Regiment Nr. 96

Appendix III

Second Army Order No. 14

(a)
Copy No. ___

Second Army Order No. 14[1]

Reference: Attack map attached
The offensive (Tenth Phase) will be resumed by the Second Army on "X" day at an hour that will be notified later.

The operation will be carried out by the II and VIII corps. The objective of each corps is shown in RED on the attached map.

For the purpose of this operation, the boundary between the II Corps and VIII Corps will be shown in BROWN on attached map. The II Corps will take over from the VIII Corps up to this boundary as soon as possible after the minor operations mentioned in para. 4 have taken placc.

As a preliminary to the operation laid down for "X" day, the VIII Corps will capture the enemy's posts situated on HILL 52 (V. 30. a) in conjunction with II Corps, who will at the same time capture VOX FARM (V. 30. a. 00. 75.). These minor operations will be undertaken as soon as possible, the date and details being arranged by the corps concerned.

(a) The artillery policy to be pursued previous to the attack on "X" day will be carried out in accordance with Artillery Instructions No. 28 already issued to all concerned.
(b) Details of the artillery for "X" day will be issued later.

The Army Report Centre will be at Locre Chateau.
Acknowledge by wire.

1 TNA WO/158/209: Second Army Operations Files.

??? Lt. Col.
for Major-General,
General Staff
Second Army
Issued at 1:30 p.m.

H.Q., Second Army
21st November, 1917

SECRET

(b)
Copy No. 1

Amendment to Second Army Operation Order No. 14[2]

Para. 4 is cancelled

Reference para. 3. The II Corps will take over from the VIII Corps up to the boundary shown on map issued with above order, on night of 24/25th November.

Acknowledge by wire.
HQ Second Army   ??? Lt. Col
22nd November 1917   for General Staff
                       Second Army

Issued at 11-30 p.m.
Copies to recipients of Order No. 14.

(c)
SECRET Copy No. 1
Second Army No. 1/2 (G).

Reference Second Army Order No. 14 [3]

The operation of the II and VIII Corps will be carried out on night of D/E [1/2 December] day an hour to be notified later.

Acknowledge by wire
H.Q., Second Army   ??? Lt. Col.
25 November 1917   for General Staff
                        Second Army

Issued at 11:00 p.m.
Copies to recipients of Order No. 14.

2   Ibid.
3   Ibid.

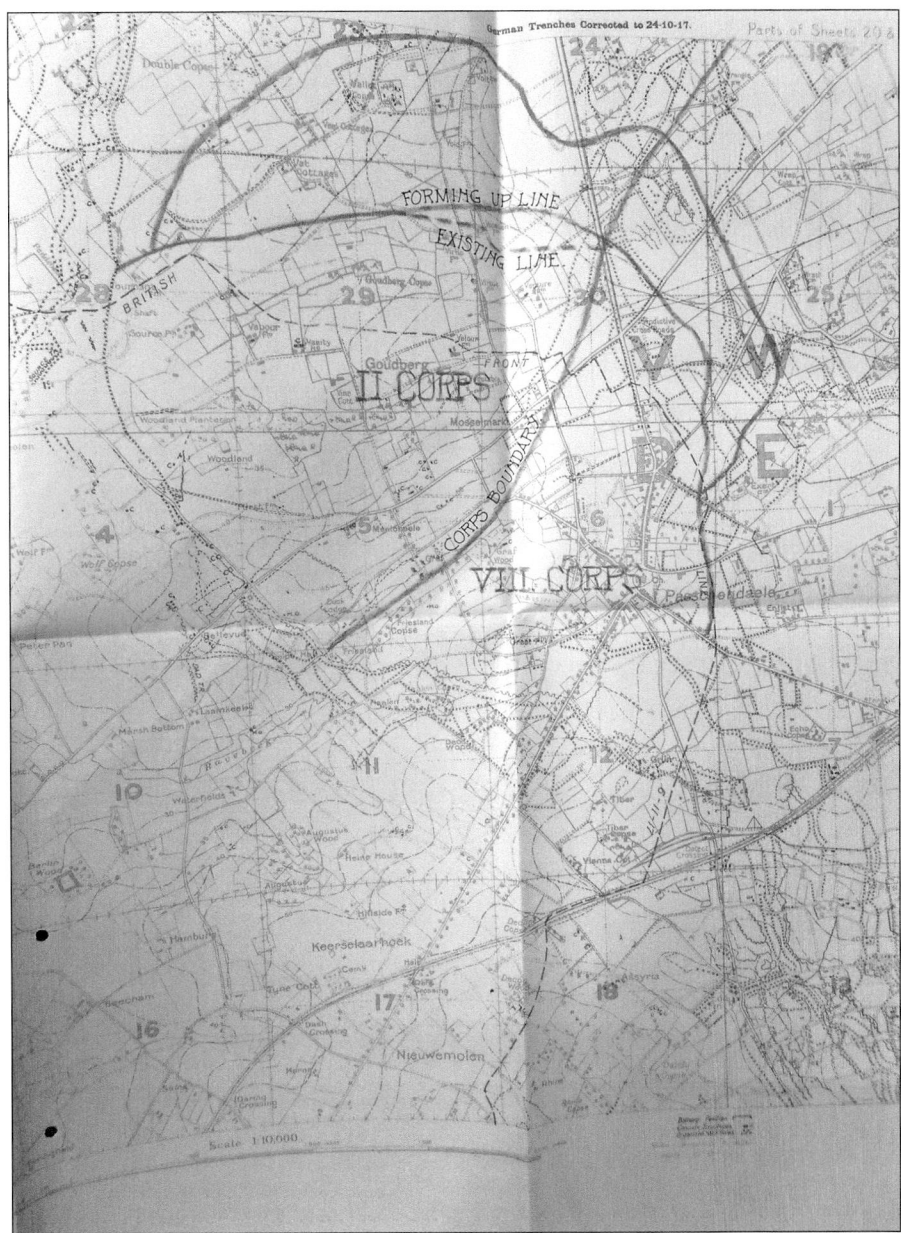

Second Army Objective Map: The area between "EXISTING LINE" and "FORMING-UP LINE" was to be secured in a preliminary operation (subsequently cancelled) scheduled for the night of 21/22 November. (TNA: WO/95/643: II Corps War Diary)

Appendix IV

VIII Corps Orders No. 52 & No. 54

(a)
SECRET
Copy No. 23

21 November 1917

VIII Corps Order No. 52[1]

1) The offensive will be resumed by the VIII Corps in cooperation with II Corps at a date [,] which has been communicated to all concerned. Zero hour will be notified later.
2) The operation will be carried out by the 8th Division (VIII Corps) and the 32nd Division (II Corps). The main objective of each division is shown in RED on the attached map.
3) The machine-gun companies of 14th, 33rd, and 39th divisions will cooperate under orders to be issued later.
4) For the purpose of this operation the boundary between II Corps and VIII Corps will be shown in Brown on attached map. The II Corps are arranging to take the frontline up to this boundary from the VIII Corps on the night following the minor operation mentioned in the next paragraph.
5) As a preliminary to the main operation, the 8th Division, in cooperation with 32nd Division, will carry out a minor operation in square V. 30. a. with a view to reaching such a line as will deny to the enemy any observation of the forming up places in that square [,] which are to be used by the 32nd Division. Details of this operation, which will take place as soon as possible after the night of 23rd/24th November, will be arranged between divisions concerned and reported to corps headquarters.
6) a) The artillery policy to be pursued previous to the main attack will be carried out in accordance with VIII Corps Artillery Instructions of today's date.

---

1 BL: VIII Corps War Diary, Hunter-Weston Papers, 48359, Vol. V.

b) Details of the artillery programme of the main attack will be issued later.
7. ACKNOWLEDGE BY WIRE

C.F. Aspinall BGGS
VIII Corps

Issued to Signals at midnight.

(b)
SECRET
Copy No. 22

23rd November 1917

VIII Corps Order No. 54[2]

1) The minor operation referred to in para. 5 of VIII Corps Order No. 52, is cancelled.
2) Para. 3 of VIII Corps Order No. 52 is cancelled. The machine-gun companies of 33rd Division will give such assistance to the attack of 8th Division as the G.O.C. 8th Division may require.
3) The temporary boundary between VIII and II Corps for the purpose of this operation, as shown on the map issued with VIII Corps Order No, 52, will be amended north-east of TEALL COTTAGE and will be a straight line drawn from Teall Cottage (inclusive to VIII Corps), to the RACKET WOOD, W. 19. a.
4) The II Corps will take over the front up to this boundary from the VIII Corps on the night of 24/25th November. Any minor adjustment of the inter-divisional boundary between 8th Division and 33rd Division will be adjusted on or after the night 24/25th November, under arrangements between divisions concerned. The date on which this adjustment will be made will be reported to Corps headquarters.
5) By arrangement with the II Corps [,] VIII Corps will retain the following accommodation on MEETCHEELE Spur after that spur has been handed over to II Corps: –
1 Battalion H.Q. at MEETCHEELE
1 Battalion H.Q. & Aid Post at MOSSELMARKT
1 Brigade H.Q. on BELLEVUE Spur
The VIII Corps will also have use of the BELLEVUE – MEETCHEELE ROAD for pack transport, except between dusk and zero on the night of the attack: also the exclusive use of the two new tracks south of MEETCHEELE.
6) ACKNOWLEDGE

V.A. Jackson
Major for BGGS VIII Corps

Issued to Signals at 4:30 p.m.

2   Ibid.

Appendix V

II Corps Operation Orders No. 167 & No. 168

(a)
<u>SECRET</u>. Copy No. 6
II Corp Headquarters
22nd November 1917

II Corps Operation Order No. 167.[1]

Reference Map
Tiendenberg Sheet.
Scale 1/10,000

1. The Second Army is, with the II and VIII corps, resuming the offensive at an early date with a view to capturing the general line VENISON TRENCH (V.30.b.) – VOLT FARM (V.24.c.) – MALLET COPSE (V.23.d.) – VEAL COTTAGES (V.23.c.). The day of the attack and the hour of zero will be notified later.
2. A summary of information regarding the enemy forces and defences in front of II Corps is attached (not reproduced).
3. The II Corps will be on the left of the attack and will, with the 32nd Division, capture the approximate line:
    V.24.d.6.2 – V.24.c.95.15 – V.24.a.25.00 – V.23.c.8.8 – V.22.d.9.2 – V.28.b.3.2 (see attached map: Scale 1/10000).
    The 8th Division (VIII Corps) will be attacking on the right of 32nd Division.
4. The boundary line between corps for the operations will be a line drawn from TEALL COTTAGE (V.30.b.1.5.) to the SE of RACKET WOOD (W.19.a.1.0.) (see attached maps: Scale 1/10000).
5. A definite, distinct and complete unit will be detailed to capture and hold each known enemy strongpoint.

---

1   TNA WO/95/643: II Corps War Diary.

6. For the purpose of coordination in arranging the barrage tables, the divisional artilleries covering the II Corps front will be under the orders of GOCRA II Corps, who will issue the necessary instructions and barrage tables.

   To each attacking infantry brigade there will be attached a RFA Battery Commander whose battery will, when required, be at the direct disposal of the brigadier.
7. Instructions regarding the artillery policy to be pursued previous to the attack are being issued separately.
8. II Corps Machine-gun Officer will prepare a machine gun scheme for making the best possible use, in cooperation with VIII Corps, of all machine guns available on the front of II Corps.
9. GOC 32nd Division will arrange for as many as practicable of the officers of each unit to meet (before the day of the attack) the officers of the units that will be operating on its flanks.
10. During the operations the usual cross attachment for liaison will be made: and in addition arrangements will be made for liaison parties from the right formation of the 32nd Division to meet similar parties from the 8th Division at fixed points to be agreed upon between the division commanders concerned.
11. Instructions are being issued separately as regards communication between infantry and aeroplanes, aeroplane to give warning of impending counter-attack, synchronization of watches and location of headquarters.
12. 32 Division will forward as early as practicable to II Corps Headquarters a detailed scheme showing how it is proposed to carry out the attack.
13. As a preliminary to the above-mentioned operation the VIII Corps is to capture the enemy's posts situated on HILL 52 (V.30.a.) and in conjunction with this attack the II Corps (32nd Division) will capture VOX FARM (V.30.a.05.75). The date for this minor operation is being communicated separately.
14. After the capture of the enemy's posts on HILL 52 and of VOX FARM the II Corps (32nd Division) will temporarily relieve the VIII Corps (8th Division) on the front between TEALL COTTAGE (inclusive) (V.30.b.1.5) and VOX FARM (exclusive) (V.30.a.05.75).

    Instructions for this relief, which will be carried out as early as practicable after the capture of Hill 52, will be issued later.
15. ACKNOWLEDGE.

S.H. Wilson
BGGS

Issued at 1:45 p.m.

(b)
SECRET. Copy No. 6
II Corps HQ
22 November 1917

II Corps Operation Order No. 168.[2]

1. Paragraph 13 of II Corps Operation Order No. 167 of the 22 November is cancelled.
The minor operation therein mentioned will not take place.
2. The jumping-off line for the main operation to be carried out by 32nd Division, will be approximately the present front line (shown in BLUE) on the map accompanying II Corps Operation Order No. 167).
3. The II Corps (32nd Division) will on the night of 24/25 November relieve the VIII Corps (8th Division) on a front between TEALL COTTAGE (inclusive) (V.30.b.1.5.) and VOX FARM (exclusive) (V.30.a.05.75).
4. All arrangements for relief will be made direct between divisions concerned; and 32nd Division will inform II Corps of the arrangements made and of the completion of the relief. Command will pass at 6:00 a.m. on 25th November.
5. Further instructions will be issued in regards the boundary line between divisions in the forward area after the completion of the relief.
6. ACKNOWLEDGE.

S.H. Wilson
BGGS

Issued at 11:55 p.m.
(Distribution overleaf)

2   Ibid.

Appendix VI

8th Division Instructions No. 1: Outline Plan of Operations

Secret 8th Division
No.G.97/1/4.

8th Division Instructions No. 1.[1]

1. The offensive will be resumed by VIII and II corps at a date which has been communicated to those directly concerned.
2. The operation will be carried out by the 25th Inf. Bde. in cooperation with the 32 Division (II Corps) on its left.
3. The objective, and the boundary between 8th and 32nd Division, are shown on the attached Map G. 31. The boundary line allots tactical responsibility for the BELLEVUE SPUR to the 32nd Division. It is understood, however, that certain rights such as sites for H.Q's. and lines of approach within 32nd Divisional area will be allotted to 8th Division. Exact details of these will be notified later.
4. (a) The 32nd Division are arranging to take over from the 8th Division for the purposes of this operation, the line as far east as TEALL COTTAGES (inclusive to 8th Division). This adjustment will take place on the night following the operation referred to in para. 5 below.
   (b) On the night following this operation, it is probable that 8th Division will take over from 33rd Division as far south as the road from D. 6. b. central – E. 1. c. 4. 8. inclusive to 8th Division.
5. As soon as possible after night of 23rd/24th November, probably 24th/25th November, the 23 Inf. Bde. will, in cooperation with 32nd Division, secure a line V. 30. b. 16 – V. 30. a. 7. 7. – V. 30. a. 50. 75 – VOX FARM (exclusive to 8th Division). Details of this operation will be notified later.
ACKNOWLEDGE.

E. Beddington
Lieut.-Colonel General Staff

22 November 1917.

1   TNA WO/95/1677: 8th Division War Diary.

Appendix VII

32nd Division Instructions No. 1: Outline Plan of Operations

SECRET

32nd DIVISION OFFENSIVE INSTRUCTIONS No. 1
OUTLINE PLAN OF OPERATIONS [1]

21st November 1917

1. <u>Future Operations</u>. The II Corps will continue operations at an early date to drive the enemy from the PASSCHENDAELE RIDGE. The VIII Corps will operate on the right of II Corps.

2. <u>Dividing Lines</u>. The dividing line between the II and VIII corps for the operation is shown on the attached map.

3. <u>1st Phase</u>. The first phase of the operations will be the capture of the RED LINE (vide attached map).[2]

4. <u>Task of 32nd Divn</u>. The capture of the RED LINE is the task of 32nd Division. The 8th Division, VIII Corps, will attack on the right of the 32nd Division. The 35th Division will be holding the line on the left of 32nd Division but will not assault.

---

1 TNA WO/95/2370: '32nd Division Offensive Instructions No. 1: Outline Plan of Operations', 21 November 1917, 32nd Division War Diary.
2 'Map to 3 Brigades & CRA only'.

5. Troops to be Employed. Cancel para 5 and substitute:³

   The assault and capture of the RED LINE on the II Corps front has been entrusted to the 97th Infantry Brigade with two battalions of the 96th Infantry Brigade attached.

   The attack will be carried out on a front of five battalions

   One battalion of the 96th Brigade will be held in reserve as a counter-counter-attacking force on the right flank in the vicinity of VIRILE FARM.

   Definite and distinct units will be told off to capture, garrison and consolidate each known strongpoint and defended locality.

   The two battalions of the 96th Infantry Brigade to take part in the attack will be holding the line on the night of the attack.

   These two battalions will come under the orders of the G.O.C. 97th Infantry Brigade on Y/Z night at an hour to be notified later.

6. General Scheme of Attack. The capture of the RED LINE will be carried out by a night attack. The essence of the operation is surprise. In order to fulfill this condition the general plan of operation is as follows:

   a) The first line of strongpoints (General line V.24.c.2.0.) – VOID FARM (inclusive) – VEAL COTTAGES (inclusive) at (V.23.c.2.0.) will be rushed at zero hour without an artillery or machine-gun barrage.

   b) At the hour which it is caculated the above line will be reached, the artillery will open fire on all known and suspected strongpoints and machine-gun positions. Lying beyond the line mentioned in (a). This barrage will lift as the attacking troops form the final objective advance, and will be specially thick on the enemy's most likely lines of counter-attack (i.e. VENISON FARM – VERSE COTTAGE – VALUATION HOUSE – MALLET WOOD (exclusive) (vide para. 9)).

   c) The exact times at which the artillery will open fire and lift off strongpoints will be notified later. This will depend upon the orders received from II Corps, the plans of the Corps on our right, and the condition of the ground at the time of the attack.

---

3   '32nd Division Instructions No. 1' (Section 5) was first issued with the following paragraph on 21 November: 'Troops to be Employed. The assault and capture of the RED LINE on II Corps front has been entrusted to 97th Brigade. The attack will be carried out on a front of four battalions. Definite distinct units will be told off to capture garrisons and consolidate each known strongpoint and defended locality. Two battalions of either the 96th or 14th (probably 96th) Brigade will be holding the line at the time of the attack. Those two battalions will come under orders of the G.O.C. 97th Infantry Brigade on Y/Z night at an hour to be notified later, and will be available as a reserve and to cover the flanks of the attack and to assist in repelling counter-attacks'. This section was amended on 24 November. See '32nd Div. No. G.S. 1499/15/3 Amendment No. 1 to 32nd Division Offensive Instructions No. 1', 24 November 1917, in TNA WO/95/2370: 32nd Division War Diary.

7. <u>Probable direction of enemy counter-attack</u>. The most likely direction from which a strong enemy counter-attack may be expected is :
   a) From the low ground about W.19. central on the south side of RACKET WOOD and south of the marshy ground in W.24.d.
   b) From the low ground about HEIDENGOED COPSE, the attack coming from the north side of RACKET WOOD and north of the marshy ground in V.24.d. and thence along the ridge via VALUATION HOUSES.
   c) A strong enemy attack is not to be expected from the area west of MALLET WOOD, as the condition of the ground would make such an attack very difficult for the enemy. Small local attacks are, however, to be guarded against in this latter area.

8. <u>Probable artillery plan</u>. As soon as the objective is reached the probable artillery plan will be:
   a) To form a protective barrage in front of the objective, which will be very thick on the enemy's most likely lines of counter-attack (vide para. 6).
   b) To search the areas where the enemy is likely to be assembling for counter-attack (vide para. 7).

9. <u>Machine-guns</u>. Machine-guns will be organized into:
   a) Close defence guns under orders of G.O.C. 97th Brigade. These will advance with the troops.
   b) Barrage gun under orders of the Corps M.G. Officer.
   c) At least two sections, and probably four sections of machine-guns will be allotted to the 97th Brigade for close defence of the captured line.
   d) The number of guns for barrage work is not yet known.

10. The task of these guns will be:
    I) To form a protective barrage in front of the objective in the area whence an attack in force may be expected.
    II) To maintain area concentrations on certain areas where the enemy is likely to be assembling for counter-attack or over which his counter-attacking troops are likely to pass. It is important that these selected areas should extend as far back as possible.
    III) To keep under fire the defensive localities on the left flank of the attack, where snipers and machine-guns may be active and which are not included in the objective.
    Detailed orders for machine-guns will be issued in due course.

11. <u>Consolidation</u>. All localities captured will be consolidated and all available machine and Lewis guns pushed up for the defence of the captured ground, the majority being advanced to the final objective.
    Strongpoints will be constructed in the vicinity of Hill 52 – VOID FARM

– VOLT FARM – MALLET COPSE – VEAL COTTAGES and enclosures at V.22.d.9.2. R.E. and Pioneers will be detailed for this duty. The number available will be notified later.

12. Routes. On the night of the attack the four assaulting battalions of the 97th brigade will move forward to the assembly position from WURST FARM (1 battalion), IRISH FARM (2 battalions), HILL TOP (1 battalion).
The routes at present available are MOUSE TRAP TRACK, No. 3 TRACK and the GRAVENSTAFEL Road.
It is hoped to get a fourth route constructed by the night of the attack, but this can not be relied on, as it must depend on the labour available.
It is essential that the times taken by units to get to our frontline from these camps should be known as accurately as possible. All brigades carrying out reliefs in the line prior to the attack will have the time taken by battalions to reach the frontline from the camps carefully checked, and report on the following morning to Divisional Headquarters.

13. Information as to the enemy's defences and dispositions was issued under 32nd Division No. G.I. 613.1/1 of 20th inst. (Issued only to three brigades, C.R.A. & 219th M.G. Coy.).

14. Headquarters.
    a) Brigade and Battalion headquarters will be selected by by the G.O.C. 97th Infantry Brigade after necessary reconnaissance. The advanced headquarters of the 97th Brigade will be in the neighbourhood of KRONPRINZ FARM and of the 14th Brigade at KANSAS. The Divsional Signal Officer will ensure that the buried cable reaches both these points.
    b) Divisional headquarters will be at the CANAL BANK C.25.d.0.0.

15. Detalied instructions will be issued later.

16. G.O.C. 97th Brigade will submit his plans based on these instructions as soon as possible.

17. ACKNOWLEDGE

A.E. McNamara
Lieut-Colonel
General Staff
32nd Division

Issued to:
14th Infantry Brigade;
96th Infantry Brigade;
97th Infantry Brigade;
C.R.A., 32nd Division;
C.R.E., 32nd Division;
A & Q.; 32nd Divl. Signal Coy.;
A.D.M.S.; D.M.G.O.

Appendix VIII

32nd Division Instructions No. 11: Special Instructions to GOC Brigade in Divisional Support [14th Infantry Brigade] and GOC Brigade in Divisional Reserve (96th Infantry Brigade)

32nd Division Instructions No. 11

32nd Divn. No. G.S. 1499/15/22

SPECIAL INSTRUCTIONS TO G.O.C. BRIGADE IN DIVISIONAL SUPPORT [14th Infantry Brigade] and G.O.C. BRIGADE IN DIVISIONAL RESERVE (96th Infantry Brigade).[1]

A. Instructions to G.O.C. 14th Infantry Brigade

1. You will be in command of the brigade in divisional support (14th Infantry Brigade, less 14th Machine-gun Company on barrage fire work) during forthcoming operations.

2. Your Brigade will be disposed at Zero as under:
   Adv. Brigade HQ. – KANSAS
   No. 1 Battalion – BELLEVUE
   No. 2 Battalion – WURST FARM
   No. 3 Battalion – HILL TOP
   No. 4 Battalion – IRISH FARM
   14 T.M. Battery (less 4 guns) – BELLEVUE
   2 guns – MEETCHEELE RIDGE
   2 guns – In vicinity of YETTA HOUSES

---

1 TNA: WO/95/2370: 32nd Division War Diary.

3. The Divisional Commander does not wish to employ your Brigade in these operations unless the enemy should make such a determined counter-attack as to endanger our present line.

4. You will be responsible for the defence of the BELLEVUE RIDGE and MEETCHEELE RIDGE. Stokes Mortars will be established in defensive positions for this purpose. Dumps of 50 rounds of ammunition for each gun must be established with each gun.

5. Your battalions will be ready to move at a notice of ¼ hour from Zero onwards. The men should, however, get as much rest as possible.

6. In the event of your Battalion at BELLEVUE being ordered forward, you will at once replace it by the Battalion at WURST FARM, and replace this latter Battalion by the Battalion at HILL TOP.

7. You will keep in close touch with the general situation and with the 97th Infantry Brigade, and have a liaison officer at the 97th Brigade Headquarters. You should establish Brigade O.Ps. in the vicinity of BELLEVUE RIDGE and send frequent reports to Divisional Headquarters as to your view of the situation and all which comes to your knowledge. The Divisional Commander does not consider it necessary for you personally to go in front of the position of your Battalion at BELLEVUE.

8. Special instructions are attached (App. A) as to action of the two Stokes Mortars at YETTA HOUSES.[2]

9. The 14th Infantry Brigade will probably relieve the 97th Infantry Brigade in the line on the night of December 3/4th, but must be prepared to do so earlier if required.

10. All units of the 14th Infantry Brigade moving forward must be supplied with 170 rounds of S.A.A. and 2 days rations.

11. In case of Brigadier General Blacklock D.S.O becoming a casualty you will be prepared to assume command of the operations.

---

2   See below.

B. Instructions to G.O.C. 96th Infantry Brigade

1. Your Brigade (less two battalions and machine-gun company) will be in divisional reserve during operations. Your Brigade at Zero will be disposed as:
Bde. HQ. – CANAL BANK
No. 1 Battalion – Attached 97th Infantry Brigade
No. 2 Battalion – Attached 97th Infantry Brigade
No. 3 Battalion – CANAL BANK
No. 4 Battalion – IRISH FARM
96th M.G. Coy. – Barrage fire/work
96th T.M. Battery – IRISH FARM

2. The units under your command will be ready to move at a maximum notice of 2 hours from Zero onwards.

3. ACKNOWLEDGE

A. E. McNamara
Lieutenant-Colonel
General Staff
32nd Division

30/11/17

Appendix 'A' Issued with 32nd Division Instructions No. 11

SPECIAL INSTRUCTIONS for the employment of TWO STOKES MORTARS of 14th Infantry Brigade[3]

1. It is possible that during the attack of the 97th Infantry Brigade, and after it has reached its objective that trouble will be experienced from snipers and machine-guns west of TOURNANT FARM, and from strongpoints about V.28.a.9.9. The enemy's battalion in the area V.22.c. and V.28.a. might also endeavour to counter-attack in spite of the condition of the ground.

2. To assist in meeting this eventuality, the 14th Infantry Brigade will place two Stokes Mortars and 50 rounds per gun at YETTA HOUSES by Zero. At Zero plus two hours the guns will move forward to the vicinity of TOURNANT FARM and the O.C. will report to the O.C. No. 5 Battalion [15th LF] of attacking force at his HQ at the pillbox at V.28.c.7.8.

3. The OC No. 5 Battalion will employ these guns if required:
    a) To open a bombardment on any strongpoint which is worrying the infantry.

---

3   TNA: WO/95/2370: 32nd Division War Diary.

>
> The strongpoint will be captured under cover of this bombardment and the objective extended to the left.
>
> b) To repel any counter-attack in force.

Care will be taken by 14th Infantry Brigade that the movement of these guns to YETTA HOUSES will not meet or cross the march of the 97th Infantry Brigade to its assembly position. Instructions to this effect have already been issued to the GOC 14th Infantry Brigade.

Appendix IX

100th Brigade Order No. 293

Secret Copy No. 5
Headquarters
100th Infantry Bde
1st December 1917

100th Infantry Brigade Order No. 293 [1]

1. The [8th] Division on our left is carrying out offensive operations tonight as explained verbally by the Brigadier General to commanding officers concerned.
2. The operation will be supported by artillery barrage and MG barrage commencing at Zero + 8.
3. At Zero + 8 an artillery barrage will be put down on the front of the 100th Infantry Bde and will be continued southward – Prior to Zero + 8 normal artillery fire will be carried out.
4. OC 16th KRRC will arrange for touch to be maintained with the 2nd Royal Berks[hire] Reg[imen]t on the left and will be ready to assist with supporting fire in the event of an enemy counter-attack. Special attention must be paid to the security of our left flank and front during the operations and until the chance of an enemy counter-attack has ceased. Headquarters 2nd Royal Berkshires will be at V.30.d.4.2.
5. The 2nd Worcestershire Reg[iment]t will similarly be ready to deal with an enemy counter-attack should one develop on our front during the operations.
6. All movement in our area is to be restricted to a minimum from Zero – 1 hour till the situation quiets down.
7. The hour of Zero will be notified later.
8. Acknowledge

G.O. Pilleau Lieut.
A/Bde Major 100th Inf. Bde.

Issued through Signals at 7.0 a.m.

---

1 TNA WO/95/2429: 100th Brigade War Diary.

Appendix X

97 Brigade Operation Order No. 181

97th Brigade Operation Order No. 181[1]

1. PRISM [97 Brigade] will establish itself on the line TEALL COTTAGE – HILL 52 – VOID FARM (inclusive) present frontline of PREFIX [11th Border Regiment] – VEALL COTT[AGES] – to enclosures at V.2.d.9.2.
2. PRINT [2nd KOYLI] will withdraw out of line at dusk.
3. PORT [16th NF] and PRAISE [16th HLI] will push forward on to HILL 52. PORT on right, PRAISE on left to VOID FARM inclusive.
4. PREFIX will consolidate their present holdings – reorganise and gain touch.
5. PRESS [17th HLI] will collect on its original tapes, reorganize, move to south of MALLET COPSE and envelope VEAL COTTAGE and VAT COTTAGE from the east in conjunction with Stokes mortars.
6. PONY [15th LF] will insure enclosures at V.22.a.9.2 are firmly consolidated, push out and join hands with PRESS.
7. PLAIN [14th Brigade] will move through PRISM and attack on the night 3rd/4th [December] after which PRISM will withdraw.
8. OCs must inform Brigadier their appropriate line early tomorrow.
9. The hour of Zero will be at 2 a.m. 3rd inst. a[t] which hour a protective machine-gun and artillery barrage will open clear of all objectives.
10. ACKNOWLEDGE. Issued at 3:50 p.m. 2/12/17

H. Wailes Capt. for Brigade Major
PRISM

---

1   TNA: WO/95/2370, 32nd Division War Diary.

Copies to:
1. PRESS
2. PRAISE
3. PREFIX
4. PONY
5. PORT
6. PANAMA
7. PLAIN
8. PROCTOR
9. PILL
10. & 11. War Diary
12. BM
13. 25th Inf. Bde.
14. Staff Capt.

Appendix XI

97th Brigade Order No. 182[1]

1. Operation Order No. 181 is cancelled.
2. Back battalions will ensure that tomorrow, they are occupying before dawn, a position at least as far forward as the original tapeline. Having gained the tapeline, every endeavour will be made to launch forward as far in advance of the line as is possible.
3. Touch, if not already gained, will be established with units on the flanks: the greatest care taken to preserve it once gained.
4. Companies & platoons will be reorganized.
5. Lewis Gun posts will be established in front of line taken up.
6. OC 97th MG Co. will post as many available guns of his own company & 8 guns of 96th MG Co. for close defence of the line.
7. Units will report to this headquarters as soon as this order has been carried out and give the following ??? ??? ??? give limits of battalions' boundaries, as much ground as possible in advance of this line will be.
8. 16th Batt. NF – TEALL COTTAGE inclusive to VIRILE [FARM]*
   16th HLI – TEALL COTTAGE inclusive to VIRILE [FARM]*
   11th Border Regiment – VIRILE FARM (enclosures) to V.29.b.1.5
   17th HLI – V.29.1.5., V.29.a.3.3
   15th LF – V.29.a.3.3 to TOURNANT FARM – area ???
   *OC 16th Batt. (NF) will be responsible for division of frontage between those two units (i.e. 16th NF and 16th HLI). Battalions may find it necessary to extend their flanks. If it is found that the number of men collected in any unit are out of all proportion to length of line taken over, this will be arranged between CO's concerned.
9. ACKNOWLEDGE

---

1   Ibid.

Issued at 9:30 p.m.
2/12/17
Capt. for B. Major
97th Inf. Bde

Copies to:
1. PANAMA
2. PLAIN
3. PROSE
4. PREFIX
5. PORT
6. PRAISE
7. PRESS
8. PONY
9. PILL
10. Staff Capt.
11. War Diary

File

Appendix XII

97 Inf. Bde. Operation Order No. 183

Copy No. <u>11</u>

97th Inf. Bde. Operation Order No. 183[1]

1. The 97th Brigade will be relieved in the frontline on night of 3/4th December by 14th Brigade in accordance with attached table.
2. All other details of relief will be arranged by OC battalions concerned.
3. On completion of relief, the command of the line will pass from GOC 97th Brigade to GOC 14th Brigade.
4. Guides will be arranged for each relieving battalions as under: –
   One per Batt. HQ
   One per Coy. HQ } To be under command of an officer
   One per Platoon

   OC 17th HLI will be responsible for finding guides in the right portion from each of the following units: – 11th Border Regt., 16th HLI (less those attached to 16th NF) and 17th HLI.
5. Relief complete will be reported to this Headquarters by code words as under –
   Relief complete HOLES
   Heavy shelling DEEP
   Slight shelling SHALLOW
6. All are reminded that soup kitchens exist – 1 off MOUSETRAP TRACK B.17.b.9.7. & 1 off No. 6 track at B.23.a.6.7.
7. ACKNOWLEDGE

H. Wailes for B[rigade] M[ajor] 97th Infantry Brigade
Issued at 2 p.m. 3/12/17

---

1 Ibid.

Copies to:
1. 15th LF
2. 16th LF
3. 11th Border Regt.
4. 16th HLI
5. 17th HLI
6. 14th Inf. Bde
7. 96th Inf. Bde
8. 32nd Division
9. Brig.
10. Staff Captain
11 & 12. War Diary
13. File

Appendix XIII

Battalion Commanders' Remarks in Response to 25 Brigade Questionnaire G1/79

Lieutenant-Colonel C.R.H. Stirling (CO 2nd Royal Berkshire)

As regards the questions contained in your G1/79 I beg to report the following:

A. Barrage
   1. Was effective as far as I can gather.
   2. But there were many shorts.
   3. Officers state that the barrage seemed to lift too quickly after the original beginning. All agree that the defensive barrage of artillery ??? ??? was excellent.

B. Assembly
   1. The duckboards were raised too high above ground, so when the men got off where there were gaps, it was difficult to get on again.
   2. A new tape should have been laid from the head of the duckboards, as the old one was hardly discoverable.

C. Enemy Fire
   1. Enemy's barrage came down from our old frontline back to behind the PASSCHENDAELE – VINDICTIVE X roads. Probably field guns on the frontline and heavy stuff on both sides of the road.

D. Forming-up
   1. 2 small tapes were all that could be desired.
   2. Yes, but some of them were not securely fastened and had moved in the wind.

E. Equipment
1. I do not think overloading was noticed except in the mud and on the duckboards, but I think the carrying of spare stores by the 3rd wave was a mistake as:
a) These never eventuated
b) The platoon would have been invaluable as a support but got it into its head that it was there to carry.
I consider a totally separate carrying party to go up when the barrage had moderated would be better.
2. No shortage.
I attribute the lack of complete success to lack of depth on my centre due to the easing off of to keep touch with the left. I should like to mention the great help given by Lt. Francis (Bde Int[elligence] Of[fice[r]) in getting us on the tapes. I consider that the forming-up could only have been done in moonlight, but the attack would have gone better if it had been darker, as the Germans could not have located where our men were and I think, in this case, we could have held on to the [Southern] redoubt.[1]

Lieutenant-Colonel N.M.S. Irwin (CO 2nd Lincolnshire)

Notes

a. (1) [Barrage]
1. Barrage when it came down was efficient.
2. One or two how[itzer]s were repeatedly firing short in S + T zones as far back as VINDICTIVE Crossroads.
3. Owing to advance being held up by MG fire from MGs on our side of the barrage line it is not possible to determine whether the pace of the barrage was suitable.

b. (2) [Assembly]
1. The continuation of the duckboard track No. 5 S [outh] was heartbreaking. There was not more than 20 yards length continuous + track was laid too high off the ground. It took an overloaded man over 3 ½ hours walk from WIELTJE to MOSSELMARKT instead of under 2 hours by road. Owing to the condition of the track, my battalion and the Berkshires were a little mixed up by the head of the track, otherwise the assembly was not worried much. Hostile fire caused an average of 10-15 casualties a company before assembly.

---

1   TNA: WO/95/1929: 'Appendix B', 5 December 1917, 2nd Royal Berkshire War Diary.

c. [Enemy Fire]
1. At about Zero + 9 fell around VINDICTIVE Crossroads westward.
2. It was his MG and rifle fire (rifle fire negligible), which stopped the advance. His MGs opened at Zero + 3 minutes.

d. [Forming-up]
1. Yes, tapes were well laid + the direction.
2. Tapes were undoubtedly useful.

e. [Equipment]
1. For the attack the men were not overloaded, although the condition of Track No. 5 made the men dead tired before Zero.
2. There was a shortage of Lewis Gun magazines + I think it would be a good thing to distribute these drums throughout assaulting troops.[2]

Lieutenant G.H.G. Anderson (Adjutant & Acting CO 2nd Rifle Brigade)

<u>Headquarters 25th Infantry Brigade</u>　　　　　　　　　　　　　　　　　　　<u>Secret</u>

In reply to your G1/79, herewith information as required: –

a. <u>BARRAGE</u>
1. Very efficient.
2. Not many shorts.
3. Pace was found suitable.

b. <u>ASSEMBLY</u>
1. Carried out with only slight interference from the enemy, although, from their subsequent action, the forming-up on the tapes was apparently observed by them.

c. <u>ENEMY'S FIRE</u>
1. No enemy barrage on our front or support lines. Searching fire from about Zero + 5 in rear of support line.
2. Machine-gun fire particularly deadly. Machine-guns firing low – about 2 feet from the ground.

2　TNA: WO/95/1730: 'Report on Action of the Battn. from 2:30 p.m. 1-12-17 – M.N. 2/3-12-17', 6 December 1917, 2nd Lincolnshire War Diary.

d. <u>FORMING-UP</u>
  1. Under the circumstances (i.e. Teall Cottage being in the hands of the enemy) the tapes were all that could be desired.
  2. The direction tapes proved useful in the advance.

e. <u>EQUIPMENT</u>
  1. The men were not overloaded in any case.
  2. There was no shortage except for very lights.[3]

---

[3] TNA: WO/95/1731: 'Report of the Part Played by the 2nd Battn. The Rifle Brigade in the Recent Operations at Passchendaele', 6 December 1917, 2nd Rifle Brigade War Diary.

Appendix XIV

GHQ Instructions for the Defence of the Flesquières and Passchendaele Salients[1]

$$\frac{64}{\text{SECRET}}$$

General Sir H.S. Rawlinson, Bt., G.V.C.O, K.C.B., Commanding Second Army
General the Hon. Sir J.H.G Byng, K.C.B., K.C.M.G., M.V.O., Commanding Third Army

----
O.A.D. 291/29

With reference to GHQ no. O.A.D. 291/29, dated the 6th December 1917, describing the policy to be pursued in the defensive organization of the British front, the following special instructions are issued as a guide to the manner of dealing with the FLESQUIÈRES and PASSCHENDAELE salients.

These salients are unsuitable to fight a decisive battle in. It is, however, desirable to retain possession of them if they are not attacked in great force; and in the event of attack in great force to use them to wear out and break up the enemy's advancing troops as much as possible before these can reach the battle zone of defence which will be sited approximately as [a] chord across the base of each salient.

In accordance with this policy the salient will be held firmly until the battle zone of defence behind each has been prepared. The defences of the salients will then be organized into advanced or "outpost" zones, and as these defences become more complete, so the garrisons can be reduced to what is required for the purpose in view.

The whole area of each salient should be organized defensively, in advance of the battle zone, with an intermediate system as well as a forward system of defence; the

---

1 TNA WO/158/209: Second Army Operations File.

object being to compel the enemy to fight for every yard of his advance to the battle zone.

For the defence of these salients, therefore, after the battle zone is ready for occupation, the ground should be held chiefly with machine-guns, supported by artillery, and aided with ample barbed wire obstacles skilfully placed and hidden. Selected machine-gun companies might be detailed for the defence of stated sectors, and kept permanently (with reliefs) for a definite purpose.

In the same way each sector should be under a specially chosen officer for preparation and defence.

In certain few portions of the area counter-attack will be possible. These must be foreseen and arranged for. At other points surprise counter-attacks with machine-gun fire will be possible. All this requires a special garrison, and leaders imbued with the offensive spirit even though forced to act on the defensive.

(Sd). *L.E. Kiggell*
Lieut. –General
Chief of the General Staff

G.H.Q.
13th December 1917

Copies addressed personally to : –
General Sir H.S. Horne K.C.B., Commanding First Army
General Sir H. de la P. Gough, K.C.B., K.C.V.O., Commanding Fifth Army

Appendix XV

Lieutenant-General Sir Aylmer Hunter-Weston's Confidential Letter [1]

Headquarters, VIII Corps
BEF December 19, 1917

I had an interesting interview this morning with Douglas Haig, the Commander-and-Chief, at the Army Commander's house. Douglas Haig came with "Curly" Birch, his chief artillery advisor, and asked Rawlinson to get me to meet him at Cassel, so that he could get my views on the situation in my area.

I went there with Ward and Aspinall, my chief gunner and chief general staff officer respectively, taking with me maps showing (i) the dispositions of our artillery; (ii) the dispositions of the enemy's artillery; (iii) our communications; (iv) our defences as they exist, and as I propose; (v) statements showing the very slow rate of progress which our plank roads, light railways, etc., are making owing to the difficulties of communication and to the effects of the enemy shelling; and (vi) a statement showing the strengths of battalions in my divisions, all of which are weak, and some, alas, desperately weak.

The Commander-and-Chief arrived about noon, and I went up to Rawlinson's own study. Curly Birch and I were sent for shortly afterwards. After a pleasant word of greeting we plunged into business, and I produced a map showing the positions of our artillery and of the enemy's artillery. I pointed out to the chief (what I had pointed out to Curly Birch (his chief artillery officer) the day before here at my headquarters at Vogeltje) that our guns were in such a position that if the enemy made even a moderately successful attack the great majority of our guns must be lost. This gave him furiously to think.

---

1   BL: 48366: Hunter-Weston to Lady Hunter-Weston dated 19 December 1917, Hunter-Weston Diary, Vol. XII. Document marginalia in Lieutenant-General Hunter-Weston's own hand noted: 'Secret. Sent by the hand of one of my own officers'.

I pointed out to him the seven-mile length of our communications from Ypres to Passchendaele, and the fact that these communications were under hostile shellfire throughout their length from both north and south; that the country has been so cut up by shellfire that with the exception of such of the German "pillboxes" as were still intact nothing remained but shell holes and mud, impassable to guns or any other vehicles, or even to men except along the plank roads, tramways or duckboards.

I showed him that my front was an almost exact semi-circle of 1300 yards radius, exposed to enemy artillery fire at easy range from almost three-quarters of a circle – from northwest by east by south.

I told him that the position at Passchendaele approximated to the position of which he had bitter experience at Lombartzyde on the coast; the swamps and the valleys behind Passchendaele corresponding to the Nieuport Canal; the Bellevue Ridge and the main Broodseinde Ridge, along which alone access to Passchendaele is possible, corresponding to the bridges over the canal; and the salient about Passchendaele corresponding to the ground that used to be held by us north of the Nieuport Canal.

I showed him that if the enemy really concentrated heavy artillery fire on to those two spurs (our only corridors of approach) and at the same time put on heavy concentrations on to our far too crowded gun positions, while they pulverized the troops and machine-guns in the Passchendaele Salient with fire, they would be able to smash up our infantry and machine-guns in the Passchendaele Salient, and having gained the ground by artillery fire, it would remain for hostile infantry to advance and occupy the ground thus won by the guns. Our defence against this advance by the hostile infantry lies in the power of our artillery to stop any such advance.

I pointed out to him, therefore, that if we wished to continue to hold the Passchendaele Salient, we must have guns in sufficient quantities and in such positions that they could mow down any hostile attacks on the salient. This necessitates having our guns forward in such positions that they were within reach of a successful minor attack by the enemy, and, indeed must form a tempting bait to him.

I furthermore pointed out how the fact of holding the salient with such long and precarious communications necessitated an immense amount of labour, and showed that owing to the great distance the labour had to go over bad communications, in order to get to the forward part of the area, the amount of work that could be done by the men in that front area was very small, even when the hostile shelling permitted any work to be done at all.

After getting him to understand this position, and making him feel very uncomfortable about the position of these guns, which, indeed, we could very ill-afford to lose, I continued to say that if my opinion were asked (my opinion had not been asked, but I felt it important to make him know my opinion politely and firmly) I should unhesitatingly recommend that the preparation of a strong position on the Pilkem – Clapham Junction Ridge should be pushed on with as rapidly as possible; an outpost or front position being prepared well ahead of it; and that as soon as ever the main Pilkem – Clapham Junction position was ready for occupation, the garrison of the Passchendaele Salient should be reduced to a negligible quantity, only sufficient to bluff the Boche, and to prevent him from coming on to take that high ground without developing some kind of attack; but that it should be clearly recognised that, as soon as the Boche did attack, that garrison, acting as a rearguard, would withdraw and leave the horrible Passchendaele Salient to the Boche. The advantage of holding it as a rearguard in that way was to delay the Boche, and prevent him getting the fine observation over our lines that he would obtain as soon as Passchendaele and the tops of the adjacent ridges, just southwest of it, were in his hands.

My words sank in, and the policy has been agreed to, which is a very good thing. But between the adoption of this policy and the possibility of having it properly carried out there is a great gulf fixed, for we are short of troops and labour. It will take a considerable time to make the Pilkem – Clapham Junction position strong, and until that main position with an outpost line in front of it is prepared, we must continue to hold Passchendaele fairly strongly, and to have a good number of guns much more forward than I would wish. If, therefore, the Boche were to attack the real strength in the immediate future, we stand a good chance of suffering loss both in men and materials. However, that cannot be helped. We must take the situation (which was none of my making) as it stands, and hope firstly: that he will not attack until we are ready, and secondly: that if he does attack now we shall be able to defeat him owing to the excellence of our artillery and the gallantry our men.

Appendix XVI

Night Operation on the Passchendaele Ridge:
The German Experience from Published Regimental Accounts [1]

25th Hessisches Division
A
Leibgarde Infanterie-Regiment Nr. 115 [2]

(1) On 6 November the first elements of *3rd Garde Division* arrived to take over positions of *Division Lokeren* in rest areas along the Dutch border. The *25th Division* supported *Gruppe Ypern*, whose area, composed of three divisional sectors, adjoined *Gruppe Wijtschate* to the north, and whose frontline, north of Ypres, ran from Becelaere to Passchendaele. Train after train rolled towards the new positions in such a way that the full strength of a division lay north of Lokeren. However, to relieve pressure on trains, the mounted troops marched to their positions.

(2) Regimental staff and the *I* and *II* battalions formed the first element for transfer. On the afternoon of 6 November they entrained at Moerbeke Station and, passing through Ghent and Dienze, arrived as early as the evening of that day at the Waereghem hub, 12 km north of Courtrai. Machine-gun companies, field and combat train elements followed by route march with a stopover at Drongen. Regimental staff were quartered in Wielsbeke, *I Battalion* in Vive St Eloi and *II Battalion* in Vive St Bavon (Vive St Baaf); all three villages were northwest of Waereghem. Damp, raw weather foretold an approaching winter.

(3) The Regiment remained in these billets for the next four days. Hardly had the *Garde-Füsiliere* arrived from Exaerde, when the regiment, now fully closed [-up],

---

1   All times related below are continental i.e., 1 hour ahead of British time.
2   Victor von Frankenberg und Ludwigsdorff, *Das Leibgarde Infanterie Regiment (1. Grossherzoglich Hessisches Nr. 115) im Weltkrieg 1914-1918* (Stuttgart: Verlagsbuchhandlung, 1921), pp.157-67.

moved to the next forward sector during the early hours of 11 November. Short rail journeys brought the battalions through Iseghem, close by Roulers, to Rumbeke; from here, new quarters, situated slightly southward, were reached: regimental staff and *Garde-Füsilier-Bataillon* in Den Hukker, *I Bataillon* in Kaiphas and *III* in Den Aap. Cramped occupation of available shelter within tiny Flemish hamlet clusters was expedient. In this area, barely 9 km from the Passchendaele front held by *44th Reserve Division*, the *25th Division* sat as *Eingreifdivisionen* for the northern *Abschnitt A* of *Gruppe Ypern* and assumed thereby the duties of *11th Division*; *Grenadier-Regiment 10* departed from the sector upon arrival of the Regiment.

(4) Attacks against this *Fourth Army* sector have raged since the battle of 4 October. The British threw themselves like wild bulls against an iron wall tenaciously held by defenders of the German U-boat bases. Twenty-sixth and 30 October, as well as 6 and 10 November, were once again days of hard fighting. The weight of our opponents was beaten back again and again. Minor adjustments of the front bore sole witness to the seesaw struggle. The German lines held in the final accounting because the tactical requirements of defensive reinforcement and relief were ably managed by the leadership. Behind almost every forward division stood a second as a counter-attack force, behind these, more often than not, another reserve.

(5) So it was here also. *Gruppe Staden* closed in from the right. In its left sector, *4th Division* was in position, the *199th Division* behind. To the left, in *Abschnitt B*, the *11th Reserve Division* held the frontline; *11th Bavarian Division* was the attack division. In a gapless chain of divisions, the *25th Division*, situated in the second echelon, sat close behind the battlefront ready to enter the fray.

(6) This assignment was filled with arduous challenges. The leadership had to consider various deployment possibilities and organise and prepare forces; it was left for units to determine and specify attack and assembly areas within the vicinity. The divisional infantry comprised three separate attack groups; *IR117*, as *Gruppe Alice*, composed a forward echelon, the Regiment was detailed to Gros as *Gruppe Ernst Ludwig* with a field artillery battery, an engineer platoon, dispatch riders and medical personnel; this deployment anticipated frontal and flanking counter-attacks in its own as well as neighbouring sectors. Depending upon the tactical situation assembly areas or, respectively, assault positions nearer the front, were to be occupied on receipt of a code word.

(7) Routes of advance and assigned areas were reconnoitered over a two-day period; battalions accustomed themselves to general terrain orientation. A counter-attack was, however, no longer required. Gradually, the enemy's reserve must have been drawn off to continue the battle elsewhere. A consequent easing of the situation took place. The front remained active and fluid. With heavy artillery concentrations massing elsewhere, the cratered fields of Flanders settled down for the winter.

(8) Strong German reserves remained in sectors for the periodic relief of frontline units. Prolonged rail transport of fresh divisions no longer being necessary, the opportunity, through frequent reliefs, afforded a balance between heightened security combat co-efficiency and necessary unit recovery.

(9) So began for the first time on 14 November, in the northern sector of *Gruppe Ypern,* the relief of *44th Reserve Division* by *25th Division*. The Regiment took over the left sector held by *RIR206*. Regiments *116* and *117* closed up from the north. The rightmost division and *gruppe* boundary began at Mosselmarkt, wound from there in a northerly direction approximately parallel to the Ypres – Roulers railway, to extend southward in a great arc around Roulers; the left division and *gruppe* boundary followed this general trace for approximately 3 to 4 km. The forward line of the entire divisional sector enclosed the village of Passchendaele in an arc, which the British probably held with their 49th Division at that time;[3] it [the village] lay directly to the northwest of the Regiment's positions.

(10) Basic regimental organisation comprised one battalion as covering force, a second in the main battle area, the third in reserve, all, for the most part, closely staggered behind each other. This organisation developed from the novel perspective that realistic assessment of the Battle of Flanders brought about. The concept of a covering force area [*Vorfeldzone*], which previously occurred during position warfare southeast of St Quentin at Neuville St Amand, had jelled here and been expanded to a defined battle zone. Major distinctions were made between the covering force and main battle zones. Weak sections of the foremost battalion, their firepower reinforced with light machine-guns, were to hold the covering force area against enemy reconnaissance and weak attacks while, in the event of serious fighting, they were to withdraw step-by-step to the so-called main line of resistance [*Hauptwiderstandslinie*] which, by manoeuvre combat from the main battle area, was to be held at all costs. Here too, only a portion of the fighting troops were committed: to the rear stood the remaining forces formed as assault companies and, according to the situation, reinforced with elements from the main battle zone ready for immediate counterattack. Security details and *Nahtkommandos*[4] remained, as before, excluded for specific defensive assignments.

(11) The Regiment commenced movement from its assault positions in order, within the set tactical scheme, to relieve *RIR206* on the afternoon of 14 November. *I Battalion* reached, following a march of almost 5 km, the sector reserve area. Its four

---

3   Passchendaele village was held by 33rd Division (VIII Corps). 49th Division was attached to the neighbouring II ANZAC Corps.
4   Seam Command or Detachment: A special command team established to control the peculiar difficulties encountered at the junction between two units.

companies lay dispersed along the little Veldebach [Velde Brook], just south of where the Moorslede – Roulers highway crossed the Ypres – Roulers railway; here the regimental command post was also established. *I* [*Battalion*] following close behind the *II*, was assigned the relief of the foremost positions.

(12) The *Garde-Füsiliere* assumed, as the trail, the main battle zone positions. Deep darkness reigned and unfamiliar terrain made relief difficult; heavy enemy barrages, with harassing fire reaching far to the rear, slowed movement. There was much scattering of units. In the end, the relief was accomplished and linkups secured on both flanks.

(13) The battleground presented a sad, and as with the severely shot up positions around Gheluvelt, affecting picture. Swamp and morass dominated the forward area and ran in broad swaths in front of and through friendly positions. The sea, only 35 kilometres distant, forced ground water to the surface of the pockmarked earth. Here also, crater upon crater. Trenches or lines with any semblance of purpose or obvious continuity did not exist. Concrete shelters were almost non-existent: the commander of the covering force area (*Kampftruppenkommandeur*) north of Moorslede could scarcely find a concrete slab to shelter his command post. Companies lay grouped in the open along the Passchendaele – Moorslede road where, in earlier days, the gas and electric works serving the 300-metre distant village provided power and light; to the rear lay the joint railway station serving both villages. Small, unit-level adjustments on the night of 16/17 November, resulting from the adjustment of sector boundaries, brought with them the former Passchendaele palace to the north and the cemetery of brave young fighters of 1914.

(14) The crater field, a tangle of impassable areas extending far into the hinterland, had unfortunate consequences. All logistic and relief efforts were confined to the railway and the few roads that led here and there, but seldom in the desired direction. The enemy, of course, immediately covered these generously and preferentially at night with harassing fire that inflicted not inconsiderable losses. The positioning of our counter-attack companies in tactically advantageous positions also caused great difficulties. They lay spread out and farther back than the situation demanded. They were, more often than not, forced to seek and occupy unfavourable terrain that predominated overall. Minor adjustments forward or backward within the framework of the new conduct of battle were generally permitted as well as demanded.[5]

(15) Enemy artillery activity remained extraordinarily lively; in varying intensities across the entire battle area as well as the rear, harassing fire of all calibres fell. Individual barrages often rose to tremendous intensity. In spite of this, communications

---

5   See Chapter 1, p. 71 , fn. 114.

channels functioned well; for the most part even the telephone connections to the *KTK* remained as a reprieve to the brave runners who required a considerable amount of time to deliver reports and orders.

(16) The battalions remained, with the exception of one relief, in this sector for six days. During the night of 20/21 November, *25th Division* was relieved by *44th Division* and, for the same period [i.e., 6 days] again withdrawn as counter-attack force. The old regimental quartering area shifted somewhat eastward; regimental staff and *II Battalion* were billeted in Oekene, *I Battalion* in the vicinity of Kaiphas-Den Hukker, *Garde-Füsiliere* in and around Bergmolens. The *6th* and *7th* companies billeted in Oekene later joined battalion machine-gun units quartered in Rumbeke. As a result, the forward attack positions and assembly areas were correspondingly adjusted, the reconnaissance of which became necessary.

(17) Major von Rettberg, severely stricken with typhus, had been on leave since the close of October. Unfortunately, the recovery took so long that he was unable to return to the Regiment that owed its many victories to his extraordinarily brilliant leadership. He was, at first, replaced by *Hauptmann* Appuhn, who on 19 November turned over command to Major von Westerhoven who, by Supreme Cabinet Order, had been named regimental commander; before the war he had been a general staff officer *5th Division*; more recently chief of the general staff *VII Reserve Korps*.

(18) On the afternoon of 26 November, the leaders of *RIR206* stood on the roads leading westward from Duivelshoeken in preparation to guide the Regiment, fresh after a six-day rest, into their former positions. With machine-gun companies attached, the battalions took possession of the sector in one night: *I Battalion* the covering force zone, *II* the main battle zone, *Garde-Füsiliere* remaining in reserve. A new regimental command post, withdrawn slightly during the occupation by *RIR206*, was established in an unprotected wooden barracks. The relief was complete by the early morning hours of 27 November.

(19) Seven difficult days followed. From innumerable gun barrels, the enemy, in his accustomed manner, shelled anything that even remotely seemed suitable for defence, quartering, advance or assembly. His superiority in munitions ate, in heavy salvos, into the aching terrain. His heavy calibre guns reached well into the reserve zone. The winter days appeared too short for enemy fliers: at night, if there was moonlight, they dived close to earth, strafed with machine-guns and dropped bombs on suspected positions. From the relief of opposing infantry, the possibility of attacks in this sector was assumed; for 28 November, heightened readiness was ordered. Two companies from the main battle area were deployed to the rail embankment south of *Bakrats-Hof*, the reserves pushed forward to the railway spur. Indeed, these by-the-book precautions proved premature. Only some days later, on the night of 2 December, did pounding denial and destructive fire from both sides commence in

overwhelming strength, descending across the Division from the north flank; firing that after pauses, increased during the afternoon. Green, yellow, red and white flares burst in colourful and indecipherable succession throughout the night, evidence of a bloody firefight. The Divisions' right sector, occupied by *IR117*, was attacked. The Regiment had to give up its *I Battalion*, which, on 30 November, had been withdrawn into reserve. Redeployed, it eked out two full days in the forward most lines of the adjacent right sector.

(20) The enemy's artillery activity resulted in loss after loss. The entire *II Battalion* had, by the start of December, barely 100 rifles (i.e., effective strength) available in the main battle area. Nevertheless, patrols traversed the forward area towards the enemy each night, reconnoitering in minute detail the trafficability of the difficult terrain and determining the enemy's foremost line began at the ruins of Passchendaele church. It lay, as did the entire area, on a high ridge that provided the British with numerous advantages. He [the enemy] sat, above the marshes, on dry ground where the rubble of Passchendaele offered welcome cover. The task organisation *II Battalion* ordered for its infantry and machine-gun sections in the battle area was exemplary.

(21) *16th Division* moved into *Abschnitt A* of *Gruppe Ypern* on the night of 3/4 December. The Regiment, fatigued by efforts over the preceding difficult days, turned over, following a successful relief, responsibility to *IR68* before withdrawing under cover of darkness to the small village of Beythem on the Menin-Roulers highway. From here it was guided to a new divisional rest area, bordered on the west by Kachtem and east through Ginste, by escort platoons.

(22) Here, situated between Courtrai and Thourout, the Division served as army reserve and remained, at first and then for an extended period, under the orders of the *Gruppe-Ypern* for Sector A. The term "Assault Division" was later supplanted by the new designation "Army Reserve". Army command was thus ceded authority over relief and combat employment. Duties remained much the same as before.

(23) Within this framework, the Regiment was assigned billets at Meulebeke and nearby hamlets for [headquarters] staff, *I* and *II* battalions, whilst the *Garde-Füsiliere* took over billets in the northern part of Ingelmünster, seat of the corps [*Gruppe Ypern*] staff. A report that mission transition from defence division to army reserve was, in future, to be every twelve days was met with joy. In this way, the well-being of the courageous Flanders fighters improved.

B
Infanterie-Regiment Nr. 116[6]

(1) The *25th Division* commenced the relief of *3rd Garde Division* on 6 November. This was accomplished in a way that ensured a full-strength division was stationed at Ghent. Transport trains carried the Division to Aersele, Waereghem and Denterghem; the regimental transport and machine-gun company, halting in Lederberg, traveled to Ghent by foot.

(2) The Division moved forward to relieve *11th Division* on 11 November. Boarding a waiting train for Rumbeke, the Regiment entrained without its transport. Following this, it traveled to Oekene and Cachtem where it relieved *IR38*. The transport was stored in Rumbeke. Designated *Eingreifdivision* for *Gruppe Ypern's* northern sector, the Division was deployed, between *Gruppe Staden* and *Gruppe Wijtschate*, to defend positions extending from Passchendaele to Becelaere.

(3) The English had, by the close of October, attacked continuously at Passchendaele, Becelaere and Gheluvelt. Passchendaele village was lost during 6 and 10 November. Further enemy attacks were imminent. The Regiment immediately sent forward an *Abteilung* to *Division Abschnitt A* in order to gather [sector] information. Preparations had to be made concerning approaches, defences and counter-attack positions. Code word "*Triarier Aufmarsch*" meant go forward [from vicinity of De Ruiter] to open the front; "*Fridericus Rex*"[7] meant to stand [about Vierkavenhoek] in readiness from south of De Ruiter. *25th Division* would advance in support of *44th Reserve Division* on receipt of these orders.

(4) *IR116* moved into *Abschnitt B* to relieve *RIR205* on 14 November. *I Battalion* was placed in reserve near Vierkavenhoek (later to Zilverberg and Le Cavalier), whilst *III Battalion* became the *Bereitschaft* [support] unit at Magermeirie; *II Battalion* became fighting battalion in the frontline position, where it sustained heavy losses from artillery fire. A grenade killed *Leutnant* d.R. Baasch[8] of *8th Company* during the relief.

(5) The frontline was in the same location it had been in October 1914. Weeks of fighting in this place of devastation occurred again. The area was similar to Gheluvelt, although there were fewer shelters. The *KTK* found, after much searching, a concrete pillbox to use as HQ. Companies lay in shell holes and there was little room for

---

6 Prof. Albert Hiss, *Infanterie-Regiment Kaiser Wilhelm (2. Grossherzoglich Hessisches) Nr. 116* (Oldenburg: Gerhard Stalling, 1924), pp. 155-59.
7 The *Triarier Raum* was the reserve assembly area; *Fridericus Rex* was the codename for the support assembly area. These zones were established east of the *Flandern I* Line.
8 d.R. = *der Reserve*.

manoeuvre. In front of the *Hauptwiderstandslinie* stretched a strip of *Vorfeldzone* to be defended elastically. Beyond was the enemy line. The Regiment, however, did not feel secure because it lacked men to defend the *Sicherungslinie*. Positions of the *Kampfbataillon* were echeloned as far as the *KTK*. The *Stosskompagnie* and *Nahtkommandos* were sent to the right and left flanks [of *IR115* and *IR117*], whilst machine-gun positions were hastily established.

(6) Two to three kilometres existed between the support and reserve battalion. The new method of defence provided for a tremendous amount of artillery fire support. Zones were now to be defended in place of trench lines; *Tiefengliederung* [distribution in depth] was the solution. The 2 to 3 kilometres distance was vital to the *Meldewesen* [signals]. This became the building block to a very important report centre under the supervision of *Leutnant* d.R. Geck.

(7) The *KTK* was near the telephone centre, which failed to function due to weather conditions. Wireless, *Luftfunker* [aerial signalman] and light signals were subsequently utilised. Messenger dogs and numerous pigeons were also utilised, but the latter were unreliable. *Ypern Siren*, bugle and flares provided connections with the artillery. This system was [more] efficient. The most reliable connection was through runners who communicated information mouth to mouth. They were primarily selected for their daring and excused duty from the immediate frontline. One of these (*Gef.* May) was indestructible and known as "*Kugelsicher*" [bulletproof]; he was totally reliable and nothing could bring him down. May was subsequently honoured with the award of Iron Cross I Class for his exploits during this period. The enemy had developed a system to listen in, so it was extremely important to use code words, acronyms and cryptographic messages when communicating through the *Meldewesen*.

(8) The fighting capacity of our infantry was limited during the first days in this position because the regiment was under strength. The area to be defended was constricted especially opposite the *Kolonnenhof* [Exert Farm]. An exchange of battalions was scheduled in two days. This proved impossible owing to severe weather conditions. The rain was so heavy that the right flank company was separated from the rest of the Regiment by a swamp. Enemy artillery was close by and bombarded the position continuously.

(9) The traditional *Sanitätspause* was maintained no matter where the English fought. There was a great deal of activity by enemy fliers who frequently strafed regimental positions. These airmen also dropped leaflets encouraging the men to vacate their shell holes [and surrender]. They thought we would give ourselves up. The English threw out leaflets near Gheluvelt announcing their tremendous successes in Flanders; this was the way our enemy perceived battlefield events.

(10) Twentieth November was the day the English attempted a breakthrough near Cambrai and *RIR208* relieved *IR116*. Following this, the regiment moved into quarters vacated six days previously. The Division was once again designated *Eingreifdivision*. This peaceful period, lasting for six days, was used to construct shelters, rest and train. On 26 November *25th Division* relieved *44th Reserve Division* as *Kampfdivision* in *Abschnitt A*. *IR116* replaced *RIR208* near Passchendaele. The positioning of battalions was identical to that of our first tour in this sector.

(11) Shell holes occupied by the infantry were rapidly filling up with water. The men were pressed for time in applying the new method of *Siegfried Unterschlupfe* [Siegfried Shelter], which worked very well. Eight to ten concave corrugated metal sheets were placed one after the other over a flat bottom supported by steel posts and then covered with 1 metre of earth. This gave four to six infantrymen protection from shell splinters, rain and cold. Positioned near the remnants of hedges, bushes or buildings, they were difficult to locate, even from the air.

(12) The fighting now increased in intensity. An officer's patrol under *Leutnant* d.R. Bode, comprising eight men of *7th Company*, reconnoitered as far as Passchendaele Church. The enemy's infantry, however, remained very quiet. An increase in hostile artillery fire led to the realization that the enemy was preparing another attack. The *KTK* was bombarded again and again. *Weidenhof* [Horne Farm] and *Grenzhof* [Greenly Corner] were also shelled on a daily basis, whilst the *Bereitschaftbataillon* [BTK] at Magermeirie was bombed from the air.

(13) On 30 November, *I Battalion* relieved *III Battalion* in the frontline, the latter moving into reserve; *II* into support. Hostile artillery fire became more severe throughout this day and the next. *Leutnant* d.R. Wust, *Vzfw.* Rothermel, and four men of *3rd Company* were killed by a direct hit.

(14) The frontline sustained a surprisingly heavy bombardment at approximately 3:00 a.m. on 2 December. The English attacked out of the right swamp in four to five waves within a quarter of an hour. They overran, despite determined resistance, the right wing boundary with *IR117* as far as the *Hauptwiderstandslinie*. Here a tremendous struggle ensued with our *2nd Company* and *IR117's 9th Company*. Men hovered around *Führer Leutnant* d.R. Schade and Fuchs. Both officers were killed and company resistance broke after bitter close-quarter fighting. The enemy was able to advance, despite fierce defensive fire, and drive the remainder of *2nd Company* into the swampy low ground beyond. Following this, *4th Company* and part of *Leib Kompagnie* from the *KTK* (*Leutnant* d.R. Albers) counter-attacked. *Leib Kompagnie* remnants, accompanied by five machine-guns, occupied Height 40. *IR117*, led by *Hauptmann* von Arnim [*Kampftruppenkommandeur*] closed the gap and resisted further attacks.

(15) *III Battalion* (in reserve) received orders to proceed to Magermeirie; *6th* and *8th* companies, rushed forward to Pottegemsgut, were shelled – 10 dead in *8th Company* – on the way. Their gallant leader, *Leutnant* d.R. Meier, was killed whilst making his way to the *KTK* for orders; *Vzfw.* Schnieder took command following this. In the meantime, *4th* and *Leib* companies arrived in place under *Leutnant* d.R. Hoffmann. *Leutnant* d.R. Plagge was one of the first to be wounded during the counter-attack. *Vzfw.* Fischer and Krichbaum (*Leib Kompagnie*) pushed on from trench to trench with hand grenades. Hard work was done and the line again in our possession at approximately 10:00 a.m. Enemy losses in dead and wounded were great with twenty prisoners remaining in our hands, but many good *Kameraden* were missed on our side.

(16) One hero of the day, subsequently killed by shellfire, was *Leutnant* d.R. Gombel, commander of *1st MG Company*. *Vzfw.* Gumbrecht, despite severe wounds, took over with rifle in hand until the struggle's victorious conclusion. Heavy artillery and air fighting continued for the remainder of the day. This caused many casualties. Losses in *3rd Company* were particularly severe.

(17) Fighting died down after nightfall. The reserve battalion was called back to Zilverberg; *II Battalion* was sent forward to replace the battered *I Battalion*. Our fliers reported a heavily occupied enemy line at the start of the next day, although the expected attack failed to materialize. The Regiment was relieved and marched to Emelgem, Cachtem and Ingelmünster on 4 December. Twelve days of peace followed. Division tactics were adjusted at this time. *25th Division's* scheduled withdrawal to Army Reserve in Gruppe *Ypern's* southern sector was postponed due to the continued training.

(18) The Regiment's next move was to Lendelede and Winkle St Eloi, where accommodation was better. Focus was, following arrival, maintained on regimental business and company training. The long period of rest and reorganisation came to an end on 16 December when the *Hessisches Division* relieved *36th Division* in *Abschnitt C*.

C
Infanterie-Leibregiment Nr. 117[9]

(1) The relief of *3rd Garde Division* commenced on 6 November. *25th Division* was now attached to *Gruppe Ypern*. *Gruppe Wijtschate*, the line of which extended from Passchendaele to Becelaere, joined *Gruppe Ypern* in the south. The *II* and *III* battalions left from St Jills at 9:00 a.m., regimental staff and *I Battalion* departing from St Nicholas at 5:00 p.m. The Regiment detrained at Meulebeke and Wareghem during

---

9   Hauptmann Kurt Offenbacher, *Die Geschichte des Infanterie-Leibregiments Grossherzogin (3. Grossherzoglich Hessisches) Nr. 117* (Oldenburg: Gerhard Stalling, 1931), pp.191-97.

the night of the 6th. It was necessary to dispatch the field kitchen and horses by rail, in order to keep transport trains as unencumbered as possible; everyone else had to march. A rest stop was made at Ghent during the move forward.

(2) Attached to OHL reserve, the regimental staff, with *I* and *III* battalions, moved to Meulebeke whilst *II Battalion* was dispatched to Oosttrosebeke. Training was intensified; *Hauptmann* von Arnim[10] and *III Battalion* demonstrating a textbook scheme based on *AOK* [*Armeeoberkommando*] *Nr. 4* guidelines for *Vorfeldzone* and *Hauptwiderstandslinie* defence. The Division was ordered, following arrival of its last elements, to the forward area on 11 November.

(3) Further English attempts to break through were, despite some minor gains, unsuccessful. The German front held fast. Behind every frontline was an *Eingreifdivision*. The Regiment moved forward as "*Eingreifstaffel Alice*." Billets for HQ Staff and *III Battalion* were found in De Ruiter; *II Battalion* in Duivelshoeken and *I Battalion* in Zilverberg.

(4) To the front, *44th Reserve Division* occupied *Abschnitt A* [east of Passchendaele] of *Gruppe Ypern*. The *199th Reserve Division* of *Gruppe Staden* was on the right with *4th Division* in support. On the left, *11th Division* occupied *Abschnitt B* with *11th Bavarian Division* in support. All future planning, intelligence and tactics were discussed with the *Eingreifgruppen*. At the code word "*Triarier Aufmarsch*", the entire Regiment would deploy south of De Ruiter; or to the front, or to the neighbouring sector. At code word "*Fridericus Rex*", it would proceed [from about Vierkavenhoek] to *Abschnitt A*. The reconnoitering of various routes and positions to be taken up for the task ahead ensured the Regiment was busy during the next two days. Plans to relieve *44th Reserve Division* in *Abschnitt A* were also under preparation. The exchange occurred during the night of 14/15 November.

(5) The *I Battalion* was deployed as *Kampfbataillon* opposite the northern exit of Passchendaele; *II Battalion* was at the ready position east of the *Grenshof*, *III Battalion* in reserve. Companies of the *Kampfbataillon* were situated in muddy shell holes without protection from the elements. The battlefield, although resembling Gheluvelt,

---

10   *Hauptmann* Achim Konstantin Rudolf von Arnim (1881-1940). Entered military service as *Fahnenjunker* (*1.Garde Regiment zu Fuß*) 1900; *Leutnant* 1901; *Kriegsakademie* 1908-11; *Oberleutnant* January 1910; Attached General Staff 1911-14; *Hauptmann* March 1914; Assigned General Staff March 1914-May 1916; assigned (successively) to General Staff *Garde Korps*, *Second Army* and as 1st General Staff Officer (Intelligence) *38th Division* August 1914-May 1916; Company Commander *Hessisches Infanterie-Regiment Nr. 115* May-July 1916; wounded and hospitalized July-December 1916; Battalion Commander *Hessisches Infanterie-Regiment Nr.115* December 1916-January 1917; Commander *III Battalion, Hessisches Infanterie-Regiment Nr. 117* January 1917.

was actually worse. It was impossible to remain in one position because of the morass. There was, other than a ruined farmhouse, no shelter or place to establish the *KTK*. The *Vorfeldzone* stretched in front of the *Hauptwiderstandslinie*. The *Sicherungslinie* protected the *Vorfeldzone*, while the *Kampfbataillon* was organised in depth. The zone extended to the *Gefechtsstand* [command post] of the *KTK*, and connected to the position of the *BTK* – 2 kilometres deep as far as the *RTK*. Shelter found in the rear zone was slightly better, the remains of houses and unsplintered planks providing cover. The Siegfried housing protected the men from rain and cold. All zone machine-guns were divided and positioned into platform positions. The battle would no longer be fought in linear trenches; zones would be defended instead.

(6) Enemy artillery fire was very active and heavy. Communications remained intact thus saving the lives of many brave runners. At 7:45 a.m. on 15 November, the enemy increased his artillery activity to drumfire on the frontline; another attack appeared imminent. Our artillery responded with destructive fire, which prevented any movement. The artillery on both sides halted at approximately 9:00 a.m. A *Sanitatspause* followed; removal of enemy wounded was then observed.

(7) The regimental commander deemed it necessary to relieve forward units after two days due to frontline conditions and continuous mortar fire. These movements occurred despite dangerous road conditions. The *II Battalion* moved to the front as *Kampfbataillon* on the night of 16/17 November. *I Battalion* was placed in reserve, whilst *III Battalion* was dispatched to the *Bereitschaftraum* [on-call or secondary zone]. *II Battalion* sustained heavy loss from enemy artillery fire after wandering into the English safety line. The HQ of the *KTK* was heavily shelled on the evening of the 18th. A direct hit killed *II Battalion* commander *Hauptmann* d.R. Schott, who had fought bravely at Bouchavesnes and Gheluvelt. *Leutnant* d.R. Brandscheid was wounded; *Obsterleutnant* Offenbacher took charge. *III Battalion* relieved *II Battalion* in the frontline that night. *3rd Company* was also dispatched by the *Bereitschaftbataillon* (*I Battalion*) as *Nahtkompagnie* to Kalve where it was placed under command of the neighbouring regiment.

(8) The high command realised the health of the Division was poor after six days [in the frontline]. *RIR205* (*44th Reserve Division*) relieved the Regiment in *Abschnitt Nord*; *44th Division* was unpopular and had a rowdy reputation; they were the worst. The *Gefechtsstand* [command post] of the *KTK* sustained a second direct hit and the *3rd MG Company* commander (*Leutnant* d.R. Gerbracht) was killed. Casualties during the six succeeding days were 2 officers and 23 men killed; 4 officers and 81 men wounded. The Regiment, on reverting to *Eingreifgruppe Alice*, returned to previously occupied billets where time was spent repairing shelters.

(9) 26 November brought another exchange with *44th Division*. The Regiment moved into the same old sector: *I Battalion* as *Kampfbataillon*, *II* as *Bereitschaft* and *III* as

reserve. It remained in the line for six days, with the exchange of battalions occurring within two days. The infantry experienced heavy fighting from the moment of arrival. This resulted from the need to enlarge the *Vorfeldzone*. The enemy was so close that lively exchanges between patrols were common. The *Sicherunglinie* was, during the next few evenings, enlarged by 300 metres. Trench and dugout construction was impossible due to steady rain that transformed the area into swampland.

(10) It rained buckets whilst *III Battalion* relieved *II Battalion* during the unusually quiet night of 1/2 December. A few grenades were found lying about the *Hauptwiderstandslinie*; otherwise it was a dark and stormy night [sic].[11] Suddenly, around 3:00 a.m., a rushing, wild *abriegellungsfeuer* [box barrage] was fired beyond the *Hauptwiderstandslinie*. At the same time enemy storm troops rushed the *Sicherungslinie*. These were followed by very strong formations advancing to assault the *Hauptwiderstandslinie*.

(11) On the right, the *11th Company*, (under the leadership of *Leutnant* d.R. Huch) withstood the assault with 25 men and 4 light machine-guns (08/15). A wide space, where *10th Company* under *Leutnant* Keiper sheltered English prisoners within *Granatlöchern* [grenade holes], existed to the left of this post. Again on the left, separated by another space, *Leutnants* d.R. Ludewig and Shuhmacher and the remainder of *12th Company* were situated. *Unteroffizier* Sudheimer and *Schutze* Ehrhardt fired, sometimes from the front and rear, a light machine-gun to avoid being overrun. Further left, the next space was occupied in strength by the enemy. Elements of *9th Company* with *Vzfw*. Scherstuhl and 12 men remained in this area. No one knew the fate of *Kompagnie Führer Leutnant* Fuchs. This small group was fully aware that the Regiment's left wing, in addition to *2nd Company IR116*, was completely surrounded.

(12) At 3:45 a.m. *Leutnant* Fuchs' young orderly stumbled into *Hauptmann* von Arnim's HQ and breathlessly announced that the left sector of *9th Company* had been unexpectedly attacked. Fuchs had been shot in the heart at very close range. *Unteroffizier* Balz bashed the assailant's head in, only to be struck down at the same moment by a bullet in the stomach; it was the same everywhere.

(13) The English had broken in on a wide front. *Hauptmann* von Arnim immediately ordered a *zug* [section] of the *1st MG Company* to occupy the *Aufnahmestellung* (assembly area). He also grabbed sections of the *2nd* and *4th* companies to meet the attack in front. *Leutnants* d.R. Lange and Hein (*2nd Company*) were severely wounded. The companies moved toward the front as far as *Kapellenhof*. *Leutnant* Hoffmann (*4th Company*) followed behind. In the swampy *trichtergelände* [shell hole terrain] the exhausted men, loaded down with heavy packs and machine-guns, were stuck

---

11 The author is mistaken about the prevailing weather conditions.

because of darkness and bad ground conditions. Only two groups eventually reached the breach. Further resistance was hopeless; defence of the remaining ground was all that could be hoped for.

(14) The morning came and with it unbelievable behaviour by the English. Troops of Sanitäts *Komp. 45* assisted with bandaging and cared for our own and the enemy wounded. English stretcher-bearers also provided succor. Our *Sanitäts* helpers discovered there were approximately 150 English in the vicinity of the breach, and altogether about 600 between and behind their own position. There was no reaction, despite considerable local superiority, when *Gef.* Speiz (*9th Company*) led eight prisoners away.

(15) *Hauptmann* von Arnim now realised he had only 80 to 90 rifles and 10 machine-guns with limited supplies of ammunition available. The enemy, however, lacked the will to continue the struggle. Leaving *Vzfw.* Woeste (*2nd Company*) in charge, he raced to the rear to organise a systematic counter-attack.[12] Woeste, having observed the enemy withdrawing under pressure from *4th Company IR116* at 12:00 p.m., seized this moment to order an all-out attack. Taking prisoners as the English hurriedly withdrew, the *Hauptwiderstandslinie* was reached and contact made with *Vzfw.* Scherstuhl and *9th Company.*

(16) In the meantime, artillery fire from both sides continued. It was very difficult for companies to maintain touch, *Gef.* Becker and *Sanität* Matzer acting as volunteer runners between units. Heavy fighting resumed at 5:00 pm. It was especially severe for *12th Company.* By sheer luck this unit had been issued new hand grenades and was thus well equipped to resist. Arrival of darkness also assisted the beleaguered men. *Stosstruppen* arrived at midnight and cleared the *Sicherungslinie* area without further loss. *I Battalion IR115* now arrived to relieve the Regiment. On the night of 3/4 December *16th Division* relieved the entire Division, *IR29* arriving in our sector to begin the relief.

(17) Trains were waiting at Beythem to transport the regiment to new quarters. *I Battalion* went to Meulebeke, *II* to Ginste and *III* to Marialoop. Losses during the previous six days were: 1 officer (Fuchs) and 59 men killed, 2 officers (Lange and Hein) and 145 men wounded, 32 missing. The Division remained an *Eingreifdivision* attached to *Gruppe Ypern* in *Abschnitt A* for the time being. On 8 December it was necessary to delay the projected move south. The Division was instead sent to *Abschnitt*

---

12 Arnim was wounded whilst making way to the rear. Full recovery was followed by participation in the 1918 spring offensive during which he earned the *Pour le Mérite* for outstanding leadership, distinguished planning and successful operations. Postwar Professor of *Wehrverfassung* (Military Science) at the *Technische Hochschule*, subsequent Third Reich activity included party membership and promotion to SA *Gruppenführer.*. Promoted *Oberstleutnant* in 1939, he was killed near Monchy Lagache on 24 May 1940.

C. Its task, however, remained the same. New quarters were taken up: regimental staff, *I* and *II* battalions to Oyghem, *III Battalion* to Wielsbeke.

38th Thüringian Division
D
Infanterie-Regiment Nr. 94[13]

(1) New positions south of the Houthulst Forest comprised some of the most difficult Flanders terrain. Our weaponry capabilities were diminished for the first time on this front. The Regiment suffered from extreme wet, cold and swampy conditions in the forward area.

(2) *Vizefeldwebel* Maier Eckhardt composed an article for *Patrouillen Zeitung* announcing a visit, during which the [38th] Division's current situation would be explained, by the Grand Duke on 24 November.[14] Greeting the officers first, the Grand Duke reviewed the Regiment. The view was, despite the clouds, the clearest experienced by the Regiment since arrival in the area. For the first time one could see the many fine parallel lines of the Flanders landscape. It was so clear that poplar trees lining the road were also discernable. All important map points could be observed. One could also view small towns and hamlets at a distance. With a telescope one could see at a greater distance, the busy railways in the English hinterland to the smallest detail. The landscape could be clearly viewed from the Kemmelberg in the SW, to the ruined cathedral at Ypres and the narrow church tower of Poperinghe.

(3) A *Patrouillen Zeitung* article described the third largest day of combat experienced by the Regiment in the World War. It took place on 2 December 1917 near Passchendaele:

The Regiment, having left the line on 25 November, hoped for a period of rest over the Christmas holidays. For the third time, however, it prepared to take over positions at Houthulst Forest. A change of orders arrived that same day; *38th Division* would take up a new section of front. *IR94* was quartered at Roulers on this day. The Division was placed on alert for the frontline early on the 28th. Relief of positions south of Westroosebeke during the evening of 30 November confirmed this would be the worst fighting encountered on the Flanders front thus far.

13 Alexander von Hartmann, *Das Infanterie Regiment Grossherzog von Sachsen (5. Thüringisches) No. 94* im *Weltkrieg* (Berlin: Verlag von Klasing & Co., 1921), pp. 235-39.
14 Grand Duke Wilhelm Ernest of Saxe Weimar Eisenach (1876-1923).

(4) The English desire to capture the Westroosebeke heights could only be achieved by frontal attack. The position had to be held at all costs. *III Battalion* relieved the frontline as planned on the night of 1 December. The will of the officers and men surmounted all difficulties as they moved forward through the hitherto unknown swampy and muddy sector. Three Englishmen were captured and important disclosures made. Artillery fire was very heavy and continued throughout the night.

(5) Enemy artillery fire decreased during the early hours of 2 December. By 2:00 a.m., it was eerily quiet over the entire area. This was a bad omen. The men continued to make their rabbit hole positions as comfortable as possible whilst maintaining good spirits and increased vigilance.

(6) Shortly before 2:00 a.m. an English patrol approached the right of *2nd Company* and was shot down. The *Vorfeldzone* reported much activity and moving about in the enemy line. At first this was thought to be only a relief in progress. Shortly before 3:00 a.m., *9th Company* recognised that an English assault was imminent. Annihilation [artillery] fire was immediately called for.

(7) The English attack commenced at 3:20 a.m. [sic]. The German defensive barrage commenced firing whilst English drumfire bombarded our line simultaneously. The enemy was very strong, attacking *IR94* with three battalions. The men in the outpost line opened strong fire with rifles and machine-guns. Artillery and *Minenwerfer* fire also inflicted great loss. The English, constantly sending more men forward, broke through the *Vorfeldzone* in two places before reaching the *Hauptwiderstandslinie* [east of Hill 52]. Like the opening of floodgates, the English came in on the right flank and in the centre of *11th Company* holding the *Vorfeldzone*. Fighting step-by-step, the Regiment withdrew, resisting with hand grenades and, in certain places, bloody bayonet and hand-to-hand combat. *9th Company* was rushed forward and resisted with continuous rifle and machine-gun fire.

(8) The attack was halted on the left wing [opposite Northern Redoubt and Teall Cottage], whilst the threat to the right wing forced a retirement to the *Hauptwiderstandslinie*. Like islands, the garrison of the *Vorfeldzone* remained in isolated groups and fought back. At 3:15 a.m. the English appeared before the *Hauptwiderstandslinie*. Well aimed fire forced them to retire. Five prisoners were captured during the withdrawal; they claimed to be intoxicated during interrogation.[15]

---

15 Accusations of intoxication amongst attacking British and Dominion troops were a common German assertion that was 'almost certainly not true.' See Nigel Cave, *Passchendaele: The Fight for the Village* (London: Leo Cooper, 1997), p. 108.

(9) The *9th Company* recaptured the *Hauptwiderstandslinie*; *2nd Company*, passing through the former, pushed on a further 20 metres before reoccupying the *Vorfeldzone*. Thus the Regiment freed itself from threat of encirclement. Serious fighting continued within the *Hauptwiderstandslinie*, as machine-gun fire from *3rd Company* forced the enemy to retreat; *12th Company* demonstrated courageous resistance also.

(10) On the right wing, the *Hauptwiderstandslinie* of the neighbouring regiment splintered under constant machine-gun fire. *Unteroffizier* Rohne, remaining like a cornerstone at his post, secured, together with *1st Company*, the position with flanking fire. This brought the attack to a standstill. A strong defence by the *KTK* and *4th Company* prevented further attacks from developing; all fighting ceased at daybreak.

(11) English medical personnel arrived around 9:00 a.m. Efforts to recover their dead and wounded were observed at many places before our line. *4th Company* removed the remaining enemy casualties from the *Vorfeldzone*. The sector of the neighbouring regiment was cleared of fallen English with the assistance of *4th Company* that afternoon.

(12) At 5:00 p.m. the English [16th NF], attacking again in many waves, attempted to capture the area on the right flank. Rifle and machine-gun fire prevented this. The *Vorfeldzone* was again secure. Forty-six prisoners and 14 machine-guns were captured. Regimental losses killed and wounded were 11 officers and 200 men. The men of *5th Company* stood sadly before a stretcher on which lay the body of their beloved *Leutnant* Junge, who had led them through many successful engagements.

(13) On 3 December the *Heeresbericht* [Army Bulletin] reported the fighting on 1/2 December: Early yesterday, after violent drumfire during a moonlight night, the English with strong forces attacked our positions at and north of Passchendaele. Thüringian and Hessian troops threw back the enemy in a sharp counter-attack and made 60 prisoners.

(14) *III Battalion's* commander invited companies to the *Kirchplatz* on 11 December for a ceremony honouring their bravery during the 2 December fighting. The Divisional Commander [*General-Leutnant* Schultheis] awarded Iron Crosses and expressed thanks during a very short address. The Regiment was also congratulated for its energy, strength and well-executed defence during which many English were killed or captured. The enemy, he concluded, did not obtain what they wished to capture; *Höhenrücken – Passendale* [and] Westroosebeke remained in our hands. All did their duty throughout the engagement.

(15) The Flanders Army was honoured by a visit from the Emperor following the close (23 December) of the great battle. Fifty select men from the Division (under the command of Major von Pfannenberg) were awarded the Iron Cross II class during the ceremony.

E
Infanterie-Regiment Nr. 95[16]

(1) The *38th Division* was assigned to *Fourth Army's* Flanders reserve. On 10 November, orders were changed and it was designated an *Eingreifdivision* attached to *Gruppe Staden* thus relieving *27th [Württemburg] Division*. Front commanders immediately proceeded to Gits, and from there to Hazewind where they joined *Grenadier Regiment Nr. 123* in *Eingreif Gruppe B* of *Division 3*. The Division would remain attached to *Gruppe Staden* throughout the great Flanders battle. Special weapons were also issued during this time.

(2) The regiment was to the rear of Houthulst Forest – once the preserve of the Belgian King – now reduced to a sea of shell holes and mud. Enormous fallen trees prevented movement. This chaos, of which more was to come, would become familiar.

(3) Divisional relief, commenced on 23 November, was complete by the 24th. The enemy, as always during reliefs, became very nervous and a night attack was anticipated by Army Group HQ. It was believed the English would attempt a *handstreich* [raid] in an attempt to gain better positions on drier ground. Companies were notified the relief would be delayed, although nothing occurred that evening. The Tommies eventually calmed down. To the south, near Westroosebeke, there appeared to be a great deal of fighting. The changeover was not complete until 25 November.

(4) Hopes that the Division had earned some rest were dashed with the relief of *4th Division* in its capacity as *Eingreifdivision* attached to *Abschnitt B* of *Gruppe Staden* (*Garde Reserve Korps*). The first thing battalions did was seek out quarters in nearby communities; *I Battalion* marched to Bevern, *II* to Ardone and *III* to Ardeppelhoek.

(5) The Regiment, thus situated, began preparations for the anticipated battle, but Tommy didn't come and the march was cancelled. Still on alert and ready, a Brigade order announced imminent relief. No one, although all were in desperate need of rest, believed this to be true. Constant wet and bad bivouacs under the open sky sickened the men. Swelling of the feet from dampness caused great suffering. The English, wearing unsuitable laced boots and *Gamaschen* [puttees] in the Flanders mud, suffered more. The German issue jackboot was much better in the prevailing conditions.

(6) Orders for the relief of the line between Passchendaele and Westroosebeke were issued on 30 November. The changeover with *IR357* was completed on 1 December.

---

16 Major A.D. Buttmann, *Kriegsgeschichte des Koninglich Preusischen 6. Thüringischen Infanterie Regiment Nr. 95: 1914-1918* (Zeulenroda, Thüringen: Verlag Bernhard Sporn, 1935), pp. 249-56.

The much fought over *Feldherrnhügel* [General's Hill] with *Nordhof* [Void Farm] on the left wing, was the position taken up by the Regiment. The battle sector was the typical Flanders landscape, with many shrubs, rows of trees and bullet-riddled farmhouses. The elevated area, extending as far as the *Hauptwiderstandslinie*, offered good observation. Mud separated the opposing lines below the slope. The enemy, undergoing a difficult time in the inundated sector, would no doubt attempt to seize the heights. English desire to reach the high ground was demonstrated by the fact that they fired every available calibre to wear the Regiment down before the next assault.

(7) A light coating of snow covered the landscape and a full moon illuminated the night sky, so one had to be careful. At around 11:00 p.m. on the evening of 1 December, not long after the Regiment settled into [new] positions, the commander of *7th Company* discovered approximately 30 to 40 English in front of the *Vorfeldzone*. Believed to be ration carriers who lost their way, they were immediately shot down.

(8) At 2:15 a.m. on 2 December, a strong twenty-man patrol was sighted opposite the *Vorfeldzone* and easily dispersed. Suddenly, in the moonlight, an unbroken enemy line was discovered approaching the *Feldherrnhügel*. Shortly before 3:00 a.m., they attacked through the deep mud. Abruptly, artillery fire, approaching the level of drumfire, bombarded the [divisional] hinterland where all the light and heavy guns were deployed. Now there was work with heavy firing by our artillery, which hailed down shells on the attackers. The full moon gave our gunners the advantage because they could observe rows and rows of the enemy and inflict many casualties. Despite all, the tough English pressed forward approximately 20 metres and threw themselves to the ground.

(9) The Regiment now underwent heavy grenade volleys which accounted for many machine-gunners and, supported by heavy artillery fire, the enemy advanced to breach the line. The brave defenders remained unperturbed. In close fighting with companions of *6th* and *7th* companies, they continued to resist at the exhortation of their officers – *Leutnants* d.R. Rossger, Dollinger, *Vzfw*. Scheler and *Vzfw*. Hess. No ground was lost despite heavy losses. Ninety to one hundred dead were counted in front of the small *Abschnitt* of *7th Company* and the English had to retreat. The enemy on the right wing had an easier avenue of retreat due to drier ground conditions.

(10) On the right wing, the English approached the front of outpost line 4. The *8th Company* fought hard – *Leutnant* d.R. Linck bleeding to death from wounds. A small group resisted from front and rear of the *Vorfeldzone* and killed many of the enemy with light machine-gun fire. They [defenders] were subsequently able to reach the safe area [behind].

(11) On the left wing, the English broke through to the *Hauptwiderstandslinie* and there made themselves secure. Heavy bayonet and grenade fighting occurred. The

enemy was too strong for the small, leaderless groups; it appeared they would conquer. *Leutnant* d.R. Rossger, recognising the danger at the last moment, gathered 15 men armed with machine-guns. Delegating command to *Vzfw*. Scheler and *Vzfw*. Hess, he threw himself and the 15 against the storming Tommies. *Feldwebel-Leutnant* Frobe[17] (commander of *5th Company*) also joined the fray with his best men. The man against man struggle halted the enemy. Not a foot of ground was lost; the gap was closed and combat came to a standstill. In the centre of the captured line was a post occupied by three brave men (*Leutnant* d. R. Vogt, *Gefreiter* Fiestner and *Gefreiter* Landwehrmann) of *IR95* who prevented the enemy from approaching.

(12) *Oberstleutnant* von Selle (HQ in Westroosebeke) recognised the critical situation at the *Feldherrnhügel*. At 8:30 a.m. he ordered *Leutnant* d.R. Martini – the most senior officer present – to attack from the left wing near *Nordhof* and force back the enemy breakthrough. The order proved extremely difficult to execute due to the fact that the enemy could observe all daylight movement. The task was only accomplished by having men crawl forward a few at a time. Martini, although delayed until the afternoon, managed to carry out this deployment. The enemy, unwilling to surrender his gains, proceeded to strengthen the newly captured positions.

(13) The enemy could redeem past failures if he captured the *Höhenrücken* of the *Feldherrnhügel*. Yes. If not for the damned Germans – the Huns; they forgot we fight for the safety of our home and country. At 3:00 in the afternoon, *Leutnant* Martini, with *Leutnant* d.R. Klopple and *12th Company*, counter-attacked the enemy. Step by step, with intense hand grenade fighting, they slowly but surely, as planned, secured the flank.

(14) The [main] counter-attack commenced in broad daylight at 5:15 p.m. when *11th* and *12th* companies with two *Truppen* of *9th Company* attacked. Annihilation fire was requested and fixed on the right positions simultaneously. The Tommies, resisting heavily at first, realised that no further headway could be made and withdrew with heavy losses. *Leutnant* d.R. Vogt and his companions [still holding out in the *Hauptwiderstandslinie*] were liberated as the enemy fell back.

(15) Not an inch of ground was gained by the English. They were thrown back to their position in the *sumpf* [mud]. The commanding heights remained in our hands. Maps discovered on the bodies of the English dead revealed the enemy had attacked with five battalions; very few of these poor souls returned. Hundreds of English dead

---

17 *Feldwebel-Leutnant* (Sergeant-Leutnant) was a wartime rank culled from NCOs (generally retired, but if active with at least six years' service) who were deemed to have the qualifications to fulfill a Lieutenant's rank, but without the qualifications to be commissioned.

lay about the *Vorfeldzone*. Our losses, however, were not few, but, thank God, more were wounded than dead. Captured booty consisted of 14 prisoners and eight Lewis Guns. On 2 December 1917 the Regiment again demonstrated, despite a lack of rest for months, great heroism. Through all this fighting it maintained its reputation with the high command.

(16) Captured maps divulged it was vital for the English to reach the commanding heights overlooking U-boat bases situated in the Brugge basin. The eastern slopes of the *Feldherrnhügel* protected the entire light and heavy artillery. It would have been a tremendous victory had the enemy succeeded. Such a success might have led to an early end of the war. That evening, *II Battalion*, having sustained the greatest losses and endured the heaviest fighting, was withdrawn into reserve and replaced by *I Battalion*. Enemy activity was confined to artillery and machine-gun barrages.

(17) At 3:00 a.m. on 5 December, the regimental *Gefechtsstand* sustained a direct hit that wounded *Obersleutnant* von Selle who, nonetheless, remained with his men. The Regiment was very much in need of rest. With subdued joy, the men received confirmation of relief. Relieved by *IR91* on the night of 7/8 December, *I Battalion* returned to Bevern, *II Battalion* to Ardone and *III Battalion* to Ardepplehoek after which the Regiment proceeded to *Roulers Nord* where it was quartered. The quiet proved short-lived, the Regiment returning to the hard-fought *Feldherrnhügel* of 2 December on the night of 12/13 December. Troops were transported by light railway to Most. The Flanders battle appeared to be over; fighting became less and less every day. Tommy, with masses of men and material, had gained nothing to speak of.

(18) On the night of 17/18 December, *Unteroffizier* Tappe and *Gefreiter* Glaser of *4th Company* led, on their own initiative, four men each from of 1st and 2nd companies, on a patrol to obtain prisoners from an enemy post known as "*Engländernest*". The post was, much to their surprise, discovered to be unoccupied. No sign of the enemy was encountered as they proceeded further along. Exiting the mud, they reached the road some 500 metres beyond the *Vorfeldlinie*. This discovery was followed by occupation and consolidation of the area. An Englishman with black and swollen feet came forward [to surrender] on 18 December. He was, like the majority of Tommies constantly walking about and standing in water, afflicted with trench foot.

(19) The Regiment was relieved on the night of 18/19 December. Christmas was celebrated at Oostkamp near Brugge. A visit by the Emperor, who wanted to spend the holiday with his Regiment in the field, was a notable event during this period. Festivities and church services took place with the Grand Duke in attendance.

F
Infanterie-Regiment Nr. 96[18]

(1) English attacks between Langemarck and Hollebeke achieved some success. Eighty-six [German] divisions were deployed during the subsequent fighting. These [formations] prevented the enemy from reaching the Flanders plain. The enemy, however, still hoped to achieve a breakthrough with partial attacks. Our front positions suffered greatly from destructive fire. *Eingreifdivisionen* encountered difficulties in reaching the forward area; a change of tactics was necessary. A *Vorfeldzone* of 500 to 1,000 metres, occupied by a thin line of machine-gun outposts, was established in front of the *Hauptwiderstandslinie*. *Vorfeldzone* outposts would retire to the *Hauptwiderstandslinie* during large-scale attacks. This defensive elasticity in the face of any attack gave the *Vorfeldkämpfer* time to await the arrival of *Eingreifdivisionen*.

(2) Constant rain created difficulties for the German defenders. Trenches and concrete shelters failed to provide refuge from the wet due to the high water table; the whole area was a complete field of mud. Men were hungry, frozen and lacked cover from artillery fire. This was the condition of *IR96* when it arrived at Deerlyk and St Louis. A new order, stating that [38th] Division would be transferred from *Gruppe Wijtschate* to *Gruppe Staden*, arrived after reorganisation.

(3) 11 November found battalions ready for entrainment at Swevegn. The train passed through Courtrai and Roulers to Gits. There was, on arrival, no [destination] order. Troops remained standing about until receipt of instructions to take up quarters at Lichtervelde. Units already billeted there having occupied all available space, quarters had to be shared with *IR120*. Additional space was arranged for following the arrival of *III Battalion* on 12 November.

(4) The Regiment was assigned to *Abschnitt 3* of *Gruppe Staden*. Two divisions, *41st Division* (*Stellung Division*) and *38th Division* (*Eingreifdivision*) were deployed in this sector. *IR94* and *IR95* were quartered at Gits. The Division, remaining in a constant state of readiness, carried out much needed machine-gun training with *Ersatzleute* [replacements]. Succeeding days were spent this way until orders to relieve *IR18* arrived on 16 November. *II Battalion* was to be *Bereitschafts* [BTK] *Battalion*; *I* and *III* battalions were designated forward and reserve battalions respectively. The Regiment proceeded to Houthulst Forest. It received, after a relatively quiet period, orders for relief by *IR18* on 24 November. The exchange was complete by the following day. An unexpected telephone message to move was received on 26 November. The

---

18 A. Bolsche, *Sturmflut: Das Erleben des 7. Thür. Infanterie-Regiments Nr. 96 im Weltkrieg: Auf Grund der Kriegstagebücher und Regimentsakten bearbeitet* (Zeulenroda, Thüringen: Verlag Bernhard Sporn, 1935), pp. 451-57.

38th Division, redesignated *Eingreifdivision,* was ordered to replace *4th Division* of *Gruppe Staden's* left wing. Billets were, on arrival at Wynendaele, scarce and unacceptable. Additional billeting arrangements, following lengthy discussions with the Town Major, were made to house the regimental staff in Roulers. Remaining in battle readiness, a degree of peace and order was now experienced by the Regiment. Arrangements were made to relieve *IR14* (*4th Division*) every six days.

(5) The *38th Division* relieved *199th Reserve Division* in *Abschnitt B* on 30 November, remaining there for six days. *IR96* replaced *IR114* SW of Westroosebeke. A small area was found for the *BTK* and *KTK* on the commanding heights. Southwest of this spot stretched the large battle sector valley as far as the Paddebeek. The depression was very muddy and, in some areas, impassable. A mid-way strip of land offered a firm footing southward as far as the Paddebeek. Divisional sector organisation was constrained by bad terrain conditions and the limited number of concrete shelters. Companies were echeloned in depth; A Company in front, B, C and D in rear.

(6) A wide *Abschnittsbesetzung* [occupied sector] of the firing line was non-existent. Contact with the right could not be established, whilst there was at least eye contact on the left. Mud prevented large-scale attacks from occurring, so companies assigned to the line at less than full strength often consisted of reduced *Kampfkompagnies* of 25 to 30 men and *Bereitschafts Kompagnies* of 30 to 40 men. It was so quiet that companies were relieved within battalions. Days spent in the line only drew heavy artillery fire. No hostile infantry assault occurred, although frontline machine-gunners were often called upon to support neighbouring sectors.

(7) Officers and *Einweisungs Kommandos* [liaison party] of *IR15* (*2nd Garde Reserve Division*) introduced themselves on 4 December. First elements of the former relieved the Regiment on the night of 6 December. *I* and *III* battalions departed first; *II Battalion* followed twenty-four hours later. Quartered in Gitsberg, Koolskamp and Eegem, six days passed before the Regiment marched to the more dangerous *Abschnitt B* on the immediate left of the previous sector.

(8) *IR96* relieved *IR77* on the night of 12/13 December. *Oberstleutnant* von Hertell proceeded on leave the following day, Major Behrens taking command in his place. *Abschnitt B* was part of the half-circle around Passchendaele. Companies were distributed as follows: *9th Company* to the *Vorfeldzone*, *10th*, *11th* and *12th* companies to the *Hauptwiderstandslinie*. The main fighting position of the *KTK* was established at *Nordhof*. The Regiment, following another quiet period, was relieved on 17 December.

Appendix XVII

Casualties: KIA & DOW 30 November-10 December 1917[1]

25 Brigade (8th Division)
2nd Royal Berkshire

Surname	Initial	Service No.	Battalion	Date of Death	Regiment
ALLEN	JJ	11579	2ND BN	01/12/1917	ROYAL BERKSHIRE REGIMENT
ASHLEY	AV	38488	2ND BN	02/12/1917	ROYAL BERKSHIRE REGIMENT
BACKWAY	AP	38489	2ND BN	02/12/1917	ROYAL BERKSHIRE REGIMENT
BARLOW	J	26065	2ND BN	02/12/1917	ROYAL BERKSHIRE REGIMENT
BEST	FW	38499	2ND BN	02/12/1917	ROYAL BERKSHIRE REGIMENT
BIRD	WG	15759	2ND BN	02/12/1917	ROYAL BERKSHIRE REGIMENT
BISHOP	WE	14474	2ND BN	02/12/1917	ROYAL BERKSHIRE REGIMENT
BURT	H	31408	2ND BN	02/12/1917	ROYAL BERKSHIRE REGIMENT
CHILDS	CH	7873	2ND BN	02/12/1917	ROYAL BERKSHIRE REGIMENT
COATES	F	27301	2ND BN	02/12/1917	ROYAL BERKSHIRE REGIMENT
COGGS	HJ	21800	C COY 2ND BN	02/12/1917	ROYAL BERKSHIRE REGIMENT
COLLINS	F	11670	2ND BN	02/12/1917	ROYAL BERKSHIRE REGIMENT

1 Commonweath War Graves Commission. <http://www.cwgc.org> and Geoff's CWGC 1914-21 Search Engine <http://www.hut-six.co.uk/cgi-bin/search14-21.php>

Surname	Initial	Service No.	Battalion	Date of Death	Regiment
DICKER	C	18732	2ND BN	02/12/1917	ROYAL BERKSHIRE REGIMENT
DOLLIN	HJ	38521	2ND BN	02/12/1917	ROYAL BERKSHIRE REGIMENT
FISHER	EE	38531	B COY 2ND BN	02/12/1917	ROYAL BERKSHIRE REGIMENT
FITZGERALD	N	38214	2ND BN	02/12/1917	ROYAL BERKSHIRE REGIMENT
GADSBY	D	38533	2ND BN	02/12/1917	ROYAL BERKSHIRE REGIMENT
GERAGHTY	T	38270	2ND BN	02/12/1917	ROYAL BERKSHIRE REGIMENT
GIDDINGS	F	2ND LT	2ND BN	02/12/1917	ROYAL BERKSHIRE REGIMENT
HARWOOD	TJ	38547	2ND BN	02/12/1917	ROYAL BERKSHIRE REGIMENT
HAYWARD	GH	9782	2ND BN	02/12/1917	ROYAL BERKSHIRE REGIMENT
HEWETT	S	16426	2ND BN	02/12/1917	ROYAL BERKSHIRE REGIMENT
HILL	EA	32863	2ND BN	02/12/1917	ROYAL BERKSHIRE REGIMENT
HOLMAN	GA	38552	2ND BN	01/12/1917	ROYAL BERKSHIRE REGIMENT
HOWARTH	H	37012	2ND BN	01/12/1917	ROYAL BERKSHIRE REGIMENT
JENKINS	H	37850	2ND BN	02/12/1917	ROYAL BERKSHIRE REGIMENT
KING	HE	17843	2ND BN	01/12/1917	ROYAL BERKSHIRE REGIMENT
KING	AS	38557	2ND BN	02/12/1917	ROYAL BERKSHIRE REGIMENT
KIRKLAND	TM	37058	2ND BN	01/12/1917	ROYAL BERKSHIRE REGIMENT
KNIGHT	S	36373	2ND BN	02/12/1917	ROYAL BERKSHIRE REGIMENT
KNOTT	F	17129	2ND BN	01/12/1917	ROYAL BERKSHIRE REGIMENT
LOCKE	N	38274	2ND BN	02/12/1917	ROYAL BERKSHIRE REGIMENT
LUCAS	T	37862	2ND BN	02/12/1917	ROYAL BERKSHIRE REGIMENT
LUFF	SC	39414	2ND BN	02/12/1917	ROYAL BERKSHIRE REGIMENT
LUING	FJ	28821	2ND BN	02/12/1917	ROYAL BERKSHIRE REGIMENT
PAGET	AW	37552	2ND BN	01/12/1917	ROYAL BERKSHIRE REGIMENT

Surname	Initial	Service No.	Battalion	Date of Death	Regiment
RAY	CE	38281	2ND BN	02/12/1917	ROYAL BERKSHIRE REGIMENT
RUDKIN	EH	37867	2ND BN	02/12/1917	ROYAL BERKSHIRE REGIMENT
RUMBLE	JW	7743	2ND BN	02/12/1917	ROYAL BERKSHIRE REGIMENT
SIMPSON	R	38597	2ND BN	02/12/1917	ROYAL BERKSHIRE REGIMENT
TAYLOR	F	36797	2ND BN	02/12/1917	ROYAL BERKSHIRE REGIMENT
TROUP	SH	LT	7TH BN ATTD 2ND BN	02/12/1917	ROYAL BERKSHIRE REGIMENT
TRUCKLE	TF	38269	2ND BN	02/12/1917	ROYAL BERKSHIRE REGIMENT
WAIT	HAV	LT	D COY 2ND BN	02/12/1917	ROYAL BERKSHIRE REGIMENT
WAKELY	FJ	38243	2ND BN	01/12/1917	ROYAL BERKSHIRE REGIMENT
WEBB	SE	15744	D COY 2ND BN	02/12/1917	ROYAL BERKSHIRE REGIMENT
WHITE	CA	38626	2ND BN	02/12/1917	ROYAL BERKSHIRE REGIMENT
WOOD	HFC	33056	2ND BN	02/12/1917	ROYAL BERKSHIRE REGIMENT
WOOD	H	37483	2ND BN	02/12/1917	ROYAL BERKSHIRE REGIMENT

Total: 3 officers and 46 ORs

2nd Lincolnshire Regiment

Surname	Initials	Service No.	Battalion	Date of Death	Regiment
AIREY	A	32990	2ND BN	02/12/1917	LINCOLNSHIRE REGIMENT
ALLSOP	GF	38012	2ND BN	02/12/1917	LINCOLNSHIRE REGIMENT
BAGWORTH	H	203894	2ND BN	02/12/1917	LINCOLNSHIRE REGIMENT
BAKER	JJ	40069	2ND BN	01/12/1917	LINCOLNSHIRE REGIMENT
BARRAN	M	202224	2ND BN	02/12/1917	LINCOLNSHIRE REGIMENT
BARROW	J	32867	2ND BN	02/12/1917	LINCOLNSHIRE REGIMENT
BARTLE	GS	1507	2ND BN	02/12/1917	LINCOLNSHIRE REGIMENT
BILLING	TW	38049	2ND BN	02/12/1917	LINCOLNSHIRE REGIMENT
BLACKBOURN	W	40708	2ND BN	02/12/1917	LINCOLNSHIRE REGIMENT
BOOTH	W	38456	2ND BN	02/12/1917	LINCOLNSHIRE REGIMENT
BRADLEY	J	18641	2ND BN	02/12/1917	LINCOLNSHIRE REGIMENT
BRAMMER	W	18533	2ND BN	02/12/1917	LINCOLNSHIRE REGIMENT
BRICE	FW	13327	2ND BN	02/12/1917	LINCOLNSHIRE REGIMENT
CARTER	E	18955	2ND BN	01/12/1917	LINCOLNSHIRE REGIMENT
CHEESEMAN	WC	265052	2ND BN	02/12/1917	LINCOLNSHIRE REGIMENT
CLARK	H	18337	2ND BN	02/12/1917	LINCOLNSHIRE REGIMENT
COGGAN	HW	21357	2ND BN	02/12/1917	LINCOLNSHIRE REGIMENT
COOPER	TH	12234	2ND BN	02/12/1917	LINCOLNSHIRE REGIMENT
COWLIN	JL	8745	2ND BN	02/12/1917	LINCOLNSHIRE REGIMENT
COWE	A	CAPT	ATTD 2ND BN LINCOLN-SHIRE REGT	02/12/1917	RAMC
CROSSLEY	CI	40380	2ND BN	01/12/1917	LINCOLNSHIRE REGIMENT

Surname	Initials	Service No.	Battalion	Date of Death	Regiment
CULLUM	AH	24985	2ND BN	02/12/1917	LINCOLNSHIRE REGIMENT
CURTIS	A	31711	2ND BN	01/12/1917	LINCOLNSHIRE REGIMENT
DICKINSON	HJ	1544	2ND BN	01/12/1917	LINCOLNSHIRE REGIMENT
DONNER	JW	R3/25059	2ND BN	02/12/1917	LINCOLNSHIRE REGIMENT
DOYLEY	F	22585	2ND BN	01/12/1917	LINCOLNSHIRE REGIMENT
EDWARDS	W	40242	2ND BN	01/12/1917	LINCOLNSHIRE REGIMENT
FENWICK	TE	31932	2ND BN	02/12/1917	LINCOLNSHIRE REGIMENT
FENWICK	E	22917	2ND BN	02/12/1917	LINCOLNSHIRE REGIMENT
FULLER	JH	8261	2ND BN	02/12/1917	LINCOLNSHIRE REGIMENT
GLAZZARD	WT	32832	2ND BN	02/12/1917	LINCOLNSHIRE REGIMENT
GRAY	JH	16279	2ND BN	02/12/1917	LINCOLNSHIRE REGIMENT
GRIFFIN	BW	2ND LT	2ND BN	02/12/1917	LINCOLNSHIRE REGIMENT
HALFORD	SH	40188	2ND BN	02/12/1917	LINCOLNSHIRE REGIMENT
HARBY	WB	27025	2ND BN	02/12/1917	LINCOLNSHIRE REGIMENT
HARRISON	R	38075	2ND BN	02/12/1917	LINCOLNSHIRE REGIMENT
HICKSON	E	41608	2ND BN	02/12/1917	LINCOLNSHIRE REGIMENT
HOLMES	A	40086	2ND BN	02/12/1917	LINCOLNSHIRE REGIMENT
KIME	A	203889	2ND BN	02/12/1917	LINCOLNSHIRE REGIMENT
LEATHERLAND	J	8357	2ND BN	02/12/1917	LINCOLNSHIRE REGIMENT
LEES	CE	40582	2ND BN	02/12/1917	LINCOLNSHIRE REGIMENT
NICHOLLS	CR	8583	2ND BN	02/12/1917	LINCOLNSHIRE REGIMENT
ODLING	FS	27699	2ND BN	02/12/1917	LINCOLNSHIRE REGIMENT
PARKER	RH	LT	2ND BN	02/12/1917	LINCOLNSHIRE REGIMENT
PEARSON	G	13658	2ND BN	02/12/1917	LINCOLNSHIRE REGIMENT

Surname	Initials	Service No.	Battalion	Date of Death	Regiment
PEART	A	41548	2ND BN	02/12/1917	LINCOLNSHIRE REGIMENT
PICARD	H	7755	2ND BN	02/12/1917	LINCOLNSHIRE REGIMENT
SENTANCE	JA	22781	2ND BN	02/12/1917	LINCOLNSHIRE REGIMENT
SMITH	FR	31272	2ND BN	02/12/1917	LINCOLNSHIRE REGIMENT
WALKER	RH	20901	2ND BN	02/12/1917	LINCOLNSHIRE REGIMENT
WILLSON	A	8471	2ND BN	01/12/1917	LINCOLNSHIRE REGIMENT
WRIGHT	WJ	203881	2ND BN	02/12/1917	LINCOLNSHIRE REGIMENT

Total: 3 officers and 49 ORs

2nd Rifle Brigade

Surname	Initials	Service No.	Battalion	Date of Death	Regiment
BARNARD	HF	S/6701	2ND BN	02/12/1917	RIFLE BRIGADE
BINGHAM	G	6201	2ND BN	02/12/1917	RIFLE BRIGADE
BLYTH	ES	S/9473	2ND BN	02/12/1917	RIFLE BRIGADE
BOTTOMLEY	T	S/28926	2ND BN	01/12/1917	RIFLE BRIGADE
BROADLEY	J	S/30853	2ND BN	02/12/1917	RIFLE BRIGADE
BROOKER	J	2ND LT	2ND BN	02/12/1917	RIFLE BRIGADE
CARR	J	S/12735	2ND BN	02/12/1917	RIFLE BRIGADE
COCKS	II	S/31983	2ND BN	02/12/1917	RIFLE BRIGADE
COOPER	JH	S/19172	2ND BN	02/12/1917	RIFLE BRIGADE
CRACK	J	S/29695	2ND BN	02/12/1917	RIFLE BRIGADE
DAVIES	TCT	S/9620	2ND BN	02/12/1917	RIFLE BRIGADE
DAY	WP	S/31377	2ND BN	02/12/1917	RIFLE BRIGADE
DUDINSKY	J	S/32173	2ND BN	02/12/1917	RIFLE BRIGADE
DUNNAGE	W	B/200434	2ND BN	02/12/1917	RIFLE BRIGADE
EASEY	AE	B/200922	2ND BN	02/12/1917	RIFLE BRIGADE
ELLIOTT	FR	S/26606	2ND BN	02/12/1917	RIFLE BRIGADE
GRIMES	W	S/26825	2ND BN	02/12/1917	RIFLE BRIGADE
HORNE	E	S/10498	2ND BN	02/12/1917	RIFLE BRIGADE
JACKSON	E	S/18125	2ND BN	01/12/1917	RIFLE BRIGADE
JEFFERY	FE	S/32157	2ND BN	02/12/1917	RIFLE BRIGADE
JOYCE	E	B/1136	2ND BN	01/12/1917	RIFLE BRIGADE
KESTER	S	S/32299	2ND BN	02/12/1917	RIFLE BRIGADE
LESTER	WT	S/33758	2ND BN	02/12/1917	RIFLE BRIGADE
MACHIN	J	Z/2193	2ND BN	02/12/1917	RIFLE BRIGADE

Surname	Initials	Service No.	Battalion	Date of Death	Regiment
MITCHLEY	HC	2978	2ND BN	02/12/1917	RIFLE BRIGADE
MOORE	A	B/1524	2ND BN	02/12/1917	RIFLE BRIGADE
MORLEY	HA	S/27831	C COY 2ND BN	01/12/1917	RIFLE BRIGADE
MORRISON	W	2ND LT	2ND BN	02/12/1917	RIFLE BRIGADE
NORMAN	RJ	S/23516	2ND BN	02/12/1917	RIFLE BRIGADE
PHILLIPS	WC	S/10504	2ND BN	01/12/1917	RIFLE BRIGADE
POYNER	A	S/11052	2ND BN	02/12/1917	RIFLE BRIGADE
PRYSE	JW	S/24279	2ND BN	02/12/1917	RIFLE BRIGADE
RATLIFF	EF	CAPT	6TH BN ATTD 2ND BN	02/12/1917	RIFLE BRIGADE
ROWE	JH	S/17413	2ND BN	02/12/1917	RIFLE BRIGADE
RULE	AE	B/200612	2ND BN	02/12/1917	RIFLE BRIGADE
RUSHBROOK	A	P/935	2ND BN	02/12/1917	RIFLE BRIGADE
RUSSELL	C	5426	2ND BN	02/12/1917	RIFLE BRIGADE
SCRUTTON	HC	S/32427	2ND BN	02/12/1917	RIFLE BRIGADE
STOTEN	HW	S/18211	2ND BN	02/12/1917	RIFLE BRIGADE
TOWNSHEND	JS	9861	2ND BN	01/12/1917	RIFLE BRIGADE
WASS	JA	S/4377	2ND BN	02/12/1917	RIFLE BRIGADE
WEBLEY	FJK	S/25854	2ND BN	02/12/1917	RIFLE BRIGADE
WOOD	GA	B/200900	2ND BN	02/12/1917	RIFLE BRIGADE
WYATT	J	S/28568	2ND BN	02/12/1917	RIFLE BRIGADE

Total 3 officers and 41 ORs

1st Royal Irish Rifles

Surname	Initials	Service No.	Battalion	Date of Death	Regiment
ADAMS	JW	9554	1ST BN	02/12/1917	ROYAL IRISH RIFLES
BOULTON	D	47410	1ST BN	30/11/1917	ROYAL IRISH RIFLES
COBB	G	47422	1ST BN	30/11/1917	ROYAL IRISH RIFLES
CONDRON	M	3956	1ST BN	02/12/1917	ROYAL IRISH RIFLES
CONNOLLY	T	11377	1ST BN	30/11/1917	ROYAL IRISH RIFLES
CONROY	W	9074	1ST BN	30/11/1917	ROYAL IRISH RIFLES
DAY	J	5228	1ST BN	30/11/1917	ROYAL IRISH RIFLES
DUNN	H	7712	1ST BN	02/12/1917	ROYAL IRISH RIFLES

Appendix XVII 449

Surname	Initials	Service No.	Battalion	Date of Death	Regiment
GILLIGAN	J	10664	1ST BN	01/12/1917	ROYAL IRISH RIFLES
GILMORE	P	9168	1ST BN	30/11/1917	ROYAL IRISH RIFLES
GLOVER	J	47300	1ST BN	30/11/1917	ROYAL IRISH RIFLES
GOUGH	CFG	43844	1ST BN	01/12/1917	ROYAL IRISH RIFLES
GREEN	S	10646	1ST BN	01/12/1917	ROYAL IRISH RIFLES
HAWKINS	A	47421	1ST BN	30/11/1917	ROYAL IRISH RIFLES
HERKES	J	47430	1ST BN	01/12/1917	ROYAL IRISH RIFLES
HICKEY	J	4253	1ST BN	02/12/1917	ROYAL IRISH RIFLES
KAYE	E	L/7355	1ST BN	30/11/1917	ROYAL IRISH RIFLES
LENNARD	EW	2ND LT	4TH BN ATTD 1ST BN	30/11/1917	ROYAL IRISH RIFLES
MCLOUGHLIN	T	5675	1ST BN	30/11/1917	ROYAL IRISH RIFLES
PARRY	RW	42426	C COY 1ST BN	30/11/1917	ROYAL IRISH RIFLES
PEPLOE	W	42423	1ST BN	01/12/1917	ROYAL IRISH RIFLES
PITTMAN	EJ	43958	1ST BN	30/11/1917	ROYAL IRISH RIFLES
WILKIE	AB	2ND LT	1ST BN	30/11/1917	ROYAL IRISH RIFLES

Total: 23 ORs

97 Brigade (32nd Division)
2nd KOYLI

Surname	Initials	Service No.	Battalion	Date of Death	Regiment
ASQUITH	GW	2ND LT	3RD BN ATTD 2ND BN	02/12/1917	KING'S OWN YORKSHIRE LIGHT INFANTRY
ABBISS	RD	2ND LT	3RD BN ATTD 2ND BN	02/12/1917	KING'S OWN YORKSHIRE LIGHT INFANTRY
ANDERTON	WT	42043	2ND BN	02/12/1917	KING'S OWN YORKSHIRE LIGHT INFANTRY

Surname	Initials	Service No.	Battalion	Date of Death	Regiment
ARMITAGE	JT	33018	2ND BN	02/12/1917	KING'S OWN YORKSHIRE LIGHT INFANTRY
BAILEY	A	20356	2ND BN	02/12/1917	KING'S OWN YORKSHIRE LIGHT INFANTRY
BAKER	H	241927	2ND BN	02/12/1917	KING'S OWN YORKSHIRE LIGHT INFANTRY
BEDFORD	WH	21334	2ND BN	02/12/1917	KING'S OWN YORKSHIRE LIGHT INFANTRY
BERRY	S	34379	2ND BN	02/12/1917	KING'S OWN YORKSHIRE LIGHT INFANTRY
CAIN	E	2ND LT	2ND BN	02/12/1917	KING'S OWN YORKSHIRE LIGHT INFANTRY
CAWDERY	J	10142	2ND BN	02/12/1917	KING'S OWN YORKSHIRE LIGHT INFANTRY
CHALLONER	A	241716	2ND/5TH BN	03/12/1917	KING'S OWN YORKSHIRE LIGHT INFANTRY
CHAPPLE	E	200920	2ND/4TH BN	01/12/1917	KING'S OWN YORKSHIRE LIGHT INFANTRY
CONNERTY	D	241515	2ND BN	02/12/1917	KING'S OWN YORKSHIRE LIGHT INFANTRY
COOKSEY	A	9280	2ND BN	02/12/1917	KING'S OWN YORKSHIRE LIGHT INFANTRY
CORCORAN	AT	2ND LT	3RD BN ATTD 2ND BN	02/12/1917	KING'S OWN YORKSHIRE LIGHT INFANTRY
COURCOUX	JH	42342	2ND BN	02/12/1917	KING'S OWN YORKSHIRE LIGHT INFANTRY
COX	H	12777	2ND BN	02/12/1917	KING'S OWN YORKSHIRE LIGHT INFANTRY
DAY	JR	235231	2ND BN	02/12/1917	KING'S OWN YORKSHIRE LIGHT INFANTRY
DEAKIN	JE	11053	A COY 2ND BN	02/12/1917	KING'S OWN YORKSHIRE LIGHT INFANTRY

Appendix XVII

Surname	Initials	Service No.	Battalion	Date of Death	Regiment
ELLIS	JN	2ND LT	3RD BN, ATTD 2ND BN	01/12/1917	KING'S OWN YORKSHIRE LIGHT INFANTRY
FORDE	HR	CAPT	D COY 2ND BN	02/12/1917	KING'S OWN YORKSHIRE LIGHT INFANTRY
FORREST	W	35797	2ND BN	02/12/1917	KING'S OWN YORKSHIRE LIGHT INFANTRY
FORREST	R	8505	2ND BN	02/12/1917	KING'S OWN YORKSHIRE LIGHT INFANTRY
FURNISS	WT	45249	2ND BN	02/12/1917	KING'S OWN YORKSHIRE LIGHT INFANTRY
GIBBONS	W	240874	2ND/5TH BN	01/12/1917	KING'S OWN YORKSHIRE LIGHT INFANTRY
HAIGH	H	33423	2ND BN	02/12/1917	KING'S OWN YORKSHIRE LIGHT INFANTRY
HANSON	W	29973	2ND BN	03/12/1917	KING'S OWN YORKSHIRE LIGHT INFANTRY
HEYWORTH	F	35708	2ND BN	02/12/1917	KING'S OWN YORKSHIRE LIGHT INFANTRY
HUTCHINSON	E	241895	2ND BN	02/12/1917	KING'S OWN YORKSHIRE LIGHT INFANTRY
KAYE	R	30941	2ND BN	02/12/1917	KING'S OWN YORKSHIRE LIGHT INFANTRY
LAKE	T	23052	2ND BN	02/12/1917	KING'S OWN YORKSHIRE LIGHT INFANTRY
MARSHALL	E	205025	2ND BN	02/12/1917	KING'S OWN YORKSHIRE LIGHT INFANTRY
MATTHEWS	F	25064	2ND BN	02/12/1917	KING'S OWN YORKSHIRE LIGHT INFANTRY
MAY	TA	14295	2ND BN	02/12/1917	KING'S OWN YORKSHIRE LIGHT INFANTRY
MCKEE	WA	23308	2ND BN	02/12/1917	KING'S OWN YORKSHIRE LIGHT INFANTRY

Surname	Initials	Service No.	Battalion	Date of Death	Regiment
MOLLOY	E	32700	2ND BN	01/12/1917	KING'S OWN YORKSHIRE LIGHT INFANTRY
NAREY	J	201957	2ND BN	02/12/1917	KING'S OWN YORKSHIRE LIGHT INFANTRY
NEILANS	TR	24688	2ND BN	02/12/1917	KING'S OWN YORKSHIRE LIGHT INFANTRY
OSBORNE	E	34815	2ND BN	02/12/1917	KING'S OWN YORKSHIRE LIGHT INFANTRY
OWEN	WE	24560	2ND BN	02/12/1917	KING'S OWN YORKSHIRE LIGHT INFANTRY
PATTERSON	EJ	235309	2ND BN	02/12/1917	KING'S OWN YORKSHIRE LIGHT INFANTRY
PATTISON	AE	202009	2ND BN	03/12/1917	KING'S OWN YORKSHIRE LIGHT INFANTRY
PERRY	AS	235294	2ND BN	02/12/1917	KING'S OWN YORKSHIRE LIGHT INFANTRY
POOLE	H	200435	2ND BN	02/12/1917	KING'S OWN YORKSHIRE LIGHT INFANTRY
RAYNE	H	22852	2ND BN	02/12/1917	KING'S OWN YORKSHIRE LIGHT INFANTRY
REANEY	J	28244	2ND BN	02/12/1917	KING'S OWN YORKSHIRE LIGHT INFANTRY
RUSHWORTH	A	30928	2ND BN	02/12/1917	KING'S OWN YORKSHIRE LIGHT INFANTRY
SHUFFLE-BOTHAM	W	202474	2ND BN	02/12/1917	KING'S OWN YORKSHIRE LIGHT INFANTRY
SIMMONETT	WH	30972	2ND BN	02/12/1917	KING'S OWN YORKSHIRE LIGHT INFANTRY
SMITH	A	41278	2ND BN	02/12/1917	KING'S OWN YORKSHIRE LIGHT INFANTRY
STEVENSON	GT	3/3616	2ND BN	02/12/1917	KING'S OWN YORKSHIRE LIGHT INFANTRY

Surname	Initials	Service No.	Battalion	Date of Death	Regiment
TURNER	C	235315	2ND BN	02/12/1917	KING'S OWN YORKSHIRE LIGHT INFANTRY
VASEY	A	42204	2ND BN	02/12/1917	KING'S OWN YORKSHIRE LIGHT INFANTRY
WAGSTAFF	J	30256	2ND BN	02/12/1917	KING'S OWN YORKSHIRE LIGHT INFANTRY
WALLACE	AE	23055	2ND BN	02/12/1917	KING'S OWN YORKSHIRE LIGHT INFANTRY
WATSON	W	15386	2ND BN	03/12/1917	KING'S OWN YORKSHIRE LIGHT INFANTRY
WEBB	F	9570	H COY 2ND BN	02/12/1917	KING'S OWN YORKSHIRE LIGHT INFANTRY
WHOMERSLEY	H	35757	2ND BN	02/12/1917	KING'S OWN YORKSHIRE LIGHT INFANTRY
WYATT	F	24653	2ND BN	02/12/1917	KING'S OWN YORKSHIRE LIGHT INFANTRY
YATES	G	20883	2ND BN	02/12/1917	KING'S OWN YORKSHIRE LIGHT INFANTRY
YERWORTH	GH	40022	2ND BN	02/12/1917	KING'S OWN YORKSHIRE LIGHT INFANTRY

Total: 6 officers and 54 ORs

16th HLI

Surname	Initials	Service No.	Battalion	Date of Death	Regiment
ALEXANDER	J	CAPT	C COY 16TH BN	02/12/1917	HIGHLAND LIGHT INFANTRY
BARNSHAW	GH	39166	16TH BN	02/12/1917	HIGHLAND LIGHT INFANTRY
BARRIE	J	27631	16TH BN	02/12/1917	HIGHLAND LIGHT INFANTRY
BELL	DSD	32453	16TH BN	02/12/1917	HIGHLAND LIGHT INFANTRY
BENNIE	WR	2ND LT	7TH BN ATTD 16TH BN	02/12/1917	HIGHLAND LIGHT INFANTRY

Surname	Initials	Service No.	Battalion	Date of Death	Regiment
BROWN	T	42221	16TH BN	02/12/1917	HIGHLAND LIGHT INFANTRY
BURNS	A	3375	16TH BN	02/12/1917	HIGHLAND LIGHT INFANTRY
BURT	WJ	43078	16TH BN	02/12/1917	HIGHLAND LIGHT INFANTRY
CAIRNS	H	350220	16TH BN	02/12/1917	HIGHLAND LIGHT INFANTRY
CAMPBELL	W	43110	16TH BN	02/12/1917	HIGHLAND LIGHT INFANTRY
CANNING	J	25924	16TH BN	02/12/1917	HIGHLAND LIGHT INFANTRY
CHUDLEY	HJ	350181	16TH BN	02/12/1917	HIGHLAND LIGHT INFANTRY
CLEWLOW	H	350154	16TH BN	02/12/1917	HIGHLAND LIGHT INFANTRY
CONNELL	J	4979	16TH BN	02/12/1917	HIGHLAND LIGHT INFANTRY
CRUICKSHANK	D	42223	16TH BN	02/12/1917	HIGHLAND LIGHT INFANTRY
DALLAS	WA	355403	16TH BN	02/12/1917	HIGHLAND LIGHT INFANTRY
DAVIDSON	GL	CAPT	4TH BN ATTD 16TH BN	02/12/1917	HIGHLAND LIGHT INFANTRY
EDGAR	W	3471	16TH BN	02/12/1917	HIGHLAND LIGHT INFANTRY
FERRIS	J	2ND LT	16TH BN	02/12/1917	HIGHLAND LIGHT INFANTRY
FORBES	W	14157	C COY 16TH BN	02/12/1917	HIGHLAND LIGHT INFANTRY
FORBES	J	1390	C COY 16TH BN	02/12/1917	HIGHLAND LIGHT INFANTRY
FRASER	J	34728	16TH BN	02/12/1917	HIGHLAND LIGHT INFANTRY
GILLESPIE	AM	26362	16TH BN	02/12/1917	HIGHLAND LIGHT INFANTRY
GRANT	JR	14165	16TH BN	02/12/1917	HIGHLAND LIGHT INFANTRY
HALLIDAY	F	12849	16TH BN	02/12/1917	HIGHLAND LIGHT INFANTRY
HART	H	31719	16TH BN	02/12/1917	HIGHLAND LIGHT INFANTRY
HATCHER	W	29418	16TH BN	02/12/1917	HIGHLAND LIGHT INFANTRY
HEPBURN	R	39185	16TH BN	02/12/1917	HIGHLAND LIGHT INFANTRY

Surname	Initials	Service No.	Battalion	Date of Death	Regiment
JOHNSON	WJ	350179	16TH BN	02/12/1917	HIGHLAND LIGHT INFANTRY
KYNOCH	J	355414	16TH BN	01/12/1917	HIGHLAND LIGHT INFANTRY
LEES	J	15002	16TH BN	02/12/1917	HIGHLAND LIGHT INFANTRY
MARR	J	33395	A COY 16TH BN	03/12/1917	HIGHLAND LIGHT INFANTRY
MARSHALL	A	355591	16TH BN	02/12/1917	HIGHLAND LIGHT INFANTRY
MARTIN	PW	39147	16TH BN	02/12/1917	HIGHLAND LIGHT INFANTRY
MCCARDLE	J	31009	16TH BN	02/12/1917	HIGHLAND LIGHT INFANTRY
MCDOUGALL	D	13909	D COY 16TH BN	03/12/1917	HIGHLAND LIGHT INFANTRY
MCDOWALL	J	39199	16TH BN	02/12/1917	HIGHLAND LIGHT INFANTRY
MCGUIRE	J	30687	16TH BN	02/12/1917	HIGHLAND LIGHT INFANTRY
MCINNES	RS	37881	16TH BN	02/12/1917	HIGHLAND LIGHT INFANTRY
MCMILLAN	DE	42323	16TH BN	02/12/1917	HIGHLAND LIGHT INFANTRY
MCVEY	W	32301	16TH BN	02/12/1917	HIGHLAND LIGHT INFANTRY
MITCHELL	C	355456	16TH BN	02/12/1917	HIGHLAND LIGHT INFANTRY
MITCHELL	J	355594	16TH BN	02/12/1917	HIGHLAND LIGHT INFANTRY
PARENT	J	40757	16TH BN	02/12/1917	HIGHLAND LIGHT INFANTRY
PATTON	ES	43068	16TH BN	03/12/1917	HIGHLAND LIGHT INFANTRY
PLUMB	S	350224	C COY 16TH BN	02/12/1917	HIGHLAND LIGHT INFANTRY
RATTRAY	R	34119	C COY 16TH BN	02/12/1917	HIGHLAND LIGHT INFANTRY
ROBERTSON	J	350202	16TH BN	02/12/1917	HIGHLAND LIGHT INFANTRY
RUSSELL	TL	25779	16TH BN	02/12/1917	HIGHLAND LIGHT INFANTRY
SCOTT	A	33371	16TH BN	02/12/1917	HIGHLAND LIGHT INFANTRY
SEMPLE	JH	37854	16TH BN	02/12/1917	HIGHLAND LIGHT INFANTRY
SHARP	JM	355602	16TH BN	02/12/1917	HIGHLAND LIGHT INFANTRY

Surname	Initials	Service No.	Battalion	Date of Death	Regiment
SMALL	J	39191	16TH BN	02/12/1917	HIGHLAND LIGHT INFANTRY
SMITH	R	30359	16TH BN	02/12/1917	HIGHLAND LIGHT INFANTRY
THOMSON	R	40073	16TH BN	02/12/1917	HIGHLAND LIGHT INFANTRY
THOMSON	LB	40912	16TH BN	02/12/1917	HIGHLAND LIGHT INFANTRY
THOMSON	A	29962	16TH BN	02/12/1917	HIGHLAND LIGHT INFANTRY
TILEY	AF	4310	16TH BN	02/12/1917	HIGHLAND LIGHT INFANTRY
TULLOCH	A	35663	16TH BN	02/12/1917	HIGHLAND LIGHT INFANTRY
WALLACE	R	43011	16TH BN	02/12/1917	HIGHLAND LIGHT INFANTRY
WENZEL	J	30121	16TH BN	02/12/1917	HIGHLAND LIGHT INFANTRY
WESTGARTH	FW	41151	16TH BN	02/12/1917	HIGHLAND LIGHT INFANTRY
WHITFIELD	J	2ND LT	16TH BN	02/12/1917	HIGHLAND LIGHT INFANTRY
WOODWARD	AA	356355	16TH BN	02/12/1917	HIGHLAND LIGHT INFANTRY
WORLING	D	14974	16TH BN	02/12/1917	HIGHLAND LIGHT INFANTRY

Total: 5 officers and 60 ORs

11th Border Regiment

Surname	Initials	Service No.	Battalion	Date of Death	Regiment
ANDERSON	R	13705	11TH BN	02/12/1917	BORDER REGIMENT
ASHCROFT	J	26005	11TH BN	02/12/1917	BORDER REGIMENT
ASHMAN	FW	28817	11TH BN	02/12/1917	BORDER REGIMENT
BAILEY	CE	28814	11TH BN	02/12/1917	BORDER REGIMENT
BAINBRIDGE	P	13680	11TH BN	02/12/1917	BORDER REGIMENT
BAINBRIDGE	E	202684	11TH BN	02/12/1917	BORDER REGIMENT
BAKER	WR	28818	11TH BN	02/12/1917	BORDER REGIMENT

Appendix XVII 457

Surname	Initials	Service No.	Battalion	Date of Death	Regiment
BARNES	H	32001	11TH BN	02/12/1917	BORDER REGIMENT
BARTON	J	28916	11TH BN	02/12/1917	BORDER REGIMENT
BENSON	I	CAPT	11TH BN	02/12/1917	BORDER REGIMENT
BICKLEY	AG	28825	11TH BN	02/12/1917	BORDER REGIMENT
BLAYLOCK	JJ	26291	11TH BN	02/12/1917	BORDER REGIMENT
BOTTOM	WB	28771	11TH BN	02/12/1917	BORDER REGIMENT
BRAMBLE	CJ	28636	11TH BN	02/12/1917	BORDER REGIMENT
BRIDGE	RJ	27670	11TH BN	02/12/1917	BORDER REGIMENT
BROADHURST	L	34511	11TH BN	02/12/1917	BORDER REGIMENT
BROUGH	TM	202879	11TH BN	02/12/1917	BORDER REGIMENT
BROWN	B	28923	11TH BN	02/12/1917	BORDER REGIMENT
BROWN	GW	241761	11TH BN	02/12/1917	BORDER REGIMENT
BURGESS	J	28765	11TH BN	02/12/1917	BORDER REGIMENT
BURGESS	EJ	25119	11TH BN	02/12/1917	BORDER REGIMENT
CADDLE	T	25588	11TH BN	02/12/1917	BORDER REGIMENT
CARMICHAEL	JR	260212	11TH BN	02/12/1917	BORDER REGIMENT
CRAKER	SE	33708	A COY 11TH BN	02/12/1917	BORDER REGIMENT
DALBY	JW	260219	11TH BN	02/12/1917	BORDER REGIMENT
DALTON	W	28928	11TH BN	03/12/1917	BORDER REGIMENT
DALZELL	W	32643	11TH BN	02/12/1917	BORDER REGIMENT
DAVIDSON	JJ	23777	11TH BN	02/12/1917	BORDER REGIMENT
DAVIDSON	F	15372	11TH BN	02/12/1917	BORDER REGIMENT
DELAHOY	GF	33344	11TH BN	02/12/1917	BORDER REGIMENT
DEMELLWEEK	J	260216	11TH BN	02/12/1917	BORDER REGIMENT

Surname	Initials	Service No.	Battalion	Date of Death	Regiment
DOBSON	W	4296	D COY 11TH BN	03/12/1917	BORDER REGIMENT
DOUGLAS	WJ	20963	11TH BN	02/12/1917	BORDER REGIMENT
EGGINTON	H	33536	11TH BN	02/12/1917	BORDER REGIMENT
FERNYHOUGH	H	28623	11TH BN	02/12/1917	BORDER REGIMENT
FLETCHER	WP	260221	11TH BN	02/12/1917	BORDER REGIMENT
FRANCIS	HG	28274	11TH BN	02/12/1917	BORDER REGIMENT
GIBSON	T	13902	B COY 11TH BN	02/12/1917	BORDER REGIMENT
GRAHAM	J	26902	11TH BN	02/12/1917	BORDER REGIMENT
GUNNING	WF	263073	11TH BN	02/12/1917	BORDER REGIMENT
HANSON	JR	26480	11TH BN	02/12/1917	BORDER REGIMENT
HARRIS	W	25083	11TH BN	02/12/1917	BORDER REGIMENT
HAYWARD	J	33484	11TH BN	03/12/1917	BORDER REGIMENT
HENDERSON	J	23690	11TH BN	02/12/1917	BORDER REGIMENT
HEPWOOD	H	28940	11TH BN	02/12/1917	BORDER REGIMENT
HEYWOOD	F	33553	11TH BN	03/12/1917	BORDER REGIMENT
HOBLEY	AW	28847	11TH BN	02/12/1917	BORDER REGIMENT
HODGSON	J	12969	11TH BN	02/12/1917	BORDER REGIMENT
HODGSON	R	263076	11TH BN	02/12/1917	BORDER REGIMENT
HOGG	RT	13746	11TH BN	02/12/1917	BORDER REGIMENT
HOWE	W	32665	11TH BN	02/12/1917	BORDER REGIMENT
HURLEY	H	26564	11TH BN	02/12/1917	BORDER REGIMENT
HYAM	J	28937	11TH BN	02/12/1917	BORDER REGIMENT
LAWS	EE	33424	11TH BN	02/12/1917	BORDER REGIMENT
LOWES	C	15396	11TH BN	02/12/1917	BORDER REGIMENT

Surname	Initials	Service No.	Battalion	Date of Death	Regiment
MACDONALD	D	17383	11TH BN	03/12/1917	BORDER REGIMENT
MACDUFF	WB	2ND LT	5TH BN ATTD 11TH BN	02/12/1917	BORDER REGIMENT
MARSH	EA	28863	11TH BN	02/12/1917	BORDER REGIMENT
MARTIN	PM	CAPT	11TH BN	02/12/1917	BORDER REGIMENT
MAYALL	H	28780	11TH BN	02/12/1917	BORDER REGIMENT
MENDHAM	G	24764	11TH BN	02/12/1917	BORDER REGIMENT
MERRYWEATHER	A	28953	11TH BN	02/12/1917	BORDER REGIMENT
MOORE	RW	33754	11TH BN	02/12/1917	BORDER REGIMENT
MORAN	J	26613	11TH BN	02/12/1917	BORDER REGIMENT
MULLARD	W	28629	11TH BN	02/12/1917	BORDER REGIMENT
OLIPHANT	T	28150	11TH BN	02/12/1917	BORDER REGIMENT
PARKIN	G	17444	11TH BN	02/12/1917	BORDER REGIMENT
PARRY	M	260254	11TH BN	02/12/1917	BORDER REGIMENT
PENNINGTON	A	35043	A COY 11TH BN	02/12/1917	BORDER REGIMENT
POLLITT	E	11919	11TH BN	02/12/1917	BORDER REGIMENT
POWELL	JT	27808	11TH BN	02/12/1917	BORDER REGIMENT
POYSER	S	34247	11TH BN	02/12/1917	BORDER REGIMENT
RAVEN	J	13373	11TH BN	02/12/1917	BORDER REGIMENT
RICHARDSON	W	28152	11TH BN	02/12/1917	BORDER REGIMENT
RICHARDSON	RC	2ND LT	3RD BN ATTD 11TH BN	02/12/1917	BORDER REGIMENT
RIDGWAY	WT	2ND LT	11TH BN	02/12/1917	BORDER REGIMENT
ROBSON	F	19666	11TH BN	02/12/1917	BORDER REGIMENT
RYAN	J	33401	A COY 11TH BN	02/12/1917	BORDER REGIMENT

Surname	Initials	Service No.	Battalion	Date of Death	Regiment
SAFFELL	E	22160	11TH BN	02/12/1917	BORDER REGIMENT
SANDEMAN	AF	CAPT	11TH BN	02/12/1917	BORDER REGIMENT
SCHOLES	W	26929	11TH BN	02/12/1917	BORDER REGIMENT
SEEKINGS	H	28215	11TH BN	02/12/1917	BORDER REGIMENT
SHORT	L	8941	11TH BN	02/12/1917	BORDER REGIMENT
SMITH	WD	32664	11TH BN	02/12/1917	BORDER REGIMENT
STEELE	BIL	15553	11TH BN	03/12/1917	BORDER REGIMENT
STEWARD	AS	28214	11TH BN	02/12/1917	BORDER REGIMENT
SWIFT	G	33144	11TH BN	02/12/1917	BORDER REGIMENT
THORNE	W	32467	11TH BN	02/12/1917	BORDER REGIMENT
TOLSON	J	202891	11TH BN	02/12/1917	BORDER REGIMENT
TRUSLER	W	32685	11TH BN	02/12/1917	BORDER REGIMENT
TYLDESLEY	E	34514	11TH BN	02/12/1917	BORDER REGIMENT
TYSON	W	13361	11TH BN	02/12/1917	BORDER REGIMENT
WALKER	T	22015	11TH BN	02/12/1917	BORDER REGIMENT
WALKER	C	30146	11TH BN	03/12/1917	BORDER REGIMENT
WATSON	B	23985	11TH BN	02/12/1917	BORDER REGIMENT
WATT	JW	17322	11TH BN	02/12/1917	BORDER REGIMENT
WHITE	B	260263	11TH BN	03/12/1917	BORDER REGIMENT
WILSON	JT	242087	11TH BN	02/12/1917	BORDER REGIMENT
WOOD	EG	26292	11TH BN	02/12/1917	BORDER REGIMENT

Total: 6 officers and 93 ORs

17th HLI

Surname	Initials	Service No.	Battalion	Date of Death	Regiment
ANKER	G	39161	17TH BN	02/12/1917	HIGHLAND LIGHT INFANTRY
ATKIN	E	37983	17TH BN	02/12/1917	HIGHLAND LIGHT INFANTRY
BAYNE	E	41195	17TH BN	02/12/1917	HIGHLAND LIGHT INFANTRY
BLACK	J	355619	17TH BN	02/12/1917	HIGHLAND LIGHT INFANTRY
BOWMAN	W	5690	17TH BN	02/12/1917	HIGHLAND LIGHT INFANTRY
BROWN	JD	2ND LT	6TH BN ATTD 17TH BN	03/12/1917	HIGHLAND LIGHT INFANTRY
CAMERON	M	2ND LT	6TH BN ATTD 17TH BN	02/12/1917	HIGHLAND LIGHT INFANTRY
CLEMENTS	J	42196	17TH BN	02/12/1917	HIGHLAND LIGHT INFANTRY
CLINES	T	2064	17TH BN	01/12/1917	HIGHLAND LIGHT INFANTRY
CLYNE	JC	353102	17TH BN	01/12/1917	HIGHLAND LIGHT INFANTRY
CONNELL	W	29801	17TH BN	02/12/1917	HIGHLAND LIGHT INFANTRY
CONNOR	D	42987	17TH BN	02/12/1917	HIGHLAND LIGHT INFANTRY
CONSTABLE	J	2868	D COY 17TH BN	02/12/1917	HIGHLAND LIGHT INFANTRY
CORMACK	HS	3456	17TH BN	02/12/1917	HIGHLAND LIGHT INFANTRY
CROSBIE	D	42018	17TH BN	02/12/1917	HIGHLAND LIGHT INFANTRY
CULLEN	J	33796	17TH BN	02/12/1917	HIGHLAND LIGHT INFANTRY
CUNNINGHAM	G	42929	17TH BN	02/12/1917	HIGHLAND LIGHT INFANTRY
CUNNINGHAM	PN	2ND LT	17TH BN	02/12/1917	HIGHLAND LIGHT INFANTRY
DARGE	JF	23055	17TH BN	02/12/1917	HIGHLAND LIGHT INFANTRY
DEUCHARS	W	353104	17TH BN	02/12/1917	HIGHLAND LIGHT INFANTRY
DICK	J	42302	17TH BN	02/12/1917	HIGHLAND LIGHT INFANTRY

Surname	Initials	Service No.	Battalion	Date of Death	Regiment
GOOCH	A	33429	17TH BN	02/12/1917	HIGHLAND LIGHT INFANTRY
GORDON	J	45008	17TH BN	01/12/1917	HIGHLAND LIGHT INFANTRY
GREER	W	42349	17TH BN	01/12/1917	HIGHLAND LIGHT INFANTRY
HANLEY	J	8720	17TH BN	02/12/1917	HIGHLAND LIGHT INFANTRY
HUNTER	R	43398	B COY 17TH BN	02/12/1917	HIGHLAND LIGHT INFANTRY
JAMIESON	J	45004	17TH BN	01/12/1917	HIGHLAND LIGHT INFANTRY
KEIR	AD	41167	17TH BN	02/12/1917	HIGHLAND LIGHT INFANTRY
KELT	J	42988	17TH BN	02/12/1917	HIGHLAND LIGHT INFANTRY
KING	A	23943	17TH BN	02/12/1917	HIGHLAND LIGHT INFANTRY
KINLOCH	A	43328	A COY 17TH BN	02/12/1917	HIGHLAND LIGHT INFANTRY
LAW	WW	41215	17TH BN	02/12/1917	HIGHLAND LIGHT INFANTRY
LEARY	O	42931	17TH BN	02/12/1917	HIGHLAND LIGHT INFANTRY
LUMSDEN	H	40895	17TH BN	01/12/1917	HIGHLAND LIGHT INFANTRY
MASON	C	41242	17TH BN	02/12/1917	HIGHLAND LIGHT INFANTRY
MCEWAN	A	39392	17TH BN	02/12/1917	HIGHLAND LIGHT INFANTRY
MCKELLAR	A	27940	17TH BN	02/12/1917	HIGHLAND LIGHT INFANTRY
MCLELLAN	J	42012	17TH BN	02/12/1917	HIGHLAND LIGHT INFANTRY
MCNEILL	P	42921	17TH BN	02/12/1917	HIGHLAND LIGHT INFANTRY
MCPHEE	C	42939	17TH BN	01/12/1917	HIGHLAND LIGHT INFANTRY
MCWHIRTER	W	42122	17TH BN	02/12/1917	HIGHLAND LIGHT INFANTRY
MEARNS	JM	356874	17TH BN	02/12/1917	HIGHLAND LIGHT INFANTRY
MILLAR	J	43375	17TH BN	02/12/1917	HIGHLAND LIGHT INFANTRY
MILLER	J	2ND LT	17TH BN	02/12/1917	HIGHLAND LIGHT INFANTRY
MILLIGAN	RB	16146	C COY 17TH BN	01/12/1917	HIGHLAND LIGHT INFANTRY

Appendix XVII 463

Surname	Initials	Service No.	Battalion	Date of Death	Regiment
MORLAND	W	2ND LT	17TH BN	02/12/1917	HIGHLAND LIGHT INFANTRY
OGILVIE	JR	33662	17TH BN	02/12/1917	HIGHLAND LIGHT INFANTRY
OSBORNE	J	2ND LT	17TH BN	02/12/1917	HIGHLAND LIGHT INFANTRY
PHILIP	DS	355173	A COY 17TH BN	02/12/1917	HIGHLAND LIGHT INFANTRY
RAMSAY	JS	42373	17TH BN	02/12/1917	HIGHLAND LIGHT INFANTRY
REID	RH	2ND LT	3RD BN ATTD 17TH BN	02/12/1917	HIGHLAND LIGHT INFANTRY
ROBERTSON	DM	2685	17TH BN	02/12/1917	HIGHLAND LIGHT INFANTRY
ROBSON	W	42979	17TH BN	02/12/1917	HIGHLAND LIGHT INFANTRY
SCULLION	R	41199	17TH BN	02/12/1917	HIGHLAND LIGHT INFANTRY
SHENTON	AW	41251	17TH BN	02/12/1917	HIGHLAND LIGHT INFANTRY
SIMPSON	T	42848	D COY 17TH BN	02/12/1917	HIGHLAND LIGHT INFANTRY
SPENCE	EH	42128	17TH BN	02/12/1917	HIGHLAND LIGHT INFANTRY
THOMSON	F	38529	17TH BN	02/12/1917	HIGHLAND LIGHT INFANTRY
WALSH	J	39516	17TH BN	02/12/1917	HIGHLAND LIGHT INFANTRY
WILSON	J	42205	17TH BN	02/12/1917	HIGHLAND LIGHT INFANTRY
WILSON	A	202497	17TH BN	03/12/1917	HIGHLAND LIGHT INFANTRY
WRIGHT	A	38513	17TH BN	02/12/1917	HIGHLAND LIGHT INFANTRY
YOUNG	J	32510	17TH BN	01/12/1917	HIGHLAND LIGHT INFANTRY

Total: 7 officers and 56 ORs

15th Lancashire Fusiliers

Surname	Initials	Service No.	Battalion	Date of Death	Regiment
ARRIES	JM	235067	15TH BN	02/12/1917	LANCASHIRE FUSILIERS
ASTIN	W	47692	15TH BN	02/12/1917	LANCASHIRE FUSILIERS
BODEN	C	39804	15TH BN	02/12/1917	LANCASHIRE FUSILIERS
BUCHAN	C	2ND LT	1ST BN ATTD 15TH BN	02/12/1917	LANCASHIRE FUSILIERS
CROPPER	JA	201126	15TH BN	02/12/1917	LANCASHIRE FUSILIERS
EARNSHAW	W	305913	15TH BN	02/12/1917	LANCASHIRE FUSILIERS
FARRINGTON	JE	2983	C COY 15TH BN	02/12/1917	LANCASHIRE FUSILIERS
GOSLING	GH	242824	15TH BN	02/12/1917	LANCASHIRE FUSILIERS
GREEN	J	39816	15TH BN	02/12/1917	LANCASHIRE FUSILIERS
HINCHEY	H	39659	15TH BN	01/12/1917	LANCASHIRE FUSILIERS
HOLDEN	J	20036	15TH BN	02/12/1917	LANCASHIRE FUSILIERS
HOPWOOD	H	27500	15TH BN	03/12/1917	LANCASHIRE FUSILIERS
HOWARD	J	202075	15TH BN	02/12/1917	LANCASHIRE FUSILIERS
ISHERWOOD	J	10199	15TH BN	02/12/1917	LANCASHIRE FUSILIERS
LAYTHAM	JH	39707	15TH BN	02/12/1917	LANCASHIRE FUSILIERS
MATHEWS	S	32585	15TH BN	02/12/1917	LANCASHIRE FUSILIERS
MONFRIES	A	32559	15TH BN	02/12/1917	LANCASHIRE FUSILIERS
NOEL	TA	306729	15TH BN	02/12/1917	LANCASHIRE FUSILIERS
ORMROD	F	12575	15TH BN	02/12/1917	LANCASHIRE FUSILIERS
OWEN	JR	39611	15TH BN	02/12/1917	LANCASHIRE FUSILIERS
PICKERING	CR	38156	15TH BN	02/12/1917	LANCASHIRE FUSILIERS
ROBINSON	GT	47125	15TH BN	02/12/1917	LANCASHIRE FUSILIERS

Appendix XVII 465

Surname	Initials	Service No.	Battalion	Date of Death	Regiment
SCRIVENER	JS	2ND LT	8TH BN ATTD 15TH BN	02/12/1917	LANCASHIRE FUSILIERS
SIMPSON	J	40296	15TH BN	02/12/1917	LANCASHIRE FUSILIERS
STEER	EA	32581	15TH BN	02/12/1917	LANCASHIRE FUSILIERS
TUSHINGHAM	T	18162	15TH BN	02/12/1917	LANCASHIRE FUSILIERS
WARBURTON	C	6053	15TH BN	02/12/1917	LANCASHIRE FUSILIERS
WOOSTER	LE	235375	15TH BN	01/12/1917	LANCASHIRE FUSILIERS
YATES	J	38412	15TH BN	02/12/1917	LANCASHIRE FUSILIERS

Total: 2 officers and 27 ORs

16th Northumberland Fusiliers

Surname	Initials	Service No.	Battalion	Date of Death	Regiment
ATKINS	E	235328	16TH BN	01/12/1917	NORTHUMBERLAND FUSILIERS
BELL	R	16/1441	D COY 16TH BN	02/12/1917	NORTHUMBERLAND FUSILIERS
BREESE	AG	36818	16TH BN	03/12/1917	NORTHUMBERLAND FUSILIERS
CEILLAMS	EG	52753	16TH BN	02/12/1917	NORTHUMBERLAND FUSILIERS
COLE	E	37049	16TH BN	03/12/1917	NORTHUMBERLAND FUSILIERS
COLLINGS	FR	2ND LT	16TH BN	03/12/1917	NORTHUMBERLAND FUSILIERS
DEVLIN	T	24090	16TH BN	03/12/1917	NORTHUMBERLAND FUSILIERS
ELLERKER	WG	54445	16TH BN	30/11/1917	NORTHUMBERLAND FUSILIERS
FATHERLEY	RT	16/732	16TH BN	03/12/1917	NORTHUMBERLAND FUSILIERS
GRAINGER	A	39752	16TH BN	03/12/1917	NORTHUMBERLAND FUSILIERS
HOOD	T	16/767	16TH BN	02/12/1917	NORTHUMBERLAND FUSILIERS
JACKSON	J	34757	B COY 16TH BN	30/11/1917	NORTHUMBERLAND FUSILIERS
JAMES	W	24041	16TH BN	03/12/1917	NORTHUMBERLAND FUSILIERS

Surname	Initials	Service No.	Battalion	Date of Death	Regiment
KIDD	RF	37035	16TH BN	03/12/1917	NORTHUMBERLAND FUSILIERS
LEYLAND	T	235448	16TH BN	03/12/1917	NORTHUMBERLAND FUSILIERS
LONG	FA	40409	16TH BN	02/12/1917	NORTHUMBERLAND FUSILIERS
NEWHAM	CT	36822	C COY 16TH BN	03/12/1917	NORTHUMBERLAND FUSILIERS
NORMAN	A	366171	16TH BN	02/12/1917	NORTHUMBERLAND FUSILIERS
OLDALE	A	17512	16TH BN	02/12/1917	NORTHUMBERLAND FUSILIERS
PYLE	GA	25/533	16TH BN	30/11/1917	NORTHUMBERLAND FUSILIERS
SHEARER	JA	16/1043	16TH BN	03/12/1917	NORTHUMBERLAND FUSILIERS
SMITH	GB	31436	16TH BN	02/12/1917	NORTHUMBERLAND FUSILIERS
THOMPSON	W	27/1268	16TH BN	03/12/1917	NORTHUMBERLAND FUSILIERS
WIGHT	F	31912	16TH BN	30/11/1917	NORTHUMBERLAND FUSILIERS

Total: 1 officer and 22 ORs

KIA or DOW 4-10 December

Surname	Initials	Service No.	Battalion	Date of Death	Regiment
DYKE	WH	38524	2ND BN	05/12/1917	ROYAL BERKSHIRE REGIMENT
HODGSON	GW	10359	2ND BN POW	10/12/1917	ROYAL BERKSHIRE REGIMENT
ROGERS	F	16308	2ND BN	04/12/1917	ROYAL BERKSHIRE REGIMENT
CONNELL	H	26499	2ND BN	07/12/1917	LINCOLNSHIRE REGIMENT
GRANTHAM	A	40212	2ND BN	05/12/1917	LINCOLNSHIRE REGIMENT
HOPPS	TJ	5510	2ND BN	05/12/1917	LINCOLNSHIRE REGIMENT
TAYLOR	JR	31917	2ND BN	04/12/1917	LINCOLNSHIRE REGIMENT
DOVE	WE	S/4547	2ND BN	09/12/1917	RIFLE BRIGADE
HIGGINBOTTOM	P	Z/738	2ND BN POW	05/12/1917	RIFLE BRIGADE
HOLLOWAY	JH	S/26623	2ND BN	06/12/1917	RIFLE BRIGADE

Appendix XVII 467

Surname	Initials	Service No.	Battalion	Date of Death	Regiment
MACE	AE	S/30798	2ND BN	09/12/1917	RIFLE BRIGADE
SHEPHERD	RWG	S/10061	2ND BN POW	07/12/1917	RIFLE BRIGADE
DIXON	J	241078	2ND BN	09/12/1917	KING'S OWN YORKSHIRE LIGHT INFANTRY
SURR	W	3/1141	2ND BN	10/12/1917	KING'S OWN YORKSHIRE LIGHT INFANTRY
WILSON	M	29334	2ND BN	04/12/1917	KING'S OWN YORKSHIRE LIGHT INFANTRY
COUTTS	AG	36546	D COY 16TH BN	06/12/1917	HIGHLAND LIGHT INFANTRY
CROSS	FA	39174	16TH BN	06/12/1917	HIGHLAND LIGHT INFANTRY
SMART	EJ	350229	16TH BN	04/12/1917	HIGHLAND LIGHT INFANTRY
SMITH	H	3426	16TH BN	04/12/1917	HIGHLAND LIGHT INFANTRY
BENT	F	260268	11TH BN POW	05/12/1917	BORDER REGIMENT
DENT	J	202882	11TH BN	04/12/1917	BORDER REGIMENT
KEMP	GH	28944	11TH BN	07/12/1917	BORDER REGIMENT
LOMAS	J	28951	11TH BN	09/12/1917	BORDER REGIMENT
NEWTON	TA	28956	B COY 11TH BN	08/12/1917	BORDER REGIMENT
REED	AJ	28869	11TH BN	08/12/1917	BORDER REGIMENT
FOSTER	J	13550	B COY 17TH BN	09/12/1917	HIGHLAND LIGHT INFANTRY
HALL	AW	202272	17TH BN	04/12/1917	HIGHLAND LIGHT INFANTRY
MAIR	AG	37916	17TH BN	10/12/1917	HIGHLAND LIGHT INFANTRY
MCFARLANE	HR	42952	17TH BN	04/12/1917	HIGHLAND LIGHT INFANTRY
ARMSTRONG	WE	38137	15TH BN	10/12/1917	LANCASHIRE FUSILIERS
BULLEN	F	32533	15TH BN KIA	05/12/1917	LANCASHIRE FUSILIERS
RATCLIFFE	C	11321	15TH BN	07/12/1917	LANCASHIRE FUSILIERS
WELLS	WA	19733	D COY 15TH BN	05/12/1917	LANCASHIRE FUSILIERS
BERESFORD	AE	4670	16TH BN	08/12/1917	NORTHUMBERLAND FUSILIERS

Surname	Initials	Service No.	Battalion	Date of Death	Regiment
COATES	WW	40166	16TH BN	10/12/1917	NORTHUMBERLAND FUSILIERS
GRACE	CE	52754	16TH BN	09/12/1917	NORTHUMBERLAND FUSILIERS
LUSTGARTEN	M	47083	16TH BN	05/12/1917	NORTHUMBERLAND FUSILIERS
MURRAY	JW	27/1145	16TH BN	04/12/1917	NORTHUMBERLAND FUSILIERS
WALSH	A	36828	16TH BN KIA	06/12/1917	NORTHUMBERLAND FUSILIERS
WINDROSS	C	41707	16TH BN	05/12/1917	NORTHUMBERLAND FUSILIERS

Total: 40 ORs

RFA, RGA, MGC & RAMC

Surname	Initials	Service No.	Battalion	Date of Death	Regiment/Corps
EDMONDSON	N	116739	C BTY 161ST BDE	02/12/1917	ROYAL FIELD ARTILLERY
HEALER	WE	152893	C BTY 161ST BDE	02/12/1917	ROYAL FIELD ARTILLERY
HORTON	VJ	2ND LT	D BTY 161ST BDE	02/12/1917	ROYAL FIELD ARTILLERY
WRIGHT	G	71569	109TH SIEGE BTY	02/12/1917	ROYAL GARRISON ARTILLERY
BANNISTER	W	64822	14TH COY	02/12/1917	MACHINE GUN CORPS (INFANTRY)
BARTON	W	7534	97TH COY	02/12/1917	MACHINE GUN CORPS (INFANTRY)
BAXTER	R	103168	218TH COY	02/12/1917	MACHINE GUN CORPS (INFANTRY)
BENNETT	JT	102782	218TH COY	02/12/1917	MACHINE GUN CORPS (INFANTRY)
BRAME	EG	86798	218TH COY	02/12/1917	MACHINE GUN CORPS (INFANTRY)
BURDOCK	AV	60306	96TH COY	03/12/1917	MACHINE GUN CORPS (INFANTRY)

Appendix XVII

Surname	Initials	Service No.	Battalion	Date of Death	Regiment/Corps
BUTTERWORTH	W	108564	96TH COY	03/12/1917	MACHINE GUN CORPS (INFANTRY)
CLAY	F	103059	218TH COY	02/12/1917	MACHINE GUN CORPS (INFANTRY)
FIDLER	S	73038	14TH COY	30/11/1917	MACHINE GUN CORPS (INFANTRY)
FOWLER	J	97618	25TH COY	01/12/1917	MACHINE GUN CORPS (INFANTRY)
GILROY	T	60464	14TH COY	02/12/1917	MACHINE GUN CORPS (INFANTRY)
HOLDEN	F	65345	96TH COY	03/12/1917	MACHINE GUN CORPS (INFANTRY)
JENKINS	HH	68529	96TH COY	02/12/1917	MACHINE GUN CORPS
KING	J	81885	218TH COY	02/12/1917	MACHINE GUN CORPS (INFANTRY)
KING	J	67924	218TH COY	02/12/1917	MACHINE GUN CORPS (INFANTRY)
KNOX	A	73022	14TH COY	02/12/1917	MACHINE GUN CORPS (INFANTRY)
MITCHELL	G	8273	14TH COY	02/12/1917	MACHINE GUN CORPS (INFANTRY)
NEAL	WG	7810	96TH COY	02/12/1917	MACHINE GUN CORPS (INFANTRY)
OSBORNE	FC	81720	97TH COY	02/12/1917	MACHINE GUN CORPS (INFANTRY)
PEARCE	W	89812	97TH COY	02/12/1917	MACHINE GUN CORPS (INFANTRY)
PEGRUM	W	47675	25TH COY	01/12/1917	MACHINE GUN CORPS (INFANTRY)
POTTER	JH	35931	96TH COY	03/12/1917	MACHINE GUN CORPS (INFANTRY)

Surname	Initials	Service No.	Battalion	Date of Death	Regiment/Corps
PRICE	WJ	67929	218TH COY	02/12/1917	MACHINE GUN CORPS (INFANTRY)
RANDALL	HE	107569	219TH COY	02/12/1917	MACHINE GUN CORPS (INFANTRY)
ROCHE	C	36383	14TH COY	03/12/1917	MACHINE GUN CORPS (INFANTRY)
ROTHWELL	H	2ND LT	14TH COY	02/12/1917	MACHINE GUN CORPS (INFANTRY)
SMEATON	H	64269	97TH COY	02/12/1917	MACHINE GUN CORPS (INFANTRY)
SMITH	E	107564	214TH COY	02/12/1917	MACHINE GUN CORPS (INFANTRY)
SOUTAR	W	7867	97TH COY	02/12/1917	MACHINE GUN CORPS (INFANTRY)
SUNDERLAND	W	27001	97TH COY	02/12/1917	MACHINE GUN CORPS (INFANTRY)
SUTTON	P	65294	97TH COY	02/12/1917	MACHINE GUN CORPS (INFANTRY)
TRIGG	JC	107565	219TH COY	02/12/1917	MACHINE GUN CORPS (INFANTRY)
WALTON	JR	106445	25TH COY	01/12/1917	MACHINE GUN CORPS (INFANTRY)
WILSON	CW	53997	25TH COY	01/12/1917	MACHINE GUN CORPS (INFANTRY)
BAKER	WH	457506	25TH FIELD AMBULANCE	02/12/1917	RAMC

Total: 2 officers and 38 ORs

Appendix XVIII

German Interrogation Report, 8 December 1917[1]

	145
A.O.K. 4	K.H.Qu. 8. XII 1917
Intelligence officer D. Nr 18379	

Interrogation
23 men of the II/R. Berks.
2 men of the II/Linc. R.

<u>25. Brig.</u>   <u>8. Div.</u>

Brought in respectively during the English attack and German counter-attack on 2 Dec. in the vicinity of Ritterhof, 500m northeast of Passchendaele[2] by J.R.116 and two men of the II/Linc. R. some 100m north of this point by J.R.117 of the 25.J.D.

Important

<u>Mission</u>: On 30 Nov., the 25.Brig. took over the front line from 23. Brig. relieving the II/R. Berks. of the II/Midd.x R. [sic].

<u>Replacements</u> : The prisoners stated that their division should have been replaced by another (unknown) division around 1am — around 9am according to other reports — on the night of 2/3 Dec. (meanwhile , according to prisoners taken from the VIII. Rif. Brig., 41. Brig. 14. Div., on 2 Dec, this was at to take place at 10pm.) The 8. Div. were due 6 weeks recuperation.

---

1   BA-MA PH 3/586: '145. Vernehmung: von 23 Mann des 2/R. Berks. R. 2 Mann 2/ Linc. R.', 8 December 1917, Vernehmungsprotokolle französischer & englischer Kriegsgefangener im Bereich des AOK 4, Bd. 3 Oct.-Dez. [1917]. Translation by Derik Hammond.
2   *Ritterhof* was approximately 200 yards north of *Kolonnenhof* (Exert Farm).

Deployment: From the south to the north on the front line: II/R.Berks.R. — II/Linc.R. —II/Rif. Brig. and from the 32.Div, the II/Yorks. L. I. Whether the I/R. Ir. Rif. were to the south of the Berks. or in reserve behind the attack battalion could not be determined.

Attack: B, D and C Companies of the II/R. Berks. attacked in the first wave from north to south. B and C Companies each consisted of 3 platoons and D Company of 1 platoon. The second mopping up wave, advanced in "artillery formation" and consisted of one platoon from each of these companies while the whole of A Company and half of D Company remained in support. The right wing lay on the marshy ground in the vicinity of Ritterhof and the left wing of the battalion at R. Pt. M (Plan Qu. F/40 Map: 10000). To render the attack a complete surprise to us, the artillery fire struck just before the start. The II/Linc. R. advanced in a line formation from north to south. In the first wave were 2 platoons from each of A, B and D Companies, in the second and third waves 1 platoon from each of these companies. C Company was held in reserve. The prisoners had no further information regarding the extent or objective of the attack.

Attack Objectives: The prisoners had no information regarding the further objectives of the attack nor were they able to offer an opinion if such were probable.

Combat performance: The prisoners are aware that their division is rated as "very good" by the British Army. The strength of the companies was given as follows: II/R. Berks. B Company, 2 officers, 75 men; D Company, 3 officers, 150 men. II/Linc.R. (amongst these were a small percentage of men who were not on this occasion involved in combat) A Company 3 officers, 65 men; D Company 6 officers, 60 men (? V.O.).

Amongst the R. Berks. were numerous 19 and 20-year-olds, as well as men over 35 and a few Regular soldiers. The younger and older age groups were, in the opinion of an old but astute sergeant, just as good soldiers as those between 20 and 30 years of age.

Capture of Prisoners

Most of the prisoners were brought in during the English attack during which they formed pockets behind our lines. The remainder were captured in the evening in shell holes in front of our lines during our successful counterattack.

Personnel

The prisoners made a good impression and the sergeants an excellent soldierly impression. Their occupations were as follows: 13 craftsmen, 6 labourers, 2 merchants, 3 agricultural workers and 1 postman. Of these 9 are under 20 years of age, 7 up to the age of 25, 4 are in the range of 25 to 30 and 5 are between 30 and 39. Eight are married and two of these are each the father of 3 children. Composition: 3 Regular soldiers, 2 Territorials, 9 Kitchener, 9 Derby and 2 conscripted. Time since enlistment: the 3 Regular soldier sergeants — 1907. 1910. 1911. For the remainder — 1914 six, 1915 four, 1916 eight, 1917 four men. With few exceptions the prisoners speak willingly and their statements comply with the facts.

Relevant Facts

Combat structure of the 8. Div. includes membership of the V.A.K. [sic] and to the 2.Army of General Rawlinson. The prisoners knew nothing of a division of M.G.K.

Commanders: 8. Div.   Major-General Hanniker [sic]
25. Brig.   Brig. General Coffin.
II/R. Berks. R.   First-Lieutenant Sterling (formerly commander of II/Yeo [?] .Rif. of 86. Brig.) [sic]
II/Linc.R.   First-Lieutenant [sic] Irwin.

Strength:
II/R. Berks. R.
B Company combat strength: 3 officers 75 men. Rationing strength: 3 officers 130 men.
D Company combat strength: 3 officers 150 men. Rationing strength: 3 officers 170 men.
A Company combat strength: 3 officers 65 men. Rationing strength: 3 officers 85 men.
C Company combat strength: 6 officers 85 men. Rationing strength 6 officers 75 men.

Losses: All prisoners of the II/Linc. R. state that the losses of dead and wounded during the attack on 2 December were slight with only D Company, while on route to the front line positions on 28 November, losing 3 dead and 6 wounded through German artillery fire. No numerical information regarding the losses during the attack was obtained although a prisoner from A Company of the II/Linc. R. knew that they suffered the loss of 20 men (which included all the officers) through machine-gun fire.

Replacements: The II /Berks. R. received 200 men in Caestre — almost all young people between the ages of 19 and 20 years of age — which were divided equally between the 4 companies. The II/Lincs. R. received in October in Steenwerck (about 9km northwest of Armentiéres) only 25 men as replacements for the whole battalion, also very young recruits.

History: From statements made in Interrogation No. 516, it possible that the 25.Brig. relieved, on 20 November, part of the 3. Kan. Div. in order to themselves, on the night of 23/24 November, to hand over the forward positions to the 24.Brig.

Attack Training: Immediately after their arrival, the 25. Brig. moved to Brandhoek, halfway between Ypres and Poperinghe on the main road. There, all 4 battalions of the brigade trained for the planned attack for a period of 8 days against realistically constructed positions with strongpoints and other obstacles specifically identified. Though it was not certain that the attack would take place by day or by night, training took place daily from 2pm until 7pm.

Staff Headquarters: The divisional staff headquarters were in Poperinghe and the battalion headquarters of the II/R.Berks. R in Fortuin just south of St. Julian.

Rear Positions: The preparatory points of the II/R. Berks. R and the II/Lincs. R. were 100m behind the front lines. These consisted of isolated shell holes. One prisoner disclosed that 26m behind the standby positions, there was a heavy-mortar battery but was not able to identify this on a map.

Gas: A prisoner from the II/Lincs. R. was, because of illness, taken to a field hospital at Poperinghe. There he encountered about 60 men of C Company of his battalion who 14 days previously were in position at Anmarach. When he asked them why they had not put on their gasmasks, they told him that because of strong winds and the heavy, general artillery fire, they noticed the detonations of the gas shells too late. The gas poisoning caused continual vomiting making it impossible to keep their food down. None of the poisoned men had succumbed to blindness or death. C Company, through this and artillery fire, had on 1 December a strength of only around 10 men.

Munitions Storage: In and around St. Jean — a good 1km north of Ypres — are, according to a credible report of a sergeant, extensive munitions stores. These are lying in great stacks and hidden from the sight of pilots by branches. From this store radiate field-railway tracks which feed nearby battery nests.[3]

Tanks: Were seen by various prisoners behind the front lines. However, they had been destroyed by artillery fire and were stuck fast in deep mud so that their removal was impossible.

Catering: Was praised.

Health Status: In both battalions is relatively good. Very few cases of "trench foot".

Insignia: Of the II/R. Berks. R. is an approximately 5cm dark-blue square with an embroidered red dragon. The general Berks. insignia is worn on the helmet this consisting of a 4cm square with vertical stripes coloured red-green-white-green-red. The insignia of the other battalions was confirmed.

---

3   See Chapter 6, p. 356, fn. 1.

Signals: The barrage fire signal is a rocket with three spheres; two red and one green.

Italians: None of the prisoners could provide information about the withdrawal of certain infantry divisions. On the other hand the statements given by many English artillery men were confirmed.

Russians: Various prisoners were aware of the peace offer made by Russia to the Central Powers. A few expressed their outrage at this "betrayal" while one wonders if the newspapers told of England's satisfaction now that Russia requires no further support.

Air Attacks: A merchant from London explained that our air attacks on London caused extensive damage. In the course of time, because of these attacks and the sacrifice of numerous lives, more and more of the inhabitants moved into the country so that one could speak of this as a formal exodus.

Distribution	*Haehle*
As for Engländer	Hauptmann and Intelligence Officer

Appendix XIX

Lieutenant-Colonel T.F. Tweed War Office Correspondence[1]

10-2-18

To: Brigadier-General Director of Personal Services

Fm: Lt-Col. T.F. Tweed MC Late XI Border Regiment BEF (31 Percy St. Liverpool)

Sir,
I have the honour to forward Arrival Report as requested.

I returned to the UK as a result of a breakdown due to over two years continuous service in an infantry unit in France, which was accentuated by the heavy losses my Bn. HQ suffered in recent fighting. I lost nearly all my experienced officers at NIEUPORT in July & Aug. of last year & lost three adjutants within 3 months the result being that I had to carry the Bn. on my back. This culminated in my Unit in the fighting at Ypres on Dec. 1/2nd after doing extraordinarily well at the offset, failed badly later when I had no officers but 3 HQ officers who were not casualties.

This bad show occasioned an Adverse Report on the part of my Brigadier coupled with a request that I should be relieved of my command.

It will serve no useful purpose in my going into the question of the future of the report of the Brigadier. The covering report of the Divisional Commander Major-General Shute is sufficient to exonerate me of incapacity. As you know, General Shute has a very high standard & his adverse reports can be of a very different nature than that of which he was good enough to give me.

My record of the war fails to justify the report. I received my commission in 1914 as Lieut., went to France as Capt. in 1915 & was promoted to my present rank of Temp. Lieut.-Colonel in Aug. 1917. I have served continuous without a break for wounds or illness up to the time of the present instance. I was awarded the MC on the Somme & was mentioned for work at Nieuport in the last list. I was frequently favourably

---

1 TNA: WO/339/21553: Lieutenant-Colonel Thomas Frederic TWEED. The Lancashire Fusiliers.

reported upon by a different Brigadier & my CO & was sent to the Senior Officers School at Aldershot. I received an excellent report from the school and recommended for command of a Battalion in France.

In General Shute's report I am recommended for employment at home for a rest & the medical board which granted me sick leave recommended the same.

I should like my services while at home to be utilised in some branch where they will be of the greatest service. My intimate knowledge of all phases of fighting on the Western Front extending over two years in a Division noted for its high standard (32nd) & the fact that Brigadier-General Kentish Commandant of the Sen[ior] Officers School urged me to take up the appointment as Chief Instructor at the Corps School – as I was particularly fitted for such an appointment suggests that I would be in the best service in being appointed to duties of an instructional character. My pre-war employment was that of an organiser on a large scale & I am an efficient lecturer and public speaker. In France I was frequently called upon to lecture at various schools, etc. on phases of warfare from an infantry point of view.

I believe I will be doing the greatest service in duties of an instructional nature & beg to apply for an appointment of such a nature. I should like to retain my present rank if possible.

It is possible that my attachment to some unit of the U.S. Army would be of service & I would like you to give this favourable consideration.

I have the honour to be yours,

Thomas Frederic Tweed
Lt. Col.

41051/3 M.S.K. Confidential

To. Military Secretary War Office

Fm. Lt. Col. T.F. Tweed MC
The Border Regiment

I have the honour to return the enclosed reports from GHQ France.

The circumstances which occasioned the original report was action of the Unit under my command failing at Ypres on the night Dec. 1st/2nd. After gaining all their objectives in the initial stage – the only battalion in the Bde to do so – the men having lost all of their company officers & most of their NCOs fell back without orders after dark on the evening of the 2nd. After this initial success, the subsequent failure was naturally a great disappointment to my Brigadier, with whom I had had personal differences previously & I fear that his natural disappointment showed itself in the character of his adverse report.

The two principle failures attributed to me are not borne out by my previous career. Lack of leadership and knowledge of my work is disproved by the fact that I have served continuously in the same Division (32nd). This Division has a very high reputation in France & yet I received continual promotion in it. My knowledge of my work is demonstrated [by] the fact that in 2 ¾ years I went from the rank of Lieutenant to substantive Lieut.-Col. I was frequently favourably reported on while serving with my original unit [,] 16th Lanc. Fus. & recommended for command during the temporary absence of the CO. I acted as CO for some weeks of the 2nd Battalion Royal Inniskilling Fusiliers & was subsequently sent to the Senior Officers School from which I received the highest possible report. During my late CO's absence, I commanded for several weeks my old Bn., the 16th Lanc. Fus. & was in the line when the enemy attacked at NIEUPORT on July 10th last. For my work on that occasion I was 'Mentioned [in Despatches]'. I was given command of the XI Border Reg. in Aug. 1917 & was frequently praised by both Brigade & Divisional commander Maj[or]-General C.D. Shute CB for my work with that unit. The difficulties with that unit were very great. It had suffered very severe losses at Nieuport & when I took it over, my Company Commanders with one exception were all 2nd Lieuts. with under 12 mo[nths] commissioned service. My 2nd in Command was only just promoted from Adjutant & my Adjutant a very junior 2nd Lieut. During the period of my command through casualties my Adjutant was changed 3 times & my RSM also 3 times. Just prior to the action which brought about the adverse report [,] I lost a Company Commander, my Intelligence Officer & my 2nd in Command went sick. I went into action with the officer next senior to me being a substantive Lieut. with less than 18 mo. service.

Though these difficulties were great, while I had the sympathy of the Brigadier, they were not inoperable [?], but when differences caused his sympathy to lessen, it was necessary for me to work night and day to keep the Unit's end up & this had the result of bringing on a breakdown.

With the report of lack of leadership [,] I can only repeat that in my Division I would not have reached my present rank without demonstrating my ability in this direction. I won the MC as a Captain on July 1st 1916 & was 'Mentioned' for work at Nieuport while commanding in July 1917.

I have the honour to request that you will favourably consider the suggestion made in the report of the General Officer commanding IV Army. I am now quite well again and have no doubt of my capacity for a command. This one adverse report is in complete disagreement with all my previous reports & the whole of my army career.

I should be glad of an opportunity to prove my fitness for command by being placed under a Brigadier-General at home for his report on my ability & fitness.

I have the honour to be your obedient servant

Thomas F. Tweed
Lt. Col.
27.2.18

Appendix XX

Official History Correspondence: General Cameron Shute[1]

10th December 1930

My Dear Edmonds,

I have read through all the papers you sent and I now return them. I made notes only in "Third Army 1st–3rd April 1918". As far as 32nd Division is concerned all that has been said is correct. Except for Ayette we had little to do.

What I should like to have looked at are:

a) Action of 59th Brigade & 20th Div. when it captured Guillemont in Aug-Sept 16.
b) Action of R. Naval Div. when I commanded it at the Battle of Beaumont Hamel & after – Oct 16 to February 17.
c) Action of 32nd Div. March-April 17 when I commanded it at the extreme British right before St Quentin.
d) Action of 19th Div. at Battle of Messines June 17 where I was sent up to command it from a week before to 3 weeks after it.
e) Action of 32nd Div. July 17 to early 18 on the Yser – Very hard fighting.
f) Action of 32nd Div. at end of Passchendaele.
g) V Corps operations April 18 to November 11th 1918.

All these are rather big shows.

(4) As an appeal came with for any papers of interest [,] I am sending a return of casualties for 6 months which I had most carefully compiled day-by-day in 32nd Div. The preparation [?] of wounds from art[ille]ry fire ??? ??? ??? rifle & MG fire make one think. I don't know of any similar return. Please don't lose it and return when done with it as I have no copy.

Yours V. Sincerely
Cameron Shute

---

1 TNA: CAB/45/187 Postwar Official History Correspondence (Third Army 1918).

Appendix XXI

How Untrained were the Troops in Late 1917?

Alison Hine

In most senior officers' eyes, the post-1914 Army could never be as well-trained as the pre-war Regular Army. This is probably true as the pre-war Regular Army, after the Boer War, had little else to do except follow the annual training programme, building up from individual training through company and battalion to brigade and divisional training and culminating in annual manoeuvres. However, even the Regular Army of August 1914 cannot have been said to have been totally well-trained, most infantry units having been brought up to strength by returning reservists, many of whom might have previously served for only three years several years before.

What the emphasis on pre-war training ignores is the reality of active service and the value of combat experience. In practice, however, senior commanders seemed to have operated a sort of "doublethink", since they certainly did recognise the value of such experience: a December 1916 Fourth Army Routine order on wastage returns noted "The replacement of trained men is a very costly business, and it is difficult to place any limit to the value to our country of the trained man who has been through the experience of the Somme Battle."[1] The pre-war Regular soldier for whom training had been honed by combat experience was indeed a valuable man but by late 1917 so too was the man with shorter service but extensive combat experience.

Training of Reinforcements at Home

By mid-1917, the training of recruits at home had been rationalized and was conducted by both the regimental reserve and training reserve. Men over 18 years and 6 months would undergo a fourteen-week syllabus and would be available for posting overseas once they reached the age of 19, so long as they fulfilled the conditions for Category A(i) in ACI 1023 of 1916:

---

1   TNA: WO/95/441: Fourth Army A & Q War Diary, December 1916.

A: General Service – able to march, see to shoot, hear well and stand active service conditions:

A1: Men actually fit for overseas service in all respects: training, physically and mentally fit.

It was laid down that care was to be taken that "no men [were] to be sent overseas who [were] not up to the standard required for the particular draft concerned, both as regards training and physical fitness."[2]

For various reasons, not least a shortage of SMLE rifles in the training units, not all men completed their training before being sent abroad and these were categorized as A(ii): recruits who should be fit for A(i) as soon as trained. When these men were required to be drafted overseas a note was placed against their name; if he had not completed the full musketry course his name was annotated "Fired only parts … GMC."[3] It was expected that the training would be completed on arrival at the base(s) of the theatres concerned.

Training of Reinforcements in France

The completion of training on arrival in France was not uncommon. In October 1916, the GS Branch GHQ informed the Inspector General of Communications:

> that a total of 15,000 recruits will be despatched gradually from England. These recruits must be trained in the use of the short rifle before proceeding up country.[4]

In the aftermath of the Somme, it was further decided:

> that all Infantry battalions be brought up to 100 men above establishment and that training of untrained men shall be completed at the Front.[5]

Training at the Front was not always easy to achieve and I am grateful to Trevor Harvey for the following extracts from 1st KRRC's war diary which indicate the difficulties encountered in training of basic skills:

> 19 March 1917: A draft of 128 untrained men and 44 returned wounded, sick etc. joined.

---

2 TNA: WO/293/6: Army Council Instruction 432, 11 March 1917.
3 Ibid, 43111 March 1917 and 533, 28 March 1917, GMC: General Musketry Course.
4 TNA: WO/95/26: AG GHQ War Diary, 16 October 1916.
5 Ibid, 19 December 1916.

> 1 April 1917: Great attention is being paid to close order drill, and the handling of arms, at both of which the untrained Draft are particularly slow. Up to the present it has not been possible to practice any bombing, though the necessity for it is great, on account of it being at present impossible to obtain bombs or rifle grenades of any description.[6]

For the GHQ manning staffs it was often a balance between the need for reinforcements to reach units as quickly as possible against time spent at the base to familiarise them with conditions in France. It also depended on the availability of trained reinforcements to meet the specific requirement:

> 11 April 1917: Owing to the necessity of rapidly bringing up to establishment Divisions which have been temporarily withdrawn from the line for training and refitting, it was decided that in certain cases it might be necessary to send reinforcements up to Divisions from the Base before completing their 9 days Base Training.[7]

Inevitably, as greater losses were incurred the time spent at the base was further reduced: three weeks into Third Ypres, on 22 August, this period was reduced to five days for all infantry drafts.[8] This would have meant that drafts of A (ii) men would not necessarily have been brought up to A (i) standard before leaving the base.

From April 1917 onwards the arrival of untrained recruits began to be annotated on the weekly strength returns submitted by divisions.[9] However, it is also apparent from reading divisional war diaries that not all reinforcements arrived "untrained". On 2 October 1917, 15th and 16th Lancashire Fusiliers respectively received 140 and 78 untrained reinforcements but on 16 October there is no indication that the reinforcements for 15th HLI (17), 17th HLI (17) and 2nd Royal Inniskilling Fusiliers were "untrained".[10]

It should also be noted that many reinforcements during 1917 were men returning having previously been wounded. In August, GHQ thanked the War Office for the arrival in June of 22,495 A3 Men (i.e. returned EF men who would be fit for A1 as soon as hardened) of whom 19,322 had been classified fit for general service immediately, with the others only temporarily unfit. It was noted that the "physique and

---

6   TNA: WO/95/1371: 1st KRRC War Diary, 19 March and 1 April 1917.
7   TNA: WO/95/26: AG GHQ War Diary, April 1917.
8   Ibid, 22 August 1917.
9   This category of reinforcement was 'institutionalised' in First Army from April 1917 onwards when First Army pro forma No. 3 i.e. strength return, was amended to include 'Column 'C' Untrained'. I owe this reference to Trevor Harvey.
10   TNA: WO/95/2373: 32nd Division A&Q War Diary, October 1917.

training of these men [were] superior to the ordinary reinforcements and [requested] that further drafts of this description may be sent when available."[11]

Many of the men sent to the front in late 1917 were also the results of the "combing out" of A1 men from the base areas. By definition, these men were categorized as suitable in all respects for general service. Whether they truly were or not probably depended on their previous employment at the base. Cavalrymen and Yeomanry had also been dismounted and required training as infantry. The basic skills did not require much time to refresh but turning them into infantrymen took a bit longer.

Absorption of new drafts could be a problem but as the Cheshires had found: "given the opportunity to get the Battalion together in a rest area, these [new] men soon became one with the unit."[12] It required a period away from the frontline in which to carry out training and other activities; almost equally important was the bonding together of the unit.

Aspects Relating Specifically to 32nd Division Prior to the 2 December Attack

This particular Division occupied the area around Coxyde, La Panne and Dunkirk areas for most of the time from the end of June onwards. Looking at the Division's war diary and strength returns for June – September 1917, many reinforcements were received by all battalions but none were shown as untrained.[13] In October the number of untrained reinforcements for 14 Brigade increased from 68 to 176 and those for 96 Brigade from 413 to 527; the 97 Brigade, however, had received only a single untrained man. In November, the numbers of untrained reinforcements for 14 and 96 brigades dropped from 165 to 124 and 523 to 330 respectively, probably as a result of all brigades in the Division having carried out training between 3-7 November. The untrained figures for 97 Brigade remained in single digits, reaching the highest sum total of 3 in 2nd KOYLI. So, it is apparent that at the end of November 1917 it was not considered that 97 Brigade had a problem with untrained reinforcements.

Looking specifically at 11th Border Regiment some 492 reinforcements had been received between 1 June – 23 September. As no nominal rolls exist it is not possible to analyse the source of these men; but they are not shown as untrained in the Divisional returns. The Battalion was not specifically in a rest area but it was able to spend a significant amount of time in training over the period August – November 1917.[14] In August some fifteen days were spent on morning training under company arrangements (with recreation in the afternoons). On 20 and 22 August the Battalion trained in the 32nd Division "attack scheme" having conducted range practice on the

11 TNA: WO/95/26: AG GHQ War Diary, 20 August 1917.
12 Colonel A. Crookenden, *History of the Cheshire Regiment in the Great War* (Uckfield: Naval & Military Press reprint of 1925 edition), p. 77.
13 TNA: WO/95/2373: 32nd Division A&Q Branch War Diary, 1 June–31 December 1917.
14 TNA: WO/95/2403: 11th Border Regiment War Diary, August–December 1917.

intervening day. On 23 and 24 August the companies practised rapid consolidation, musketry and firing. September was spent in and out of the line but once back at Teteghem on 7 October training continued. On 10 October the companies carried out rifle firing practice and specialized training. Throughout the rest of the month a further thirteen days were spent on training including platoons in attack and deployment for the attack, musketry, specialist training and a battalion practice attack on 27 October. After 2 November company training gave way to a total of thirteen days battalion training before the Battalion moved to Hill Top Farm on 22 November. There is obviously no indication of the quality of all this training but in terms of time spent on it this Battalion could not be considered untrained. Whether the training was appropriately targeted is another matter.

The composition of 11th Border Regiment at this time may be gauged to some extent by analysis of 91 men killed on 2 December. Of these 36 had enlisted in the Border Regiment's recruiting area of Cumberland and Westmorland. A further 30 had enlisted in No 3 District (Lancashire, Cumberland and Westmorland) and 5 from No 4 District, thus making 71 men or 78% drawn from Western Command. Thus there was still a large degree of regional homogeneity within the battalion.

Some 40% of those who died had been with the battalion since before November 1916. Of those who joined in 1917, some will have been recruits but many will also have been returners or men from other Border Regiment battalions. Some medal index cards show previous service with other cap badges but this is likely to have been in many cases only the length of time spent at the base before being transferred to the Border Regiment. Although 11th Border Regiment was a Regular (Service) battalion, many of its men had started life as Territorial Force soldiers and had been transferred under authority of the Military Service Acts of 1916. Whatever their origins, the Divisional A & Q Branch War Diary did not consider any of the men assigned to the Battalion after mid-1917 to have arrived "untrained" from the base.

The Leadership Aspect

In comparison with pre-war soldiers, the soldiers of 1917 had not gone through years of set-piece training – but their concentrated combat experience would more than have made up for that. Their basic training was shorter and this inevitably leant itself to descriptions of untrained troops, even though that is a simplistic view. As Gordon Corrigan, himself an experienced infantry officer and trainer of recruits, notes:

> It was and is possible to train a man to a standard where he can take his place in a rifle section in a few weeks. In the Great War he needed to be able to march, to shoot and to perform tactical manoeuvres directed by his officers and NCOs.

To produce those officers and NCOs takes far longer. They cannot be made; they must be grown, and growing takes time.[15]

The lack of trained officers and NCOs coincides with a common thread in many Great War extracts. For example, the "Fourth Army Tactical Notes" of May 1916 emphasised the inexperience and lack of previous training of officers and troops which meant that they lacked the military skills which should have become second nature to them, and could thus be applied in unforeseen circumstances. Specific training was needed in the actions required of subordinate commanders in unexpected situations.[16] In early 1918, the Cambrai enquiry also sensed "a certain lack of efficiency in subordinate leadership" which was subsequently echoed by General Smuts noting that the training of junior officers and NCOs needed immediate attention.[17]

The heavy losses and rapid promotions also meant that far too few officers and NCOs had had time to grow into their positions and then have had the experience to pass on in their training. A further aspect relating to training is that apart from the very basics, responsibility for enabling appropriate training would have lain above sub-unit or even unit level.

Conclusion

Reinforcements arriving in units were probably as trained as they ever had been during the war but would always have required combat experience to become truly part of the unit. Given sufficient time for training and the necessary facilities there was no need for troops to be untrained – so long as the training was well-run and appropriate to the task in hand; inevitably, some units were better and/or more appropriately trained than others. It seems to have become common practice, however, to refer to troops as untrained as an easy excuse for inadequacies higher up in planning and execution.

---

15 Gordon Corrigan, *Mud, Blood and Poppycock* (London: Cassell, 2003) p. 259
16 Sir J.E. Edmonds, *Military Operations: France and Belgium 1916 Vol. 1* (London: Macmillan & Co., 1932), Appendix XVIII.
17 Miles, *Military Operations: France and Belgium Vol. 3*, p. 296.

Bibliography

I. ARCHIVE SOURCES

I.1 Cabinet Papers, The National Archives of the United Kingdom (Kew)

CAB/45/134	Post-war Official History Correspondence (Somme 1916)
CAB/45/116	Post-war Official History Correspondence (Arras 1917)
CAB/45/140	Post-war Official History Correspondence (Ypres 1917)
CAB/45/187	Post-war Official History Correspondence (Third Army 1918)

I.2 War Office Papers, The National Archives of the United Kingdom (Kew)

a. War Diaries

WO/95/15	GHQ
WO/95/26	Branches and Services: Adjutant General
WO/95/275	Second Army War Diary
WO/95/473	47th HAG (Brigade) RGA
WO/95/643	II Corps
WO/95/652	II Corps Artillery
WO/95/655	II Corps Heavy Artillery
WO/95/821	VIII Corps
WO/95/825	VIII Corps Heavy Artillery
WO/95/1232	1st Division
WO/95/1677	8th Division
WO/95/1873	14th Division
WO/95/2370	32nd Division
WO/95/2371	32nd Division
WO/95/2373	32nd Division Adjutant & Quartermaster
WO/95/2376	32nd Division Artillery
WO/95/2406	33rd Division
WO/95/3659	New Zealand Division
WO/95/3729	1st Canadian Division
WO/95/1274	1st Brigade

WO/95/1275	2nd Brigade
WO/95/1276	3rd Brigade
WO/95/2391	14th Brigade
WO/95/1710	23rd Brigade
WO/95/1718	24th Brigade
WO/95/1727	25th Brigade
WO/95/1894	41st Brigade
WO/95/2396	96th Brigade
WO/95/2400	97th Brigade
WO/95/2398	96th Brigade MGC
WO/95/2429	100th Brigade
WO/95/1712	2nd Devonshire
WO/95/1714	2nd West Yorkshire
WO/95/1730	2nd Lincolnshire
WO/95/1929	2nd Royal Berkshire
WO/95/1731	2nd Rifle Brigade
WO/95/2397	2nd Royal Inniskilling Fusiliers
WO/95/2397	15th Lancashire Fusiliers
WO/95/2402	2nd KOYLI
WO/95/2403	11th Border Regiment
WO/95/2398	16th Northumberland Fusiliers
WO/95/2404	16th HLI
WO/95/2405	17th HLI
AIR 1/1186/204/5/259 RFC	

b. Operation & Intelligence Files

WO/157/120	Second Army Intelligence
WO/157/121	Second Army Intelligence
WO/157/287	II Corps Intelligence
WO/157/288	II Corps Intelligence
WO/157/289	II Corps Intelligence
WO/157/423	VIII Corps Intelligence
WO/157/593	II ANZAC Corps Intelligence
WO/158/209	Second Army Operations
WO/158/210	Fourth Army Operations
WO/158/251	Fifth Army Operations

c. Maps

WO/153 261-69: 'German Artillery Groupings & Raids (British & German) Nov. to Dec. 1917' Confidential [Map] 1st-31st December 1917, Press 16, Drawer 3, YPRES 1917'

WO/297/4903: Sheet name and no: Oostnieuwkerke Edition No: 1 Production: FS Co (1291)

WO/297/4907: Sheet name and no: Oostnieuwkerke Edition No: 1 Lines: A Production: FS Co (1450)

d. *Officers' Services, First World War, Long Number Papers (numerical)*

WO/339/1191: Captain Henry Rawson FORDE. The King's Own (Yorkshire Light Infantry)

WO/339/24923: Lieutenant Rupert Hardy PARKER. The Lincolnshire Regiment

WO/339/7031: Lieutenant-Colonel Arthur John SCULLY. The Manchester Regiment

WO/339/8873: Captain Colin Robert Hoste STIRLING. The Cameronians (Scottish Rifles)

WO/339/21553: Lieutenant-Colonel Thomas Frederic TWEED. The Lancashire Fusiliers

WO/374/70307: UTTERSON, Major H K

II. OFFICIAL PUBLICATIONS

Generalstab, *Ausbildungsvorschrift für die Fusstruppen im Kriege (A.V.F.), 2. Entwurf.; Januar 1918*.

General Staff, *S.S. 135 Instructions for the Training of Divisions for Offensive Action* (December 1916).

——. *S.S. 143 Instructions for the Training of Platoons for Offensive Action, 1917* (14 February 1917).

——. *S.S. 631.A Illustrations to Accompany Notes on the Interpretation of Aeroplane Photographs* (1918).

——. *German Army Handbook April 1918* (London: Arms & Armour Press 1977 reprint of 1918 edition).

——. (Intelligence), *Vocabulary of German Military Terms and Abbreviations (Second Edition) July 1918* (Nashville, Tennessee: Battery Press reprint of 1918 edition).

Historical Sub-section. General Staff, AEF, *A Survey of German Tactics, 1918* (Washington DC: War Department, December 1918).

House of Commons, *The Parliamentary Debates: Official Report, Fifth Series – Volume 100 H.C.* (London: HMSO, 1917).

——. *The Parliamentary Debates: Official Report, Fifth Series – Volume 101* (London: HMSO, 1918).

House of Lords, *The Parliamentary Debates: Official Report, Fifth Series – Volume XLIX* (London: HMSO, 1922).

Brigadier-General Alfred Toppe, *CMH Pub 104-3 Historical Study: Night Combat* (Washington DC: Center of Military History United States Army, 1986).

War Cabinet, *Report for the Year 1917* (London: HMSO, 1918).

War Office, *The Army List for the Quarter Ending 31st December 1917 Vols 1-3* (London: HMSO, 1918).

——. *Field Service Regulations Part I: Operations 1909 (Reprinted with Amendments, 1912)* (London: HMSO, 1914).

III. PRIVATE PAPERS, DIARIES & DOCUMENTS

III.1 Imperial War Museum, London

General Sir W.G.C. Heneker
General Sir R.J. Pinney
General Sir E.P. Strickland
Brigadier-General T.S. Lambert
Lieutenant-Colonel J.H. MacDonell
Lieutenant P.A. Ledward
Private Albert Elshaw
Composition of the British Army Headquarters 1914-1918

III. 2 Others

Field Marshal Sir Douglas Haig, 'The First World War Political, Social and Military Manuscript Sources: Series One: The Haig Papers from the National Library of Scotland, Part I Haig's Autograph Great War Diary', Parts 7-12 1916-19, Reels No. 4, 5 and 6 (Brighton: Harvester Press Microfilm Publications LTD, 1987)
Field Marshal Sir Archibald Montgomery-Massingberd, Liddell Hart Centre for Military Archives, King's College, London
General Sir Henry Rawlinson, Churchill College, Cambridge
General Sir Aylmer Hunter-Weston, British Library, London
General Cecil Faber Aspinall-Oglander, Newport Record Office, Newport, Isle of Wight
Major-General A.H. Marindin, Joint Services and Command Staff College, Shrivenham
Lieutenant-Colonel Cuthbert Headlam, Durham County Record Office, Durham
Heeresgruppe Kronprinz Rupprecht, Bayerisch Kriegsarchiv, Munich
Kronprinz Rupprecht Manuscript Diary, Bayerisches Geheimes Hausarchiv, Munich
PH3 Series, Bundesarchiv-Militärarchiv, Freiberg

IV. PRINTED SOURCES

Air Historical Branch, *The Royal Air Force in the Great War* (Nashville, Tennessee: Battery Press Inc., 1996 reprint of 1936 edition).
Anonymous, *The Roll of Honour of the Empire's Heroes* (London: Queenhithe Publishing Co., 1919).
——. *With the Forty-Fourths: Being a record of the doings of the 44th Field Ambulance (14th Division)* (London: Spottiswoode, Ballantyne & Co., 1922).
J.W. Arthur & I.S. Munro (eds), *The Seventeenth Highland Light Infantry (Glasgow Chamber of Commerce Battalion): Record of War Service 1914–1918* (Glasgow: David J. Clark, 1920).

George Ashurst, *My Bit: A Lancashire Fusilier at War 1914–18* (Ramsbury: Crowood Press, 1987).
Brigadier-General Cecil F. Aspinall-Oglander, *Military Operations: Gallipoli Vo1.1* (London: Heinemann, 1929).
C.T. Atkinson, *The Devonshire Regiment 1914-1918* (London: Eland Brothers, 1926).
——. *The History of the South Wales Borderers 1914-1918* (London: The Medici Society, 1931).
Captain P.G. Bales MC, *The History of the 1/4th Battalion Duke of Wellington's (West Riding) Regiment 1914-1919* (Halifax: Edward Mortimer, 1920).
Stuart Ball (ed), *Parliament and Politics in the Age of Churchill and Attlee: The Headlam Diaries 1935-1951* (Cambridge: Cambridge University Press, 2000).
Arthur Banks, *A Military Atlas of the First World War* (London: Heinemann, 1975).
Colin Bardgett, *The Lonsdale Battalion 1914-1918* (Melksham: Cromwell Press, 1993).
Peter Barton, *The Battlefields of the First World War: The Unseen Panoramas of the Western Front* (London: Constable & Robinson, 2005).
——. *Passchendaele: Unseen Panoramas of the Third Battle of Ypres* (London: Constable, 2007).
John Baynes, *Far From a Donkey: The Life of General Sir Ivor Maxse KCB, CVO, DSO* (London: Brassey's, 1995).
C.E.W. Bean, *The Australian Imperial Force in France 1917 Vol. IV* (Sydney: Angus & Robertson, 1936).
——. *The Australian Imperial Force in France 1918 Vol V.* (Sydney: Angus & Robertson, 1943).
Major A.F. Becke, *Order of Battle of Divisions, Part 1 – The Regular British Divisions* (London: HMSO, 1934).
——. *Order of Battle Divisions, Part 3B – New Army Divisions (30-41); and 63rd (RN) Division* (London: HMSO, 1945).
——. *Order of Battle Divisions, Part 4 – The Army Council, GHQ's, Armies and Corps* (London: HMSO, 1945).
Ian Beckett & Keith Simpson, *A Nation in Arms: A Social Study of the British Army in the First World War* (Manchester: Manchester University Press, 1985).
——. & Steven Corvi (eds), *Haig's Generals* (Barnsley: Pen & Sword, 2006).
——. (ed) *The Memoirs of Sir James Edmonds* (Brighton: Tom Donovan, 2013).
Edward Beddington, 'My Life' (UK: Privately printed, 1960).
Bellahouston Academy, *Bellahouston War Memorial Volume August 4th 1914 – 28th June 1919* (Glasgow: J. Cossar, 1919).
Werner Beumelburg, *Flandern 1917* (Oldenburg: Gerhard Stalling, 1928).
Shelford Bidwell & Dominick Graham, *Fire-Power: The British Army Weapons & Theories of War 1904-1945* (Barnsley: Pen & Sword, 2004).
Robert Blake (ed), *The Private Papers of Douglas Haig 1914-1919* (London: Eyre & Spottiswoode, 1952).
Edmund Blunden, *Undertones of War* (London: Cobden-Sanderson, 1930).

Eleonore von Bojanowski, et al, *Thüringen im Weltkrieg: Vaterländisches Kriegsgedenkbuch im Wort und Bild für die Thüringischen Staaten Vols. 1 & 2* (Leipzig: Verlag der Literatur "Minerva" R. Max Lippold, 1919).

A. Bolsche, *Sturmflut: Das Erleben des 7. Thür. Infanterie-Regiments Nr. 96 im Weltkrieg: Auf Grund der Kriegstagebücher und Regimentsakten bearbeitet* (Zeulenroda, Thüringen: Verlag Bernhard Sporn, 1935).

Brian Bond, et al, *'Look to Your Front': Studies in the First World War by the British Commission for Military History* (Staplehurst: Spellmount, 1999).

——. (ed), *The War Memoirs of Earl Stanhope: General Staff Officer in France 1914-1918* (Brighton: Tom Donovan Editions, 2006).

——. & Simon Robbins (eds), *Staff Officer: The Diaries of Walter Guinness (First Lord Moyne) 1914-1918* (London: Leo Cooper, 1987).

Lieutenant-Colonel Reginald C. Bond DSO, *The King's Own Yorkshire Light Infantry in the Great War Vol. 3* (London: Percy Lund, Humphries & Co., 1929).

Lieutenant-Colonel J.H. Boraston, *Sir Douglas Haig's Despatches: December 1915- April 1919* (London: J.M. Dent & Sons, 1919).

——. & Captain Cyril E.O. Bax, *The Eighth Division 1914-1918* (London: Naval & Military Press reprint of 1926 edition).

Jonathan Boff, *Haig's Enemy: Crown Prince Rupprecht and Germany's War on the Western Front* (Oxford: Oxford University Press, 2018).

Franky Bostyn, Kristof Blieck, Freddy Declerck, Frans Descamps, Jan Van der Fraenen, *Passchendaele 1917: The Story of the Fallen at Tyne Cot Cemetery* (West-Vlaanderen: Roularta Books, 2007).

Ian Malcolm Brown, *British Logistics on the Western Front 1914-1919* (Westport, Connecticut: Praeger, 1998).

J.M. Bruce, *The Aeroplanes of the Royal Flying Corps: Military Wing* (London: Putnam, 1992).

Christopher M. Burgess (ed), *The Diary and Letters of a World War I Fighter Pilot: 2nd Lieutenant Guy Mainwaring Knocker's accounts of his experiences in 1917-1918 while serving in the RFC/RAF* (Barnsley: Pen & Sword, 2008).

Major A.D. Buttmann, *Kriegsgeschichte des Koninglich Preusischen 6. Thüringischen Infanterie Regiment Nr. 95: 1914-1918* (Zeulenroda, Thüringen: Verlag Bernhard Sporn, 1935).

John Campbell, *If Love Were All: The Story of Frances Stevenson and David Lloyd George* (London: Jonathan Cape, 2006).

Terry Carter, *Birmingham Pals: 14th, 15th & 16th (Service) Battalions of the Royal Warwickshire Regiment: A History of the Three City Battalions Raised in Birmingham in World War I* (Barnsley: Pen & Sword, 1997).

Nigel Cave, *Passchendaele: The Fight for the Village* (London: Leo Cooper, 1997).

——. *Polygon Wood* (London: Leo Cooper, 1999).

Thomas Chalmers (ed), *A Saga of Scotland: History of the 16th Battalion Highland Light Infantry (City of Glasgow Regiment)* (Glasgow: John M'Callum & Co, 1930).

Guy Chapman, *A Passionate Prodigality* (New York: Holt, Rinehart & Winston, 1966).

Mike Chappell, *British Battle Insignia (I): 1914-1918* (London: Osprey Publishing, 1986).
——. *The British Army in World War I (2): The Western Front 1916-18* (Oxford: Osprey Publishing, 2005).
——. *The British Soldier in the 20th Century 4: Light Machine Guns* (Hatherleigh: Wessex Military Publishing, 1988).
——. *The British Soldier in the 20th Century 8: The Vickers Machine Gun* (Okehampton: Wessex Military Publishing, 1989).
Peter Chasseaud, *Artillery's Astrologers: A History of British Survey and Mapping on the Western Front 1914-1918* (Lewes: Map Books, 1999).
Randolph S. Churchill, *Lord Derby: 'King of Lancashire'* (London: Heinemann, 1959).
Dale Clarke & Brian Delf, *British Artillery 1914-1919: Heavy Artillery* (Oxford: Osprey Publishing, 2005).
R.A. Colwill, *Through Hell to Victory: From Passchendaele to Mons with the 2nd Devons in 1918* (London: Naval & Military Press reprint of 1927 edition).
Captain C.H. Cooke, *Historical Records of the 16th (Service) Battalion Northumberland Fusiliers* (Newcastle-upon-Tyne: Council of the Newcastle and Gateshead Incorporated Chamber of Commerce, 1923).
Messrs. Cox & Co., *List of Officers taken prisoner in the Various Theatres of War between August 1914, and November 1918* (London: London Stamp Exchange, 1988 reprint of 1919 edition).
Sir O'Moore Creagh VC, GCB, GCSI & E.M. Humphris, *The Distinguished Service Order 1886-1923: A Complete Record of the Recipients of the Distinguished Service Order from its Institution in 1886 to the 12th June 1923, with Descriptions of the Deeds and Services for which the Award was Given and with Many Biographical and Other Details* (London: J.B. Hayward & Son, 1978).
Hermann Cron, *Imperial German Army 1914-18: Organization, Structure, Orders-of-Battle* (Solihull: Helion & Company, 2002).
Ian Cull, *The 2nd Battalion Royal Berkshire Regiment in World War One: The China Dragon's Tale* (Stroud: Tempus, 2005).
Daniel G. Dancocks, *Legacy of Valour: The Canadians at Passchendaele* (Edmonton: Hurtig Publishers, 1986).
——. *Gallant Canadians: The Story of the Tenth Canadian Infantry Battalion 1914-1919* (Calgary: Calgary Highlanders Regimental Funds Foundation, 1990).
Lieutenant-Colonel H.M. Davson, *The History of the 35th Division in the Great War* (London: Sifton & Praed, 1926).
——. *Memoirs of the Great War* (Aldershot: Gale & Polden, 1964).
Major a.D. Ernst Demmler, et al., *Das K. B. Reserve-Infanterie-Regiment 12* (Munich: Verlag Max Schid, 1934).
Peter Dennis & Jeffery Grey (eds), *1918: Defining Victory: Proceedings of the Chief of Army's History Conference Held at the National Convention Centre, Canberra 29 September 1998* (Canberra: Army History Unit, 1999).

———. *1917: Tactics, Training and Technology* (Commonwealth of Australia: Australian History Military Publications, 2007).
Marquis De Ruvigny, *De Ruvigny's Roll of Honour 1914-1918 Vol. IV* (London: Naval & Military Press reprint of 1922 edition).
Mabel Desborough Allardyce (ed), *University of Aberdeen: Roll of Service in the Great War 1914-1919* (Aberdeen: Aberdeen University Press, 1921).
Michael Dockrill & David French (eds), *Strategy and Intelligence: British Policy During the First World War* (London: Hambeldon Press, 1996).
Charles Douie, *The Weary Road: Recollections of a Subaltern of Infantry* (Stevenage: Tom Donovan Publishing, 1988 reprint of 1929 edition).
Peter Doyle & Matthew Bennett (eds), *Fields of Battle: Terrain in Military History* (Dordrecht, Boston, London: Kluwer Academic Publishers, 2002).
J.C. Dunn, *The War the Infantry Knew: 1914-1919. A Chronicle of Service in France and Belgium with the Second Battalion His Majesty's Twenty-Third of Foot, The Royal Welch Fusiliers: founded on personal records, recollections and reflections, assembled, edited and partly written by One of their Medical Officers* (London: Jane's, 1987 reprint of 1938 edition).
Christopher Duffy, *Through German Eyes: The British and the Somme 1916* (London: Weidenfeld & Nicolson, 2006).
Charles Edmonds (Pseud.), *A Subaltern's War* (London: Anthony Mott, 1984 reprint of 1929 edition).
Sir J.E. Edmonds, *Military Operations: France and Belgium 1917 Vol. 2* (London: HMSO, 1948).
———. *Military Operations: France and Belgium 1918 Vol. 1* (London: Macmillan & Co., 1935).
———. *Military Operations: France and Belgium 1918 Vol. 2* (London: Macmillan & Co., 1937).
———. *Military Operations: France and Belgium 1918 Vol. 5* (London: HMSO, 1947).
H. Essame, *The Battle for Europe 1918* (London: B.T. Batsford, 1972).
Major John Ewing MC, *The Royal Scots 1914-1919 Vol. 2* (Edinburgh: Oliver & Boyd, 1925).
Captain Cyril Falls, *The History of the First Seven Battalions the Royal Irish Rifles (Now the Royal Ulster Rifles) in the Great War Vol. 2* (Aldershot: Gale & Polden, 1925).
———. *Military Operations: France and Belgium 1917 Vol. 1* (London: Macmillan & Co., 1940).
Captain David Ferguson MC, *The History of the Canterbury Regiment NZEF 1914-1919* (Auckland: Whitcombe & Tombs, 1921).
John Ferris (ed), *The British Army and Signals Intelligence During the First World War* (Stroud: Alan Sutton & Army Records Society, 1992).
Colin Fox, *Monchy le Preux* (Barnsley: Leo Cooper, 2000).
Frank Fox, *The Royal Inniskilling Fusiliers in the World War: A record of war service as seen by the Royal Inniskilling Regiment of Fusiliers, thirteen battalions of which served* (London: Constable, 1928).

Hubert C. Fox (ed), *Infantry Officer 1914-1918: The Record of Service as a Young Officer in the First World War of Lt. General N.M.S. Irwin, CB, DSO, MC, Member of the British Legion* (Southampton: Pearson & Lloyd, 1995).
Victor von Frankenberg und Ludwigsdorff, *Das Leibgarde Infanterie Regiment (1. Grossherzoglich Hessisches) Nr. 115 im Weltkrieg 1914-1918* (Stuttgart: Verlagsbuchhandlung, 1921).
David French, *The Strategy of the Lloyd George Coalition* (Oxford: Clarendon Press, 1995).
George Heriot's School, *George Heriot's School Roll of Honour 1914-1919* (Edinburgh: War Memorial Committee, 1921).
Philip Gibbs, *Open Warfare: The Way to Victory* (London: William Heinemann, 1919).
Martin Gilbert, *British History Atlas* (London: Weidenfeld & Nicolson, 1968).
John Giles, *The Ypres Salient: Flanders Then and Now* (London: Picardy Press, 1979).
Major-General Lord Edward Gleichen, *Chronology of the Great War* (London: Greenhill, 1988 omnibus reprint of 1918-20 editions).
Gerald Gliddon, *VCs of the First World War: Arras & Messines 1917* (Stroud: Sutton, 1998).
Major G. Goold Walker DSO (ed), *The Honourable Artillery Company in the Great War 1914-1919* (London: Seeley, Service & Co., 1930).
General Sir Hubert Gough, *Soldiering On* (London: Arthur Barker, 1954).
Neil Grant, *The Lewis Gun* (Oxford: Osprey Publishing, 2014).
Randall Gray & Christopher Argyle, *Chronicle of the First World War Vol. 2 1917-1921* (Oxford: Facts on File, 1991).
Andrew Green, *Writing the Great War: Sir James Edmonds and the Official Histories 1915-1948* (London: Frank Cass, 2003).
Keith Grieves, *The Politics of Manpower 1914-18* (Manchester: Manchester University Press, 1988).
Paddy Griffith, *Battle Tactics on the Western Front: The British Army's Art of Attack 1914-1918* (New Haven/London: Yale University Press, 1994).
——. (ed), *British Fighting Methods in the Great War* (London: Frank Cass & Co., 1996).
John Grigg, *Lloyd George: War Leader 1916-1918* (London: Penguin Books, 2003).
Bruce Gudmundsson, *Stormtroop Tactics: Innovation in the German Army 1914-1918* (New York: Praeger, 1989).
Paul Guinn, *British Strategy and Politics 1914 to 1918* (Oxford: Clarendon Press, 1965).
Brian N. Hall, *Communications and British Operations on the Western Front, 1914-1918* (Cambridge: Cambridge University Press, 2017).
Sir John Hammerton (ed), *'The Great War… I Was There!' Undying Memories of 1914-1918 Vol. 2* (London: Amalgamated Press, 1939).
Lieutenant-Colonel A.A. Hanbury-Sparrow, *The Land-Locked Lake* (London: Arthur Barker, 1932).
General Sir Charles Harington, *Plumer of Messines* (London: John Murray, 1935).
Glyn Harper, *Massacre at Passchendaele: The New Zealand Story* (Auckland: Harper Collins, 2000).

Alexander von Hartmann, *Das Infanterie Regiment Grossherzog von Sachsen (5. Thüringisches) Nr. 94 im Weltkrieg* (Berlin: Verlag von Klasing & Co., 1921).
Trevor Henshaw, *The Sky Their Battlefield: Air Fighting and the Complete List of Allied Air Casualties from Enemy Action in the First War: British, Commonwealth and United States Air Services 1914 to 1918* (London: Grub Street, 1995).
Hillhead High School, *Hillhead High School War Memorial Volume* (Glasgow: William Hodge & Co., 1919).
Alison Hine, *Refilling Haig's Army: The Replacement of British Infantry Casualties on the Western Front, 1916-18* (Warwick: Helion & Company, 2018).
Prof. Albert Hiss, *Infanterie-Regiment Kaiser Wilhelm (2. Grossherzoglich Hessisches) Nr.116* (Oldenburg: Gerhard Stalling, 1924).
Richard Holmes, *Tommy: The British Soldier on the Western Front 1914-1918* (London: Harper Perennial, 2005).
Matthew Hughes & Matthew Seligmann (eds), *Leadership in Conflict 1914-1918* (Barnsley: Leo Cooper, 2000).
Mark Osborne Humphries & John Maker (eds), *Germany's Western Front: Translations from the German Official History of the Great War 1914 Part 1. The Battle of the Frontiers and Pursuit to the Marne* (Waterloo, Ontario: Wilfred Laurier University Press, 2013).
Lieutenant-Colonel Graham Seton Hutchison, *The Thirty-Third Division in France and Flanders 1915-1919* (London: Warlow & Sons, 1921).
———. *Footslogger: An Autobiography* (London: Hutchinson & Co., 1931).
Captain V.F. Inglefield, *The History of the Twentieth (Light) Division* (London: Nisbet, 1922).
Intelligence Section of the General Staff, American Expeditionary Forces, *Histories of Two Hundred and Fifty-One Divisions of the German Army Which Participated in the War 1914-1918* (London: London Stamp Exchange, 1989 reprint of 1920 edition).
Captain E.A. James, *A Record of the Battles and Engagements of the British Army in France and Flanders, 1914-1918* (Aldershot: Gale & Polden, 1924).
Brigadier-General ---------- *British Regiments 1914-1918* (Dallington: Naval & Military Press, 1998 reprint of 1929 edition).
Douglas Jerrold, *The Royal Naval Division* (London: Hutchinson & Co., 1923).
———. *Georgian Adventure* (London: The "Right Book" Club, 1938).
Lieutenant-Colonel H.S. Jervis, *The 2nd Munsters in France* (Aldershot: Gale & Polden, 1922).
Ian Johnson, *Newcastle Commercials: 16th Service Battalion Northumberland Fusiliers* (Privately published, 2016).
H.A. Jones, *The War in the Air: Being the Story of the Part played in the Great War by the Royal Air Force Vol. 4* (Nashville, Tennessee: Battery Press reprint of 1934 edition).
Ernst Junger, *Storm of Steel* (London: Penguin Books, 2003).

W.R. Kingham, *London Gunners: The Story of the H.A.C. Siege Battery in Action* (London: Methuen & Co., 1919).

Paul Knight (ed), *Lessons from the Mud: 55th (West Lancashire) Division at the Third Battle of Ypres* (Warwick: Helion & Company, 2019).

General Hermann von Kuhl, *Der Weltkrieg 1914-1918* (Berlin: Verlag Wilhelm Kohl, 1929).

Major-General J.C. Latter, *The History of the Lancashire Fusiliers in Two Volumes, Vol. 1* (Aldershot: Gale & Polden, 1949).

Peter H. Liddle (ed), *Passchendaele in Perspective: The Third Battle of Ypres* (London: Leo Cooper, 1997).

Nick Lloyd, *Passchendaele: A New History* (London: Viking, 2017).

David Lloyd George, *War Memoirs Vol. 2* (London: Odhams Press abridged edition, 1937).

Fritz von Lossberg, *Meine Tätigkeit im Weltkriege 1914-1918* (Berlin: Mittler und Sohn, 1939).

Timothy T. Lupfer, *The Dynamics of Doctrine: The Changes in German Tactical Doctrine During the First World War* (Leavenworth, Kansas: Combat Studies Institute, US Army Command and General Staff College, 1981).

Andrew MacDonald, *Passchendaele: The Anatomy of a Tragedy* (Auckland: Harper Collins, 2013).

Lyn Macdonald, *They Called it Passchendaele: The Story of the Third Battle of Ypres and of the Men Who Fought in it* (London: Michael Joseph, 1978).

——. *Somme* (London: Michael Joseph, 1983).

Compton Mackenzie, *Gallipoli Memories* (London: Cassell & Company, 1929).

Sanders Marble, *'The Infantry Cannot Do with a Gun Less': The Place of the Artillery in the British Expeditionary Force 1914-18* (New York: Columbia University Press, 2003).

Martin Matrix Evans, *Passchendaele: The Hollow Victory* (Barnsley: Pen & Sword, 2005).

Major-General Sir Frederick Maurice, *Soldier, Artist, Sportsman: The Life of General Lord Rawlinson of Trent* (Boston & New York: Houghton Mifflin Co., 1928).

Captain S. McCance, *History of the Royal Munster Fusiliers from 1861 to 1922 (Disbandment), Vol. 2* (Aldershot: Gale & Polden, 1927).

Chris McCarthy, *Passchendaele: The Day-by-Day Account* (London: Arms & Armour Press, 1996).

Elaine McFarland, *'A Slashing Man of Action': The Life of Lieutenant-General Sir Aylmer Hunter-Weston MP* (Bern: Peter Lang, 2014).

Joanna Meacock, Fiona Hayes, Alan Greenlees and Mark Roberts, *Fred A. Farrell: Glasgow's War Artist* (Glasgow: I.B. Tauris & Co. Ltd, 2014).

H.E.L. Mellersh, *Schoolboy Into War* (London: William Kimber, 1978).

Charles Messenger, *Call-To-Arms: The British Army 1914-18* (London: Cassell, 2006).

K.W. Mitchinson, *Pioneer Battalions in the Great War: Organised and Intelligent Labour* (Barnsley: Leo Cooper, 1997).

Captain Wilfred Miles, *Military Operations: France and Belgium 1917 Vol. 3* (London: HMSO, 1948).
Brock Millman, *Pessimism and British War Policy 1916-1918* (London: Frank Cass, 2001).
William Moore, *See How They Ran: The British Retreat of 1918* (London: Sphere Books, 1975).
——. *A Wood Called Bourlon: The Cover-up after Cambrai* (London: Leo Cooper, 1988).
D.B. Nash, *Imperial German Army Handbook 1914-1918* (London: Ian Allan, 1980).
John Nettleton, *The Anger of the Guns: An Infantry Officer on the Western Front* (London: William Kimber, 1979).
Sir Cecil Lothian Nicholson, *History of the East Lancashire Regiment in the Great War 1914-1918 Vol. 1* (Doncaster: D. P. & G., 2002 reprint of 1936 edition).
G.W.L. Nicholson, *Canadian Expeditionary Force: 1914-1919* (Ottawa: Queen's Printer, 1962).
Michael Occelshaw, *Armour Against Fate: British Military Intelligence in the First World War* (London: Columbus Books, 1989).
Hauptmann Kurt Offenbacher, *Die Geschichte des Infanterie-Leibregiments Grossherzogin (3. Grossherzoglich Hessisches) Nr. 117* (Oldenburg: Gerhard Stalling, 1931).
Peter Oldham, *Pill Boxes on the Western Front: A Guide to the Design, Construction and Use of Concrete Pill Boxes 1914-1918* (London: Leo Cooper, 1995).
Brigadier-General A.W. Pagan, *Infantry: An Account of the 1st Gloucestershire Regiment During the War 1914-1918* (Aldershot: Gale & Polden, 1951).
Christopher Page, *Command in the Royal Naval Division: A Military Biography of Brigadier General A.M. Asquith DSO* (Staplehurst: Spellmount, 1999).
Major H.G. Parkyn (ed), *The Rifle Brigade Chronicle for 1936* (London: The Rifle Brigade Club and Association, 1937).
Robert A. Perry, *To Play a Giant's Part: The Role of the British Army at Passchendaele* (Uckfield: Naval & Military Press, 2014).
F. Loraine Petre, *The Royal Berkshire Regiment Vol. 2* (Reading: The Reading Barracks, 1925).
R.E. Priestley, *The Signal Service in the European War of 1914 to 1918 (France)*, (Chatham: The Institution of Royal Engineers & Signals Association, 1921).
Robin Prior, *Gallipoli: The End of the Myth* (New Haven/London: Yale University Press, 2009).
Robin Prior & Trevor Wilson, *Command on the Western Front: The Military Career of Sir Henry Rawlinson 1914-18* (Oxford: Blackwells, 1992).
——. *Passchendaele: the Untold Story* (New Haven/London: Yale University Press, 1996).
——. *The Somme* (New Haven/London: Yale University Press, 2005).
Prussia Armee. Grosser Generalstab, *Die Schlachten und Gefechte des Grossen Krieges 1914-1918: Quellenwerk, nach den Amtlichen Bezeichnungen/Zusammengestellt vom Grossen Generalstab* (Berlin: Verlag von Hermann Sack, 1919).
M.A. Ramsay, *Command and Cohesion: The Citizen Soldier and Minor Tactics in the British Army 1870-1918* (Westport, Connecticut: Praeger, 2002).

Andrew Rawson, *British Army Handbook 1914-1918* (Thrupp-Stroud: Sutton, 2006).
——. *The Passchendaele Campaign 1917* (Barnsley: Pen & Sword, 2017).
Regimental History Committee, *History of the Dorsetshire Regiment 1914-1919 Vol. 1* (London: Henry Ling, 1932).
Regimental Publication Committee, *The Fifth Battalion the Cameronians (Scottish Rifles) 1914-1919* (Glasgow: Jackson, Son & Co., 1936).
Lieutenant-Colonel C. À Court Repington, *The First World War 1914-1918 Vol. 2* (London: Constable & Co., 1920).
Robert Rhodes James, *Gallipoli* (London: Pan Books, 1984)
Simon Robbins, *British Generalship on the Western Front 1914-1918: Defeat into Victory* (London: Frank Cass, 2005).
Sidney Rogerson, *Twelve Days on the Somme: A Memoir of the Trenches 1916* (London: Frontline Books, 2009 reprint of 1933 edition).
Kronprinz Rupprecht von Bayern, *In Treue Fest – Mein Kriegstagebuch Vol. 2* (Munich: Deutscher National Verlag, 1929).
A.B. Scott, R.E. Grice-Hutchison, et al., *Artillery & Trench Mortar Memories: 32nd Division* (London: Unwin Brothers, 1932).
Leonard Sellers, *Hood Battalion: The Royal Naval Division: Antwerp, Gallipoli, France 1914-1918* (London: Leo Cooper, 1995).
W.W. Seymour, *The History of the Rifle Brigade in the War of 1914-1918 Vol. 2* (London: Rifle Brigade Club, 1927).
Gary Sheffield, *Leadership in the Trenches: Officer-Man Relations, Morale and Discipline in the British Army in the Era of the First World War* (Basingstoke: Macmillan Press, 2000).
——. & Dan Todman (eds), *Command and Control on the Western Front: The British Army's Experience 1914-18* (Staplehurst: Spellmount, 2004).
——. & John Bourne (eds), *Douglas Haig: War Diaries and Letters 1914-1918* (London: Weidenfeld & Nicolson, 2005).
Jack Sheldon, *The German Army at Passchendaele* (Barnsley: Pen & Sword, 2007).
Dennis Showalter (ed), *History in Dispute Vol. 8: World War I* (Detroit: St James Press, 2004).
Andy Simpson, *Directing Operations: British Corps Command on the Western Front 1914-18* (Stroud: Spellmount, 2006).
Major-General C.R. Simpson (ed), *The History of the Lincolnshire Regiment 1914-1918* (London: Medici Society, 1931).
Stephen Snelling, *VCs of the First World War: Passchendaele 1917* (Thrupp-Stroud: Sutton, 1998).
Society of Telegraph Engineers, *The Roll of Honour of the Institution of Electrical Engineers* (London: W.A.J. O'Meara, 1924).
Captain H. FitzM. Stacke MC, *The Worcestershire Regiment in the Great War Vol. 1* (Kidderminster: G.T. Cheshire & Sons, 1928).
Brigadier-General F.C. Stanley, *The History of the 89th Brigade 1914-1918* (Liverpool: 'Daily Post' Printers, 1919).

Michael Stedman, *Salford Pals: A History of the Salford Brigade – The 15th, 16th, 19th, and 20th (Service) Battalions the Lancashire Fusiliers 1914-19* (London: Leo Cooper, 1993).
Nigel Steel & Peter Hart, *Passchendaele: The Sacrificial Ground* (London: Cassell & Co., 2000).
Lieutenant-Colonel H. Stewart, *The New Zealand Division 1914-1919: A Popular History based on Official Records* (Auckland: Whitcombe & Tombs, 1921).
Pat Swinburne, et al, *Tingewick's Fallen Soldiers of the Great War* (Tingewick: Tingewick Historical Society, 2014).
James W. Taylor, *The 1st Royal Irish Rifles in the Great War* (Dublin: Four Courts Press, 2002).
John Terraine, *The Road to Passchendaele: The Flanders Offensive of 1917: A Study in Inevitability* (London: Leo Cooper, 1977).
——. (ed) *General Jack's Diary: The Trench Diary of Brigadier General J. L. Jack DSO* (London: Cassell, 2000).
Nigel Thomas & Ramiro Bujeiro, *The German Army in World War I (3): 1917-18* (Oxford: Osprey Publishing, 2004).
J. Lee Thompson, *Northcliffe: Press Baron in Politics 1865-1922* (London: John Murray, 2000).
Colonel E.G.L. Thurlow D.S.O., *The Pill-Boxes of Flanders* (London: Ivor Nicholson & Watson, 1933).
Tim Travers, *The Killing Ground: The British Army, the Western Front, and the Emergence of Modern Warfare 1900-1918* (London: Allen & Unwin, 1987).
——. *How the War Was Won: Command and Technology in the British Army on the Western Front 1917-1918* (London/New York: Routledge, 2001).
——. *Gallipoli 1915* (Stroud: Tempus, 2001).
University Court of the University of Glasgow, *Members of the University of Glasgow and the University Contingent of the Officers' Training Corps Who Served With the Forces of the Crown 1914-1919* (Glasgow: Maclehose, Jackson & Co., 1922).
University of Edinburgh, *University of Edinburgh Roll of Honour 1914-1919* (London: Oliver & Boyd, 1921).
Jan Vancoillie & Kristof Blieck, *Defending the Ypres Front 1914-1918: Trenches, Shelters & Bunkers of the German Army* (Barnsley: Pen & Sword, 2018).
Aubrey Wade, *The War of the Guns* (London: Batsford, 1936).
Achiel Van Wallenghem, *1917. The Passchendaele Year: The British Army in Flanders* (Brighton: EER, 2017).
War Office, *Statistics of the Military Effort of the British Empire During the Great War 1914-1920* (London: HMSO, 1922).
Andrew A. Wiest, *Passchendaele and the Royal Navy* (Westport, Connecticut: Greenwood Press, 1995).
Jeffery Williams, *Byng of Vimy: General and Governor General* (London: Leo Cooper, 1983).
Keith Wilson (ed), *The Rasp of War: The Letters of H.A. Gwynne to the Countess Bathhurst 1914-1918* (London: Sidgwick & Jackson, 1988).

David Woodward, *Lloyd George and the Generals* (East Brunswick NJ: Associated University Presses, 1983).
Colonel H.C. Wylly, *The Border Regiment in the Great War* (Aldershot: Gale & Polden, 1924).
——. *History of the Manchester Regiment (Late 63rd and 96th Foot) Vol. 2* (London: Foster Groom & Co., 1925).
Llewellyn Wyn Griffth, *Up to Mametz* (Norwich: Gliddon Books, 1988 reprint of 1931 edition).
Captain G.C. Wynne, *If Germany Attacks: The Battle in Depth in the West* (Brighton: Tom Donovan unexpurgated edition, 2008).
Everard Wyrall, *The Die-Hards in the Great War: A History of the Duke of Cambridge's Own (Middlesex Regiment), 1914-1919, Compiled from the Records of the Line, Special Reserve, Service and Territorial Battalions Vol. II 1916-1919* (London: Harrison & Sons Ltd, 1926).

V. JOURNALS & PERIODICALS

Richard Baumgartner (ed), 'Death's Fugue in Flanders', *Der Angriff: A Journal of World War I Military History* (November 1982).
John Cooksey, 'Visiting the Western Front 2: Slaughter by Moonlight: The Passendale – Westrozebeke Road north of Passendale, Belgium', *Britain at War* (November 2012).
——. Editorial, *Stand To!* (September 2013).
Lieutenant-Colonel J. H. Dyer, 'A Holding Operation in September 1917', *Gun Fire No. 6*, Series 2 (date unknown) reprint of June 1939 *Royal Engineers Journal* article.
David French, '"Official but not History?" Sir James Edmonds and the Official History of the Great War', *RUSI: Royal United Services Institute for Defence Studies Journal*, 131:1 (March 1986).
Great War Committee, 'Report of the Committee on the Lessons of the Great War (The Kirke Report)', *The British Army Review Special Edition* (April 2001).
John Hussey, 'The Movement of German Divisions to the Western Front, Winter 1917-1918', *War in Society*, Volume 4, Number 2 (April 1997).
Lieutenant E.A. James, 'A Record of the Battles and Engagements of the British Armies in France and Flanders 1914-1918', *RUSI: Royal United Services Institute Journal*, Volume 68:1 (February 1923).
Roger Noble, 'Raising the White Flag: The Surrender of Australian Soldiers on the Western Front', *Revue Internationale d'Histoire Militaire*, No. 72 (1990).
Brigadier-General Sir H.S. Rawlinson, Bart., CVO, CB, psc, commanding 2nd Infantry Brigade, Aldershot Command, 'Night Operations', *RUSI: Royal United Services Institute Journal*, 52:1 (June 1908).
M. Royburt, Y. Epstein, Z. Solomon, J. Shemer, 'Long-term Psychological and Physiological Effects of Heat Stroke', *Physiology & Behavior*, 54:2 (August 1993).
David Schurman, 'Passchendaele: The Final Phase', *History of the First World War*, London: BPC Publishing, Vol. 6. No. 5 (1971).

Leonard Sellers (ed), "Western Front: Report on Operations During the Third Battle of Ypres: Passchendaele, 24th October to 5th November 1917", *R.N.D.: Royal Naval Division. Antwerp, Gallipoli & Western Front 1914-1918*, Issue Number 22 (September 2002).

VI. THESES & PAPERS

James Beach, 'Intelligence and the German Army, 1914-1918' (PhD Thesis. London: University College, 2004).

Aimée Fox, '"The word 'retire' is never to be used": The performance of the 9th Brigade, AIF, at First Passchendaele, 1917', Australian War Memorial Summer Vacation Scholarship Scheme Research Paper (Canberra: AWM, 2011).

David John Jordan, 'The Army Co-operation Missions of the Royal Flying Corps/Royal Air Force 1914-1918' (PhD Thesis. Birmingham: University of Birmingham, 1997).

Stuart Mitchell, 'An Inter-disciplinary Study of Learning in the 32nd Division on the Western Front 1916-18' (PhD Thesis. Birmingham: University of Birmingham, 2013).

Michael Rauer, 'Yanks in the King's Forces: American Physicians Serving with the British Expeditionary Force during World War I' (Paper. Washington DC: Office of Medical History, Office of the Surgeon General United States Army, date unknown).

Alun Thomas, 'British 8th Infantry Division on the Western Front 1914-18' (PhD Thesis. Birmingham: University of Birmingham, 2010).

VII. NEWSPAPERS

Buckinghamshire Advertiser
Illustrated London News
Le Petit Journal
The Outpost
The Sphere
The Times

VIII. ELECTRONIC SOURCES

Air of Authority – A History of RAF Organization. <http. rafweb.org/Sqn021-25.htm>

Commonweath War Graves Commission. <http://www.cwgc.org>

Flandernland <http.//www.flandernland.de/>

Geoff's CWGC 1914-21 Search Engine <http://www.hut-six.co.uk/cgi-bin/search14-21.php>

Glasgow's Forgotten War: Artist Fred Farrell <http://www.heraldscotland.com/arts-ents/visual/glasgows-forgotten-war-artist-fred-farrell.1400900405>

Great War Forum <http://1914-1918.invisionzone.com/forums/>
Imperial War Museum, Burke, Lieutenant Ulick Bernard (interview), Reel 16, <http://www.iwm.org.uk/collections/item/object/80000565>
The Long, Long Trail: The British Army in the First World War <http://www.1914-1918.net/index.htm>
The Lonsdale Pals Battalion, 11th Service Battalion Border Regiment 1914-1918 <www.freewebs.com/granatloch/>
National Schools Observatory, Universe Now: A Month of the Moon, National Grid for Learning. <http://www.schoolsobservatory.org.uk/ngfl.htm>
Ossett – The History of a Yorkshire Town <www.ossett.net>
The People of Tingewick, Buckinghamshire (England) <http://freepages.genealogy.rootweb.com/~tingewick/>
RAMC in the Great War < http://www.ramc-ww1.com/index.html>
Sons of Penicuik < http://www.sonsofpenicuik.com/>
Stevenage at War <http://www.stevenageatwar.com/nsindex.html>
Understanding Society: Innovative Thinking about Social Agency and Structure in a Global World <understandingsociety.blogspot.com/2008/11/narrative-history.html>
University of Glasgow, Archive Services: Roll of Honour <http://www.gla.ac.uk/honour/>
Wereldoorlog 1 in de Westhoek <www.wo1.be>
McMaster University, Libraries: World War I Military Maps & Aerial Photography: France & Belgium < http://library.mcmaster.ca/maps/ww1/home.htm>

IX. MISCELLANEOUS SOURCES

Anonymous, 'The Biscuit Boys', Section 272, The Third Battle of Ypres, 2nd Battalion [Royal Berkshire Regiment], July-December 1917 (RBGW Project PDF, 2007).
Great War Digital, 'Lines Man: NGI Belgium: 1:25,000 & 1:50,000 scale modern Belgian map data and aerial photography in association with NGI Belgium' (2008).
IWM Film & Video Archives: Film Nos. 416 & 1100 'British Regiments' series (Topical Film Company for War Office Cinema Committee 1918). Two short films depicting 2nd Rifle Brigade and 2nd Lincolnshire Regiment prior to deployment (autumn 1917) at Passchendaele.
Alan Ridgway, 'The Road from Passchendaele' (December 2002) Ridgeway Routes (Privately circulated family journal).

Index

INDEX OF PEOPLE

Abbiss, R.D. 2nd Lieutenant 226, 449
Albers, *Leutnant* 427
Alexander, H.R. Colonel 352
Alexander, J.A. Captain 230, 266
Allenby, Sir Edmund General 316
Amoradhat, Prince 83
Anderson, G.H.G. Lieutenant 182, 215-217, 219-220, 258, 260, 284, 337-338, 412-413
von Arnim, K.R. *Hauptmann* 261, 293, 427, 429, 431-432
Aspinall, C.F. Brigadier-General 51-52, 56-57, 60, 80, 96, 100, 122-123, 169, 244, 246, 307, 355, 361, 389, 416
Ashurst, George Corporal 163
Asquith G.W., 2nd Lieutenant 224, 449
Atkinson, H.V. Private, 240

Baasch, *Leutnant* 425
Baird, A.W.F. Brigadier-General 220, 383
Balz, *Unteroffizier*
Bax, C.E.O. Captain, 339,372
Bean, C.E.W. 42
Becker, *Gefreiter* 432
Beddington, E.H.L Lieutenant-Colonel 60, 91-92, 101-102, 124, 174, 333, 340, 393
Bennie, W.R. 2nd Lieutenant 229
von der Bense, *Leutnant* 321
Bent, Frederick. F. Private 372
Birch, N. Lieutenant-General 416

Blacklock C.A., Brigadier-General 109-111, 125, 139, 141-142, 153, 160, 184-186, 191, 195, 200, 205, 247, 251, 253, 265, 270-271, 273, 276-281, 283, 285, 287, 291, 300-305, 308, 342-346, 349, 382, 400
Bode, *Leutnant* 427
Bolton, H.W. Major 351
Bonham Carter, Charles Brigadier-General 112
Boraston, J.H. Lieutenant-Colonel 339, 372
Bradburn, A. Private 240
Brand, Hon. R Lieutenant-Colonel 125, 182, 215, 312, 337-338
Brandscheid, *Leutnant* 430
Braithwaite, W.G. Brigadier-General 324,326
Brigham, H.L. 2nd Lieutenant 216, 223
Brockman, J.W. Lieutenant 238
Brooker J., 2nd Lieutenant 218
Buchan, C. 2nd Lieutenant 239, 464
Burman, A.H. 2nd Lieutenant 181
Burne, Lieutenant 306
Byng, Hon. Sir Julian General 39, 60, 414

Cain, E. 2nd Lieutenant 266
Cairns, H. Private 192-193, 335, 375, 377, 379-380, 454
Cameron, M. 2nd Lieutenant 236
Carrington, Charles Lieutenant 172
Carson, Sir Edward 189
Chapman, Guy Captain 363

Charlton, D.V. Lieutenant 230, 294-295
Chichester-Constable, R.C. Captain 110
Chivers, A. Corporal 212
Christison, A.F.P Colonel 367
Coffin, C. Brigadier-General 92, 107-108, 111, 125, 132-134, 169, 174, 186, 260, 262, 264, 282-283, 291, 293, 301, 306, 312, 338, 382, 473
Collings, F.R. 2nd Lieutenant 309, 465
Cooksey, A. Private 189, 335, 375-376
Corcoran, A.T. 2nd Lieutenant 249, 266
Cowe, A. Captain 259, 261
Cundall C. Captain 164
Cunningham, P.N. 2nd Lieutenant 236
Currie, Sir A. Lieutenant-General 43

Davidson G.L. Captain G.L 229-230
Davidson, J.H. Brigadier-General 57, 316-317, 368
Davies, Sergeant 216, 223
De Lisle, H. Major-General 103
Derby, Lord 317-318, 473
von Dresler und Scharfenstein, *General-Major* 214
Dyer, J.H. Lieutenant-Colonel 123

Eckhardt, M. *Vizefeldwebel* 433
Edmonds, Sir J.E. 79, 318, 479
Ehrhardt, *Schutze* 431
Ellis, J.N 2nd Lieutenant 225-226
Elshaw, A Private 88-89, 199-200
Essame, H. Captain 90, 369
Evelegh, E.E. Major 146, 248, 269, 315, 351

Fagan, E.A. Brigadier-General 91
Falls, Cyril Captain, 84, 96
Fanshawe, Sir E. Lieutenant-General 101
Ferrier, J.A. Major-General 189
Ferris, J. 2nd Lieutenant 292
Fiestner, *Gefreiter* 438
Fischer, *Vizefeldwebel* 428
Flint, Captain 212, 256, 262
Forde, H.R. Captain 187-189, 225, 376
Francis, O.S. Lieutenant 177, 179
Franks, G. Major-General 240, 383

Forde, H.R. Captain 187-189, 224-226, 375-377
Fraser, Captain A. 207-208, 314
Frobe, *Leutnant* 438
Fuchs, *Leutnant* 431
Fuller, C.G. Lieutenant-Colonel, 350

Geck, *Leutnant* 426
Geddes, Sir Auckland 318
Gerbracht, *Leutnant* 430
Giddings, F. 2nd Lieutenant 177, 210, 443
Gilmour, Corporal 192
Gilmour, W. Private 192, 314
Girdwood, A.C. Brigadier-General 84, 161, 184, 382
Glaser, *Gefreiter* 439
Godley, Sir A. Lieutenant-General 105
Gombel, *Leutnant* 428
Gough, Sir Hubert General 39, 41, 78, 83, 415, 449
Greenhill, R.F. Captain 238
Grice-Hutchison, R.E. Reverend 319-320
Griffin, B.W. 2nd Lieutenant 257
Grogan, G.W. St. G. Brigadier-General 108, 132, 381
Gumbrecht, *Vizefeldwebel* 428

Haig, Sir Douglas Field Marshal 37-39, 41, 43-44, 49, 54, 57, 61, 82, 88, 93-94, 120, 311, 316-318, 329, 339, 349, 358, 364-369, 416
Haig, R. Brigadier-General 91, 177, 382
Halliday, C.P. 2nd Lieutenant 223
Hamilton Gordon, A. Lieutenant-General 349
Hamilton, Sir Ian General 79-80, 246
Hampden, Second Viscount 125
Hanbury-Sparrow, A.A. Lieutenant-Colonel 89-91, 106, 108, 172, 177
Harington, C.H. Major-General 41, 351
Hassell, J. Captain 226, 249-250, 265-266, 288, 291
Hearst, William Randolph 346
Heathcoat-Amory, L. Major 172

Hein, *Leutnant* 431-32
Heneker, W.C.G. Major-General 60, 89-92, 96-97, 99-101, 107-108, 113, 118, 121-124, 137, 161, 170, 174, 176, 208, 216, 220, 260, 264, 283, 301, 307, 311-312, 333, 337-339, 353, 355, 381
Herbert, A.P. 87
von Hertell, *Oberstleutnant* 441
Hess, *Vizefeldwebel* 437-438
Higginbottom, P. Rifleman 371
Hilley, Corporal 192
Hislop-Reid, R.H. 2nd Lieutenant 236
Hood, T. QMS 309
Hodgson, W. Private 371
Hoffmann, *Leutnant* 428
Horne, Sergeant 224, 226, 250
Hooton, A. Rifleman 217
Horton, J.W. Corporal 240
Horton, V.J. 2nd Lieutenant 292, 319
Howard, J.H. Captain 222, 224
Huch, *Leutnant* 431
Hunter-Weston, Sir A. Lieutenant-General 39, 58, 60, 79-83, 101, 170, 175, 220, 243, 246-247, 252, 254, 260, 262-263, 283, 285, 298-299, 301, 307, 311-312, 315-316, 353, 357-359, 363, 368, 375, 388, 416
Hunter-Weston, Lady 83, 358, 416
Hurst, 2nd Lieutenant, 240

Inglis, J. Lieutenant-Colonel 198, 250
Irwin, N.M.S. Lieutenant-Colonel 100, 181, 255, 257-258, 260, 262, 293, 308, 336-338, 473
Ivey, T.H. Major 217

Jacob, Sir C Lieutenant-General 39, 58, 76-79, 86, 353
Jerrold, Douglas 87-88
Junge, *Leutnant* 435

Keiper, *Leutnant* 431
Kerr, Lieutenant 230, 266, 348
Kiggell, Sir L.E. Brigadier-General 57, 361, 415
Klopple, *Leutnant* 291, 438

Klotz, *Oberstleutnant* 212
Kirby, A.D. Brigadier-General 114
Krichbaum, *Vizefeldwebel* 428
Knight, H.J. Second Lieutenant 223
Knott, F. Private 375
Knox, Captain, 271, 278, 281, 286-287, 299-300
von Kuhl, H. *General* 67

Lambert, P. Captain 224
Lamotte, L. Lieutenant-Colonel 190, 166
Lange, *Leutnant* 431-32
Ledward, P. Lieutenant 108
Lee, W. Rifleman, 217
Linck, *Leutnant* 437
Lloyd George, D. 38-40, 57, 173, 317, 346, 360, 365, 367, 369
Lloyd, H.G. Brigadier-General 132
Longford, Jennifer 346
Lonsdale, Earl of 193
Lumm, J.W. Lieutenant, 230
Lumsden, F.W. Brigadier-General 84, 160, 275, 280-283, 285, 304-306, 309, 327, 382, 462
von Ludendorff, E. *Generalquartiermeister* 65, 67, 93

Macdonell, I.H. Lieutenant-Colonel I.H. 85
Macduff, W.B. 2nd Lieutenant 232-233, 459
Machado, Bernardino 83
Macready, Sir N. Lieutenant-General 317
Maddison, Captain 266
Malcolm, N. Major-General 41
Mandleberg, L.C. Captain 238
Martin, P.M. Captain 233
Martini, *Leutnant* 289, 291, 293-294, 438
Maxse, F.I. Lieutenant-General 112, 185
Maxwell, J. Major 313
McLellan, J. Lieutenant 192, 292
McNamara, A.E. Lieutenant-Colonel 84, 138, 305, 352, 397
McConnan, Captain 233

Meier, *Leutnant* 428
Miller, J. 2nd Lieutenant 230, 235
Montgomery, B. Lieutenant-Colonel 352
Morland, W. 2nd Lieutenant 235
Morris, C. 2nd Lieutenant 177
Morrison, W. 2nd Lieutenant 218

Nettleton, J. Lieutenant 182, 187, 215, 333
Nicholas, H.J. Private 326
Nicholson, R.D.W. 236
Nosworthy, Major 209, 312

Offenbacher, *Oberstleutnant* 430
Osborne, J. 2nd Lieutenant 236

Pannett, Sergeant 223
Parker, R.H. Lieutenant 180, 335, 375-376
Paterson, A.K. Sergeant 84
Pereira, C.E. Major-General 58
Pinney, R.J. Major-General 220, 383
von Pfannenberg, *Major* 435
Philips, L.F. Brigadier-General 88
Pile, F. Brigadier-General 352-353
Plagge, *Leutnant* 428
Poole, H.R. Private 239
Pollard, G.C. Lieutenant-Colonel 140, 162, 271, 281, 351
Plumer, Sir Herbert General 40-41, 120, 293, 363
Pollitt, 2nd Lieutenant 240

Ratliff, E.F. Captain 218
Rawlinson, Sir Henry General 39-40, 44-45, 48-49, 57-61, 82, 93, 102-105, 116-117, 161-162, 167, 169, 201, 206, 274, 283, 310-311, 316, 329, 358, 360-361, 363, 414, 416, 473
Repington. C.A. Colonel 57
von Rettberg, *Major* 423
Rice, 2nd Lieutenant 177
Richardson, R.C. 2nd Lieutenant 233
Ridgway, W.T. 2nd Lieutenant 195, 197, 233, 335, 375. 377-78, 459
Ridgway, F. 197, 377
Roberts, S.M. Lieutenant 193

Robertson, R.B. Lieutenant 230
Robertson, Sir W. General 37
Rogerson, S. Captain 89
Rossger, *Leutnant* 438
Rupprecht, Crown Prince 331
Russell, A. Major-General 324

Sandeman, A.F. Captain 232-233, 266, 240
Scott, A.B. Lieutenant 106, 252-253, 340, 343
Scott, Major W.D. 228, 292, 302-303, 309, 346
Schade, *Leutnant* 427
Scheler, *Vizefeldwebel* 437-438
Scherstuhl, *Vizefeldwebel* 431-432
Scholes, 2nd Lieutenant 240
Schott, *Hauptmann* 430
Schultheis, *General-Leutnant* 435
Scrivener, J.S. 2nd Lieutenant 200, 239, 465
Scully, A.J. Lieutenant-Colonel 165, 208, 222, 229, 248, 252-253, 269, 288, 295-296, 301-302, 310, 314, 341, 346-347
von Selle, *Oberstleutnant* 240, 289, 438-439
Seton Hutchison, G. Lieutenant-Colonel 50, 81
Shepherd, R.W.G Rifleman 371
Shoubridge, T.H. Brigadier-General 93
Shute, C.D. Major-General 59, 84-89, 93-97, 100-103, 109-110, 139, 149, 151, 161, 163, 172, 186, 206, 208, 236, 242, 244-245, 249-251, 264-265, 267, 270-272, 274-277, 280, 282-283, 285-288, 294-295, 299-301, 304-306, 308-309, 311-312, 316-318, 341, 344-355, 382, 476-479
Skinner, P.C.B. Brigadier-General 307, 382
Smith, 2nd Lieutenant 212
Smith, D.H. Lieutenant 238
Solly-Flood, A. Brigadier-General 112
Somervail, W.F. Captain 215
Speiz, *Gefreiter* 374
Spottiswoode, Lieutenant 227, 249
Stanhope, Major Earl 58, 76-78, 86-87
Stark, A.W. 2nd Lieutenant 266

Stevenson, Frances 346
Stirling, C.R.H. Lieutenant-Colonel 177-178, 208, 210, 245, 255-256, 260, 262, 284, 293, 306-307, 335-338, 382
Strickland, E.P. Major-General 48, 381
Sturgess, A. Sergeant 212
Sudheimer, *Unteroffizier* 431
Sutherland, C.S. 2nd Lieutenant 166

Tappe, *Unteroffizier* 439
von Taysen, *Oberstleutnant* 227
von Thaer, Albrecht 42
Thom G. St. C. Colonel 322
Tillett, A. Lieutenant-Colonel 312, 338
Toppe, A. Brigadier-General 355
Tremellan, 2nd Lieutenant 177, 214
Troup, S.H. Lieutenant 210
Tweed, T.F. Lieutenant-Colonel 193-195, 344-346, 354, 476-478
Tyler, J.A, Brigadier-General 249, 299

Uniacke, H.C.C. Lieutenant-General, 95
Upton, 2nd Lieutenant 177, 210, 212, 214, 245-246, 255, 257, 260, 262, 284, 293, 307

Utterson, H.K. Major, 238, 267, 306, 310, 327, 341

Vogt, *Leutnant* 438

Wailes, H. Captain 281, 404, 408
Wait, H.A.V. 2nd Lieutenant 210
Wakely, F.J. Private 178-179, 335, 375, 378, 380, 444
Ward, H.D.O. Brigadier-General 113
Waters, Major 163
Watt, G. Private 233
Watt, W. Private 233
Wavell, A.P. Brigadier-General 352
Webb, J.V. 2nd Lieutenant 223
Wedgwood, Josiah 365
von Westernhagen, *Oberstleutnant* 212
von Westerhoven, *Major* 423
Westwater, J.O. Captain 236
Wilson, S. Brigadier-General 86, 281
Woeste, *Vizefeldwebel* 261, 432
Wylly, H.C. Colonel 231, 327
Wilson, J.S. 2nd Lieutenant 226
Wust, *Leutnant* 427

INDEX OF PLACES

Abraham Heights 53, 114, 170
Abschnitt A 63, 373, 420, 424-425, 427, 429, 432
Abschnitt B 68, 227, 420, 425, 429, 436, 441
Abschnitt Nord 430
Adler Farm 156
Aersele 425
Ancre, Battle of the 101
Antwerp 44, 98, 133, 156, 227
Ardeppelhoek 436
Ardone 436, 439
Arras 38, 110, 121, 160, 281, 316, 354, 368
Ayette 479

Bakrats-Hof 423
Bazentin Ridge, Battle of 102
Becelaere 419, 425, 428
Bellevue Spur 42-43, 50, 52-53, 59, 122-130, 133-134, 141-142, 146, 156, 159-160, 162, 167, 181-182, 187, 190, 192-194, 208, 244, 246, 270, 275, 306, 308, 313, 319, 327, 389, 399-400, 417
Beythem 424, 432
Boeteleer 53, 114
Boisdinghem 333
Bouchavesnes 99, 113, 430
Brandhoek 108, 473
Bridge House 161, 322
Broodseinde 40-42, 50, 68, 104, 173, 361, 367, 417
Brugge. 332, 357, 439
Bucquoy 363
Buffs Road 187

Cachtem 425, 428
Cambrai 39, 44, 57-58, 60-62, 105, 117, 121, 318, 323, 329, 349, 357-358, 360, 364-366, 368-369, 372, 427, 485
Cambridge Road 53
Cambridge University 81, 197
Cameron House 240

Canal Bank 128-130, 132, 141, 144, 147-148, 156, 161, 163, 172, 244, 270, 273, 286, 311, 397, 401
Caporetto 38, 40, 58, 205, 317
Chateau Lovie 59, 61
Cheddar Villa 144, 146-147, 156, 320
Christ Church College Oxford 180, 376
Clifton College 187-188
Collierolenhoek 320
Courtrai 419, 424, 440
Coxyde 483
Crest Farm 50, 368

Dambre Camp 111, 132, 141, 148, 333
De Ruiter 212, 425, 429
Den Aap 420
Den Hukker 420, 423
Denterghem 425
Devil's Crossing 53
Double Copse 46, 233, 279-280, 282
Doullens 358
Droogenbroodhoek 283
Duhallow ADS Cemetery 249, 292
Duivelshoeken 423, 429

Emelgem 428
Exaerde 419
Exert Farm 167, 174-175, 202, 207, 209, 211-212, 214, 253, 331, 375, 426, 471

Fayet 84, 109
Feldherrnhügel 205, 289, 291, 332, 437-439
Fins 113
Flandern I 40, 74, 363, 425
Flandern II 40, 63, 74, 363
Flandern III 40
Flesquières 360, 414
Frezenberg 53, 367

Gallipoli 52, 79-83, 98, 246
Gallipoli Dugouts 128-130
Gheluvelt 40-41, 43, 79, 104-105, 324-326, 422, 425-426, 429-430

Ghent 357, 419, 425, 429
Ginste 424, 432
Gits 436, 440
Gitsberg 441
Godley Road 53
Goudberg 45, 48, 52, 74, 79, 116, 244, 246, 307, 323, 327, 333, 359
Goudbergstraat 184, 231, 379-380
Gouzeaucourt 113
Gravenstafel 50, 53, 127-128, 141, 159, 161, 171, 181, 184, 187, 190, 192-193, 301, 313
Grensshof 429

Hannixbeek 328
Haringstraat 228, 379-380
Heidengoed 139, 320-321, 329, 396
Hill 50 47-48, 59, 62, 205, 263
Hill 52 48, 59, 68, 70-71, 94, 124, 138, 140, 149, 153, 164, 184, 206, 221-222, 224, 226-229, 245, 247, 249-251, 254, 264-265, 270, 272-277, 279-281, 285, 287-289, 291, 293, 296, 298-305, 307-309, 311-312, 315, 319, 333, 343-344, 354, 359, 361, 365, 376, 385, 434
Hill Top Farm 156, 198-199, 334, 397, 399-400, 484
Hindenburg Line 39, 84, 113, 134, 354
Hinton Farm 240
Höhenrücken 69, 227, 291, 435, 438
Hollebeke 440
Holnon Wood 84
Houthulst Forest 42, 44, 48, 50, 58, 115-116, 171, 221, 227, 328-329, 354, 433, 436, 440
Hubner Farm 103, 273, 277

Ingelmünster 424, 428
Irish Farm 140-141, 148, 156, 160-161, 187, 275, 308-309, 333, 397, 399, 401
Iseghem 420
Italy 40, 58, 60-61, 117, 366

Kachtem 424
Kaiphas 420, 423

Kalve 212, 430
Kansas Cross 53, 103, 129-130, 141, 146-147, 161, 172, 190, 275, 283, 285, 309, 322, 359, 397, 399
Kapellenhof 431
Keiberg Spur 164
Kemmelberg 433
Klercken Ridge 50
Kolonnenhof (Exert Farm) 212, 214, 331, 426, 471
Koolskamp 441
Korek 128-130, 301
Krithia 82
Kronprinz Farm 129, 141-142, 146-147, 149, 161-162, 172, 200, 266, 279, 281, 397
Kronprinz Track 162, 271

La Lovie Chateau 128, 311
La Panne 483
Langemarck 40-41, 108, 114, 277, 351, 359, 363, 440
Lederberg 425
Lederzeele 59
Lekkerboterbeek 45-47, 62, 209, 240, 328
Lichtervelde 440
Lille 57
Lind Cottage 151, 240
Lokeren. 419
Lump House 161
Lys 123

Magermeirie 75, 212, 425, 427-428
Mallet Copse 71, 140, 148, 153, 184, 229-231, 234, 248, 250-251, 264, 267-269, 276, 279-282, 285-289, 293-295, 299, 302-303, 345, 347, 359, 378
Mallet Wood 46, 60, 71, 139, 187, 231, 233, 248, 251, 264-265, 267, 299, 378, 395-396
Marialoop 432
Marlborough College 125
Meetcheele 50, 122, 124, 128-130, 132, 161, 165, 171, 175-177, 187, 191, 244, 258, 270, 300, 302, 308, 389, 399-400

Mendinghem Military Cemetery 226
Menin 41, 52, 55, 116, 123, 326, 367, 424
Messines 38-39, 83, 88, 121, 160, 368
Meulebeke 424, 428-429, 432
Middle Copse 46
Middlekirke 38

Moerbeke Station 419
Mohmand Expedition 52, 161
Moislains 99
Monchy Front 221
Monchy-le-Preux 103
Moorslede 55, 75, 212, 422
Mosselmarkt 50, 100, 124, 127-130, 132, 161, 179, 181, 184, 187, 190, 192, 217, 244, 255, 260, 308, 389, 411, 421
Mousetrap Track 149, 162, 193, 198, 281
Mullet Farm 46-47, 59, 294
Mullet Wood 46
Murray Switch 271

Netheravon 128
Newcastle-upon-Tyne 186
Newcastle-under-Lyme 365
Nieuport 38, 85, 92, 195, 228, 252, 274, 354, 417, 476, 478
Nivelle Offensive 38
Noir Carme 333
Nordhof (Void Farm) 203, 289, 321, 437-438, 441
Northern Redoubt 63, 68, 71, 164, 174, 207, 214, 217-219, 222, 227, 260, 264, 301, 312, 315-316, 337, 378, 434

Oekene 423, 425
Oostkamp 439
Oostnieuwkerke 50, 62, 70, 75, 106, 139, 184, 212, 253, 320, 331, 361
Osselstraat 187, 227-228
Ostend 38, 42, 57, 357
Oyghem 433

Paddebeek 45-49, 59, 97, 242, 302, 441
Palestine 352
Passchendaele 38-44, 46, 48-50, 52-63, 65, 67-71, 74-75, 78, 81, 83, 92, 94, 97-99, 104-106, 108, 111, 113-117, 120-121, 123, 127-128, 130, 133, 137-138, 156-157, 161-162, 164, 166-167, 169-170, 172-173, 175, 178-179, 182, 184, 201, 203, 206, 209-212, 217-220, 222-224, 227-228, 233, 237, 243, 246-247, 252-255, 258-260, 262-263, 265, 270, 276, 283-285, 288, 290-293, 298-299, 301, 303, 307-308, 310-324, 326, 328-329, 331-334, 336-338, 340, 343, 350-351, 354, 357-365, 367-370, 374-375, 377-378, 394, 410, 413-414, 417-422, 424-425, 427-429, 433-436, 441, 471
Passchendaele, First Battle of 62
Passchendaele, Second Battle of 40, 44, 70, 361, 363
Penicuik Public School 259
Penrith 193, 233
Peter Pan Track 159, 162, 187
Pilckem Ridge 56, 108
Ploegsteert 92
Poelcappelle 41-42, 45, 47, 50, 55, 79, 236, 253, 363, 365
Poezelhoek 326
Point 83 194, 198, 201
Polderhoek 104-105, 117, 317-318, 324-325, 329, 350, 360, 362
Polders Wood 171
Polygon Wood 40-41, 55, 360, 367
Poperinghe 172, 433, 473-474
Potijze 53
Pottegemsgut 428
Puisieux 86, 88, 96

Racket Wood 59, 139, 396
Ravebeek 50, 123, 164
Reutelbeek 55, 324, 324, 326
Roodkruis 75, 139, 212
Roulers 38-39, 43, 53, 57, 75, 202, 212, 214, 263, 314, 320, 357, 361, 365, 368, 420-422, 424, 433, 439-441
Royston 189, 377
Rumbeke 420, 423, 425
Russia 357-358, 475

Salford 194, 200
Sandhurst 188
Scarpe, Third Battle of the 96
Scherriabeek 325, 360
Shaw Wood 171
Somme 37-38, 62, 83-84, 87, 90, 93, 102, 112-113, 118, 127, 134, 161, 195, 204, 233, 353, 365, 476, 480-481
Sorel 113
Source Farm 162, 193, 198, 227
Sourd Farm 46
Southern Redoubt 63, 71, 74, 122, 209, 211-214, 220, 245-246, 254-255, 262, 289, 293, 301, 311, 315-316, 338, 359, 378
Spriet 46-48, 58-59, 62, 184, 270, 273, 365
St Jills 428
St Julian 133
St Louis 440
St Nicholas 428
St Omer 333
St Quentin 109-110, 214, 421
St. Jean 122, 474
Staden 58, 59
Steenbeek Valley 103, 140, 359
Stroombeek 200, 282
Suvla Bay 246
Swevegn 440

Tagliamento 205
Teall Cottage 68, 116, 142, 163-167, 179, 181, 187, 191, 207, 215-217, 220, 222-223, 247, 251, 259-260, 264-266, 270, 274-275, 279-280, 283, 286-288, 298-301, 303, 305, 309, 311-312, 315, 337-338, 344, 359, 376, 378, 413, 434
Thiepval 194
Thourout 38-39, 43, 57, 424
Tiber 52, 55, 74
Tiendenberg 390
Tingewick 195, 197, 377
Tombola Farm 184
Tournant Farm 45, 49, 60, 74, 98, 116, 153, 160, 167, 187, 200, 207, 234, 237, 239, 286, 298, 303, 306, 327, 359, 401

Trinity College Cambridge 197
Tyne Cot 165, 210, 218, 224-225, 229, 233, 236, 239, 257, 259, 266, 292, 309, 375-378

Valour Farm 245, 309
Valuation Houses 46-47, 59, 139, 184, 228, 245, 251, 263-265, 270, 273, 277, 286, 288-290, 300, 395-396
Vapour Farm 45, 162, 271
Vat Cottages 45-46, 48-50, 60, 62, 71, 93-95, 97, 114, 116, 138-139, 141, 148, 153, 170, 184, 197, 203, 206, 221, 231, 233-234, 236, 238, 240-241, 253, 265, 267, 270-272, 279, 281-282, 286-287, 289, 293-296, 299-300, 302, 305, 308, 311, 319, 328, 343, 354, 361
Vat Cottages Ridge 45-46, 48, 50, 60, 62, 71, 93-95, 97, 114, 138-139, 141, 148, 153, 170, 184, 197, 203, 206, 231, 233-234, 240-241, 253, 294, 302, 308, 319, 361
Veal Cottages 46, 49, 71, 139-140, 148-149, 153, 184, 227, 234, 236, 248, 250-251, 264-265, 267, 269-272, 274, 279-281, 286-289, 295, 298-299, 303, 359, 395
Veldt Farm 202, 228, 231, 248, 251, 281-282, 299
Venison Trench 60, 63-64, 68-69, 71, 97, 100, 114, 122, 133-134, 137164, 170, 203, 210, 214, 220, 222-224, 246-247, 249, 253-255, 257, 260, 262-265, 273, 278, 280-281, 283-284, 293, 306-307, 315, 318, 337, 340, 361, 369, 378.
Venison Farm 139, 395
Venture Farm 70, 116, 165, 187, 192
Versailles 318
Verse Cottage 139, 395
Vierkavenhoek 75, 212, 425, 429
Vindictive Crossroads 50, 62, 69-70, 123-124, 141, 210, 215, 217, 220, 246, 300, 336, 359, 361, 410-412
Vine Cottage 245, 271
Virile Farm 139, 144, 146-147, 149, 162, 165, 184, 186-187, 201, 208, 229, 248,

265, 269, 271, 275, 277, 288, 295-296, 300-301, 307, 309-310, 327, 343, 346, 380
Vive St Eloi 419
Vlamertinghe 111, 132, 141, 147, 167, 333
Vocation Farm 59, 163, 165, 184, 192, 229, 279, 296, 303, 346
Vogeltje Chateau 416
Void Farm 46, 71,139-140, 148, 153, 203, 217, 223, 228-230, 247-248, 264, 266, 269, 272-274, 276, 278-279, 281-282, 285-287, 289, 291, 293, 295-296, 299-300, 302-303, 309, 314, 321, 346-348, 359, 377, 395, 437
Volgeltje Chateau 307
Volt Farm 60, 71, 140, 148, 153, 184, 222, 228-229, 273, 277, 288, 294
Vox Farm 49, 59, 71, 97, 116, 124, 184, 228-230, 263, 266, 269, 273, 276, 280, 282, 286, 296, 299, 304-305, 310, 315, 327, 359, 385

Waereghem 419, 425, 428
Wallemolen 161, 281
Waterloo Farm 126-127, 161, 181, 307
Wellington College 180, 376
West Wood 46
Westhoek 41, 56, 379
Westroosebeke 41-42, 44, 46-48, 50-51, 55, 58-62, 68, 70, 75, 97, 105, 114, 116-117, 139, 151, 166, 171, 184, 200, 203, 205, 221-224, 229, 231, 244, 253, 255, 262, 264-265, 270, 283-284, 289, 310, 313, 318, 320-323, 328, 331, 340, 351, 361, 377, 433-436, 438, 441

Westwood House 46, 59, 184
Whisk Farm 217
Wielsbeke 419, 433
Wieltje 122, 127-128, 133, 135, 156, 161, 179, 181, 187, 285, 322, 411
Windmill Cabaret Ridge 53, 114
Winkle St Eloi 428
Winnipeg 114, 162-163, 351
Wizernes 333
Wrangle Farm 59, 132, 219
Wrap Cottage 132
Wrath Farm 132, 175, 219
Written Farm 132
Wurst Farm 140-142, 148, 160, 167, 193, 198, 231, 275, 308, 397, 399-400
Wynendaele 441

Yetta Houses 156, 399-402
Ypres 38-40, 42, 44, 53, 57-58, 60-62, 65, 69, 75, 78, 83, 92, 94-95, 98, 106, 108, 115, 123, 126-127, 133, 156, 161-162, 173, 185-186, 214, 227, 239, 313, 317, 323, 326, 340, 350, 354, 356, 359, 361, 363-369, 417, 419, 421-422, 433, 473-474, 476-477, 482
Ypres, Third Battle of 38, 40, 42, 44, 53, 57, 62, 65, 75, 78, 83, 92, 95, 98, 108, 115, 123, 133,173, 185-186, 227, 317, 350, 356, 359, 363-365, 366-369, 482
Ypres Prison 127
Ypres Reservoir Cemetery 239, 313

Zeebrugge 38, 42, 57
Zilverberg 75, 212, 321, 425, 428-429
Zonnebeke 53, 277
Zudausque 333

INDEX OF BRITISH & DOMINION FORMATIONS AND UNITS

British Army 37, 58, 78, 82, 109, 112, 125, 146, 194, 197, 215, 229, 244, 352, 472
BEF 38, 56-57, 80, 92, 95, 108-109, 111-112, 119, 121, 185, 197, 199, 215, 317, 335, 365-366, 368-369, 416, 476
First Army 39, 77, 415, 482
Second Army 39-42, 44, 46, 49, 52, 57-62, 70, 74, 79, 93, 102-103, 105, 114, 116-117, 120-121, 141, 162-163, 166-167, 169, 173, 186, 202, 206, 209, 221, 254, 263-264, 284, 289, 291, 301, 306, 311-312, 314, 316-317, 321-322, 329, 340, 348, 350-351, 356-363, 365, 368, 374-375, 385-387, 414, 429
Third Army 39, 57-58, 60-61, 96, 121, 316, 323, 365, 414, 479
Fourth Army 102, 134, 345, 361, 480
Fifth Army 39-42, 44-45, 50, 78-79, 83, 95-96, 185, 333, 363, 415

I ANZAC Corps 55, 79
II ANZAC Corps 55, 104-105, 116, 123, 164, 326, 360, 421
Canadian Corps 43, 46, 48-49, 58, 60, 70, 112
II Corps 44-48, 50, 52, 58-60, 62-63, 69-71, 74, 76-79, 86, 92, 96-97, 100, 102, 105-106, 113-116, 122-124, 134, 138-139, 141-142, 144, 146-147, 149, 153, 158-159, 161-162, 164, 166-167, 171, 185, 202, 204, 206, 209, 217, 227, 231, 234, 240, 242, 244, 247, 251, 262, 264-265, 272-274, 276-277, 280-281, 286-289, 293, 298-299, 301, 304, 306-307, 309, 311-312, 314-316, 322, 345, 357, 359, 362-363, 375, 385-387, 390, 392, 394-395
V Corps 353, 479
VIII Corps 39, 51-53, 55, 57-60, 62, 70, 79-83, 92, 96-97, 100, 105-108, 113-117, 121-124, 126-128, 130, 134-135, 138-139, 141, 144, 146, 149, 164, 167, 169-170, 175, 220, 243-244, 246-247, 252, 254, 260, 262-264, 281, 283-285, 298-299, 301, 307, 311-312, 315-316, 319, 357-359, 363, 375, 385-386, 388-390, 394, 416, 421
IX Corps 104-105, 324-325, 349, 360
X Corps 79, 104
XV Corps 113, 274
XVIII Corps 44, 79, 112, 185, 214
XIX Corps 116, 286

1st Division 45-48, 71, 97, 107, 163, 381
1st Canadian Division 46, 48-49, 69-70
3rd Canadian Division 106, 132
8th Division 58, 60-61, 89-94, 96-97, 99-101, 106-108, 113, 121-137, 141-142, 153, 155, 159, 162, 164, 166-168, 170, 174-176, 179, 181-182, 186, 206-207, 210, 212, 216, 219, 220, 223, 243, 245-246, 254-255, 259-260, 262, 264, 272-273, 277, 282-284, 287-288, 293, 298-302, 306-308, 311-313, 315-316, 322, 333, 336-340, 356, 369, 371-372, 375, 381, 390, 393-394
14th Division 127, 134, 306-308, 313, 318-319, 333
19th Division 88, 329
21st Division 107, 353
29th Division 79, 103, 350
32nd Division 47, 58-60, 68, 71, 74, 84-86, 88, 92-97, 100-101, 103-104, 106, 109-111, 113-114, 116, 121, 124-125, 127, 129-130, 134-135, 137-167, 171-172, 181, 184, 186-187, 191-192, 194, 198, 200-201, 203-204, 206, 208, 216-217, 222, 230, 233, 236, 240, 242, 244-245, 247-252, 254, 264-265, 269-273, 275-284, 286-289, 293, 295-308, 310-313, 315, 318-319, 322, 327-328, 330, 333, 338, 340-341, 343-349, 351-354, 372-373, 382-383, 390, 394-395, 397-402, 404, 468-470, 479, 482-483
33rd Division 80, 123, 125, 129, 134-135, 164, 220, 256, 299, 307, 315, 383, 421

35th Division 138, 158, 171, 240, 274, 277, 287, 394
37th Division 103
49th Division 421
58th Division 45
63rd (Royal Naval) Division 44, 87, 89, 97-99, 101, 133, 142, 144, 156, 158, 163, 171, 329
New Zealand Division 55, 104-105, 317-318, 324-326, 360, 378

3 Brigade 94, 381
14 Brigade 84, 141, 146, 149, 153, 159-161, 172, 244, 248, 275-276, 280, 282-283, 285-288, 300, 302, 304-306, 308, 318, 322, 327-328, 341, 382, 354, 397-402, 483
23 Brigade 91-92, 97, 106, 108, 127, 132, 163-164, 167, 181, 203, 369, 371, 381
24 Brigade 91, 106, 135, 166, 177, 369, 371-372, 382
25 Brigade 91-92, 101, 106-108, 122, 125-128, 130, 132-135, 142, 144, 146, 167, 169, 174, 176, 179, 181-182, 186, 203, 207, 220, 223, 243, 245-246, 254, 259-260, 262, 264, 273, 278-279, 282-284, 289, 291, 293, 299, 301-302, 306-307, 311, 313, 333, 335, 338, 369, 371, 382, 412
41 Brigade 306-308, 313, 318, 382
96 Brigade 84, 106, 111, 138, 141, 149, 153, 161, 163-164, 167, 172, 184, 231, 269, 273, 276, 286-287, 301, 304, 308, 333, 382, 398-399, 483
97 Brigade 89, 106, 109-111, 125, 130, 132, 138-139, 141-142, 144, 146, 149, 151, 153, 155, 159-161, 167, 172, 182, 184-186, 187, 191-194, 198, 200-201, 203, 207, 221-222, 226-229, 231, 234, 238, 242, 244-245, 247-251, 259, 265-266, 269-283, 285-288, 293, 295-296, 298-305, 308-309, 311, 313, 315, 326-328, 333, 341-344, 346-349, 372-373, 382, 395-397, 400-402, 407-408, 483
100 Brigade 220, 331, 383, 403

11th Border Regiment 110, 138, 142, 161, 167, 184, 192-195, 197-198, 200-201, 221, 228-233, 240, 247, 250-251, 265-266, 267, 269, 273-274, 276, 278-281, 286, 288-289, 293-295, 299-300, 302-303, 310, 333, 335, 341-342, 344-346, 349, 354, 372, 373, 382, 456-460, 467, 476-477, 483-484
2nd Cameronians 177, 215, 381
10th Canadian Battalion 70
1st Canterbury Regiment 325-326
2nd Devonshire Regiment 97, 163-164, 203, 312, 338, 381
1st Dorsetshire Regiment 85, 160, 286, 327-328, 382
22nd Durham Light Infantry 126, 382
2nd East Lancashire Regiment 99, 177, 370-372, 382
Hawke Battalion 87
15th HLI 300, 302, 308, 328, 382, 482
16th HLI 138, 140, 142, 157, 167, 184, 186, 192-193, 201, 220-221, 223, 226, 228-231, 233-234, 238, 240, 247-248, 249-251, 265-266, 269-276, 278, 280-282, 286-288, 291-296, 299, 302-303, 309-310, 314, 319, 333, 335, 341-342, 346, 350, 372, 380, 382
17th HLI 88, 138, 184, 198-201, 221, 233-240, 245, 248, 250-251, 267, 269, 271, 273-274, 278-280, 289, 293, 296, 298-300, 302-303, 310, 333-335, 341-342, 372-373, 382, 461-463, 467, 482
2nd KOYLI 125, 130, 132, 138, 140, 142, 182, 184, 186-193, 201, 203, 205, 215-216, 219-227, 229-230, 238, 244, 247, 249-251, 265-266, 269-270, 272-276, 279-280, 282, 284, 288, 291, 293, 295-296, 309, 333, 335, 341-342, 372-373, 376, 449-453, 467, 382, 483
1st KRRC 482
7th KRRC 306
8th KRRC 307, 313, 382
15th Lancashire Fusiliers 138, 160, 167, 172, 184, 194, 200-201, 221, 234, 237-240, 248, 250-251, 264, 267, 273-274, 279-280, 298, 300, 302, 306,

Index 515

310, 327, 333, 335, 341-342, 372-373, 382, 401, 464-465, 467,476, 482
16th Lancashire Fusiliers 161, 163-164, 167, 194-195, 382, 482
2nd Lincolnshire Regiment 100, 127, 133, 135, 175, 178-182, 208, 210, 213-214, 217, 220, 246, 255, 257-260, 262, 273, 284, 293, 307-308, 333, 336-338, 369, 371, 375-76, 382, 412, 445-447, 466, 471-475
3rd Lincolnshire Regiment 180, 375
2nd Manchester Regiment 160, 327, 382
2nd Northamptonshire Regiment 369, 371, 382
16th Northumberland Fusiliers 138, 142, 165-167, 172, 184, 186-187, 191, 203, 222, 229, 248, 252, 265, 269, 271, 273, 275, 288, 295-297, 302, 309-310, 333, 341-342, 346-347, 372-373, 382, 435, 465-468
17th Northumberland Fusiliers 149, 382
1st Otago Regiment 325
2nd Rifle Brigade 84, 125, 127, 130, 132-133, 135, 142, 175, 178-179, 181-182, 205, 214-220, 222-224, 227, 247, 255, 257-258, 260, 273, 279, 284-285, 301, 308, 312, 333, 337-338, 369, 371, 382, 413
7th Rifle Brigade 306, 313, 382
8th Rifle Brigade 306, 308, 313, 319, 382
2nd Royal Berkshire Regiment 89, 108, 127, 133, 167-168, 172, 175-179, 182, 208-210, 212, 214, 220, 245, 254-257, 260, 262, 284, 293, 307-308, 333, 335-338, 369, 371, 375, 381-382, 411, 442-444, 466, 471-475
13th Royal Fusiliers 121
2nd Royal Inniskilling Fusiliers 88, 122, 161, 163-165, 167, 181, 191, 203, 288, 336, 382, 411, 441, 472-473, 478, 482
1st Royal Irish Rifles 127, 132-133, 167-168, 175, 179, 181-182, 217, 255, 308, 333, 369, 371, 382
2nd Royal Munster Fusiliers 48-49, 52, 60, 140, 381
5/6th Royal Scots 160, 327, 382

1st Royal Scots Fusiliers 192
10th (Works) Royal Scots Fusiliers 192
1/5th Royal Warwickshire Regiment 173
1st South Wales Borderers 48-49, 94, 140, 381
1/5th Welsh Regiment 163
2nd West Yorkshire Regiment 89, 97, 181, 306, 381, 306
1st Worcestershire Regiment 166, 371, 382
14th Worcestershire Regiment 149, 163

62nd HAG 113, 121, 336
309th Siege Battery 117, 328
RFA 130, 153, 248, 252, 352, 369, 371-372, 468
22 Brigade RFA 117
161 Brigade RFA 319
168 Brigade RFA 252
Royal Marine Artillery 114, 160
No. 2 FOO Group 307
No. 4 FOO Group 277

Heavy Branch MGC 178
MGC 301, 369, 371-373
1st MG Company 428, 431
14th MG Company 139, 144, 160
24th MG Company 135
25th MG Company 122
96th MG Company 139, 144, 161
97th MG Company 139, 144, 372
188th MG Company 144
189th MG Company 144
223rd MG Company 144
218th MG Company 122, 135
219th MG Company 139

14th TMB 399
96th TMB 401
97th TMB 226, 292

Royal Engineers 119, 368
2nd Field Company RE 132
206th Field Company RE 149
218th Field Company RE 149, 163, 271
219th Field Company RE 140, 227, 249-250, 266, 309

247th Field Company RE 149
248th Field Company RE 149
249th Field Company RE 149

2nd Field Survey Company RE 162
5th Field Survey Company RE 162

RAMC 197, 470

25th Field Ambulance 127, 322
90th Field Ambulance 322
91st Field Ambulance 322
92nd Field Ambulance 161, 322

No. 7 Squadron RFC 147-148, 132, 298
No. 21 Squadron RFC 128, 254
No. 65 Squadron RFC 252

INDEX OF GERMAN FORMATIONS AND UNITS

Westheer 65, 369
Heeresgruppe Kronprinz Rupprecht 42, 67, 203, 283, 310, 326, 331-332
Fourth Army 39-42, 62-63, 70, 75, 93, 166, 171, 203, 252-253, 281, 283, 308, 310, 314, 326, 329, 331-332, 351, 356, 374, 420, 436, 480, 485

Gruppe Staden 62-63, 68, 71-72, 74-75, 227, 253, 310, 329, 331, 333, 351, 374, 420, 425, 429, 436, 440-441
Gruppe Wijtschate 42, 419, 425, 428, 440
Gruppe Ypern 62-63, 74-75, 253, 331, 333, 351, 374, 419-424, 428-429
3rd Garde Division 419, 425, 428
4th Division 62, 420, 429, 436, 441
11th Division 98, 420, 425, 429
11th Bavarian Division 420, 429
16th Division 424, 432
17th Reserve Division 360
25th Division 202-203, 205, 212, 214, 217, 283, 293, 321, 332, 373, 384, 419-421, 423, 425, 427-428
38th Division 202, 204, 217, 221, 227, 240, 281, 283, 291, 299, 321, 329, 373, 384, 427-429, 430, 433, 435-436, 440-441
44th Reserve Division 62, 420-421, 423, 425, 427, 429-430
199th Reserve Division 62, 164, 263, 420, 429, 441
204th Division 209

Grenadier-Regiment 10 420
Grenadier-Regiment 123 436
IR18 440
IR29 432
IR68 424
IR77 441
IR91 439
IR94 202, 204, 217, 220, 227, 259, 285, 296, 357, 373-374, 384, 427-428, 430, 433-435, 440
IR95 204-205, 227, 240, 251, 289, 291, 293-294, 320, 331-332, 373-374, 384, 436-439, 440
IR96 221, 227, 240, 384, 440-441
IR115 164, 201-202, 214, 321, 331, 374, 419-424, 432, 384
IR116 43, 205, 212, 214, 245-246, 255, 261, 289, 316, 321, 373-374, 384, 425-428, 431-432, 434-435
IR117 202, 212, 214, 217, 246, 260-261, 289, 315, 321, 373-374, 384, 420, 424-31, 439-440
IR120 440
IR162 360
IR357 436
RIR205 425, 430
RIR206 421, 423
RIR208 427
25th Sturmabteilung 321

Luftstreitkräfte (German Army Air Service) 321

INDEX OF MISCELLANEOUS TERMS

Eingreifdivisionen 63-65, 68, 75, 264, 289, 420, 425, 427, 429, 432, 436, 440-441
Grosskampfzone 65, 67-68, 71, 74
Hauptwiderstandslinie 67-68, 71, 74-75, 93, 97, 184, 207, 219, 228-229, 230-231, 262, 283, 293, 295, 315, 321, 331, 421, 426-427, 429-432, 434-435, 437-438, 440-441
Kampftruppenkommandeur 75-76, 246, 321, 329, 423, 425-428, 430, 435, 441
London Gazette 164, 181, 189, 197, 212
Nahtkommandos 421, 430, 426
POWs 126, 202-204, 314, 356, 374, 471-475
Sicherungslinie 67, 321, 426, 430-432
S.S. 119 118
S.S. 135 118-119, 120-121, 125-126, 138, 155, 162, 362
S.S. 143 111-112
S.S. 144 112
S.S. 148 121, 144, 153
S.S. 158 121
S.S.185 112
St John Ambulance Brigade 195
Stellungsdivisionen 63-65, 68, 74-75
Times, The 43, 323
Vorfeldzone 65, 67-68, 71, 74-75, 93, 95-97, 113, 123, 139, 163, 166, 184, 202, 204-207, 209, 214, 217, 227-228, 230-231, 236, 238, 259, 265, 278, 283, 293, 296, 306, 331-332, 340, 421, 426, 429-431, 434-435, 437, 439-441
War Cabinet 57, 317-318, 360, 365, 367, 369
War Council 317, 364

Wolverhampton Military Studies

www.helion.co.uk/wolverhamptonmilitarystudies

Editorial board

Professor Stephen Badsey
Wolverhampton University

Professor Michael Bechthold
Wilfred Laurier University

Professor John Buckley
Wolverhampton University

Major General (Retired) John Drewienkiewicz

Ashley Ekins
Australian War Memorial

Dr Howard Fuller
Wolverhampton University

Dr Spencer Jones
Wolverhampton University

Nigel de Lee
Norwegian War Academy

Major General (Retired) Mungo Melvin
President of the British Commission for Military History

Dr Michael Neiberg
US Army War College

Dr Eamonn O'Kane
Wolverhampton University

Professor Fransjohan Pretorius
University of Pretoria

Dr Simon Robbins
Imperial War Museum

Professor Gary Sheffield
Wolverhampton University

Commander Steve Tatham PhD
Royal Navy
The Influence Advisory Panel

Professor Malcolm Wanklyn
Wolverhampton University

Professor Andrew Wiest
University of Southern Mississippi

Submissions

The publishers would be pleased to receive submissions for this series. Please contact us via email (info@helion.co.uk), or in writing to Helion & Company Limited, 26 Willow Road, Solihull, West Midlands, B91 1UE.

Titles

No.1 *Stemming the Tide. Officers and Leadership in the British Expeditionary Force 1914* Edited by Spencer Jones (ISBN 978-1-909384-45-3)

No.2 *'Theirs Not To Reason Why': Horsing the British Army 1875–1925* Graham Winton (ISBN 978-1-909384-48-4)

No.3 *A Military Transformed? Adaptation and Innovation in the British Military, 1792–1945* Edited by Michael LoCicero, Ross Mahoney and Stuart Mitchell (ISBN 978-1-909384-46-0)

No.4 *Get Tough Stay Tough. Shaping the Canadian Corps, 1914–1918* Kenneth Radley (ISBN 978-1-909982-86-4)

No.5 *A Moonlight Massacre: The Night Operation on the Passchendaele Ridge, 2 December 1917. The Forgotten Last Act of the Third Battle of Ypres* Michael LoCicero (ISBN 978-1-909982-92-5)

No.6 *Shellshocked Prophets. Former Anglican Army Chaplains in Interwar Britain* Linda Parker (ISBN 978-1-909982-25-3)

No.7 *Flight Plan Africa: Portuguese Airpower in Counterinsurgency, 1961–1974* John P. Cann (ISBN 978-1-909982-06-2)

No.8 *Mud, Blood and Determination. The History of the 46th (North Midland) Division in the Great War* Simon Peaple (ISBN 978 1 910294 66 6)

No.9 *Commanding Far Eastern Skies. A Critical Analysis of the Royal Air Force Superiority Campaign in India, Burma and Malaya 1941–1945* Peter Preston-Hough (ISBN 978 1 910294 44 4)

No.10 *Courage Without Glory. The British Army on the Western Front 1915* Edited by Spencer Jones (ISBN 978 1 910777 18 3)

No.11 *The Airborne Forces Experimental Establishment: The Development of British Airborne Technology 1940–1950* Tim Jenkins (ISBN 978-1-910777-06-0)

No.12 *'Allies are a Tiresome Lot' – The British Army in Italy in the First World War* John Dillon (ISBN 978 1 910777 32 9)

No.13 *Monty's Functional Doctrine: Combined Arms Doctrine in British 21st Army Group in Northwest Europe, 1944–45* Charles Forrester (ISBN 978-1-910777-26-8)

No.14 *Early Modern Systems of Command: Queen Anne's Generals, Staff Officers and the Direction of Allied Warfare in the Low Countries and Germany, 1702–11* Stewart Stansfield (ISBN 978 1 910294 47 5)

No.15 *They Didn't Want To Die Virgins: Sex and Morale in the British Army on the Western Front 1914–1918* Bruce Cherry (ISBN 978-1-910777-70-1)

No.16 *From Tobruk to Tunis: The Impact of Terrain on British Operations and Doctrine in North Africa, 1940–1943* Neal Dando (ISBN 978-1-910294-00-0)

No.17 *Crossing No Man's Land: Experience and Learning with the Northumberland Fusiliers in the Great War* Tony Ball (ISBN 978-1-910777-73-2)

No.18 *"Everything worked like clockwork": The Mechanization of the British Cavalry between the Two World Wars* Roger E Salmon (ISBN 978-1-910777-96-1)

No.19 *Attack on the Somme: 1st Anzac Corps and the Battle of Pozi.res Ridge, 1916* Meleah Hampton (ISBN 978-1-910777-65-7)

No.20 *Operation Market Garden: The Campaign for the Low Countries, Autumn 1944: Seventy Years On* Edited by John Buckley & Peter Preston Hough (ISBN 978 1 910777 15 2)

No.21 *Enduring the Whirlwind: The German Army and the Russo-German War 1941-1943* Gregory Liedtke (ISBN 978-1-910777-75-6)

No.22 *'Glum Heroes': Hardship, fear and death – Resilience and Coping in the British Army on the Western Front 1914–1918* Peter E. Hodgkinson (ISBN 978-1-910777-78-7)

No.23 *Much Embarrassed: Civil War Intelligence and the Gettysburg Campaign* George Donne (ISBN 978-1-910777-86-2)

No.24 *They Called It Shell Shock: Combat Stress in the First World War* Stefanie Linden (ISBN 978-1-911096-35-1)

No. 25 *New Approaches to the Military History of the English Civil War. Proceedings of the First Helion & Company 'Century of the Soldier' Conference* Ismini Pells (editor) (ISBN 978-1-911096-44-3)

No.26 *Reconographers: Intelligence and Reconnaissance in British Tank Operations on the Western Front 1916-18* Colin Hardy (ISBN: 978-1-911096-28-3)

No.27 *Britain's Quest for Oil: The First World War and the Peace Conferences* Martin Gibson (ISBN: 978-1-911512-07-3)

No.28 *Unfailing Gallantry: 8th (Regular) Division in the Great War 1914–1919* Alun Thomas (ISBN: 978-1-910777-61-9)

No.29 *An Army of Brigadiers: British Brigade Commanders at the Battle of Arras 1917* Trevor Harvey (ISBN: 978-1-911512-00-4)

No.30 *At All Costs: The British Army on the Western Front 1916* Edited by Spencer Jones (ISBN 978-1-912174-88-1)

No.31 *The German Corpse Factory: A Study in First World War Propaganda* Stephen Badsey (ISBN 978-1-911628-27-9)

No.32 *Bull Run to Boer War: How the American Civil War Changed the Victorian British Army* Michael Somerville (ISBN 978-1-912866-25-0)

No.33 *Turret versus Broadside: An Anatomy of British Naval Prestige, Revolution and Disaster, 1860-1870* Howard J. Fuller (ISBN 978-1-913336-22-6)

No.34 *A Moonlight Massacre: The Night Operation on the Passchendaele Ridge, 2 December 1917. The Forgotten Last Act of the Third Battle of Ypres* Second Edition, paperback Michael LoCicero (ISBN 978-1-911628-72-9)